MINISTRY

Lay Ministry in the Roman Catholic Church: Its History and Theology

KENAN B. OSBORNE, O.F.M.

Wipf and Stock Publishers
EUGENE, OREGON

Wipf and Stock Publishers
199 West 8th Avenue, Suite 3
Eugene, Oregon 97401

Ministry
Lay Ministry in the Roman Catholic Church: Its History and Theology
By Osborne, Kenan B.
Copyright© January, 1993 Osborne, Kenan B.
ISBN: 1-59244-1572
Publication date: February, 2003
Previously published by Paulist Press, January, 1993 .

Contents

PART TWO
THE RISE OF THE LAY MOVEMENT WITHIN THE WESTERN CHURCH AND THE DECLINE OF CLERICAL DOMINANCE: 1000–2000 A.D.

Preface

This volume on the ministry of the non-ordained is a companion volume to my other book, *Priesthood, A History of the Ordained Ministry in the Roman Catholic Church.* On the one hand, these two aspects of ministry, the ordained aspect and the non-ordained aspect, cannot be studied apart, since they mutually identify and define each other. On the other hand, I found that, at least as far as my own talents were concerned, I could not deal with them in a concomitant way. I could not write a single volume, dealing at one and the same time with both the ordained and the non-ordained aspects of ministry. This separation into two volumes, however, should not be interpreted as if these two themes are mutually exclusive. Indeed, one of the fundamental reasons why the theological understanding of ministry is complicated rests in the fact that these two aspects are so intrinsically united.

The documents of Vatican II have given great emphasis to this connection between the unordained and the ordained ministries. As we know well, the bishops at Vatican II reworked the preliminary draft of the document on the church, *Lumen Gentium,* so that the fundamental importance of the entire people of God, the *Christifideles,* became paramount for all Christian ministry. Only on the basis of this fundamental significance of all baptized Christians (chapter two) did the bishops then discuss both the ordained and the non-ordained ministry (chapters three and four). Thus, we can speak of a mutual relationship between ordained and non-ordained ministry, but the lynch pin must be seen in the baptismal-eucharistic sacrament of initiation. This integration of the sacrament of initiation (baptism-confirmation-eucharist) into the fundamental structure of church ministry is key to the understanding both of the church itself and of the various church ministries, which one finds throughout the Vatican II documents.

1

Vatican II has, as a result, intensified the theological research and discussion on certain key issues regarding lay ministry. The first of these key issues is, quite simply, the very meaning of the "lay Christian." In a most notable way, Yves Congar, prior to the council, had already written at great length on this subject. Since Vatican II numerous other theologians and many canon lawyers as well have dealt with this subject: What is a lay Christian? Even before Congar, however, the modern lay movements which had taken shape in the nineteenth century, particularly during the papacy of Pius IX, began to advance the position and status of the lay Christian in the church. As we shall see in a later chapter, neither Pius IX nor any of the subsequent popes who bore the name Pius were overly enthusiastic about such movements, if these movements were not under the control of the clergy. Nonetheless, the chain of events, which included the rise of highly independent political parties, as well as lay congresses and lay organizations, both under clerical control and those not under clerical control, increasingly demanded of church authority, i.e. clergy, a better recognition and evaluation of the lay role in the church.

A second modern issue which arose concomitantly with this interest in the lay Christian was the role of women both in the church and in society. At times this issue has been rather disdainfully called "the American issue," or, even worse, an "American problem." However, it is neither a problem nor a specifically American issue. It is in itself not a problem, since the role of women in the church finds its rootage in the gospels themselves. It is a problem, however, for a church authority and policy which might make male domination an ideological issue. In this volume we will explore the history of this issue of women and ministry, as it moved from century to century in the history of the Roman Catholic Church. No complete resolution of the tensions which this issue has raised and continues to raise can be expected. My aim is more modest: to offer some guiding principles, based on scripture, history and theology, which hopefully will further the discussion both on the role of women in the church and on the actual participation of women in decision-making bodies within the church structures.

A third issue is that of ministry and religious life. Although Vatican II did consider religious life and issued a decree on the subject, namely, *Perfectae Caritatis,* the interrelationship of the ordained, the non-ordained, and the religious, as far as ministry is concerned, is still not clear. It is my hope that some of the historical considerations on this issue, which appear in this volume, will help orient the discussion in a more cogent way.

From time to time, reference will be made to the volume *Priesthood.* It would be uncalled for to repeat some of the sections from that previous book in this present volume, and although this means that the readership must, at times, have two books in hand, it also means that the readership will see more clearly (so it is hoped) the intrinsic interdependence of ordained ministry and non-ordained ministry.

It would be ungracious if I did not express my appreciation to so many people who have helped to make this volume possible. Over the years the many students at the Franciscan School of Theology and the Graduate Theological Union at Berkeley, California, have actually been my teachers during the almost annual course on the sacraments which I have tried to teach them. In any sacraments course, the issue of ministry is central, and the many discussions we have had in class have helped shape my ideas on this theme. The insights and the experiences of these students, lay and cleric, masculine and feminine, in various religious communities and without, have helped in no small way the very shaping of this present volume. To all of them I owe an enormous debt of gratitude.

A number of my academic peers both at the Graduate Theological Union and at other positions carefully and painstakingly read parts of the manuscript and provided me with a number of helpful observations and emendations. Among these I wish to mention in a special and grateful way: Dr. Michael Guinan, O.F.M., and Dr. Linda Mahoney, professors in biblical theology; Dr. Alan McCoy, O.F.M., professor emeritus in canon law; Dr. William Short, O.F.M., and Dr. Mary Ann Donovan, S.C., professors in early church history.

PART ONE

The Establishment
of the Clerical Position
and
The Disestablishment
of the Lay Position:
30–1000 A.D.

1

The First Point of Departure: The Origin and Significance of the Terms, Lay/Cleric, in the Early Christian Churches

The theme of the lay person in the Roman Catholic Church, as well as that of lay ministry in the church, has engendered an enormous amount of literature in the past fifty years. In this mass of material, there have been several points of departure. Within the Roman Catholic literature, in a special way, certain of these points of departure have been used with a frequent intensity. One's point of departure, in so many ways, determines the entire direction of a topic, and thus some care should be exerted both in the selection and in the explanation of one's point of departure. Often this can only be done in a comparative way, namely through a contrast with other points of departure.

In this present chapter and the two chapters following, I would like to study two of the more frequent Roman Catholic starting points, which in my judgment are theologically insufficient for our theme of the lay person in the church, and then present the point of departure which I believe is theologically more valid. I will use this point of departure throughout the remainder of this book, not only as a point of departure, but as a criterion for the ways in which various centuries of church life have developed a position, whether positive or negative, on the role of the lay person in the church.

This present chapter, which focuses basically on only one of these points of departure, is arranged as follows:

1. Three different points of departure for the study of the role of the lay person in the church

1. THREE DIFFERENT POINTS OF DEPARTURE FOR THE STUDY OF THE ROLE OF THE LAY PERSON IN THE CHURCH

The first point of departure, which many authors take, focuses on the first Christian usage of the terms *klerikos/laikos*. Although this point of departure involves highly technical analysis, it continues to appear in one way or another in many contemporary studies on the lay person in the church. It will be my thesis that the first Christian usages of *klerikos/laikos* do not offer a solid base for a theology of the lay person in the church or even lay ministry in the church. The terms *klerikos/laikos,* in earliest Christian literature, are most often used independently, i.e. they are not used in ways through which one clarifies the other. If all one had were the few instances of these terms in that early literature, one would have no clear understanding of the terms cleric and lay. Rather, only when the church leadership began to pattern its structures along the lines of the Graeco-Roman social and political *ordines* and coordinate both *klerikos* and *laikos* around the term *ordo* (*tyche*) did the interpretation of the terms *klerikos/laikos* assume an ecclesiastical status along the lines of later interpretation. In other words, the exploration should not center only on *klerikos/laikos,* but should also include the first Christian usage of *ordo* (*ordinatio, ordinare*). It seems to me that some of the conclusions which certain authors have derived from the study of only the two terms *klerikos/laikos* go far beyond the data. In fact, the conclusions are more dependent on the usage of *ordo* than on the usage of *klerikos/laikos.*

A second point of departure, which one finds among Roman Catholic authors, is the code of canon law. Since this code was revised in 1983, there has been a plethora of literature dealing with canonical issues. One of these issues is the role of the lay person in the church. The small section on canon law in this volume offers nothing new. Indeed, the chapter is more like an excursus than anything else. To make no mention of canon law, however, would be an oversight of no small measure; to restate a few basic issues seemed to be wise, since here and there one finds a tendency, among some Roman Catholic theologians and canonists, to make canon law normative for theology itself. Canon law, like all law, is meant to be normative, of course, but canon law cannot be seen as either a normative source of faith or as a normative source of theology. The opposite is true. Faith and theology are the normative sources for law. Whenever one makes law the origin of faith and theology, a total misreading and misuse of all three factors: faith, theology and law, take place. Given this *caveat,* one can reflect on the efforts of the revised code of canon law to incorporate the lay person into church life and structure, efforts which arise from the very aims of those canonists who revised the code, for they attempted to incorporate into the code both the basic and traditional tenets of Christian faith and the aspects of Christian theology which the documents of Vatican II highlighted. Nonetheless, it is quite possible to develop certain theological aspects on the role of the lay person in the church which go beyond the 1983 revised code of canon law. One can make such further steps, since, as we shall see, the very theology on which some of the canons relating to the laity are based is no more and no less than a "theology," not a dogma. In the field of theology, there are vast areas which can only be considered the views of certain theological schools or of certain theologians themselves. This holds true for biblical theology, systematic theology and moral theology. These areas have, in the past, been called by such names as: *certa in theologia, doctrina communis, doctrina communior,* etc. Whenever a canon is based on and reflects these areas of theological endeavor, then the canon is no more normative than the theology on which it is based. In virtue of this, canon law as such cannot be unconditionally presented as a theological point of departure for any theme, including a presentation on the lay person in the church, nor as a limit beyond which theological thinking cannot pass. We shall see that on the matter of the lay person in the church, many canons of the revised code are ambiguous, sometimes even deliberately so, precisely because the theology which underlies these canons is based on theological opinions, not on dogmatic positions of the Roman Catholic Church.

The third point of departure in current discussion on the lay person in the church is the study of scripture, particularly the New Testament, and in a special way the gospels. In contemporary Roman Catholic theology, greater emphasis has been given to the scriptures, greater than one finds, for instance, in counter-reformation theology or in the manual theology of the nineteenth and early twentieth centuries. It will be my contention that the better point of departure on the issue of the lay person in the church is the study of the scriptures, particularly the New Testament, on the topic of discipleship. Only on the basis of a solid scriptural understanding both of the *kerygma* and *didache* of Jesus, including the *kerygma* and *didache* of his very life, death and resurrection, and of the New Testament meaning of discipleship, can one understand the meaning of "hierarchy," "cleric," "lay," "ministry," "leadership," "priesthood of all believers," etc. When one begins with the study of early Christian usage of *klerikos/laikos,* or of *ordo,* or when one begins with the various canons on the lay person in the church, one is beginning *mediis in rebus.* There is a prior need to establish: (1) the christological basis of our Christian life, which is found in both what Jesus preached and the way in which he lived, died and rose; (2) the meaning of discipleship, which is based on the word of God, in particular the New Testament. These two foundational elements determine the very shape of ministry, whether it is clerical or lay. These two foundational elements determine the very structures of a church community. These two foundational elements determine the formulae of any Christian code of law. It will be the thesis of this entire book that only within a gospel theology of discipleship is it possible to develop the meaning of church and therefore the meaning of lay and cleric.

2. ETYMOLOGICAL ISSUES REGARDING THE TERMS: *KLEROS/LAIKOS*

Ever since 1953, when the Dominican Yves Congar published his book on the lay person in the church, *Jalons pour une théologie du laïcat,*[1] Catholic theologians have argued both for and against many of his positions on the role of the lay person in the church. Among the articles and studies which developed from this discussion, a number of them have dealt specifically with the first extant uses of the term *laikos* in early patristic literature, as also the connection which *laikos* has with the biblical term *laos* (people). These etymological studies, however, were only possible on the basis of a concomitant study, namely that of the twin term: *kleros,* cleric. The debate, of course, is still going on, but the material which has so far been developed helps us evaluate both the significance of the terms "lay/cleric," as these pertain to theology generally, and also the significance of the terms "lay/cleric," as these pertain to an ecclesiology which has been so dominant from the end of the third century A.D. to the present.

This etymological discussion of both *laikos* and *klerikos* has been one of the primary methodologies which Roman Catholic theologians especially, but some Protestant theologians as well, have currently used to focus on the issues of a lay/cleric church. There is, of course, a limited value to this methodology and to its conclusions, but since it has been fairly dominant in current theological literature and has been used to substantiate claims made for the very meaning of lay/cleric in the Christian church, it is necessary to spend not a little time on the issue. In this chapter we will consider the etymological issues first and then turn to the ecclesiological ramifications which these etymological considerations engender.

There are serious methodological problems which confront anyone who wishes to discuss the etymology and use of the terms lay/cleric in early Christian literature. These problems have both positive and negative implications: positive in the sense that the very study helps us to understand the meaning and scope of the "non-ordained" ministry in the church; negative in the sense that these very problems prevent us from understanding clearly the meaning and scope of the "non-ordained" ministry.

The negative implications are almost entirely involved with the non-scriptural use of the word *laikos* and with the quite limited scriptural use of the term *kleros*. Moreover, the New Testament does not use the terms: ordained, ordination, non-ordained at all. However, it would be wrong to surmise that the issues involved are merely semantic. Semantic issues are indeed present, but at a far deeper level there are issues of serious theological and historical implications which go far beyond any quibbling about particular words, their precise meaning, and their application. One must attempt to study the usage of these words in their philological and historical context and at the same time explore their theological and ecclesiological ramifications.

The primary reason why these particular words, *laikos, kleros,* ordained and non-ordained, present a negative methodological problem lies, as we have just mentioned, in the fact that *laikos* is not a scriptural term at all, and that *kleros,* which is used, but only in a briefest of ways, has a very limited meaning. Because of this, it becomes difficult to indicate those precise areas or those specific people or those precise functions in the scriptures to which this *later* ecclesiastical terminology of cleric/lay, ordained/non-ordained, might refer. The danger of *eisegesis,* i.e. reading into texts, is serious, and so, too, is the danger of interpreting the scriptural texts on the basis of pre-conceived and/or dogmatic ideas.

A. THE TERM: "KLEROS"

The use of the term *kleros,* in both the Old and the New Testaments, has been rather thoroughly reviewed.[2] In the Septuagint, *kleros* is used some one hundred and twenty-nine times; sixty-two times it translates the Hebrew word, *goral,* which is translated in English as "lot." *Goral* means both the stone dice and the portion or inheritance one obtains. In English as well, the word "lot" means both the dice which are cast, as in "throwing lots," and also the land, the acreage, the portion, the inheritance, and therefore the "lot," which one at times might receive by winning at the throw of dice. The Greek word *kleros* also means both dice and a space, such as a lot. A derivative word, *kleronomia,* or inheritance, indicates this verbal intertwining of both an apportionment through the throwing of dice and a resultant ownership or a claim to a place, a lot.[3] The *Book of Jubilees,* a pseudepigraphal work of post-exilic Judaism, describes how Noah apportioned the earth to his sons by the throwing of dice (8, 11ff; 10, 28, 31). In this process Canaan falls to Shem, not to Ham. Werner Foerster remarks: "The point of the story is obvious. It is designed to show that God has legitimately assigned Canaan to Israel, for God speaks through the lot."[4] Because of this idea, not because of the precise story in the *Book of Jubilees,* Israel is at times called "God's portion" in various Old Testament writings (Dt 9:29; Est 4:17h; also Dt 32:8ff).

Kleros in the Septuagint is used forty-nine times to translate the Hebrew word *nahala,* possession, property, inheritance (cf. Job 20:29; 27:13; 31:2; Ps 16:6). Eleven times *kleros* is used for words deriving from *yarash* (to inherit; to possess). The remaining few times, in which *kleros* is used in the LXX, it translates derivatives from the Hebrew words *pur, helaq, hebel* and *qurban.* Possession and inheritance dominate the meaning behind the usage of these terms. Casting lots was one way in which possession and inheritance were determined.

In post-exilic Judaism and in the New Testament this same dual meaning continued: the casting of lots on the one hand, and the apportioned lot or space on the other. More often than not, however, the apportioned "space" in the literature of post-exilic Judaism and in the New Testament refers to an eschatological "space" rather than an earthly space. It is the "lot" which one will have in the new Jerusalem, i.e., in the messianic times.

In the New Testament itself, we find *kleros* used for the throwing of dice on two occasions: in Mark 15:24 and par., and in Acts 1:26. Mark 15:24 reports: "Then they crucified him and shared out his clothing, casting lots [*kleron*] to decide what each should get."

In this verse of Mark, repeated almost verbatim by Matthew, Luke and John, the dice are thrown to decide who would receive the garments of Jesus.[5] It is obvious that the usage of *kleros* in this context (Mk, Mt, Lk, and Jn) has no reference to a ministry or to a category of special people within the Jewish community or the Christian church.

In the passage from Acts, however, the term *kleros* is used at least in the context in which an "ecclesial" function is described. In this section of Acts, the author presents by name each of the eleven who are gathered in the upper room. Mention is also made of the women gathered in that room with the eleven, and the author pointedly names Mary, the mother of Jesus, as one of these women. The author also states that Jesus' brothers were likewise present. E. Haenchen offers the following names of people as the more likely members of this unnamed group: Mary of Magdala, Joanna, the wife of Chuza, Susanna, and, on the basis of Luke 8, perhaps other women as well; among the men, Jesus' brothers, James, Joses, Judas and Simon (cf. Mt 6).[6] At this particular time, namely immediately after the resurrection of Jesus, one cannot call this group of people assembled in the upper room "church," since these disciples of Jesus still considered themselves to be a part of Israel, worshiping in the temple and proclaiming themselves in fact as the true Israel. At this particular time, these women and men, in their self-identity, were at best a sect within the larger Jewish community. It is precisely for this reason, i.e. their identity with Judaism, that one must be careful when speaking of "ministry" within the context of Acts 1:24–26. The Jewish religion of that precise period had its official ministers, and this group of Jewish disciples of Jesus is not portrayed as though it were setting up an alternative ministerial group to the official Jewish ministerial group. The people involved were not setting up a group of "priests" as an alternative to the Jewish high priest and his subservient priests. They were not establishing a new "clergy" which would function within the Jesus community in lieu of the duly appointed Jewish priesthood. Had they been doing this, they would not be subsequently portrayed as worshiping in the temple and in the synagogues. Rather, they would immediately be portrayed as a splinter-group, much like the Essenes, who had rebelled against the temple priests and had set up a counter-priesthood in their own enclaves. This small Jesus-community, gathered in the upper room, are not yet self-identified as a "Christian church," separate from Judaism. This stage comes many years later. As a result of this self-identity, one must be quite circumspect in attributing an intra-community "ministry" significance to the selection of a successor of Judas and, more broadly, to the significance of the twelve as such in this early stage of the Jesus-community.

This handful of disciples was, indeed, a small community. Nevertheless, as in every form of community, it had its own leadership. Mary, the mother of Jesus, had some sort of leadership role, undoubtedly as the most respected member of this group. Peter, for his part, is portrayed as a leader or spokesman. It is he who addresses the group of brothers (*adelphoi*), and in calling these people "brothers" he is speaking to all, not merely to the eleven.[7]

In his address, Peter, basing himself on scripture (Ps 69:25 and Ps 109:8), recalls that Judas, before he had betrayed Jesus, had been "numbered among us and had received the lot of this service" (*kai elachen ton kleron tes diakonias tautes*). Haenchen notes that throughout Acts, any community task, *Gemeindeamt*, from serving at the tables to the preaching of the apostles, can be called a ministry, *diakonia*, since all of this is service for God in the community. "The play on words between 'lot' [*kleros*] and 'service' [*diakonia*] belongs to the special rhetoric with which

Luke adorns the words of an apostle."[8] Luke emphasizes that service among the Christians comes from the Lord (God has assigned the lot) and it involves service rather than hegemony. During the lifetime of Jesus, Judas had received this lot or share of service.

Next, Peter recites a prayer to the Lord who is able to read everyone's heart, asking that the Lord indicate which of the two candidates, Barsabbas or Matthias, ought to be selected to receive the "place" (*topos*) of this ministry and apostolate [*labein ton topon tes diakonias tautes kai apostoles*]. It is interesting to note that in the Greek we find the term *topos* or place.[9] There is a place of ministry and of apostolate. In the same verse Peter continues on, saying that Judas had abandoned this place of ministry and apostolate, i.e. with the Lord Jesus, and went off into his own place (*topos*). This second use of *topos* or place helps to clarify the first use of *topos* or place. There is a place of ministry with Jesus, and there is one's own place. Outside of Acts and within early Christian literature, the interrelationship of these two words: *topos* and *kleros*, can be found, at least in a rudimentary way, in *I Clement* (40 and 44), in the letters of Ignatius of Antioch (*Smyrn.* 6, 1; and *Poly.* 1, 2), and in the letter of *Polycarp* (11, 1). In a much more determined way, however, we find this interrelationship in the *Apostolic Constitutions* of the fourth century (c. 1 and c. 23). The very word "place" [*topos*] and the spatial concept of "lot" in the sense of acreage [*kleros*] provide the linkage. Eventually, as in the *Apostolic Constitutions*, we have established positions [*topoi*], higher and lower, of honor, merit and authority, which become an integral part of the later clerical world. One cannot, of course, read these later developments into this section of Acts.

They then cast lots (*kai edoken klerous autois*) and the lots fell in Matthias' favor (*kai epesen ho kleros epi Matthian*). Neither the first nor the second usage of *kleros* in this verse refers to a specific minister or to a specific ministry; the two occasions in which this term *kleros* is used apply to a *procedure*, which was rather commonly used in Judaism, as also in the Greek world generally, in order to settle an issue.[10] *Kleros* in this verse means the throwing of dice; it has no connection with "cleric" or "clergy," nor does it even indicate a clerical activity in contrast to a "lay" activity. On the basis of this text one could not say that Matthias is assumed into the "clergy." Much less can one say that by the throwing of the dice we have a ritual of ordination!

The closest Acts 1:26 comes to a connection of ministry and *kleros* is the phrase: "the lot of this service." We see that this means "the place (*topos*) of service." It is the Greek word *diakonia*, however, not *topos* and not *kleros*, which refers to ministry. The word *kleros* focuses on the place, i.e. a place with Jesus, and, as used subsequently, on the procedure for assigning one to this place. Matthias takes his place with the eleven, thus becoming one of the "twelve."

Some nuancing of "twelve" and "apostle" is, however, necessary. The "twelve" and the "apostles" in the New Testament, according to the best scriptural studies, are not coextensive, for there are more New Testament apostles than simply twelve. Consequently, the task or role of the twelve is not coextensive or identical to the role and task of the apostles. The Christian churches, and the Roman Catholic Church in particular, have emphasized this distinction between the twelve and the apostles, for many Christian leaders and theologians over the centuries have said again and again that the college of bishops (*episkopoi*) succeeds to the college of the apostles. *Episkopoi* do not succeed to the twelve. Were one to argue that in Acts 1:26 we have a New Testament statement establishing a "clergy," then one must immediately add that with the death of the last of the "twelve" this "clergy" also perished, for there is no continuation beyond this indication in Acts of the early Christian community continuing a group of "twelve." However, Acts 1:26 does not call the eleven nor the assigned Matthias "clergy." None of these is called *kleros.* This passage of Acts simply states that the twelve had been given an assignment, a lot, of service (*diakonia*) with Jesus.

In Acts 8:21 *kleros* is used once again. Peter rebukes Simon the magician who wanted to buy Peter's miraculous powers. Peter says to Simon:

> May your silver be lost forever and you with it, for thinking that money could buy what God has given for nothing! You have no share (*meris*), no inheritance (*kleros*), in this word.

The juxtaposition of share (*meris*) and inheritance (*kleros*) appears off and on in both biblical and later Christian literature, so that the meaning of one term clarifies the other term (cf. Is 17:14; 57:6; Jer 13:25). *Kleros* in this context of Acts clearly refers to the eschatological inheritance. It has no connection at all with either a minister or a ministry.

In Acts 26:18, *kleros* is again used. In this context, Paul is presenting the account of his conversion before King Agrippa. In recounting this experience, Paul says that he had asked: "Who are you, Lord?" and the Lord had answered, "I am Jesus, and you are persecuting me." Jesus, in this version, continues on, telling Paul that he has been chosen to bring the gospel to the non-Jews so that they might "receive, through faith in me [Jesus], forgiveness of their sins and a share in the saints [*kai kleron en tois hagiasmenois*]." *Kleros* here is translated as "share," corresponding to the meaning of both the Hebrew (*goral*) and the Greek as portion, inheritance, and therefore share. In the later books of the Old Testament, *kleros* is used for the "lot" of the individual (cf. Prv 1:14; Wis 2:9; 5:5; Sir 25:19). As we noted above, Foerster indicated that in both post-exilic Judaism and in the New Testament, *kleros* most often had an eschatological meaning. The meaning of *kleros* in this passage of Acts is clearly eschatological: one's lot in the messianic kingdom. The passage in Acts has no reference either to a minister or to a ministry in the incipient Jesus community.

One can conclude, then, that in Acts the term *kleros* never indicates either a minister or a ministry. Rather it is:

(a) an *act* or procedure for determining a choice;
(b) a *place* within the following of Jesus rather than in the following of one's own desires;
(c) a *place* with the saints in the eschatological kingdom.

In Colossians 1:12 the term *kleros* is found again: "thanking the Father who has enabled you to have a share [*meris*] in the lot [*kleros*] of the saints in the light." In this passage, which again is eschatological in intent, we find conjoined the two Greek words *meris* and *kleros,* a share and a portion, and these two words mutually interpret one another. In this text the recipients of the *kleros* cannot be seen as a specified or officially deputed group, e.g. a ministerial group, a "clergy," but rather the recipients are all those who have come to believe in Jesus, whether in a leadership role or not.

In this eschatological meaning of *kleros,* which one finds in the New Testament writings, the term is never restricted to a "ministerial few," a "clergy." Actually, one might say, though anachronistically, that in this eschatological sense, as used in Colossians, all the persevering followers of Jesus are "clerics," i.e. all have been chosen and set apart, all share in the *kleros* of the end-time.

In 1 Peter 5:3 this same eschatological use of *kleros* appears once more. The presbyters (*presbyteroi*) are told not to be dictators over those chosen (*med' hos katakurieuontes ton kleron*). The meaning of the term *kleros* here is evident: those who have been called, i.e. those who have been selected for the eschatological kingdom. This is confirmed by the very next phrase: "but be examples for the flock" (*tupoi ginomenoi tou poimniou*). The "flock" and the "called" are parallel. In this letter of Peter, the Jesus community has indeed reached a stage of incipient self-identity apart from Judaism, and in this community there are leaders or ministers of the community. It is nonetheless interesting to see that the term *kleros* in 1 Peter is applied not to the leaders or the ministers, but to the larger community, whereas in subsequent centuries the term *kleros* will apply only to the leadership, never to the larger community.

The New Testament offers us no other use of the term *kleros*. In all of these New Testament passages, *kleros* is never used for either a minister or a ministry. Only with the *Apostolic Tradition* of Hippolytus (c. 215) do we have the first instance in early Christian literature of the use of the term *kleros* for a clearly defined circle of officially positioned ecclesiastical ministers.[11] W. Nauck, on the basis of his research, states: "We have to surmise that the beginnings of the ecclesiastical 'kleros-notion' goes back to the period at the end of the second century."[12] The beginning of the ecclesiastical "kleros-notion" does not go back to the New Testament.

This material on the use of the term *kleros* and its cognates as also its use in the translation of the various Hebrew terms in the Septuagint has been fairly well established. The development of this term, which was never used for an office or ministry in either the Old or the New Testament, nor in the sub-apostolic church writings, has been traced with a strong degree of historical certainty. Moreover, since the word *kleros* is not used at all for a "clerical group of Christian ministers" in early patristic literature up to the time of Hippolytus (215), one can only say that such a term became the referent to a church ministry sometime about a century and a half after the resurrection of Jesus. However, when one goes from a later period, in which the term *kleros* meant a defined group of church ministers, back to the New Testament, problems, both methodological and theological, arise.

In the book *Priesthood* I presented a listing of New Testament titles for ministers, together with the specific passages of the New Testament writings in which such titles or names appeared.[13] The listing included the following:

The Twelve	Overseer	Episkopos
Apostle	Leitourgos	Presbyteros
Prophet	Neoteros	Evangelist
Teacher	Shepherd	Preacher
Deacon	Father	Servant

If one approaches the New Testament writings, and these ministries in particular, with the question: Who are the "clerics" among these New Testament ministers? what answer can be expected? Several answers are possible:

1. **POSITION NO. ONE:**
   The above-mentioned ministers are all clerics. If so, then are they not all clerics *by divine right*, since the scriptures mention them specifically? However, were this the case, should not all Christians

who are engaged in any of the above ministries be considered clerics, e.g. the teachers are clerics, the prophets are clerics, etc.?

2. **POSITION NO. TWO:**

   Or perhaps one could say that none of them are clerics. If so, are they all "lay" people? If this were so, would they not all be lay people *by divine right,* since these are all mentioned in scripture? Should not such Christians who today are engaged in the ministries mentioned above be considered "lay"? If so, would we then have "lay" bishops, "lay" presbyters, and "lay" deacons, etc.?

3. **POSITION NO. THREE:**

   Neither of the two approaches mentioned above has ever been approved or defended in an official way by church leadership or church theologians. More often than not, a selective process takes over, i.e. from the list given above certain of the ministries are called "clerical" (e.g. episkopos, presbyter, deacon, etc.), while others in the above ministries are called "lay" (e.g. teacher, liturgist). In making such a distinction, however, some new criterion has had to be introduced in order to determine which of the above should be considered "cleric" and which should be considered "lay." The addition of a new criterion only further complicates the matter, both methodologically and theologically.

This new criterion deserves special attention, since it is a criterion which is not intrinsically connected with the terms *laikos* and *kleros.* We might, however, gain a better grasp of the significance of this "new criterion," once we have considered the correlative of *kleros,* namely, *laikos,* and have attempted to find some reference for *laikos* to the New Testament.

B. THE TERM: "LAIKOS"

When one takes up the theme of the term *laikos,* "lay," in reference to scripture, the major difficulty is crystal-clear: the scriptures, both Old and New, never use the term *laikos.* "Lay" and "laity," in the sense of the non-cleric, is a later idea and cannot be superimposed on scriptural texts. The current investigation of the origin of *laikos* in Christian literature has been discussed and debated far more extensively in Roman Catholic theology than in Protestant theology. In a number of Roman Catholic writings of the nineteenth and early twentieth centuries, the very term "lay" connoted anti-clericalism, rejection of the Catholic Church, a prolongation of the secularistic ideas which church leadership associated with the French Revolution.[14] As such, nineteenth and early twentieth century Roman Catholic discussion of the term "lay" tended to be negative and critical.

Against this rather negative and hostile background, Y. Congar's study on the role of the lay person in the church, *Jalons pour une théologie du laïcat,* could certainly appear to many Roman Catholics, at least at first blush, as quite controversial.[15] Congar's positive evaluation of the laity was based on the association of the Christian usage of *laikos* with the Old Testament notion of *laos,* the people.

> Our word, laic, then, is connected to the word, which in the Jewish language and later in the Christian language, specifically designated the consecrated people, in opposition to the profane people: a nuance which has been present in the meaning, at least when it has been used in Greek, during the first four centuries, and even beyond.[16]

I. de la Potterie, in 1958, took issue with Congar's approach, gathering together further refinements on the origin of the term *laikos* in early Christian literature.[17] J.B. Bauer, in the succeeding year, published an article, "Die Wortgeschichte von 'Laicus.' "[18] In Bauer's article, which basically concurs with de la Potterie, some additional, early material on the use of *laikos* was presented. De la Potterie, in a later article, agreed with the nuances Bauer made.[19] F. Wulf contributed a short article to this discussion,[20] and A. Barruffo added another brief comment.[21] These articles were then followed by M. Jourjon's "Les premiers emplois du mot laïc dans la littérature patristique" in 1963.[22] All of these articles tended to reinforce de la Potterie's argument to some degree and raise questions about Congar's position. In 1973 J. Hervada published a lengthy study, *La definición nominal del laico.*[23] In 1977 the essays of L. Pizzolato and G. Picasso appeared in the volume *Laicità: problemi e prosepettive,* which further nuanced the early Christian usage and meaning of this term.[24] Pizzolato notes that "laicità e laicato" are fundamental positions of the Christian message, but historically the coordinating of "lay" and "priest" remains difficult. Nonetheless, Pizzolato maintains that the Christian meaning of *laikos* cannot be based on the Judaeo-Christian usage of *laos* [people]. In this he continues the thesis of de la Potterie. Since Pizzolato's essay covers the earliest usage of *laikos* in Christian writings down to the beginnings of the Carolingian period, many of his suggestions will be taken up again in the section of this book which deals with the patristic period. G. Picasso's article focuses almost exclusively on the middle ages.[25]

G. Wingren addressed the same questions in "Der Begriff 'Laie' " in 1982.[26] G. Magnani in his article "Does the So-Called Theology of the Laity Possess a Theological Status?" has continued the debate with Congar as regards the origin and meaning of the term *laikos* in early Christian literature.[27] For Magnani, the theological meaning of the term *laikos* cannot be seen in its derivation from *laos*. This kind of argument, he says, is the "so-called theology of the laity." Rather, he argues, *laikos,* as used in the primitive Christian world, is one of categorization and of contrast, not one of derivation and exemplification. "The theological content [of *laikos*] remains indirect, as we said above, and is dominated by the prevalent semantic usage expressing contrast."[28] From another point of view, A. Faivre, in *Les laïcs aux origines de l'Église,* has reviewed the material on the origins of the term *laikos* and its usage in early Christian literature only to come up with conclusions quite different than those of de la Potterie and Magnani.[29] He argues primarily from the first appearance of this term, as one finds it in the *Letter of Clement* to the church of Corinth, and concludes his presentation by stating that "the lay Christian is, then, at the time of Clement, only a mirage, a literary fiction."[30] In other words, one cannot really speak about "laikos" in the Christian church, Faivre argues, until the third century, when the term *kleros* begins to be used rather frequently. It is this usage of *kleros* which gives rise to the concomitant Christian use of *laikos.* It is only at this particular period of time that one can speak meaningfully of *laikos* as found in Christian documents as a term of contrast and category (de la Potterie). Finally, Juan Chapa, in 1987, at the eighth international theological symposium at the University of Navarra, Spain, presented both a lengthy review of the debate and his own suggestions for it.[31]

As one can see there has been no little discussion on this issue of the etymological origin of *laikos* and its first appearance in Christian literature by Catholic authors. Indeed, in recent times the term *laikos* has been far more frequently submitted to scholarly study than the polar term *klerikos.* We will return to the theological ramifications of this debate when we deal with the *Letter of Clement,* which is the first time that the term *laikos* appears in both biblical and Christian literature. At this juncture of our presentation, it is simply necessary to realize that from a methodological and terminological framework the term *laikos,* as regards both its origin and its meaning within the Christian tradition, is still highly debated. All authors are well aware, however, and are in full agreement that the word *laikos* does not appear in either the Old or New Testament. They disagree, however, on two major issues: first, the way in which the later ecclesiastical term *laikos* relates to the scriptural material, and, second, on the significance which some of these later appearances of the term *laikos* might carry. The disagreement over the significance and interpretation of these patristic texts is important, since the various authors depend on the interpretations to substantiate their positions. In both of these areas, however, we are dealing with interpretation and with judgment, and consequently with areas which are perhaps not unquestionably established.

Let us consider for a moment the usage of the term *laos* (people). Without any doubt the noun *laos* is a major term in the scriptures. The research of H. Strathmann and R. Meyer presents a compact overview of the term *laos* both in the Greek and the Jewish world up to the time of Jesus.[32] In this literature one finds that *laos* has several layers of meanings:

(a) a crowd, a population, a people;
(b) a nation (*ethne*);
(c) Israel as a nation;
(d) the Jesus community itself which is called at times a new people, *laos kainos.*

This last understanding (d) is evident particularly in the early patristic period, with Justin (*Apologia,* 1, 67, 5) and Clement of Alexandria (*Strom.* VI, 5, 42, 2). The new people gathered in worship was also seen as *laos.* It is precisely in this latter context of the gathered worshiping community that we begin to see a use of *laos* for those other than the leaders of the worshiping community. In Justin's *Apology,* we see that it is the people, *laos,* who say "Amen" to the prayer of the leader. A similar use is found in Clement of Alexandria, *Strom.* I, 1, 5. 1. Strathmann notes: "It [this use of *laos* for the worshiping community] is an adaptation of popular use to the specific relationships of the congregation, and the idea of the 'laity' developed from it later."[33] In other words, in the later Christian community the assembly of disciples began to be called *laos,* and it is from this later nomenclature for the worshiping community that the distinction in the Christian community between the people and the leadership (laity and clergy) began to arise. The specific distinction of lay-cleric originates, therefore, in a post-apostolic church, not in the New Testament itself. The specific distinction also originates on the basis of a pastoral situation (i.e. liturgical celebration) and not on the basis of any formalized dogmatic stance. The dogmatic or theological rationalization is given to this specific distinction of laity and clergy in a post-200 A.D. church.

One must also turn to non-canonical literature to find the usage and the meaning of the term *laikos* in the early centuries. The work of F. Preisigke on various papyri has been valuable.[34] In these Greek papyri, dating from the Ptolomaic period, i.e. the third century B.C., *laos* is used in administrative kinds of documents to describe, first of all, the Egyptian people, the natives, as opposed to those who are immigrants, aliens, slaves, and strangers. Secondly, as Nephtali Lewis has pointed out, the Egyptians had quite early in their history developed a sacerdotal class or caste, in contrast to the peasants, the artisans, the minor land-owners, the merchants. Most of these latter were poor, although a small few of them were, indeed, rich.[35] In the papyri of that time, the non-sacerdotal Egyptians themselves were called *laos*. The adjective *laikos* shares in this dual meaning. It is used for the native Egyptian people in general, in contrast to the sacerdotal authorities. In his dictionary on Greek papyri, Preisigke writes: "*Laikos,* pertaining to Egyptian civilians (in contrast to royal officials, liege lords, royal farm lords, etc.)."[36] Note should be made of the phrase "pertaining to *Egyptian civilians.*" This is set first, and it is a key detail, for the aliens, the immigrants, the strangers in Egypt at that time were also under the royal officials, etc., but they were not part of the *laos,* and therefore could not be described as *laikoi.* Some authors from de la Potterie down to Chapa tend to stress the second phrase, namely, "in contrast to" of Preisigke's description, but the more basic meaning of *laikos* is that one belongs to the *laos,* i.e. one is an Egyptian civilian, an Egyptian native. One is not a foreigner, an alien, an immigrant. Those who were foreigners in Egypt, such as the Jews under Sethos I and Ramesses II, would not have been called *laikoi.* Rather, since one belongs to the *laos* (in this instance the Egyptians), one can be called *laikos.* This "belonging to" aspect of *laikos* is more fundamental, and as such this usage strengthens Congar's view that *laikos* must be understood, in its primary stratum, on the basis of *laos.* This is quite different from de la Potterie's position, namely: because one is subservient to a leadership, therefore one is called *laikos.* Within the Egyptian people, *laos,* there were indeed leaders. However, it is only at this secondary stratum that one can speak of subservient and authoritative categories: the *laikoi* and the *hegoumenoi.* This notion of being a "people," in contrast to other tribes, groups, clans, etc., who are called: strangers, non-people, is replicated in many cultures. It is even found in Old Testament passages as well, in which the Gentiles are considered: "not Yahweh's people."[37] The study of Egyptian papyri by Preisigke helps us see, at best, the way in which the term *laikos* was used in the Greek-speaking Egyptian world of the early centuries. As such, it serves only as an oblique testimonial on the eventual Christian meaning and usage of the term.[38] It would be difficult, if not impossible, to trace historically the relationship between the use of *laikos* in these papyri and the use of *laikos* in early patristic literature.

Still another source of knowledge are three Greek translations of the Old Testament which were made by Jews in the second century A.D., namely, those of Aquila, Symmachus and Theodotion.[39] Theodotion, it should be pointed out, is actually not a totally new Greek translation, but rather a revision of the work of Aquila and to some degree that of Symmachus. When these three Greek translations are compared with the Greek of the Septuagint, the use of various words and phrases are quite helpful. Scholars point out that these three second-century Greek translations do use the term *laikos,* but only in three Old Testament passages:

OT PASSAGE	USE OF LAIKOS IN
1 Sam. 21:5;	Aquila, Symmachus, Theodotion
cf. 1 Sam 21:6	Symmachus
Ez. 48:15	Symmachus, Theodotion
Ez. 22:16	Theodotion

1. In 1 Samuel 21:5 we read:

I have no ordinary bread (LXX: *artoi bebeloi*); there is only holy bread (LXX: *artoi hagioi*).

In this passage the ordinary and the blessed bread are contrasted. In v. 5 the three authors mentioned above use the word *laikos* instead of *bebelos,* which is found in the LXX. In v. 6 David assures the priest that he is on an ordinary trip (LXX: *odos bebelos*), which Symmachus alone translates with *odos laike,* i.e. the rules against sexual intercourse do not apply. Because these rules do not apply to David and his followers, eating of the holy bread would not constitute a legal or ceremonial disobedience to the prescribed ceremonial laws. The connection of *laikos* to *bebelos* indicates that in Greek usage of the second century A.D. the two words meant common, ordinary, not blessed. However, one must also take into account that for the Jewish people, particularly those who were quite religious, there really was no profane or unblessed area. There was a religious quality about every facet of life. In other words, the ordinary bread has its own holiness, and the specially blessed bread for temple use has its own holiness as well. The reading of Jewish meal prayers, the *Berekah,* clearly indicates this holiness of the ordinary bread. At table fellowship, ordinary bread is blessed, indicating a holiness which the ordinary bread indeed has. It would be misleading to think that "ordinary" and "holy" are totally opposed. If they were so opposed, why would one bless God for the gift of ordinary bread? Rather one blesses God for the gift of ordinary bread precisely because it is, in its ordinariness, a gift of God and therefore it has a distinctive holiness about it.

2. In Ezekiel 48:15 we read:

> As regards the remainder, an area of five thousand cubits by twenty-five thousand, this is to be for the common use of the city, for houses and pastures.

In the LXX the Greek word for "common" is *proteichisma,* which Symmachus and Theodotion translate as *laikos.* Aquila translates it as *bebelos.* The meaning appears to be "profane." Nonetheless, care must be taken to see that "profane" in this context is not totally opposed to "sacred." As Tkacik notes: "The profane land of v. 15 simply means land put to ordinary use, as distinct from land used exclusively for worship of Yahweh. The whole land is sacred because it is Yahweh's land and he is in its midst; at the same time, it is totally separated from the sanctuary by the land of the priests."[40] It might be noted that although this part of the book of Ezekiel is generally considered to be the work of an alien author, not that of the prophet Ezekiel, the view that there is a holiness about everything is clearly part of the theology which Ezekiel himself maintains.

3. In Ezekiel 22:26 we read:

> They have drawn no distinction between sacred and profane.

The LXX reads *ana meson hagiou kai bebelou* (distinction between sacred and profane). Theodotion, and only he, uses the term *laikos* instead of *bebelos.* Tkacik notes: " 'Sacred' (Hebr *qodesh*) is that which belongs in a positive way to God and partakes of his holiness. 'Profane' (Hebr *hol*) is the opposite of sacred, because of its association with man; it is 'common,' i.e., at man's disposal. Sometimes God and man are both involved in certain affairs. To put at man's disposal for furthering his affairs, that which pertains to God, is to profane it."[41] *Laikos* would mean, then, what is common to both the divine and the human. Its opposite is that which belongs to God alone. In both situations, it should be noted, God is involved, and because God is involved, there is a holiness to both situations. In the Jewish mind, therefore, one cannot say that "bebelos," "laikos" and "proteichisma" are purely secular terms, i.e. terms which do not involve holiness. This modern view of the sacred and the lay does not correspond to the theological insights of these Old Testament passages. As a result, a totally secular interpretation of *laikos* cannot be justified.

The influence of these translations on early patristic writers is quite scattered and not very extensive. Origen uses all three in his *Hexapla,* and Jerome apparently consulted the lone manuscript of this document by Origen, which was kept in the library at Caesarea. Origen likewise uses the text of Theodotion as regards the pericope of Susanna in his letter to Julius Africanus. Hippolytus, for his part, uses Theodotion's Greek version of Daniel in his own *Commentary on Daniel.* John Chrysostom in his *Homilies on the Psalms* uses, at times, the translations of Aquila, of Symmachus and of Theodotion. Beyond these few references, which really do not directly focus in any way on the use of *laikos,* the influence of these three Jewish translations is rather thin among patristic writers. At best we have an oblique testimonial of the way in which some Jewish authors used, though sparingly, the term *laikos,* and the way in which some Christian writers of the early patristic period also used the term *laikos,* in dependence on these three Jewish authors: Origen, namely, in the *Hexapla* and Jerome, whose Latin translation of the Old Testament uses the Latin term *laicus* in places that these three translators used the Greek *laikos.*

Outside of these few Old Testament passages in which the Greek translation, made in early Christian times, uses the term *laikos,* there is no further biblical data on this term. We have already considered the term *klerikos,* and the end result, from a biblical standpoint, is one of thin data, beyond which any deduction is at most hypothetical.[42] Actually, if all we had as our workable data were the few instances of *klerikos/laikos* from the first two centuries, few deductions could be made. The real hermeneutical key is not found in either of those two terms, but rather in the term *ordo* and its hermeneutical influence on *klerikos/laikos.*

C. THE TERMS: ORDO/ORDAINED/NON-ORDAINED

One of the major ways by which some theologians confront the New Testament statements on ministry involves the understanding of ordination. These writers have almost a presupposition that there are some ministers, mentioned in the various New Testament texts, who are ordained, while all other ministers are non-ordained.[43] From the biblical data alone, such a position is difficult, if not impossible, to maintain. The various New Testament texts, which have, here and there, been adduced for possible instances of ordination, are listed in the book *Priesthood.* It is not necessary to repeat this analysis here.[44] However, it should be restated that there is no passage in the entire New Testament which authors advance as an instance of ordination which is not disputed by biblical scholars of solid repute. Moreover, there are in the New Testament major silences on the issue of ordination, for example:

a. Nowhere are the twelve ordained.
b. Nowhere are the apostles ordained.
c. Nowhere are the apostles or the twelve described as ordaining.
d. Nowhere is there a command of Jesus to ordain.
e. Nowhere are *episkopoi* ordained.
f. Nowhere are *episkopoi* described as ordaining.

It may sound strange to our contemporary ears, but could one not say on the basis of New Testament data that the twelve were unordained, that the apostles were unordained, that *episkopoi* were unordained, etc.? To presuppose that the twelve, the apostles, the *episkopoi* or even others *had to be ordained* is a dogmatic presupposition, which neither historical data nor scriptural data support. To maintain an ordination of the twelve, the apostles, the *episkopoi*, etc., is possible only on the basis of a presupposed dogmatic stance, a stance which a later theology would find ordinary, but which a scriptural theology would find alien. One cannot even maintain in an undisputed way that the twelve and the apostles are coterminous, nor that either the apostles or the twelve were *episkopoi*.

What has happened over the centuries—and happened step by step and not all at once—is that a structural and subsequently a theological view has been developed, ontologizing the issue of ordination, so that one is apparently unable to think of the twelve, the apostles or *episkopoi* except in the terminology of ordination. This kind of later theologizing is then applied to the very beginning of the Jesus community. This latter step is, of course, *eisegesis.*

Ordination as such makes sense only if there is an *ordo* into which one is ordained. An understanding of *ordo* precedes either an understanding or ritualization of ordination. Because there are orders in the church, there are ordination rituals. The opposite makes no sense: because there are ordinations in the church, there are orders in the church. In the historical part of this study, we will see how the church society of the third century began to imitate the socio-political society of the Graeco-Roman world. In the Graeco-Roman world there were established *ordines:* the order of senators, *ordo senatorius;* the order of decurions, *ordo decurionum;* the order of knights, *ordo equester.* These various orders in the socio-political world of the Graeco-Roman times had deep roots in the histories of those peoples. The people in these orders were highly respected, and the orders themselves were considered, in many ways, sacrosanct. As the Christian church began structuring itself, it modeled itself on this "ordered" society. The very term *ordo* was gradually used in ecclesiastical literature, and there arose an order of episkopoi, an order of presbyters, and an order of deacons. Here and there we also find an order of people, but this last designation never took hold. Nor did the idea of an *ordo plebeius* become popular in the socio-political world. A distinction was generally made between those in an *ordo* and the remainder of the populace. In the Graeco-Roman world, one found and still finds the SPQR, *senatus populusque romanus:* the senate and the people. Only here and there in Latin literature does one find that the *populus romanus* were called an *ordo*. More often, one finds that there was the socio-political order, e.g. the senate, and the people.[45] This, too, became the model for the structuring of the Christian churches. The orders were distinguished from the *populus*. One became a member of the Christian orders, not by birth or by imperial decree, but by an ordination. Those not in these ecclesiastical orders were called the people.[46]

Once this "ordering" of the Christian structure began, it is easy to see the next step. Those in the various ecclesiastical orders were the *kleros,* and those not in such ecclesiastical orders were the *laikoi*. The real distinguishing mark to distinguish *klerikoi* from *laikoi* developed because of the insertion of *ordo* into church structures. The meaning and use of *klerikoi/laikoi* did not give rise to *ordines;* rather, the incorporation of *ordines* into the church structures gave rise to the meaning and subsequent usage of *klerikoi/laikoi*. *Ordo* became the hermeneutic through which *klerikoi/laikoi* received their ecclesiastical meaning.

The structuring of the churches along the lines of *ordines* gave rise, in turn, to the theologizing of these various *ordines*. This theology developed slowly, and, as we shall see below, received enormous impetus from two sources: (a) the theological description of the Christian priest on the basis of the Old Testament priest; (b) the description of divine order, both in creation and redemption, portrayed by Gregory the Great and Dionysius the Areopagite. Still, we must realize that we do not find the term "order" as a description of Christian ministry in the New Testament, nor do we find this term "order" in the apostolic fathers as a description of Christian ministry. In both sources we find ministry and leadership, and in this sense alone could one speak of an "order." However, since the term "order" has both in the Graeco-Roman culture of the early centuries of this millennium and in later church history generally taken on so many nuances and meanings, one must also say that the ordering found, either in the New Testament or in the apostolic fathers, does not totally correspond to the nuances and meanings which the term *ordo* has gained in later Christian life. As one moves into the late second and early third centuries, with such writers as Origen, Tertullian, Cyprian, and Hippolytus, the theologizing of church orders moves steadily into those hierarchical interpretations of church order, which became co-terminous with so many Christian churches. The theological validation for this hierarchical interpretation of such *ordines* was not based on the New Testament data, but rather on the Levitical priesthood or the priesthood of Aaron in the Old Testament and on the socio-political structures of the Graeco-Roman world. The bases for this theology of order are not endemic to the message of Jesus. Oddly enough, the bases for this theology are found in the very areas which New Testament documents had repudiated. In the letter to the Hebrews, the priesthood of Jesus is not in line with the Levitical or Aaronic priesthood. The priesthood of Jesus, like that of Melchizedek, is a unique priesthood, and so unique and so overpowering that the Jewish Levitical priesthood has been invalidated. Nonetheless, it was precisely this invalidated Levitical priesthood which served Christian authors in the late second and subsequent centuries with their attempts to theologize sacred orders within the priestly people of Jesus. *Ordo* gave rise to ordination, and once ordination became standard, the Christian interpretation of *klerikoi/laikoi* became somewhat fixed.

T. O'Meara notes that a "theology of orders begins with its underlying reality as Church service as well as with its development in the Roman and medieval worlds."[47] That there is ministry and leadership in the New Testament portrayal of the Jesus community is a given. The Jesus community did not start off as a totally egalitarian and democratic group. O'Meara takes to task such authors as Harnack and H.G. von Campenhausen, who urged that there was a "devolution from a golden age of democratic equality" to an explicitness of structure. "Organic structure," O'Meara reminds us," is a condition of life; we would expect it in the Church." What O'Meara finds puzzling is not a growth in development of church structures in the early church, but rather "the marked decline of diversity and broad ministerial involvement within the churches."[48]

> The reduction of church life during the second and third centuries—necessary perhaps at that time of expansion—prepared for the unfortunate separation of the christian community into a large, passive laity directed in word and sacrament by a very small separate group, who alone were publicly constituted in fulltime service, i.e., ordained.[49]

Harnack and von Campenhausen might be cited as proponents of an exaggerated development in the church from an early democracy to a later aristocracy, a development which in these authors' minds was a sort of "devolution." T. O'Meara, for his part, uses different descriptive terms;

he speaks of an "unfortunate separation," a "reduction," a "severe delineation" between *klerikoi/laikoi,* and an ordained diversity which became "fixed, sparse and prominent." In many ways, this kind of descriptive terminology, however, indicates some form of "devolution," so that O'Meara's language, although less harsh, refers to the same kind of process, which both Harnack and von Campenhausen described as a "devolution." O'Meara suggests that this ministerial delineation and reduction of ministry in the churches of the third and fourth centuries was influenced by "a general social move towards organization stimulated by the reforms of Trajan in the second century," and also that the "Constantinian appropriation of the higher clergy intensified this development." The very language which O'Meara uses, and his analysis of the historical data, indicate that the adoption, usage and interpretation of *ordo* with the Christian churches had deep roots in the Graeco-Roman world of that early period, and that the interpretation of such terms as *ordo, ordinare,* etc. was far more influenced by the Graeco-Roman world than by the New Testament writings themselves.

> The church could not help but be modified in its self-understanding by the powerful and useful thought-forms and political institutions of the Roman world bestowing fixed positions and subordinate arrangement. This Roman, social appropriation of order into church polity was intensified by the influence of Pseudo-Dionysius in the Middle Ages. There a neo-platonic canonization of a taxonomy of higher and lower orders took place.[50]

Actually, it is only with Hippolytus' *Apostolic Tradition* that we have the first extant and clear indication of ordination in the Christian community. This occurs at the end of the second century and the beginning of the third century. Dupuy's comment on this situation is very apropos: "How someone in the early church is called to ecclesial ministry is not described in the New Testament, so that theories relative to ordination have in part a hypothetical quality about them."[51] The dogmatic presupposition on ordination which has almost created an ontological situation for the ordained is clearly one of those "theories" which has in part a hypothetical quality about it.

The terms *ordo* and *taxis* are not the problematic issues. The use of such terms could easily be considered acceptable. That there should be some sort of order and arrangement within a society such as the Christian community cannot be faulted. The terms themselves are not the problem, even though the terms are not biblical. Rather, it is the interpretation that was given to these terms which brought on the problem. The orders in the Christian community were given a "status" similar to those in the socio-political world of that time. They became Christian "castes." This was problematic enough, but very quickly a new hermeneutical aspect emerged, namely, the perception that the "orders" within the Christian community reflected the orders within creation itself and originated from the very orderliness of God's nature. The next step, namely the ontologizing of these Christian orders, followed quickly on the heels of this creational theologizing of *ordo.* When one begins to hear that there is an "ontological" difference between the ordinary Christian and those who were *in ordines,* one has moved in directions which far surpass the grid of discipleship as found in the New Testament.

The terms *ordinatio* and *cheirothesia,* taken as terms, are by no means problematic. Since the ministers of the Christian community were *personae publicae in ecclesia,* some perceptible and ritualized installation process has its rightful place. Such a ritualization is both the public acknowledgement of such ministerial leadership and the celebration by the community that God has given such a grace to a particular community. Ordination is one way to acknowledge in a communal and public way what the Lord has done for his church. Ordination is a sort of publicly celebrated ritual of discernment. None of this, so far, causes much concern. The concern arises when the ordination ritual is interpreted to mean:

a. a conferment of sacred power,
b. based on a conferment of an ontological repositioning.

Both of these factors have contributed to the problematic issues of ordination; one without the other tends to be meaningless. Together, the notions of sacred power and ontological change have created the almost unsolvable problems of *klerikos/laikos.*

We will probe this issue of *ordo* (*ordinatio, taxis, cheirothesia*) more at length in the historical part of this volume, namely, in the patristic period around the time of Tertullian. The focus of the issues, which are indicated here, simply intend to move the field of discourse away from the important but still ineffectual discussion on *klerikos/laikos,* a discussion which remains barren unless the issues of *ordo* are included in the field of discourse.

If one cannot find in the New Testament writings clear and indisputable instances of ordination, then it is equally difficult to speak clearly and indisputably about the "non-ordained" in the New Testament. One cannot search through the various New Testament writings on the issue of ministry and indicate that some ministries were taken care of by "ordained" people, while other ministries were provided for by "non-ordained" people. The very questions "Who in the New Testament are ordained?" and "Who in the New Testament are unordained?" are textually and contextually meaningless, since they cannot be indisputably answered. The further attempt to find in the New Testament instances of women being ordained is rendered fruitless, since one cannot even find instances of men being ordained. Ordination/non-ordination are not biblical terms, nor are they part of the apostolic and sub-apostolic Christian community. From Hippolytus onward there can be no doubt that ordination gradually became the standard way in which Christians were placed into certain ecclesial offices or ministries. Prior to Hippolytus, one cannot make apodictical statements. It is the issue of *ordo* and then ordination which appears to be added as the special "criterion" whereby some authors judge which ministries in the New Testament correspond to the later "clerical" ministries, and which ministries in the New Testament correspond to the later "lay" ministry or even "lay" structure. However, the criterion itself is not organic to the New Testament in any clear way, and as a result the criterion itself cannot be seen as based on the word of God, revealed to us in the Jesus event.

3. ECCLESIAL IMPLICATIONS

The documents of Vatican II center the entire mission and ministry of the church itself and of each and every specific mission and ministry in the church (bishop, priest, lay minister, etc.) in the mission and ministry of Jesus. In this sense, Jesus is the primordial sacrament of all and every mission and ministry within the Christian community. This conciliar position provides us with a positive methodology as regards the meaning of *laikos/klerikos.* It is true that the documents of Vatican II nowhere state that Jesus, in his humanity, is the primordial sacrament. Rather, the documents of Vatican II state only that the church is a fundamental sacrament. However, the theology which involves the church as a sacrament is unintelligible unless it is connected with the wider sacramental theology which presents Jesus as the primordial sacrament. The sacramentality of the church is, therefore, theologically united to the sacramentality of Jesus. The documents of Vatican II base all mission and ministry in the Christian church on Jesus' own mission and ministry. This christocentric center of all ecclesial mission and ministry provides the basis for both the later clerical and lay mission and ministry.[52]

From a methodological point of view, we can establish the following steps, based on the theology presented in the documents of Vatican II:

1. FOUNDATION	=	Jesus, the primordial minister
2. BASE	=	Church, the basic sacrament (the ministry and mission that comes from the sacrament of initiation: baptism-eucharist)
3. SUPERSTRUCTURE	=	Each and every ministry in the church (bishop, priest, deacon, lay minister, etc.)

A. JESUS THE BASIC SACRAMENT OF ALL CHRISTIAN MINISTRY

Jesus, in his humanness, is the primordial basis or sacrament for all Christian ministry and mission. Without this mission and ministry of Jesus, there would be no mission or ministry in the church; there would be no mission and ministry by individuals in the church. Jesus is the fundamental or primordial infrastructure. All other missions and ministries in the Christian community are sacraments of his mission and ministry.

The church, as the people of God, sacramentalizes and continues this mission and ministry of Jesus. Vatican II speaks of this as a continuation of the *tria munera:* prophet, priest and king. The documents of Vatican II are quite clear on this matter: through the sacrament of initiation, baptism (though one should more rightfully say: baptism-eucharist), every Christian shares in the *tria munera* of Jesus. Every Christian shares in the mission and ministry of Jesus as prophet, priest and king.

Because of this foundation in Jesus of all ministry, one can only conclude:

Jesus himself is neither cleric nor lay.
Jesus' mission is itself neither clerical nor lay.
Jesus' ministry is itself neither clerical nor lay.

For those who have generally considered Jesus as "high priest" and therefore, to a certain extent, clerical, this may sound strange. But if Jesus himself is a "cleric," then in what way can the documents of Vatican II base the mission and ministry of the lay Christian in Jesus himself? How can lay ministry arise from a clerical foundation? If Jesus' ministry is "clerical," then how is it possible for the documents of Vatican II to consider lay ministry a part of Jesus' own *tria munera?* Would not the *tria munera,* as found in Jesus, be clerical? If they are clerical, how can "lay" people share in them, without becoming to some extent "clerical"? If Jesus' mission is a "clerical mission," how can the documents of Vatican

II describe the mission of the lay Christian as sharing in Jesus' own mission? Again, would not a "lay" Christian be sharing in a "clerical" mission, and thereby become to some extent clerical himself or herself?

The opposite, however, would be equally cogent: if Jesus is lay only, then in what way can the documents of Vatican II base the mission and ministry of the "cleric" in Jesus? Would not the "cleric," by sharing in the mission and ministry of a "lay Jesus," be somehow "laicized"? How can the cleric's mission be a participation in the very mission of the "lay Jesus"? Again, would not the cleric, by sharing in Jesus' mission, be sharing in a "lay mission"? What then would the clerical mission be, as far as the church is concerned? Third, how can the clerical ministry be a sharing in the "lay ministry" of Jesus? Would not the ministry of the "cleric" likewise be essentially a "laicized" ministry.

The root produces certain specific flowers, vegetables, fruits, leaves, etc. What is not in the root cannot appear later on, or at least what is not in the grafting into the root cannot appear later on. This rather natural phenomenon has found its counterpart in philosophy: for example, *ex nihilo nihil fit*. Nothing can come from nothing. Again, *bonum est sui diffusivum* [goodness gives rise to goodness]. In moral theology, one argues that the end cannot justify the means. The basic or fundamental *telos* cannot allow for any and all means: good does not give rise to evil. *Mutatis mutandis,* if Jesus is seen in theology as the root, the foundation, the basis, the ground, the original sacrament, the primordial sacrament, etc., of all Christian mission and ministry, then theologians must face the issue: How can both lay and clerical missions and ministries derive from the same root? Some authors might argue that the lay aspects of mission and ministry are present in Jesus' mission and ministry only *analogically,* or in a *spiritualized* way, or in a *metaphorical* way, while the clerical aspects of mission and ministry are present in the mission and ministry of Jesus in a real way, a true way, an *actual* way, etc.[53] These kinds of arguments, however, fly in the face of the theological position that Jesus' mission and ministry are root, primordial, ground, etc. of all Christian mission and ministry. Even more serious a charge can be leveled against such a position, since the analogical, metaphorical, spiritual interpretation hardly does justice to the conciliar statements that the church is a basic sacrament. It is difficult to see how the theological position of an analogous or metaphorical approach to this christocentric theology of sacrament and ministry, which has received an endorsement from Vatican II, does not essentially compromise the very meaning of Jesus as the primordial or ground sacrament, or the very meaning of the documents of Vatican II, which clearly makes Jesus' own mission and ministry the foundations for all mission and ministry within the church, lay or clerical. If Jesus' very mission and ministry, the *tria munera,* are the basis of all ecclesial mission and ministry—and this is clearly presented throughout the documents of Vatican II—then both clerical and lay mission and ministry must find their basis, their *raison d'être,* in this christocentric center. Both the clerical and lay aspects of church mission and ministry are essentially, not analogously, not metaphorically, not spiritually, related to the mission and ministry of Jesus. Even more, both are related essentially, not analogously, not metaphorically, not spiritually, to the mission and ministry of the church. This latter argument raises an entirely new ecclesiological issue: Is the very mission and ministry of the church clerical or lay?

B. THE CHURCH: A FUNDAMENTAL SACRAMENT
OF ALL CHRISTIAN MINISTRY

One does not go directly from a given clerical or lay mission and ministry to Jesus. One goes to Jesus, the christocentric center, through the mission and ministry of the church itself. Once again, the question arises: Is the church's *mission* clerical or lay? Is the church's *ministry* clerical or lay? If the church's own mission and ministry is the motherlode (with Jesus as the primordial foundation) of all ecclesial mission and ministry, then it, too, can be neither clerical nor lay. How can a clerical motherlode give rise to a non-clerical mission and ministry? Or vice versa, how can a lay motherlode produce a clerical mission and ministry? In other words, how can the motherlode be either clerical or lay, if both clerical and lay mission and ministry derive from this source? Such terms as clerical and lay appear meaningless when applied to Jesus and to the church itself. The terms cleric and lay, ordained and non-ordained, have meaning only in the particularized manifestation of specific Christians for specific missions and ministries, which exemplify in part the *tria munera* of Jesus and the church itself. This will, of course, be the core of the problem, which has focused so intensely in our own day and age, and which we will discuss far more thoroughly in the final chapters of these volumes.[54]

Even as conservative an author as J. Galot admits that in the teaching of Vatican II, Jesus is seen as the source of the church's mission and ministry. In his article, "Christ: Revealer, Founder of the Church and Source of Ecclesial Life,"[55] which presents his summation of the role of Jesus in the various documents of Vatican II, he begins with the very term *Lumen Gentium,* or Jesus, as the light for the whole world. This application of the title to Jesus is the clear intent of the bishops. "The whole of the message of salvation addressed to humanity is found in Christ, and it can be neither added to nor modified. The Church can only draw on this fullness."[56] The Jesus we know is the Jesus of scripture, preserved in the church community. There is a clear priority to the word of God, which we find in the New Testament. Galot stresses that Jesus is fundamental for an understanding of the Christian community and its various ministries.

> [Jesus] pours his life into this body, especially through the sacraments of baptism and the eucharist. He is the source of unity, the universal head, the model to which each person must be conformed. He makes his body grow by constantly bestowing gifts of ministry. The doctrine of the mystical body of Christ explains the action of Christ as the source of the vital growth of the Church in all areas.[57]

On this basis, Galot concludes his essay with the conciliar ideas of Jesus as (a) source of priestly activity; (b) source of consecrated life; (c) source of liturgical life; (d) source of apostolic activity; (e) source of unity.[58] That Jesus, according to the documents of Vatican II, is the source of all of these various activities and forms of Christian life is a given. In a far more nuanced and careful way, Gérard Philips lines up the various interpretations in which one can say that Jesus is the source of the unordained ministry and the ordained ministry.[59] Among the distinctions that were mentioned during the debates at Vatican II, Philips notes the following:

a. Is one speaking about a real priesthood for the ordained and only a figurative priesthood, when one speaks of the baptized as sharing in the priestly mission and ministry of Jesus on the one hand, and the ordained sharing in the same priestly mission and ministry of Jesus?

b. Or is the distinction made on the basis of a real priestly sharing as far as the ordained are concerned and only a spiritual sharing in the case of the non-ordained?

c. Or is there perhaps a distinction based on an external sharing in the priestly mission and ministry of Jesus by all Christians on the one hand and on the other hand an internal sharing in that same ministry by the ordained members of the Church?

d. Or is the one sacramental (the ordained) and the other non-sacramental (the non-ordained)?

e. A further possibility debated at Vatican II was: is one a lay priesthood and the other a hierarchical one?

f. Other bishops described the one as full (for the ordained) and the other as incomplete (for the unordained).

g. Philips even notes that some bishops proposed the distinction between a masculine sharing in the priesthood of Christ (the ordained) and a feminine sharing in this mission and ministry of Jesus (for the unordained).

Philips concludes his discussion on this matter as follows:

> The problem of terminology was not deliberately avoided. The long list of cited terms could give the impression that the theologians gave themselves over to pointless discussion. But the question of vocabulary, to which we have dedicated so many paragraphs, offers us the occasion to describe quite in detail the dogmatic significance of the Christian vocation, and to analyze it in depth. Only after mature reflection, did the council decide to select the terms which seemed to be closest of all to revelation, namely, the common priesthood, developed on the basis of baptism [one should add as well eucharist], and the ministerial or hierarchic priesthood, established on sacramental ordination in view of an organized ministry.[60]

This unity within some sort of diversity between the ordained and the non-ordained, as expressed in Vatican II, attests to the common origin of all mission and ministry: Jesus the Lord. In the book on *Priesthood,* the first chapter dealt with the ministry of Jesus,[61] and it was noted that all ministry should reflect the characteristics of Jesus' own ministry, namely, that Jesus' own ministry was (a) from God; (b) a ministry of love; (c) a ministry of service; (d) to some degree political; (e) a ministry of preaching. Every disciple of Jesus, then, must strive to incorporate these aspects of Jesus' ministry into his or her own ministerial work.

The mission and ministry of Jesus not only had special characteristics, but there was a message in this mission and ministry. This message focused on the kingdom, its incipient presence and its eschatological fulfillment. This message of kingdom must be central to each and every mission and ministry within the church, whether ordained or not. The kingdom, however, which Jesus preached included in a strong way the saving and forgiving love of God for the marginated peoples of our society. It would be difficult to think of a Christian mission and ministry which did not include this option, even at times a preferential one, for the poor and the marginated. Where the kingdom of God begins to be present in our human lives, evil is slowly being eradicated and the Spirit of God, a spirit of healing and peace, of life and strength, begins to take over. The mission and ministry of every Christian minister, ordained and non-ordained, must in a most central way incorporate this message of Jesus.

After the resurrection, the community of Jesus began to proclaim: Jesus is Lord. This catch-phrase has two sides: the first says that there is no salvation outside of Jesus.

> I am glad to tell you all, and would indeed be glad to tell the whole people of Israel, that it was by the name of Jesus Christ the Nazarene, the one you crucified, whom God raised from the dead, by this name and by no other that this man is able to stand up perfectly healthy, here in your presence, today. This is the stone rejected by you the builders, but which has proved to be the keystone. For of all the names in the world given to men, this is the only one by which we can be saved. (Acts 4:10–12)

Jesus alone is the savior of the world. Outside of Jesus there is no salvation. In our Christian tradition there have been and still are several different ways to understand this message of the centrality of Jesus for salvation, but in all of these theological views, Jesus, and he alone, is the key to the salvation of all men and women. This centrality of Jesus for the salvation of the world must also be central to every Christian mission and ministry, ordained and non-ordained.

The second issue is the divinity of Jesus. "And the word was made flesh and dwelt among us" (Jn 1:14). Jesus is not only an exemplary human being alongside of many other exemplary men and women. There is a uniqueness about Jesus, because in Jesus God is present, or as the Council of Chalcedon stated it: Jesus is truly God and truly human. This proclamation of Jesus' divinity is, as well, a central part of every Christian mission and ministry, ordained and non-ordained alike.

4. CONCLUSIONS FROM THE DATA

This chapter presents one of the points of departure, which many scholars have used, to elucidate the issue of *klerikos/laikos.* Having considered the data, one can legitimately ask: What conclusions can be drawn from all this textual and historical material? In my judgment, the study of the origin and significance of these terms within the early Christian world, with the intent of determining the origins of a lay/cleric church as understood by later generations, seems, first of all, to be counter-productive. At the earliest strata of Christian writings, both terms are used so sparingly that no generalized conclusion is possible. Secondly, the term *laikos* does indeed mean, in its most fundamental sense, a connectedness to a people. The term is clearly connected to *laos.* One can proudly be called a *laikos,* in contradistinction to the "alien," the "foreigner," the "outsider." This line of thought, naturally, reinforces Congar's position. The term *laikos* can also be seen, but only secondarily, as a description of a member of a people (*laos*) who are not in some ruling position. At this secondary level, *laikos* is defined not by the alien, the foreigner, the outsider, but by the person of the same laos who has a regulatory position of some official nature. This is the emphasis which de la Potterie prefers, but it is a secondary and derived meaning of the term *laikos*.

The term *klerikos* did not originally develop historically and etymologically as a counterpart to *laikos*. This term *klerikos* had a history and an etymology all its own. In time, the two terms began to be used in a complementary way. However, the study of these terms within early Christian literature shows that the more fundamental term which engendered the eventual ecclesiastical and canonical meaning of these two terms was *ordo*. Without this term *ordo*, the terms *klerikos/laikos* would not have taken on the meanings which they subsequently received. The emergence of this term *ordo* into ecclesiastical vocabulary and thought colored the meaning of both *laikos* and *klerikos*. There would have been no ordination in the Christian community if there was not an understanding of church leadership as an *ordo*, both in the society called church and eventually in the society called empire. The reality and the term "ordination" are based on *ordo; ordo* is not based on ordination. Thus, the true focus for an understanding of the eventual lay/cleric church should be sought not in the terms lay and cleric, but in the origin, usage and validity of church leadership as an *ordo*. As regards the term and usage of *ordo*, one should keep in mind that there were several hermeneutical stages, which occasioned its acceptance within the Christian community. These stages can be outlined in a general fashion as follows:

a. The emergence of the term *ordo* within the Christian community, denoting those in ministerial, leadership positions.
b. The functional description of *ordo*, i.e. authors describe what those in these various orders do and how they function within the community.
c. The theological description of *ordo*, beginning with a connection to the ordering of Old Testament priesthood: Aaron, Levi, Sadoq, as also the theological description of *ordo* on the basis of the order in God and the order of creation: Gregory the Great, Dionysius the Areopagite.
d. The gradual inclusion of the ministerial *ordo* into the sociopolitical structures of the Graeco-Roman world, then the Frankish world, then the world of Holy Roman Empire.

e. The description of *ordo* with a structure of "being," with an emphasis on the "ontological" difference between those in such orders and those without such orders.

As the term *ordo* moved from one stage to the other, its nuanced and even changed meaning colored the way in which the terms *klerikos/laikos* were understood. Were one to remove this consideration of the term *ordo* from the field of discourse, the meaning of the terms *klerikos/laikos,* even at the stage of their earliest Christian appearance, would provide little to substantiate the eventual understanding of the clerical/lay church.

We have also seen in this chapter that Jesus, both in his own mission and ministry and in the way through which the apostolic church proclaimed and continued his mission and ministry, is the source, origin, model and measure of all Christian ministry. Whether one is ordained or not makes no difference at this basic level of source, origin, model, and measure. If Jesus is the source, origin, model and measure of all Christian leadership, then Jesus himself cannot be seen as either lay or cleric. A clerical Jesus cannot be called the source, origin, model and measure of lay Christian ministry, and, vice versa, a lay Jesus cannot be seen as the source, origin, model and measure of a clerical church ministry. In other words, christology itself does not provide a base for the lay/cleric church. The reason for *klerikos* and *laikos* must be found in some other area. It is this "other area" which we begin to find in the late second century and the early third centuries. This "other area" again appears to be the Christian use of the term *ordo.* Once the various Christian communities began to model themselves on the Graeco-Roman social structures of differing orders, *ordines,* those who were raised to the higher orders associated with the church were called *klerikoi,* while those who were in no order were called *laikoi.* It is not so much the use of the terms *laikos/klerikos* which created a socially caste-divided Christian group, but rather the use of the term *ordo* which created such class-distinguished groups. Once we find the appearance of socially recognizable orders within the Christian community, we also find that a process of theologizing begins to take place. This theologizing—the presentation of a theological rationale for the various orders—was based far more on Old Testament patterns of priesthood than on the gospels and the other New Testament writings. In other words, the later patristic theology of orders, which began to substantiate the clerical/lay church structure, is itself somewhat suspect, since the basis for that theological rationale is in many ways devoid of a gospel foundation. As a result, the etymological analysis of *klerikos, laikos* and even *ordo,* together with their resultant ecclesiological implications, does not provide an adequate point of departure, since too many extraneous, non-

Christian, socio-political, neo-platonic elements are involved. Conclusions, which to some degree or another are based on these extraneous factors, cannot be the point of departure to determine the meaning of either various Christian ministries or baptismal-eucharistic ministry as such. To find this meaning we must turn to other foundations.

2

The Second Point of Departure: The Use of Lay/Cleric in Roman Catholic Canon Law

Since Roman Catholic canon law has incorporated some notions on the lay/cleric church, which have been based on the origin of these terms and categories within the Christian community, let us consider the canonical data, which at times is used as a point of departure or at least as a framework beyond which Roman Catholic authors should not stray. Historically, from the third century A.D. onward, as we shall see presently, one finds a lay/cleric structuralized positioning in the church, but not a structuralized dichotomy of the Christian community, i.e. a division of the Christian community into two sections: lay and cleric. In the Constantinian and early medieval church, the role of the monks and women religious was seen as a third area of Christian life, and likewise the role of the emperor/empress and their immediate consorts was a fourth area of Christian strata. Only from the time of Gratian onward does one find, specifically in the Roman or Latin church, both a legalized justification of a dichotomized lay/cleric structure and a generalized attempt to understand all Christians from the twofold framework of lay/cleric. This complex history has found its expression both in the code of canon law, promulgated in 1917, and in the revised code of 1983.

1. THE CANONICAL TEXTS

In the 1917 code of canon law, canon 107 reads:

Ex divina institutione sunt in Ecclesia *clerici* a *laicis* distincti, licet non omnes clerici sint divinae institutionis; utrique autem possunt esse *religiosi.*

41

By divine institution there are in the Church *clerics* distinct from *the laity,* although not all clerics are of divine institution; both clerics and laity may be *religious.*

The footnote for this canon refers to *1 Clement,* c. 40, in which we find for the first time in Christian literature the term *laikos.* Besides this patristic reference, there is a reference to the Council of Trent, session 23, a section which deals with holy order, and in the 1917 code of canon law the footnote specifically refers to canon 4 of the Tridentine decree on the sacrament of holy order, which reads:

If anyone says that by holy ordination the Holy Spirit is not given and thus it is useless for bishops to say, "Receive the Holy Spirit"; or if anyone says that no character is imprinted by ordination; or that he who was once a priest can become a layman again, let him be anathema.

It is difficult to see, on the basis of either the *Letter of Clement* or of canon 4, session 23 of the Council of Trent, that the distinction of cleric/ lay is *of divine institution.* This canon in the 1917 code provides absolutely no references to scriptural texts, primarily because none exist to prove the divine institution of a lay/cleric church. Moreover, both the Clementine and Tridentine references are, at best, oblique indicators, regarding the ecclesial use of these terms. The Tridentine canon does not even use the term "cleric"; rather, it uses the term "ordained" and, even more particularly, ordination to priesthood. The term "layman," which it does use, is in contrast to the ordained priest.

At the time of Trent, tonsure marked the entry into the "clerical state," even though tonsure was not an ordination, with the result that those who were ordained and those who were clerics were not co-terminous. In the sixteenth century, the term "lay" was not used technically as the opposite of "ordained." It was used as the opposite of cleric.[1] As regards ordination, there were minor orders and major orders. The latter, the major orders, at least deacon and priesthood, were considered of divine institution.[2] The minor orders were generally considered to be of ecclesiastical institution. Nor can one argue that the lesser orders, though often called by the term "ordination," were considered of divine institution. At the time of Trent, not all clerics were "ordained," since some clerics had merely received tonsure, and not all ordained were ordained through an ordination which was of divine institution.[3] Even though the canon states that not all clerics are of divine institution, thus maintaining the distinction between minor orders and major orders, the Tridentine reference, to which it refers as its basis, indicates that there is a distinction, namely between lay, on the one hand, and the ordained priest, on the other. Beyond that distinction, which is found in the Tridentine passage, further distinctions are only surmised. As a result, neither the Tridentine nor the Clementine textual references furnish any proof of a divine institution of a specifically lay/cleric church.[4]

The commentary on the 1917 code of canon law by P. Wernz and P. Vidal, *Ius Canonicum,* is typical of the numerous commentaries which developed, although the Wernz-Vidal commentary does spend more time on canon 107 than is usually found in such volumes, and so let us use this typical commentary as a voice for many. For Wernz-Vidal, lay persons are "baptized Christians (*fideles baptizati*) who lack a certain status in the ecclesiatical hierarchy, particularly the status of order."[5] In clear scholastic fashion, the authors state that there is a generic and positive element as regards the definition of lay, namely baptism, and that there is a specific and negative denomination, namely the lack of order. The specific difference, it should be noted, is negative, not positive.

> Perfectissima igitur ratione laicus dicitur qui utraque potestate et ordinis et jurisdictionis caret sed sensu maxime stricto laicus appellatur, cui ne infimus quidem gradus et initiatio hierarchia competit, quamvis fortasse aliquo gradu iurisdictionis ecclesiastica sit instructus. . . . Quare laicus et subditus ecclesiasticus opponuntur clero et Praelato ecclesiastico.[6]

Basing themselves on Gratian (C. 7, C XII, q. 1) the authors proceed to state that this division comes from Christ, *ex ordinatione Christi,* and therefore the laity exist (note the ontological language) outside the church's hierarchical arena. The result is that the lay person has no power of sacrificing and sanctifying, teaching and ruling, within the Catholic Church.[7]

This line of thinking as regards the 1917 code was typical. A. Ledesma notes: "The second book of the *Codex* (of 1917), *de personis,* was conceived from a sharply hierarchical standpoint, dealing with persons in the Church in so far as they relate to the hierarchy or form part of it."[8] Major issues came to the fore in the period between these two editions of the code; one can say that with Vatican II the panoramic vision changed radically.[9] The corresponding canon in the revised 1983 code of canon law, consequently, is worded in a far more cautious way. One reads in this revised code the following canon (207):

Ex divina institutione, inter christifideles sunt in Ecclesia ministri sacri, qui in iure et clerici vocantur; ceteri autem et laici nuncupantur.

Among the Christian faithful by divine institution there exist in the Church sacred ministers, who are called clerics in law, and other Christian faithful, who are also called laity.

The *Code of Canon Law: A Text and Commentary,* published by the Canon Law Society of America, presents some background material for the deliberations and changes which occurred in the reconstruction of this particular canon.[10] The language, i.e. the phraseology, of the 1917 canon is kept, but in the later rendition "the distinction is said to be based on sacred ministers—not on the canonically determined status of clergy and laity."[11] Historical studies have occasioned this change: the New Testament speaks about ministers to the community, whereas the legal organization, which one finds in the code, is more a reflection of the pseudo-Dionysian ideal of *taxis* or perfect order in society, including the society of the church.[12]

The commentary notes that the medieval worldview of a class society was reflected in almost all the legal documents of the church, and eventually became codified in the 1917 text. The documents of Vatican II attempted to change this juridical class approach: "What is significant is that after centuries of attempting to implement such a system [the class system], the magisterium at the Second Vatican Council rejected such institutional clericalism and sought to locate sacred ministry within the people of God and the common condition of all the Christian faithful."[13]

Vatican II stressed this notion of the people of God (*LG,* 18, 32), as is well known, and the framers of the new code made great efforts to integrate the teaching of Vatican II into the revised text.[14] It is clear, from this new canon, that the terms "cleric/lay," as well as their specific meanings, are only juridical. The terms are clearly *not of divine institution,* and therefore the technical meaning of these juridical terms is likewise not of divine institution. "The juridical status of sacred ministers is not necessarily divinely given but is determined in church law and is changeable (as indeed it has been changed in several respects by this Code)."[15] There are, however, ministers in the Christian community, and such ministry is seen as divinely given, for we find "ministry" and "service leadership" present in the New Testament itself. The revised code, however, merely states this situation of the juridical position of lay/cleric, but it does not go into any more detail. Moreover, the use of the terms "cleric/lay" in the new code is to be understood as merely typological: that is, the code describes what clerics presently do and what lay people presently do. Any effort to turn this typological description into an ontological one goes beyond the intent of the revised code. *How* a cleric or lay person is described in the code is not necessarily *what* a cleric or lay person has to be. Pastoral necessity might easily occasion a change in these typological descriptions.[16] It appears that those who revised the code did not want to take on the role of biblical exegete, church historian or systematic theologian. On the other hand, these editors did inherit a text from 1917 to be revised, and they inherited as well a background in Roman Catholic exegetical, historical and theological thought. In the wording of the 1983 code, one senses a much more careful and sensitive approach to the various exegetical, historical and theological issues than one finds in the wording of the 1917 code.

The authors of this commentary, however, go on to list certain ways in which theologians have attempted to base the distinction between the divinely established minister, on the one hand, and on the other hand the divinely established Christian people. One should note from the very start that both are *ex divina institutione,* i.e. intra-ecclesial ministry or service leadership is of divine origin, and the people of God is of divine origin. However, one can legitimately ask: What distinguishes these two aspects of church life? Some of the bases for distinction, which were actually and seriously considered in the deliberations for the revised code, were as follows:

a. The lay person is in the world = a secular character. The minister is in the church = a sacred character.
b. All the faithful are members of the priesthood of all believers; the ministers are *also* members of an ordained priesthood.
c. The faithful participate in the *tria munera* of Jesus in a different way than that of the ministers. This different way was not further specified.
d. Sacred ministers have the power of jurisdiction and the power of orders; the ordinary Christian does not have the latter, and, for some authors, does not have the former either.

All of these "differences" were discussed by the framers of the new code, but the final position of the code regarding each of them resolved nothing. "The code has not attempted to go beyond stating the distinction."[17] That there are *Christifideles* and that some *Christifideles* are also *ministri* is presented as a given. What makes these two groups different is left undetermined, and, as we shall see, this lack of determination has been the theme of serious and abundant theological and canonical discussion ever since Vatican II and ever since the promulgation of the revised code.[18]

In summary, we can say that the terms "cleric/lay" with an ecclesial and ministerial meaning are foreign to New Testament terminology. The terms *began* to be employed for ecclesial ministry at the end of the second century and the beginning of the third century. Since each of the terms has specific historical overtones and meanings not found in scripture, one cannot say that a juridically institutionalized class-structure of the Christian church is of divine institution. Rather, this specific terminology "lay/cleric," with its juridically institutionalized overtones and meanings, arises from a later theology and is therefore of church origin. As a result, canon law cannot be used as a point of departure on the issue of *klerikos/laikos.* The code of canon law, presently in effect within the Roman Catholic Church, describes typologically the way the church is currently structured. The canon on the lay/cleric differentiation presents only a juridical and typological description of the lay person and the cleric, a description which cannot be considered as unchangeable. Therefore, scholars may indeed, at least theologically and academically, move far beyond the constraints of law. In other words, theological discussion, though taking note of the code, cannot be boxed in by the limitations of the code.

Beyond the particular canon in question, one must also realize that canon law is not the vehicle through which dogmas and doctrines are defined. Nor is the code of canon law the vehicle in which infallible statements are made. Even more, canon law is neither the vehicle in and through which theology is formulated, nor is it the vehicle in and through which the scriptures are interpreted. Individual canons in the code might evidence such issues as (a) scriptural teaching, (b) defined dogmas and doctrines, (c) various theological positions, and (d) various scriptural interpretations. The appearance of any or all of these positions in a given canon does not provide the positions with any greater foundation or authoritative weight than these various positions already have, independent of their appearance in the code. The role of the code of canon law itself indicates that it should be used neither as a point of departure nor as a framework within which one must of necessity operate in the matter of scriptural exegesis, historical study, and theological discussion.

2. CONCLUSIONS FROM THE DATA

Catholic theological thought at the end of the nineteenth and throughout the first half of the twentieth century often used canon law as a court of final appeal. Many textbooks on moral theology were really books on canonical legislation, dealing with moral issues. During this time of textbook theology, canon law appeared to have the final word. For many reasons, this approach to canon law has ended, although there are still some church leaders and teachers who continue to emphasize this "canonization" of canon law. With the code of canon law published in 1917 and its revision published in 1983, we can chart various changes which the revised volume makes. One of these changes, as noted above, is the codex's approach to the issue of lay/cleric. No longer does it state that this division is of divine institution. There are, the new code states, sacred ministries in the church which are of divine institution. Only in a later age, *ex institutione humana,* however, are the *christifidelis* and the minister set apart by a lay/cleric framework. This lay/cleric distinction was shaped in a fundamental way by the introduction of *ordo* into church structure. When the fathers of the church and other theologians of the patristic period attempted to provide a theological base for *ordo,* they did so, not on the basis of New Testament data, but on the basis of a theological position: namely, that there is an *ordo* connected with God and with the entire created universe. They did not argue that Jesus himself established the church's ministry as a specific *ordo.*

The second conclusion which is important to keep in mind is that the framers of the revised code did not adopt any of the reasons for a lay/cleric division, which had been a part of their debate. The framers declined to take a stance on this matter. The issue is obviously an open issue, one which can be freely debated by Catholic scholarship. However, even if the framers of the new code had taken a stance, the closure of the issue would not rest on canon law alone. It would rest on something quite extrinsic to canon law and something which is far more fundamental to Christian truth than canon law. For instance, canon law presupposes the divinity of Jesus, but the dogma on the divinity of Jesus does not depend on its incorporation into canon law. The basis for this teaching on Jesus is fundamentally scripture and, on that basis, the constant and even solemn teaching of the church. Christian canon law has to be based on such a teaching, but the incorporation of such teaching into canon law does not make canon law, even indirectly, the source or foundation for the teaching. The theological position of Jesus in the Christian community did not fundamentally change from the code of 1917 to that of 1983. However, the understanding of lay/cleric did, which signifies, on the one hand, the very fragility or non-immutability of such terms as lay/cleric, and on the other hand the scope and the limit of canon law itself.

3

The Third Point of Departure:
The Meaning of Discipleship
in the New Testament Writings

Contemporary Roman Catholic theology deliberately tends to be far more scripturally based than its predecessor: the Tridentine and counter-reformation theology. To understand the meaning of a "lay person" in the Christian church, many scholars make the scriptural data, particularly the New Testament, the point of departure. This way of beginning has caused a certain change in perspective. If one reads the counter-reformation and nineteenth century literature on either priestly life or on religious life, one finds that certain New Testament passages have often been almost exclusively interpreted and used to portray either the meaning of a priest or the meaning of a vowed religious. Such New Testament passages, as a result, were not seen as directly applicable to the non-ordained or to the non-religious. In other words, several key passages or key themes in the New Testament became a sort of scriptural justification for clerical life or a scriptural justification for religious life. The non-ordained and the non-religious could not see themselves reflected in these specific passages. It is the contention of this chapter that such a reading of the New Testament can no longer be upheld. The authors of the various New Testament writings, with the exception, perhaps, of 2 Timothy, were addressing Christian communities as such. They were not addressing a leadership in-group, nor a cadre of vowed religious. The picture of discipleship which these New Testament authors present is meant for all followers of Jesus. If and when the New Testament authors wished to direct their ideas to a leadership group within the community, both the text and the context make this quite clear, as we shall see. Otherwise, the various

48

New Testament writers developed their description of the disciple of Jesus for all those who have followed the Lord.

In this chapter we will consider author by author the New Testament data concerning discipleship. It would be anachronistic, however, to search this material with the following pre-determined questions: Which of these disciples, mentioned in the New Testament, are portrayed as "clerics" and which are portrayed as "lay"? It would be equally anachronistic to search this same material with the pre-determined questions: Which of these disciples are portrayed as "ordained" and which are portrayed as "unordained"? Neither the lay/cleric pattern nor the ordained/non-ordained pattern is discernible in the New Testament.[1]

This is a lengthy chapter, consisting of many sub-sections. The length of this chapter, however, is key to the theme of this entire volume. In contemporary Roman Catholic theology, one of the questions, dealing with the issue of the laity, has been formulated as follows: What is the difference between the priesthood of all believers and the ordained or ministerial priesthood? The attempt to describe or define either of these two "priesthoods" by comparing and contrasting one with the other seems to lead nowhere. Rather, it seems to me, one should search out the theological basis or foundation which provides the very meaning of both priesthoods, and this theological foundation or base is that of discipleship. The following diagram attempts to clarify the situation.

CHRISTIAN DISCIPLESHIP

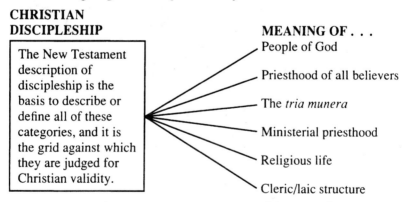

MEANING OF . . .

People of God

Priesthood of all believers

The *tria munera*

Ministerial priesthood

Religious life

Cleric/laic structure

The New Testament description of discipleship is the basis to describe or define all of these categories, and it is the grid against which they are judged for Christian validity.

We will consider the New Testament material systematically by gathering the data from each of the major New Testament sources, namely:

1. **The disciples in the gospel of Mark**
2. **The disciples in the gospel of Luke**
3. **The disciples in the gospel of Matthew**
4. **The disciples in the Johannine writings**

1. THE DISCIPLES IN THE GOSPEL OF MARK

D. Harrington states, in his essay on Mark, that the focus of Mark's theology is the same focus as that of Jesus' theology, namely, the kingdom of God.[2] The kingdom of God centralizes all of Marcan theology. It centralizes what Mark teaches about christology, i.e. Mark's answer to the question: Who is Jesus? It centralizes what Mark wishes to say in answer to the question: Who is the follower of Jesus?[3] Mark's understanding of the kingdom of God is the framework in which the person of Jesus makes sense, and it is likewise the framework in which the disciple of Jesus makes sense. This kingdom of God meant, to the Jews of Jesus' time, the "definitive display of God's lordship at the end of history and its acknowledgement by all creation."[4] Jesus' teaching in the Marcan gospel expands on this understanding of God's kingdom. His healings anticipate the eventual life with God in the kingdom. His parables describe both the hiddenness and the presence of this kingdom. Above all, Jesus' own life, death and resurrection was, in Mark's view, the clearest expression of what God's kingdom was and is all about. "Mark's message is that whoever wishes to understand the kingdom must look at Jesus the healer, the teacher, and the crucified-and-the-risen one."[5]

The disciples, that is, all those who are portrayed in Mark's gospel as following Jesus, must be seen first of all as those who were with Jesus, sharing his mission of preaching and healing (3:14–15). In the first section of Mark's gospel, these disciples are presented as possible examples of discipleship who might be imitated, but in the second and latter part of Mark's gospel the disciples are presented as examples to be avoided, since they continually misunderstood who Jesus truly was. In this way, Mark highlights "the person of Jesus as the only one who deserves imitation."[6] Thus the Marcan portrait of the disciples of Jesus indicates both what discipleship means and what it should not mean. Like Janus, the disciples present two distinct and opposing pictures: one to be imitated and one not to be imitated. Jesus alone is seen as the true focus of discipleship.

However, for whom is Mark writing? Who is to find in the early picture of the disciples an example for imitation, and in the later picture of the disciples an example not to be imitated? Who is to find in Jesus alone the real example for imitation? The answer is clear, and in the introduction of almost every commentary on Mark's gospel one finds the standardized question: Who are the addressees of this gospel? The scholars' answers vary. Irenaeus in *Adv. haereses* (3, 1, 1) and quoted in Eusebius (*Hist. eccl.* V, 8, 2–4) believed that Rome was the place of origin, and this view has had a long history. Others have suggested a Jewish/Gentile community, living outside of Palestine, perhaps in Syria around the year 70 to 80 A.D. Currently, there seems to be a trend among the scholars to place the origin of this writing in a community in the southern part of Syria, neighboring on Palestine.[7] There are, of course, many nuances to this description, as well as other minority answers which either in date or place deviate from this generalized description. Still, in all of the descriptions of the addressees for Mark's gospel, none indicates that the gospel has been written for a small, intramural leadership group of such a community, nor for a cadre of "religious" ascetics within that same community. If the addressees are the community in its totality, then the portrait of discipleship, which is presented by Mark, is meant to warn/inspire all such Christians. With these addressees in mind, namely, all the members of Mark's community, let us walk through the gospel of Mark, considering step by step the picture of disciple which Mark presents.

It is also important to emphasize that in Mark's gospel it is the kingdom of God which is the framework, not the church. Mark is, indeed, writing both for and out of a given Jesus community, but this is a community which at the time of Mark still is very much a part of Judaism. From Mark's gospel alone, one could not say that the Jesus community has separated itself from the Jewish community; rather, one would have to say that in the Marcan account, the Jesus community is seen as the true meaning of the Jewish community. In other words, at the time of Mark, one cannot speak about two religions: a Christian religion and a Jewish religion. At the time of Mark, one still must speak about one Israel, which in the author's view is clearly found within the Jesus community. This distinction has a very important bearing on the issue of discipleship, for disciples of Jesus, including the twelve whom Mark mentions, are not presented within a "church framework" but within a "kingdom framework." To describe the men and women disciples in Mark's gospel in ecclesial or ecclesiastical terminology, in the sense of a distinct church-community which is not the Jewish community, is clearly an imposition of a later view on these gospel texts. In many ways there is nothing "churchy" about Mark's presentation of the followers of Jesus.

In Mark 1:16–20 we find the calling of the first disciples: Simon and Andrew, James the son of Zebedee and John, his brother. All four were in the fishing business, at that time a major industry in Galilee. Simon and Andrew owned nets (1:16) and John and James' father had employees (1:20). In other words, they were in a rather secure job and, given the society of that day and age, they were moderately well-off. James and John were likewise engaged in a profitable business. Their father was active in this fishing enterprise, and the family business had, as well, employees, whom they paid (1:20). These four first disciples were all Jewish, of course, and apparently all Galileans. They had no specific preparation which would warrant their following of Jesus, except their Jewish religious background. They believed in God, as pious Jews of that time would do, and were evidently serious about the spiritual dimension of their life. Otherwise, it is inconceivable that they would have so suddenly left jobs and security to follow this itinerant, as yet unknown, spiritual preacher. Mark in no way indicates that they "gave up" their Jewish faith in order to embrace a "Jesus faith." Quite the contrary. Mark clearly indicates that the following of Jesus flowed from their Jewish spiritual rootage.

The next specific person we hear about in Mark's gospel is Simon Peter's mother-in-law (1:29–31). Jesus is present within the home of Simon and Andrew, and James and John are there as well. Simon Peter and Andrew have evidently opened their house to Jesus and to these two others. No mention is made of Simon Peter's wife, but he was evidently married. There is even some reason to believe that Simon Peter's wife stayed with him, both during the time of Jesus' earthly life and during the time after the resurrection (cf. 1 Cor 9:5). Once Jesus had cured Simon Peter's mother-in-law, she begins to serve them. Is this merely the service of hospitality, or does Mark want to indicate a more protracted service, which would have included some form of discipleship? The text and context are not clear.

In the initial chapters of Mark's gospel, which deal with the first of Jesus' healings and his preaching, there are also present a large, undifferentiated group, called "the crowd," the "many," "all." Jesus is presented as quite successful, and these crowds of people, these many people, all of them Jewish, came to hear him. His message was a spiritual message, focusing on the kingdom of God, and these Jewish people evidently found in his words something which touched their religious rootage in a deep way. In other words, Jesus was not preaching a message which contradicted their Jewish faith; rather, his message confirmed and deepened their Jewish faith. Both in the message of his words and in the message of his healing, it was a Jew speaking to Jews, *cor ad cor loquitur*. Subsequently, in the initial Marcan chapters, Jesus moves from Capernaum to the wider Galilee. His mission is extended, but still within a Jewish framework.

In 2:13–17 Mark presents the call of Levi, the son of Alphaeus. Levi is a toll collector, serving Herod Antipas. Such toll collectors, even though they were not Roman but Jewish, were considered by many Jewish leaders of that time as sinners, though this "sinfulness" might be more socially than morally interpreted. Levi's call, like that of Simon and Andrew, James and John, took place by the sea, and in a similar way is presented with a brief: "Come, follow me." Levi, like the others, immediately left his rather secure and lucrative business and followed Jesus. Like Simon and Andrew, he opened his home to Jesus and to his disciples (2:15 *mathetai*), inviting them to a meal. At this meal other tax collectors and sinners were also invited. Levi is presented as a very welcoming and gracious host to Jesus and his disciples. He is also presented as a disciple of Jesus.

After mentioning the meal and those invited, the author adds an additional sentence (2:15), which is to some degree parenthetical and to some degree ambiguous. We read: "For they were many (*polloi*) and they followed him." The "they" might refer to sinners and tax collectors, but more likely it refers to disciples (*mathetai*), indicating that besides Simon and Andrew, James and John, and now Levi, there were other disciples of Jesus, and enough "others" to be considered "many," who were also at this dinner. If this reference of *polloi* to *mathetai* is correct, then Mark is indicating to us that beside the "crowd" who came to hear Jesus, there were "many" who in a special way were considered disciples of Jesus, *mathetai*. Thus, at Levi's dinner, we have not only Jesus and the five named disciples, but other "many" unnamed disciples as well. One must add even further to this group of dinner invitees the number of additional tax collectors and sinners.

Who is this Levi? Not only do we find his call in Mark 2:14, but also in Luke 5:27. On the other hand, Matthew 9:9 speaks about the call of a tax collector, but this man is named Matthew. Levi does not seem to be one of the twelve, although in some of the mss evidence for the gospels one finds an attempt to link him with the twelve.[8] In the Marcan text, Levi, though not one of the twelve, nonetheless is clearly a disciple of Jesus.

The next occasion in which the gospel of Mark presents us with named disciples of Jesus is found in 3:13–19, the choosing of the twelve. Mark's list of these twelve reads as follows and in this order:

Simon Peter
James of Zebedee
John of Zebedee
Andrew, brother of Peter

Philip
Bartholomew
Matthew
Thomas

James of Alphaeus
Thaddeus
Simon the Zealot
Judas Iscariot

There are three groups of four, and this same threefold grouping of four is found in the parallels: Matthew 10:1–4; Luke 6:12–16; Acts 1:13. Each of these four lists breaks down into three groups of four, and although within each of the groups the order of names might vary, the names within each group never pass from one group to another. Brown arranges the naming and ordering of the twelve in these four accounts as follows:[9]

NAME	MARK	MATTHEW	LUKE	ACTS
Simon Peter	1	1	1	1
James of Zebedee	2	3	3	3
John of Zebedee	3	4	4	2
Andrew	4	2	2	4
Philip	5	5	5	5
Bartholomew	6	6	6	7
Matthew	7	8	7	8
Thomas	8	7	8	6
James of Alphaeus	9	9	9	9
Thaddeus	10	10		
Lebbaeus		10*		
Judas (Jude) of James			11	11
Simon the Zealot	11	11	10	10
Judas Iscariot	12	12	12	

In each of the accounts, Simon Peter is placed first, and in Matthew's account the author even states: "First of all, Simon." Some of these men are mentioned in the New Testament on other occasions as well. As early as the time of F. Schleiermacher and F.C. Baur, critics have argued that Jesus himself had not chosen the twelve, but that this was a later addition by the early church to substantiate its emerging authority structures.[10] The arguments against the historicity of the twelve seem to have run their course, and today the more reputable biblical scholars do not hesitate to make the selection of the twelve part of the historical data of Jesus' own life. However, it is evident that at the time when the gospels and Acts were being written, the name of "the twelve" was still venerated, but some of the members of the twelve were not that well remembered. This is reason why, it seems, that there is the discrepancy in the various listings. "It seems more probable that Thaddeus, Lebbaeus and Jude (all Semitic names) do not refer to the same person, but rather the difference of names means that by the time the Gospels were written the historical memory of who among the disciples of Jesus belonged to the Twelve was already hazy."[11]

The gospel of Mark does not permit us to see in this selection of the twelve an establishment of a new "priestly" or clerical group, since Mark frequently makes reference to the established Jewish priesthood without any indication that it had been supplanted. In 1:44 Jesus told the cured leper to go to the priest, in accordance with Mosaic law. In 8:31, the first prophecy of his suffering, he mentions the rejection he will have by the chief priests. The reference to the chief priests is repeated in the third prophecy (10:33). After the expulsion of the dealers from the temple, the chief priests confronted Jesus: "What authority have you for acting like this?" (11:28). In 12:12 the subject of the sentence, "they," is clearly the chief priests as well as the scribes of 11:27. The same reference of "they" must be seen in 12:13: "Next *they* sent to him some Pharisees and some Herodians. . . ." Throughout Mark's account of the arrest, trial and death of Jesus, the chief priests are again mentioned, naturally in an adversarial role; cf. 14:1, 10, 47, 53, 54, 55, 60, 61, 63; 15:1, 3, 11, 31. Had Jesus intended to supplant the Jewish priesthood, one would expect that the author would simply say that the Jewish priesthood had come to an end, that it had no validity, that the twelve were the new "priests" of Israel. None of this, however, is the case. Even though Mark presents the chief priests in an adversarial role, and in a role which compromises their own status as the religious leadership of the Jews, he nowhere states that the Jewish high priests had been removed from their office because Jesus had selected the twelve. Nowhere does the author indicate that a "rival religion," a "rival clergy," had been established with the election of the twelve. One cannot therefore read, either textually or contextually, in Mark's account the election of the twelve as the establishment of a new priestly hierarchy. The meaning of the twelve in this gospel appears to be quite different.[12]

Are the twelve, then, in Mark's gospel portrayed in any way akin to the later Christian cleric? As noted above, to present the disciples (*mathe-tai*) of Jesus, as found in the gospels, as either cleric or lay is anachronistic. That the twelve were held in great esteem by the Marcan community can be clearly drawn from the Marcan text, but the very fact that the names had become hazy is indicative that the twelve, as the name of a group, were much more a matter of history than of contemporary (to Mark) leadership. The twelve do not seem to have any leadership role within the Marcan community. The twelve seem to have a symbolic and modeling role. It should also be noted that the twelve are never called "apostles" in the Marcan text.

The twelve in 3:13–19 are indeed sent out (*apostelle*) by Jesus to preach and to have power to expel demons. In other words they are to do the same things which Jesus is doing: preaching the kingdom and making the kingdom present by healing and expelling demons. In 6:6b–13 Mark speaks about the mission of the twelve again. They are sent out (*apostel-lein*) two by two. Harrington, in his comments on this passage, reiterates what he has said above: namely, that the mission of the disciples was the same as the mission of Jesus, that is, to preach the kingdom. Harrington sees certain parts of these few verses as an editorial framework within which Mark describes what it means to be a disciple of Jesus: 6:6b–7, 12–13. They were to preach so that people might repent and they were to cast out many demons and anoint with oil many sick people.[13] These men were sent out to preach a revival (*metanoia*) of their Jewish faith and Jewish spirituality. The kingdom of God, which lies at the center of this Jewish faith and Jewish spirituality, demands a renewed spirit, a revival, a conversion. The twelve were not sent out, in Mark's accounting, to preach a "new religion." They were not sent out to preach that Jesus was messiah, nor that he was the Son of God. They were not to preach Jesus, but to preach the kingdom. In 6:8–9 the twelve are told (and through them the disciples of Mark's own community) not to take with them material com-forts. This highlights the urgency of Jesus' mission and by prolongation their own mission. Since traveling missionaries depended on local hospi-tality, they were to enter a house and stay there. As Harrington notes, this was to prevent social climbing.[14] Undoubtedly Mark has in mind, in writ-ing this passage on traveling missionaries, a group of similar people in his own community. Mark in this passage alludes to a smaller group than just disciples, and the implications of his descriptions seemingly bear on this service-leadership group. However, the traveling missionaries of Mark's own time and place, to which the author seems to allude, are not pre-sented as the "successors" to the twelve. The Marcan description of the sending out of the twelve, on the other hand, does offer to these later traveling missionaries a model for their own behavior and style.

In 3:21, 31–35 Mark mentions the mother and brothers of Jesus. In many ways it appears that the brothers of Jesus are not portrayed in Mark's gospel as Jesus' disciples. There is also a mention of his mother Mary, and his brothers, James and Joses, Judas and Simon, in 6:3, but again with no indication that they were "disciples." As relatives, of course, they were concerned about Jesus.[15]

In 4:10, Jesus explains to the twelve and the "others with him" the parable of the sower, which he had just told to the crowds. This passage indicates that besides the twelve there were other disciples close to Jesus. The true disciple, Jesus tells these people, is one who hears the word of God, accepts it and acts in accordance with the word of God.

In 8:14, we find mention of a smaller group of disciples, namely those who were in the boat with Jesus. In 8:27 Jesus with some disciples (*mathetai*) were leaving the villages around Caesarea Philippi, and on the way Jesus asks these disciples who they think he might be. Peter's response, "You are the Christ (messiah)," is immediately followed by (a) Jesus' command not to tell anyone about him, and (b) his first prediction about his upcoming suffering. Peter, again the spokesman, remonstrates with him, only to be called "Satan!" by Jesus himself. A turning point in Mark's gospel is being made. Up to this point the disciples have been generally presented as imitable. Now they begin to appear as non-imitable.

In 8:34 the crowd and his disciples have been called together once more, and Jesus explains to them the conditions for those who wish to be among his followers (*opiso mou elthein*). This emphasis on the suffering and death forms the turning point as regards imitable and non-imitable discipleship. But it is only a turning point, for Mark immediately presents a more positive picture of Jesus and discipleship in 9:2ff, as Jesus invites Peter and James and John to the mountain, where he is transfigured and then discloses to them the meaning of this transfiguration and its relationship to the figure of the Son of Man. Disciples, in imitation of Peter, James and John, should be able to see this transfigured Jesus. Yet no sooner has the transfiguration taken place than the theme changes once more. In 9:14ff this small group rejoins the disciples (*mathetai*) and all find themselves within a crowd of people. Jesus is asked (9:28–29) by a man to cure his son who is possessed by a demon (perhaps an epileptic). The father had asked the disciples to cure his son, but they could not do it. Jesus cures the boy, and when Jesus and the disciples had entered into the house, they asked him why they had been unable to cure the boy. Jesus' answer simply notes that this is the kind of demon which can only be driven out by prayer, a subtle way of saying either that these disciples themselves were not very prayerful, or that some of the disciples of Jesus in Mark's own community were not very prayerful. Mark's point may not be totally directed against the historical disciples of Jesus, but more against some members of his own Jesus community.

In 9:30–31, which follows, Jesus teaches his disciples privately, and the message of this teaching is again the upcoming suffering and death of the Son of Man. The disciples, however, did not understand him. The structure of Mark's gospel as regards imitable and non-imitable disciples continues to change. In a very marked way, from chapter 9 onward, the Marcan portrait of the disciples is presented in ever heavier negative overtones: namely, Mark portrays people acting precisely the way a disciple of Jesus should not be: thick-headed, not prayerful, fearful, afraid of suffering, disloyal, etc.

In 9:33–36 the issue of which disciple is the greatest arises. Jesus responds in two ways. First, he says that the greatest should be the last of all, the servant of all. How powerful a statement this answer of Jesus is can be seen in the fact that in the remainder of Mark's gospel Jesus is presented precisely as the last of all, the servant of all. "The ideal of leadership as service will be exemplified by Jesus as the Gospel story continues."[16]

In 10:23 Jesus again speaks to his disciples (*mathetai*), warning them that riches can easily deter one from entering the kingdom of God. The disciples (*mathetai*) were astonished at this saying, but Jesus continued: "It is easier for a camel to pass through the eye of a needle than for a rich person to enter the kingdom of God." But at this, the disciples became even more astonished. Jesus is clearly saying: riches and wealth can easily be an obstacle to discipleship.

Peter, once again, a spokesman for the *mathetai,* says: "Look at us! We have left everything and followed you" (10:28). Peter and the others are not like the man who refused to give up his wealth and follow Jesus. Jesus answers Peter: "No one who has left home or brothers or sisters or mothers or fathers or children or lands for my sake and for the sake of the kingdom will not be repaid a hundred times over, houses, brothers, sisters, mothers, children and lands—as also sufferings—now in this present time and in the age to come, eternal life" (10:29–31).[17]

In this entire episode Jesus is not speaking about a certain specialized group of disciples. In later generations of Christians, these words have too often been applied to religious and even to clergy, but Mark intends them to be guidelines for each and every disciple of Jesus. No doubt, through this narrative Mark is also speaking to his own community of Jesus disciples. The issue of wealth and its power, more specifically the misuse of both wealth and its power, presents major challenges to each and every disciple of Jesus. One finds this same issue of the misuse of both wealth and its power in the Lucan writings.

In 10:32–34, Jesus mentions to the twelve his third prophecy of the passion. In this third prediction the twelve are specifically mentioned, whereas in the first two predictions Mark had used the generic term "disciples." Moreover, the twelve are taken aside. In this third prediction, however, the twelve make no response.

Mark's narrative immediately focuses on the request of both James and John for special places in heaven. Mark once more makes the disciples' obtuseness center-stage. Jesus answers in a threefold way: (a) a place in the kingdom demands suffering; (b) not Jesus but God gives such places; (c) leadership in the Jesus community means service. Among the Gentiles, Jesus tells them, there is the use of raw power; in the kingdom of God, service is foremost. Mark uses first the word *diakonos* (servant), and then the stronger term, *doulos* (slave). This is immediately applied to Jesus himself: "For the Son of Man did not come to be served but to serve and to give his life as a ransom for all" (10:45). The author presents Jesus, and him alone, as the true model for all discipleship.

In 11:2 two of his disciples are sent to a village to get a young horse. When this was done, Jesus entered Jerusalem on the horse with the crowds cheering him. Jesus went to the temple and then with the twelve withdrew to Bethany. In 13:4 Peter, James, John and Andrew, strikingly three of his very first disciples, ask Jesus about the end of the world and the signs that will herald this moment. Mark uses this question to draw together all the eschatological ideas which we find in this same chapter.

In chapter 14 when his disciples (*mathetai*) ask about the passover, two were sent into Jerusalem with instruction on how to find a place in the city for them to celebrate the feast. These two are then said to have "prepared the passover" (14:16). Then, at evening time, Jesus arrives with the twelve. Were the two disciples part of the twelve or separate from them? It is difficult to make a solid conclusion on the basis of the text or the context. This passage in Mark does reopen the question whether the last supper was celebrated by Jesus only with the twelve or whether there were others as well at this supper. Since past theological history has emphasized so strongly the "clerical" aspect of this supper, based precisely on the presupposition that only the twelve were there with Jesus, the exegetical possibility of additional people at this supper raises many questions about the "clerical" interpretation of the last supper. At any rate, there is the celebration of the last supper, with its eucharistic interpretation, followed by the prediction of Peter's triple denial and of the fact that all of the disciples would be scandalized. All of this comes true. At Gethsemane the disciples, with Peter singled out, all slept, while Jesus prayed. When Judas [pointedly called one of the twelve] and the troupe of men arrived to arrest Jesus, we find the following: at first one of the bystanders (undoubtedly one of the disciples) drew a sword and cut off the ear of the high priest's servant, but they, i.e. the disciples, all abandoned him and ran away. A young man who had followed Jesus and was wearing only a linen cloth was grabbed by the soldiers, but he slipped out of the garment and ran away naked.[18] Who this might have been has never been decided. The total picture, however, is clear: the disciples abandoned Jesus in his hour of suffering. Mark climactically presents the very disciples of Jesus as the non-imitable disciples of Jesus.

Peter fares no better (14:66–72), for although he is at the courtyard of the high priest's house, he denies Jesus three times. This is the last we hear of the twelve and these disciples until mention is made of them, although rather obliquely, in regard to the women at the tomb on the day of resurrection. Mark has clearly painted a negative picture of Jesus' male disciples, and in particular of the twelve.[19] With all of the pictures and statues of the "twelve apostles," and with all the liturgical celebration of their feasts, it is sobering to realize that Mark is telling his own community: Do not imitate the twelve. He takes the focus off of the twelve and places it solely upon Jesus, the Lord.

In 15:40–41 mention is made of the women disciples: Mary of Magdala, Mary who was the mother of James the younger and Joses, and Salome. "These used to follow him and look after him when he was in Galilee. And there were many other women there who had come up to Jerusalem with him." In Mark's gospel this is the first time we have reference to the women disciples of Jesus. Up to this point, the disciples, who have been named, were all male, with the possible exception of Peter's mother-in-law, who is named only indirectly. In 14:3–9 an unnamed woman is mentioned who anointed the feet of Jesus when he was having dinner in the house of Simon the leper. Now, however, we hear about women who had followed Jesus and had served him. Mary Magdalene and Mary the mother of Joses not only were present when Jesus died, but these two women also saw where he was buried (15:47). These two women and also Salome are the ones who come to the tomb on the first day of the week (16:1), and at the tomb the young man points out that they are seeking "Jesus of Nazareth, the one who was crucified. He has been raised; he is not here. But go and tell his disciples and Peter, 'He is going before you into Galilee and there you will see him, just as he told you' " (16:6–7). The women, however, do not do this. They flee from the tomb, deeply frightened and say nothing to anyone. Even with this presence of women at the death, the burial and the tomb, the human disciple comes out both positive and negative: positive, since these women remained close to Jesus, but negative, since they, too, failed to understand Jesus. In the last part of Mark's gospel, it is Jesus alone who is the focus of discipleship.

Throughout this entire Marcan presentation of the disciples of Jesus, there is, besides the named individuals and unnamed individuals and groups, another group of disciples who are never mentioned, but are clearly present on every page of this gospel. These are the disciples in the Jesus community of Mark himself, the addressees of his gospel. Where this community, of which the author himself was a part and for which he wrote the gospel, was actually situated, may never be decided. It is clear, however, that the author is writing an account of Jesus for a definite group of people, who already believe in Jesus. The author is not writing for a group of people who do not believe in Jesus. Mark, then, is writing "to deepen the faith of the members of his community. By showing them how the traditions about Jesus related to their belief in the saving significance of the cross and resurrection, the evangelist equipped them to face persecution and resist the temptations of their world."[20] The author portrays the discipleship of Jesus both positively and negatively, that is, the disciples in the gospels are presented at first in a positive way, imitable, and this portrait is meant to show his own community certain characteristics which they themselves should deepen. The author also presents the negative side of these same disciples in the latter half of the gospel, indicating to his own community that they should not be like these men, that is, the twelve and the disciples, nor even like the women disciples. Jesus alone should be their real model.

In this sense there is something "ecclesial" about this gospel. It is written to make the Jesus community, of which the author is a part, that is, the *ekklesia* of his home base, much more imbued with the ideals of the kingdom. The addressees of this entire gospel are not an "hierarchical in-group." They are not a cadre of "religious professionals." The addressees are the many and various men and women who make up this Jesus community. To them Mark is saying on each and every page: This is what discipleship is all about.

Still another disciple hovers in the wings of this gospel and is found likewise on every page, and that is the author himself. The author of this gospel is a very careful and intriguing writer. He develops issues and events with set purposes, as for instance his use of geography, his use of specific terms, and the format we have just mentioned on the positive/negative side of the disciples. In all of this the author is indicating his own ideals of discipleship. He is ardently telling his community [and us] what his own faith in Jesus is all about, what his own understanding of the kingdom of God and discipleship in this kingdom is all about. In a very oblique way the readership of this gospel can catch a glimpse of the hopes and dreams, the ideals and spirituality, of the man who wrote this account of Jesus' life, death and resurrection.

I have spent a great deal of time on Mark's portrait of the disciples of Jesus. The theme is central to his gospel, as biblical scholars tell us again and again. When all the pieces are placed before us, we do *not* have a picture of what a good cleric should be. The disciple in Mark, even through the way he describes the twelve, cannot be limited to the later "cleric" or "episkopos" or "presbyter." The portrait of the twelve in Mark's gospel has a message, both positive and negative, for each and every follower of Jesus. *Nor* does Mark describe in this picture of discipleship what a later generation would call the ideal "religious." Even less can one find in Mark's gospel what a later Christian generation would call a good "lay" person in the church. Rather, the author describes what each and every follower or disciple of Jesus, male or female, rich or poor, leader or non-leader, should be and should not be. Mark's centering on Jesus himself, not on a disciple, not even on the twelve, nor on the special three, Simon Peter, James and John, but only on Jesus, is key to the intent of this author, who makes the model for discipleship, as found in this gospel, the life, death and resurrection of Jesus, and this model is meant for all who would follow Jesus, the Lord.

2. THE DISCIPLES IN THE GOSPEL OF LUKE

The theology of both the Lucan gospel and the Acts of the Apostles builds on, but in major ways differs from, the theology one finds in the gospel of Mark. In the first place the material in Luke–Acts covers not only the life, death and resurrection of Jesus, but also, in a detailed way, the growth of the early Jesus community. The material in Luke's gospel is necessary to understand Acts, and vice versa the material in Acts is necessary to see what Luke is attempting to present in his gospel. The gospel of Luke and the Acts of the Apostles have come to be seen more and more in their togetherness, rather than in their separateness.

J. Fitzmyer, in his commentary on Luke's gospel, presents a lengthy introduction on Lucan theology. He notes that this kind of essay, a sort of theological synthesis, has been common for the Pauline and the Johannine material, but not for the Lucan material.[21] M. Goguel in 1946, he notes, presented a very negative judgment on Lucan theology. H. Conzelmann in 1954 presented only a very "attenuated sense of Lucan theology." H. Flender,[22] I.H. Marshall,[23] E. Franklin,[24] and J. Fitzmyer himself have made serious efforts to turn this view of Luke into a more positive evaluation.

It is not the place here to present the totality of Lucan theology, as it is being developed by these scholars. Rather, presuming their work, let us consider only one aspect of this Lucan theology: the theology of discipleship. Such a limited goal, however, indicates to us that we must first ask the basic question: For whom is this material written? When one combs the scholars with this question in mind, one is faced almost immediately with the issue: Was the readership "a Gentile Christian audience, or at least one that was predominantly Gentile Christian"?[25] Or was the readership Jewish-Christian? The first view is the more common, and the second view is an older, more traditional position.[26] It would seem that contemporary scholarship envisions the readership of both the gospel and of Acts as basically Gentile, with only some Jews and Jewish Christians within its readership. Contemporary scholarship also indicates that there were some problems besetting this community or communities of addressees, some arising from within the community itself, such as Jewish Christians who wanted to retain many Old Testament features, and some arising from without the community, such as harassment from the local Jewish synagogue leaders.

It is also important to note that the author is writing for a definite group of people who believed in Jesus, a group who were living close to the years 80–85 for the gospel,[27] and 85–90 for Acts.[28] These two New Testament writings were clearly not written out of a Palestinian Christian community, but the exact location of this predominantly Gentile Christian community (or even a grouping of such communities), to which Luke belonged, is not known. Every page of these Lucan writings, however, has been penned for this specific Christian group. Since the author himself had a fairly definite audience in mind, and since he wanted to convey to this group of Christians some basic aspect of the good news, the way in which the author emphasizes his material, shapes and focuses his material, and selects certain details while not mentioning others might be described as Luke's own kerygma.[29] In this kerygma of Luke, we hear, of course, the kerygma of Jesus: what Jesus himself preached and what Jesus himself taught.

Luke certainly understood Jesus as a teacher and as a preacher. In the New Testament generally no distinction is made between kerygma and didache, preaching and teaching. Both terms indicate the proclamation which Jesus brought. Luke follows this usage of these terms, frequently portraying Jesus as a teacher. In the gospel of Luke, Jesus is called "teacher," *didaskalos,* thirteen times and called "master," *epistata,* six times. Jesus is said to teach (*didaskein*) fourteen times, and often Luke has Jesus teaching in the synagogue and temple, the very areas in which the professional teachers of Israel held forth.[30] We also find in the Lucan material the kerygma which Jesus' disciples were to proclaim, namely that of the twelve (9:1-6, 10), that of the seventy (-two) (10:1-16), as well as that encapsulated in the final missionary charge, given by the risen Jesus to his disciples (24:47). Acts, for its part, portrays the earliest disciples preaching this same kerygma, teaching this same didache. The various speeches in Acts, for instance, contain this early kerygma. Naturally, the author may have reworked some of his material, but the material is clearly presented as the kerygma which the disciples of Jesus should proclaim.[31]

Luke himself, however, is also personally preaching and teaching through these two writings. He has, it might be said, his own agenda. He is attempting to proclaim, tell, instruct his own community about Jesus himself, about his message, and about the way his own community should "follow" Jesus, that is, how to be disciples of Jesus. One could approach the gospel and Acts with such questions as: Whom does Luke name as the disciples of Jesus? What are their qualities and characteristics? But a mere cataloguing of named people who appear in these New Testament pages and a mere description of their "way" of life would not exhaust the Lucan account of discipleship. Luke himself appears in the wings of these writings, for it is this author who has selected, emphasized, and nuanced the portrait of Jesus' disciple. It is this author himself who has, to some degree, shaped and honed the very kerygma and didache which one finds expressed in these writings. This kerygma and didache is not totally the work of Luke, for he has used sources, such as Mark and Q, as well as others, but Luke has subtly contextualized this kerygma and didache into the structure of his own works. In doing this, he indirectly indicates to his readership those aspects of the Jesus message which he himself considers paramount as far as discipleship is concerned. Luke indicates what he himself believes a disciple of Jesus should be. Luke indicates his own ideals and his own goals, as far as he understands discipleship of the Lord.

Secondly, this highlighted and subtly nuanced picture of a Jesus disciple which Luke presents is not only indicative of his own aspirations, but it is precisely what he hopes the readers, i.e. the predominantly Gentile community, will make their own as well. Again, besides the people who appear in the pages of Luke as disciples of Jesus, we have, in the wings, but very present to each page, the disciples of Jesus who make up the community out of which Luke is writing. These disciples are both men and women, both leaders and followers, both Gentiles and Jews. This predominantly Gentile, but secondarily Jewish community to which he is writing is not differentiated in the following way: Luke is not writing only to the *men* in his community. He is not writing only to the *leaders* in his community. He is not writing only to a *sectarian few* within his community. He seems to be writing to his total community, which means that the ideal of disciple that Luke presents is an ideal for all the members of his intended audience.

The discussion on the identity of the "most distinguished Theophilus," mentioned in the prologue of the gospel (1:3-4) and in the prologue to Acts (1:1), brings out this character of a public writing. As Fitzmyer notes: "Because Luke dedicates the two volumes to Theophilus, it means that his opus is not a private writing; Theophilus stands for the Christian readers of Luke's own day and thereafter."[32] Luke wanted his writings to be read by a wide audience, and not only read—he wanted his audience to find in his presentation of the ideal disciple of Jesus the ideal which the men and women of his audience should incorporate into their own Christian lives.

Naturally, during the course of these two volumes Luke writes passages here and there which are pointedly addressed to the Christian leadership of his own day. It is clear, for instance, that he singles out the twelve. Mark had already done this, and we find a similar situation in Matthew. Luke emphasizes that the origins of this group must be traced to Jesus himself (6:12-16). Jesus, in Luke, summons his disciples (*mathetai*) and selects twelve of them. In the Lucan account and only in this account, it is Jesus himself who calls them "apostles." This addition of the term "apostle" is probably a retrojection by Luke of a post-resurrection term into a pre-resurrection event. Luke clearly wants to associate an apostle with Jesus himself, and this association to the life and death of Jesus is echoed in the account of Acts 1:21-22. "For Luke, these special disciples were not simply to 'be with him' (Mark 3:14), but they were to be his 'emissaries' (*apostoloi*, i.e. persons sent out), indeed, even witnesses to him."[33] For instance, they are with Jesus in his Galilean mission as is seen in 8:1, but the twelve are with Jesus together with some women: Mary called Magdalene, Joanna, Susanna and "many others" (8:2-3). However, it is clear in this latter passage that there is a distinction between the twelve and the women. Luke does not here, nor anywhere, place the women on a par with the twelve, nor does he place any other group of Christians, male or female, on a par with the twelve. Luke sees the twelve as a special group of Jesus' followers. Can we, however, from the standpoint of a later Christian generation see in the twelve the later *episkopoi* of the church? Can we even see in the twelve an ecclesiastical office? That Luke sees the twelve as a special group among the disciples of Jesus is evident; the role of the twelve within this community, as we shall see, is not that evident.

After Jesus tells the parable of the sower and the seed (8:4-8), his disciples ask him: "What is the meaning of this parable?" (8:9). The disciples, asking this question, are the twelve *and* the women.[34] Jesus then explains that these disciples (the twelve *and* the women) have been granted a knowledge of the secrets (*mysteria*) of the kingdom of God. The center of the good news is, of course, the kingdom of God. These disciples have been given a knowledge of its mysteries which the "others" do not share. This is not a knowledge to be treasured in private in a gnostic sort of way. Rather, it is a knowledge which one should proclaim from the roof-tops, praying that the "others" will hear as well. How does Luke present these mysteries, these hidden insights in the parable?[35] Luke emphasizes that there are four different groups of hearers of the word of God, for "The seed is the word of God." These four groups of hearers or disciples are:

    a. Those on the edge of the path, who indeed have the word of God, but the devil comes and carries the word out of their hearts so that they do not believe and cannot be saved.

    b. Those on the rock who hear the word of God with joy, but who have no rootage, and so they only believe for a while, and in time of trial fall away.

    c. Those who are found among the thorns, and who, though they hear, are choked by worries, riches, and pleasures of life and so do not reach maturity.

    d. Those who in rich soil hear the word with a noble and generous heart, and who make it a part of themselves, yielding a great harvest because they persevere.

This insight into the parable is given to the twelve and the women. By indicating this audience, Luke is clearly speaking, at least indirectly, to his own predominantly Gentile community, holding up for their view a mirror of discipleship. In the Jesus community discipleship takes on many forms, and not all of them are ultimately saving. Even the twelve must see themselves in this fourfold mirror, for not all the twelve are in the last category. Judas, one of the twelve, betrayed Jesus, as Luke notes often enough (6:16; 22:3, 47). Judas had heard the word of God, but worries and riches and the pleasures of life choked him.

Moreover, Luke emphasizes the issue of trial and suffering. To be a disciple of Jesus involves one in persecution and trial. The seed that falls in rich soil produces great results but only through perseverance (*hypomene*). Only a disciple of generous and noble heart will persevere. This is borne out in the many episodes in Acts in which the disciples of Jesus undergo imprisonment, persecution, even death. Many of these early followers of Jesus had to persevere even to the point of death.

In this same eighth chapter, we hear that Jesus' mother and brothers are waiting to see him (8:20). Whereas Mark excludes the mother and the brothers of Jesus from the role of disciples (Mk 3:31–35; cf. the harsher statement in Jn 7:5), Luke and Matthew avoid any such negative judgment. In fact, for Luke "they are the prime examples of those who listen to the Word of God 'with a noble and generous mind' (8:15)."[36] Again, the author presents the true disciple of Jesus, and Mary certainly has a primacy of place.[37]

In 9:1–6 Luke recounts the mission of the twelve.

> One now sees the purpose behind the choosing of the Twelve in 6:13: they are to be given a share in Jesus' own mission of preaching the kingdom of God. He has already told them that they have been granted the favor of knowing the secrets of the kingdom (8:10) and that what is secret will become known (8:17). Now he bestows on them "power and authority," yet it is not restricted to preaching, but involves the care of the physical and mental health of human beings. In this passage Luke, more carefully than Mark, distinguishes between healing and exorcism, but both are to be in their ability. But Luke has not only prepared for this commission, but it is in itself a foreshadowing of a greater commission to be given in 24:46–47. Now, during his own Galilean ministry, his commission gives them a share in his "power" and "authority"; later, they will be commissioned in a different way.[38]

Although this narrative section appears rather straightforward, the sending of the seventy (-two) in 10:1–12, which in so many ways parallels this very section on the twelve, raises serious questions about the difference between the mission of the twelve and the mission of the seventy (-two). The reprise of these instructions which one finds in the Lucan account of the last supper (22:35–36) again raises the question: To whom is Jesus presenting these instructions? In 10:1–12 do we not see the "purpose" behind the choosing of the seventy (-two), just as we do for the twelve in 9:1–6? Are not the seventy (-two) given a "share in Jesus' own mission of preaching the kingdom of God"? Do not the seventy (-two) receive "power and authority" just as the twelve had? In other words, from either the text or the context of Luke's writings, how does one distinguish the twelve and the seventy (-two)?[39] Moreover, the fact that there is no sending of the disciples during the lifetime of Jesus in the Johannine tradition raises the question of the very historicity of this event. That Jesus might have empowered his disciples to share his preaching and healing ministry is possible; that it actually occurred remains questionable. Because it remains exegetically questionable, one would be well cautioned not to construct an ecclesiology on its base.

The twelve continue to play a role in the gospel of Luke. Peter makes his profession of faith, namely that Jesus was "The Messiah of God." This is followed by the first prophecy of the passion and death. Luke includes Peter, John and James in the transfiguration (9:28–36). The day after the transfiguration there is a cure of an epileptic demoniac, and while everyone is full of admiration for him, Jesus tells his disciples for a second time that he must suffer and die. But they did not understand him. In these pericopes there is that strange juxtaposition of admiration, suffering, incredulity.

In 17:5 the apostles (*apostoloi*) say to the Lord, "Increase our faith." Jesus points out that faith can be as tiny as a mustard seed, but it has nevertheless great power. In 18:28, Peter asks about the reward for those who had left everything, and Jesus promises them an abundance both in the present time and in the world to come. Yet with this promise, Jesus, in Luke's account, immediately adds the third prophecy of his suffering. Again, one finds that odd juxtaposition: reward and promise on the one hand, suffering and even death on the other.

The twelve continue in Luke's gospel to act in ways similar to those one finds in Mark: at the last supper, at the arrest in Gethsemane, at Peter's denial in the house of the high priest. As in Mark, they are conspicuously absent at Golgotha. Unlike the Marcan account, however, the eleven are present in Jerusalem after the resurrection, and Jesus appears both to Peter and to the eleven with his final instructions (24:44–49).

These final instructions, however, are not given to the eleven only. The text indicates otherwise, for the two disciples had returned to Jerusalem from Emmaus, and had found the eleven and "those with them." In the next episode, Luke makes no change as regards the *dramatis personae*. The risen Lord appears to this group: namely, the eleven, "those with them," and the two disciples who had returned from Emmaus. Karris notes that this episode seems to be a "new" episode, tied in to the one which has the disciples returning from Emmaus and the one in which Jesus appeared to Simon. Oddly, no mention is made in this "new episode" that Jesus had already appeared to these disciples.[40] However, had Luke wanted he could have made the disciples in this "new episode" only the eleven, but he makes no effort to narrow the audience. It is, as far as the text itself is concerned, to this larger group that Jesus then speaks, giving them his farewell address. From 24:36 to 24:53, no mention is made that only the eleven are being addressed; no mention is made that only "apostles" are being addressed.[41] This final section of Luke's gospel appears to be an address to a fairly wide group of disciples, and through them to the disciples of Luke's own community. These final words become, then, a message for all disciples of Jesus, not only for a leadership group. All followers of Jesus, men and women, those of Gentile origin and those of Jewish origin, those in a leadership position and those not in a leadership position, are enjoined: (a) to be witnesses (24:48); (b) to be given what the Father has promised (24:49); (c) to be clothed with power from on high (24:49).

If one had only the gospel of Luke, the role of the twelve could only be understood as a symbol for the reconstitution of Israel, i.e. the formation of the new Israel. Just as there were twelve patriarchs and twelve tribes, who again and again throughout the Old Testament symbolize the whole of Israel, so too in the new Israel of Jesus there are the twelve, symbolizing a totality, yet one which is not exclusive, but inclusive, which is not hemmed in by barriers, but which is boundary-breaking, as we shall see. A connection of the twelve to an episcopal office or an ecclesiastical office can hardly be made on the basis of the material in the Lucan gospel. Does the material in Acts, however, alter this view? Does it specify more clearly the role of the twelve?

In Acts the apostles are instructed by Jesus during the forty days (1:3); they are witnesses to the ascension (1:9–11); they return from the Mount of Olives to Jerusalem and gather in the upper room. The eleven are then mentioned by name, and although the Lucan gospel list of names is the same as that in Acts, the positioning of the names is not the same, as we have seen. Under the leadership of Peter they—and Luke adds, *together with others*—reconstitute the twelve through the election of Matthias. This never happens again; when James dies (12:2), there is apparently no need to elect a successor to him. After this election of Matthias, Peter and the eleven are mentioned in 2:14, and the twelve as such are mentioned only on one other occasion in Acts, namely in 6:2–6, for the institution of the seven. Fitzmyer asks: "How does one account for the ephemeral existence of this group? Why does its influence disappear in Acts? Why is its only function, after the testimony to Israel on Pentecost, to change the community-structure by overseeing the democratic appointment of the seven table servers?"[42] These are major questions put to the scriptural texts, which have far-reaching ecclesiological implications.[43] In Mark we saw a shadow side of the twelve. In the final section of Mark they were presented as non-models of discipleship. In Luke's writings we have an imposing portrait of the twelve; they alone merit, in Luke's view, the name of apostle, but after the initial preaching of the risen Jesus as Lord and Messiah (Acts 2:4, 2:11), and after the two incidents in which they share in a structuring of the Jesus community, the twelve simply vanish. The twelve play no further role. Luke evidently does not see them as a necessary component of the Jesus community as it struggles to maintain itself in spite of the delay of the parousia.

I have spent this time on the twelve and their role in the Lucan writings to indicate that, even though there is a special position attributed to this group, Luke does not make its role crystal-clear. Moreover, the writings of Luke cannot be seen as though they were written for such a group. In Luke's accounts, even in those sections which specifically mention the twelve, we do not have a "manual for episkopoi" nor a "manual for presbyteroi," nor can Luke's gospel be seen as a "manual for the twelve." Jesus is not presented as a teacher who spent his time instructing a small in-group. Even when he speaks to the twelve, the audience seems to be wider than just that limited number of a dozen persons. Luke is writing for his community, and his gospel is meant to be a manual for his community. Mention, indeed, is made of intramural, Christian leadership, particularly in Acts, but only here and there and in a passing sort of way. That there is a leadership group in the early Christian community out of which Luke comes and for which he writes is clear. But Luke is not writing directly or exclusively for this leadership group. Nor do we have any indication in the entire Lucan material that there is a distinction between the leadership group, even the Twelve, on the one hand, and the remaining disciples of Jesus, on the other, which has its basis in an ordination ritual. Nor is there a distinction between leadership and non-leadership, based on some *klerikoi/laikoi* structure. In fact, we are not given, even in Acts, a very clear indication in what way the early Christian communities arrived at their leadership, established their leadership, or even named their leadership. Luke's presentation of the twelve, both in the gospel and in Acts, offers no clear basis for the so-called "apostolic succession," a concept which later generations of Christians would develop and even wrangle over. Rather, the focus of Luke's two presentations, the gospel and Acts, is on Jesus himself and on discipleship as it affects every follower of Jesus, male or female, leader or non-leader, Greek or Jewish. From Luke's writings, one cannot deduce that there are two ways of following Jesus: one a general way for the undifferentiated group of the baptized and another for an inner-circle of leadership. Both the inner-circle of community leadership and the wider-circle of the baptized-eucharistic community find foundationally their purposes and goals, their ideals and values, in precisely the same source: the meaning of Christian discipleship. Luke makes every effort to describe this disciple of Jesus.

When Fitzmyer draws up his description of discipleship, as presented in Luke, he mentions three main characteristics:

a. Faith in Jesus.
b. Repentance and conversion.
c. Baptism.

To these he adds others, but they are not primary:

d. An identification in Jesus' very way of living.
e. The task of bearing witness to the risen Christ.
f. A serious commitment to prayer.
g. A correct way of using material possessions to help those less fortunate.

For Luke this Christian "way" of life (*hodos*), this discipleship, is not a matter of an individual's way of life. There is an organized and communal framework as well, a *koinonia*, an *ekklesia*. We are not Christians individually; we are Christians collectively. We are the new Israel, the reconstituted Israel. However, when Fitzmyer enumerates these qualities of discipleship, he does not begin with belonging to the community, but rather with belonging in faith to Jesus, with a life of metanoia or conversion, and with a public acknowledgement of this faith-acceptance of Jesus and this turning about of one's life through the ritual of baptism.[44]

Karris, in his own commentary, highlights in a different way those aspects of Lucan theology, which have a direct bearing on discipleship.

1. Jesus' mission is an inclusive one as he seeks out the lost and sinners and restores them to union with God.[45]

At the very start of his public ministry, Luke presents Jesus proclaiming the good news of the kingdom to Nazareth, to Capernaum, and then to other towns (4:14–44). This section begins with the verse from Isaiah, in which Jesus says of himself that he is to bring good news to the poor, to proclaim liberty to captives, give sight to the blind, bring release for those downtrodden. There is an openness, an inclusiveness to the Lucan presentation of Jesus' message. Men and women are restored to wholeness (4:31–44). His ministry to the outcasts is boundary-breaking, stepping across the religiously and socially accepted division of clean and unclean.[46] Jesus' power over sin (5:17–26), his mission to sinners (5:27–32), the newness of his message (5:33–39), his subordination of the sabbath to mercy and kindness (6:1–11), all attest to this "boundary-breaking" kerygma of Jesus.

In a way that is quite different from Mark, Luke does not present the first disciples as following Jesus on the spur of the moment. Only after Peter, James and John have heard the teaching of Jesus, described in the preceding paragraph, and have seen his mighty works, and are overwhelmed by Jesus, does Jesus invite them to be his disciples (5:1–11). Only after instances of boundary-breaking kerygma does Jesus, in Luke, select twelve out of his many disciples. "For Luke, the Twelve become the bond of continuity between Jesus' kingdom proclamation and the Church's preaching of God's word."[47] In Luke's account, the first disciples of Jesus, the twelve themselves, the many followers of the way, which we find in Acts, are all bonds between Jesus' proclamation of the kingdom and the preaching of the church community. This means that the church communities, the disciples, must reflect this inclusive mission of Jesus. Otherwise the bond is lost.

Nonetheless, both the choosing of the twelve and the restoration of the twelve in Acts 1:15–26 cannot be interpreted as "ecclesiastical office. The basic 'service' of the Twelve is the 'ingathering of Israel,' which Jesus had begun and which their own number prophetically symbolized."[48] All the disciples of Jesus, but in a highly symbolic way the twelve as well, were to manifest this reconstituted Israel, which is meant to be inclusive to all, step over religious and social boundaries of clean and unclean, and be a boundary-breaking group.

2. Jesus' kingdom message is for men and women and shatters the boundaries of clean and unclean.[49]

This sentence of Karris categorizes the Lucan section from 7:1 to 9:6. In these episodes the centurion's servant is healed; the widow's son is brought back to life at Naim; Jesus answers the messengers of John the Baptist by noting that the blind see, the deaf hear, the lame walk, lepers are cleansed, the dead are raised to life, and the poor have good news preached to them. In this section as well, a woman washes his feet while he is eating in the home of a Pharisee, and women, such as Mary of Magdala, Joanna and Susanna, as well as many others (*heterai pollai*), follow him. The parable of the sower is recounted, a parable of discipleship, as is also the parable of the lamp. Jesus calms the storm, cures the demoniac in the Gerasenes, brings health to the woman with a hemorrhage and life to Jairus' daughter. Only after all this does Luke mention that the twelve were sent out with "power and authority" over devils, and they were to cure and to proclaim the kingdom of God and to heal. The meaning of these terms: cure, heal, proclaim, authority, power, has to be understood against the preceding material which can be summarized as a message for both men and women and a message which shatters the boundaries of what is clean and what is unclean. The reconstituted Israel, in Luke, is a kingdom of peace, reconciliation, openness, inclusiveness. It is a reconstituted kingdom for sinners, for the poor, for the sick, for the dying, for the oppressed, for the downtrodden. It is a kingdom open to Gentiles and Jews, which means it is a kingdom open to all. When one begins to see in the terms "power" and "authority" something other than the power of God's boundary-breaking and inclusive love, when one begins to move into areas of power such as "jurisdiction," "power of the keys," "power of order," etc., these latter so-called powers must be interpreted by the power of God's boundary-breaking love and inclusive mercy which Luke presents, and not vice versa.

In Luke's account, Jesus really begins his own exodus from the time of his conception and birth onward, but this exodus becomes a major moment in Lucan theology, when from 9:51 to 24:53 Jesus journeys (*exodus*) to Jerusalem, undergoes his arrest, suffering, and death, but then rises from the dead. In Luke's presentation this exodus of Jesus incorporates his life, his death and his resurrection, but it also incorporates his leaving the north of Palestine and steadily moving southward to Jerusalem, only to bring about in Jerusalem itself the deconstitution of Israel and the reconstitution of Israel.

On this journey, Jesus in the Lucan account provides an instruction on the meaning of the Christian "way." He tells his many disciples that there is a cost to this discipleship (9:57–62), that it is a discipleship meant for both men and women (10:38–42), that opposition will not undo the growth of God's kingdom (13:18–21). In a second part of this instruction, 13:22–17:10, we find the need for repentance, we find the inclusive nature of Jesus' banquet of the kingdom, we find the need to carry one's cross (14:27) and the need to share with those in want (16:1–31). In a third part of this same instruction (17:11–19:27) fidelity to God and to Jesus and also the need to take a risk are part of a disciple's life.

In this "exodus instruction" of Jesus, covering several chapters of Luke's gospel, one finds an instruction not for the twelve alone, nor for a small group of Jesus' disciples. One finds, rather, a description of discipleship which applies to all those who wish to follow Jesus. This exodus from Galilee to Jerusalem ends, as we know, in the death and resurrection of Jesus. Key to an understanding of this death and resurrection, however, is the supper which the Lord shared with his disciples on the very eve of his arrest.

3. **Luke does not describe a supper with just Jesus and the twelve apostles present. He is painting on a much larger**

canvas with many more subjects—women and men of his own communities who continue Jesus' ministry of feeding people.[50]

Luke's presentation of the final supper of Jesus shatters the picture of Jesus and only the twelve, a picture which Leonardo da Vinci's last supper painting has made almost canonical. Jesus, in Luke, celebrates this supper in an inn (*katalyma*). At his birth there was no room in the inn (*katalyma*) (2:7). In Jerusalem he finds another inn (*katalyma*) in which he holds this supper (22:11). The Greek word is the same in both instances. At his birth there was no hospitality, no room for him in the inn; in the center of Israel's world, Jerusalem, there is hospitality for Jesus at an inn. In the account of this supper, the Lucan language varies considerably as regards who are present: from Judas, one of the twelve, to disciples generally, to apostles. The picture which Luke offers is not a meal with the twelve alone, but a meal with a mixture of his disciples.

At this meal we hear once again the Lucan description of a disciple: Jesus settles the dispute among them (i.e. the many disciples at the meal) about who is the greatest. The dispute focuses on discipleship, and, even more, on the acme of discipleship. Mark and Matthew do not include this episode in their accounts of the last supper. John presents the same idea, but in a quite different way, namely, that of the washing of the feet. Luke deliberately includes this episode here. Since a final supper is a time for final reminders, the theme of discipleship is basic. Since the portrait is that of Jesus speaking to a wide spectrum of disciples, the theme of discipleship is meant for all the listeners. Once again we see Luke moving beyond a message to the twelve, moving to a message for all Jesus' followers. To these Jesus says: "The greatest among you must behave as if he were the youngest, the leader as if he were the one who serves. For who is the greater: the one at table or the one who serves? The one at table, surely? Yet here am I among you as the one who serves" (22:26–27). To this same group, i.e. all the various disciples at the meal, Jesus confers his kingdom, and promises that they will sit on thrones, judging the twelve tribes of Israel (22:28–30).

The servant Jesus, the model of discipleship, then moves to the Mount of Olives to pray, but the disciples can only sleep. When the men came to arrest him, Luke mentions that one disciple, with a sword, tried to defend Jesus.[51] It is the last we hear of these disciples until after the resurrection, with the single exception of Peter's threefold denial (22:54–62). Nonetheless, the theme of discipleship is not left to one side. Jesus, throughout the account of his trial, condemnation, march to Golgotha and death, is portrayed by Luke as the model for all disciples. Everything which Jesus has preached about the kingdom—its inclusiveness, its mercy, its boundary-breaking love—finds echoes throughout the account of the death of Jesus. Beyond this riveting picture of Jesus, there are minor incidents which touch briefly on the issue of discipleship.

Luke is more gracious to the followers of Jesus than Mark is, for in 22:49 he notes that all those who had known Jesus (*pantes hoi gnostoi*) stood at a distance, and in a pointed way Luke adds: "And the women who had accompanied him from Galilee saw all." Luke's theological use of geography does not allow for the disciples to return to Galilee. Jerusalem is central to the deconstitution and reconstitution of Israel. For Luke, all the resurrection episodes take place in the area around Jerusalem, not in Galilee, since it is in the religious center of Israel itself that the religious renewal of Israel takes place.

Only in Luke's account do we find that "large numbers of people followed him, and of women, too, who mourned and lamented for him" (23:27). The words of Jesus to these daughters of Jerusalem are really words about the immanence of God's judgment and the need to repent and accept the presence of God's kingdom. The description of Simon from Cyrene is also worded in the phraseology of discipleship, for he shouldered the cross and carried it behind Jesus. There may be more symbolism than historical reality in these details of Luke, but Luke deftly weaves these details into the theme of discipleship. Joseph of Arimathea is likewise in this category of an upright and virtuous person, living in hope of seeing the kingdom of God. For Luke, the disciple of Jesus will be involved in trial and even death, and the presence of these rather cameo figures indicates that even in the trial and death of Jesus discipleship is not totally obscured.

In 23:56 Luke mentions the women disciples, who had come from Galilee with Jesus, once more. They noted where Jesus was buried and went home to prepare spices and ointments. These are the same women who arrive at the tomb on Easter morning, hear the message of the two men about the risen Jesus and bring the message of a risen Jesus to the eleven and all the others. However, the apostles and these other disciples do not believe the women. Peter runs to the tomb, notes everything, and is amazed, but nothing more.

The episode concerning the two disciples on the way to Emmaus covers almost one-half of Luke's account of the resurrection. Evidently this episode is highly significant for Luke, since the allocation of so much space to it is overwhelmingly out of proportion to every other resurrection episode in the Lucan material. These two disciples represent, at least indirectly, the disciples of Luke's own community: questioning, doubting, hesitant, perplexed. Luke presents Jesus explaining to them the meaning of Moses and the prophets (24:27), a similar approach which Jesus offers to all the disciples in his final instructions (24:44). Discipleship of Jesus, with its trials, persecutions, and death, is part of the total plan of salvation. At the end of these final instructions, the disciples are blessed by Jesus and they worship him.

In Acts we see Luke presenting again and again, by means of historical narrative and various speeches, these same characteristics of discipleship. We find the early disciples proclaiming the message of Jesus and the kingdom in an ever-expanding inclusive way. We see them breaking down new boundaries as they present the same kerygma and didache. We see them moving the edges of this message out of Jerusalem to the ends of the world, to Rome itself. Acts is a vibrant reprise of Luke's gospel message on the kingdom and on discipleship, lived and proclaimed by the fledgling church communities. These early followers of Jesus can say: "For this reason the whole house of Israel can be certain that God has made this Jesus whom you crucified both Lord and Christ" (Acts 2:36). Whatever role the Jesus community, the *koinonia,* the *ekklesia,* the church, might play, it too must reflect this one Lord and Savior (Acts 4:12; 5:31–32) who brought and lived a message of reconciling and open love.

In the volume on *Priesthood* I have discussed the many passages in Acts in which one finds organizational terms such as *episkopos, presbyteros,* and the seven, as well as passages dealing with the imposition of hands.[52] There is no need to discuss anew the various issues involved on this matter of church organization and church leadership. Between the gospel of Luke and Acts there is no difference in the portrayal of discipleship, and the authors mentioned above, such as Fitzmyer and Karris, describe the Lucan theology of a disciple which can be found in both writings. There is no doubt that the example of Paul offers Luke the best portrait of discipleship, and even though Luke's picture of Paul may differ from Paul's own self-imaging, nonetheless Luke presents Paul as the disciple of Jesus *par excellence.* In Acts, Luke does not portray Paul as an example for church leadership only. Rather, Luke presents Paul as an example for every follower of Jesus. From Paul's conversion (9:1–31) down to Paul's two-year stay in Rome (28:17–31) Luke presents his hero as one who truly understood the connection between the Israel of old and Jesus on the one hand, and between Jesus and the Christian community on the other. The many speeches in Acts really have "Luke as the author and his readers as their audience; whether the audience on the scene would have grasped the argument is often beside the point."[53] It is the community of Luke as such which needs to hear the message of these speeches, not simply a leadership group.

Luke clearly indicates to us that in the apostolic church a servant leadership, a ministry, was part of the structure of the community. This is a given. One does not find evidence of a non-ministerial church in the various apostolic communities. One does not find evidence of a totally egalitarian, democratic, or congregational community. Rather, one finds a community in which there is a ministry. One does not find, however, a two-tiered community. One does not find a *klerikos/laikos* community. One does not find a community with a "sacred order" in it, much less an order that is ontologically different from the remainder. All of these theological descriptions come later and cannot really be argued textually or contextually from Acts. There is indeed a ministry in Acts, but that ministry reflects the meaning of discipleship, as explained above, and its purpose is to make the total community a reflection of that same discipleship. Paul is not the center. Peter is not the center. Jesus is, for Luke, the center. Jesus, for Luke, is the center for all, minister or non-minister.

In many ways, Luke has made the disciples in his gospel and in Acts genuine models in a way that is far more positive than in Mark. The disciples of Jesus, in both the gospel and Acts, are not without flaws, of course; Jesus alone remains the real model of discipleship. On the other hand, Luke, more clearly than Mark, makes those disciples of Jesus beyond the twelve central to his presentation. Pointedly, and at crucial areas, Luke reaches out to include this wider audience of disciples. In this wider audience, the men and women of Luke's own community can find images of themselves, models for their own lives, portraits of their own strengths and weaknesses. Further distinguishing of the followers of Jesus, whether this be done in a hierarchical structure, or in a *klerikos/laikos* structure, or in a priesthood of all believers/ministerial priesthood structure, must begin on this central emphasis of the Lucan material: Jesus as the model of discipleship, and discipleship which each and every follower of Jesus is called to attain.

3. THE DISCIPLES IN THE GOSPEL OF MATTHEW

The gospel of Matthew has a twofold focus: (a) Jesus as the Christ, and (b) the near approach of the kingdom of God which Jesus proclaims. These two focuses, however, should not be separated; indeed, the entire gospel of Matthew could be read with either focus in view.[54] Similar to the gospel of Mark, this gospel has as its center the kingdom of God, a kingdom in which Jesus himself is central. B. Viviano notes that there are two additional "characteristic features" of this gospel: namely (a) Matthew's concern for the church, and (b) Matthew's special use of the Old Testament.[55] In this gospel there is certainly a relationship between the kingdom of God, on the one hand, and the church, on the other, but it would be contrary to the text and to the context of the gospel to equate the two. Certainly, those in the church or Jesus community are, in Matthew's view, part of the kingdom of God, but God's kingdom does not seem to be limited to the parameters of the church, as 25:31–40 might indicate. This passage—when I was hungry, you fed me, etc.—has been a focus of argument on the part of many biblical scholars. Does it come originally from Jesus himself? Did Jesus say this or at least something quite similar? Is it perhaps a description which comes from Matthew himself? Or has the early church developed this description on the basis of the ethos of Jesus' teaching? Might it even stem from a non-Christian source, perhaps from pre-Christian Judaism?[56]

> This much-loved text presents a practical religion of deeds of loving-kindness, love of neighbor. It has been overinterpreted to say that neither faith in Christ nor membership in the church is necessary for salvation; but, in fact, it is addressed to Christian disciples, and discipleship is understood in a very bold way as identical with care of the needy. This is not a denial of faith; it is of the essence of faith.[57]

This particular passage from Matthew's gospel, which seems so particularly open to any and all who are in need, should be correlated with the issue whether the gospel itself should be preached only to Israel or also to the world at large, i.e. the Gentiles. This clash of perspective on the inclusion of Gentiles into the Jesus community was a major point of debate in the community of Matthew, and the debate finds expression in Matthew's gospel, as we shall see. This passage on the hungry, thirsty, naked, etc., which seems so open-ended, is clearly addressed to the followers of Jesus, i.e. to Christians and not to people indiscriminately. On the other hand, it does say: whenever you did it to one of these, the least of my brothers and sisters, you did it to me. The community out of which Matthew is writing is struggling to find the meaning of the kingdom of God within the pluralistic make-up of its own community, a pluralistic make-up which has ramifications in the pluralistic society of Antioch and its environs in which the community appears to be located.

It seems to be the more probable view that this gospel was written in Antioch somewhere between 80 and 90 A.D. If we at least provisionally accept this position, then an analysis of the Antiochene society and the Jesus community at Antioch helps us understand some of the thought-currents we find in this particular gospel. J.P. Meier lists a number of issues which colored the church at Antioch at that time.[58] These issues are:

1. The first Jewish War, along with the incidents preceding and following it. This includes the death of James in Jerusalem and the destruction of Jerusalem, particularly the temple, in 70 A.D.
2. The resumed fellowship of a circumcision-free mission. The Pauline literature, as well as Acts, indicates this continuing struggle with the more traditional Jewish-Christian element in the early Church.
3. The various streams, both written and oral, of traditional material on Jesus, such as Mark's gospel, the so-called Q source and the so-called M source. Matthew inherited not only these traditions, but also the work of the scribal schools. It was his task to reinterpret and synthesize these various, often competing, traditions, and make them meaningful for the Christian community at Antioch.
4. There were significant instances of crisis inherent in the Antioch church. This church had once been quite Jewish, but now major symbols of Judaism had crumbled: the temple, the very city of Jerusalem, even the local synagogue. With the breakdown of both Jerusalem and the synagogue together with their leadership, the question of leadership within the Antiochene Christian community had become acute.

These four issues apparently raised troubling questions for the Christian community at Antioch. Issues, however, generally are promoted by a leadership group, and consequently the issue of competing leaderships and competing authorities engendered questions. In the gospel of Matthew, then, we find traces of these issues, and we find mention of leadership.

As long as the Church was tied to the synagogue, the authority of the Mosaic Law and the authority of the Jewish teachers in the synagogue could act as a support for moral teaching among Jewish Christians as well. Consequently, the question of authority, especially in moral matters, was not at first acute for christians who belonged to a church with a markedly Jewish coloration. But, at the very time when the church saw an increasing number of Gentiles at her door seeking entrance, she also saw herself cut off from the synagogue, the bastion of traditional morality. How were the moral teaching and the authority to teach morality in the church to receive a theological justification and basis?[59]

This gospel, then, addresses the double crisis of church identity and moral authority in the church. Because of this, we find in Matthew's gospel a stress on church leadership which we do not find in either Mark or Luke. The Johannine writings, similar to Matthew, are concerned rather pointedly with authority, but the response of the Johannine writings is quite different from the response one finds in Matthew's gospel. The Johannine writings base authority on a christological purity of doctrine; the gospel of Matthew does not bypass the christological focus, as we noted above, but it stresses a more structural side of church life.

Not only do we find in Matthew's gospel a presentation of what a follower or disciple of Jesus ought to be, but we also find a presentation of what a leader among and for these disciples ought to be. Ministry internal to the church is a major theme of this gospel, but this aspect must be seen constantly against the framework of (a) the kingdom of God and its near approach, and (b) the belief that Jesus is the Christ, the Lord, the Son of God. In other words, the internal church leadership aspect of Matthew's gospel is meaningful only in a relativized framework. To absolutize the passages on internal church leadership which one finds in this gospel is to misinterpret the very intent of the gospel.

Since the gospel of Matthew is based on Mark's gospel in so many fundamental ways,[60] the picture of the disciple of Jesus remains quite similar. The nearness of the final days, which Matthew stresses, does heighten the need for even greater efforts to realize this discipleship, but it does not alter the nature of such discipleship. The portrait of disciple in both Mark and Matthew tend to coincide.

In the organization of his gospel, Matthew gathers together an enormous amount of material in the section called the sermon on the mount (4:23–7:29). One finds in this particular set of materials a portrait of the true disciple of Jesus. Every disciple of Jesus, male or female, of Jewish origin or of Gentile origin, leader or non-leader, is presented with the ideal of this "sermon on the mount." The intention of Matthew in organizing this material is not to present a portrait or an ideal of a community leader (a so-called "clerical" group). Rather, his intent is to present to every disciple of Jesus a portrait and an ideal of what his or her life in Christ ought to be.

This gathering of material begins with the beatitudes. Who are the "blessed" (makarioi) if not the followers of Jesus? These followers are to be the poor in spirit, the meek, those who mourn, the merciful, the pure in heart, the peacemakers, those who are persecuted for the sake of justice. Jesus' disciples will be like salt and light; they will live by a higher ethic; they will share with the poor, but do it quietly; they will be men and women of prayer, but in a non-ostentatious way; they will fast, but again in a private manner; they will have true treasures and trust completely in a God who feeds sparrows and arrays the fields. They will not be judgmental on others, particularly brothers and sisters [fellow Christians?]. They will follow the golden rule of charity, and they will center their life in Jesus. In a way that has amazed so many generations of Christians, these chapters of Matthew's gospel present a portrait of the ideal disciple of Jesus. "*Everyone* [i.e. every disciple] who listens to these words of mine and acts on them. . . ."

In presenting this picture of a disciple, Matthew is really presenting a picture of Jesus himself. The chapters of the sermon on the mount must be seen against the christology of Matthew's entire gospel. The portrait of Jesus, from conception to resurrection, which Matthew spreads before his readers, presents in a living-dying-rising way all that the sermon on the mount proposes.

The Jewishness of Matthew's gospel is likewise more outspoken than that in Mark or Luke. The entire New Testament, of course, is based on and grows out of a Jewish foundation, but the gospel of Matthew evidences both the incorporation and the adaptation of Jewish religious elements on the one hand, and the tensions and even antipathies of this interplay on the other hand. Matthew's response to this deconstitution and reconstitution of Israel revolves around his picture of salvation history. He divides salvation history into the following three areas:

1. The time of prophecy in the Old Testament.
2. The time of fulfillment by the earthly Jesus.
3. The time of universal mission by the church.

Luke's division of salvation history is rather similar to this. Matthew, however, stresses the prophecy/fulfillment aspect far more strongly than Luke does. For Matthew, who has high respect for Jewish traditions, the law and the writings of the prophets are sacrosanct. These writings, understood as the revealed word of God, Matthew stresses, foreshadowed and promised Jesus. During his earthly life Jesus fulfilled precisely what the law and the prophets had proclaimed. In stressing this earthly phase of Jesus, Matthew is able to maintain some rather stringent Jewish material, such as one finds in 10:5–6 and 15:24, which prohibits a mission to the Gentile world. However, with the death and resurrection of Jesus, which Matthew describes in strong apocalyptic terminology, there is an end of the former age and the beginning of the new age, the deconstitution and reconstitution of Israel. This new age or reconstituted Israel allows Matthew to make room for new and innovative forms. For Matthew, "Israel [as it had existed] has ceased to be the people of God" and the community of Jesus, the church, has taken Israel's place.[61]

In the gospel, then, we find injunctions to obey the scribes and Pharisees as the successors of Moses (13:2–3), since Jesus freely accepted the Jewish structures of his day. Given the death-resurrection of Jesus, the beginning of the new age, Matthew can equally say: "Beware of the teaching of the Pharisees and the Sadducees" (16:12); the Pharisees are "a plant . . . [which] my Father has not planted, [which] shall be uprooted; leave them" (15:12–14); "the kingdom of God shall be taken from you and given to a people bearing its fruit" (21:43). On the basis of the tripartite structure of salvation history in Matthew's gospel, not only must one be cautious in interpreting the role of the scribes and Pharisees during the lifetime of Jesus, a role which is acknowledged, but one must also be cautious not to find an alternate leadership group established during the lifetime of Jesus.[62] In other words, the way in which Matthew has structured salvation history does not allow one to see in the twelve, for instance, the establishment of a leadership group in opposition to the priests, scribes, and Pharisees. The Petrine passage in 16:13–20, if historically placed in the lifetime of Jesus, must be seen within the context of an intra-Israel mission. If it originates in a post-resurrection situation and is only proleptically inserted into a pre-resurrection narrative, then it can be seen within the reconstituted Israel. In the lifetime of Jesus, Peter evidently made some sort of confession of belief in Jesus, an episode which one finds in Mark and in Luke. Jesus' response, which is so heightened in Matthew's account, cannot be seen historically, that is, in the actual lifetime of Jesus, as an establishment of Peter as a pope or as the chief leader of a group which stands in an oppositional posture to Judaism. This Petrine passage must be seen against the background of Jesus' intra-Jewish mission during his lifetime. Only against the background of the risen Jesus can one see this Petrine passage in any broader way. This means of course that the passage itself, taken at face value, probably does not reflect the actual historical words of Jesus during his lifetime.

From chapter 11 onward the gospel of Matthew heightens the tension between Jesus and Israel. He condemns his contemporaries (11:16–19); he laments over the cities of Israel (11:20–24). He openly confronts the Pharisees when his disciples pick corn and when the man with a withered hand is cured (12:1–14). He is accused by the Pharisees of casting out devils in the name of Beelzebul (12:22–32). In a challenging way, Jesus offers the scribes and Pharisees but a single sign, namely, the sign of Jonah (12:38–42). In all of these confrontational narratives, Matthew is presenting the flow of salvation history as it moves toward the confrontation of Jesus and the small but highly powerful group of Jewish leadership.

In the trial and death of Jesus, Matthew shows how the crowds of Jewish people generally (27:22–24) and more specifically all the groups who make up the Sanhedrin, priests, scribes and elders (26:47–48, 57–68;

27:1–2, 20, 41) reject Jesus. He shows how the Roman officials reject him as well (27:11–31). It is only the centurion "and those standing guard with him" who say, "Truly, this one is the Son of God." This symbolism of some Gentiles, proclaiming what Jews and Romans reject, corresponds to the opening of Matthew's gospel in which the magi, a small group of Gentiles, come to Bethlehem and acknowledge (adore) the newborn Jesus, while Herod and others reject this birth. With the death of Jesus and with the resurrection, Matthew says, a new, reconstituted Israel has begun.

In this new Israel, there were at first Jewish scribes and leaders, who accepted Jesus, and these men [presumably all were men] continued as leaders in this new Israel. With the passage of time, with the split between synagogue and followers of Jesus, and with the growing number of Gentiles within the Jesus community, changes of leadership roles began to take place, and these changes began both to create havoc and to bring about the creation of leadership structures.

> It is only natural that a group which is experiencing both rapid growth and a crisis of identity and function, and which moreover is interacting dialectically with other organized groups, should develop institutional organs of its own.[63]

Much has been made of the term *ekklesia* in Matthew. But this gospel is the only gospel which employs the term *ekklesia,* although this term is found twenty-seven times in Paul, twenty-three times in Acts, three times in 1 Timothy, and twenty times in Revelation. In all of these usages of *ekklesia* the Jesus community is attempting to spell out its own identity, and it does this with reference to the exodus event. Just as the Israel of old was called out of Egypt (*ekklesia*) into the promised land and became a people (*laos*), so too the Jesus community has been called both from the Israel of old and from the Gentile world to be the new people of God (*laos*). This term *ekklesia,* then, should be seen throughout the New Testament with reference to its original Jewish usage, and not merely as a structure or an institution. The new people of God have been called in virtue of a second exodus event, brought about by God's initiative in and through Jesus, the Christ.[64] Even in the infancy chapters, Matthew uses this exodus image through his description of the flight into Egypt and then the calling of the holy family out of Egypt and back to Palestine.

In his description of the leadership for this new people, *ekklesia,* Matthew raises a warning about the desire for ostentatious religious clothing and symbols (23:5), about seeking the first seats at a gathering (23:6), about special titles and names (23:7–10). Why would the author have singled these out so strongly, if he did not see some of the leadership people in the church at Antioch moving in this direction? Meier along with others indicates that the church at Antioch seems to have been led by a group of prophets and teachers (Acts 13:1) from its earliest days onward. This group appears to be present in Matthew's gospel as well (13:52; 23:34).[65] It might be said, but with some terminological hesitation, that there appears to be a nascent "clericalism," which Matthew wishes to eradicate.[66] In Matthew's view the emerging Christian leaders should not strive for domination, monopoly, places of prestige or gaudy trappings of office. Rather, the Christian leader must look at himself/herself again and again both in the mirror of chapters 5–7, the sermon on the mount, and in the mirror of Jesus himself, who in a living-dying-rising way exemplifies all that the sermon on the mount portrays. These Christian leaders must themselves be poor in spirit, meek, merciful, non-judgmental, etc. They must be the salt and the light; they must love others as they wish others to love them; they must share with the poor, pray, and fast, but always in a quiet, unnoticed way. They must live by a higher ethic. Above all, they must listen to the words of Jesus and act on them. If, however, they have listened to Jesus' words but not acted on them, they and whatever they have built will have no foundation and fall into ruin (7:24–27).

The picture according to which Matthew urges his community leadership to measure itself is nothing other than the measure of discipleship, which every follower of Jesus must follow. There is not a twofold way of following Jesus: one for disciples generally, and one for an elite leadership group. Nor is there a twofold way: one for disciples generally and one for a cadre of professional religious. Latter-day popes, bishops, priests and deacons must measure themselves by the very same standards which each and every follower of Jesus uses, and latter-day religious must follow those same standards of measurement as well. In other words, one will not find in Matthew's gospel any foundation for a "clergy group" or for a "religious group" which has a different standard of measurement from that of each and every disciple of the Lord. Latter-day religious and latter-day clerics might indeed be held to live up to the standards more stringently than other disciples, precisely because they have accepted leadership roles within the community, but these groups do not operate with a different set of standards. In other words, there is not in the Christian community a clerical spirituality distinct from a general spirituality, nor is there a religious-life spirituality distinct from a general spirituality. There is neither a "higher way" nor a "more perfect life." Later Christian writings which begin to see both the clerical group and the "religious" group in theological terms of something higher, more perfect, better, etc., have a difficult task in showing how their position conforms to the gospel of Matthew.

We actually have no clear insight into who these Antiochene leaders might be. There is absolutely no mention of *episkopos, presbyteros,* and *diakonos* in Matthew's gospel. There is, perhaps, a suggestion that at Antioch some of them were Christian scribes (13:52), as also Christian prophets, wise men and scribes (23:34). At this particular period of time, some sort of group leadership at Antioch seems more likely than a leadership by a single individual. Matthew 18:18 speaks about a communal act of binding and loosing, and this might well be a reflection of a practice in his own community.

But, one might say, what about Peter? Is he not singled out in a special way as we see in 16:18–19? "Matthew, writing to meet the problems of a Church in Syrian Antioch about A.D. 85, is certainly not concerned with the problem of whether a single-bishop in Rome is the successor of Simon Peter, especially since both Rome and Antioch around 85 do not seem to have known the single-bishop structure."[67] The enormous amount of discussion which relates this passage from Matthew's gospel to the Petrine office at Rome is by and large both textually and contextually without foundation. A Roman Petrine office is not the intent of this particular passage. Nor can we even say that Peter was the sole community leader in Antioch. Matthew is not attempting to uphold a Petrine office and authority in Antioch. Nonetheless, it is obvious that Matthew does see Peter as the rock on which Jesus built his church: Peter, for Matthew, is the bridge-figure, the moderate center, a norm for all churches, in contrast to the dissident and factious churches which press their views.[68] This Petrine role fits in well with Matthew's whole approach: he is open to the newness which comes through the Jesus event as a way to understand the old teachings of the Jewish religion, but he is also "firm on the need of preserving the old."[69] Christ is central to Matthew's understanding of the reconstituted Israel, but he often, in contrast to Mark, heightens the christological element and immediately brings in an ecclesiological aspect.

> In the context of moral teaching, it is important to notice that Christ shares with his church his authority to teach, to make decisions, and to forgive sins. At the end of the healing of the paralytic, which vindicates the authority (*exousia*) of the Son of Man to forgive sins, Matthew reworks the Marcan conclusion to indicate that men in the church share this authority: "the crowds glorified God, who gives such authority *to men*" (9:8). The phrase "to men," which does not make too much sense in the

narrative, is used by Matthew to stress that people in the church share the Son of Man's power to forgive sin.[70]

Peter represents both a leadership figure in the church and a moderate voice among shrill demands. In this sense Peter is held up by Matthew as a model of leadership within the community, a leadership which Jesus himself is portrayed as establishing. The precise form of leadership at Antioch is not clearly presented by Matthew, although he does express, as we have seen, what he does not want that leadership to manifest. The term "nascent clericalism" which Meier uses cannot be pressed in any literal way. *Kleros* and *klerikos,* in the latter part of the first century A.D., did not have the connotation which these words would receive in the latter part of the third and throughout the fourth centuries. The undue quest for position and status, for recognition and power, for pomp and circumstance, based on one's leadership role, which Matthew finds reprehensible, not only in the Jewish leadership of his day, but also and even more in the incipient Christian leadership of his day, follows the same patterns which a later "clericalism" will evidence. However, in the gospel of Matthew we have no trace of a *klerikos/laikos* division with the Jesus community. We do have an indication of a community, an *ekklesia,* on the one hand, and a ministry of service leadership within and for this community, on the other hand. A theological rationale of this Christian ministry on the basis of a *klerikos/laikos* framework or on the basis of a hierarchical *ordo,* much less on the basis of an ordination, is not present in this gospel.

The twelve in Matthew's gospel do not seem to have any greater meaning than what one finds in Mark's gospel. In the parallel passages, Matthew does not make any substantial changes. In 10:2 the twelve are called apostles (*ton dodeka apostolon*), but nowhere else in the gospel does the author use this term.[71] In 10:1, the preceding verse, the twelve are called the twelve disciples (*tous dodeka mathetas*). One might jump to the conclusion that disciple and apostle are thereby equated, although in the year 85 it would seem, from other sources, that apostle in the Christian communities was a term which Christian communities used in a fairly limited way, while the term disciple had a far wider application. Since this is the only instance in which the term *apostolos* is found in Matthew's gospel, it would be more than either the text or the context might bear to develop a wide-ranging theological interpretation of this *hapax legoumenon.* In 10:5–16 the twelve are commissioned to go out to the Jewish towns and villages in the same way and for the same reasons which one finds in Mark: namely, to heal and to preach. Matthew, however, speaks directly about healing and only indirectly mentions the aspect of preaching. Since in this commissioning the twelve are sent only to Jewish towns and villages, the question arises: How can chapter 10 be reconciled with the final section of the gospel, 28:16–20, in which not merely Jews but all peoples of the earth are to become disciples of Jesus? Once more we see that with the death and resurrection of Jesus, the new age, in Matthew's view, has arrived, and what was restricted during the earthly life of Jesus is now unrestricted in this new exodus event, this new people of God, this apocalyptic period of salvation history. In the final section of the gospel, the twelve (called the eleven) and the new Israel, the new people, are presented in a very symbolic way. In the old Israel, there were twelve, and in this new Israel, promised and described already in Daniel 7, a passage from the prophets, which Matthew quite obviously is using in this final pericope,[72] there are also twelve, the symbol of universality.

One might also take into account the women in Matthew's gospel. In the infancy narrative of the gospel, the emphasis is, of course, on Jesus, and his birth is presented with strong references to the birth of Moses. In many ways Joseph, with all his dreams, plays a more prominent role than Mary, the mother of Jesus, but Mary is clearly integral to Matthew's theology of this infancy narrative. For Matthew, Mary is indeed a key person in salvation history, and his citation from Isaiah makes this eminently clear (1:22–23). She is, however, only briefly mentioned in the magi episode, and in both the flight into Egypt and the return from Egypt, Mary is also a peripheral figure.

The four Old Testament women mentioned by Matthew in a rather specific way in his genealogy of Jesus have occasioned considerable speculation over the centuries. Perhaps the fact that all four of these women showed initiative and played an important role in God's plan of salvation history, and the fact that there was something extraordinary in their relationships to their partners, as also the fact that they were either Gentiles themselves or quite closely connected to Gentiles, were important issues to Matthew, as he constructed the genealogy.[73] However the scholars might determine this appearance of women in Jesus' genealogy, their presence in the listing is not routine. Matthew goes out of his way to mention these four women. Is he addressing some issue with which the church of Antioch was struggling, perhaps an issue about the role of women within the Jesus community? Neither the various texts nor the contexts are clear on this matter, but there must have been some issue within the Jesus community at Antioch which Matthew wanted to address at least indirectly by his frequent mention of women. The precise nature of this issue, however, cannot be determined in any clear fashion, and any further determinations can only be conjectural at best.

In the public ministry of Jesus, Matthew mentions a number of women associated with Jesus and his ministry: Peter's mother-in-law (8:14–15); the woman with a hemorrhage, as also the daughter of the official (9:18–26); his mother and brothers (12:46–50; 13:53–58); the woman as part of the parable of the yeast (13:33); the daughter of the Canaanite woman (15:21–28); the mother of James and John (20:20–23); the parable about the wedding and the ten bridesmaids (25:1–13); the anointing at Bethany (26:6–13); the women at Calvary (27:55–56); the women at the tomb (28:1–8); the appearance to two of these women after the resurrection (28:9–10). From genealogy to resurrection, Matthew indicates the presence of women in salvation history. In the reconstituted Israel, the new Israel, which we find in the post-resurrection material, women play key roles. They are the first "evangelists" of this good news, and they are the first presented by the gospel to whom the risen Lord appears. One cannot, of course, overburden these texts, but for Matthew in the third period of salvation history, namely that which comes after the death and resurrection of Jesus, the kingdom of God becomes all-inclusive: not only Jews but Gentiles are part of the ecclesia, and, one must add, there is a new inclusiveness for women in the Jesus community as well.

With all the material on leadership in the community, with all the emphasis on the Jesus community, even with the specific emphasis on Peter, Matthew nowhere indicates that a leader has a different standard of measurement than that of any other disciple of Jesus. The tendency to rank oneself above another, particularly through domination, monopoly and gaudy trappings of office—a tendency which certain forms of later hierarchical theology have at times attempted to justify—is censured by this author. There is clearly power and authority in Matthew's church and in the service leadership of that church, but in Matthew's view one must look to Jesus to see how such power and authority should be employed. One finds the model, the principles and the standards for using such power and authority in the words of the sermon on the mount, and more importantly in the life, death, and resurrection of Jesus himself.

4. THE DISCIPLES IN THE JOHANNINE WRITINGS

In contemporary Johannine studies, the issue of the Johannine community has played a major role. The gospel of John stems from a community; it is different from the synoptics, and although there are some links in the gospel to Mark, Luke, and to some degree Matthew, it is not clear that the author or authors of this Johannine gospel relied on one or any of these other gospels. Perhaps the appearance and use of the other gospels in other communities provided the impetus for the author to draw up this particular gospel, but it seems he might have done this using his own set of traditions, not those found in the synoptics. The resolution of these questions on dependency/non-dependency, use/non-use, etc., has not yet been found, but the very question indicates that the Johannine author and the Johannine community are integral to an understanding of this fourth gospel.

Pheme Perkins notes that the Johannine community "had drawn its boundaries against: (a) followers of John the Baptist (1:35–37; 3:22–30; 4:1–3; 10:40–42); (b) the Jews, who had taken measures to expel those who believed in Jesus from the synagogues (9:22–23; 16:1–4a); and (c) other 'Christians,' who had been followers of Jesus but who have now separated themselves from the community, apparently over the christological affirmations of the divinity of Jesus (6:60–65)."[74] Other factors are also involved in delineating this Johannine community. (1) There seems to have been a strong and successful missionary movement among the Samaritans, and Samaritans who have accepted Jesus are a visible part of the Johannine community. (2) The conflict with certain Jewish elements (synagogues) which rejected the claims of Jesus did not eliminate a Jewish element within the Johannine community, nor did this conflict eliminate a group of sympathetic Jews within the Jewish synagogues themselves. Nonetheless, the antagonism, perhaps even an expulsion, may have caused a migration of the Johannine community from the area of Palestine to Ephesus or some other area.[75] (3) Peter appears to represent the Jesus communities outside the Johannine community. However, the Johannine community, although respecting Peter, appears to have distanced itself from a Petrine form of leadership. In all of this, many questions remain unanswered; many issues are to some degree hypothetical. Nonetheless,

> the "writing down" of Johannine traditions was clearly part of the ongoing life of the community. It may have been the result of a "Johannine school" of disciples of the Beloved Disciple and teachers within the Johannine churches. There is a sufficient unity in the literary composition and the narrated point of view in the Gospel to justify the claim that a single individual was responsible for the structure of the gospel narrative. But the importance of the community's history of faith in shaping the Johannine tradition makes preoccupation with a single Johannine author inappropriate today.[76]

The saga of this Johannine community, however, continues, for we see in the Johannine letters that there is a fracturing of the Johannine community itself. In the gospel the opponents seem to be the three groups mentioned above. In the epistles the focus is more on dissident groups within the Johannine community itself. The strong insistence in the letters on tradition: "Hold on to what you have heard from the beginning," both forges a link with the gospel, that material which the community had already heard, and indicates the schismatic element, namely, some members of the community itself were moving in new and uncharted directions. Both 1 John and 2 John mention persons who have been part of the Johannine community but who were now separatists (1 Jn 2:19; 4:1; 2 Jn 7). The reason is clearly stated: these persons do not confess Jesus, and therefore they are deceivers and antichrists.

Brown enumerates the various groups who were, to some degree, at odds with the core Johannine community, in the following way:[77]

I. Those who do not believe in Jesus:

a. **The world:** This is a wider term than the Jews, but includes them, for it includes all those who prefer darkness to light. By their own choice they are already condemned.

b. **The Jews:** Those within the synagogues who did not accept Jesus and who had decided that the followers of Jesus were excommunicated.

c. **The followers of John the Baptist:** Those who had followed the Baptist, but had not joined those who believe in Jesus.

II. Those who [claim] to believe in Jesus:

a. **Crypto-Christians:** Jews who remained in the synagogues, but secretly accepted Jesus as Messiah.

b. **Jewish Christians:** Those who had left the synagogues but whose faith was inadequate by Johannine standards. Basically these people professed a low christology, not accepting the divine character of Jesus.

c. **Christians of apostolic Churches:** The non-Johannine communities of the followers of Jesus, particularly those who regarded themselves as the heirs of Peter and other members of the Twelve.

The Johannine community clearly has leadership or ministerial roles. The "beloved disciple" appears in a rather commanding way. The authors both of the gospel itself and of the various letters speak in an authoritative way. The *tessera fidei*, however, is clearly focused (a) on a belief in the divinity of Jesus, and (b) on a community which unfolds this belief in brotherly and sisterly love.

> Gradually they developed an independent understanding of the primacy of love rather than of authority (the reason for the continual 'upstaging' of Peter by the Beloved Disciple: see esp. 13:21–26 and 20:2–10). The Johannine community became more aggressive in its gradual development of a new and higher christology (Jesus as the Logos, the Son of God, "sent" by the Father from "above" to "below" in a way quite unknown to Synoptic Gospels), a unique Paraclete pneumatology, and an ethic based on a law of love, without emphasizing the restrictions of a final, end-of-time judgment on behavior (there is no Johannine scene to parallel Matt 25:31–46).[78]

In all of this, however, there is no theological rationale based on a *klerikos/laikos* model, nor is there a portrayal of sacred orders within the community. The letters indicate that the Johannine community had formed "house churches" clustered around a central area but linked together by traveling missionaries.[79] Leadership and ministry are part of these communities, but status and position based on such roles is downplayed. We are not told how any of those in leadership roles came to be accepted as such. There is no indication at all of any "ordination" or "sacred order." There is no indication of any clerical/lay distinction. We see this, for instance, in the way in which the gospel portrays the women disciples of Jesus. In the wedding feast at Cana (2:1–12) the mother of Jesus (she is never named in this gospel) is presented as one who believes in her Son. In 2:12 it mentions that Jesus then went to Capernaum together with his mother, his brothers and his disciples, where they remained for several days. Mother, brothers and disciples are drawn together in this verse.

In the conversion of the Samaritans (4:4–42) the woman is presented as the first missionary of Jesus. The discourse with the Samaritan woman leads to Jesus' statement: "I am" (4:26). The ease with which Jesus speaks to this woman, and the fact that both the woman and the disciples are amazed at his ease in such conversation is not presented as a mere curiosity. When the many instances of the presence of women in the Johannine gospel are drawn together, the pattern emerges: women who believe in Jesus as the Messiah and Son of God are equal to any male who also so believes.

In the raising of Lazarus (11:1–44) Mary and Martha appear as though the readership already knows about them. They are the sisters of Lazarus, and Mary is the one who anointed Jesus. In 11:5 we read that Jesus loved Martha and her sister and Lazarus (cf. 11:4)—strong words from the author, but words which fit in well with the whole program of the Johannine gospel on the centrality of love within the Christian framework. Martha, rather than Mary, is the focal figure, next to Jesus and Lazarus. Martha confesses her faith in Jesus: "If you had been here, my brother would not have died, but now I know that whatever you ask God, God will give to you" (4:21–22). Martha is not like one of the doubting followers of Jesus; she acknowledges the closeness Jesus has with God. Jesus' response, however, places the issue at a deeper level: "Your brother will rise again." Martha expresses a belief in the afterlife which some Jews of that period accepted: "I know that he will rise again at the resurrection on the last day." Jesus then places the issue at an even deeper level: "I am the resurrection and the life. Whoever believes in me, even though already dead, will live. Whoever lives and believes in me will never die. Do you believe this?" Martha then makes a profession of faith that rivals that of Peter in Mark 8:29, Matthew 16:16, and Luke 9:20. Martha says: "Yes, Lord, I believe that you are the Christ, the Son of God, the one who was to come into this world." Brown notes that the author of the gospel might have deliberately placed this confession of faith in the mouth of a woman, to indicate that neither position, nor status, nor leadership, nor sex is the basis for discipleship. Faith in Jesus and love are the only two criteria. Just as the synoptics had used the confession of Peter at Caesarea Philippi to illustrate the faith of the disciples, John uses the confession of faith by Martha for the very same purpose.

Martha's sister Mary is also presented as one who believes in Jesus. When she comes to Jesus, her first words are: "Lord, if you had been here, my brother would not have died," the very same words which Martha had used. There is no doubt that this entire episode about Jesus, who is called life and life-giving throughout the gospel, namely, Jesus' raising Lazarus from the tomb, is a pivotal one for the gospel. The centrality of women in this episode is clearly indicative of the entire Johannine view of discipleship.

Mary and Martha are presented again in the episode of the anointing at Bethany (12:1–11). The woman who anoints Jesus is none other than Mary, the sister of Martha. A woman—and one whom Jesus, as the gospel says, especially loved—plays a central symbolic role in the preparation of Jesus' burial.

At the supper, the circle of participants in John's gospel is left rather open, when one compares the description of the Johannine participants to those mentioned in Mark (14:17, 20), where one finds an explicit mention of "the twelve." In 22:11 Luke calls the participants disciples, but in 22:14 he uses the term "the apostles," indicating that the Lucan author had this particular group in mind. Matthew (26:17–20) describes more participants than the twelve at the supper. "John, who knows of the existence of the Twelve as a group led by Peter (see 6:67–68), maintains the more indeterminate circle of 'disciples' (13:5, 22–23), a group not limited to the Twelve, as the presence of the Beloved Disciple shows."[80] The exclusion of women from the supper is generally motivated by a desire to include/exclude certain people, in this instance women, from "ordination." Neither the text nor the context of John's pericope on the supper supports such a basis for an inclusion/exclusion regarding the disciples whom Jesus loved.

The mother of Jesus is mentioned in a very key way after Jesus has been crucified (19:25–27). She is mentioned together with her sister, Mary the wife of Clopas, and also with Mary of Magdala. The "disciple he loved" stands near the mother of Jesus. Scholars are still not at one on the way in which the relationship between this tradition of Mary and the beloved disciple and the tradition of Mary in the upper room with the brothers of Jesus and the twelve (Acts 1:14) should be interpreted. Nor is the meaning of Jesus' entrustment of Mary to the beloved disciple totally clear. That Jesus, at the hour of his own death, wanted to provide care for his mother seems evident enough. Only in later centuries, particularly in the middle ages, do we find additional and symbolic interpretations of this pericope: namely, Mary is the new Eve, Mary is the mother of the new Jerusalem, etc.

One aspect does stand out in John's gospel, however, and this is the symbolism of those who surround the cross of Jesus. Roman soldiers are there, and, through them, a symbol of Roman rule, including Pilate. They are in an adversarial role. The Jewish chief priests too are mentioned (19:21), and they are also mentioned in an adversarial role. Scribes and Pharisees are not mentioned in the Johannine account of Jesus' death.[81] On the other side of this symbolic picture we find Mary, the mother of Jesus, two other women and one male disciple.[82] If the author is making some sort of symbolic statement on all of these various groups of people standing around the cross of Jesus, it more than likely has something to do with those who accept Jesus and those who do not. Pointedly, there are more women in this latter category than there are men. "The reader of the Gospel is already well aware that Jesus' death is not a humiliation or defeat but a glorious return to the Father."[83] There are those who perceive this victory, and there are those who do not. Among those who do not are: Pilate and the Roman soldiers; the Jewish leaders, portrayed in the gospel of John as claiming Caesar as their king (a remarkable situation in itself) and abetting the entire process of Jesus' arrest, trial, and death; Peter, who disowns Jesus three times (13:36–38; 18:15–27); Judas Iscariot who betrays Jesus; and the remainder of the twelve who simply disappear from the gospel in silence.

In the resurrection account of chapter 20, Mary of Magdala, and she alone, is portrayed.[84] She is the first to come to the tomb, only to find it empty; she is the one who announces this to Simon Peter and the beloved disciple. It is not insignificant that her message to them is: "They have taken the Lord out of the tomb and we do not know where they have put him." Who are the "they" in this sentence? She repeats this "they" in 20:13 to the angels. In 20:15 the "they" becomes "you," namely, the "apparent gardener." Neither Mary nor the disciples know where Jesus' body has now been buried.[85] She is also the first to whom the risen Jesus appears. Jesus tells her to go and tell the brothers (*adelphoi*) that Jesus is ascending to his Father and their Father, to his God and their God. Mary of Magdala fulfills this command, for she goes to the disciples (*mathetai*) and says that she has already seen the risen Jesus, the Lord, and she conveys to them his message.

This insertion of women in significant stages of the gospel does indicate that discipleship in the Johannine community has a certain egalitarian role about it.[86] But other aspects of both the gospel and the letters indicate that there is a leadership role involved. The only leadership word we find in the gospel itself which indicates a ministerial role is the "twelve." The term "apostle" is used only on a rare occasion.[87] In 2 John and 3 John we find the title "presbyter."[88] "The presbyter to the chosen one, to the lady and to her children" (2 Jn 1). "The presbyter to Gaius, the beloved" (3 Jn 1). In the first letter, one finds a "we," that is, the author(s), and a "you" who are called, children (*teknia*), brothers (*adelphoi*), and beloved (*agapetoi*). The presbyter in 2 John at times says "I" and at times says "we" in the way he addresses the lady, "you." In 3 John there is also an "I" and a "you" (the addressee). Mention is made of a certain Diotrephes, who is part of a church, and who "seems to enjoy being in charge of it and refuses to accept us" (v. 9). He also seems to expel some from the church (v. 11). A certain Demetrius is also mentioned (v. 12) but in an unspecified way. In all of this we find a leadership (the "we" and the "I" and the presbyter) and the larger group of true believers. One cannot therefore speak of a totally democratic or egalitarian Johannine church. Can one speak of a clerical/lay church? Certainly one cannot speak in these terms with definitions which only a later Christian age applies to the words *klerikos/laikos.* Certainly one cannot apply to these leadership people the term of "ordination" and "sacred order." These terms, too, gained a specific meaning within the Christian community only at a much later era. How one came to be a presbyter or a leader is never specified in any of the Johannine writings.

There is some sort of prophetic leadership in the book of Revelation. Whoever this "John" might be, he speaks with some authority to the seven churches, not on the basis of being a member of the twelve, or on the basis of being a *presbyteros,* but on the basis of the vision he has seen. If the work stems from the time of Domitian (c. 95), we have other instances in early Christian literature which mention "prophets." These prophets had a certain leadership within various Christian communities, but not on the basis of ordination nor on that of a clerical/lay division.

Nonetheless, even with this evidence of various incipient structures of church leadership, the Johannine material has as its major goal the formation of a true disciple of Jesus. It does not have as its major goal the formation of a true leader in the church. In other words, all of these writings present to us and to the readers for which they were intended the qualities and traits of a true disciple of Jesus. They do not present either to us or to the readership of their times a picture of a Christian leader. These writings were directed to the Christian disciple generally. They are not guidebooks for a cadre of Christian leaders. What they portray, then, applies to all followers of Jesus, male and female, slave and free, Jew and Greek. Only indirectly, and as a sort of *obiter dicta,* are there indications of Christian leadership.

The Johannine gospel and letters (and the book of Revelation as well) were not written as some sort of "manual for seminarians" or "manual for priests," which in much later generations attempted to portray the ideal seminarian and the ideal priest and the ideal cleric. These writings rather present us with the ideal disciple. Naturally, Christian leaders should exemplify the same qualities and traits, but these qualities and traits are not presented in a way that would be exclusively the domain of church leadership. These qualities and traits are presented rather as the essential marks of the followers of Jesus, his disciples, no matter who they are, either in society or in the ecclesial structure. The various Johannine authors are attempting to tell the readership of their day, and by extension subsequent generations of Christians who might read these letters, what it means to be a disciple of the Lord.

5. THE DISCIPLES IN THE PAULINE WRITINGS

Unlike the gospels, together with Acts and the Johannine material, which present in a sustained and quite developed way particular themes or theological positions, the letters of Paul by and large are merely occasional writings, written rather independently of each other, and focused on particular situations rather than on lengthy, well-developed issues. As a result, one must find in the individual issues, which Paul treats, indications of wider considerations. For instance, it is quite true to say that Paul is thoroughly christocentric, but his view of Christ is not presented as systematically as the evangelists present their views of Jesus, when they wrote the rather lengthy gospel presentations of the life, death and resurrection of Jesus. Justification, another theme, is central to Pauline thought, but justification is not presented in any lengthy, speculative way, even in the letter to the Romans. Justification shows up now and again, at times in a fairly strong way, such as one finds in the opening section of the letter to the Romans, but more often only in a passing sort of way, as we find in the letters to the Galatians and Corinthians.

Besides the content of each letter, it is evident that Paul communicates with particular churches in a way that expresses both his own presence to them and his authority among them. The author, Paul himself, is very much an integral part of the content of each of these letters. He is, however, not writing to these communities, as though all the members of the communities together with himself are equals. Paul writes his letters from a self-identity of Christian leadership. Moreover, here and there in the letters he makes mention of other leadership or ministerial individuals—Timothy, Sylvanus, Sosthenes—and in various passages of his letters we find several names and titles of community leadership, such as apostle, the twelve, teacher, prophet, evangelist, *episkopos* (once only), *diakonos* (twice), *hyperetes* (servant), and shepherd, to cite only the major ones. For Paul the apostles have a primacy of place in communal leadership, and he includes himself very outspokenly among the apostles. However, from the Pauline letters themselves, it is not crystal-clear how individual church communities, house churches and city-wide churches, are structured, nor is there any indication of the way in which one becomes a part of this church leadership, with the exception of himself. Paul clearly states that he was called to be an apostle by the risen Lord. Indirectly he bears witness to a similar calling by the Lord as regards the pillars of the church: Peter, James, and John. In a more general way this calling by the Lord would apply, so it seems from his writings, to the twelve, the five hundred in 1 Corinthians 15:6, and Junia (Rom 16:7).

Paul's letters, however, are not directly addressed to leadership people. Rather, the letters are addressed to Jesus communities, gathered together in various cities. Since they are not specifically addressed to the leadership group, the Pauline letters cannot be seen as letters, addressed to a group, which we, at some later date of Christian history, might relate to or even call *klerikoi*. In other words the letters are not communications sent by a leadership person, in this case Paul, to other leadership people, who in turn are instructed to share the contents of the letters with their communities. In later Christian times, popes and the Vatican curia have communicated to bishops, who in turn have communicated to pastors, who then share the material with the parish community. This is not the pattern one finds in Paul. Rather, the letters are sent to a local community as such. The leadership in the community is of course an integral part of the community and, at times, mentioned in a fairly specific way. However, Paul seems to be addressing, in each of his letters, the community as such. The precise leadership of these communities is not the direct or exclusive addressee of the letters.

Similarly, one does not find in Paul's letters any indication that the non-leaders, or non-ministers, correspond to the later-appearing name of *laikoi.* Since there is no indication that the Christian leaders belong to an *ordo,* and since there is no mention of any ordination ritual in these letters, it would be difficult to describe the distinction between the leadership group on the one hand, and the gathered Christians on the other, both of which are clearly evident in the Pauline corpus, in terms such as ordained, non-ordained, or *klerikoi/laikoi. That* there is a distinction between leadership people and the larger community is clearly presented in the Pauline material. *How* these two Christian groups should be differentiated and named is not clear.

Pauline studies in recent times have focused on very concrete issues. J. Murphy-O'Connor studies Corinth archaeologically to understand Paul's writings to the Corinthians.[89] Murphy-O'Connor studies the city history of Corinth and gives ancient text after ancient text which is descriptive of this city. He measures early Graeco-Roman dining rooms and studies textual data on the size and usage of such dining rooms. In doing all this he helps us understand the way Corinthians lived, and more particularly the way Corinthian Christians lived. His analyses help us see some of the socio-political and physical background for the problems which Paul addresses in his letters to the Corinthian community. W. Meeks' volume, *The First Urban Christians: The Social World of the Apostle Paul,* moves in the same direction that Murphy-O'Connor takes.[90] The studies by H. Koester,[91] V. Branick,[92] G. Theissen,[93] and M. Hengel[94] could also be mentioned. In all of this, materials, external to Paul and even to Christian origins in such cities as Corinth, are highly important for an understanding of Paul, and the sometimes passing statements in the Pauline letters, which refer to fairly concrete situations, when taken with this socio-political data, help us today to come to grips with the situations Paul is attempting to address.

A second focus of contemporary Pauline studies is on the internal make-up of the Christian communities addressed by Paul. Who are the various people mentioned by Paul? What is their task within the community? Who are the leadership people? Who are the members of the larger *ekklesia?* In these studies the socio-political factors also play an enormous role, and thereby the leadership people within the Pauline churches as well as the Christian community members are contextualized in a way which has not been possible until the appearance of these current studies. Generalized and even idealized portraits of Pauline leadership roles and Pauline community membership have been fleshed out in a much more graphic way than ever before, and generalizations and idealizations of these Pauline churches have been radically rethought.

All of these studies have made Pauline scholarship somewhat more complicated, and it would be far beyond the scope of the next few pages to summarize or recapitulate these highly technical materials. Rather, the intent of the following pages on the Pauline letters is much more modest. I wish to offer some of the key issues which contemporary Pauline research considers central to the theological core of Paul's vision. In his letters this vision is presented by Paul as a benchmark for each and every follower of Jesus. It is also presented as a benchmark for those in community leadership roles. Paul writes to a given Christian community, and consequently we are able to catch some glimpse of this *ekklesia,* a gathering of men and women who believe in Jesus. Paul mentions leadership people, and so we also are able to catch a glimpse of men and women who have a leadership role in these same *ekklesiai.*

Helen Doohan in her volume *Paul's Vision of the Church*[95] draws up the key areas of Pauline spirituality and in doing so she presents the key aspects of discipleship which Paul stresses. The key areas are the following:

1. **A central focus on God.** Paul clearly sees the world as a creation of God, and even more he sees that God is concerned about the world. Salvation history is the grid in which all of Paul's religious beliefs find meaning and value.

2. **The centrality of Christ.** God has communicated most clearly in and through Jesus. One preaches Jesus (2 Cor 4:5). Believers must put on the mind of Christ (1 Cor 2:16; Phil 1:21; 4:13). Christ is the model of church life (Phil 2:6). This centrality of Christ and the Christian's union with Christ dominate Paul's thought and action.

3. **The mystery of the church.** For Paul, one does not enter into either salvation history or into the Jesus event alone. One enters

the mystery of God and the mystery of Jesus only in a community, and this community so shares in both God and Jesus that it is
the mystery of the *ekklesia:* those called.

4. **The role of prayer.** Prayer is central to the daily life of a follower of
Jesus. Paul indicates his own continuous prayer for the church
(Rom 8:26); he wants the churches to pray continuously as well
(Rom 12:12; 1 Thess 3:10; Phil 4:6).

5. **A life of high moral values.** Life in Jesus, for Paul, is not only
knowledge, it is also praxis. Paul's ethics are highly christocentric,
for in Christ we find the motive for one's pattern of life. Often the
exact answer to a difficult moral situation is not given by Paul, but
he does present each church with the principles and motives to
struggle for some resolution.

These key areas of Paul's vision lead each church and the members of
each church into a daily effort to live out the dying and rising with Jesus,
to live out a scope of forgiveness that has as its paradigm the gift of justification which God has bestowed on us in and through Jesus. Values are
turned upside down, so that weaknesses become strengths, and strengths
become weaknesses (1 Cor 1:25; 4:10; 2 Cor 11:30; 12:10). Service of
others takes as its model Jesus himself (Phil 2:1–11). The good news,
moreover, is not something one keeps to oneself. Rather, one must proclaim and announce the good news to all who listen. In this good news,
boundaries are broken, even socio-political boundaries. Being Jew or being Gentile ultimately has no meaning, for the life in Jesus is open to all.
Being either male or female ultimately has no advantage, since, in Christ,
through baptism all are one.

Paul's vision is placed before the churches, and Paul cajoles, urges,
upbraids, scolds, encourages each community to realize this vision in an
ever deeper way. When he turns to local leadership, finding at times its
failure to respond, he offers no additional or special vision. As leaders,
however, they should incorporate this vision in a public and pastoral way.
If one takes this vision of Paul—and the above description is only one way
to draw it together[96]—one finds a portrait of discipleship. One finds: (a)
those ideals which Paul himself found so powerful for his own personal
life; (b) those ideals which he preached to group upon group, usually Jew
first and then Gentile; (c) those ideals for which, when they are present, he
praises the churches, and for which, when they are absent, he roundly
chides and scolds the churches. He holds himself to this vision, just as he

holds others to it as well, even when those others are held up as leaders of the churches.

It is interesting to see that in Paul, when the christocentric focus is the strongest, the distinction of leader and non-leader disappears. Leadership is not at the heart of the *ekklesia;* Jesus is. In a later age, when *klerikoi/ laikoi* distinctions take on strongly separatist interpretations, when *ordo* structures the church into a class or caste society, we will begin to hear that the "church urges the faithful" to do something. In this latter-day view, the "church" will be the "church leadership"; all the faithful will not be in such leadership. One never hears in Paul that he is the "church" speaking to the "faithful." Rather, he is a leadership person, urging the church to put on Christ, a task and hope which he himself is attempting to do. His vision of Jesus and church calls into question some of the later interpretations given both to *klerikoi/laikoi* and to *ordo.*

Fitzmyer continually stresses the Pauline view of the divine plan of salvation, made known to us in a most definitive way through the life, death and resurrection of Jesus.[97] His "gospel" focuses on the Jesus event that brings to all men and women justification, salvation, reconciliation, expiation of sin, and redemption. This "gospel," which is not a book but an active event in the life of the world, sanctifies, transforms and glorifies those who believe. Indeed, Paul can even speak of a new creation.

The image of God's plan, made real in the humanity of Jesus, shows each of us what human life is all about.[98] The light of Christ indicates the meaning even in the dark mystery of sin. But sin cannot even be partially understood except in the light of God's grace, the gift of love, the gift of himself, the gift of the Spirit. Neither the Torah nor the prophets came close to imaging the height and depth of God's activity in Jesus. Indeed, in Paul's mind, human beings had misused both the Torah and the prophets. Human life in Jesus is one of faith and one of love, and on this earth it is through the community of Jesus, that is, through baptismal-eucharistic life, through life in the *ekklesia theou,* that one begins to live truly.

Only on the basis of God's mystery for the world, and God's mystery in Christ, and God's mystery of the *ekklesia,* can one begin to talk about an ethical dimension to one's life. Discipleship is not in the first place the following out of a series of commands. Discipleship is first of all a call by God into the mystery of salvation. It is a call into the mystery of Jesus, his life, his death and his resurrection. Through this call and one's response in faith, one is a disciple, and only because of this call and one's response in faith does a man or woman begin to see ways to answer the ethical aspects of daily life.[99] For Paul the disciple is not simply one who follows Jesus. Rather, he or she is one who through no merit has been quite graciously called out of the nothingness of sin by God himself. The disciple is one to whom this call has been answered through faith, which itself is a gracious gift of this same loving and forgiving God. Only a man or woman who meditates deeply on this call, this gift, this love of the transcendent God in and through Jesus, will begin to understand the way in which Paul sees the meaning of discipleship.

6. THE DISCIPLES IN THE DEUTERO-PAULINE EPISTLES AND THE CATHOLIC EPISTLES

In this section we will consider the notion of disciple in the deutero-Pauline letters and the so-called Catholic epistles. Even these titles, however, are not unanimously clear, since a document such as the letter to the Hebrews might not even be a letter at all. Nonetheless, this section will consider the following New Testament writings.

a. 1 Timothy

b. 2 Timothy

c. Titus   There is considerable debate on the authors, the dates and the places of composition for these three letters, all of which have many common characteristics. It seems that a fairly acceptable position would maintain that these three letters were written somewhere around the year 100 A.D., and since they all focus on Christian communities in the Aegean and Asia Minor area, one might think of Ephesus as a place of composition. The authors, consequently, are not the Timothy and Titus mentioned in the genuine Pauline letters.

d. 1 Peter   The author, the place of composition, and the time of composition of 1 Peter are all matters of debate. A fairly acceptable position is that it is a pseudonymous letter written between 90 and 100 A.D.

e. 2 Peter   This letter appears to be clearly a pseudonymous letter, written between 100 and 110 A.D. The place of composition cannot be determined with any degree of certainty.

f. James   Though much debated, it would appear that this letter, too, is pseudonymous, written perhaps around 80 A.D. in either Alexandria or Antioch.

g. Jude   No certain date or place of composition can be given to this pseudonymous letter, but it represents a Christian community after 80 A.D.

h. Hebrews   The author, time, and place of composition of this "letter" are all disputed. The work is pastoral in tone, written by someone who does not have first-hand knowledge of Jewish temple worship, and who is addressing in a very pastoral way a second generation Christian community that has become tired in its faith.

Roughly speaking, one could say that all of these letters or writings stem from the end of the first century, with perhaps some of them moving into the first part of the second century. To say that they are representative of "early Catholicism" seems to be too sweeping, but the various Christian communities to which these writings are either addressed or to which the addressee of the letter is attached appear to be fairly well established communities, with some degree of mature community structure. One finds, for instance, more definite details about the leadership of the community in 1 and 2 Timothy and Titus. The remaining letters or writings are less detailed. In general, however, one can say that if and when the individual authors wished to address themselves directly to the community leadership, they do so in a way that is quite apparent.

We see this in the letter to Titus. Titus himself (the name of the addressee) is considered by the author as a community leader. The author even enjoins him to appoint *presbyteroi*, a function which involves some sort of leadership capacity.[100] The qualities of such *presbyteroi* are likewise mentioned (1:5–9), although the ethical qualities themselves, which the author mentions, are basic to every disciple of Jesus. Mention, however, is made of leadership qualities: the *presbyteros/episkopos* is called *theou oikonomos,* the "steward of God's house," a task which a servant performed in the households of the wealthy. This same servant-leader of the community must have a grasp of the word of faith which is found in the teaching, *didache,* so that he can present sound doctrine and refute false doctrine (1:9). This verse provides us with a small window through which we can see that the teaching/preaching of this early community was at least beginning to be seen as having a somewhat established and traditional teaching/preaching nucleus. The *presbyteros/episkopos* whom Titus might appoint is expected to maintain this traditional teaching/preaching. In the eyes of the author of this letter, leadership people had a teaching/preaching function.

The passage also indicates that there are some teachers within the community who are presenting something different, and the author indicates that these "false" teachers in the community should be silenced. It appears that Titus has some sort of authority to bring about this silencing. However, there is no indication in this letter that he could do this by himself, for there is no indication that Titus exercises the position of a single *episkopos/presbyteros* for the community. The mono-episcopacy or mono-presbyterate is a second century development.

After this initial discussion on the moral and administrative qualities of the presbyteral/episcopal leader, the remainder of the letter, and therefore the bulk of the letter, addresses the correct conduct of all true followers of Jesus (2:1–3:15). In other words, the major part of the letter deals with the theme of discipleship, not leadership. The letter indicates that Titus himself should preach and teach the same kind of moral behavior which the bulk of the letter prescribes for all members of his community (2:1–10, 15; 3:1, 8–11). The letter to Titus clearly indicates leadership within the Christian community. The author, whoever he might be, speaks from some leadership position. The person called Titus is described as a leader in the community. The *presbyteroi/episkopoi,* whom Titus is enjoined to appoint, are presented as leaders. This leadership involves (a) stewardship, (b) moral integrity, (c) a grasp of solid teaching, (d) the task of preaching/teaching what discipleship of Jesus truly means, and (e) the task of refuting false doctrine. Besides the leaders, there are as well the various men and women who make up the Christian community, and who are to hear and put into practice this teaching and preaching.

The same kind of fairly organized Christian community is apparent in 1 Timothy. Besides the so-called Timothy, the addressee of this letter, there are other teachers who are affecting the community, but in a harmful and erroneous way. No indication is given by the text or context as to the precise nature of these "teachers." However, these "false teachers" apparently belong to the Christian community and have some influence within the community itself. Since the author speaks of them as "doctors of the law" (*nomodidaskaloi*), they seem to be part of the Jewish-Christian element in the community. The author opposes their teachings with "sound doctrine" (1:10), a phrase which Titus also used to indicate traditional Christian teaching. Christian leadership, which is at least implied in this section of the letter, involves teaching/preaching on the one hand, but based on a sound corpus of *didache.* Evidently the precise form of that *didache* was still being debated, since the author speaks about false teachers.

Another indication of a structured community can be ascertained from the mention of (a) communal or liturgical prayer (2:1–2), (b) an *episkopos,* and one who desires the task of *episkope* (3:1–2), (c) the qualities of such a leader (3:2–7), (d) a *diakonos,* with the qualities of such a minister (3:8–13), (e) a specific and clearly visible ministry of widows (5:9), and (f) presiding *presbyteroi* (5:17). In all of these sections of the letter one finds mention of both community leadership and community structures. None of these leadership positions or structural forms are spelled out in any detail, but their very mention indicates their presence. It is not at all clear, however, that the tasks for these leadership Christians have been well delineated. The difference between *diakonos, episkopos,* and *presbyteros* remains fuzzy. No indication of a lay/cleric division, or of an ordained/non-ordained division, can be drawn from either the text or the context. Such terminology, with its concomitant theological overtones, is a later development.

2 Timothy is addressed to a pseudonymous individual, namely "Timothy," precisely in his capacity as a leader of a Christian community. In many ways the author of this letter presents to this "Timothy" the picture of an ideal leader of a Christian community, namely Paul himself. Jesus, of course, is mentioned, but Paul's own procedures are given extensive center stage (1:11–13; 2:2–10; 3:10–17). Paul is presented to "Timothy" as the model Christian leader, and Timothy, as a Christian leader, should reflect the Pauline image. The author indicates his own ideal of Christian leadership by selecting and describing Paul. But this is not the extent of leadership which one finds in this writing. There are as well the "reliable people" (*pistois anthropois*) who will be teachers of "others." We have, then, a sort of three-generation vision: Paul himself, then the addressee of the letter (Timothy), and then those whom he instructs and who will instruct others. No mention of leadership names is applied to these "others." They are given only the generic term: reliable people, true believers. This handing down of solid teaching, a sort of rudimentary form of a "deposit of faith," is important, since the end time is at hand, and all must be strong and steadfast in their faith in Jesus. As in 1 Timothy there are false teachers besetting the community, but once more we have no indication who these false teachers might be, although it is clear that they are in the Christian community, not outside the Christian community. In spite of the indications of leadership and structure, this letter indicates internal turmoil and non-homogeneity.

1 Peter is very informative as regards discipleship, since it is directed clearly to the Christian community at large. There is no single person to whom the letter is addressed. Whether or not it is, in origin, a baptismal homily, a position which many exegetes since the time of Harnack have espoused, remains a matter of debate. That it might even appear to be so, however, indicates that the thrust of the letter corresponds well to an address which might have been given to newly baptized Christians, urging

them to become ever more profoundly disciples of the Lord. W.J. Dalton, who represents a rather conservative approach to this New Testament writing, mentions:

> 1 Pet is a pastoral document. By emphasizing the dignity of the Christian vocation, which provides a God-given "home" (*oikos*, 2:5; 4:17) for the "homeless" (*paroikoi*, 2:11; cf. 1:17), and the positive value of sharing the passion of Christ through persecution, the writer encourages his readers to remain faithful. These two themes run through the whole letter, but reach high points in texts such as 2:4–10 (the "spiritual house") and 2:18–25 (directly dealing with slaves but valid for all Christians). The climax of the letter seems to come in 3:18–4:6, where Christians' confidence in persecution is seen as based on the story of Christ's salvific acts.[101]

Whoever the author might be, and whatever title he might have borne, are of little consequence. That the author has some sort of leadership role seems both logical and correct, but the entire letter focuses not on any twofold church structure: *laikos/klerikos*, but rather on the kind of person each and every follower of Jesus should strive to be. If this writing has nothing to do with a baptismal liturgy, then it is even more striking, since it is addressed not simply to the newly baptized, but to all who have accepted Jesus as their Lord and Savior, that is, all who are disciples of the Lord.

2 Peter is quite a different work. Some few have even argued that its date of composition lies in the middle of the second century. Is this writing an apology for eschatology, as Käsemann has argued,[102] or is it a "typical debate over God's providence and just judgment," that is, an argument focused on "theodicy," as J. Neyrey has argued?[103]

We find in 1:12–15 and 3:1–2 mention of a leadership role, which the author claims. The community is highly Greek in nature and background, and the argument which the author uses throughout is quite sophisticated. Many ideas which support theodicy, over against the Epicureans (and perhaps some Jews) who denied providence, judgment and afterlife, are skillfully presented. Since christology is fairly minimal throughout this document, there is even some debate on its Christian character. In some ways, however, we gain a small window into an early Christian community: a community, rather conversant with opposing Greek views, rather open to philosophical debate, rather at home in a pluralistic community and a pluralistic social setting. In other words, the document has as its addressees not a small in-group of church leaders, but a fairly wide group of educated Christians who are quite at home in the Greek world of that period.

The letter of James is a long exhortative document, not too well organized, intended for a Jewish-Christian community outside of Palestine. It is not addressed to any leadership group, but like 1 Peter to the community of disciples as such. T. Leahy notes:

> The one common trait, which gives the letter its distinctive quality, is a concern that the faith of the recipients be not merely theoretical or abstract, but implemented in action, in every aspect of their lives. In a situation where trials and temptations abound and where the poor suffer at the hands of the rich, Jas exhorts them to joy, endurance, wisdom, confident prayer, and faithful response to the liberating word of God in a hostile world, as they wait for the coming of the Lord.[104]

The writer has some sense of authority, for he calls himself the servant of God, an Old Testament title used for such leaders as Abraham, Moses, Jacob and some of the prophets. He has authority not only as the "servant of God," but also as the servant of the "Lord Jesus Christ." His authority stems from the God who has revealed himself in Jesus, the Christ. He calls the disciples of Jesus, often referred to in the letter as the "brothers," the twelve tribes of the dispersion. This Jewish manner of speaking had been used since the Assyrian captivity for the ten northern tribes of Israel, in order to represent the eschatological hope of the new Israel. The author applies this symbolism to the Christian community he is addressing, indicating a self-identity of the Jesus community as distinct from the Jewish community. The separation of these two communities, particularly after the destruction of Jerusalem, began to give Christians the identity of the new Israel, the true Israel, the new people of God, etc. It is to this newly called people, the *ekklesia,* that the author directs his words. Only in a few brief passages does the writer indicate leadership roles: in 3:1 he notes that not many should be teachers, and he speaks of the small group of teachers as one with him, for he immediately adds, "knowing that we [teachers] will receive a stricter judgment." But he does not tarry over the scope and position of the "teacher," for he immediately takes up another moral issue, namely that of uncontrolled language, which applies to all the disciples. In 4:1–12 the writer speaks of disunity in the community and the remedies for this disunity. The squabbling in the community, the sinfulness of some brothers (4:8), and the slandering and judging of one another are mentioned, but there is absolutely no mention of church leaders as "judges" or "reconcilers" in these cases. The disciples themselves should bring about the peaceful solutions. In 5:14 the presbyters of the church, *presbyteroi tes ekklesias,* are mentioned only in connection with the sick. The sick person himself or herself calls them. That these presbyters are leadership people in the church is evident; what their precise role might be is not evident. In the situation of a sick Christian, the author indicates that they are to pray over the sick individual, and they are to anoint the sick person with oil in the name of the Lord. Much has been written on this passage, and some have even attempted to see in this text the "institution" or "promulgation" of a sacrament of anointing. Neither the text nor the context allows such a detailed exegesis. Nor can one draw from this text that the anointing with oil is a forgiveness of sin, for in 5:16 the Christians, particularly those who are sick, are urged to confess their sinfulness *to one another, to pray for one another,* and this confession and prayer will cure them. In the preceding verse (5:15) we read that the prayer of faith will save the sick man and the Lord will raise him up again, and if he has committed any sin, he will be forgiven. Issues such as "priestly power," "jurisdiction," and the "power to forgive sins by an official of the church" are all extraneous to this passage. Nonetheless, the few verses do indicate that there were leadership people, called *presbyteroi,* in the church to which the letter is addressed. We also see that sickness was an issue which the church as an organized community (the twelve tribes in the diaspora, the *ekklesia*) dealt with in some sort of prayerful form.

The letter of Jude is a general exhortation to the "beloved," the ones called and kept safe in Christ Jesus. It is not addressed to an individual, to a leadership group, but rather to a community of disciples generally. False teaching appears to be the cause for this communication, but the description of this false teaching is so general that scholars cannot identify it clearly. Mention is made of a special leadership group: the "apostles of our Lord Jesus Christ" (v. 17). Their teaching is to be recalled and heeded. The letter even cites a portion of this message of the apostles, namely: "At the end of time there are going to be people who sneer at religion and follow nothing but their own desires for wickedness" (v. 18). This is an apostolic logion whose source remains unknown. Nor is it clear from the text or context that "apostles" can be restricted merely to the twelve.

The letter to the Hebrews is addressed to the followers of Jesus generally, not to a specific leadership group. That the author has some sort of authority or leadership comes out in the letter itself, but who he is or what his title and function might be is a matter only of speculation. Of interest to the issue of church leadership is the author's denial of the need for any other "priest" (*hiereus*) once Jesus appeared and offered his sacrifice once and for all. The Levitical and Aaronic priesthoods have been terminated.

When one realizes that the early church, up to the beginning of the third century, did not use the term *hiereus* for the Christian leadership, the focusing of a single, new priesthood in Jesus, and the focusing of a single new sacrifice in Jesus' salvific life, death and resurrection, can be seen as part of a general pattern in the apostolic and sub-apostolic community. Only when the church leadership was considered an *ordo* within the *ekklesia,* and only when the *klerikoi/laikoi* division was emphasized, do we begin to find the *episkopos,* first of all, and then, somewhat later, the *presbyteros* and even *diakonos,* described in Old Testament Levitical and Aaronic priestly language. In other words, when hierarchical structures began to take on a sort of socio-political form within the ecclesiastical organization, theologians did not go back to the letter to the Hebrews, or even to the New Testament generally, for their theological understanding of church leadership, but rather they went back to the Old Testament, to the Levitical and Aaronic descriptions of Jewish priesthood, for their theological justification. This letter to the Hebrews, however, indicates just the opposite: namely that those kinds of priesthood have ended with Jesus, and that the Christian community has need of only one priest, Jesus, and of only one sacrifice, his own. The theological rationale based on the Old Testament, which developed at a later period of church history, and which continued to be used in church documents and in theological discussion throughout Christian history, clearly clashes with the approach taken by the canonical letter, the letter to the Hebrews. In the matter of *klerikos/laikos* and church *ordo,* it is theologically difficult to maintain a Levitical and Aaronic description of Christian ministry, when the New Testament clearly indicates the demise of such priesthoods. There is no doubt that the Levitical and Aaronic descriptions of priestliness support many aspects of a *klerikos/laikos* structure and substantiates many aspects of ecclesiastical *ordines,* but when one is confronted with the revealed word of God in the New Testament writings, one cannot cling to Old Testament positions, no matter how supportive and substantiating they might be, if these Old Testament positions stand in opposition to the New Testament revelation.

Nor can one derive much understanding of "priestly" ministry in the passing allusion to "baptisms" [in the plural] and the laying on of hands in 6:2. Only in this single New Testament passage do we have the plural form "baptisms," a usage which scholars have noted and debated.[105] The single phrase "laying on of hands" is also left in the text both unqualified and unclarified, so that we have no possible way of identifying what it refers to. Every attempt to see in it an "ordination," a "confirmation," a "baptismal rite," is purely conjectural.

In this letter, the priestliness of Jesus is not presented by the author to a small hierarchical in-group for their own edification. Rather, the author presents the priestliness of Jesus to the followers of Jesus generally. These disciples of the Lord are to see in the priesthood of Jesus something which will deepen their own faith and love, their own energies to follow Christ, their own endeavors to grow in the Christian life. Indeed, the splendid portrayal of Jesus the priest relates, both textually and contextually, more to the priesthood of all believers than to an ordained priesthood. Textually and contextually, the presentation of Jesus as priest (*hiereus*) has *per se* no direct relationship to a hierarchical Christian in-group. In other words, this document cannot be utilized in any direct way as a "manual for seminarians" or a "manual for priests." The author uses the priestliness of Jesus more as a "manual for discipleship."

In all of these so-called "pastoral letters," we find, with the exception of 2 Timothy, that they are written with the broader Christian community in mind. Individually, each letter does provide some evidence, here and there, of the presence, the naming (to some degree) and the function (again to some degree) of an internal Christian leadership. Nothing in these letters, however, indicates a *klerikoi/laikoi* situation, not only because these very terms themselves are not used, but also because the later interpretation of *klerikoi/laikoi* does not fit well with the portrayal in these letters of Christian disciples generally and service leadership in particular. The term "hierarchy" is also not used in any of these writings, nor is the term *ordo*. From these letters and writings, it would be impossible to deduce that there are in the various Christian communities a structure similar to the Graeco-Roman socio-political structure, involving various *ordines*. Service leadership within the community is clearly evident; that this service leadership involves a structure of *ordo* is not evident.

7. CONCLUSIONS FROM THE DATA

The New Testament overwhelmingly speaks about discipleship. In the gospels and Acts, in the Johannine writings, in the Pauline corpus, in the additional epistolary material, we are presented again and again and again with the meaning of discipleship. Only here and there are we presented with small windows on church leadership. The New Testament, accordingly, instructs us overwhelmingly on the way in which we can become followers of Jesus; it instructs us on the very meaning of what a baptized-eucharistic disciple of the Lord should be. Only in a quite limited way do we find, here and there, pointed statements on what a leader in the Christian community should be. Even in these few places on leadership, however, one does not find that there are two ways of discipleship: one for leaders and one for followers. Rather, we are presented with a powerful portrait of true discipleship, which all who believe in Jesus must strive to replicate in their own lives. If one is a leader in the community, then he or she must clearly evidence this discipleship, and if one is not a leader, one must likewise reflect the same image of discipleship. The New Testament as such is much more a manual of discipleship for all Christians. It is not a manual of discipleship, written in an exclusive way for Christian leaders. The New Testament could be described in contemporary language as the "people's book," not the "hierarchy's book."

As we move through the history of the lay person in the church, the New Testament picture of disciple will serve as a sort of norm by which one can measure the validity or invalidity of certain ecclesiastical situations. Since the goal of the church, the *ekklesia,* is to make disciples of all nations, our task will be this: to discover whether or not, in post-New-Testament Christianity, men and women are imaging and are being encouraged to image the ideal of disciple which one finds so powerfully portrayed on every page of the New Testament. Discipleship, as found in the New Testament, is the point of departure for an investigation of the lay person in the church, for only if Christian lay men and women exist in a community that fosters such discipleship do we even have an *ekklesia.* Without Jesus, of course, there is no church; but without disciples of this same Jesus, we also have no church.

In the material we have just studied, a detailed consideration was not given to the issue of Christian women and early ministry. B. Witherington, in *Women in the Earliest Churches,* presents a healthy overview of women in first century Mediterranean cultures.[106] Culturally the role of women was not uniform throughout the Graeco-Roman world of Jesus' time. Athens, Sparta, Corinth, Macedonia, Asia Minor, Egypt and Rome each had differing ways in which women engaged or did not engage in the academic, political, cultural and religious aspects of everyday life. There was also the Jewish milieu of Jesus' time and its openness and non-openness to women's roles. The role of a disciple of Jesus was shaped not only by the gospel living of Marcan, Lucan, Matthaean, Johannine, etc., communities, but also by the various cultures in which these communities lived. In the Pauline communities as we see in Romans 16:1–16 and in Philippians 4:2–3, there appears to be an "abundance of women . . . involved in some form of ministry."[107] Women both prayed and prophesied as we see in 1 Corinthians 11:2ff.

> There is certainly nothing in the undisputed Paulines that would rule out a woman from teaching or preaching. Paul, however, did apply restrictions when new roles in the Christian communities were taken to imply a repudiation of women's traditional roles and the importance of maintaining sexual distinctions.[108]

Paul appears clearly to affirm new religious roles for women, based on the Jesus event. He affirms Christian modifications of the role of a woman in the family. One could not describe Paul as a "feminist," however, nor could one say that he is a "male chauvinist." Such epithets are too simplistic and do an injustice to the hermeneutics involved in studying the Pauline texts. At times Paul seems to have a somewhat moralistic and conservative bent; at other times he seems to have a more open and liberal stance. Perhaps much of the difficulty arises from the rather occasional ways in which topics are treated. One can certainly say, nonetheless, that even in Paul's time his positions were not warmly received, neither by the more conservative elements in the various Christian communities, nor by certain women themselves.

In the letters of Timothy there appears to be no generalized ban on women speaking in the church. At best, perhaps, one might say that at Ephesus the author(s) of these letters found some women teaching "false doctrine," and therefore these particular individuals should be banned from such teaching. However, these letters cannot be adduced to reject in an outright way the role of women in the ministry of the word.

What one does see in all this is the struggle of these communities to make the teachings of Jesus on the equality of every follower as meaningful as possible in the milieu in which they found themselves. In the gospel material, this same struggle reappears. Women and men are placed in parallel situations, something quite noticeable in the gospel of Luke, but also in John. Women are exemplars of faith. Women are genuine witnesses to major events in the life, death and resurrection of Jesus.[109] Certainly a plausible reason for the emphasis on the role of women, which one finds so strongly both in Luke and John, but also to some extent in Matthew and Mark, is this: part of their agenda was to "give significant attention to women and their roles . . . because when they wrote there was significant resistance to such ideas perhaps especially amongst Jewish Christians."[110]

The role of women disciples in the subsequent period of the Christian community, namely from about 100 to 325, has been studied at great length by a number of significant writers.[111] Various factors began to play a part in the reduction of women from ministerial positions: factors such as views which gave prominence to celibacy over married life, thereby devaluating human sexuality; views which were influenced by gnostic positions, in which the feminine principle was clearly rejected; the views of the Montanist movement which took a strong position on women in leadership, especially after the death of Montanus and the influence of Maximilla became keenly obvious. This role of women in groups which stressed prophecy found a strong reaction from the mainline Christian groups which were beginning to stress orthodoxy and maintenance of set traditions. New prophecies had little space in their understanding of the church. In all of these vying factors, the role of discipleship was often not held up as the criterion; rather, the role of leadership, especially a leadership which claimed apostolic succession, began to become the dominant criterion.

The portrait of discipleship from the New Testament, however, will make us ask hard questions, as we walk through history. We will have to face such questions as: Does a given *klerikos/laikos* structure allow Christians to realize this New Testament portrait of disciple? Does a given theological interpretation of *ordo* in the church also allow for such realization? Does a given era's church leadership foster and sponsor such discipleship? The presentation of discipleship not only is a critique of an era's church leadership and its use of leadership within the Christian community, but is also a critique for the non-leadership sector of the community, for the non-leadership sector is held as strongly as the leadership sector to put on the Lord Jesus, that is, to follow him, to walk in his footsteps, to be his disciple. Indeed, is not discipleship by each and every follower of Jesus more basic to New Testament thought than ministerial structure? If the answer to this question is yes, then how can one position hierarchy within the ecclesial community "higher" or "more important" than the non-ordained disciples? Has there not been, in the development of Church history, a misreading of the gospels and therefore a misapplication of the gospels whenever the ordained hierarchy are presented as an "ontologically" superior group of disciples, compared to the non-ordained group of disciples? The gospels nowhere present us with a double standard of discipleship. Greater and lesser disciples, and therefore higher and lower disciples, are distinguished neither by an *ordo* nor by a hierarchical position. Even more, are male disciples superior to female disciples? Does male discipleship have its privileges which female discipleship does not? Do these ideas square with the New Testament presentation of discipleship? Each era of church history presents us not with a "perfect" ecclesial community or a "perfect" ministerial structure. Each era, rather, presents us with a community and a ministerial structure which are both perfect and imperfect: perfect, insofar as they manifest what discipleship truly is, and imperfect, insofar as they camouflage what gospel discipleship means. *No era of church history, then, is totally normative;* indeed, each era of church history must be seen, to a certain degree, as dis-normative. One looks to the scriptures for the norm, but the only scripture we have is a scripture which has come down to us in a variety of historical attempts to make such a norm existentially actual at a given place and in a given time. Nonetheless, with this portrait from the New Testament of discipleship as a guiding norm, let us walk through the pages of Christian history, noting when and where and how such discipleship strove to find expression year after year, century after century, and noting, as well, when and where and how such discipleship found warped expression, year after year, century after century.[112]

4

The Patristic Period:
The Apostolic Church to 325 A.D.

The history of the lay person within the Roman Catholic Church has been studied, at least in general terms, by a number of scholarly authors. The following chapters will pursue this theme in a much more intense manner. Needless to say, the early patristic period remains the more difficult period, primarily due to the thinness of the sources. Because of the poverty of source material, almost every conclusion derived from the early patristic period involves some aspect of conjecture, my own conclusions as well. Unfortunately, too often the early church period has been read with quasi-dogmatic eyes, with which certain "dogmatic" positions are presupposed. Such presuppositions fall under the same judgment of "conjectural," and therefore must be considered only "quasi-dogmatic," which means, in the long run, not dogma at all.

For the sake of clarity this chapter is divided into the following sections:

1. **Situating the Early Patristic Period Within the Post-New Testament Periods of Church History**
2. **The Church at Rome**
3. **The Church in Egypt**
4. **The Church in North Africa**
5. **The Church in Asia Minor, Syria, and Palestine**
6. **The Acts and Accounts of the Martyrs**
7. **The Ecclesial Role of Women**
8. **General Overview**
9. **Conclusions from the Data**

1. SITUATING THE EARLY PATRISTIC PERIOD WITHIN THE POST-NEW TESTAMENT PERIODS OF CHURCH HISTORY

A. THE SIX PERIODS OF CHURCH HISTORY

1. The Early Church Up to the Beginning of the Fourth Century

In this period of church history, the major emphasis for the followers of Jesus was not so much on the difference between a cleric and a lay person within the church structures, but rather on the difference between the Christian environment and the "world." Internal Christian division, such as the cleric/lay, appeared only tangentially, while the center of attention focused on the difference between those who had accepted the Christian faith and those who had not. The Christian community was a minority community, and one which was subject to pogroms and persecutions.

2. The Emergence of the Clerical Church from 300 to 1000

In this period of time, the Christian church gradually became the only acceptable religious group within the socio-cultural world of the western empire. This happened in the so-called Constantinian church, when east and west were still united, but even more so in the Frankish and Saxon empires of the early middle ages. Clerics, and particularly the higher echelon of clerics, the bishops, not only became leaders, administrators and directors of the church, but also became integral to the socio-political structures of the government. To speak of church and state in this particular period, however, is anachronistic, since the European world did not develop such a dichotomy until the high middle ages. Throughout this period of time there was a religious state, and from the edict of Theodosius I onward there was a Christian religious state. The highest leaders in the governmental structures came to be considered as integral to the Christian religious sphere, and the highest leaders in the Christian church structure came to be considered integral to the socio-political sphere.

The flip-side of this development was the disempowering of the lay person. "Disempowering" might not be the correct term, however, and some authors prefer terms such as disenfranchising, displacement, denigrating, diminishment, etc. Even though the most acceptable term for this repositioning of the lay person in the church remains to some degree a matter of dispute, the overwhelming usage of terms which include a prefix of "dis" or "de," and therefore a negative prefix, is clear. The rise of clergy both in the church itself and in the socio-political world during this period of time had as its side-effect the displacement of lay people in the church and in the socio-political framework. This process took place from the beginning of the fourth century and lasted until the twelfth century.

We might consider these two sections of church history as a time when certain situations regarding church structure took place: namely, (a) an established naming, i.e. cleric/lay; an established positioning, i.e. *ordo* and *ordinatio;* (b) an established socio-political structuring, i.e. the role of higher clergy within the government; (c) an established theologizing, i.e. the presentation of a theology of celestial orders and terrestrial orders; followed eventually by (d) an established ontologizing, i.e. the cleric is "ontologically" different from the lay person. None of this occurred overnight, but took decades, even centuries, to formulate, yet in retrospect we can see a clear line of movement from the first appearance of *ordo* down to the first appearance of some "ontological" difference between major cleric and lay.

Since this created a "dis"establishmentarian situation for the ordinary lay person in the church, the remainder of the sections of church history attended to in this volume can be considered as eras of lay attempts to reposition themselves both ecclesiastically and socio-politically. These various attempts by differing lay groups resemble an incoming tide: there is a momentary invasion of the beachhead, but then a reversal. This is followed by another inward movement which presses further into the shoreline and the subsequent retreat is less extensive. Each succeeding attempt by the lay groups within the Christian church from 900 onward to reestablish themselves crashed against the established position of the cleric. Each attempt was, to some extent, rejected, but not completely. The next attempt brought new strength and new staying-power. This new strength and power, as we shall see, came in these lay movements through the addition of new factors: e.g. (a) the spirituality of the eleventh century lay movements; (b) the widespread education of lay people in the fifteenth and sixteenth centuries; (c) the appreciation of individual rights at the time of the French and American revolutions; (d) the equality of women and the issue of religious freedom in the movements of the twentieth century.

3. The First Resurgence of the Lay Person: 1000–1600

In this particular period of time we find in our Christian history a resurgence, or at least an attempted resurgence, of lay importance. Some of the early movements toward lay involvement were considered heretical and were at times strongly rejected by both the church and the government. This resurgence of the "lay" dimension of Christian life is documented in disparate ways. One finds this resurgence within the monastic renewals of the eleventh and twelfth centuries. One finds this resurgence in the appearance of apostolic lay groups of preachers in the twelfth and thirteenth centuries. One finds this resurgence in the enthusiastic lay response to the various crusades and the accompanying esteem for the crusaders. One finds this resurgence in the burgeoning literacy and educational opportunities for lay men and women in the twelfth, thirteenth and fourteenth centuries, an educational development of the lay person which did not cease at the end of these centuries but has continued on to the present century. However, it was in these medieval centuries that the number of educated lay men and women geometrically increased, with the consequence that such educated men and women began to find powerful positions both in government and in church circles. We find this resurgence of the lay person in the renewal of humanistic learning in the fourteenth, fifteenth and sixteenth centuries, a renewal which the European clerical church found threatening.

The Protestant reformations were, in many ways, a reassertion of the lay person in the church. Not all the reformations were anti-clerical, since a clerical caste can be found in a number of reformation churches immediately after the break with Rome. Nonetheless, in all of these reformation churches a common characteristic was an increased involvement of the lay person both in ecclesiastical and in ecclesial matters. The response of the Roman Catholic Church, however, was an increased emphasis on clerical authority. This is seen both in the doctrinal positions of the Council of Trent and in the pastoral reforms which the Tridentine movement engendered.

4. From 1600 to the French and the American Revolutions

In the *Conciliorum Oecumenicorum Decreta,* under the rubric *Laici,* there is no reference at all to the decrees of Trent, although here and there the Tridentine documents do use the term. Under the rubric *Clerici,* there are many references. There is, however, a cross reference indicated, namely, *saeculares potestates,* and under this rubric there are a number of Tridentine references. The issue which Trent seems to have faced on this matter of the laity focused rather strongly not on the lay person in the church generally, but on those specific lay people who wielded political power and seemed to encroach into the ecclesial sphere. With the principle *cuius regio illius religio,* the rights of the Roman Catholic Church were at stake, and these rights could only be maintained if the religious powers, that is, the hierarchy, were not controlled by the secular powers, particularly in regions which were not considered Roman Catholic, and conversely, in the Roman Catholic regions, if the religious leadership morally and ethically directed the secular powers. This remained the basic pattern of intent for the counter-reformation church.

5. From the French and American Revolutions to Vatican II

With the French Revolution, and its anti-royal and anti-clerical stances, the lay person in society reached a new plateau. Both the French royalists and the Roman Catholic Church took a dim view of this assertion of lay and popular power. In the American Revolution, there are also anti-church strands, besides the anti-governmental strands. The persecution of non-conformist churches in England gave rise to a number of the colonies and cities in the eastern part of the United States and Canada. In many of these church groups, lay people held important and at times dominant positions. The history of Roman Catholicism in the United States, during the period from the revolution down to the issue of lay trusteeism and the so-called Americanism, indicates a continuous struggle between the clerical and the lay element of the church.

After the French Revolution, the term "lay" in European circles often meant anti-clerical, and consequently the leadership of the Roman Catholic Church took a dim view of lay movements. They were almost automatically suspect on the grounds of being anti-clerical. When the various revolutions of 1848 stunned the entire European world, a reactionary position in both governments and churches became immediately evident. Populace movements became highly suspect, not only because they were perceived as anti-clerical, but also because they were perceived as anti-social.

In the Roman Catholic Church, from Pius IX to Pius XII, the official attitude of the church leadership toward the laity was one of suspicion, even hostility, with the exception of an official openness toward those lay groups which were under the firm control of the hierarchy.

6. Contemporary Lay Involvement in the Church

Long before Vatican II, lay groups of Roman Catholics were quite outspoken on the issue of the position of lay people in the church. One also finds in the twentieth century a growing demand by women for a more significant role within the church. In this sense Vatican II did not give rise to the contemporary interest and positive evaluation of the lay person in the church. Rather, Vatican II gave an official endorsement of a movement which was already in progress. This official endorsement, on the other hand, was not merely a small nod of approval. It was, quite the contrary, a major endorsement and a furthering of such lay resurgence.

Vatican II engendered an enormous literature and discussion on the very meaning of the lay person, but in doing so it engendered an enormous literature and discussion on the meaning of a church which is overwhelmingly lay. Indirectly, more than directly, Vatican II called into question the clerical dimension of the church, since, in its official documents, issues were raised on the meaning of the priesthood of all believers which challenged the settled positions on the priesthood of a clerical group. The use of the *tria munera* by the documents of Vatican II, not only for Jesus, but for all baptized, and then for all special ministry in the church, including the episcopal, presbyteral and lay, raised the issue of the difference between the ordained and the non-ordained. Even though the documents state clearly at times that there is an essential difference, no effort was made to clarify the meaning of this "essential" difference, with the result that the efforts to clarify this essential difference remain a matter of heated discussion to the present moment.

The contemporary lay positioning in the church has been called by some authors the maturation of the lay person in the church. It is the age when the lay person has reached adulthood. Such a metaphor is found again and again, but the question arises: Why has it taken almost two thousand years for the lay person in the church to reach adulthood? What are the causes for this lengthy, even over-extended period of childhood and minority status? When one begins to ferret out the reasons why lay men and women were kept in a position of minority and childhood for so long, the activities of many clerical groups do not appear, on many occasions, in good form.

These six very generalized divisions seem to portray quite accurately the way in which lay men and women within the church, particularly the Roman Catholic Church, have found themselves over the past two thousand years. In these six generalized periods unordained men and women played major roles within Christian life, although not at times within "official" Christian life. In contemporary literature, a focus on the presence and/or absence of women in the churches' various activities during all these six generalized periods has certainly developed, with various authors approaching this focus differently. My focus will be on the factors which brought about the repositioning and depositioning of the lay person, both male and female. This repositioning and depositioning affected Christian women more strongly, however, than men. The factors for the repositioning and depositioning of Christian women based on gender will also have to be considered, and these factors will move us into a consideration of societal factors as well. To say, however, that the church leadership simply accommodated itself to the way in which a given society considered women may be factually correct in a superficial way, but it leaves aside the critical dimension which the church leadership should have had regarding the dignity and freedom of all human beings, men and women. The strong rise of feminist theology in the late twentieth century is not simply a critique of the late twentieth century. Rather it is a critique of almost twenty centuries of theology, and therefore the major reasons for the contemporary critique by feminist theologians must be retrojected into each of the preceding centuries.

B. *LAIKOS/KLERIKOS* IN THE EARLY PATRISTIC PERIOD

From the resurrection onward, the Jesus community became aware of itself, but only gradually, as "church" in contrast to Judaism. This began to occur in a noticeable way after the destruction of the temple in Jerusalem in the year 70 A.D.[1] Once the separation from the rabbinical Jewish religion began to take place, the Christian dependence on the structures of Judaism was gradually abandoned, and in their place the Christian community began to form its own institutional structures. We find this initial development particularly in the second, third and fourth centuries. In this lengthy, post-apostolic period, various church ministries became institutionalized and the naming of the major institutionalized ministries gradually became common throughout the Christian world, both east and west. This process of internal organization and naming affected the entire Christian community, and from the beginning of the third century onward we find, sporadically at first, and then as the years go by more commonly, the use of the term *kleros* referring to an established group of Christian leaders, i.e. the "clergy," while those in the Christian community who were not of this leadership group were increasingly referred to as "lay" and "laity." In other words, the earliest Christian community did not start with these names or even with these specific categories; only in the course of time did Christian communities, at first here and there, adopt the terms: cleric/lay, and only in the course of time did the specific meaning of these terms receive theological import.

The goal of this chapter is not to present an over-arching view of Christian life, particularly non-leadership Christian life in the early patristic period. Such a task would require a volume of its own.[2] Rather, this chapter will focus directly on the material, which indicates the emergence and usage of the terms *laikos/klerikos* in the post-apostolic period. By the year 325 church structure has become clerical, and church leadership is referred to as *klerikoi*. To a lesser degree, however, the extant literature indicates that the non-leadership group is called *laikos*. By the year 325, however, one cannot say that ministry and those who are *klerikoi* are identified, while Christians not involved in ministry are referred to as *laikoi.* Christian ministry was far more extensive than the leadership by the *klerikoi.* Consequently, a study on the emergence and meaning of these two terms *laikos/klerikos* does not adequately represent the ministry/non-ministry development in the church. Nonetheless, such a study of the appearance and meaning of these terms indicates the pattern or trend which will continue beyond 325, a trend that increasingly divided the church into cleric and lay, and even at times into official ministry and non-official ministry.[3]

Secondly, in the patristic period up to 325, there was no monolithic structure either to leadership or to ministry. Regional differences are not only evident but are the very source of growth and development. We possess more specific data about four regions of this burgeoning Christian world than we have of the many other sectors of the Christian world: namely, Rome, North Africa, Egypt, and Asia Minor/Syria/Palestine. However, even with this wider data-base, our understanding of these early centuries is quite limited. The data offers only small windows into the geographically diverse Christian life of that period. The structure of this chapter, nonetheless, will consider the data from these four geographical perspectives.

Finally, since this chapter is part of a larger framework, the focus on the emergence of terms *klerikos/laikos* as also of *ordo,* as its hermeneutical principle, is to discover some of the reasons because of which the western church developed not only into such a dominantly clerical church, but into a church which repositioned and depositioned the ordinary lay Christian. Once one begins to see the complex set of causes that occasioned this lay repositioning and depositioning, one is better able both to evaluate the situation and to rectify, where necessary, such a situation.

In this chapter we will not consider the references to *kleros* in the New Testament, which we have already traced, but only those instances in the patristic literature up to 325 in which the *kleros/laikos* image is in evidence. Scholars have established a few basic facts regarding the Christian usage of *kleros* and/or *laikos* during this period.

1. The term *kleros* is not used at all during the first two centuries to refer to a specific Christian minister or ministry. Only at the beginning of the third century is the term *kleros* used for specific Christian ministers and ministries.

2. The term *laikos* is used up to 220 A.D. very infrequently. In the Greek literature there is one passage in Clement of Rome, three in Clement of Alexandria, and one in Origen. In the Latin literature we have the Latin translation of the letter of Clement with its one

passage. Only with Tertullian does one again find the Latin term *laicus* but used only in a very limited way. After 220 the term is used more often.

This small amount of literary data has received an enormous amount of attention. On the one hand, there are authors who see in this meager data something quite astonishing. De la Potterie, for instance, says: "We begin by emphasizing a detail which is quite astonishing [the infrequency of the use of *laikos*]."[4] De la Potterie is astounded that the word *laikos* is not used more frequently in these first two centuries. One might just as well say, however, that it is quite astonishing to find the opposite, namely that such a word takes on rather suddenly a major importance for the Christian church at the beginning of the third century. If one is astonished at *not* finding such a word prior to this time, it might mean that one was expecting to find it. That expectation, however, might easily be due to dogmatic presuppositions on the part of the reader. Other scholars, for their part, find in these few passages an early justification for the clergy/ lay development in the later Christian church.[5] There are still other scholars who consider this meager data in a much more tentative and cautious way.[6] Let us consider each of these early patristic passages in some detail, since in many ways they have been the focus of detailed scholarly study and have been used to argue several conflicting ecclesiologies.

2. THE CHURCH AT ROME

The small volume *Antioch and Rome* by R. Brown and J.P. Meier, is illustrative of the many issues involved in discussing the origins of Catholic Christianity in both areas.[7] Not without good reason does Brown begin his reflections on the Roman cradle of Christianity with a study of Jewish groups who were in Rome just prior to the appearance of Roman Jesus communities. With no strong centralized leadership among the various Jewish groups, early followers of Jesus seem to have moved somewhat randomly into various synagogues with the message of Jesus, the Messiah. Some of these Jewish groups were more receptive than others, but there was clearly no city-wide, organized Jewish position against the preaching of these early disciples of Jesus at Rome. Gradually, a Jesus community, or, better, several Jesus communities, developed at Rome, with decidedly Jewish elements. By the year 50, at least an inchoative Jesus community existed in Rome. Roman Gentile converts to the Jesus message would have been so influenced by the Jewish aspects of this Jesus community that it is, in retrospect, often difficult to separate the specifically Jewish and specifically Gentile factors of the Roman community at this early date.

A few years later, Paul wrote a letter to the Roman community, and from an analysis of the letter one can justly conclude that the Roman Jesus community had become a fairly strong community, no longer a fledgling one. In *Antioch and Rome,* Brown also analyzes both 1 Peter and Hebrews, in order to understand the Jesus community of Rome at the end of the first century. In these two writings he sees the "second generation" of Roman disciples of Jesus. When he comes to the first non-canonical writing, 1 Clement, he sees a "third generation" of such disciples. It is in the midst of this third generation of Roman disciples of Jesus that we begin our present observations.

A. CLEMENT OF ROME

This *Letter of Clement* to the Corinthian community is one of the writings of the apostolic fathers which was fairly well known in the early church. Ignatius of Antioch (*Rom.* 3:1) and, according to some, even perhaps 1 Peter (5:10) seem to allude to it. The letter of Polycarp makes several allusions to it. It was treasured by the church of Corinth, as we read in Hegesippus and Dionysius. Irenaeus makes a sort of summary of it in his writings, and Clement of Alexandria quotes from it on several occasions in his *Stromata.* When one moves into the later patristic writers, the names abound: in the east, Origen, Eusebius of Caesarea, Cyril of Jerusalem, Basil of Caesarea, and Epiphanius, and, in the west where it was less known, we find quotations from this letter in Jerome and John the Deacon.[8] In the late Byzantine times and in the middle ages, however, Clement's letter was almost unknown. Only in 1633 did western Christendom begin to utilize this letter. The Codex Alexandrinus of the letter, written in the fifth century, was presented by the Orthodox patriarch of Constantinople, Cyril Lucar, to the English crown, and Patrick Young, librarian to Charles I, published an edition of the letter at Oxford in 1633. Since then, this letter has played a major role in the historian's evaluation of the sub-apostolic period of church history.[9]

This letter is actually a letter from the Roman community of Christians to the Corinthian Christian community, as we read in the opening salutation, rather than from a single individual.[10] It seems that the letter was written during the reign of Domitian (81–96). Moreover, it is difficult to call Clement the *episkopos* of Rome, as though Rome at this time had an *episkopos.* Rather, Clement seems to belong to the "episkopos-presbyteros" *group* at Rome, and it is in their name that he is sending this letter to the Christian community at Corinth.[11]

The letter advocates peace and order, whereas in the Corinthian community "a few rash and self-willed individuals" (1:1) had set aside the duly established "presbyters" of the Corinthian community. Who these individuals might have been is by no means clear.[12] Many attempts have been made to identify these instigators: for instance, were they a particular social group, or were they an heretical faction, or were they a pneumatic group? Harnack's view that it was a "quarrel among cliques" at Corinth still has some strength, since it seems that there was an intra-community struggle among the Christians at Corinth, and that this Corinthian intra-community difficulty found an echo in other Christian communities as well, which likewise had some sort of intra-community struggle. The fact that there was this echo-effect would help validate its early notoriety and popularity. Barbara Ellen Bowe concludes her analysis of these instigators as follows:

> Despite these other views, I must conclude that, given the evidence present in I Clement, the actual causes and motivation both for the deposition of the presbyters and for the general state of *stasis* ("communal strife") in Corinth cannot be known. None of the attempts to identify the leaders of the dissenting group, either as a social subgroup or as an heretical faction has proved convincing.[13]

Since the dissidents are not easily identified, the cause of the strife is, as a consequence, equally unidentifiable. Generally, Roman Catholic scholars have focused on the issue of ministry and office. It is odd, however, that Clement only broaches this subject when he comes to no. 44 of the letter.[14] Bowe argues that the author intends to press for a more generalized status of peace and order within the Corinthian church than simply one that is related exclusively to ministry and office. The author of the letter, Bowe argues, attempts to confront the pervading envy and self-seeking individualism of the Corinthian community. This wider concern is the real motive for the letter, and the issue of the deposed presbyters is more or less an occasion for the church at Rome to raise these wider issues.[15]

In the section apropos to our theme on *laikos* (37–42), the author presents a picture of ordered worship, described on the basis of the Old Testament, as a model which the Corinthian church should follow. First, though, he uses the imagery of an army with all its various chains of command (37:1–3); then the imagery of the human body with its various members (37:5–38:1–4). The author next cites a lengthy doxology (39:1–9), drawing from many passages from the LXX translation of Job. Having described all this, he turns to the divine origin of church order, which is precisely the place where the term *laikos* appears twice:

> Thus to the high priest have been appointed his proper services (*idiai leitourgiai*), to the priests their own place assigned (*idios ho topos*), upon the Levites their proper duties imposed (*idiai diakoniai*), and the layman (*ho laikos anthropos*) is bound by the rules for laymen (*tois laikois prostagmasin*) (40:5).[16]

Clement is clearly speaking about the need for order, and this need for order comes from God, for it is God who has "commanded sacrifices and services to be performed, not in a careless and haphazard way, but at the designated seasons and hours."[17] It is the Old Testament in particular which provides Clement with this idea of a divinely established order. The adjective *laikos* is used here for a person, the lay individual (*ho anthropos laikos*), and this seems to be the first time in extant literature that this adjective *laikos* is applied to a person. Generally, in the few literary instances we know of, the Greek usage was to employ the term *laikos* only for things. Clement's second usage of the term, "the lay rules," is in keeping with this generally accepted Greek usage of this term.[18]

Nonetheless, Clement is describing liturgical tasks assigned by God to: (a) the high priest; (b) the priests; (c) the levites; (d) the others. Clearly the ranking indicates that the lay individual is not as exalted as the high priest, the priest, or the levite, and in this sense there is a negative quality about the term *laikos*. Faivre, however, notes: "One should not forget that the most important issue perhaps is not that Clement mentions the lay individual at the lowest rank of the hierarchy, but rather that he did not omit mentioning lay people."[19] In this context, their very inclusion in the assigned tasks for liturgy is far more important than their ranking. On the other hand, the author writes, there are liturgical offices which the high priest should do, there are set places for the priests, there are services which the levites should do, and there are regulated activities (*laikois prostagmasin*) which the lay individual should do. In this sense, it should be emphasized, there is a positive aspect to the term *laikos*.

Before one makes a hasty judgment on the value of this text, one should keep in mind that Clement does not use the term *laikos* in any other section of his letter. He does, however, refer to Christians generally with a plethora of other terms: beloved (1:1; 12:8; 21:1; 24:1; 35:5; 36:1; 47:6), brotherhood (2:3), the elect of God (2:3; 46:4; 64:1), beloved brothers (7:1), brothers (13:1; 14:1; 33:1; 38:3; 41:1, 2, 3; 45:1; 46:1; 50:1; 52:1; 56:2, 16), a holy portion (30:1), those called in Christ (32:4), men and brothers (37:1; 62:1). On many of these occasions, when Clement is speaking directly to the Corinthian group, he is advocating that "they" reinstate the presbyters who had been ejected. The "they" seems to refer to all members of the community at Corinth. Only in the specific context of liturgy does Clement use the terms levite, high priest, and the lay individual. Only in the context of liturgy does Clement use the term *laikos* for specific tasks. In other words, there is no ontologizing of this term; rather, the term *laikos* is used in a functional or typological way, just as high priest and levite are used functionally and typologically. If there is to be any indication of an ontologizing, then one must look at the other terms which Clement uses to describe the very status of a Christian: namely, beloved, brother, chosen by God in Christ, etc. These terms are the ones nearest to something ontological in this letter of Clement; the term *laikos,* like levite, priest, and high priest, is at best functional and used merely in a typological way.

One should also note that the reference of *laikos* in Clement's letter is to a Jewish individual, not a Christian individual. So also, Clement's mention of a high priest is clearly Jewish, since at the time of Clement no leader of the Christian community was called high priest (*archiereus*), nor were any Christian leaders at this time called priests (*hiereus*), nor did any leader among the Christians of Clement's time correspond to the levite. *Pari passu* no Christian at the time of Clement corresponded to the term *laikos anthropos.*

> Does the lay person in the Old Testament liturgy find his exact correspondent in the Christian cult? The text says nothing which resembles this.[20]

> Actually, the lay person in the letter of Clement is not a Christian, but a Jew. Or more precisely stated, this lay person is a hybrid and synthetic creature. The lay person is presented to us, as exercising a specific function within a framework of Jewish worship, which is totally artificial and corresponds only to the image of a simply baptized who participates really in Christian worship and brings a spiritual offering of a life regulated by the Christian ideal. In this way, there is a distortion of the Old-Testament image in virtue of the Christian reality.[21]

Even though Clement's letter was popular in the early church and was circulated rather widely, there is no evidence that his use of *laikos* played any role effecting its appearance in the lay/cleric usage of the early third century. In many ways Clement's use of *laikos* is an *obiter dictum* of this period. Moreover the Latin translation of this letter, which originally was made in the second or third century, is known to us on the basis of an eleventh century manuscript, discovered by G. Morin and published in the *Analecta Maredsolana* in 1894. One of the problems of this Latin manuscript is that the medieval copier altered Clement's text here and there, as Harnack mentioned.[22] Probably this particular section was not altered in the eleventh century, but represents the original translation of the second or third century. The Latin translation of n. 40, 5 reads: "*Plebeius homo laicis praeceptis datus est.*" Clement's first use of *laikos* is thus translated by the Latin *plebeius,* not by the Latin *laicus,* while in the second occurrence the translator uses the Latinized Greek word *laicus.* For the person, *plebeius* is used; for things, *laicus* is used. Someone knowledgable in Greek at the end of the second and beginning of the third century would indeed have realized that *laikos* was not used in reference to persons, and this may have been the reason for the Latin translator's change of words.[23]

One cannot overburden the text of Clement with theological ideas and implications of a later period. Clement's letter is the first instance of a Christian use of the term *laikos.* It is also the first instance in which the term is applied to a person, not to a thing. It is used only in the context of liturgical tasks and is found nowhere else in the letter. Clement's usage of *laikos* engendered no subsequent Christian development as regards the use of this term. For all practical purposes it is an *obiter dictum.*[24]

> The notion of the lay-individual, which appears in the writings of Clement of Rome at the end of the first century, is inserted with difficulty into the Christian thought of that era. During the entire second century, the major preoccupation of Christians is to define their relationship to Christ, rather than define their relationship with one another.[25]

B. TRADITIO APOSTOLICA

A span of one hundred years lies between the letter of Clement and the *Traditio apostolica.* In that period the Christian community at Rome had gone through a number of generations and had experienced diverse situations. Ignatius of Antioch had written an important letter to the community at Rome, a community he expected to meet on his arrival at Rome for trial and perhaps death. Justin, a prominent scholar who was born at Flavia Neapolis in the province of Syria, had, after his conversion to Christ, come to Rome about the mid-second century and, as Eusebius tells us, established a school there. Tatian, it seems, was one of his students, although when Tatian returned to his native east, he does not reflect the openness to Graeco-Roman literature and philosophy which he had surely learned from Justin. Crescens, a Cynic philosopher, was one of the most outspoken opponents of Justin. In a cautious way, R. Norris remarks: "He was a sort of Christian intellectual who taught the doctrines of Christianity in much the same way as other philosophical preachers of the time taught those of the Cynics or Stoics."[26] In the various writings of Justin, we see a well-educated and subtle mind addressing controversial issues which arose between the philosophical thought of the day and Christian positions, between Jewish thinking and Christian thinking. To some degree, the persecution and killing of Roman Christians had begun to take place, and Justin raises a thoughtful voice against such official procedures. That Justin, through his academic role both in Rome and elsewhere, was certainly involved in Christian ministry can hardly be denied. That Justin, again because of his academic position, was a Christian leader, a man respected by his co-religionists and by his opponents, is also undeniable. The *Acts of Justin and His Companions* were official Roman documents on the trial of these Christians. That these *acta* have been preserved is itself indicative of the respect that the Roman Christian community had for Justin in particular, and for the six other martyrs of the faith.

Some fifteen to twenty years later (180–185), another well-known and educated Christian, Apollonius, presented at Rome his personal defense or *apologia* for the Christian faith, only to be condemned to death.[27] Once again, even in this brief, cameo appearance of a Christianized scholar, we see a Christian leader, not one who is "ordained" but one who was intellectually quite sterling and one who was willing to pursue his discipleship of Jesus to martyrdom. Had he not been such a man, the *acta* of his death would not have survived nor would his writings, which Harnack once called the noblest Christian apology in antiquity.

The *Shepherd* of Hermas, written about mid-second century, is a work that had profound influence on the early church. It is quite akin to other apocryphal apocalyptic writings of that period. The author was not a "cleric" nor an official church leader, but rather a Christian husband who found his wife with all her jabbering rather unbearable, who was deeply hurt by the apostasy of his own children during the time of persecution and whose lives were less than respectable. His writings have a sermon quality about them, as well as a feverish and visionary aspect. The author, however, seems quite at home, writing in such an exhortatory and ministerial way to his fellow Christians, and in many ways these very writings indicate to us the author's own sense of personal vocation to ministry.

When we arrive at the end of the second century and move into the beginning of the third century, the Roman Christian community has much to its credit. It is an organized community with a sense of tradition. It is also a community which is facing issues, for which the tradition offers few answers. There is a need for stability, but there is an equal need for creativity. It is precisely in this kind of community that Hippolytus, another scholarly gentleman, struggles to lead his Christian life.

The *Traditio apostolica*, which scholars generally attribute to Hippolytus of Rome, a contemporary of Tertullian, is a major book emanating from this early patristic period. In it we have the first extant ordination rituals for *episkopos, presbyteros* and *diakonos*.[28] It is clear from this work that the local church which it describes has by this time a leadership of a single *episkopos*, as well as a group of presbyters and some deacons. The laity are not defined in any positive way, while these leadership positions are clearly defined and their tasks are, in general terms, spelled out in the ordination prayers. All other positions in the church are secondary to these three and are quite distinct from them.

This situation can best be seen in the section of the *Traditio apostolica* which deals with the widows:

When one institutes a widow, one does not ordain, but she is designated by this title.

The author clearly makes a distinction between ordination (*cheirotonein*) and institution (*kathistasthai*). Ordination is reserved for the clerics (*kleros*) in view of liturgical service (*leitourgia*), and consequently the widow is neither ordained nor is she involved in *leitourgia*. This is crystal-clear from the text.[29] Nonetheless, she is instituted in a way in which the ordinary baptized Christian is not, and this institution is a dedication to prayer which, however, is common to all. One might rightfully ask: What is the reason for a special institution? There appears to be some ambiguity here as regards the status of widows, an ambiguity which one already finds in the first letter to Timothy. On the other hand, although the triad of *episkopos, presbyteros,* and *diakonos* form an *ordo,* so, too, we find an *ordo* of widows. By installation into this *ordo* of widows, do these women cease to be *laikai?* Are they still *laikai?*[30] In other words, at this particular period of time, is the distinction between *klerikos/laikos* clearly established? It seems not to be the case, but rather that at the beginning of the third century we are still in a period of flux, in which the terms *klerikos/laikos* are as yet finding their later, more technical meaning. The Roman church, at this period of time, is not a church clearly divided into cleric/lay.

It should be noted, however, that in the so-called *Canons of Hippolytus,* compiled about 340, we have not only the *klerikos/laikos* distinction but, in a quite emphatic way, the male/female distinction. These canons clearly state: "One is not to ordain the widows who are appointed—they are in effect for them the precepts of the Apostle. They are not to be ordained, but one is to pray over them, because ordination is for men."[31] These canons, however, stem from a different region, namely, Egypt, and from a different period of church history, namely, the first half of the fourth century. Textually analyzed, these canons indicate substantial rewriting of the sources which they used, including the *Traditio apostolica.*

The distinction between those ordained and those not ordained, as presented by the *Traditio apostolica,* is based on the issue of liturgy, *leitourgia,* which at this period of time would have meant baptism-eucharist, and to some degree reconciliation. With the mention of the *prosphora,* it is clear that the central focus is on the eucharist. The original Christian matrix for the evolution of the terms *klerikos/laikos,* then, must be seen within the context of liturgy. Later this liturgical context will be enlarged and even given a certain "ontological" status. We do not, however, find any such "ontological" considerations of *klerikos/laikos* throughout this patristic period.

The *Traditio apostolica,* in the section on baptism, states that the teacher or catechumenist, whether cleric or lay, prays and imposes hands after an instruction. We will soon note in the discussion on Origen that at the very time the *Traditio apostolica* was written, some churches found lay teaching questionable. Again, one notes the fluctuating circumstances of these particular decades of church history.

The *Traditio apostolica* also mentions the lector: "The lector is instituted (*kathistasthai*) when the *episkopos* gives him the book, but he does not receive the imposition of hands (*cheirotenie*)" (n. 12). Is the lector a cleric or a layman? On the basis of the entire tenor of the *Traditio apostolica,* it might be better to classify him as a *laikos,* since the author clearly emphasizes the distinction between ordination (*cheirotenie*) and installation (*kathistasthai*). On the other hand, the lector enjoys a liturgical role, a role which the author had denied the widow.[32]

The document also mentions the instance of the confessor-martyr (n. 16) and we are told not to "impose hands on him either for the diaconate or for the presbyterate, for he possesses the honor of the presbyter by his confession. If however he is made an *episkopos,* then one should impose hands on him." The Christian belief that such a confessor-martyr, already filled with the holy Spirit, did not need presbyteral ordination once again raises the issue of the boundary between *klerikos/laikos.*

In the section on baptism, the *Traditio apostolica* indicates the many professions which are incompatible with either a catechumen or a baptized Christian: someone who runs a house of prostitution, an actor, a gladiator, a keeper of animals, etc. Those outside the people of God, the new *laos,* were not referred to as *laikoi.* One had to belong to the people of God to be a *laikos,* and in this differentiation of acceptable and non-acceptable careers, one finds a positive assessment of *laikoi,* or better the baptized. Within this people of God, however, the *klerikoi* were the spiritual leaders, and this clerical leadership was based on ordination, which in turn was based on ecclesial leadership. This portrait of an early church, which the *Traditio apostolica* describes, is not presented as something new. One sees in the ordination prayers, for instance, a certain liturgical maturity. One sees in the church's baptismal structure a developed format. In other words, the portrait which we find in the *Traditio apostolica* is not a fledgling one; it has its own *traditio.* One cannot, of course, take this format back to the apostles as the title of the work might indicate. One can, however, see in this church structure a format of perhaps several generations of Christian living. On the other hand, one must also note the tendential aspect of the document. The author does stress, for instance, that widows are neither to be ordained nor considered *klerikai.* Can one read between the lines that certain widows were pushing for ordination-status or for clerical-status? The fact that the author stresses the issue is indicative; it is not clear, however, how far one can establish the reason for such a stress. The author, however, does not deny either ordination or clerical status to the widows on the basis of their sex; rather, the basis is their non-liturgical role. In the *Canons of Hippolytus,* however, written only a few years later and in connection with the *Traditio apostolica,* the exclusion is indeed based on gender.

3. THE CHURCH IN EGYPT

Eusebius informs us that he found nothing in his sources about the primitive history of Christianity in Alexandria.[33] To this day, scholars still struggle to piece together a picture of early Christian origins in the area of Alexandria. Philo mentions nothing about Christians in Egypt. The wispy tradition of Mark as the first of many Alexandrian bishops remains merely a will-o'-the-wisp. Was Apollos already a Christian while in Alexandria, and did he even preach Christian teachings to the Alexandrians, as codex D of Acts indicates? Or is this annotation part of an early wish list? Was it the emperor Hadrian who wrote to the consul Servianus, or is this a concocted letter by Phlegon, a freedman of Hadrian? In this letter a clear mention is made of Christians in Alexandria, and even were the letter to be falsely attributed to Hadrian, there is a certain daring in the very act of such falsification. The *Epistle of Barnabas,* which may have Egyptian origins, raises a host of problems because of its gnostic overtones. This gnostic aspect is apparent in other coptic-gnostic writings: the *Pistis Sophia,* the *Odes of Solomon,* the *Books of Jeû.* Add to this the manichean literature in Coptic, the *Gospel of the Egyptians,* which is at times mentioned by Alexandrians along with the *Gospel of the Hebrews,* and the Jesus-logia of the Oxyrhynchus papyri.

Each of these sources has raised a wide spectrum of scholarly debate, and when all is said and done, the origins of Alexandrian and Egyptian Jesus communities remain uncertain. By the beginning of the second century, and perhaps earlier, there seem to have been Jesus communities in Alexandria, but it is only in the Alexandria of the last decade of the second century onward that we catch a glimpse of "ecclesiastical" Christianity at Alexandria.[34] It is precisely in this somewhat established ecclesiastical Alexandrian milieu that we resume the focus of our search.

A. CLEMENT OF ALEXANDRIA

In his *Stromata* Clement of Alexandria (c. 150–215) uses the term *laikos* two times.

> He [St. Paul] allows a man to marry one woman, be he a priest, or deacon, or a laic (*Strom.* III, 12, 90, 1).[35]

> Therefore the curtain [in the temple] is a barrier to lay disbelief (*laikes apistias*) (*Strom* V, 6, 33, 3).[36]

In the *Tutor* he uses the term *laikos* once:

> The lay task is assigned, both what is right and what is required (*Tutor* II, 10, 93, 2).[37]

Beyond these three instances, Clement does not use this term again. In his discussion of Clement of Alexandria, Luigi Pizzolato contextualizes the thought of Clement within the framework of Greco-Roman cosmology. For the Greco-Roman philosophers, the world, he writes, had become theological, i.e. a place in which one contemplated the divine. For the Christian philosopher such as Clement, the world is a free creation of God and has its own *laicità* or lay quality. As Clement states at times in his various writings, we are only *paroikoi* in this world, transient individuals.[38] Diognetus, in his letter, had said the same thing, namely, that we are *xenoi* or strangers in this world. Pizzolato is arguing for a certain independence of the world vis-à-vis the divine, since only in this qualified independence can there be any value to something lay.

Certainly, Clement of Alexandria moves in this direction, not, however, in any conscious way of developing a "theology of the laity." Actually, the infrequency of the term *laikos* in his writings leads one to frame his intent more in terms of the Christian *gnosis* and the Greco-Roman *gnosis.*

In the first instance above, Clement is defending legitimate marriage, which is allowed to a *presbyteros,* a *diakonos* and a *laikos.* The *presbyteroi* and *diakonoi* of Alexandria at this time were by and large married men. It would also seem that in Clement's time, Alexandria had already developed a single-*episkopos* system, with the *presbyteroi* acting as a group of consultors. Likewise, there were a number of *diakonoi* who aided the *episkopos* in a pastoral and administrative way. The writings of Origen on the *episkopos* certainly bear this out.[39] Clement uses the term *laikos* as a category, in contrast to *presbyteroi* and *diakonoi,* just as *diakonoi* and *presbyteroi* are contrasted with each other. We do not have, however, a clergy-lay contrast *per se.* Clement does not speak in terms of *kleros/laikos.* He speaks in terms of *presbyteroi, diakonoi* and *laikoi.* His point, however, is not to stress the issue of ecclesiastical office, but to stress the issue of the dignity and validity of marriage within the Christian *gnosis.* Marriage is an acceptable way of life for *all* Christians.[40] In this context of marriage, Clement's use of *laikos* cannot be understood, except as a passing way to speak about people generally. To develop a lay-cleric theology from this citation is an overburdening of the text.

In the second instance in which Clement uses *laikos,* he speaks about "lay disbelief." De la Potterie notes that we have here a case of metonomy, and that by "lay disbelief" one is actually speaking about an unbelieving people: *laos apistos.*[41] *Laikos,* in this context, therefore refers to the non-Christian over against the Christian people, i.e. the believing people. Thus the use of *laikos* in this passage in no way addresses the issue of *klerikos/laikos.*

The third instance of *laikos* in Clement, this time in *The Tutor,* is within a context, describing libertine behavior, a manner of life which an aristocratic or elite group would in no way follow. In this passage, *laikos* is clearly not contrasted to *kleros,* but to the aristocratic and cultured approach to life. It has nothing to do with the *klerikos/laikos* aspect of the church.

There is no doubt that Clement used the term *laikos* for certain categories of people. Indeed, this is generally the case with Greek adjectives ending in "ikos." To move from this rather generalized description of *laikos,* namely, a given category, to his concrete instances, one sees that the categorization is not between lay/cleric, but (a) between one way of life in which people respect marriage and a gnostic way in which marriage is disdained, or (b) between a non-Christian people who have no faith and Christian people who have faith, or (c) between the libertine behavior of the masses and the cultured and considered behavior of the artisto-cratic elite.

It is difficult to see that Clement, in his meager use of the term *laikos*, advances the thinking of "lay person" within a church-office context. That there is a fairly well established church leadership at Alexandria at the time of Clement is clear; that there is any developed cleric/lay termi-nology and theology is unsubstantiated by Clement's writings.

B. ORIGEN

Origen (c. 185–253), as we noted above, transmits the Greek transla-tions of Aquila, Symmachus and Theodotion in his *Hexapla*. In these translations, one finds the term *laikos*. Outside of this use of *laikos*, which Origen merely reproduces from other authors, he employs the term *laikos* only on one occasion in his own extant and prolific spate of writings. We find this in his *Homilies on Jeremiah*.[42]

Before citing this passage, however, it would be wise to recall that from Origen's many writings we realize that the mono-episcopacy, as the main church leadership in a given area, seems to have become standard, at least in the areas he himself knew.[43] Under the *episkopos* there are other leaders of the community: *presbyteroi, diakonoi, diakonissai* and other so-called minor orders. In his writings, allusions to church ministry are frequent enough, as also his use of *kleros* in reference to this organized and institutionalized church leadership.[44] Origen's abundant material on church leadership, with the above established names for this leadership (*episkopos, presbyteros, diakonos, diakonissai*), makes the single occa-sion when he uses *laikos* a *hapax legoumenon*. This is significant, not because it points to any "theology of the laity," but rather because it appears that in Origen's situation *laikos* had not yet become the custom-ary word to contrast with *kleros*. In other words, Origen's single occasion of the word *laikos* offers no evidence of a clergy/laity understanding of Church ministry in Alexandria at the beginning of the third century. Nonetheless, at the very same time in which Origen is writing his *Homi-lies on Jeremiah*, there appears to be both stabilized names and stabilized functions for church ministry in the areas with which he was acquainted, and which he called *kleros*. A "clergy class" had indeed begun to take hold, and Origen utilizes many terms and imagery of the Old Testament to provide a theology of ordained Christian ministry.[45] He does not, how-ever, present us with a specific model of the church with the terminology *klerikos/laikos*.

Indeed, to understand Origen's position, one must approach his writings not with the questions: Who are the "laity"? Who are the "clergy"? Rather one must first consider his numerous statements that respond to the questions: Who is a Christian? What is the meaning of the "baptized" person? What is the priesthood of all believers? Origen refers to this priesthood of all believers in a quite abundant way; one needs only to read, for instance, *Homilies in Leviticus,* 9, 1; 9, 9; 7, 2; *Homilies in Numbers,* 4, 3; *Contra Celsum,* 8, 73; *Commentary on Romans, 4, 7; 7, 5.* In the *Contra Celsum,* Origen compares every baptized Christian to the priests in the pagan world and gives them all the privileges of these pagan priests.[46] Origen, however, also compares the baptized Christian to the Jewish priests. The Jewish priests were but shadows and image, entering into a temple that was built from stones, while the baptized Christian, together with Jesus, enters into the true holy of holies, the heavenly temple.[47] The baptized Christian is the "spiritual Jew," not simply a genealogical Jew,[48] and the baptized is the "true Israelite of the coming world."[49] The baptized form a truly spiritual priesthood.[50] For Origen, of course, this spiritual priesthood is a real priesthood, more real than the priesthood of the Graeco-Roman pagan religions and more real than the Jewish priesthood of the Old Testament. Because of this priestly role the baptized were present at church councils.[51] The baptized share in the kingship of Jesus, for they are a kingly and priestly group (*Homilies on Judges* 6, 3; *Homilies on Numbers,* 12, 2; *Homilies on 1 Peter,* 2, 9). Through baptism every Christian is a member of the priestly body of Christ (*Homilies on Leviticus,* 7, 2; *Commentary on Romans,* 4, 7; 7, 5).

Although Origen is well aware that the ordained ministry has a significant place in the role of the church, he never uses the word *hierarchy.* In fact, the first time this word occurs in Christian literature is with Pseudo-Dionysius, and in this writing it appears with a vengeance. Origen, however, does state in other language that there are differing grades within the ordained ministry.[52] It is precisely when he is speaking about this role of the various ordained ministries that he uses, on the one and only occasion, the term *laikos,* which one finds in the *Homilies on Jeremiah.* The text reads as follows:

> "Their functions (*kleroi*) are of no help to them." Others before us have interpreted these words, and since we ourselves do not reject their interpretation, we willingly repeat it here, not as if we ourselves discovered it, but as one who has received a good teaching. This passage (*houtos ho logos*), if we pay attention to what is written, will be helpful both to you and to us—we who seem to be by our function (*apo klerou*) seated above some of you to such an extent that some of you wish to have this very

function (*kleron*). Realize, however, that the function (*kleros*) does not always avail, for many presbyters are lost, and many laics (*laikoi*) will be declared blessed. There are those in the function (*en klero*) who do not live so as to draw profit from and fulfill the function (*kleron*), and for this reason the interpreters say: it is written "Their functions are of no help to them." What is advantageous is not to be seated in the presbyterion, but living worthily of the place (*topos*) as the Word asks [of us]. The Word asks of both you and us that we live well (*kalos*), but it is also necessary to speak thus: "Those in power will be tested strenuously." More is asked of me than the deacon, more of the deacon than the lay person (*laikon*); as for the one who has been entrusted with ecclesiastical leadership (*arche*) above all of us, even more will be asked of him.[53]

Origen also uses the concept of *taxis* (order) to distinguish between all the baptized and the ministerial or ordained priestly class. All the baptized, Origen writes, constitute a *taxis* in the church.[54] *Taxis,* for Origen, clearly indicates a group. In the *Peri archon* (*On First Principles*) he speaks of the *taxis* of angels and the *taxis* of saints.[55] This idea of a *taxis* or order of all Christians can be found here and there in other early church fathers, but this way of speaking never became a common Christian way of describing the baptized. Besides this *taxis* of the baptized, Origen also mentions a *taxis* of priestly ministry. In many ways, Origen's use of *taxis* corresponds at times to his use of *kleros,* so that we see that *taxis* and *kleros* mutually interpret one another.[56] Nonetheless, the ordained priesthood is not seen, in Origen's writings, as the opposite of the priesthood of the baptized. Rather, the priesthood of the baptized is the base for the ordained priesthood.[57]

In Origen we have a fairly detailed description of the ordained ministry in the church, as he knew it in his day and age, at least in certain churches. On the other hand, we have a powerful description of the priesthood of all believers. Origen's description of the baptized Christian is deeply theological and strongly christological. In fact, one could never understand the ordained priesthood in Origen if one did not first understand his teaching on the priesthood of all believers. The documents of Vatican II have provided, for our day and age, a major statement on the dignity and theological depth of the baptized. These contemporary documents emphasize that every baptized person shares in the prophetic, priestly and kingly mission and ministry of Jesus. Origen, for his day and age, presented a very similar in-depth portrait. Origen does this, not by any contrast of *laikos/klerikos,* but through his teaching on the very meaning of priesthood: namely, the foundational priesthood of all believers on the one hand, and, on the other, the ecclesial ordained priesthood of *episkopos, presbyteros* and *diakonos.*

Nonetheless, Origen clearly contributes to the distinguishing between cleric and "lay" even though he only uses the term *laikos* once. We see this in the following ways:

1. **The forgiveness of sins:** The ritual of reconciliation was in its foundational stages at the time of Origen, but Origen clearly states that the baptized needs to be forgiven by the high priest (*episkopos*).[58] In other words, as far as the forgiveness of sin is concerned, the *kleros* (more specifically the *episkopos*) has a power which the baptized do not have.

2. **The eucharist:** Origen follows the lines of Clement of Rome, according to whom there are different roles which Christians perform at a eucharistic gathering. Faivre describes Origen's position as follows: "Between clerics and the baptized, there is not only a difference in the practical distribution of roles, there is also a distinction in the distribution of powers at the very heart of the eucharistic assembly; Christians participating in this liturgy are not all equal."[59]

3. **Teaching:** Origen, for a major part of his life, was not ordained, and on one occasion (c. 216) when he preached before the gathered community at the invitation of the *episkopoi* of Caesarea and of Jerusalem, the *episkopos* of Alexandria, Demetrios, was incensed that a non-ordained gave a homily in the presence of *episkopoi.*[60] This occasion was not an isolated one, for the question of lay people teaching had vexed several major churches during this same period. Although Origen defended his position, and therefore the position that a qualified baptized person should clearly be allowed to teach and even preach, the arguments pro and con tended to separate the clergy from the baptized more and more. Eventually, teaching and preaching was reserved to the clergy.[61]

4. **Holiness:** Although Origen clearly states that holiness is not the prerogative of the clerical class, and that many baptized surpass the ordained in holiness, he nevertheless also states that holiness is demanded of all baptized, but is demanded in an even greater way of the clergy. There seems to be, in his writings, a progression of perfection, as one moves from baptized to the various ranks of

ordination. This, too, contributes to the growing distinction between the baptized and the ordained.[62] Even though almost all the writers at the beginning of the third century tended to relativize the titles and dignities of the clergy, stating that all are called to holiness, nonetheless there was an opposite tendency, namely to see perfection culminating in the priestly service.

5. **Maintenance:** Origen mentions that the baptized have an obligation to provide for the maintenance of the clergy so that they can have adequate time for ministerial service. "Without doubt," Faivre says, "we have here the concrete and true knot (*noeud*) of the distinction between cleric and lay."[63]

6. **Celibacy:** The issue of celibacy played a role in the historical separation of clergy and laity, even at this early date when most of the clergy were married. The montanists were depreciating marriage. People such as Clement and Origen upheld the holiness of marriage, but they had harsh words for those who remarried.[64] A widowed person is a better Christian if he or she never remarries. Naturally, the next step would be that anyone who is not married at all will be in a "better" state.

One must add, however, that at the beginning of the third century, the clerics and the "lay" are not as yet absolutely separated. We find ourselves, rather, at a time when the theological writers are attempting to articulate the differences between various leadership roles within the Christian community. This articulation is primarily done by way of describing functions (a typological description) rather than by way of describing an entitative status (an ontological description). One of the reasons, perhaps, why one cannot speak of an "ontological difference" between the ordained and the unordained in Origen is the fact that he really did not have such a theological vocabulary for this. More importantly, in Origen there is not an equation between the baptized and the "laity." For Origen, the term "baptized" does not correspond to *laikos,* but corresponds more pointedly to priesthood, since it is in the priesthood of all the baptized that Origen locates the roots of ministerial priesthood. However, as the word *laikos* becomes more and more common in later generations, as we shall see, the split between *laikos/klerikos* becomes more and more pronounced, and as a result an ontologizing theology gradually begins to take shape. To cite Faivre once again: "Thus the laics belong to the people of priests, but they will become very quickly the people of the priests."[65]

4. THE CHURCH IN NORTH AFRICA

A. TERTULLIAN

At the end of the second century and the beginning of the third century, our knowledge of the early Christian church depends in a strong way on the data regarding three local churches: Alexandria, Rome, and Carthage.[66] Perhaps the most important author on the precise issue of cleric/lay at that time is Tertullian, even though he only uses the word *laicus* in five texts:[67]

De baptismo, written c. 189–200.
De exhortatione castitatis, written between 204 and 212.
De fuga in persecutione, written in 212.
De monogamia, written probably in 217.
De praescriptione haereticorum, written around 200.

Even though he uses the term *laicus* rather seldom, given the volume of his work, Tertullian exhibits a clear distinction between "clergy" and the Christian "lay" people. The terms "cleric" and "lay" may not be that frequent, but in Tertullian there appears to be a functional distinction, at least, between those who are the church leaders (*episcopus, presbyter, diaconus*) and those who are not in such leadership positions.

1. The Five Texts

Let us consider the five texts first, and then consider the context of church leadership within the writings of Tertullian.

a. De baptismo:

Of giving it [baptism], the chief priest (who is the bishop) has the right; in the next place the presbyters and deacons, yet not without the bishop's authority, on account of the honour of the Church, which being preserved, peace is preserved. Beside these, even laymen have the right; for what is equally received can be equally given. Unless bishops, or priests, or deacons, be on the spot, other disciples are called, i.e., to the work. The word of the Lord ought not to be hidden by any; in like manner, too, baptism, which is equally God's property, can be administered by all. But how much more is the rule of reverence and modesty incumbent on laymen—seeing that these powers belong to their superiors—lest they assume to themselves the specific function of the bishop.[68]

b. De exhortatione castitatis:

It would be folly to imagine that lay people may do what priests may not. For are not we lay people also priests? It is written: He hath made us also a kingdom, and priests to God and His father. It is ecclesiastical authority which distinguishes clergy and laity, this and the dignity which sets a man apart by reason of membership in the hierarchy. Hence, where there is no such hierarchy, you yourself offer sacrifice, you baptize, and you are your own priest. Obviously, where there are three gathered together, even though they are lay persons, there is a Church. For, as the Apostle also says, each man liveth by faith nor is there respect of persons with God, since not the hearers of the law are justified by the Lord, but the doers. Therefore, if in time of necessity you have the right to exercise a priestly power, you must also needs be living accordingly to priestly discipline even when it is not necessary for you to exercise priestly powers. As a digamist will you baptize? As a digamist will you offer sacrifice? How much more serious a crime is it for a lay digamist to perform sacerdotal functions, when a priest who becomes a digamist is removed from his priestly office. . . . There is one God, one faith—let there be one discipline also. So true is this that we may ask how we shall ever obtain priests from among the laity, if laymen fail to lead the kind of life demanded of those who are chosen for the priesthood. Therefore, we must insist that the obligation of avoiding second marriages rests first of all on the laity, since no man can become a priest except one who as a layman, lived in monogamy.[69]

Note: Tertullian uses *laicus* eight times in this section.

c. De fuga in persecutione:

But when those in authority—I mean deacons, priests, and bishops—take flight, how is the mere layman to understand the sense in which it was said: 'Flee from city to city'?[70]

d. De monogamia:

If he wills us to iterate conjugal connections, how does he maintain that "our seed is called" in the but once married Isaac as its author? How does he make monogamy the base of his disposition of the whole Ecclesiastical Order, if this rule does not antecedently hold good in the case of laics, from whose ranks the Ecclesiastical Order proceeds?[71]

For if bishops have a law of their own teaching monogamy, the other [characteristics] likewise, which will be the fitting concomitants of monogamy, will have been written [exclusively] for bishops. With laics, however, to whom monogamy is not suitable, the other [characteristics] also have nothing to do.[72]

e. De praescriptione haereticorum:

And so it comes to pass that to-day one man is their bishop, to-morrow another; to-day he is a presbyter who to-morrow is a reader; to-day he is a presbyter who to-morrow is a layman. For even on laymen do they impose the functions of priesthood.[73]

2. The Context

M. Jourjon, in his concluding remarks, notes that Tertullian is not a father of the church in the strict sense of this term, and consequently one must retain a certain reserve regarding his formulations.[74] This may be so, but his testimony regarding the church in North Africa at the end of the second and the beginning of the third century is invaluable.

In the North African colony it had been a tradition to have a society of various orders, *ordines.* The power of these ruling groups had threatened Rome, and in 146 B.C. Carthage was destroyed by the Romans. From then on, the Romans had deliberately thwarted, as best they could, any revival of the Carthaginian position. In 123 B.C. Gaius Gracchus had attempted to establish a *colonia iunonia,* but the opposition of the Roman senate prevented any lasting outcome for this venture. The plan of C. Gracchus had envisioned a colony with clearly defined social ranks. It was, however, in 44 B.C. that C. Julius Caesar reestablished a Roman colony in Carthage. Still, the beginnings were not peaceful. Roman antagonism remained strong and deadly. Gradually, however, Carthage and the North African colony developed into a major area. In the second and third centuries A.D. there was an economic boom in North Africa, not only in Carthage itself, but also in many of the interior towns as well. Corn and olives were the main products, then wine, figs, livestock and horse-breeding. As the economy of the area developed, so, too, the social structures. The *ordo decurionum,* which had been totally removed during the Punic Wars, gradually reemerged in Carthaginian society. Wealth produced upward mobility, and many newly rich Carthaginians became members of this *ordo.* A similar upward mobility is found in the *ordo equester,* particularly in the second and third centuries. Of far more consequence, however, is the *ordo senatorius.* Under Trajan, only three Roman senators were of African heritage (two percent of the total senate). Under Hadrian there were twelve (eight percent). Under Antoninus Pius there were nineteen (eleven percent). Under Marcus Aurelius there were twenty-five (fourteen percent). Under Commodus there were fifteen (thirteen percent). And under Septimius Severus there were seventy-three (fifteen percent). The tendency moves upward in the years that follow.[75]

By the time of Tertullian (c. 155–220) Carthage was a flourishing and major center. The three social *ordines* were an established fact of life, so that we find such Latin expressions as *ordo et populus*, or *ordo et plebs*. People who were in these various *ordines* tended to be the social and political leaders of the community. We cannot say that Tertullian was the first to apply this notion of *ordo* to the church structure (from which eventually we have the theology of sacred orders), but we can say that his writings were very influential in making this manner of speaking not only popular but terminologically and theologically technical. The *episkopi* and the *presbyteri* became, in the church, an *ordo;* soon *diakoni* and others eventually were included and the entire group was called clergy, the *kleros,* the sacred order. Just as the political structure had its *ordines,* on the one hand, and the *populus* or *plebs* on the other, so, too, the church had its *ordo,* on the one hand, and its *populus* or *plebs* on the other as well. This latter group gradually came to be described rather commonly by the adjective *laicus.* Had Tertullian not used these terms: *ordo, clericus, laicus,* another writer would surely have done so, since this kind of socio-ecclesial structure reflected so well the socio-political culture of the day. We see a similar development of such Church language during the Holy Roman Empire with its formalized monarchical language. In that period, the political monarchical language began to be mirrored in church structures as well, at both a papal and an episcopal level, so that one hears of a monarchical papacy and a monarchical episcopacy. We see this pattern again in the contemporary discussion on the people of God and the issue of religious freedom, with its democratic overtones, taken from the contemporary cultures of our own age. The emphasis on the equality of all the baptized, found in the documents of Vatican II and the *Instrumentum laboris* for the synod on the laity, and the effort by some of the popes to remove some of the more regal symbols of papal behavior, indicate this contemporary tendency.

At the time of Tertullian, it should be recalled, some sort of ordination ritual had begun to develop. We see this in our first extant ordination ritual of a contemporary of Tertullian, Hippolytus of Rome. The emergence of a ritual of ordination—and it was in many ways Tertullian who provided the Latin church with the very name of this ritual, *ordination*—is indicative of the sacralization of church leadership and its resultant "laicization" of the rank and file Christian. In other words, the church's use of the terms "cleric/lay" cannot be understood except against the socio-political background of the Greco-Roman world at the end of the second and beginning of the third century. Without this cultural context, the distinction in the church of *ordo* and *populus* would never have taken on the meaning it did. As the term *ordo* came to be used more and more for the church leaders, the terms "klerikos/laikos" began to take on new shades of meaning. Clericalization may be the usual term to express the process which began to occur at the end of the second and beginning of the third centuries, but the linchpin is not the term *klerikos,* nor the term *laikos,* but the term *ordo.* Both the use of the term *ordo* and the socio-political meaning of this term, which was assumed into the ecclesiastical usage, gave rise to what we call clericalization. Perhaps it would be more accurate to speak of "ordinization." Once the church leaders took on the identity of an *ordo,* and once the Christians generally perceived their leaders in terms of an *ordo,* the theological justification of this status began. The early writers, however, did not go back to the gospels and to Jesus, but they went back to the Levitical and Aaronic priesthood of the Old Testament, for the tribe of Levi had a special place, an order, within the twelve tribes. Theological descriptions of the church leaders were cast more and more in Old Testament terms, thus sacralizing the *ordo* itself. This Old Testament sacralization of church leadership, which has no foundation at all in the New Testament, began to reshape the meaning of the term *klerikos,* and once this process began, the reshaping of the term *laikos* also occurred.

B. CYPRIAN

A brief mention of Cyprian of Carthage (c. 200–258) might be made at this juncture. Although he appreciated Tertullian in an eminent way, he did not develop the *laicus/clericus* approach which Tertullian somewhat gingerly began. *Laicus* is never used in the writings of Cyprian, and the term *clericus* is used only once in his *De Unitate Ecclesiae* (17, 480).[76] Even in the middle of the third century, one can see that there remains in the churches a hesitation on these terms. Terms, however, reflect a reality, and so the hesitant and ambiguous use of these terms *laikos/klerikos* indicates to some extent the hesitant and ambiguous underlying meaning they had at that time. Cyprian's writings name specific church leaders, of course: such terms as *episcopus, presbyter* and *diaconus* appear frequently in his writings, as also, here and there, one finds mention of sub-deacons (*Epistulae* 8, 1; 9, 1, 2; 34, 4), of acolytes (*Epistula* 34. 4), of exorcists (*Epistula* 23), and of lectors (*Epistulae* 38 and 39). The main religious leader of the community, the *episcopus,* ranked high: "You should understand that the bishop is in the church and the church in the bishop and that whoever is not with the bishop is not in the church."[77] When Cyprian speaks about the role of the baptized in such matters as the election of bishops, he says that it should include the participation of the people (*plebs*) (cf. e.g. *Epistulae* 10, 8; 67, 3 and 5). The *plebs* and the *ordo*, which one finds in Tertullian, is maintained in Cyprian, but *ordo* had not been ontologically interpreted at this time. *Plebs*, on the other hand, meaning the baptized-eucharistized Christian, had been, to some degree, ontologized, for these people belonged to the new Israel, the saved; they were a priestly people, the true believers. In their very existence and being, Christians were not the same as pagans (i.e. all the non-baptized), nor were they the same, exactly, as the catechumens. They were a people set apart, and this *status* was not merely interpreted sociologically or functionally. These baptized-eucharistized Christians were quite different from all others in their very being. Perhaps the authors of these early centuries did not use ontological language for the meaning of *plebs*, but they certainly used language which indicated a different *status*, both in creation and in redemption.[78] We do not find this kind of interpretation of *ordo* at this early time. The interpretation of *ordo* remains merely sociological, typological and functional. It is modeled after the *ordines* of civil society, and it had not yet been described in terms of the angelic and celestial hierarchy. This comes much later in theological history. Thus, one cannot equate the *plebs/ordo* distinction of this early, pre-Nicene period with the *laikos/klerikos* understanding of the fourth, fifth and sixth centuries. When one says, therefore, that an author such as Cyprian does not use *laicus* and uses *clericus* only once, the response cannot be made: "But of course he used *plebs/ordo*, which meant precisely the same thing." This would be pressing the *plebs/ordo* terms in Cyprian beyond both their text and their context. The same can be said of Tertullian and Origen, who use the terms *laikos/klerikos* so sparingly. Again, one cannot say in Tertullian's case: "But he uses *plebs/ordo* which means the same thing," for in Tertullian this cannot in any way be substantiated. Much less would this be true in Origen, as we have seen above.

Cyprian's Carthaginian and North African Christian communities were communities which suffered enormously in the Roman persecutions, and this persecution gave rise to many troubling and new situations which desperately called for guidance and even resolution. The suave, educated, competent Cyprian probably never thought that he would be involved in so many difficult issues, when he was pressed into the office of *episcopus*. One of the issues which he had to face was the issue of the *pax* given by confessor-martyrs. This was not an exclusively North African situation, for the martyr's privilege is noted in the letter from the churches of Lyons and Vienne, in the writings of Dionysius of Alexandria, and in Tertullian's *Ad martyres*. However, the vehemence of the Decian persecution in North Africa created a martyr-privilege situation which at times got out of hand. In 250 Cyprian forbade his priests and deacons to reconcile apostates on the basis of a document by a confessor-martyr, but this order was broadly ignored. The subsequent letters of Cyprian raise the identical issue again and again, and his overall plan to resolve the apostasy issue by a synod is thwarted again and again. In the end, even those with a certificate from a martyr-confessor must become part of the reconciliation process in vogue at that time; otherwise, no hope, not even on their deathbed, can be given to them.[79] Still, in spite of Cyprian's intransigence on the matter, the issue of forgiveness by someone who is considered a model of Christian discipleship, rather than by someone who is officially a leader of the church, will remain a strong factor not only in the North African church and its Donatist division, but throughout the Christian world.

5. THE CHURCHES IN ASIA MINOR, SYRIA AND PALESTINE

Much of the New Testament provides us with an assortment of views on the formation and development of the early Jesus communities. The work of J. Meier on Antioch helps clarify the way in which this particular church community began.[80] The extant data of early Christianity owes much to the genius of this area; one thinks of the *Didache,* more than likely compiled in the Syrian region. One thinks of the letters of Ignatius to churches in Asia Minor, as well as the letter of Polycarp of Smyrna and the writings of Papias of Hierapolis. One thinks of the various apocryphal writings: the *Acts of Paul,* the *Acts of Peter,* the *Acts of John,* the *Acts of Thomas,* the *Acts of Thaddeus,* all of which might be of Syriac origin. The abundance of early literature is indicative of an educated, literate, creative and certainly diverse Christian community. We will consider, however, only two major documents from this area which have major bearing on our theme.

A. THE DIDASCALIA APOSTOLORUM

The *Didascalia apostolorum* is another highly important document from this early patristic period. Scholars seem to place its origin in either Syria or Palestine. The dating of the document has been even more contested than the argument over the locale of its origin. Some have assigned the document to the early part of the third century (Harnack, to some degree, Funk, early on, Zahn); others prefer a later date, toward the end of the third century (Kattenbusch); others like Achelis and Connolly take no stand, *non liquet,* as Achelis comments. Connolly suggests some time prior to the Decian persecution, but after the grant of toleration by Gallienus.[81]

In this work we have a portrait of another local church. The work is primarily ethical; theological issues are treated, at best, in a tangential way. As a result, there are only passing allusions to sacramental actions (baptism, eucharist and reconciliation), but the allusions are quite helpful insofar as they indicate to us some of the liturgical issues of that particular church as regards these three rites. There are also certain dogmatic issues which the author mentions, again in a sort of occasional way: namely, allusions to the Trinity or to the divinity of Jesus. There are long sections on the validity of the old law which indicate a certain confrontation with Jewish thought.

For our present purposes the document offers us a portrait of this particular church's structure. The *episkopos,* and only one, is the main spiritual leader. Eight chapters are devoted to describing his role, and indeed he is central and pivotal. He stands in the place of God himself. He is father, mediator, high priest, leader, king, judge, guardian, guide and teacher. The paternalism and monarchialism of the *episkopos* is evident. In contrast to the description of the *episkopos,* the presbyters (plural) are mentioned only in a casual way. The deacon is, however, described at length, and his position vis-à-vis the *episkopos* is enormous. He is the immediate delegate of the *episkopos;* he has the full confidence of the *episkopos;* he is the hearing, the mouth, the heart and the soul of the *episkopos.*[82] Generally one deacon is presented, but the number of deacons will depend on the size of the community (chap. 26).

A brief and only single mention is made of both subdeacon and lector. Achelis believes that the single reference to the subdeacon is a later textual interpolation, while Connolly tends to regard it as original.[83] In any case, the subdeacon is hardly more than a servant to the deacon. The lector is mentioned along with the presbyters, but only in the context of remuneration for their duties. There is a longer section on the deaconesses (chap. 16), in which both deacon and deaconess are described. It mentions that the deaconess is meant for the ministry to women, a ministry which included house-visiting, going into the baptismal water with other women, and anointing women at baptism. This ministry is called "especially needful and important." The image of Jesus is presented as a basis for this feminine ministry: "For our Lord and Saviour also was ministered unto by women ministers."[84]

Widows are described in chapters 14 and 15. Armitage Robinson describes these widows of the *Didascalia* as follows: "The widows were a numerous and somewhat troublesome body of Church pensioners. Among their besetting sins were grumbling at their fellow-widows who happened to receive larger doles, and making begging expeditions instead of being content with the supplies that reached them in the normal way."[85] The author of the *Didascalia* notes that at times they are not widows (*cherai*) but wallets (*perai*). Not every woman whose husband died was a "widow" in the ecclesiastical sense. There seems to be an *ordo,* at least incipiently, of such women, which indicates that some women whose husbands have died became a sort of permanent group within the church structures. Care for younger widows is encouraged, lest they feel the need to marry a second time. One sees here another instance of the early church's hesitation on second marriages. This group or *ordo* of widows, like orphans, are supported by the church community. The *episkopos,* however, either personally or through the deacon, receives the funds and distributes them; the faithful do not make contributions to the widows directly. Since these widows are compared to the altar, only the baptized can make contributions for their care. The proper task of the widows is prayer and fasting; however they also visit the sick and lay hands on them, but again only under the supervision of the *episkopos* or deacon. They are not to teach and they are not involved in the baptismal liturgy.

Are the subdeacon, the lector, the deaconess and the widow *laikos* or *klerikos?* It would be difficult to say: the single mention of both subdeacon and lector offers us no clue at all. The *Didascalia* does not mention an ordination of the presbyters or the deacons, only an imposition of hands for the *episkopos,* which the Latin translates as "ordinetur" (chap. 4). The deacons and deaconesses are said to be appointed (chap. 16). At this juncture of church history, the *laikoi/klerikoi* division is neither clearly established nor technically developed.

However, the *Didascalia* does use the term *laikos.* In chapter 6 the *episkopos* is warned: "For it behooves thee not, O bishop, that being the head thou shouldst obey the tail, that is, a layman (*laico*)."[86] This quotation is certainly not a positive evaluation of the layperson. In chapter 7 we read:

> Hear, then, ye bishops, and hear, ye laymen, how the Lord saith: I will judge between ram and ram, and between ewe and ewe; that is between bishop and bishop, and between layman and layman: whether layman loves layman and whether again the layman loves the bishop and honors and fears him as father and lord and (as) God after God Almighty.[87]

The Greek is extant for this section, and the term *laikos* is clearly used. In another place, chapter IX, there is an exhortation to the people to honor the *episkopos;* it begins:

> Hear these things then, ye laymen also, the elect of the Church of God. For the former people was also called a Church, but you are the Catholic Church, the holy and perfect, a royal priesthood, a holy multitude, a people for inheritance the great Church, the bride adorned for the Lord God.[88]

These are praising terms for the lay people, but immediately these same people are exhorted to provide for the ministers and to honor them, especially the *episkopos,* for he is their high priest, their minister of the word and mediator, their teacher and father after God, their chief and their leader, their mighty king, who rules in the place of the Almighty. The *episkopos* should be honored by the lay persons as God, "for the bishop sits for you in the place of God Almighty." Although the lay person is honored in this passage, the *episkopos* is given even more honor, but in ways which make the lay person totally subservient and secondary.

In the same chapter we are told that if one calls a layman "fool" or *raca,* he is liable to the assembly, for one is calling his brother empty who is filled with Christ; he is calling his brother a fool who is the dwelling place of the Spirit. These, too, are very positive words, but immediately they are placed in a relativized position, for the text adds that if one says these things to a layman and is found condemned, "how much more if he should dare to say aught against the deacon or against the bishop."[89]

Still in this same chapter, the layman "is not permitted to judge his neighbour nor to lay upon himself a burden that is not his. For the weight of this burden is not for the laymen but for the bishop."[90]

In chapter 12, there is mention of a definite place for the lay men and a definite place for the lay women within the church building. After the *episkopos* stands to pray, the rulers stand up next, then the lay men, then the lay women. Indeed, the liturgical picture we receive from this chapter is that there are definite places in church for men, women, children, fathers, mothers, young women, aged and the widows. All in all, a very organized and structured congregation! On the other hand, in chapter 12, in which we once again read about the seating arrangements for the liturgy, the *episkopos* is reminded:

> But if a poor man or woman should come (whether of the same district) or of another congregation, and especially if they are stricken in years, and there be no place for such, do thou, O

bishop, with all thy heart provide a place for them, even if thou have to sit upon the ground; that thou be not as one who respects the persons of men, but that thy ministry may be acceptable to God.[91]

On many occasions throughout the *Didascalia* the term "brother" is preferred to *laikos;* indeed, brother is far more frequently used, and it generally means all those who have been baptized, but not the *episkopos,* presbyters or deacon. In the *Didascalia* the portrait of the church, on the one hand, indicates the grandeur of the *episkopos.* There is a paternalism and monarchialism which pervades his position in the church. On the other hand, the brothers (the *laikoi*) are presented at times in a negative way but more often in a secondary or relativized way. Even the moments of praise as regards their own grandeur are quickly tempered by the overriding grandeur of the *episkopos.* We have here a description of a church which is finding its way ministerially and in leadership. The *episkopos* is most clearly presented as a leader, but the deacon, too, is described in a leadership role. All other leadership people, such as the presbyters, do not appear with a clear role, but rather in a somewhat ambivalent, still undefined role.

The gradual development of a clergy/lay ordering of church structure was not confined, as we have seen, to the African churches, but found its echo slowly but surely throughout the entire Graeco-Roman empire, not always in the same way or with the same emphases. In the times and in the places of Clement of Rome, Cyprian, Tertullian, Clement of Alexandria, Origen, the *Traditio apostolica* and the *Didascalia apostolorum,* one should note, the process of clericalization, which eventually assumed almost all church power into the clerical domain, had only begun to take place, and this process was by no means either regionally or temporally uniform. At this juncture of our study, we are only at the multimorphic beginning of the process, not at one of its monolithic terminal points.

B. THE COUNCIL OF NICAEA: 325 A.D.

At the Council of Nicaea in 325, we have some official statements of the church leadership. In the canons of the council, we find that the terms *klerikos/laikos* had taken on a more uniform and technical meaning. In canon 2 we read:

If in the process of time, some internal sin is found concerning such a person [recently baptized] and is so accused by two or three witnesses, such a person should refrain from the clericate (*tou klerou*). One who continues beyond this, raising himself in opposition to this great synod, will be endangering his own clergy (*tou klerou tou idiou*).[92]

In canon 3, we read:

This great synod universally forbids that either an episkopos or a presbyter or a deacon or anyone else in the clergy (*en te klero*). . . .

In canon 8 we hear about ordination (*cheirotonethentes*) and clergy (*en to klero*). Ordination (*cheirotonia*) is also mentioned in canon 16, and the title of canon 17 reads: On clerics who accept usury (*peri klerikon tokithonton*). In canon 19, the council takes up those who were involved in the schism of Paul of Samosata. If they return to the Catholic Church, then they are to be baptized anew, and if they were in the clergy (*en to klero*) of Paul's group, and these are found blameless, they are to be ordained anew (*cheirotoneisthesan*). In this same canon we hear a word about deaconesses, but the synod notes: they are not ordained and they are to be regarded as lay (*en tois laikois*).

In this synod of Nicaea, the usage of *kleros* and *klerikos* is fairly abundant, and it is connected with the laying on of hands (ordination). The term *laikos,* however, is used only once, but it is connected to those on whom hands have not been laid (i.e. the non-ordained). Given the diversity of *episkopoi* who were gathered at this synod, even though almost all were from the eastern churches, the fact that these terms and their meanings could so easily be used indicates that the terms had by 325 attained a fairly widespread coinage and acceptance. *Kleros* had taken on a technical interpretation, so as to include those in specially designated church leadership, particularly the triad, *episkopos,* presbyter, and deacon, but there is an openness to other not specifically named ministers as well. The deaconesses are, however, not included among the clerical group.

6. THE ACTS AND ACCOUNTS OF THE MARTYRS

In this same period, that is, from apostolic times to 250 A.D., the periodic threat and actuality of martyrdom created an impressive list of heroes of the faith: men and women who had died for their Christian faith, as also men and women who had suffered deeply for the faith, the so-called "martyr-confessor." These heroines and heroes of the faith are found in all the regions we have just considered, but it seems wise to focus on these martyrs in a special way, since these women and men represented an ideal of discipleship, an ideal of Christian life, which others, including the official leadership of various Christian communities, could and would never provide.

Many of these men and women were "lay" people, as a later age would categorize them.[93] Official court records, as we noted above, tell us of Justin and his companions, who died at Rome c. 165. Justin was a prominent "lay" Christian (to use a term from a later era). In Africa there are the records for the martyrs of Scilli: namely, Namphano, Madaura, Miggin, Sanam and six other Numidian Christians, beheaded in 180. There are likewise the letter of the churches of Vienne and of Lyons to the churches of Asia and Phrygia, describing in a most moving way the martyrdom of Christians at Lyons in either 177 or 178. Blandina, a female slave, was a courageous example of a faith-filled Christian. So, too, Maturus, a neophyte, Alexander, a physician, and the young boy Ponticus. The sufferings of Perpetua and Felicitas, as also three catechumens, Saturus, Saturninus and Revocatus, all martyred at Carthage in 202, were recorded in one of the more exquisite writings of this early patristic period. One could add the names of Agathonika, who died at Pergamon between 161 and 169. With her were Karpos and Papylus. A learned philosopher, Apollonius, was beheaded during the reign of Commodus (180–185). In Rome there are the *Acta* of such martyrs as Agnes, Cecilia, Felicitas and her seven sons, as also Sebastian, Cosmas and Damian, perhaps John and Paul. During this same period there were also *episkopoi, presbyteroi* and *diakonoi,* who were martyred as well: perhaps Clement of Rome, perhaps Ignatius of Antioch, surely Cyprian of Carthage, Hippolytus of Rome, Lawrence, and Sixtus. Nonetheless, all of these latter people were honored in a special way by the Christian community, not because they were leaders of a church, but because they confessed their faith through martyrdom. They were held in the same esteem as those mentioned first, who were not deputed leaders in the Christian community. The large number of "lay" men and women (using again a term from a later period) who belong to this group of honored martyrs indicates the major role which such "lay" people had in the church; they were the examples of the true meaning of discipleship. Not office but faith commitment was exalted by this early church, and in dying for one's faith, belonging to leadership or not played no role. Still, it should be remembered that one of the Donatists' complaints was precisely the lack of faith by many African church leaders (*episkopoi* in particular). These had given up the chalices and patens, the books and holy objects, to the Romans. These were called by the Donatists *traditores,* a name that could not help but conjure up the passages in the gospels which refer to Judas.[94] A leader of the church was supposed to be a leader of faith and a leader even into martyrdom. The reverence paid at this time to the many non-leaders who gave up their lives for the faith is indicative of the way in which this early church viewed discipleship. Not office but faith was the telling criterion.

Given this high profile of many martyred men and women, who were not in leadership roles in the church, we must admit that one does not find a negative evaluation of "lay" people. Behind the actual cases of martyrdom, however, one finds Christian men and women who spoke out strongly for their belief in Christ. Celsus, a pagan opponent of the Christian way, has become one of the most cogent witnesses on this "lay" history. "In private houses, also," Celsus writes,

> we see wool-workers, cobblers, laundry-workers, and the most illiterate and bucolic yokels, who would not dare to say anything at all in front of their elders and more intelligent masters. But when they get hold of children in private and some little old women with them, they let out some astounding statements as, for example, that they must not pay any attention to their father and school-teachers, but must obey them; they say that these talk nonsense and have no understanding, and that in reality they neither know nor are able to do anything good, but are taken up with mere empty chatter. But they alone, they say, know the right way to live, and if the children would believe them, they would become happy and make their home happy as well.[95]

It is obvious that the wool-workers, the cobblers, and the laundry-workers were baptized Christians, but not *episkopoi, presbyteroi* and *diakonoi,* and though not ordinarily called at that time "lay," they correspond to the laity which gradually and generally became their "name" in the hundred years following both Celsus and Origen. Even though we have scant extant, written evidence of any "lay missionary activity" in the first three centuries of the Christian community, there can be no doubt that the spread of the community was not due merely to "clerical" leadership during those years. K.S. Latourette noted: "It would probably be a misconception to think of every Christian of the first three hundred years after Christ as aggressively seeking converts."[96] Nonetheless, as G.H. Williams wisely points out:

> But if none rose up with the same vocation as the first apostles and evangelists, the fact remains that the expansion of Christianity in the hostile environment of the first three centuries and its eventual conquest of the seats of political authority has ever

since been considered so phenomenal as to be one of the clearest proofs of the divine credentials of this new people, this third race under God, neither Jew nor Barbarian.[97]

Once the martyrdom ceased, however, and church leadership (*episkopoi, presbyteroi* and *diakonoi* particularly) began to move upward in the social and political world of the Roman empire, those who were not in their functions or place (*kleros*) began to receive a much stronger negative valency. This becomes ever more evident as one moves into the so-called Constantinian church.

7. THE ECCLESIAL ROLE OF WOMEN

To address the issue of women in a special section might imply that one is rethinking the above material to see if and where, if not and where not, women were involved. This is not my intention, and hopefully it will not be taken as such. In all the regions mentioned above, women were an integral part of the Christian community and many of them were leaders in their communities. Since the later division of cleric/lay had not yet become a part of ecclesiastical thought, and since the exclusion of women from a clerical position had as well not yet become a part of ecclesiastical thought, the very terms "cleric/lay" provide a disservice to an understanding of Christian life in this early period. Leadership might be a better term, but only if by leadership one does not mean only "official" leadership, but that unqualified leadership which a man or woman has through his or her deeply lived discipleship. As we have seen in the discussion of martyrs the gender issue and the "official" leadership issue were quite secondary to the higher dignity of martyrdom. Martyred women and men as well as martyred "ordained" and "unordained" were venerated as disciples of Jesus, because they fulfilled in both their life and their death the very meaning of the following of Jesus. One was not "more" a martyr because of his/her sex; one was not "more" a martyr because of his/her ecclesiastical position.

On the other hand, the rather exhaustive compilation drawn up by Elisabeth Clarke on early patristic discussion of women raises, at least to me, enormous concern, since Clarke combs the material well, only to end up with a handful of citations.[98] The way in which patristic writers of this period spoke of "cleric," "lay," and "*ordo*" seems to reflect the fact that a "male bias in Roman attitude and custom had always been conspicuous in respect to sexual activity."[99] This sexual bias affected not only marriage and family, but the social life generally. If Christian discipleship, as we saw in the chapter on the New Testament material, was to a great extent gender-negative, and barrier-breaking, why were Christians of this early patristic period, and particularly those in official leadership positions, not more in tune with the discipleship issue?

When the so-called non-canonical literature is investigated as well as the canonical and "orthodox" early patristic literature, one finds a more comprehensive view of discipleship. W. Schneemelcher makes the observations that "the apocryphal literature . . . comes in the main from circles in which the development was different from, and took place in areas other than, that in the circle usually designated that of the great Church."[100] Particular attention should be given to those apocryphal writings which date from the earliest period of church history. Schneemelcher's advice on this matter is very apropos to our discussion:

> In its early period Christianity was no uniform phenomenon, and the churches which called themselves Christian in this early period, i.e., in the 1st and 2nd centuries, were quite diverse institutions especially in the matter of their doctrine. One of the motives to the formation of the apocryphal literature must be seen in this diversity of views. This diversity in doctrine and belief (which at first was not at all felt as 'splitting the church,' as some in our day would willingly make us believe) brought with it the emergence of different presentations of the gospel and of the doings of the apostles, which time and again tallied with the ideas of the churches concerned. The relationships of the churches to Christ as Saviour and Redeemer, their attitudes to the world and their dispositions towards 'history' were too different for different gospels and acts of apostles not to come into being.[101]

This divergence can be seen in the presentation of women. Earlier apocryphal writings often present women in a more ecclesial fashion than later apocryphal texts. In the *Gospel of Peter,* probably written in the second half of the second century, Mary Magdalene is called a woman disciple of the Lord (12.50). In the early part of this same second century, one hears of important women: "Jezabel," the head of the prophetic school of Thyatira, and Alce of Smyrna, who Ignatius says "is dear to me," as well as the family of the woman, Tavia, for whom he prays (*Letter to the Smyrnaeans,* 13). Among the followers of Montanus we have Priscilla and Maximilla, who were held in esteem. Thecla, as one reads in the *Acts of Paul and Thecla,* was sentenced to death, not directly for her Christianity, but because through her acceptance of Christianity she had renounced her role as daughter, wife, mother and mistress. Her own mother demanded of the governor: "Burn the lawless one. Burn her so that all the women who have been taught by this man may be afraid" (3. 203–205).[102] It is evident, in this episode about Thecla, that Christianity's impact on women stood in strong contradiction to the ethos of the Graeco-Roman world of that time. In the *Epistola Apostolorum*, another second century document, Mary of Magdala and Sara (Ethiopic text) or Martha and Mary (Coptic text) are sent to announce to the apostles that Jesus had risen. In the *Sophia Iesu Christi* Jesus appears both to the twelve and to seven women disciples, of whom Mary of Magdala is the only woman mentioned by name. She is also one of those who pose questions to Jesus, just as Thomas, Matthew or Bartholomew, and who then receive a dominical answer. Schüssler-Fiorenza concludes that when the "disciples" in the *Sophia Iesu Christi,* on the basis of Jesus' command, went out to preach [the concluding words of the document], the disciples were both the women and the men.[103] She goes on to add other examples:

> The *Gospel of Philip* and the *Dialogue of The Redeemer* mention Mary Magdalene with two other Marys, whereas the *Gospel of the Egyptians* gives a prominent role to Salome. In the *Great Questions of Mary,* Christ gives revelations and secret teachings to his privileged disciple, Mary Magdalene, whereas the *Gospel of Thomas* alludes to the antagonism between Peter and Mary Magdalene, a theme more fully developed in the *Pistis Sophia* and in the *Gospel of Mary* (Magdalene).[104]

Both in the *Apostolic Church Order* and in the *Questions of Bartholomew,*[105] one finds an indication that the active presence of women in ecclesial leadership was not always accepted. This is even more apparent in the *Dialogue Between a Montanist and an Orthodox.* Other apocryphal examples from these first three Christian centuries might be adduced.

Just as the Jewish world at the time of Jesus was not a monolithic or unified world, but rather a world in which one can find several different, even opposing, strands of Jewish thought and practice, so, too, the Jesus world from the resurrection down through this early patristic period was not a monolithic or unified world. The various gospels, the writings of Paul, the Johannine epistles, the pastoral letters of Timothy, Titus and Peter—all attest to this divergence, even at times suspicion, between one Jesus community and the next. In the course of early church history, a variety of Christian positions were being stressed, argued, and, as historical data indicates, even at times furthered by questionable methods.[106] Just as there was not a unified naming of early ecclesial leaders, for the names of church leadership varied from Jesus community to Jesus community, and just as there was no set description of the tasks of individual leadership roles, for which only one group or another could provide, so, too, one finds fluidity and even divergence, not "orthodoxy" and canonical nicety, in matters such as the meaning of the death of Jesus, the meaning of the "divinity" of Jesus, and the meaning of discipleship. On the issue of cleric/lay, as we have stressed, the fluidity is more apparent prior to the emergence of *ordo* in the Christian communities. The emergence of a leadership *ordo* tended to make the boundaries between cleric and lay more defined. The fact that many of the details about women during this period, at least as one moves away from the acts of martyrs, derive from "apocryphal" literature should not be discounted. To quote Schneemelcher again:

> Only when what had precipitated itself in the NT as kerygma had gained ground as orthodoxy, being interpreted uniformly in the early catholic sense, did this literature gradually disappear or become literature of a heretical tendency.[107]

Using a term from Alex Haley, Schüssler-Fiorenza notes that history was by and large written by the "winners."[108] Montanism, for instance, has come down to us almost exclusively through the eyes of the "winners." The apocryphal literature never gained a standing in the eventual "winner's circle." As one moves into the second and third centuries, one notices a growing "patriarchal approach" in the so-called "orthodox" communities, which speaks at times, though not often, against the presence of women in ecclesial leadership. In some of the apocryphal and non-orthodox literature, on the other hand, there appears, again not to any great extent, an approach which is more open to women in ecclesial leadership roles. To understand this openness/non-openness to women, however, one must unite it to the growing separation between clerical leadership, as an *ordo,* and those not in this order, whether male or female.[109] The apocryphal and non-orthodox literature, however, provides us with a window into that period, so that we catch a glimpse of the widely divergent ways of structuring the Christian communities, existent at that time. One sees, dimly of course, a divergence far greater than one would surmise from the study of only "orthodox" sources.

It would seem that the issue of dividing the Christian community into two sectors, based on *ordo* and called *klerikoi/laikoi,* did not find immediate acceptance in each and every community. The role of the non-ordained, including women, appears to have been one of the issues which clouded any immediate acceptance of such a division. The apocryphal and non-orthodox literature of this period presents us with a host of positions with which the orthodox communities took issue. Although the role of women and the role of the non-ordained generally appear to be somewhat tangential issues, when compared with the christological and trinitarian themes and positions, the secondary appearance of these issues in this apocryphal literature seems to indicate no little divergence in the way early Christian communities took to heart the very meaning of Christian discipleship.

8. GENERAL OVERVIEW

Prior to the Constantinian church, that is, in the ante-Nicene period of church history, one could, with Williams, describe the role of the baptized under the following headings:[110]

A. THE LITURGY

From the *Didache,* from Clement of Rome, Justin, Hippolytus and Tertullian, from *The Testament of Our Lord,* and from the Council of Elvira (306), we see that baptized Christians play significant liturgical roles. They could baptize catechumens in the hour of death when no other church leaders were present. This ministry of "baptismal ordination" belongs to all the baptized and must be positively valued. A term which we find in Justin, *prospherontes,* i.e. the ones who brought the gifts to the table of the Lord, were the baptized Christians. At the liturgy, the baptized were not the same as the catechumens, who were generally dismissed after the homilies and prayers. Nor were they the same as the unbaptized or non-catechumen, who eventually came to be called, at times, an "observer" and "hearer" of the Christian liturgy. Unfortunately, as the liturgy developed into a more clerically dominated format, such as we find in the late fourth and fifth centuries, all the "observers," whether baptized, catechumen or pagan, tended to be amalgamated into the "people." They were preached to and they were prayed over. The liturgical role of the baptized became minimalized.

B. DISCIPLINE

In the ante-Nicene church, the baptized played a role in the reacceptance of sinners, especially those who had apostatized. We find this in Tertullian[111] and in Cyprian.[112] Even the confessor-martyr at the time of Cyprian played a significant role in the exomologesis. In some of the Syriac churches, the confessor-martyr celebrated eucharist without "ordination." In many facets, church discipline varied from region to region, and at times more room was accorded to charism rather than structure.

C. CHURCH LEADERSHIP

In the selection of *episkopoi* and *presbyteroi* the baptized had a significant role. In Origen the *episkopos* must be established in the presence of all.[113] Cyprian writes in a similar way.[114] He even states that the laity have the "power either of choosing (*eligere*) worthy priests or of rejecting (*recusare*) unworthy ones."[115] Gradually we begin to hear a more differentiating language: there was a divine vocation at the heart of all ministry, of course, but then there were various stages of discernment: the lay recognition of the call or of the election; the liturgical installation or eventually ordination. The first of these, the lay recognition, was then seen merely as part of the selection process; the second of these, the ordination, was eventually seen as the conferral of power and status. This eventual differentiation reduced the role of the people of God to observers.[116] As we shall see later, one exception lingered on, namely, the royal lay person continued to play a major role in the selection of episcopal candidates (and therefore papal candidates) and in some ways in the installation role as well. This eventually became a source of strife: the so-called lay-investiture strife. Nonetheless, we find in the pre-Nicene Christian literature a clear indication that the people of God, i.e. the "laity," were to be involved in the process in a significant way.

D. CHURCH MAINTENANCE

In Tertullian and Origen one finds urging of the baptized to contribute to the maintenance of the Christian leadership. However, church maintenance went far beyond this, for mention is also made of support for the poor, of care for orphans, of assistance to the elderly and to those who suddenly find themselves in a crisis (e.g. shipwreck or banishment by political rulers), of support for those in prison. Irenaeus mentions that the baptized laid hands on the sick and healed them, drove out demons, spoke of things to come, uttered prophetic statements.[117] In this area of care for the sick, the elderly, and those in crisis situations, Christian-inspired charism, more than codified regulations, was the source of one's response. Immediate and intense pastoral needs cried out for immediate and intense pastoral responses, and even less immediate and intense pastoral situations found more often than not a charismatic response by the Christian community rather than an officially programmed response.

E. PROFESSIONAL TEACHING

We have already made mention of the difficulty Origen experienced as a lay teacher, and similar hesitations about lay teaching can be found in Tertullian. The *Ambrosiaster,* at the end of the fourth century, indicates in a rather sanguine way that "everyone taught" in the early period of the church. There was never a leaderless Christian community, however, or a sort of early congregational, almost democratic gathering. There were, from the very beginning, leadership roles, but even with these early leadership roles, the baptized, particularly those who were competent, were teachers. The *Didache* speaks of prophets and teachers. We have noted that the bishops of Jerusalem and Caesarea responded to the rebuke of Demetrios, the bishop of Alexandria, pointing out several instances of lay people preaching and teaching, while *episkopoi* were in attendance. In the debate between Origen and Heraclides we find that lay people attended synods and took part in the formulation of doctrinal texts.[118] We also find lay people actively present at the synod of Carthage in 256.[119] Justin and Tatian were teachers, not because of a *missio canonica,* but because of their academic standing in the wider community.

9. CONCLUSIONS FROM THE DATA

What can one conclude from the data which this period of church history has left for us on the issue of the lay person in the church? Perhaps, the following points sum up the most important issues:

1. From apostolic times down to the beginning of the fourth century, the overriding issues which confronted the Christian communities were:

> (a) How does a follower of Jesus relate to Judaism, and conversely how did the various co-temporaneous Judaic movements square with the centrality of Jesus? At the beginning of the apostolic period the relationship to the many groups of Judaism, and subsequently, after the destruction of Jerusalem, the relationship to the new leadership of pharisaical Judaism centered in Jamnia, was very central to the Jesus communities. When the Christian communities became overwhelmingly non-Jewish, this issue began to fade.
>
> (b) Who is Jesus of Nazareth? Christological issues came to the fore, not only as regards Jesus as messiah, but the further understanding of Jesus as Son of God. There is a crescendo effect on this matter of christology, since the issue continued to build right down to the Arianism of the early fourth century. A lion's share of Christian thought and energy went into the issues of christology.
>
> (c) Christological thought is the rootage for Christian thought on the trinity. How could Jesus be God, if monotheism is to be maintained? The beginnings of trinitarian theology became an increas-

ingly developed doctrine during this period, and more and more
scholars began to spend their time and energies on this trinitarian theme.

(d) How can one be a follower of Jesus and live within the known
Graeco-Roman world of that age, especially with its hostility to
the followers of Jesus? The Christian-Jewish relationship was
quickly supplanted by the Christian-world relationship. Roman
persecutions only intensified the issue. This question began to
fade at the end of the third century, when it became more acceptable to be a Christian. Constantine's own favor toward the Christian religion made this more possible in the west than in the east
during the last decades of the third century. It is precisely in the
material concerning this particular issue, however, that one sees
the way in which these early Christians perceived the centrality of
the question: Who is a disciple of Jesus? This question on discipleship is not found in the materials of this era, which describe
klerikos/laikos.

2. At the same time, but in a somewhat secondary level of importance, the inner-community life of the Christians needed to be developed.[120] This was done primarily in the area of liturgy: namely, the baptismal liturgy, i.e. who should be accepted as disciples of Jesus; the
eucharistic liturgy, i.e. both as an integral part of the baptismal liturgy on
the one hand, and as the liturgy for the regular gathering of full-fledged
disciples of Jesus on the other; the reconciliation liturgy, i.e. how does the
community handle the post-baptismal/eucharistic serious and substantive failures of its membership, particularly such failures as public apostasy, adultery and murder; finally, the leadership liturgy, i.e. the public
and religious way in which various Christians were selected and consecrated for leadership roles within the community. Thus in this period we
see, in a marked degree, the growth and development of these four liturgical rituals.

3. As a sort of tertiary theme, i.e. something which arises only on the
basis of the questions and developments just enumerated, was the distinction between the Christians who were in leadership positions and those
Christians not in leadership positions. From the beginning, i.e. from the
resurrection event onward, the Jesus community had a ministry of service
leadership. This issue was not debated in any serious way from apostolic
times down to the beginning of the fourth century. Names for Christians
in ministry developed only gradually and were by no means the same for
every region. This includes the later, monolithic terms: *episkopos, presbyteros* and *diakonos*. Functions for Christians in such ministries were dif-

ferentiated only gradually as well. One cannot find, at the earliest period of Christian life, a functioning of an *episkopos, presbyteros* and *diakonos* which was universal, that is, the same in every part of the Christian region. *Episkopoi* functioned differently in different regions; so, too, *presbyteroi* and *diakonoi.* The early Christian usage of the terms *klerikos/laikos* exemplifies this searching for names. Until roughly the time of Tertullian, Origen, and Hippolytus, i.e. the beginning of the third century, the use of *klerikos/laikos* did not present any clear theological distinction between Christian minister and Christian follower. There is no doubt that in this early period when the terms *laikos* and *klerikos* were being assimilated into the Christian vocabulary, ambiguity should be expected. *Kleros* became a theologically technical term only as we move close to the Council of Nicaea. *Laikos,* on the other hand, began to be used as a theologically technical term only later than Nicaea. Up until that time, the frontier between the lay and the cleric was still rather fluid, as Lanne notes.[121] On the other hand, one must add that when an author of this period discussed in a positive way the most profound religious quality of each baptized, i.e. his or her holiness, the stress, more often than not, was not focused so much on a place (*topos*) or a function (*kleros*), but on an individual's response to the Spirit of Jesus in his or her life. The esteem for martyrs throughout this period of time bears witness to this manner of evaluating holiness, which was simply another way the early church used to express what Christian discipleship was all about. With the gradual introduction, at least in the west, of the term *ordo* (*ordinatio, ordinare,* etc.) in connection with the *clerici,* a new basis for distinguishing leader/led was brought into the theological discussion, and this way of thinking issued in a different way of looking at holiness and perfection, namely the perfection which one received by "advancing" into a higher "*ordo.*" One must add to this the socio-political aspects of the *ordo clericorum,* which were beginning to influence the way in which Christian leadership was perceived. In the east, installation into church leadership was called the laying on of hands, *cheirotenia,* which linguistically is not connected with order, *taxis* or *tagma.* This does not mean, however, that in the east, position within the community and within the socio-political world was not important, or that such a positioning did not begin to provide a basis for the understanding of the clerical world. Indeed, it did, so that both east and west presented a similar interpretation of the clerical world. Nonetheless, Christian holiness on the basis of personal discipleship (e.g. martyrdom and, later, monasticism) and Christian holiness on the basis of *ordo* or status in the church must be seen as part of the context in which the church/world question was developed.

4. At the end of the third century and the beginning of the fourth

century, the most practical issue which confronted the Christian church was the way in which a Christian should relate to the socio-political world. This issue, in many ways, dominated the energies of that time. Three diverse responses began to develop and reached a certain strength as the fourth century unfolded. The first was a strict separation of Christianity from government. This was the response of the Donatist churches. The second was personal retreat from the world as such. The rise of the monastic movement and its rather spectacular success was a major example of this Christian response. The third response was to form some sort of marriage between Christianity and the government. This was by far the overwhelming choice of the Christian leadership, both east and west, and on the tails of this response, one finds the beginnings, though cautious, of a theological stance on this issue in Augustine's well-known *City of God.* This third Christian response is characterized as one of mutual assimilation between church and government, followed rather swiftly by the church's domination of the religious aspect of the Graeco-Roman socio-political world. This issue of church/government, with its three rather diverse answers, affected the way in which christology was then developed; it affected the way in which church leadership then developed, and as a consequence the way in which those not in church leadership developed; it affected the way in which Christians viewed the very meaning of discipleship, the grid against which all such relationships should be evaluated; and it affected the structuring of Christian liturgy. It also affected the role of Christian women as far as church leadership was concerned. Other questions, many of great importance, were left to one side or given only tangential focus, as this issue of church/government was faced, debated, and tentatively resolved. But this is the focus of the next chapter.[122]

5

The Lay Person in the High Patristic Period: 324 to 731 A.D.

In this chapter we will consider a rather lengthy period of church history, generally called by ecclesiastical historians the high patristic period, since a majority of the more influential fathers of the church lived and wrote during this time. Because of the length of this period of church history and the number of patristic authors involved, there exists a wide-ranging corpus of Christian writings, and some of this written patristic material relates in a theological and analytical way to the status of the non-ordained or lay person in the ecclesial communities. However, in all honesty it must be admitted that the issue of the lay Christian precisely from a theological and analytical perspective was not a central issue to the fathers of the church during this period. That these same fathers were concerned about the spiritual and moral life of the Christian community cannot be denied, and that consequently there was a great pastoral concern for the baptized is abundantly evident. Nonetheless, these authors were not focused on the lay/cleric issue in the same theological ways which one finds, for instance, in the middle ages, in the reformation period, and in the nineteenth and twentieth centuries. It would be impossible, even given this lack of detailed patristic focus on the lay person, to cover each and every angle regarding the non-ordained, which was either mentioned by these writers or was the result of the historical circumstances of that period of time. Rather, we will focus on a few key issues of this period which affected in a major way the meaning and status of the lay Christian.

Before we consider these major issues, it should be stated that there is no clear data, during this entire period, of any deliberate attempt by church leadership to play down the *laikoi*. One exception to this can be found, perhaps, in Gregory the Great who deliberately removed from the Lateran curia both lay people and presbyters and systematically filled their vacant roles with monks.[1] Gregory did this out of his high esteem for monks, but also, "given Gregory's distrust of the clergy, his suspicions that they are easily prey to flattery, ambition and careless discipline."[2] If one looks beyond Gregory's preference to have monks as his co-workers, it would seem that the key factors which shaped the positioning of the significant lay persons in church structures had little to do with any ideological program on the status of "laity." A few lay people became significant in church structures, not because they were "lay," but for other factors. The status of the ordinary lay person, however, was established, indirectly, by a directly ideological and theological positioning of the major cleric within both church and socio-political structures.

In the pre-Constantinian period, as we have seen in the preceding chapters, it was the emergence of a technical term, *ordo,* and subsequently the actuality of an ecclesiastical *ordo* to which only clerics belonged that caused the increasingly negative aspects of lay status in the church. In the Constantinian church, that is the church in the Graeco-Roman empire with which this present chapter begins, it is the gradual, and often sporadic incorporation of this same *ordo clericorum* into the socio-political structures of the empire, which again gradually and often sporadically intensified the negative positioning of the ordinary lay person, not only in the church structures but concomitantly in the socio-political structures as well. In other words, the deliberate and focused, though somewhat haphazardly and even at times quite circumstantially, executed elevation of the *ordo clericorum* into the social structures of the day, and the subsequent political, ideological and theological validation of this elevation, indirectly brought about the de-evaluation of the ordinary lay person both in the church structures and in the social structures of those times.

There are two "theses" or positions which I hope not only to suggest but also to some extent establish in the following chapter:

A. I want to show that the precise manner in which church leadership gradually structured the relationship of both church leadership and church community to the Graeco-Roman governmental structures intensified in a major way the repositioning and subsequent depositioning of the ordinary, non-ordained Christian within the church. There is, in this view, a continuous line between the cozying by Christian leaders to Constantine and his successors, and the eventual western form of this relationship, which raised the question of *regnum et sacerdotium* in the middle ages.

B. When one asks, however, what was the main reason why such a warm relationship brought about this eventual repositioning and depositioning of the lay person in the church, the answer seems to lie in the fact that the hierarchical-positioning or power-positioning of church leadership slowly but ever-increasingly became the hermeneutical instrument to interpret Christian discipleship, rather than Christian discipleship itself serving as the hermeneutical instrument to interpret the role of church leadership within governmental structures. When the issue of church and governmental structure in the west became the intense issue of *regnum et sacerdotium,* the cycle was complete: *regnum et sacerdotium* determined the meaning of discipleship, not vice versa. Such a situation marginated the ordinary lay person to an extreme within the *societas christiana.*

Methodologically, there are several ways in which such positions might be tested. I have selected simply one of these methodological procedures: namely, I will use, by and large, the documentation based on church writings. One might also attempt to focus on the lay person at this period of time by sifting through non-ecclesiastical documentary material, a method which is often called socio-historical, drawing out details which provide some sort of picture of ordinary lay life presented by ordinary lay people themselves. Such material is less than abundant at this particular period of time and it becomes increasingly rarer as one moves into the Merovingian era.[3] Other methodological processes might focus more pointedly than the way in which I use the material on the role of women during this time. Each methodology has its potential and its limitation, and the methodology I have decided to employ is no exception. There are limitations connected to it, but there are also dimensions of strong potential.

In this chapter, then, we will review those issues which elevated the *ordo clericorum,* but only insofar as they affected the ordinary lay person. The term "ordinary" is key, since there were a few lay men and women who continued to play quite extensive roles of power within the church. These few lay people, however, had this kind of influence, not because they were "lay," but because of other factors, such as governmental connections, education, wealth, etc. We will consider these momentarily.

For the purpose of organization, then, this chapter has been arranged under the following six headings.

1. **The Reasons for the Dating of This Period.**
2. **Ecclesial Options as Regards the Issue of a Relationship to the Political Structures**
3. **The Privileged Lay People During This Period**
4. **The Christian Missionary Movement**
5. **Gregory the Great and Dionysius Areopagita**
6. **Conclusions from the Data**

1. THE REASONS FOR THE DATING OF THIS PERIOD

The precise dating of certain periods of historical importance can often be questioned, and rightfully so. Why does one begin with a particular date? Why does one end with a particular date? This kind of questioning applies to our present chapter. Why does it begin with 324? Why does it end with 731? What relationship do such beginning and ending dates have with the issue of lay status in the Christian church?

At the end of the year 324 Constantine was acknowledged as the sole ruler of the entire empire and was called the "Chosen One of God." From the extant literature of that time, we see that Constantine's inauguration as sole ruler of the entire empire had been regarded as a momentous event, and Constantine was celebrated throughout the empire with an almost unprecedented fanfare of acclaim, some of which in written form has been preserved. Christians particularly celebrated the occasion, for Constantine had already shown a favorable preference for the Christian religion,[4] and many characteristics of his later governmental relationship to the Christian communities had to some extent been operative. Constantine's accession to sole leadership of the entire empire in 324 did not immediately make these already operative Christian-government relationships universal throughout the empire, but his accession did indicate that a relationship to the Christian church, which Constantine favored, might soon become in some ways standard throughout the empire to the disfavoring, naturally, of non-Christian religions. "From 324 on, he [Constantine] made no effort to conceal his ever growing contempt for the pagan religion."[5] Constantine's clear and eventually univocal preference for the Christian faith can even be seen in a foreshadowed way in his letter to the inhabitants of Palestine, written in the autumn of 324.[6]

The Roman empire in 324 was quite different from the empire of Augustus and even of Diocletian. The empire was in one of its stages of disintegration. The date for the so-called "fall of the Roman empire" has been disputed by historians. In the middle of the fifteenth century, Flavio Biondo, in the writing of his history of Italy, penned the phrase *ab inclinatione Romanorum imperii*. For Biondo the turning point was the sack of

Rome by the Goths in 410. Since Biondo penned this memorable phrase, scholars have argued about the turning point of Roman imperial history. Machiavelli and Paruta focused on the initial constitution of Rome. Montesquieu stressed the power of the army, on the one hand, and the Roman aristocratic love of luxury, on the other. Voltaire and Gibbons zeroed in on Christianity, making it the whipping boy. Toynbee, in his own remarkable way, saw the end of Rome four centuries before Rome was even born! More recently, however, Pirenne and Dopsch have argued on the continuity/discontinuity of the Roman empire, with Pirenne stressing discontinuity, primarily due to the Arab invasions.[7] There may be no answer to the question regarding the fall of Rome *ab inclinatione Romanorum imperii,* but what is clear from all this is that the Roman empire of Constantine and his successors was not unified. Indeed, it was in the process of division, restructuring, and even falling apart. Historians struggle to find the correct word or term to describe what was happening to the Graeco-Roman world at the time of Constantine. Are the terms "fall" and "disintegration" too strong? Would "restructuring" or simply "division" be a better term? J. Herrin, for her part, states: "In the fifth century A.D., the western half of the Roman Empire finally ceased to have a formal existence."[8] Perhaps the phrase "the western cessation of a formal, imperial existence" better describes the actual situation of that time. Something was clearly taking place which eventually left the western part of the empire in a quite different situation than its eastern counterpart.

The reasons for this shift are multiform. Scholars note that the large empire had become more and more a complex unity of Roman and non-Roman groups, with the latter's allegiances and loyalties often not centered in Roman history and Roman culture. The many Germanic tribes which were brought into the empire through payments, treaties, and hostages diluted the *Romanitá* of the empire. In the more populated eastern sphere of the empire, the incursion of the Germanic tribes did not create the same havoc which the tribes brought to the western sphere. In part, the Germanic tribes tended (and were encouraged) to move westward, where uninhabited land was more abundant. In the Roman empire of these times, the west certainly experienced a break-up in a way which the eastern sphere never did. The eventual strength of the Byzantine empire bears this out, while the history of the western region, at that very same time, indicates the threadbare quality of the empire. These non-Roman loyalties and allegiances to local customs, tribal customs, and these non-Roman family ties will play a major role throughout this high patristic period, as Christian leaders, i.e. bishops, who often came from these non-Roman blood lines, will become loyal leaders of local areas, rather than loyal leaders of some imperial program.

The Christian community, at the accession of Constantine as sole ruler of the empire, was also a complex situation. One might speak more precisely of Christian communities, rather than a single entity. There was at that period of time no overarching, theological expression of beliefs, beyond a rather broad rule of faith, which one finds in the inchoative baptismal creeds.[9] Rather, because of the regional character of Christian communities, there were, de facto, many competing ways of expressing Christian belief. There were, for instance, many inchoative forms of christology, each of which had strong points and each of which had *lacunae*. There were differing ways of computing the major Christian feast of Easter. Even with the definitions and canons of the Council of Nicaea, this complexity of theology and liturgical practice did not go away. The term *homoousios,* though accepted at the Council of Nicaea, lacked precise definition. The continued fragmentation of christologies which surfaced in the wake of Nicaea, Ephesus, Constantinople and Chalcedon was indicative of the complexity and the division within the various Christian communities, when it came to a clear and detailed theological explanation of their tenets.[10]

In all of this complexity, on both the empire's and the church's side, there was no established "program" regarding the relationship of church and government. As ecclesial and imperial leaders changed, so, too, did the nuances of this relationship. From 324 to 731 there is, however, a clear, basic trend or pattern on the part of the mainstream leadership of both sides: namely, a trend toward a strong, mutual relationship, a sort of marriage, if you will. However, this was not merely a marriage of convenience. It was a liaison, deliberately nurtured by both sides, even if, at times, for different reasons. Clearly all Christian communities had developed existentially within a particular space and time, even prior to Constantine, and therefore these communities had structured themselves in one way or another so as to relate to the particular socio-political and economic forms of human society in which they lived. The early Christian communities did not exist in a space-time vacuum, a sort of a-historical or meta-historical situation. The issue, consequently, in each era was not whether the Christian community and the governmental structures should relate, but rather the manner in which the Christian communities might relate to the governmental structures of the respective Graeco-Roman society and vice versa.

Some of the rootage for the Constantinian relationship of church and empire can be found, for instance, in Hippolytus' *Commentary on Daniel,* in which there is a conjunction of empire and church, but for Hippolytus only the church has a true universal mission.[11] Melito of Sardis, for his part, joins the salvation which comes from Christ with a "synchronism of

Christ and Augustus and the association of the well-being of the empire with the growth of Christianity."[12] Origen, likewise, but in a limited way, saw a connection between the unification of the "world" by Augustus and the correct time for the arrival of the Christian message.[13] There existed, in pre-Constantinian Christian literature, a strand of thought, stressing the divine economy, and this view of the divine economy provided a certain theological evaluation of world history, particularly for those writers the "world" history of the Roman empire and the peace of Augustus.

The situation for the Christians at the time of Constantine, accordingly, was not totally new. The earliest Jesus community needed to relate to the multiform Jewish world of its day. The Jesus communities, after the destruction of the temple, needed to relate to various Jewish diaspora societies. Later generations of Christian communities had to find ways to exist within the Roman empire, when officially the Roman administration was adversely persecuting the Christian groups. In the literature from that period of time, there was on the one hand the tenacity of the martyred Christians, who refused to bend to Roman demands, and on the other hand a series of *Apologies,* which argued for a "place in the sun," that is, an acceptance into the complex structure of the Graeco-Roman world. In this situation we see conflicting forms of a relationship between Christians and governmental structures: first, in the martyrs, a relationship of intransigent refusal, even if this meant arrest, torture and even death; second, in some of the *Apologies* a relationship which sought to maintain Christian religious uniqueness and at the same time find a way to co-exist with the given socio-political structure.

With the edict of toleration by Constantine, such a mode of co-existence was given to the Christian communities, but officially the toleration of Christians was neither more nor less than the toleration of the Persian cult of Mithras, or the cult of Serapis and other Egyptian gods. The mainline worship of Graeco-Roman gods and goddesses continued, of course, and maintained a certain official status. At this stage, however, we see a new form of relationship between Christian community and governmental structures, namely a relationship based on toleration, although not on any privileged status, that is, a status of being the only tolerated religious group within the empire.

Nonetheless, one must also acknowledge that there eventuated at the beginning of Constantine's reign a competition between Christian church and the pagan establishment in Roman society. When the Christian church eventually became the imperial church, which took place under Theodosius, a new dimension of this competition arose, namely, that between the main figures of the imperial leadership and those of the ecclesiastical leadership, for the ecclesiastical leadership began pressing the imperial leadership for a suppression, not a toleration, of Graeco-Roman religious practices and other sundry religious practices which one found within the widespread empire. At times this pressure from the Christian side placed the imperial leadership on a collision course with some of the major figures of the Graeco-Roman society, who had remained stalwartly within the official Roman religion of their progenitors. These intensified forms of competition had repercussions in the ways in which, recipro-cally, church leadership and imperial leadership danced with each other. With the edict of Theodosius, this particular stage of the Christian com-munity's status as the sole, official imperial religion is a markedly differ-ent form of relationship from those mentioned above, and during this period of time Christian leadership, both ecclesiastical and to a degree imperial, became increasingly intolerant of any other rival religious group. With the prominence of the church in socio-political structures, a variety of factors, including imperial and ecclesiastical politics, pushed toward more unification of expression. One church, one empire became an increasingly important factor, and this union gradually shaped the way in which the church itself became structured and expressed various theo-logical teachings.

> Eusebius of Caesarea is the real theologian of the association of
> Christianity with the Roman empire; indeed he is its 'publicist'
> (E. Peterson). However, this happens only after 313. In his writ-
> ings a *political* theology seems more and more to have gained
> the upper hand over a *doctrine of the economy* and a *theology of
> history*. Eusebius primarily saw the encounter between Chris-
> tianity and Rome from a *moral* perspective: Hellenistic-Roman
> civilization has brought about an undeniable moral progress for
> mankind. The event of the incarnation takes place in a condi-
> tion of humanity which has been prepared for in this way.[14]

From the time of Constantine on, however, there was on both sides a fundamental option for a positive relationship, even a marriage, even though such a relationship created situations of competition. An odd conjuncture, one might say, but a conjuncture which is key to interpreting this period of history, 324–731. It is particularly key to an understanding of the positioning of the lay person in the western church, for the eventual relationship of the western Christian communities to Charles the Great and the Frankish empire was patterned, in so many ways, on the manner in which the Christian communities had related to Constantine and the Constantinian empire. In the Frankish situation, however, as we shall see, this relationship took on a different focus, for it became a question of *regnum et sacerdotium,* that is, a relationship not with the Christian community as such, but only with the *sacerdotium* of the Christian community. As this began to unfold during the Frankish period, the lay person in the west, that is, the one not in the *sacerdotium,* was not considered a major figure in this *regnum/sacerdotium* debate and was therefore further repositioned and even depositioned. The several ways in which the Christian leadership, during the course of these early centuries, related to the socio-political and governmental structures of the times affected the various ways in which the lay person in the church historically found his or her changing positions and roles.

The year 324, however, is at best a "peg year," indicating that a different governmental relationship between the Graeco-Roman empire as such and the Christian faith communities had both already begun and had, in 324, received a new, though incipient, pan-imperial status. This governmental relationship to the Christian community in turn began to give enormous prestige to the ranking leaders of the Christian community, that is, to the ranking clerics, the *ordo clericorum.* More as a consequence of all this, than as any deliberative act, the ordinary non-cleric, or the ordinary lay person, generally lost prestige.

The second date, 731, marks the death of Pope Gregory II. It was he who had written to the emperor at Constantinople, Leo III, noting that the center of gravity of the Christian world had begun to shift to the inner west (*epi ten esoteran choran tes duseos*).[15] In a premonitionary way, this phrase of his suggests that the western and Latin world, and particularly its center at Rome, was beginning to disassociate itself from the Byzantine empire. Nothing dramatically irrevocable had happened when Gregory II died, and Gregory, for his part, had considered himself as an integral part of the empire. However, the momentum of a disassociation had certainly begun, as one can see from a later historical perspective, and within a very short time after Gregory's death the western and Latin world definitively became separated from Byzantium.

The roots for this separation can be traced to Diocletian's formal division of the Roman empire into two areas, with two equal emperors, each aided by a junior emperor, the so-called tetrarchy. A major sign of separation can be seen in Constantine's construction of his capital in Constantinople, and his subsequent move of the imperial government to this "new Rome." However, the roots can also be traced to the continuous struggle with the non-Roman groups: particularly, at first, the Gothic tribes on the north and east sides of the Black Sea. Both the Rhine and Danube provinces of the Roman empire continually struggled with haphazard Germanic invasions. The death of Valens I, at Adrianople in 378, was a dramatic signal that the Romans were not dealing well with the non-Romans. The advance of the Huns, from 370 on, opened the weakening wounds of the Roman empire only more and more. Judith Herrin, in *The Formation of Christendom,* carefully knits together the various incidents, which eventually made the Roman empire an empire of mixed blood, Roman and non-Roman, and which made the non-Roman element more predominant in the western sphere of the empire rather than in the eastern sphere.[16]

Perhaps one of the clearest symbolic indications of this separation took place only a few decades after Gregory II's death in 774, not because in that year Charles the Great had come to Rome, but because in that year both the coinage, which Rome produced, as well as the papal documents, which emanated from the Lateran, no longer bore either the emperor's name and image or the imperial regnal years, but the pope's name and image and the years of his pontificate. In the decades around 731 a major change in the eastern-western worlds was taking place. An old era was coming to an end, and a new era was beginning to arise. This change involved a new set of relationships between the western Christian communities and the western government, or better, at the beginning of this era, the various western governments.

The eventual rise of the papal states also affected not only the position of the most important western cleric, the pope, but also the position of other high-ranking western clerics, the bishops. Once again these kinds of changes in western clerical status had repercussions on the western lay status, so that in the years after 731, when the west was becoming independent of Byzantium, there arose a new positioning of cleric/lay, both in western society and in the western Church.

This period of time, then, 324–731, when the Roman empire was still to some degree unified both in the East and in the West but in a decreasing way as this period unfolds, was a significant one for an understanding of the lay person in the Christian church for the following reasons:

A. In this period of time the Christian church became ever more thoroughly the church of the empire. An imperial church emerged from this wedding of government and church, which affected both the ordinary Christian's role in such a society and the Christian leadership's role in the same society. At the time of Theodosius, this imperial church was found both in the east and in the west.

B. At the same time, and in ways which often were quite subtle, the western world began gradually and sporadically to find itself disassociated from the center at Constantinople. As Herrin noted, the west eventually, in the fifth century, ceased to have a formal existence within the empire. In this turn of events, western societal and governmental structures fluctuated widely, as various non-Roman groups, such as Ostrogoths and Vandals, Visigoths and Lombards, created profound societal changes throughout the western world.

C. In the west, the bishops of Rome gradually but not in any orthogenetic way began to relate to these various non-Roman political leaders in significant ways, which one does not find in the eastern relationship between bishops and patriarchs on the one hand and Byzantine emperors on the other. The position of the bishop of Rome, as regards his relationship to the socio-political structures, varied considerably during this period. There was no preconceived, ideological pattern that governed the development of the Roman bishop's role in the socio-political arena. Eventually, in the struggle over *regnum et sacerdotium,* an ideological positioning of the bishop of Rome was formulated, and even enjoyed a certain period of time in which this ideological view was considered sacrosanct.

D. The formation during this period of "one empire-one church" provided the church leadership not only with moral and persuasive powers, but also with socio-political powers. Because of this, church leadership (bishops) had extensive influence both on the governmental leadership itself, and on the citizenry as well, i.e. the lay element of both church and society.

E. During this same period of time, 324–731, western church leadership, both the bishop of Rome and other regional bishops, began to affect both governmental leadership and the western citizenry in ways which do not correspond to similar relationships in the eastern church. This was occasioned, of course, by the process of western separation from Constantinople. In spite of these differences, however, one finds traces of similarity: a similarity based on the desire of church leadership to form, when possible, strong ties to a governmental structure, and when this eventually became a major reality with the Frankish leaders, the example of Constantine was dominant, not only as regards the position of the Frankish leader, but also as regards the position of the bishop of Rome.

F. The interfacing of church leadership to the governmental leaders (the emperor and his immediate entourage) and to the citizenry at large established a generalized pattern which was echoed and reechoed in the western church from Merovingian times down through the Saxon dynasty, beginning with Henry I (919–936) to Otto III, who died in 1002. This generalized pattern of church-government interfacing included a way of perceiving the status of the ordinary lay person in the church: namely, the ordinary lay person had little influence as far as church issues were concerned.[17]

G. Thus, in this period we find the formation of a church position on the status of the ordinary lay person, a position which subsequent theological reasoning will attempt to substantiate, based on an inner-church class system (*ordo*), which is described at first with functional and typological language, based on the order in human society, and then on the order in creation itself. The theological substantiation of church *ordo,* which is rooted in the order of being (creation), paved the way for the philosophical substantiation that the ordained are "ontologically" distinct from the unordained. This secondary positioning of the unordained is basically one of subservience and passivity.[18]

H. In this period, we also find the weaknesses of these same positions, weaknesses which at first did not seem to be major. There is a weakness in the ways in which church leadership and highest governmental figures (emperor, king) related, since the boundaries of both leaderships were not clear. In the medieval period one can begin to speak of "two spheres," and this eventually led to the late-medieval theory of church and state. Such precision of terms cannot be expected at this early period, of course, but the undefined character of boundaries between these two leaderships led to many *de facto* situations in which at times co-leadership roles were welcomed by both sides, and at other times when disputes over leadership prerogatives were bitterly contested. The incursions into one another's domain, by both church and governmental leadership, and the resultant disputes and competition for perceived areas of influence, were the seeds of eventual disharmony, particularly the so-called lay-investiture dispute of the later middle ages. The roots of this dispute were already present in the ambiguity and fluidity of the interrelationship of church leadership with both the Roman emperors and the later Merovingian, Frankish and Ottonian kings.

I. There is also a weakness in the way in which church leadership, through its process of clericalism, overtly and inovertly, reduced the position of ordinary lay persons. Even though the nonordained constituted a majority of the church membership, the repositioning of this group to virtual passivity vis-à-vis church decisions contained the seeds for the several eventual attempts by the lay world to find a stronger place within the church community.

J. The major weakness in this entire set of relationships was the way in which the discipleship of Jesus was theologically and pastorally presented. This weakness lay in the growing tendency to narrow discipleship to an unqualified adherence to church leadership. Only that kind of discipleship which agreed with the judgments of the leadership of the church became "orthodox." The grid for discipleship was *not* a return to the New Testament base, i.e. the christological base, but a return to an ecclesiological base, i.e. a hierarchically understood ecclesiological base, which in some ways offered a distortion of the New Testament meaning of discipleship. Throughout this period, the "real" or ideal disciple of Jesus, so it was taught, could be found either in the monk-cleric or in the clerical prelate. The ordinary lay person was viewed as a disciple of Jesus, but at a secondary or inferior level. The *ordo clericorum* became the *ordo discipulorum,* and the monastic orders likewise came to be considered orders of true disciples. This distortion of the very meaning of gospel discipleship is the root-cause for the various attempts by lay groups, starting in the eleventh century, to reposition themselves within the *societas Christiana.* This issue of discipleship can be considered the second part of my thesis for this chapter, and in many respects it is more fundamental than the first part, namely, the thesis regarding the relationship of the Christian community to the governmental structure. But the way in which church leadership came to relate to the socio-political structures caused, in no small measure, the lack of focus on the meaning of discipleship.

All of these issues became established during this period, at least in a strong rudimentary way, and for these reasons, this period of time can be seen as trend-setting or pattern-setting for major segments of subsequent church history.

Historians have sometimes exaggerated the importance of Constantine's conversion for the history of the Christian institutions. But it is certain that from the year 320 the situation of the Christian groups was modified. The clerics very soon became "privileged persons"; the bishops were to change their bishoprics on receiving "promotions," sometimes distancing themselves in the process from the local communities. The 4th century was the golden age of administration and civil bureaucracy. It was also a golden age for the clergy: these two bodies grew and increased in number. Thus the layman, the "ordinary baptized Christian," once again found himself dependent on, and made to feel inferior to, two parallel hierarchies: the civil authorities and the religious authorities.[19]

If the third century was, in the words of A. Faivre, *le siècle de la grand mutation cléricale* (the century of extensive clerical mutation),[20] the fourth to the eighth centuries was a time of strongly establishing the religious and socio-political relationships between church leadership, i.e. the clerical area of the church, and imperial government, between ruler and ruled, and indirectly, therefore, between cleric and ordinary lay person.

2. ECCLESIAL OPTIONS AS REGARDS THE ISSUE OF A RELATIONSHIP TO THE POLITICAL STRUCTURES

From the resurrection of Jesus onward, the Christian community had had to face, in varying ways, its manner of relating to the socio-political and governmental structures in the cultural world in which this Christian community found itself. Between 30 and 70 A.D. there was the lengthy and difficult task of finding a way to relate to the socio-political structures of the Jewish world in which the Jesus communities first arose. When separation from the Jewish structures became inevitable, both from the external forces caused by the Jewish revolts around the year 70, and from the internal forces caused in a special way by the post-70 A.D. rift with the emerging Pharisaical Jewish leadership, stemming from Jamnia, the Jesus community had to situate itself within the Graeco-Roman socio-political structures and thereby develop some relationship to the Graeco-Roman governmental structures as well. Since the Graeco-Roman governmental structures were essentially hostile to the Christian communities, as we see in the various pogroms and persecutions which these communities suffered from the end of the first century down to the beginning of the fourth century, the relationship of the Christian community tended to be one of isolation and non-involvement. The various *Apologiae* written in these centuries are evidence of the way in which some of the Christian leaders and communities attempted to present themselves to the wider world as respectable groups within the empire. Once the Christian communities become respectable (after Constantine), one does not find, except here and there and for quite other reasons, such *Apologies.*[21]

When Constantine, in the western part of the empire, began to show an acceptance of the Christian communities, the communities themselves, particularly through their leadership, had to reconsider the ways in which they might live within the socio-political structures of the empire and the ways in which they might relate to the imperial government.

There was no "orthodox" ecclesiology which provided the Christian world with a plan for these various moments of rethinking the church/world relationship. In fact, there was no ecclesiology of any kind. Ecclesiology is basically a creature of the reformation and post-reformation eras. Nonetheless, in the latter part of the third century and throughout the period of church history which we are considering in this chapter, there were three major ways which the Christian leadership groups could and did follow. Choices were indeed made by various Christian leaderships of that time, so that one cannot read this period of history, with the presupposition that there were no alternatives open to the leadership of the various Christian communities as regards its relationship to governmental structures, a position which Baus presents.[22] These three major alternatives (and there were other minor ones as well) were the following:

A. THE ALTERNATIVE TO CONFRONT AND RELATE TO THE IMPERIAL GOVERNMENT IN A BASICALLY HOSTILE WAY

This alternative has been rightfully centered on the North African Donatist church. The alternative did not arise because Constantine, even before he was the supreme emperor of the total empire, began to show a favorable stance to the Christian world. Rather, it had taken root during the century and a half prior to Constantine, when wave after wave of persecution had rocked so much of North Africa. The imperial government was viewed by such North African Christian leaders as Tertullian and Cyprian, and quite understandably so, as "the enemy." However, because many North African bishops became, to one degree or another, a "traditor," these same Christian "traditor" bishops also came to be seen as the "enemy."[23] When one adds to this "Christian" element of persecution the imperial antagonism of the Romans toward the Carthaginians and the long history of an "anti-Punic" stance by Rome toward North Africa, one sees very clearly that Donatism was not simply a matter of "the spiritual integrity of the Christian minister." W.H.C. Frend's volume *The Donatist Church* was and is a major rewriting of that period of history.[24] So, too, is the earlier-appearing, multi-volume work of P. Monceaux, *Histoire littéraire de l'Afrique chrétienne.*[25] Frend, for his part, and more clearly than Monceaux, painstakingly showed that there were socio-political and demographic factors involved in this struggle called Donatism. Frend has, no doubt, overstated the position that the struggle was a sort of "class struggle" between the lower class stratum of North Africa, which used an early Libyan dialect, and the upper class, Latin-speaking stratum of North Africa, or between the inland districts and the maritime cities of North Africa. The subsequent works of such authors as S.L. Greenslade, E. Tengström, A. Pincherle, A. Mandouze and B. Krieg-baum have certainly modified this somewhat simplistic view. These authors have all pointed out that the issue was at heart a religious or theological issue, namely one that focused on the relationship of the integrity of faith and adherence to the Holy Spirit. But they also stress that second-arily the Donatist crisis was a socio-political event, though certainly not a "class struggle," as Frend had proposed. It was, rather, a socio-political event, insofar as certain areas of both church leadership and church membership began to consort amicably with the enemy: i.e. the enemy of Christians, because of the persecutions, and the enemy of North Africa, which the Roman government had again and again evidenced from the destruction of Carthage in 146 B.C. down to the blockade of the Cartha-ginian harbor in 308 A.D. and the invasion of Maxentius' troops in 310/311. That this Roman government had been the same government which had oppressed so ruthlessly the peoples of North Africa, that this same government had ruthlessly persecuted Christians in North Africa, that this same government was basically Latin-speaking, while many followers of the Donatist party were of an early Libyan dialect—certainly all this played a role, but the key issue of the crisis remained at a theological or religious level. The purity or spiritual integrity of the Christian minister and the purity and integrity of the Christian community became major touchstones: neither a Christian minister nor a Christian community should cozy up to such a government, and above all Christians should not capitulate (*traditor*) to such a government. The execution of Bishop Don-atus of Bagai in 347, after the Roman soldiers crushed the rebellious Circumcellions, and the execution of Bishop Marculus by the Romans had created martyrs for the Donatist cause. The Roman edict of August 15, 347, uniting the schismatic churches of Carthage under the non-Don-atist Gratus, the successor of Caecilian, created havoc. Those in the Dona-tist community at Carthage who submitted to this Roman edict were themselves viewed as *traditores* and *lapsi*. This was the same issue which the election and installation of Caecilian at Carthage had earlier on brought to a head. Caecilian had openly catered to the Roman imperial officials; he had become a "traditor," in the eyes of these followers of the Donatist movement, and he had made no public retraction of his stance. He was clearly the opposite of Cyprian, who had given up his life rather than surrender to imperial pressure (although in an earlier persecution

Cyprian had fled from the persecutors, which was viewed as another acceptable position). Alongside the fundamental theological issues of integrity and purity in the church, a secondary issue for the Donatists, because of the long-standing hostility of the Roman government to the Christian faith and to North Africa generally, was this: the Christian church cannot become a puppet of the imperial state.[26]

The position of the Donatists vis-à-vis Rome should not be dismissed as simply "non-orthodox," nor can the political factors be separated from the theological issues, e.g., the purity and spiritual integrity of the minister. In fact, in itself there was nothing heretical about the Donatist stance toward Roman government, and the stance had existed in North Africa (and elsewhere) long before the appearance of Donatus. Moreover, in North Africa a "Donatist" negative trend toward the government lasted for decades, even after Donatism had been officially suppressed by the Roman political powers. Whether a later reference to Donatists in North Africa, made by Gregory I, is accurate or only an attempt to discredit his opponents is a matter of debate. Gregory may have simply so labeled his opponents in North Africa "Donatists" to discredit them. One finds, nonetheless, a long-standing independence of the North African bishops vis-à-vis the bishop of Rome, an independence which lasted down to the destruction of the North African church by the Islamic invaders of the seventh century.

Moreover, this "Donatist" ecclesiological position between church and government, in one way or another, has resurfaced in church history, whenever there was a government which was antithetical to the Christian faith. The attitude in this "Donatist" position received a slogan from Donatus himself: "What has Caesar to do with the church?" It is an attitude of entrenchment: there is a rightful domain for government (Caesar) and there is a rightful domain for the church, and the two are separate.[27] Whenever in the course of western church history a particular government was open to Christianity, such a "Donatist" stance did not appear applicable, but whenever a particular government was antithetical to Christianity or at least not open to a particular form of Christianity, either an independent "you-go-your-way/we-go-our-way" or an adversarial stance by the minority church has surfaced again and again, both in Catholicism and in Protestantism.[28]

At the end of the third century and throughout the fourth century this "Donatist" alternative was quite available to the wider church leadership of that day. Some church leadership did indeed opt for this kind of stance, which, of course, is most notably seen in North Africa, in which roughly one-half of the North African episcopal leadership preferred the option. On the other hand, the episcopal and intellectual leadership in Rome and Milan, in Antioch and Alexandria, in Constantinople and Caesarea preferred a different form of relationship to imperial Rome (namely, the alternative discussed in section C below). It is important to note in this matter that the issue on the holiness and integrity of both the minister and the community, which lingered on in the debates over rebaptism and reordination, can be separated from the issue of a church-government stance. The two issues are not intrinsically interrelated. Some of the opposition to the church-government stance of the Donatists was, at the time of Augustine, intermingled with the opposition to the theological issue of spiritual integrity, but the church-government issue was clearly a distinct issue and an alternative position for the Christians of that particular time.[29] Certainly it can be viewed and was indeed viewed as an "extreme" alternative, and one which for that period of time appeared to many as counter-productive to the stability and growth of Christian communities. At other periods of church history, such an approach, however, was not viewed as "extreme" and was considered the more productive way to stabilize a Christian community, given the governmental structures operative at the time. To classify the Donatist position as "extreme" must be seen in its relativity. It is not per se extreme, as subsequent church history indicates. Once a doctrine of church and state develops in the late middle ages, some sort of separation gradually takes place and is even advocated officially. On the other hand, it is also correct to note that throughout much of subsequent church history, the marriage of the Christian church to a particular government has seemed to many a church leader and church theologian as the "ideal." All other forms of church-state relationships are, consequently, judged by this "ideal." On the basis of such a judgment, the Donatist position appears to be per se extreme. The response to this judgment, however, is q.e.d.

B. THE ALTERNATIVE TO RETIRE FROM THE WORLD AND LIVE A LIFE TOTALLY DEDICATED TO THE CHRISTIAN PRINCIPLES

The second alternative, namely, to leave the culture of the cities and towns and move to an anchoritic or monastic form of Christian existence, began to take place at the end of the third century and the beginning of the fourth century. It was not occasioned by the favorable stance of Constantine toward the church, but appeared around the same time that Constantine was moving in a direction which favored the Christian faith. We will explore this facet of Christian life to a greater extent in the next chapter.

Unlike the position of the Donatists, this option was not fiercely anti-government nor was it opposed by the episcopal and intellectual leadership of the Christian community itself. In fact, almost from the beginning the episcopal leadership and to some extent the intellectual leadership approved of this option. Even the imperial leadership at times took great pains to protect monks and nuns. There are as well many recorded instances in which the anchoritic and monastic life was presented by various bishops as a "perfect way" to be a disciple of Jesus. Nonetheless, with the exception of a few bishops in northern Italy, and the monastic communities of bishop and priest which one finds, for instance, at Vercelli with Eusebius, at Hippo with Augustine, and in the Lateran with Gregory the Great, the entire monastic movement was basically non-episcopal, non-presbyteral and non-clerical. It was clearly at its origins a lay-movement, and the non-involvement of the cleric in most of the early monastic enterprises may have been one of the reasons why this alternative, in contrast to the Donatist option, which did indeed involve bishops and lesser clergy, remained acceptable in itself. Nonetheless, the monastic alternative did not become the official stance of the episcopal leadership of that time. It, too, could be considered "extreme," but even though it might be so named, the monastic movement was by and large warmly allowed to co-exist with the episcopally directed churches, even though in this issue of church/government the monastic movement took a quite opposite stance to that of the church/government stance of the "wider" episcopal church. The Donatist faction with its many bishops, which held a different stance than that of the "wider" episcopal church, was not, however, generally considered an acceptable ecclesial alternative as regards the relationship of church and government.

C. THE ALTERNATIVE TO FORM A STRONG RELATIONSHIP WITH THE IMPERIAL ROMAN GOVERNMENT

The third alternative, namely, to form a strong relationship with the imperial Roman government, was the one which the majority of the church leaders took at this time. For some the relationship was hailed as the "new paradise," while others were more cautious. There were, of course, no internal precedents on the part of the Christian community for this kind of alternative, and thus from 324 to 731 we see various and groping attempts to stabilize the relationship. The boundaries between government and church were not fixed, and there were incursions made by both sides, as each struggled to find equilibrium. The motives for this mutual relationship at times coincided, but at other times the motives which the government had were different from those of the church, and likewise the motives which the church leadership had were at times quite distinct from those of the government. On both sides, however, there was a clear, growing perspective that an open relationship both of the Christian church to Roman government and of the Roman government to the

Christian church was beneficial and should be encouraged. There was never a view that the religious world of the Christian community could live totally apart from the socio-political and governmental structures of the age. Even the monks became, in short order, dependent on the economics of a given region for their basic sustenance, and therefore dependent on the peace and stability of the empire. Nor could the governmental structures of that time ignore the rather widespread and increasingly numerous Christian sector of the realm. The issue was not an either/or one, but rather how cozy the Christian leadership and the governmental leadership should become. It is the fundamental stance of openness, from both sides, to this relationship which lies at the heart of this particular alternative.

In the development of this relationship between the Christian church and the Roman imperial leadership, the episcopal leadership of the Christian community began to form, first of all, in practice, and eventually in theory formulations of the so-called "church-state" relationship. One must be very cautious with this phrase "church-state," since only in the thirteenth century is the church-state theory really developed. Prior to the thirteenth century, one finds only scattered building-blocks for this eventual theory. In other words, the church leadership did not develop its stance toward the civil government on the basis of a pre-conceived plan or program. Rather, there was a general acceptance that a church-government marriage was desirable. On the basis of this fundamental stance, the delicate balances and positions were gradually worked out. The histories both of this period and of the middle ages as well indicate that there were many trial-and-error efforts, on the part of both church leadership and governmental leadership in this effort to set boundaries and to balance power. Still, one finds in those same periods of church history definite trends and patterns, and when the center of gravity began shifting to the inner west, both the episcopal and papal leadership utilized many of the trends and stances which had developed between church leadership and the imperial government. One finds, then, similarities in the patterning of balances which had played such a role between church leadership and the imperial government at Constantinople, and which western church leadership began to exhibit in its relationship to the various western governments: to the Goths and the Ostrogoths in northern Italy, to the Visigoths in Spain, eventually to the Anglo-Saxons in England, and above all, in a most developed and fostered way, to the Frankish kingdom in the Gallo-Roman areas of central Europe.

In this latter relationship, that is with the Frankish rulers (and subsequently with the Saxons), the theologizing of the status of the western emperor took on religious and theological dimensions which far surpassed the theological descriptions of any Byzantine emperor. We will consider in detail this theologizing of the western emperor in a section below.

Such were the three major alternatives open to the church leadership as Constantine began to solidify the Roman empire under his sole control. By and large, the episcopal leadership at that time deliberately selected the third alternative. Although a marriage with the government was not the only alternative they had, it was the form of co-existence which these episcopal leaders, by and large, fostered. I wish to argue that there was a deliberate move in this regard by the mainline church leadership of that time. Eusebius of Caesarea, more than any other figure, provided the church with a *political* theology, as Grillmeier well describes it.[30] Many of his positions in this regard were absorbed into the mainstream of Christian practice and thought. In doing so, episcopal, and therefore by extension, clerical leadership moved into the socio-political arena, precisely as a socio-political leadership group (an *ordo*). Unity was based on two foundations: the unity which comes from the incarnation, and the unity which comes from the *Imperium Romanum* through the monarchy. From the standpoint of the major theme of this present volume, namely, the role of the lay person in the church, the importance of this church-government relationship is crucial, for:

The repositioning of the clerical group within the socio-political structures had, as its effect, the depositioning of the ordinary lay person not only in the socio-political structures but in the ecclesial structures as well.

Had the church leadership selected one of the other options, or even modified its relationship to the *Imperium Romanum,* this depositioning of the lay person would not have occurred in the way it did, which indicates that there is no "divine plan" that ordinary lay people should be in such a depositioned situation, politically and ecclesiastically. Nor is there any "divine plan" that clerics, even the pope, should be in the socio-political repositioned situation characteristic of the Roman empire and the Carolingian empire, with its consequent effects on their ecclesiastical status.

3. THE PRIVILEGED LAY PEOPLE DURING THIS PERIOD

The reduction of the ordinary *laikos* to a position in the church which had little authority did not happen overnight. The process was a gradual one and affected the *laikoi* in differing ways. From 324 to 731, however, some *laikoi* continued to exercise a privileged position within the Christian community, not because they were *laikoi,* but because of other factors. We will consider some of the major groups of these privileged lay people, both men and women, and indicate the bases for their position of privilege within the church structures.

A. SENIORES LAICI

In the fourth century, particularly but not only in the North African churches, the "seniores laici" continued to wield an enormous presence within the local church structures.[31] The *Ambrosiaster* (c. 375) compares this group to the synagogue. However, even the names for this group varied in different regions: one finds, for instance, *fideles seniores,*[32] *seniores plebis,*[33] *seniores locorum,*[34] and *seniores Christiani populi.*[35] These "elder laymen" had, in varying ways, a voice within the Christian communities, but they were quite distinct from the presbyterium, which also had a voice, in varying ways, within the Christian communities. In the *Codex canonum Africae ecclesiae* we learn that "in Catholic Churches, they took precedence over the *clerici,* coming immediately after the deacons."[36]

> Their functions were both administrative and disciplinary. Among the former duties, they co-operated with the bishop in administering and safeguarding church property. . . . The seniores of Citra in Numidia and Apthunga in Byzacena seem to have formed an administrative council for their churches. . . . Apart from these duties were others of a judicial and disciplinary character, which allowed the seniores a check even on the conduct of their bishop.[37]

These *seniores laici,* however, indicate that a new distinction was being made within the organization of the churches, namely a distinction between the ordinary lay person, on the one hand, and a few privileged lay individuals, on the other. In other words, there were the generalized Christian people, the laity, but there were also "special lay members" who exercised a degree of power within the church. These "special lay people," the *seniores laici,* continued to play an ecclesial role throughout the first part of the historical period under investigation in this present chapter.

The *seniores laici* were in this privileged position because of their aristocratic family ties, because of their wealth, because of their governmental positions, because of their education and learning. However, no data indicates that there was any attempt on their part to claim a lay voice, *qua* lay, in church administration. At this early period of history, such an idea would have had no meaning at all. These *seniores laici* are present in church administration in virtue of nobility of family, in virtue of a governmental position, in virtue of extensive education, etc. In the course of time, however, this group of *seniores laici* disappeared. The reason for the disappearance was, of course, the gradual clericalization of all church structures, including the *seniores laici.*

B. LAY PEOPLE IN POWERFUL POSITIONS OF GOVERNMENT

From 324 to 731 we find, as a matter of course, a few privileged Christian lay people in powerful positions of government, and precisely because these lay people were powerful within the government, some of them became powerful within the church as well. On the other hand, the opposite also happened, although with less frequency, namely, a few privileged lay people found an important role within the structure of the church and as a result gained a position of strength within the imperial government as well. We might outline these kinds of non-ordained Christians who fell into these governmental positions of power.

1. The emperor plays a singular and special role for this privileged status, and the aura of his office enhances the ecclesial status both of his family, and of his closest associates in government. The emperor himself, however, enjoyed a singular ecclesial status, difficult to describe exactly, but one which in many ways was neither lay nor cleric. We will treat the position of the emperor in a separate section.

2. Regional and local government officials also find a special position within the church structures. This is evident in such cases as the Roman senate, but it is also seen in the appearance of the leaders of the Germanic tribes, such as the Goths and the Ostrogoths, the Lombards and the Gauls. Again, the aura of the main leader enhances the position within the church of his or her immediate family and also his or her close governmental associates. These privileged regional and local government officials appear even while there is a unified emperor and an empire.

3. Lay men held curial positions within the bishops' offices, particularly in the curias of the bishops of Rome, Constantinople, Alex-

andria, Antioch, and Milan-Ravenna. The role of *apocrisarios*
was often held by a lay person, who possessed thereby considerable church prestige. In time such lay men were replaced by clerics, but at the beginning of this period these lay men were found in
privileged and powerful church positions.

Leaving the position of the emperor to one side for the moment, let
us review some instances of these privileged lay men and women from
324 to 731. On the one hand, this review is not meant to be exhaustive;
rather, it is meant to be representative. On the other hand, this review will
indicate that the number of such Christian lay men and women are relatively few. In other words, the sparcity of names is another indication that
in the structure of the high patristic church only a few privileged lay
people played any role in the church's decision-making or leadership processes. The following instances, then, are indicative, not taxative, of this
presence of a few lay men and women in privileged positions within the
church.

1. At the Council of Serdica in 342, two officials of the government
accompanied the eastern delegation. It is true that Athanasius objected to
their presence, but it is also true that they exerted no little influence over
the proceedings of this council, and did this in virtue of their official status
as representatives of the government in an official way. The Council of
Serdica was touted in a special way by the western church leadership.
Indeed, the Chieti manuscript connects the Nicene and Serdican canons
under a single heading, giving the impression that all the canons emanated from Nicaea. Pope Zosimus, for instance, cites the Serdican canons
as Nicene.[38]

2. Constantia, the step-sister of Constantine, lived in Nicomedia and
because of her position was highly instrumental in bringing Eusebius,
bishop of Nicomedia, into prominence at the imperial court, where he
eventually became the patriarch. In a similar way, in 357 at Rome, aristocratic and powerful Christian women lobbied to have Liberius reinstated.
Through their efforts his reinstatement eventually, although not with any
unanimous acclaim, did take place. These instances are noteworthy, since
they indicate the power of lay women in church matters. However, it was
not because they were "lay" that they had influence, but because they
were related either to the eastern emperor or to powerful, aristocratic
families at Rome.

3. In the court of Constantius II senior officials played major roles in
church government. Eutropius, for instance, was instrumental in bringing
John Chrysostom into the patriarchate of Constantinople. The three
counts, Candidian, John, and Irenaeus, were behind-the-scene figures at

the Council of Ephesus in 431. In his struggle against the Nestorians, Cyril of Alexandria did not hesitate to bribe Chrysoretus, a chamberlain, and Eutyches himself was under the patronage of the chamberlain Chrysaphicus. Similarly, Augustine, at the Council of Carthage in 411, asked Count Marcellinus to be the moderator in the discussions between the Donatists and the orthodox bishops.

4. The imperial court is asked by the African church, c. 400, to establish *defensores ecclesiae* for the church. These men were to be selected from lawyers, *scholastici,* and they were to be advocates in the socio-political realm for the needs of Christians. Note that the Church asks the government to establish such officials, who would have oversight of ecclesial matters. Although the subsequent destruction of the North African churches by the Vandals brought an end to this program, it indicates again the presence of governmental lay men within church administrative structures. In the Roman church, the *defensores ecclesiae* continued to have great power, particularly over the patrimony of St. Peter. Only at a later date did Gregory the Great replace the Roman *defensores ecclesiae* with monks and clerics. Through this replacement, the lay character of this office disappeared, but prior to the replacement there were indeed lay men involved in the affairs of the Roman church.

5. At the Council of Nicaea, it was a governmental official, Philumenos, either a *magister militum* or *magister officiorum,* who personally presented the *biblion* for the bishops to sign. If they did not sign there was an explicit understanding that they would be deposed. Although the debate of the bishops had been sharply divided on several key issues and although many bishops were opposed to some of the conclusions, only two of the two hundred and twenty some bishops present, Secundus of Ptolemais and Thonas of Marmarica, refused to sign, and were immediately mandated into exile. Philumenos might be seen as a powerful figure at this general council, but his power stemmed from the fact that he was acting in the name of Constantine I.[39]

6. At the Council of Ephesus, 431, Count Candidian reacted strongly against the strong-arming of Cyril of Alexandria. Although his reaction had little avail, still his intervention indicates the strong presence of state officials in the workings of the church. After the so-called latrocinium council at Ephesus in 449, Pope Leo I did not hesitate to write not only to Theodosius II, but also to Pulcheria, his sister, and urge a new council. He also wrote to the monks at Constantinople, who were overwhelmingly lay, urging the same goals. When these efforts failed, he contacted the empress, Galla Placidia. One asks, however: Why is Leo writing to such lay people? The answer is clear: they have influence, particularly in this instance, as regards the calling of a church council. In all of these

situations we see the role of governmentally influential lay people in a privileged position as regards the role of the church.

7. With the emperors Justin I (518–527) and above all Justinian (527–565) we have a new era of governmental influence in the structures of the church. Even more so than Constantine, Justinian was a major church figure: "Whether or not he consciously competed with the Old Testament lawgivers and judges, Moses and Solomon, his determination to be measured by their scale and achievement is very clear."[40] One must also take into account the amount of control which Empress Theodora exercised. Quite apart from the imperial figures themselves, people close to both of them had considerable ecclesiastical and ecclesial influence. This same respect for governmental figures is found, in a hesitating way at first, with the western kings. Theodoric, the Visigoth at Ravenna, sent Pope John I to mediate the issue of the Gothic Arian churches. The bishop of Rome was a dutiful citizen, it appears, even to the Goths who had overrun much of Italy at that time, and therefore he went on the orders of Theodoric. Justin, however, did not give in to this pressure from Gothic arianism, and Theodoric therefore imprisoned John I when he returned to Ravenna. Justinian's goal was one empire, one church, and one emperor, and even though he respected the bishop of Rome, that same bishop was well advised to make decisions in accordance with the imperial decrees.

8. After the Frankish-Visigothic war (507–511) a Catholic area in Gaul was formed, and out of this collaboration of Gallo-Frankish bishops arose the Frankish "national church." In 511 Clovis called all the bishops of the Frankish territory to meet at Orléans for the first council of the Merovingian kingdom. The agenda was set by Clovis, and the bishops, highly influenced by Clovis' wishes, established the basic laws for the Merovingian church. One notes that it was a lay person, Clovis, who dominated this ecclesial synod, and this set a precedent for future Merovingian and other Gallic synods.

9. In the election of bishops, one finds from 549 on, within the Merovingian world, the phrase: *cum voluntate regis iuxta electionem cleri ac plebis* (with the will of the king beside the election of clergy and people). The Latin terminology should be carefully noted: one finds *clerus* (clergy), *plebs* (people, i.e. the ordinary lay man or woman), and *rex* (king). The king is not simply a lay person, *plebs*, nor is he a cleric; rather he is a quite special person. In 549, it must be recalled, there was an emperor at Byzantium; in the Merovingian sector there was only a king, *rex*. Nonetheless, this king, in a way similar to the emperor, was distinct from both lay and cleric. In this instance we see that the pattern developed in the imperial

court at Constantinople as regards the position of the governmental leader is being transferred to the royal court of the west.

10. Proprietary churches, in the Merovingian world, displaced the episcopal church, so that the idea that all churches, even those founded by lay people, should be placed in the hands of the bishop became inoperative. Rather, the lay person, such as a king, a prince or other aristocrat, continued to "own" the church and have a right of appointment thereto.[41] Both the rise and the development of the proprietary churches attest to the power which special lay or non-cleric individuals had over inner-church activities.

11. Pope Gelasius I, an African, became pope in 492. The Goths under Odeacer had almost total control over northern and central Italy. At Odeacer's death, Theodoric, an individual who was more open to Christianity though not personally a Christian, established himself as king of Italy. Gelasius often turned to Theodoric for assistance, and did so particularly in his struggles with the emperor, Anastasios I. Theodoric cannot even be considered "lay," since he was neither catechumen nor baptized. Nonetheless, he involved himself, at the invitation of Gelasius, in inner-church matters.

12. The synod at Rome, which Gelasius held in 495, notes in a special way that members of the lay nobility were present.[42] This synod dealt with inner-church matters, and a few privileged lay people took part in these proceedings. Gelasius, however, is the author of several letters which stress not only the separation of the ecclesiastical from the imperial, but also the superiority of the former over the latter, an issue which we will consider shortly.

13. When one thinks of Ambrose, Augustine, John Chrysostom, and Basil, one also thinks of a pious Christian mother or sister who influenced these men in profound ways. Such family relationships are recorded for the noted church fathers mentioned above, but similar familial relationships cannot be discounted *a priori* for other church leaders who never made a mark in history in a way similar to Ambrose, Augustine, John Chrysostom and Basil.

14. The church of St. Polyeuktos, rivaling Justinian's church of Santa Sophia in Constantinople, was constructed by Juliana Anicia, one of the wealthiest persons in that city, and a member of one of the wealthiest and most distinguished families of Rome itself. Her church was built according to the specifications of the original temple in Jerusalem, and aroused the envy of Justinian.[43]

15. Olympias was a wealthy young widow and a close friend of John Chrysostom. She used some of her money to construct a monastery for

women in the neighborhood of Constantinople.[44] She was, during her widowed life, ordained as a deaconess, and thus she might rather be considered not as lay but as cleric. Still, she represents, even before her ordination, a prominent lay person.

These are some of the more pronounced indications that lay people, both men and women, played varying roles within the church structures. Most of the instances of such lay involvement are due to the privileged governmental positions of the lay people, while only a few cases are due to more incidental reasons. Nonetheless, in the relationship of church structure and governmental structure a pattern of interplay developed which indicated that a strict lay/cleric interfacing had not yet been established. This fluidity has significant value for our contemporary study of the lay person in the church, since this fluidity argues strongly against any iron-clad position that the "constant teaching of the church" has demanded clerical control over all forms of lay activity.

One of the reasons for this fluidity is the relationship of the church to the governmental structures of that time. Throughout this period of history there was no clear division between church and state, as we find at some later period of western history. Rather, there are ordained church officials and non-ordained governmental officials, and since both have a religious nature about them, there is great fluidity. Church officials self-consciously move into governmental areas, and governmental officials self-consciously move into ecclesial areas. At times there are cries of trespassing, but generally not.

This pattern of fluidity between government and church structures deliberately shaped the way in which church officials in the west dealt with the various new groups which were making inroads, such as the Goths, the Ostrogoths, the Visigoths, the Burgundians, the Franks, etc. One finds again and again, in the historical data, instances in which church officials, the pope included, not only worked with the leadership of some of these groups, but also willingly allowed "lay" involvement in church matters. Some of the leaders of these various groups also allowed church officials to share in governmental structures. In other words, the very pattern of church-government interrelationship, which developed in the Graeco-Roman empire, became operative in the new relationships which the western world began to experience as these various tribes moved into Europe and gained socio-political power.

Historians have over and over again struggled to find the correct term for the relationship between the Graeco-Roman empire and the church. Baus, for instance, has used the phrase "church of the empire" to describe the relationship, but he has felt constrained to define this phrase.

Fundamental to this relationship was the fact that the State's power and the Church agreed in principle on a close collaboration in the public sphere. This became possible because the Emperor, personally and as a representative of the State's authority, professed the faith which the Church preached and the majority of the Empire's inhabitants accepted.[45]

The church officials stressed that the power of the emperor came from God and depended on God. "The extraordinarily close union of the two was not questioned [by church authority], especially since in the thought of the day an alternative to it was not known and could scarcely be understood."[46] As noted above, however, there were indeed other alternatives which some bishops and many lay people did indeed understand and deliberately selected. It seems to me that there is a false reading of history if one claims, as Baus does, that the actual church-government relationship was the only possible one. Baus attempts, however, to cover his position, by insisting that the church leadership realized that in its innermost essence the church belonged to another area, "namely to that reality of the order of grace which was bestowed on mankind through Christ's redemptive act."[47]

From a theological standpoint, however, one must nuance Baus' *caveat*. That the church leaders of that particular time realized that the church was a mystery is without question; nonetheless, the same leaders of the church at that time did not have a precisely formulated ecclesiology. Ecclesiology is a fairly modern theological study, and in the centuries we are studying there was no clearly enunciated ecclesiology. J.N.D. Kelly, describing the church of this early period, speaks about the ecclesiology of the east as somewhat immature, perhaps archaic.[48] The western fathers were somewhat more pointed on this issue of ecclesiology, for two reasons: the emphasis on the position of Rome and the Donatist controversy. Kelly elaborates on the position of Augustine, but Augustine was writing when the west was beginning to fall under the invasions of the Germanic tribes. Moreover, Kelly notes, Augustine never resolved several basic ecclesiological problems.[49] In their relationship to the Roman-Byzantine emperors, the fathers of the church saw the empire as part of the order of grace, and the emperors as instruments of God's grace. Because of this, the order of the church and the order of the empire were intimately united, and this in a theologically articulated way, and not merely in an external way. What later generations understood by the phrase "church and state" is not really applicable at this time. This is why Baus rightfully attempts to recast this relationship in his coinage of "church of the empire." Perhaps no phrase is all that clarifying, but what is clear is this: the Church and the empire were so deeply intertwined that one without the other became existentially almost unintelligible.[50] Nonetheless, it should be remembered again and again that this basic determination for some sort of "marriage" was a deliberate and contingent move on the part of the leadership of both empire and church.

C. LAY PEOPLE IN POSITIONS OF WEALTH

Christian lay men and women who were wealthy were also privileged lay persons in the church. Wealth by itself did not, of course, mean an automatic privileged position in the church, but wealth at times did provide a lay person with power internal to the church community itself.

Constantine's mother Helena raised great interest in Palestine by her own pilgrimages there and by her lavish contributions to shrines in Palestine. Basil the Great speaks about the amount of money and assets which wealthy lay people had bequeathed to the church. He also indicates that a fixed sum should be determined, perhaps one-half of one's estate, to be given to the church and to the poor before the remainder of the estate is divided among the heirs.[51] Paulinus of Nola does the same. In North Africa mention is made of Melania and Pinianus, who had enormous estates from which they gave large endowments to the church. Etheria makes note of a church near Jerusalem which had been constructed by a tribune.[52] The Code of Theodosian[53] and a letter of Jerome[54] make note of bishops actively engaged in legacy-hunting. Neill notes that "the foundations of the immense wealth of the medieval Church were laid in the century after the conversion of Constantine."[55] In Rome, however, there is an anomalous situation. The senatorial leadership in Rome remained conservatively pagan, and therefore they did not build Christian churches. Outsiders, at first, were the ones who financed the church buildings in Rome. As the senatorial families of Rome began to move downward in influence, the bishops of Rome began to move upward. Celestine, Sixtus III, Leo I and Hilary, often with money from the emperor, were responsible for the most important church buildings; these men also began to rebuild public monuments which the senatorial families had allowed to disintegrate; they also attended to the flood walls along the Tiber and the restoration of hostels in Rome itself. Innocent I helped to negotiate with Alaric in 409, and Leo I in 452 led the mission to negotiate with Attila.[56] All of these building enterprises and diplomatic negotiations cost money, and those who gave money to the Roman church clearly were giving money to power. Bishops elsewhere in the empire were doing exactly the same thing: Severinus on the Danube frontier, as well as many bishops in the Gallo-Roman areas.

In every age, people with wealth also have power, and wealthy lay people have continued to exert a powerful influence within the church. As we move from the Byzantine church into the early medieval church, wealthy aristocracy will continue to influence church structures. On the other hand, since the majority of lay people were not in the moneyed class, it remains true to say that the lay people, by and large, were effectively removed from this particular sphere of influence within the church. Historical instances of wealthy lay people influencing the church only emphasizes the issue that it is not the lay quality as such but the money quality which allowed this kind of influence.

D. INFLUENTIALLY EDUCATED LAY MEN AND WOMEN

In the same era, we find lay people of strong educational background playing a role in the church, particularly in the area of theology. However, as one moves into the end of the Byzantine church in the west and the emergence of the early middle ages, such educated lay people become few and far between.

1. Didymus the Blind, 313–398, was one of the foremost teachers in the catechetical school at Alexandria. Blind from the age of four onward, he nevertheless became a man of prodigious learning. He was the teacher of both Jerome and Rufinus. His personal style of life was austere, even monastic, and he was consulted by both Anthony the Hermit and Palladius. He was a lay person, but one of great influence.

2. Asterius, the sophist and a lay person, was apparently allowed to preach in Syrian churches between 331 and 335 and to attend synods of bishops, even though there were clear church prohibitions against such a practice.[57]

3. Synesius of Cyrene (c. 370–413) was a neo-platonist philosopher, highly educated, and active in governmental circles. His writings date basically from the time when he was a lay person. Only in 405/406, in other words after his career as an educated lay man, was he elected bishop and metropolitan of the Pentapolis.

4. In 350/370 the two lay men, father and son, both named Appolinarios, paraphrased the Pentateuch into heroic verse. Other Christian poets who were lay men were Prudentius (348–410) and Tarragona.

5. Synesius became a bishop in 409, but prior to his ordination he was a lay theologian. His ordination to the episcopate was, in part, an effect of his prominence as an educated lay person.

6. Marius Victorinus was also a Christian scholar of note, and a teacher at Rome. He was acquainted with the *Enneads* and the idea of an eternal generation which Plotinus had developed. His *Adversus Arium* was an influential volume for early trinitarian doctrine.[58]

7. Tyconius' writings had a fundamental influence on Augustine's *City of God*, even though Tyconius was of Donatist leaning.

8. The *Ambrosiaster*, perhaps written by Hilarius Hilarianus (370–410), seems to be the work of a lay person.

9. Diodore of Tarsus was a brilliant intellectual, with a caustic tongue. It was as a lay person that he wrote most of his treatises, although in 378 he became bishop of Tarsus in Cilicia.

10. Philostorgius, born at Borissus in Cappadocia Secunda around 368, was a layman who spent most of his life in Constantinople. Between 425 and 433 he wrote a history of the church in twelve books, covering the period from 300 to 425.

11. Another layman, Socrates, was born at Constantinople c. 380. He wrote a church history, which starts with the abdication of Diocletian in 305 and extends to 439. He uses sources well: Rufinus, Eusebius, Athanasius, Gelasius of Caesarea, Eutropius, as also the acts of various councils. Many of these sources he represents verbally, which gives his works a great deal of importance. He even revised his text in a second edition, since he had discovered that some of his quoted sources had been unreliable.

12. Another historically-minded layman, Salaminius Hermias Sozomen, who lived at the same time as Socrates, wrote a church history covering the period from 324 to 425. These historians, together with the cleric, Eusebius, indicate that there was a strong desire to put the history of the church into writing for posterity. All felt that the church was moving into a period of extreme importance, perhaps not quite a golden age, but at least an age of profound significance. It is also worthy of note that in these works the state and the church continually intertwine.

13. Augustine, for his part, experienced and lived the church, until his ordination, as a lay person, and his own monastic experience at Cassiciacum was basically a lay experience. Nonetheless, because of his erudition and his leadership abilities, as well as his Christian life, he was well known in North Africa. As a layman, Augustine himself avoided travel, lest he be made a cleric. On one occasion, however, when he was in Hippo, he was ordained a priest. His reputation had indeed gone ahead of him, and this reputation was that of a laic, not a cleric.

14. At the end of the fifth century, Cresconius, a lay person, a grammarian, a teacher of young children, and a Donatist, wrote a lengthy defense of the faith, arguing with Augustine's book against Petilian of Constantine. It was so well done that Augustine himself felt he had to respond and did so in his own work, *Contra Cresconium*. In this episode there is an *episkopos* answering the arguments of an educated lay person.

15. Boethius (523) and Cassiodorus (584), both lay men, should be mentioned since they affected Christian theological thought in no small measure. Boethius was also a powerful figure in the imperial court at Ravenna. Cassiodorus eventually became a monk and then a bishop, but his training and much of his immediate influence, particularly at Constantinople and in his working with Junilius, an African civil servant, came about during his days as a non-ordained, non-monastic individual. Cassiodorus wrote his *Institutiones* as a monk at Vivarium, but he gained his background when he was not a monk.

Other lay scholars could also be mentioned. Pelagius was a lay monk, and his followers, James, Timasius, and Celestius, were all lay. Arnobius, Firmicius Maternus, Helvidius, and Evagrius of Pontus are also lay men and scholars who have been remembered by historians. Celantia, Demetrias, Marcella and Claudia were all aristocratic lay people who supported Pelagius, and Pelagius himself was a non-ordained individual until late in his career. Jerome, a presbyter, was aided in no small measure by the educated lay women, Paula the Elder, Melania the Elder and Melania the Younger. Marcella is mentioned by Jerome for her opposition to Origen. Faltonia Betitia Proba, an aristocratic Roman woman, wrote a Cento, with lines borrowed from the Aenaeid, Eclogues and Georgics.[59] Egeria, a nun who journeyed from western Europe to Palestine in the late fourth century, wrote her famous travelogue. Sidonius Appolinaris did become the bishop of Clermont, but prior to this task he was an outstanding non-ordained scholar.

When all is said and done, however, such a litany of names is thin. In many ways, these names and a few others that might be added are number-wise minuscule. Each of these people, however, had received an education, so that one can clearly assume, if not many, at least some unnamed other Christian lay men and women who were also well educated and were their teachers. It is clear that education at this time was not "mass education." It is clear that more often than not education was basically a sort of shop-keeper literacy, and little more. Still, in the heyday of the empire, education of the elite was a major priority, and an educated leadership was socially fostered. Educational leadership within the church throughout this high patristic period remained a task at first shared by lay and cleric, but with the bishops' growing antagonism toward "pagan" literature, philosophy and academic material of any kind, clerics, primarily the bishops, began to eliminate even the limited lay presence in the classroom. A clerical presence was considered a safeguard against paganism of any kind. The closer one is to the fourth century, the more names of educated lay men and women occur, while the closer one is to the end of the seventh century, the fewer names of educated lay men and women appear, while at the same time the names of educated clerics and monks appear with greater and greater frequency. The clerical world and the monastic world gradually cornered the educational arena, with a few exceptions, such as the imperial and royal families and their close associates. The result was, for a period of time, not only an uneducated mass of ordinary lay people, but also in large part an uneducated wealthy and ruling group. Without solid education, the ordinary lay person was at a disadvantage; only from the thirteenth century onward, when universities were attracting lay men and women, did a small but significant percentage of the generalized lay sector of both society and the church gain a major advantage: namely, education.

When one looks throughout the patristic period in a specific way for the situation of women, one finds that unordained women, far more than unordained men, were depositioned. Elizabeth Clarke, who has rather thoroughly combed the patristic writings of this time for material on women, comes to the following conclusion:

> We have come full circle in our exploration of the Church Fathers' ambivalence toward women. Women are extravagantly lauded and are inordinately denounced for the world's woes by one and the same author: rarely are they seen as persons with the same virtues and weaknesses as men. Time had to pass before male religious authorities could view women involved in the world of sexual functioning and reproduction as worthy of the same respect as women who chose the celibate course. Much also remained—and still remains—to open the avenues to women that the Church Fathers blocked, even as they hesitantly sanctioned new roles and opportunities for some members of the female sex.[60]

We will return to the situation of the religious woman and her possibilities in the next chapter, which deals with the monastic movement. Clarke's judgment bears out the view that the unordained generally had diminishing power. Clarke notes that the women who are mentioned in the patristic texts are from educated or aristocratic families. Little or nothing is found in these sources about those from lower social classes.[61]

E. THE STATUS OF THE EMPEROR

A uniquely privileged situation arose as regards the emperor, especially from the time of Constantine, the first Christian emperor, and this unique position of the emperor was maintained both in the east and in the west down to the end of the middle ages. The emperor (and by extension, as we shall see, certain kings) cannot be categorized as either "cleric" or "lay." He (or at times an empress or a queen) defied such a simplistic or legal division of the Christian people. Even though authors in this patristic time did not divide the Christian world into cleric, lay, emperor and monk, these four divisions were the de facto divisions of Christian life. Even though there were special "lay" people, as we have just enumerated, that is, lay people who were a cut above other lay people in virtue of education, position, family ties, etc., and even though there were at times special names for such differentiated, non-ordained people, e.g. *seniores laici, defensores ecclesiae,* these special groups of non-ordained never attained in actuality the status of "monk," or of "emperor." Nor were they ever equated to "cleric."

With the emphasis on apostolic succession, which developed strongly in the late second century onward, the clerics, particularly the major bishops or patriarchs, were described as "apostolic," which at first was meant to establish legitimacy to various sees, various bishops, various theological positions. At a later date, apostolic succession was gradually connected to a "divine institution" theory. In this same early period of church history the theological emphasis on the Christians as the chosen people of God, a name given to all baptized/eucharistic Christians, indicates that this people, too, were "apostolic." The church itself was, as the creeds say, one, holy, catholic and apostolic, and this meant that the church community, that is, the total people of God, were apostolic. The "apostolic succession" of the individual baptized Christian, however, never entered into the technical, theological language of that era. The church was apostolic, baptism was apostolic, the leadership in the church was apostolic, but an ordinary Christian was not called apostolic.

Although the monks and nuns, for their part, only gradually developed a theological language which included references to divine institution as far as their own status was concerned, both church leaders and church followers, from the earliest stages of the anchoritic and monastic life, regarded the monk and nun as a very special disciple of Christ. On the other hand, neither Christian leader nor ordinary Christian considered the monk or nun as either a cleric, in the same sense as bishop or presbyter, or as an ordinary lay person, in the same way as they viewed the married, the artisans, the farmers, etc. Above all, they did not consider the monk or nun as imperial, as if they were equal to the emperor. Monks and nuns were, however, close to God, were filled with the Holy Spirit, were sacred, were the ideal followers or disciples of Jesus. They represented in their austere lives precisely what the apostles had preached. They led an *apostolic* life. They were the visible successors of the apostolic community in Jerusalem. Still, the idea of "apostolic succession," even though these monks and nuns were continuing the apostolic life in such a radical way, did not enter into the technical theological language of that period.

The same cannot be said, however, as regards the emperor. The theological and ecclesiastical language which developed in this same period to describe the status of the emperor is filled with the idea of divine institution. The emperor is emperor by God's decision, by the grace of God. The emperor is the vicar of God. In the Frankish world he will be described as almost a co-ruler with Jesus. He is the divinely appointed defender of the world and of the church, with the precise purpose that the apostolic message and apostolic life might have successors throughout the world. The emperor's task is to enable the very existence of apostolic succession in the church and in the world to take place. Nonetheless, he is not precisely described as succeeding the apostles, in the same way as the bishops, but he is clearly present in the church and in society with a divinely instituted Christian role.

Thus, from the patristic period down to the end of the middle ages, the Christian world was divided de facto, not into two groups: lay/cleric, but into four: emperor, cleric, monk, lay. This is the first conclusion one must draw from an analysis of imperial material during this patristic age. However, the study of the emperor/king of this period of church history does not simply end with a de facto fourfold division in the Christian community. Oddly enough, both the history of the questioning and then the history behind the struggle to answer "What is the origin of the emperor or king?" affected in a substantial way the positioning of the ordinary lay person in the church. Since there are various answers to this question, there are also various ways in which these answers affected the positioning of the ordinary lay person.

For this reason, it is important for our study to consider both the emperor's status and the monk's status in detail. Let us pursue the issue of the emperor's status within the Christian world, leaving the status of the monk to the subsequent chapter. For the sake of my argument, it seems necessary to present a short, preliminary excursus ranging far beyond the focusing dates of this chapter; otherwise, the drift of the argument may not be clear. Let us begin this excursus or review with the crucial issue, namely what the precise issue is and what it is not.

IT IS NOT: The issue of church and state.

The issue of temporal government and spiritual government.

IT IS: The issue of the *status* of the emperor/king.

The issue of the *origin* of imperial or regal power, and consequently its impact on the issue of sacerdotal and papal power.

Only after the year 1200 does the issue of church and state, church and government, political power and spiritual power, *qua tale,* truly begin to be the focus of discussion. Prior to that development, the issue focuses on persons, with the person of the emperor (king) very often at center stage. There are three major positions on this matter of the status and origin of the emperor/king which developed from the Constantinian period onward, through Gregory VII, Alexander III, Innocent III and Boniface VIII, and to some degree have perdured even to the end of the twentieth century. There is also a fourth position, which has developed only in the last two centuries, but which recasts one's view of these medieval debates in a much different framework.

The First Position: Papal Monism

There are various interpretations as regards when, how and why the primacy of the Roman pontiff occurred.[62] Emphasis has been clearly placed on statements by Leo I (440–461) who was quite anxious to establish the *principatus* of the Roman see, which meant the *principatus* of the Roman bishop himself.[63] Gelasius I, with his statement of two powers, "consecrated the word *principatus*," as Battifol once remarked.[64] For Gelasius, God has placed this spiritual and ecclesial *principatus* in the *totum corpus ecclesiae,* but particularly in the bishop of Rome.[65]

In the reign of Charles the Great, the relationship of pope to emperor and emperor to pope was described in a well-known statement made in a letter of Charles to Leo III. In this letter Charles acknowledges his wish to enter into a compact with Leo III, specifying:

He, on the one hand, would defend the Church everywhere from external attacks and fortify it internally by knowledge of the orthodox faith, and that the Pope, on the other, would assist the royal forces to victory through his intercessory prayers.[66]

Leo III considered Charles the Great as the guardian of the holy church, and he enhanced the office of the emperor with many spiritual honors. Trials of clerics were placed under his jurisdiction; he was consulted on matters of faith, and bishops were to be in his service.[67] Still, Leo

III attempted to distinguish in a rather generalized way between the spiritual and the political.

It is perhaps Gregory IV (827–844) who first stated that the spiritual government of the church, i.e. the pope, was superior to the temporal government, *even in temporal matters.* This was something new in the way that the bishops of Rome presented themselves.[68] Gregory's threat of excommunicating Louis the Pious included a threat to depose him. Leo IV (847–855) in a letter to Emperor Louis II claimed that he had the charge "of all who are in the world."[69] In Benedict III (855–858) we hear that the pope is the overseer "of all who believe in Christ," the mediator for peace among all earthly princes and the monitor of all their laws.[70] Nicholas I (858–867) and John VIII (872–882) further developed this approach of papal monism.[71]

The Roman church in and through the Roman bishop claimed *principatus* over the entire *societas Christiana.*[72] Although Gelasius' position was not made use of in any overarching way at first, in time it came to be cited again and again. To these and other papal statements there was added a wide range of theological discussions, such as those of Isidore of Seville, and, later on, those of Honorius of Canterbury, John of Salisbury, Bernard of Clairvaux, and Hugh of St. Victor. Canonical literature, with even some forged documentation, contributed to the presentation of this view.

The basic argument of this hierocratic view, when it reached full term, runs as follows: the universal church or the *populus Christianus* is a single and inseparable unit, and it consists of both *sacerdotium* and *regnum.* Such a unified body must be fundamentally ruled by a single force, and the scriptures, the very word of God, indicate that this fundamental ruling force is the *sacerdotium,* and therefore the king, representing the *regnum,* functions in the role of a lieutenant, who is appointed by the head (*caput*) of the *sacerdotium.* This is why the papal crowning of the emperor became successively more important. If, at first, the crowning of the emperor (e.g. Charles the Great) was seen as one of several symbolic acts, in later centuries the crowning of the emperor by the pope came to mean for the advocates of papal monism (at times only these) the conferral of imperial power. For this group, advocating papal monism, the emperor received his imperial position from the papal or sacerdotal power, but this was neither uniformly nor duly accepted by the imperial personages and their followers. At a later stage, it was even argued by similar-minded theologians that the pope actually, through divine right, combined in himself personally both *sacerdotium* and *regnum,* sacerdotal and regal powers. Both theoretically and actually, he could be both emperor and pope of the entire *societas Christiana,* but "in humility" he deferred the regal tasks to a king.[73] On the basis of this radical possession of both powers, it was argued, at still a later stage of the development of this view, that the twofold power of the pope provided one of the major reasons why he might depose a ruler or release subjects from fealty to a king or emperor, a position spelled out baldly in the *Dictatus Gregorii VII*.[74]

In this progressively established view, not only is the emperor/king reduced to the lay state, to the role of a "lieutenant" under the sacerdotal leadership, but the priests (*sacerdotes*) and particularly the head of the priests, the pope, is given an omnicompetence, not only in spiritual matters pertaining to the church, but also in societal issues as well. As a consequence of this extolling of the *sacerdotium*, the "lay" element in the church was further reduced. The struggle of popes and papal theologians to establish this papal monism throughout the Christian world, but particularly the western world, centered around the issues of both *regnum* and *sacerdotium*, not, it should be noted, around the issues of *regnum* and *ecclesia*. In such a view, the church, *ecclesia*, was basically equated with the *sacerdotium*. The widespread lay constituency of the church was not directly considered, for the focus of attention was on both the status of the emperor/king and the origin of imperial and regal power, on the one hand, and the status of the pope and the origin and scope of papal power, on the other. The focus was not on the status of the lay person nor on the origin of lay power. In this position of papal monism, the status and origin of the emperor/king ultimately does not arise from the *societas Christiana*, which would include the laity, but only from the *sacerdotium*, and more specifically the *caput sacerdotii*, the pope. It is clear that in the entire historical discussion and struggle to establish papal monism, especially in its most radical form, there took place a massive repositioning of the *sacerdotium* within the *societas Christiana*, and in particular a repositioning of the *caput sacerdotii*, with an inevitable depositioning not just of the king or emperor, but of the ordinary lay person as well.

In the high middle ages this theory reached a peak, but it did so at a price, for though kings, in the eyes of key church leadership, were in a secondary position, there were many scholars who began to develop in a theoretical way the elements, which later formed the theory of church and state, so prevalent in modern and contemporary history. In the developed church-state theory, a significant sector of society is removed from any direct active church governance, and this sector is increasingly seen as "lay." However, in the view of papal monism, there is a but a single sphere: *societas Christiana*, in which the *sacerdotium* is supreme in every area. In this view there can be no sector of the *societas Christiana* which is not under the *principatus* of the pope. In the church-state view, which began to develop during the later middle ages, there were two separate spheres: the church, on the one hand, and an independent *societas saecularis,* on the other. With the secularization of the state in the modern period, the idea that a pope was a universal civil ruler in theory and, if he so wished, in practice became obsolete. Neither in theory nor in practice could popes appoint kings and other civil leaders, much less depose them. In a secularized state the pope might enjoy personal prestige as a spiritual leader, but he has no inherent right to act beyond that. Within the papal states, of course, the pope continued to be both spiritual ruler and political ruler. In theory, however, the idea of the pope as the one who had *principatus* over the entire world, or that the world was even co-extensive with the *societas Christiana,* became anachronistic.[75] This historical development indicates the relativity of many medieval positions held by papal monism.

The Second Position: Imperial Monism

In this view, the emperor or the king is the chosen one of God and has been divinely appointed to rule the *societas Christiana.* As vicar of God himself, the emperor has the responsibility to make sure that the church not only exists, but exists well. To accomplish this, it is incumbent on the emperor to oversee the leadership of the church, preventing false leadership and fostering orthodox leadership. In this view the *sacerdotium* is, at least to some degree, clearly under the purview of the imperial throne. J.H. Aufhauser, in his essay "Die sakrale Kaiseridee in Byzanz," outlines this monistic view of a *Kaiser-Mystik,* presenting a series of descriptive historical documentation: insignia and titles, art work of all kinds, mosaics, coins, seals, clothing, golden edicts and imperial signatures in red ink, as also in the gestures of acclamations, adorations and ceremonies.[76] The imperial leadership of Justinian in many ways offers us an extreme example of this view in practice. It would, however, be incorrect to associate this view exclusively to the eastern part of the empire. If radical papal monism, however, threatened the *societas Christiana* in the west, radical imperial monism threatened the *societas Christiana* in the east, but it must be stated that both papal monism and imperial monism affected each sector of the church, though in different ways. Papal monism is not an exclusively western phenomenon, nor is imperial monism an exclusively eastern phenomenon.

In the west, Henry IV attempted a modification of this view with his notion of two distinct areas: the regal and the sacerdotal. He and his counselors argued that the pope, Gregory VII, had no claim over kingship, which had been given by God to Henry himself. Key to this stage of imperial monism is the idea that a king or emperor rules *Deo volente,* or that such a person has been appointed by God himself to his regent position. At the time of the Avignon papacy and the tripartite split of the papacy, many Christians in the western *societas Christiana* looked to the German king, Sigismund, to resolve the papal crisis, which he did by convoking a council.[77] In what capacity, however, did the council act? Fink pinpoints the issue in a terse but accurate way: "At the basis of the conciliar idea . . . lay the concept that the Pope is not the absolute master of the Church."[78] Many forms of this non-absoluteness of the pope began to surface. Besides the notion that a general council of the church might adjudicate the situation, another idea, current at that time, focused on the power of the college of cardinals: namely a theological view, rather widespread as well, that the college of cardinals were the true successors of the apostles, not the bishops themselves.[79] But who should call a council? The Council of Pisa (1409) was called by the cardinals, not by any of the three rival popes, and its agenda clearly included the task to begin proceedings against all contenders of the papal throne. This council, however, by and large failed. As we know, it was Sigismund who then summoned a council to be held at Constance. Although thinly attended at first, the episcopal attendance at the council mushroomed with his own arrival at Constance on Christmas, 1414.[80] Questions, however, abound. Was the king acting under the aegis of imperial monism? Was he going beyond his power of *principatus?* On the other hand, if he had not exerted his power of *principatus,* there was at that time no papal *principatus* which could do anything, with the result that the disintegration of the papacy (and to some degree the empire) would have continued. Sigismund's centralizing position was quite key at this time, but the explanation of his key role remains controverted, with theologians at times taking a very dogmatic stance as they interpret history, and historians taking a more factual approach in their interpretation, while canonists scurry to find legal precedents which dovetail with both theological presuppositions and also historical data.

In the aftermath of the reformation period, and with the French and American revolutions, the emergence of the secularized state continued apace, leading to the de facto end of an imperial monistic position in the west. Since these two revolutions, and the subsequent revolutions of 1848, western rulers make no direct claims over church activities. However, again and again, even today, governments often do tread or appear to tread into the religious area. Governmental leaders here and there have even assumed a sort of spiritual aura, a spiritual *principatus.*[81] Rarely today is an appeal made to a position of imperial monism for the entire society, including the religious area; rather there has arisen a monistic imperialism for everything "secular," and a complete *principatus* over the entire *res publica.*[82] The effect of this omnicompetent governmental positioning is the privatization or position of public irrelevancy of anything "religious." At best, civil religion alone, with its civil leadership in either individual rulers or democratic ruling bodies, claims any generalized "religious" voice. Organized religion has been shunted to a publicly ineffective area of private concern. In this situation, the *sacerdotium* is to play an effective role only in the areas of private concern, and equally the Christian lay element of the church, *qua* Christian, is reduced to an area of private lay spirituality and private religious practice. One is not expected to bring one's "religious" issues into the arena of government.

Imperial monism was again a struggle between *regnum* and *sacerdotium*, that is, between royal and imperial leadership and priestly or papal leadership. It was not a struggle between *regnum* and *ecclesia*. The emperor or king thought of himself as the protector of the entire *societas Christiana*, including the clerical sphere of this Christian society. In other words, the *regnum* was superior, in a number of areas, to the *sacerdotium*, and if the emperor was superior to the clerics, he was certainly superior to the laity. The descent of dignity in this view was: emperor (king), then pope and clerics, then monks, then ordinary lay men and women. Imperial monism thus contributed to the depositioning of the ordinary lay person to some degree, just as papal monism contributed to the depositioning as well.

Third Position: Dualism

In this view, and one that the Gallic bishops of the early middle ages tended to espouse, society is both spiritual and temporal, and supremacy in each domain was held respectively by the episcopal and royal offices.[83] In this view, even though the king is not reduced to a "lay" state, but given due honor and respect as the one who was appointed by God to rule over the temporal or political aspects of society without sacerdotal hegemony or interference, the king remained singularly distinct from the ordinary lay person. The Carolingian world was at heart a Christian society, and in this Christian society every major role, including that of the king, was sanctified by God and by Christ. The king, therefore, remained a sacred person, even though his role was in the area of the socio-political.

> For the Franks, sovereignty—and thus the resolution of dualistic tensions—was inconceivable: the burden of their thought was that there was no sovereignty except the direct government of God.[84]

Secondly, in this view the *regnum* is in the hands of the king, and the church is in the hands of the *sacerdotium*. In later Frankish thought, the offices of church and the offices of government were seen as two juridic entities, differing from one another, yet irreparably united within a single Christian society. Only as Hincmar of Rheims in the middle of the ninth century began to employ principles from both Roman law and Frankish law, albeit in a very nuanced way, can one really speak about an initial, major building block of a "church-state" theory. Nonetheless, in the entire effort to make the dualistic process work, the ordinary lay man and woman was rendered second-rate by the regent positionings of both king and priest/bishop. In the church the priests, particularly the bishops, were the highest rulers. In the realm the king, together with his chief consultants, was the highest ruler. Nonetheless, in this view the church leadership and the leaders of the realm do not constitute separate or independent entities; both are able to exist only through a polar relationship. As regards both the *regnum* and the *sacerdotium*, the ordinary lay person should obey, provide maintenance, and render respect. The dualistic approach, just as the two monistic approaches, tended to deposition the ordinary lay person within both Church and kingdom.

This form of dualism, however, is not the same as the secularized church-state position which one finds in the late eighteenth and nineteenth centuries. This form of dualism implies a mutual relationship between *sacerdotium* and *regnum*. It implies, actually, a state church. In the dualistic framework, it is the bishops rather than the pope who represent the *sacerdotium*, and it is this episcopal, non-papal, element which distinguishes this form of dualism, as far as the church situation is concerned. In this form of Frankish dualism, the papal issue was an important but secondary issue. The dualistic approach was strong throughout the Frankish world, and one can certainly see in it a rootage of later Gallicanism, as well as a rootage of the entire cis-alpine/trans-alpine competition of modern European history.

Fourth Position: The Wider World

All the medieval writers who advocated the views mentioned above perceived the world from the western and narrowly Christian approach. Even contemporary books on church history and books on "profane" or church history often get caught up with this *Sitz im Leben*. Given our current knowledge of the wider world during the eighth to the sixteenth centuries, we know that the *societas humana* was enormously larger than the *societas Christiana* in which medieval kings and clerics, writers and theologians, played out their lives. When we read that a medieval pope or emperor claimed that he was the ruler of the entire world, what meaning does this have for those of us today who know that at the very same time such a claim was made, the "entire world" was gigantically larger than they even dreamed of.

One might inquire, for instance: What about the Vandals, the Vikings, the Jutes, the Picts? Even more significantly, one might ask: What about the Islamic people?[85] These groups were all on the edges of the early medieval *societas Christiana*. Officially they were not in the bark of Peter, a bark which rested in the bosom of the emperor, as Charles the Great once described it.[86] As far as these "pagans" were concerned, what was the role of the *regnum* and the *sacerdotium?* Could the pope, in virtue of papal monism, with its view that the pope was the *rex et sacerdos* of the entire world, depose Vandal kings and Viking rulers, or depose the Islamic rulers, who in 630 moved against the Christian east? At stake is not a practical problem, one which deals with political clout or martial resources. At stake is an ideological question. Is the pope, in the view of papal monism, only the *rex et sacerdos* of the *societas Christiana*, and not of the whole world, which included the *societas non Christiana?* If the answer is that the pope, by divine right, is *rex et sacerdos* of the entire world, then the Vandals, Vikings, Jutes and Picts, as well as the Islamic rulers, would fall under his *principatus*. But has such a view any validity at all?

Beyond these edges of the early medieval European world, there were other worlds as yet at that time unknown to kings and popes, or unknown in any significant way. Far to the east, past the Persians, the Chinese were developing a civilization far superior to any western counterpart. Could the pope have deposed any of the leaders of the Sui or T'ang dynasties? Could the king have demanded that they become part of the *regnum*, over which he was the divinely established sole leader? Far to the west, beyond the ocean, the Aztecs, the Incas and the Mayans were developing unbelievably sophisticated societies. In the Roman, Byzantine and Carolingian times, these societies played no role whatever. Had they been known, they would have fallen undoubtedly under the rubric: conquer them and baptize them, i.e. make them a part of the *societas Christiana*.[87] But they were not known, so again one might ask: Is there any validity in a medieval papal claim or a medieval imperial claim to "rule" the entire world?

When placed against the backdrop of this actual wider world, the three positions mentioned above cannot help but become very relativized. In the middle ages, popes and kings, theologians and canonists, argued their various cases from a quite absolute standpoint. God had created the world, and in the Christian dispensation the entire world was the *societas Christiana* with both *regnum et sacerdotium*. With an emphasis on *regnum* or an emphasis on *sacerdotium*, or with an emphasis on a dialectic between the two, such writers and leaders advocated a fairly absolutist stance, either for the king, or for the pope, or for a dualistic position, involving kings and regional bishops. The world, however, was much larger than the then-known *societas Christiana* in which and for which they argued their positions. From our standpoint of this wider but mostly unknown-at-that-time world, we can only conclude that their "absolute" ways of arguing their respective cases were in actuality quite relativized.

Today most people readily admit that secular leaders have a relativized sphere of influence. No secular leader is "king of the world." But what about papal power, episcopal power, and priestly power? If these powers are relativized, then major questions arise. For example, the ordinary priest generally has a certain position within a local ecclesiastical framework, i.e. the parish and the diocese. One does not find a "priest of/for the entire world." Within the Catholic Church, the ordained individual is, indeed, a priest, but among the non-Christians who live in his parish he has, technically, no *priestly* relationship at all. He is not, technically, a priest for them. He is not "their priest," even though sociologically and as a matter of courtesy he will be addressed as "Father . . ." Catholic bishops, too, have a large framework in which their episcopal role has meaning. In their dioceses they are the main spiritual leaders for the Catholic population. Nonetheless, even though the boundaries of their dioceses are most often co-extensive with civic boundaries, the many non-Christians who also live within these "diocesan" or "civic" boundaries do not technically consider the bishop their "spiritual leader." Theologically, the local Catholic bishop has no episcopal relationship to them *qua episcopus*. Theologically, he is not their bishop. He will, of course, be addressed as "Bishop," but this is done on a merely sociological and cultural basis, a "courtesy" of good protocol, but no more than that. The same situation affects the pope of Rome. Several eastern churches have their own pope. Roman Catholicism has its pope. Within the Latin church the Roman pope has a special meaning, one with deep theological implications. The pope at Rome is, however, not a "pope of/for the entire world." Technically and theologically, he has no jurisdiction, *qua* pope, among non-Christian sectors. He is generally respected as the Christian pope by non-Christians, but he is clearly not "their" pope. Even among the wide framework of Christians, the role of the pope at Rome varies, as one considers the different eastern churches, the Anglican churches and the many Protestant churches.

The view of the *regnum/sacerdotium* struggle in the early middle ages from the standpoint of the wider world, in both its historical and its contemporaneous implications, renders the issues so ardently stressed in the debates over papal monism, imperial monism, and Gallic dualism quite relative. Although the medieval individuals saw their respective positions, at times, from an absolutist standpoint, our current understanding of the wider world disallows such an over-extended form of argument. What is vital to our study of the lay/cleric issue, however, is this: the medieval argument was focused on two sectors: a royal or imperial sector, on the one hand, and a sacerdotal sector, on the other. The issue was not on individual persons, i.e. the person of a given emperor/king or the person of a given pope/bishop. The issue was on "kingship" and "priestship": *regnum et sacerdotium.* If it were not for a Christian *sacerdotium,* the claims made in papal monism would have had no cogency. Because a given pope was the *caput sacerdotii,* and because *sacerdotium* was higher, both spiritually and socio-politically, than *regnum,* therefore the pope could press his claims. The same cogency was needed for the claims made in imperial monism. Because a given emperor or king was *caput regni,* and because the *regnum* was divinely established to preserve the church, in which *sacerdotium* was the rightful leadership, the imperial throne could press its claims. The same cogency was demanded of dualism. Because there exists through divine institution both *regnum* and *sacerdotium,* and the two in virtue of this divine institution are mutually interdependent, though individually different, the claims of the Gallic dualists could be pressed. In all three situations, the ecclesial key was *sacerdotium,* not discipleship, not the church in general, not a lay-cleric base. Since the key was *sacerdotium,* the lay element played no direct role.

The proponents of papal monism, gradually as the medieval period went on, changed the dichotomy: no longer did the argument focus on *regnum et sacerdotium,* but on lay-cleric. The later argument, which one hears throughout the lay investiture controversy, involves a "reduction" of the king and therefore the *regnum* to the lay state. As long as the king as *caput regni* was considered the "vicar of Christ," as long as the king as *caput regni* was considered divinely instituted, the proponents of papal monism made little headway. When kingship was seen as a "part" of the lay world, then, and then only, did the proponents strike a key blow against the tenets of imperial monism and even against those of Gallic dualism. However, in this entire struggle it was the lay element in the church which was increasingly set to one side. *Sacerdotium* alone is seen as the key issue.

However, the dignity of the lay Christian is not, from a theological standpoint, established and founded on *sacerdotium.* In particular, the dignity of the lay Christian does not, theologically, depend on the *caput sacerdotii.* There are many eastern lay Christians, many Anglican lay

Christians, many Protestant lay Christians, whose dignity and value as "lay" involves no relationship to the pope at Rome. Secondly, the dignity of the lay Christian is not, theologically, dependent on an episcopal or presbyteral *sacerdotium*. A lay Christian does not have his or her status and dignity within the church *because there exists a sacerdotium within that same church*. Rather, the dignity of the lay Christian has its foundation primarily and originally in Jesus, more specifically in a Christian's grace of discipleship. Discipleship is the basis for the dignity and status of both the lay and the clerical Christian. The clerical Christian is not the mediator through whom the lay person receives his or her status.

In the wider historical view of the world, the first issue that must be taken into account is this: the meaning of the lay person does not depend on some papal positioning, or some episcopal positioning, or some presbyteral positioning. It depends, rather, on the point of departure mentioned in an earlier chapter, namely the meaning of discipleship. For this reason, the entire positioning and repositioning of the lay person which took place during these early medieval years, when finding a balance or a status of either pope or king or both became the overarching issue, has unfortunately skewed the very basic question: What is a disciple of the Lord. The questions of these early medieval authors were: What is an emperor? What is a king? What is a pope? What are bishops? What is the *sacerdotium?* Both the struggle to find the self-identities of these individuals, and the interrelationship which these various self-identities might have with one another, over and over again bypassed a far more profound issue which is at the very basis of why there might be a pope or bishop or priest or emperor at all in a *societas Christiana,* namely: What does it mean to be a disciple of Jesus?

From a wider historical worldview, a second issue arises which asks us today to rethink these arguments on papal monism, imperial monism, and Gallic dualism. When the question about the rights and freedoms of the non-Christian arose at Vatican II—the first time this theme was officially debated in a conciliar way—echoes of these three views could be heard in the council chambers. The resultant decree on religious freedom acknowledged the relativization both of socio-political power (*regnum*) and also, though quite indirectly, of papal or episcopal power (*sacerdotium*), as far as basic human freedoms and the freedom of conscience were concerned, and these freedoms include religious freedom as well. Once one acknowledges that *outside* the *societas Christiana* papal, episcopal and presbyteral power is relativized, one must then ask whether or not there remains a similar human freedom, a fundamental freedom of conscience and a basic religious freedom *within* the *societas Christiana* as well? Do Christians as such enjoy the basic human freedoms which the decree on religious freedom acknowledges for the non-Christian? If so, is there not a basic human and religious freedom for all Roman Christians, including the lay person, including in a special way today the Christian lay woman, which the Roman Catholic *sacerdotium* must honor and respect?

This fourth position, although only fairly recent in its appearance in the western world, clearly affects the way one should evaluate the medieval discussions on papal monism, imperial monism, and imperial/episcopal dualism. Presenting these three views solely from a European stance or from a Roman Catholic stance, even on the basis of presenting a history of the middle ages, without taking into consideration the very relativity of such stances, does not appear to be adequate. Even though the early medieval world either was unaware of the existence of these other worlds and cultures or was aware of them only in a tangential way, still our contemporary awareness of this "wider world" makes the historical recounting of this western and European medieval period a relativized recounting, namely, a recounting of only one of the actual "worlds" within the many worlds of that particular time span.

With this excursus summarily stated, let us move to the issue of the king and the struggle to establish the source of regal power.

Although he was baptized only on his deathbed, May 22, 337, Constantine, throughout his imperial life, played an enormous role in the church. In the decade prior to his defeat of Licinius, Constantine had already "assured to the Christian religion freedom to profess and proclaim its faith, and, after giving it an initial equality with paganism, had shown it an ever more undeniable benevolence."[88]

Once Constantine becomes the sole ruler of the Roman empire, we find his imperial presence strongly affecting the internal life of the church as well as its external life. Legislation which Constantine brought about openly favored the Christian.[89] It was Constantine who convoked the Council of Arles in 314 and the even more famous Council of Nicaea in 325. It was he who set the agenda for these councils. It was he who, in a formal speech to the bishops at Nicaea, suggested the very term *homoousios,* a term which some bishops found questionable, since Paul of Samosata, a man suspected of heresy, had once used it. It was he who promulgated and enforced the creed of Nicaea.

There is an opposite side of this position of Constantine within the church structures, namely, the position of the episcopacy within the social structures:

> The Catholic episcopate gradually stepped into the place which the pagan upper class had hitherto occupied. The most intimate entourage of the Emperor at court [i.e., the bishops] reflected this new picture, an unmistakable sign of a changing world.[90]

Constantine clearly influenced the episcopal leadership of the church, but the episcopal leadership of the church, under the emperors, moved steadily into positions of power and influence within the government. Other clerics as well found places of influence in the imperial court.[91] This socio-political enhancement of the bishops and other clergy affected the way in which their *ordo* was regarded by both the clergy themselves and by the non-ordained segments of the Christian community.

Constantine, for his part, is even called by church leaders a *pontifex maximus,* which almost implies a "clerical" status.[92] Eusebius of Caesarea called him, certainly in a hyperbolic way, the thirteenth apostle and an *episkopos ton ektos,*[93] a bishop instituted by God to look after the people of his kingdom, even in matters of the religious area. Constantine fully concurred "when Christian writers compared him to Abraham and Moses and addressed him as God's vicar on earth, whose palace was the earthly reflection of the heavenly throne room."[94] Constantine was called "peer of the apostles," *isapostolos,* and was buried in the church dedicated to the twelve apostles in Constantinople. Although unbaptized until the moment of his death, he was clearly, during his long and busy life, involved in the church and at the highest level of church leadership.

> With the constitutional recognition of Christianity (313) . . . the emperor's legislative activity in religious affairs became enormous, as is seen, for instance, in the documents emanating from Constantine I (306–337), the first Christian emperor, who even considered himself as a kind of lay bishop and, as a bishop is supposed to be the shepherd of his sheep, so busied himself with often careful, but occasionally careless, cultivation of spiritual matters on an ecumenical basis.[95]

It is true that a successor of Constantine, Valentinian I, is reported to have said to some bishops who were seeking a synod: "I am only a laic and do not therefore have the right to occupy myself with such matters."[96] In many other ways, however, that same emperor, Valentinian, certainly did not consider himself "merely a lay person" in the matters of the church but involved himself deliberately in church matters precisely because he was the emperor, not because he was lay.[97] Ambrose, in particular, who had a great deal of influence in the imperial court, reminded Valentinian II of a letter of Valentinian I, in which bishops were not to be judged for any cause by non-bishops. Ambrose writes: "In case of faith or of any ecclesiastical rank he who is neither unequal in office nor dissimilar in legal right ought to judge."[98] Although this citation is often used to indicate that Ambrose should not appear before the imperial consistory in 386 because of the dispute with Auxentius, bishop of Silistria, regarding the possession of the Portian Basilica in Milan, and by extension that no bishops for any cause should be under scrutiny of any except an episcopal tribunal, the appeal Ambrose makes is to an *imperial* statement. Ambrose tells Valentinian II that his father, an emperor, had decreed otherwise. Ambrose argues not that God has determined this, but that an emperor had issued such an edict. Ambrose, not only here but elsewhere during his career, treated the emperor in a way quite different from any other "lay person."[99]

Not only in the case of Constantine himself, but throughout the centuries of Graeco-Roman rule, it is difficult to say that the emperor was "only a lay person." But, if he were not *laikos,* was he then *klerikos?* At first such a question was never posed. As long as the emperor at Constantinople was in power, such a question had no meaning. There were lay people, there were clergy, there were monks and nuns, and there was an emperor or empress. The emperor had a singular position. This singular position, both in society and in the church, continued with succeeding Graeco-Roman emperors who were hailed at their ascendency to the throne as *Neos Konstantinos,* the "new Constantine." This privilege of imperial status, moreover, had repercussions, as we shall see, far beyond the Byzantine empire, affecting both the Merovingian church and the Holy Roman Empire of the medieval period. In these latter empires, we will find again the non-lay status of the emperor, at least in the sense that he is certainly no lay man like any other lay man.

From the time of Constantine to the so-called lay investiture struggle, the church in reality was not divided into two groups: clerics and lay people. Although authors such as Gregory the Great attempted to divide the Christian world, at least on paper, into cleric/lay or cleric/monk/lay, the reality of Christian life appears to be otherwise. This reality appears to be a mixture of the following:

(a) a small but powerful group of clerics;
(b) an emperor or king together with his closest governmental leaders;

(c) a growing number of monks and nuns;

(d) and the remainder, the vast majority of "lay" men and women.

These four groups were all within the Christian world. One might wish to add to these four groups still a fifth group: those people of any and every rank outside the Christian world. These latter were called at various times the "pagans," the "unbaptized," the "unsaved," and, if they had once been Christian, the "heretics."[100] Such people were surely not clerical, certainly not imperial in the same way as the Christian emperors and kings, and they were not monks or nuns either. However, they were not *laici* either. One had to belong to the *laos,* the people of God, to merit the term "lay."

It is, however, the emperor and the immediate group which surrounds him that is the focus of this present section. Christian writers in those early times began to develop a special language and a distinctive theology for the emperor. Eventually this theology spoke of the divine right of emperors or kings. *Ex divina institutione,* a person was an emperor or a king, which made him quite different from the cleric, on the one hand, and from the ordinary lay person on the other. This way of theological thought, which began with Constantine, moved rapidly forward. At the end of 751, for instance, when Pepin was elected king by the Franks, the role of the king within the church reached a significant stage.

The anointing of Pepin as King was of decisive importance for the development of the Christian notion of the king in the West. The ruler's position in the Church was thereafter sacramentally justified, for the royal anointing was regarded as a sacrament until the Investiture Controversy.[101]

Although we are ahead of our chronology, the crowning of Pepin was simply one of many steps in this ecclesial sacramentalizing of the king. At the crowning of Charles the Great, the formula *Dei gratia rex* appears. A liturgical coronation rite gradually developed in which the apostles were called on for the pope, Mary and the angels for the king, and the martyrs for the imperial army. In the liturgical prayers of Visigothic Spain, these three groups were related to the three divine Persons: the angels to the retinue of the Father, the apostles to that of the Son, and the martyrs to that of the Spirit. Kingship began to be seen more and more as belonging to the very order of creation (the Father), while priesthood belonged to the order of redemption (the Son).[102]

In the early medieval period, the emphasis, theologically and politically, was to enhance the emperor, and, with him, those who were the closest to him in government. Only at a much later date, when difficulties arose between ruler and bishop (pope), did the higher clergy of the church strike out at this privileged position of the ruler. It is only at this later date that both western canon law and, to some degree, western theology not only formulated a strict cleric/lay division in the church, but attempted to make such a division *ex institutione divina.* One does not find such an iron-clad division of cleric/lay at the time of Constantine and his successors in Byzantium or at the time of Pepin, Charlemagne and their successors. This iron-clad division of cleric/lay began to appear when the fluidity of government and church relationships reached a chafing stage. When this period of history arrived, the non-ordained element, even if that non-ordained element were imperial, regal, or princely, was excluded from the clerical element, and this exclusion came to be described, even officially, as *ex institutione divina.* No attempt was ever made, however, to square this idea of a divine institution of the *klerikos/laikos* division of Christianity with the centuries of historical data, much of it generated by church officials, which presented the origin of the imperial or regal office as *ex institutione divina* or *Dei gratia,* i.e. by the grace and institution of God himself one is made a king. These Latin phrases, which clearly stated a divine institution for the emperor/king, had been honored by church leadership throughout the early medieval period, and the notion of God's direct providence in raising up kings had been applied to many kings of the Gallo-Roman world, and in a special way to the Frankish kings, who eventually became, also by divine grace, the Holy Roman Emperors. When *regnum* and *sacerdotium* collided, the *sacerdotium* began to maintain that *regnum* was *ex institutione sacerdotii,* even *ex institutione papali.*

During the patristic period, a "trenchant separation between the spiritual and temporal powers was still unborn."[103] The theory of the two swords, which one finds at a later date, for instance, in Boniface VIII's bull *Unam Sanctam,* developed only at a very slow pace. One often, however, is referred to the letters of Pope Gelasius I to the emperor Anastasios I.[104] When Gelasius, prior to his election as pope, was in the Lateran curia under Felix III, he had already written to the emperor Zeno in much the same way he writes to Anastasios after his election as pope.[105] Gelasius' letter is, in part, reprinted in *Denziger* (347), and the letter notes that the world is ruled by two powers: the sacred authority of bishops (*pontifices*) and the royal power. Far greater weight is awarded to the power of the bishops (*sacerdotes*) than to the emperor, for the emperor is called on to submit his neck to the leaders of the divine (*praesules divinarum*). This was written in 494. One hundred years prior to this, Optatus of Mileve had written that "the State is not in the Church, the Church is in the State, that is, in the Roman Empire."[106] At almost the same time, Ambrose had written just the opposite: "The emperor is within the Church, not over the Church."[107] One might argue that at the time of Optatus/Ambrose the issues were not as clear as they were at the time of Gelasius. However, even after Gelasius, not only will Pepin, and then Charlemagne, and then Charlemagne's successors act in ways which run counter to Gelasian thought, but church leadership will provide these regal and imperial figures with an authority that extends beyond the two-power distinction of Gelasius. Charlemagne, for instance, will be regarded and named "the vicar of Christ"; the pope, for his part, will be regarded and named only as "the vicar of Peter." This way of referring to the pope was not disputed until the late middle ages, namely the twelfth century, when the pope, for the first time ever, assumed to himself as pope the title "vicar of Christ." One finds similar attributions, which were given to the imperial/royal power by the Frankish church officials, transferred to the pope at a later date.

One can say, however, that in the post-Nicene period the rank-and-file lay Christian gradually took on a more and more negative or passive role within the church as far as leadership and liturgical participation were concerned, for the rank-and-file Christian was *not* a cleric, *not* a voice in church elections, *not* a theological teacher, *not* a church administrator, and even *not* as holy as the cleric. He was certainly not a king or emperor. K. Baus, in his description of the lay person in this patristic period, attempted to maintain some sense of the positive value for the lay person; he writes:

> Because of the differentiation of functions and still more because of the expansion of its tasks and authority in the care of souls and administration, the clergy gained such a power in authority and public respect that the previous position of the laity could not remain uninfluenced by it.[108]

There is considerable understatement in this citation, and Baus goes on to say that the consequences of these changes were not uniform throughout the Christian world of that time. Nor "was there always a question of a merely negative repudiation of lay influence, but often a shifting within its previous spheres of duty."[109] It is hard to see, however, in this shifting of previous spheres of duty, that the lay person was not shifted into a more negative situation. Baus himself does not elaborate, but immediately proceeds to note that in the basilica the place of the people became clearly distinct from the place of the clergy, and since this place of the clergy was considered "holy," no lay person was supposed to

enter it.[110] In processions, he notes, there was a definite order of precedence: clergy first, then monks, then virgins, then widows, and last of all
the "people."[111] An emperor/king also had a position of honor. By no
means did an emperor/king join the procession after monks, virgins and
widows. In some areas he was superior to all clergy; in other areas he was
second to none except the pope.

Lay persons continued to play some role in preparing the catechumens, and in case of necessity lay men might baptize, and even lay women
(if no lay men were present!) might also baptize.[112] Baus likewise notes
that the ancient right of the people to cooperate in the election of the
clergy continued in principle, but at times this meant only the acclama-
tion of the people to the candidate presented.[113] At other times, the emperor *qua* emperor, not *qua* laicus, intervened in these elections, totally
disregarding this right of the Christian people. At times the imperial intervention overrode the clerical choice of candidate as well.

4. THE CHRISTIAN MISSIONARY MOVEMENT

The missionary activity of the church, once the Constantinian period
began, is very apropos to our theme of the laity, because in this missionary
work we see the way in which new church structures were established and
the way in which lay Christians were positioned. "The term 'mission' and
its derivatives appear only in early modern times,"[114] but one finds at this
early stage of Christian life an attempt to convert neighbors and friends,
relatives and acquaintances, warring and unwarring tribes. As Christians
moved from a persecuted church to a recognized church, the impetus was
both developed and fostered to make the Christian church the *only acceptable religious group* within the empire, a situation which officially came
to pass only with Theodosius I in 380. Nonetheless, until 380 both the
emperors (with the exception of Julian) moved in this same direction, as
did the mainline Christian leadership, that is, the bishops. To attain this
goal of one empire and one church, clergy, but bishops particularly, became more and more a part of the socio-political structure. In the reformation period we hear the phrase *cuius regio illius religio.* After Theodosius'
edict, *Cunctos populos,* this same idea dominates the Byzantine empire
and this same idea is later taken over in the west by the Frankish government. The *regio* is the empire, presided over, of course, by a Christian
ruler. Therefore, only the Christian *religio* [and only the correct Christian
religio] is acceptable. In spite of the earlier edicts which allowed religious
toleration, the idea of a plurality of religious affiliation and therefore
toleration was dutifully eliminated. Christian missionary activity, in particular, was aimed during the high patristic period not only at making

people Christian, but also at eradicating, or at least neutralizing, all non-Christian elements within the missionized areas. In the several centuries in which this post-Constantine missionary movement of the Christian world took place, we find no data which acknowledges a "freedom of religion" status.[115] We find no data by church leadership which acknowledges the right of a religious body, other than the Christian one, to co-exist with the Christian community, with the exception of a certain tolerance, at times, for the Jewish (but not Samaritan) communities. On the part of the emperors, the data for this period indicates more tolerance for the Graeco-Roman religious communities to co-exist, but the data also indicates that from Constantine to Justinian the course of imperial action toward these non-Christian religions, even the traditional Roman religious forms of worship, was one of ever-decreasing tolerance, until, with Justinian, there are clear laws which totally disallow paganism. This missionary procedure, fostered by the government and pursued by the Christian leadership, was one of the major reasons why clerical status, both within the church structures and within the governmental structures, advanced during this period of time, for this leadership again and again informed the ordinary citizen what was culturally, educationally, and artistically permissible within a Christian community. This was more easily done in the west, for in the west only Latin became the *lingua franca,* with the result that only a minimum of people were exposed to the wealth of Greek culture. In the east everyone spoke, and to some degree read and wrote, the very language of the great Greek scholars, so that their writings were available on a daily basis. Education among the non-ordained in the east was easier to maintain than it was in the west.

In some instances we find that the earliest missionaries were not clerics, but lay men and women. For instance, the earliest Christian missionaries in Ethiopia (*asum*) were Frumentius and Edessus, both lay men.[116] Similarly Nivea, a lay woman, missionized at Iberia in the Black Sea. Longinus, a Christian lay man, did the same at Merewe near Khartoum. When these Christian lay men and women came to these areas, no clerics had been there. Accordingly, it was lay men and women who first established incipient Christian communities in such areas. In some cases the lay people had even constructed churches, even though there were no clerics. Nonetheless, after the establishment of these lay Christian communities, the clerical members of the church appeared, and the clerical figures almost immediately became the local Christian leaders, setting to one side the lay people who had previously been seen as the Christian leaders.

A missionizing effort took place in the central cities as well. This was a missionary effort against the Graeco-Roman pagan culture and religion. The data is abundant and clear. A few instances will indicate the intensity of this missionary effort. In 391 Christians and pagans clashed at Alexandria, since Christians had ridiculed the pagans at one of their processions. In the end the government closed the temple of Serapis and gave it to the Christians, who made it into a Christian church. Shortly after this, the temple of Isis at Menuthis was transferred by government decree to Christian ownership, and it too became a Christian sanctuary. In 415, the outstanding woman philosopher Hypatia was murdered by a fanatical mob of Christians. Abbot Schenute, head of the White Monastery in Sohag in upper Egypt, inflamed not only the monks but the Christian populace to destroy temples.[117] Rome, however, remained a sort of anomaly, for the senatorial families maintained the symbols of Roman religion, and the bishop of Rome was unable to do much about it. Only when the senatorial families began to withdraw from Rome did the bishops of Rome gain ascendancy and the Christianizing of Rome begin to take place.

Christians and their leaders, who only a few decades earlier had been the object of Roman persecution, now at times became the persecutors. There was to be no room for pagans. In the codex of Justinian, every pagan must have himself and his family instructed in the Christian faith and baptized. The penalty for not obeying this law was confiscation of property. In the same code, a Christian who reverts to a pagan religion should be punished with death. Because of Justinian's anti-pagan legislation, the neo-platonic school at Athens was closed. In Constantinople educated people, grammarians, sophists and physicians, even if these were among the aristocratic circles, were arrested, flogged, or even executed, while others were forced to convert to Christianity. In the same Justinian code we find that Jews could not testify in court in cases with Christians, nor could they purchase church property. Justinian himself interfered with their synagogue worship and forced them to use Greek or Latin translations of their writings. Samaritans, however, were summarily treated like pagans. Only rarely did Christian leadership oppose this pan-Christianizing effort, and in the few recorded instances when bishops protested, it was due to the ferocity of punishment, never to the principle of one empire/one church itself.

In all the areas where Christianity became dominant, bishops were established as the main religious leaders, together with the lesser clergy. Since these ecclesiastical leaders also had power—moral power certainly, but also at times political power—within the governmental structures, the ordinary lay person, *plebs,* was systematically set to one side. Only those lay people, connected to government, connected to wealth, and, in ever decreasing fashion, connected to learning, continued to play a role in these newly Christianized areas. If the Christian community had become simply one of several legitimized religious groups within the empire, and by no means the dominant or only religious group, the form of Christian episcopacy would have been structured in a quite different way. A differently structured episcopacy would have meant, as well, a differently structured clericalism. In turn, the ordinary lay element in the Christian community would have also been differently structured. This is not, however, the way it happened. History clearly shows that the marriage of the empire and the Christian church affected both the understanding of imperial leadership and ecclesial leadership. This marriage shaped the leadership of both sides and thereby, more indirectly than directly, shaped the *plebs,* the followers, of both sides.

As this missionary activity was going on, and more and more people joined the Christian church, the liturgy also adapted itself to new situations. From the second century on, the catechumenate was developed, with a longer period for those who either postponed baptism itself or were not ready for baptism. On this matter one should not only mention the cases of Constantine and Theodosius, who postponed their baptism, the usually cited cases, but also John Chrysostom, Gregory of Nazianz, and Basil, who also postponed their baptisms, even though they came from very pious Christian homes. John Chrysostom was about twenty-two, while Gregory and Basil were twenty-six. Not only those who might not be able to live up to the baptismal promises, but also persons who were renowned for their wisdom and holiness, postponed baptism, which indicates that such postponement was not all that negative. In the course of history, however, baptism here and there became almost a sacrament of the dying.[118] After Augustine's writings on original sin, infant baptism gradually showed an increase. Both the ordinary lay person and the catechumen celebrated the eucharistic liturgy, at least the liturgy of the word, in much the same way. Their roles during this first part of eucharistic worship were almost identical, i.e. hearers, a situation which de facto helped deposition the baptized lay man and woman. The liturgy of the word at the eucharist became highly developed, and the homilies of the great fathers of the church indicate a high level of teaching and moral persuasion presented to the non-ordained. However, as this eucharistic liturgy developed, the lay people in an ever increasing way "attended" the liturgy, even though efforts were made to involve the non-ordained through the introduction of antiphonal singing, e.g. the *Kyrie eleison,* the *Trisagion* and other responsorial songs.

The development of the ritual of reconciliation, however, was strict and kept sinners, both lay and cleric, away from any profound participation in the central life of the church. These restrictions on sinners lasted, at times, for three years, ten years, and even longer. Second relapses into post-baptismal sin brought on a lifelong separation from church participation. In the west the prohibition of marital sex after such ritualized reconciliation only increased the separation, since lay people more frequently refused to enter into the penitential discipline which disallowed them their marital privileges. The harshness of this reconciliation liturgy separated the ordinary Christian even further from the "perfect" Christians: the clerics and the monks.

The liturgical development, however, must be seen within the process of clericalization, for the various liturgies came to be more and more the enclave of the clerics, and the participation of non-clerics was systematically moved to the edges of worship.

The Christian inner-city missionary activity affected the social and recreational areas of life, for the many games which the government sponsored were also Christianized, at least in this sense, that at these *ludi* incense was not offered to the emperors or to the gods. Gladiatorial games were discontinued in part by Constantine, but only with Emperor Honorius II were they completely outlawed. Many a bishop complained, however, that when the games were in full swing, the churches were empty. The theater, too, came under clerical criticism, since the theater was at that time highly pornographic. In all of this one sees that the Christianizing of the empire affected all parts of one's life, including the religious, the social, the economic, and the recreational. The goal of both bishop and emperor, though perhaps for different emphases, was indeed that expressed so clearly by Justinian: one empire, one church, one emperor.

The Christian missionary movement provides one with the following framework:

A. TIME OF PERSECUTIONS   Christian writers and leaders seek the right of co-existence, or Christians prefer martyrdom.

B. TIME OF TOLERATION   Christian writers and leaders move more and more into the socio-political power structures.

C. TIME OF THE RELIGION OF THE EMPIRE   Christian leaders become intolerant of any religion other than Christianity.

If one were to expand the idea of "mission" somewhat so as to include the care of the poor, one would have another key element of this period of church history and the positioning of the lay person. At the time of Constantine down to Justinian, the eastern part of the empire experienced urban poverty, often in extreme ways. In the western part of the empire, in that same time-span, rural poverty was rife. Roman emperors, prior to Constantine, had already given examples of governmental care for the poor, and this same royal task was continued after 324. As the Christian church became central to the imperial structures, bishops and monks became co-workers with the emperor in this matter of care for the poor. "The fact that Julian thought of setting up pagan charitable institutions shows the extent to which social aid institutions had by this time become firmly established under Christian influence."[119] The sermons of Chrysostom, Basil, Gregory of Nyssa, Ambrose and Gregory the Great urged care for the indigent, and these speakers also castigated those who oppressed them. In this respect the gospel ideals are powerfully present in the patristic church. Little insight into the structural causes of poverty, however, were noted, either by church leader or by imperial leader.[120]

In the early Merovingian period and then into the beginnings of the Frankish period, the western church experienced poverty and plague in an enormous way. The growing numbers of people, artisans and farmers, who became *pauperes* and *vagi,* must be seen as another major factor in the repositioning of the lay person. Although the stress in this chapter is on the repositioning effects due to the socio-political and ecclesiastical structuring of clergy, this stress represents only one of several major causes why the lay person was repositioned and depositioned.

5. GREGORY THE GREAT AND DIONYSIUS AREOPAGITA

These two important Christian figures are linked together, not because they worked in tandem or even knew each other, not because they might possibly have lived at least in times close to one another, but because they both wrote about the ordering of the universe in a way which profoundly influenced the western Christian worlds which succeeded them. The emphasis on *ordo,* which both writers made so central to their vision, provided the subsequent Christian generations with a theological basis for the *ordines* in church structure, and indirectly provided a still later Christian generation of theologians with an "ontological" base for the distinction between those in orders and those who were not ordained.

Carole Straw, in the introduction to her work on Gregory, paints a quite subtle portrait of this quite subtle man.[121] Gregory is both monk and competent church administrator. He has a "breadth of personality and vocation that has intrigued and, on occasion, baffled historians."[122] He is artless, honest, practical; he is deeply pious and monastic, but well trained in the Latin world of stoicism, neo-platonism, pythagoreanism and hippocratism. His knowledge of Greek appears to be non-existent, but in translation he appears to have read Origen, Gregory of Nazianz and Gregory of Nyssa.[123]

Gregory, first of all, saw the world as highly integrated: the earthly and heavenly, the carnal and the spiritual, the divine and the diabolical. The highly transcendent world of Christian antiquity is replaced by Gregory with a far more immanent or sacramental world. Based on this sacramental worldview, Gregory moves to a description of society. This society, like God himself, is ordered and organized.

> For he who marvelously created all things ordered all creation so that it would harmonize with itself. Where the Creator is resisted, the peace of harmony is dissipated, since things cannot be ordered which lose the management of heavenly government. For the things that are subject to God remain in tranquility, and those that have been abandoned to themselves bring disorder and confusion upon themselves.[124]

Life, for Gregory, is a hierarchical continuum. "The Church, however, is not without orderly degrees of distinction. If hierarchical order keeps peace and tranquility in secular affairs, how much the more must it exist in the Church to avoid discord and confusion?"[125] Just as God both in himself and in his creation is orderly, so, too, the church and society are ordered in a hierarchical way. At the time of Gregory, the major obligation of a monk was obedience, and through such obedience monastic life was an orderly life. A similar obedience was to characterize the Christian within the church's hierarchical structure: "Through obedience to another, one needs neither to judge nor to examine the decisions of one's superiors, but simply execute them happily."[126]

In Gregory's writings one finds a strong theological justification for a hierarchical order, both in the socio-political world and in the ecclesiastical world. When one realizes that throughout much of the middle ages the ordinary parish priest simply read passages from Gregory as his Sunday homily, one can appreciate the extent of Gregory's influence through his writings. If one adds to this the way in which medieval theologians used the writings of Gregory to bolster their positions, then one is equally astounded at the influence of this man.[127]

For Gregory, the ideal church would have the leader, rector, a holy man or saint. The Gregorian saint is, however, the monk.[128] In the ideal church the episcopal ordering and the monastic ordering would be almost identical. In the ideal world the ideal social structure would have only holy rulers, so that the ruler would reflect monastic saintliness as well.[129] In the real world, however, neither the church nor the government is ideal, so that the *rectores* of the church exhibit non-saintly characteristics, which Gregory sees as the "secularism" of the church, and the governmental structures are perceived as antithetical to Christian holiness (i.e. monastic holiness). Ideally, church and government should work hand in hand, and in this Gregory longs for a continued marriage of the two. Practically, at times, the aims of the church and the aims of government are dissimilar, and so Gregory advocates a stance of hostility, i.e. the position which the Donatists favored. Although Gregory at times urges the leaders of the church to eschew the ways of the society world, nonetheless the ideal which he pursues and places before both church and society is one of confluence. Thus, he continues the goals of the so-called Constantinian church.

His theologizing on order within both society and ecclesial hierarchy provides later theologians with a basis to distinguish the church on the basis of hierarchy. The holy person who is filled with the wisdom of the Inward Teacher is a rarity.[130] "Gregory's achievement in the *Dialogues* lies in placing these servants of God with their real power of divine inspiration firmly with the Church's hierarchy."[131] There is order in holiness, and this holiness can be found in the order within the church. This order in the church is based on the order of creation.[132] Once creation becomes central, the foundation for an ontology of sacred orders has been set in place. Sacred orders (eventually) will be seen on the basis of being, i.e. creation, which reflects Being, i.e. the "ordered" deity.

Gregory the Great did not see the Christian world and therefore the secular world as well divided into two: cleric and lay. Rather, his view was tripartite: the ordained cleric, the monk, and the lay person. It was this view of Gregory which dominated theoretically the entire middle ages until Gratian's twofold division: cleric/lay. Practically, however, there are four distinct areas: cleric, emperor, monk and lay. One finds this fourfold *praxis* even in Gregory as he dealt with the emperors at Constantinople, with the exarch at Ravenna,[133] with the leaders of the Lombards. Gregory did not deal with governmental leadership nor view governmental leadership in the same way he dealt with and viewed the ordinary lay persons in the church.

Dionysius Areopagita remains even today a mysterious individual. H.-G. Beck, basing himself on U. Riedinger, implies that this man is none other than Peter the Fuller.[134] Even this position is filled with problems. Whoever Dionysius might be and whenever the exact time of his life may have been remain somewhat secondary to the fact that he, like Gregory, influenced the middle ages in no small degree.[135] Dionysius wrote, somewhat mystically at times, about the hierarchical structures of both heaven and earth. Earthly hierarchies reflect divine hierarchies, but this implies that earthly hierarchies have the blessing, the endorsement, the power, to some degree, of the divine hierarchies.

> He [Denis] has three levels of reality: God, the angelic (or celestial) hierarchy, and the ecclesiastical hierarchy, in descending order. . . . The ecclesiastical hierarchy (itself seen as being midway between the 'legal' hierarchy of the Old Testament and the celestial hierarchy) consists again of three ranks of three: first the rank of the mysteries into which we are initiated . . . [baptism, eucharist, holy oil]; secondly the rank of those who perform the mysteries . . . [episkopoi, presbyters, deacons]; thirdly the rank of those who are being initiated . . . [monks, laity, and the catechumens/penitents].[136]

To oppose earthly hierarchies is to oppose divine hierarchies. Dionysius himself describes hierarchy as "sacred order and knowledge and activity which is being assimilated as much as possible to likeness with God and, in response to the illuminations that are given it from God, raises itself to the imitation of him in its own measure."[137] All these hierarchies are divided into various orders, *tychai*, and the positioning of these various orders must be respected. For Dionysius they reflect not merely reality, but above all divine reality. To stand in opposition to these *tychai* is to stand in opposition to being and to the source of being, God.

Like Gregory, Dionysius brought together church hierarchy and civil hierarchy, church hierarchy and the hierarchy of creation, and church hierarchy and the orderliness of God. In synthesizing these various orders, we have a clear attempt to theologize the *ordines* (*tychai*) of the church, and this theological attempt because of its basis in creation (being) indirectly provides the later scholastic theologians with their proposed "ontological" base to distinguish those who are ordained from those not ordained.[138] The mystical element in Dionysius, reminiscent of both Plotinus and Proclus, involves a series of withdrawals "first from involvement in civil society, then from the tyranny of sense, and finally through a process of introversion and self-knowledge to the knowledge of the supreme being."[139] Nonetheless, the ecclesiastical hierarchy and the civil hierarchy, if they work together, are powerful means to lead one into the higher orders. For Dionysius, there is no essential antagonism toward the civil area, nor toward a union of the civil and the ecclesiastical per se.

6. CONCLUSIONS FROM THE DATA

The following conclusions are not meant to be a summary of the material which we have just considered. Rather, these conclusions are meant to indicate the significance of this important period in Christian church history.

1. From 324 to 731 the Christian church, through its leaders and its educated members, developed a *modus vivendi* with the socio-political rulers of that era. From a minority group, struggling to maintain itself physically and to present itself as trustworthy within a hostile rulership, the Christian community was at first awarded, through acts of toleration, the right to exist, and then, as time went on, this religious group came to be the only religious group with an official right to exist in the empire.

In the high patristic period, 324 to 731, as the clergy, particularly the upper clergy, became more and more an integral part of the socio-political world, church leadership deliberately developed a position of intolerance toward other religious movements, and this same leadership justified this intolerance on the basis of the gospel. During the time of the persecutions, on the other hand, that is, the centuries preceding this Constantinian church, when being a Christian was not a socio-political asset, we find, among the apologists particularly, an effort to make the Christian faith acceptable or tolerable within the larger social world. In other words, there was an effort to present Christianity in a way which allowed Christians a sort of equal position, or at least a minority position, within a predominantly non-Christian world. In this earlier period there was a strong effort to present the characteristics of the way in which a disciple of Jesus should live within a world that was not exclusively or even predominantly Christian. To do this, for instance, Aristides' *Apology* described a Christian in a way that his readers might be happy to have him or her live next door.[140] Justin's first *Apology* opens (cc. 4–12) with a censure of the government's attitude toward and procedures against the Christians; the second part (cc. 13–67) is a presentation of the doctrine and worship of the Christians, written in a way in which governmental leaders might find such Christians acceptable members within the non-Christian, Graeco-Roman world. Athanagoras' *Supplication for the Christians* is equally a document of persuasion for the legitimacy of the Christian community.[141] The rather well-known passage from the *Epistle to Diognetus* follows the same pattern. Christians are fine people, indeed excellent people, and enhance the fabric of the Graeco-Roman world.[142]

A totally new situation, however, developed with the Constantinian period. The Christian community had to come to grips in a new way with the socio-political cadre which had only recently set up pogroms against it, and which was now making positive overtures to it. The key to understand this era, for our purposes, is this: to explain both how and why the Christian community related eventually in such an intimate way with the political and social world in which it lived.

2. As we have seen, there were several alternatives open to the Christian community as regards the relationship between church and the socio-political world. The Constantinian emperors saw in an open, positive relationship great benefits for the unity of the empire, and the church leadership, for its part, saw in the same open, positive relationship the benefit of making the church viable and strong. Both imperial leadership and church leadership opted, in general and in substance, for a marriage. Frontiers, boundaries, spheres of influence were not delineated at first, and the next few centuries saw each side setting boundaries and breaking boundaries, opening boundaries and closing boundaries. Neither mainline church leader nor imperial leader, however, with the exception of Julian, proposed anything other than a close relationship between church and empire.

3. The church leaders, through this union, gained enormous power within the socio-economic structures of the empire. Per se, they had no immediate official status as a civil servant, but the church leaders clearly felt a responsibility to exert moral pressure on both emperor and subject alike, in all matters which related to doctrine and right living (faith and morals, as the terms eventually came to be called). Since the empire in short time came to be seen as a Christian empire, the Christian leadership influenced not only the emperors in their decision-making activities, but also the rank and file citizenry whose lives were led within this Christian world. *Ubi Christianitas, ibi auctoritas ecclesiae.* Since every aspect of one's life was supposedly Christian, church authority, that is, the clerical authority, could consequently make itself felt in every aspect of a person's life. At this time, there was no conceivable area open to a "lay autonomy" or to a "lay independence." Clerical intervention in ordinary lay life became part and parcel of the *societas Christiana,* and this was given a theological basis in the hierarchical thinking developed by Gregory and Dionysius. The opposite, however, was not true. The ordinary lay Christian had no entry into the clerical areas, no way of influencing decision-making processes. Those lay Christians who did have such influence had this potential not in virtue of their lay status, but in virtue of their status as

emperor or connection to the emperor, or in virtue of their economic status.

4. This new position of the church within the socio-political world gave rise to a description of discipleship which had distinctive social over-tones. One came to be a disciple of Jesus in all aspects of the Roman world: in family, in work, in recreation, in government. Being a disciple included the obligation to be a "missionary," i.e. make disciples of all nations. Conversion of those not yet Christian, or not yet Christian in an orthodox way, was incumbent on all. In this missionary obligation, Christian discipleship was not only a religious issue, but also a social issue. Non-Christian elements had to be made ineffectual within the empire, at times even through force. One empire, one religion came to be seen as the logical outcome of the gospels. The goal of a *societas Christiana* was to be achieved by all Christians, but especially by the leaders of such a society, both socio-political leaders and ecclesiastical leaders. To work for this goal was an essential element of discipleship.

5. This union of church/empire developed gradually, and the con-tours of this union created a pattern which the western Roman church made normative for its own purposes during many subsequent centuries. We see this normative structure, one empire-one religion, in the western world as it has unfolded down to present times:

a. The way in which the western Church comported itself to the Merovingian, the Frankish and the Ottonian empires.

b. The claims of both Innocent III and Boniface VIII that the pope is supreme over any and every state.

c. The negative reaction on the part of Roman Catholic leadership to the reformation principle: *cuius regio illius religio,* at least when the *regio* was not governed by a member of the Roman Catholic *religio.*

d. The apprehension among Roman Catholic Church leadership at the time of the French and American revolutions. Both the auton-omy of the lay area and the pluralistic forms of co-existence were viewed with alarm and decried as theologically incorrect. Evil and error, it was claimed, had no rights, including no civil rights.

e. The dispute over religious freedom at Vatican II, which created the most strident and shrill debates, and which reflected, even in the twentieth century, the pattern of the patristic period as regards the normative way for a government and a church to interrelate.

f. The response by Roman Catholic Church leadership to the open-ing of eastern Europe to the west, which is taking place in our own day and age. The call for a "Christian Europe" does not seem to include either the Orthodox, the Protestants or the Anglicans. The call appears to be a return to one empire and one religion, i.e. Roman Catholic religion.

Again and again, Roman Catholic leadership appears to indicate that the ideal relationship between the church and any socio-political entity is one in which the Roman Catholic Church is the only religion, and in which government furthers both the doctrines and the morals of this one and only religious structure. In doing this, the patristic period, which we have just considered, is, directly or indirectly, used as "normative." This is why, in my view, an understanding of the church/socio-political relationship of the patristic period is so important for the study of the lay/cleric church. Central to this patristic view is (a) the issue that there must be hierarchical order, both in church and in government, and (b) the view that whenever these two hierarchical orders are of one mind, the world will be closer to its ideal. This means that the ideal world order is a *societas Christiana Romana Catholica.* Such reasoning, however, is questionable today. First of all, one must be careful as regards any hierarchical structuring, for such structuring often implies the "perfect" and the "less perfect," the "rulers" and the "ruled," the "ones who know" and the "ones who are ignorant." When one searches for the criteria to distinguish one from the other in this hierarchic framework, one finds a variety of such criteria: knowledge, sex, race, economic position, divine choice. Too often a given status in society, whether socio-political or ecclesiastical, has been endowed with a theological basis, and this theologizing of a given hierarchical structure then tends to make it untouchable. We see this, for instance, in the way that a theology of holy order, with its "ontological difference" between ordained and non-ordained, makes the sacrament of holy order in many ways superior to the sacrament of initiation (baptism/confirmation/eucharist). Baptized/eucharistic people are ontologically not different, followed by the next step: they are ontologically inferior to the ordained. Secondly, care must be taken when one describes the "ideal world." Most portraits of an ideal world derive from a single view, even a single theological view, which is seen not only as orthodox but also as mono-orthodox, i.e. the only orthodox position. In a pluralistic world such as ours, a mono-orthodoxy like this can lead to a disdain of any other competing presentation of an "ideal world," including even the positive elements within such a competing view.

6. There are, however, additional factors which stem from this normative valuing of the patristic position, and some of these other factors involve the status of the lay person in the church. In the pattern and program of the patristic period, the church's clerical leadership—bishops,

patriarchs, and popes, in particular—not only had a position within the church itself, but also wielded enormous moral and suasive power within the governmental structures. Church leadership, in this format, could speak out on any and all issues which involved either doctrinal matters or moral matters. Since the ideal was a Christian government, this left in actuality no governmental or socio-political area which was autonomous or untouchable by the church's leadership. However, this leadership of the clerical element within the socio-political field was not only directed to the socio-political leaders, but was also directed to the ordinary lay person. In this normative construct of church and society, the ordinary lay person had his or her place, and it was a secondary place as far as the clerical position was concerned. In the tenth and eleventh centuries, when the lay brothers attempted to reassert themselves within the monastic framework, the response was a renewed clericalizing of the monastic life.

In the twelfth and thirteenth centuries, in which lay men and women attempted to reassert themselves through the various *vita evangelica* movements, the church leadership responded by bringing such movements under clerical control or by evicting them from the church. In the reassertion of the lay person in the church, which was a part of the intellectual fomentation of the late medieval world with its many lay intellectuals and which spilled over into the Protestant reformation, the response of the Roman Catholic Church was to denounce the "priesthood of all believers" as inconsistent with true Catholic doctrine, to emphasize anew the position of the cleric, and to place theological thought almost exclusively into the post-tridentine seminary system. In the reassertion of the lay person in the French and American revolutions with their emphases on the dignity, freedom and equality of each human individual, the response of the Catholic leadership was fierce. The very term "lay" came to mean "anti-clerical," not anti-human-dignity, not anti-human-freedom, not anti-human-equality. All lay movements in the nineteenth and early twentieth centuries which were not under clerical control were regarded as both anti-Catholic and anti-clerical, and these two "anti" issues were seen as one: to be Catholic one had to be clerical. In the rise of the lay movements in the twentieth century only those lay movements which were under the control of the hierarchy were given the endorsing title "lay apostolate." All others were officially disallowed by church leadership.

7. The recent feminist movements, with their reevaluation of historical data, finds opposition from mainline orthodox Catholic theology on the basis of the time-honored and consequently normative positioning of church leadership vis-à-vis both ecclesiastical and socio-political structures. By this I mean, that the standard view of the *societas Christiana*, as developed in the early patristic period, precludes *a priori* the demands of

contemporary feminist thinkers. These feminist demands are, it seems, considered "out of line," because the image of this so-called normative *societas Christiana* is not open to such feminist demands. In the hierarchical position which the patristic period developed, and which set both a pattern and eventually a program for subsequent Christian generations, the position of women was not central. The few instances in which a woman came to the fore during the first millennium were most often not due to her womanly person within this structure, but due to the fact (a) that she was an empress or queen or close to the imperial/royal family, (b) that she was an educated person of unique credentials, (c) that she was (as we shall see in the next chapter) a powerful leader within the monastic life, or (d) that she was a woman of independent wealth. Not her person, but other factors, accounted for her position of strength within this church-government structure. That some women, particularly in the later middle ages, attempted to break out of these constraints and exert themselves precisely as women cannot be denied, but it is also interesting to note that these efforts often went aground because they moved against the normative positioning in both church and socio-political structures. The negative response to these feminist endeavors may not be due, in the first place, to an anti-feminine stance, but rather to a defense of a perceived normative structure, which one might call the idealized *societas Christiana*. The fundamental argument by many feminist theologians against this defense of structure is based on a contemporary reexamination of the meaning of gospel-discipleship.

8. So, too, the current movements of and for the poor, namely the various liberation theologies of the African poor, the South American poor, and the black religious movements in the United States, must be seen against this same so-called normative positioning of the church vis-à-vis socio-political structures. In those areas where Christianity has made deep roots, the poor too often have been set to one side, on the pretext that social and ecclesial order must be maintained. The current rising of the poor, not only against economic and social discrimination, but even more so against the very causes of this discrimination, causes which can at times be located in the stance of certain clerical hierarchies, are indeed a rising against a view of "order," even church order, which has been justified with both theological and ontological theories. The justification of this protest by the poor and their leaders against a given view of hierarchical church structure is based on a most firm foundation: a return to the gospel portrait of discipleship. "Return to your sources" was a command of the bishops at Vatican II to religious communities. "Return to your sources" is a command to all who follow Jesus, and those sources include in a most

basic way the New Testament, with its amazing boundary-breaking inclusivity.

As noted above, there were two "theses" which have governed the presentation of this chapter. First of all, there was the precise manner in which church leadership gradually structured the relationship of both church leadership and church community to the governmental structures; this fostered relationship of church leadership to governmental structures subsequently intensified the repositioning and subsequent depositioning of the ordinary, non-ordained Christian within the church. This pattern is a major aetiological base to the central medieval question of *regnum et sacerdotium.* Hopefully, I have indicated the multidimensional ways in which this structuring came about. Second, as this issue of church-empire, and then *regnum et sacerdotium,* became so centralizing, it began to shape the way in which discipleship was understood. Discipleship, as found in the New Testament, gradually ceased to be the primary criterion for the way in which this relationship of church/empire developed; rather, the way in which the relationship of church to empire developed became the primary criterion that was used to present a theology of discipleship. If, on the other hand, the church/empire and the later *regnum et sacerdotium* issue is seen as a highly relativized issue, given a view of a much wider world than any Constantinian or early western medievalist person dreamed of, then the way in which church and empire related can itself only be seen as a highly relativized criterion for discipleship, and certainly not the primary criterion. Clinging to this relativized position, church leadership over the last centuries has attempted to maintain a positioning of the ordinary Christian which is anachronistic. Church leadership, by using this criterion to interpret discipleship, cannot be seen today as a true gauge of measurement.

No period in church history, the apostolic or sub-apostolic periods included, is normative in any absolute way. One finds in each and every period of church history elements which are of value, and elements which are detrimental. Each period of church history has a relative quality about it. This applies to the pattern and program of church/empire relationships of the high patristic period. This relationship cannot be seen in an absolute way; it has profound values and it has severe limitations. One cannot maintain a view of "one empire/one religion" as the ideal. There will never be an ideal form of "empire" and there will never be an ideal form of "religion."

Rather, Christian communities must, in each period of church history, return to the issue of discipleship. Each generation of Christians must return to the New Testament, the very word of God, and ask anew:

How does it portray a disciple of Jesus? Each generation of Christians must review its multiple histories, its manifold traditions, and ask again: How have past generations attempted to live out gospel discipleship? In this historical review, care must be taken to assess candidly the strengths and the weakness which belong to each generation's attempt at gospel discipleship. Such a review allows us to see the insights and the smallness of former generations of Christians.

In the period 324–731 it was this socio-political aspect of church/empire which in so many ways dominated and in one form or another became normative. However, it is important to realize that there was another movement which arose at this very time, namely, monasticism, and this movement, though not contributing directly to the church/empire relationship, did contribute a way of viewing discipleship which has remained both enriching and enigmatic to the church structures down to the present day. Let us consider this movement in detail.

6

Monasticism to 600 A.D.

The rise of the anchoritic and monastic life within the Christian church was, in its own time, a far-reaching and powerful phenomenon, and in the ensuing centuries of church history, both in the east and in the west, this ascetical movement has had a continued reverberation. As far as the role of the lay person in the church is concerned, both its beginnings and its continued history are of enormous consequence. On the one hand, the first few centuries of both the anchoritic and the monastic movements were overwhelmingly non-clerical, and for the male religious this lasted, more or less, down to the ninth century in western church history. The word to note is "overwhelming." In this early period the few clerics who joined these monastic groups generally remained, percentage-wise, small in numbers, and by no means did they play a commanding administrative role within monasticism itself. The non-clerical character of early religious life, both male and female, is historically well documented and highly significant for an understanding of the "lay" person in the church.

On the other hand, the emergence of the monastic form of religious life created a sort of "alternative church." This term "alternative Church" does not mean that monastic life developed because of any antagonism to the official, episcopal or clerical church structures. Such an antagonism does not appear in the earliest literature of the monastic movement. On the contrary, there was at first a mutual respect and honor, and, on the part of the monastic communities, a deference to the local bishops. One finds this spirit of respect for episcopal churches throughout the early monastic period. Only gradually and only here and there, throughout the period 250 to 600 A.D., does one find a growing tension, even at times an hostility, between episcopal authority and inner-monastic authority. The meaning of an "alternative church," which at first blush might seem to play bishop against abbot, is used in this present context to refer more to an alternative style of Christian life. Why is it that at the end of the third and the beginning of the fourth centuries, men like Anthony and Pachomias, who wanted to follow Christ and be his disciple in a thoroughgoing way, did not enter into the clerical structures of the church? Why is it that there were so many similar-minded Christian men who preferred to follow the path of discipleship found in the anchoritic and monastic world, rather than in the world of the clerical or episcopal churches? Evidently the form of discipleship which the clerical or episcopal church structure offered was not seen as the only form of discipleship, nor even as the more desirable form of discipleship. In this sense, then, there was an alternative church—namely, an alternative way of being a disciple of the Lord.

Historically one might say that there were two ways of being "lay" in the church during these centuries. The first way was that of the ordinary husband and wife, mother and father, artisan and farmer. The second way was the ascetic and celibate monk or nun. In time this second way came to be viewed as the "better" way. The first hermits, monks and nuns, however, did not in any deliberate way set out to "out-do" the other lay people. Yet with time the notion of an elite or "perfect" Christian life within monasticism began to mature. Naturally, if there was an elite group of Christians, there was as well a "non-elite" group of Christians. If there was a "perfect" group of Christians, then there had to be an "imperfect" or "less-perfect" group of Christians. In comparison with the hermits, monks and nuns, the non-elite group or imperfect group of Christians came to be identified at times with either the ordinary Christian or even the ordained Christian, with either cleric or non-cleric. The "religious" were considered to be in a special class of Christian discipleship, a sort of *tertium quid.*

It is precisely this *tertium quid* factor of the monastic group which slowly but quite clearly (along with the positioning of the emperor) began to becloud any over-arching and sharp distinction as regards the incipient appearance of a *klerikos/laikos* church. From Gratian onward, that is, from the twelfth century onward, canonists and theologians, as well as church officials, have made every effort to understand the church by means of a rather absolute cleric/laic prism. Nonetheless, the presence in the church of "religious" men and women has been part of a continuing critique of this *klerikos/laikos* form of thinking. There is a *klerikos* way of discipleship of the Lord, there is a *laikos* way of discipleship, and there is a *monastic* or religious way of discipleship. We have even seen, in the preceding chapter, that there was an *imperial* way of discipleship as well. Try as one may to cram the entire Christian world into the two boxes of cleric/lay, the historical data on Christian discipleship continually critiques such a simplistic and ideological position.

In the following few pages, a complete history of the anchoritic and monastic movements, and therefore of religious life, would be an impossible task. Other authors have presented this material at great length, and in contemporary literature there have been major studies on this history.[1] My aim is far more modest but hopefully of value. I would like to present a sort of two part "thesis," or working hypothesis, namely:

PART ONE:
The presence, development and variety of the anchoritic and monastic movements within the church, both east and west, undermine the monolithic, either-or form and definition, which a *klerikos/laikos* model of Church structure has bequeathed to us.

PART TWO:
As a second aspect of this thesis, I would like to show that "religious life" at its inception was not in itself a monolithic structure, with an "essence" that one can find thereafter in every religious community.

PART ONE

The undermining process cannot be found at the very origins of the anchoritic and monastic movements, because at the time of its inception the general way of understanding the church, i.e. the self-consciousness of the church, was not molded by the *klerikos/laikos* model. Nonetheless, the rootage of the *klerikos/laikos* model was indeed already present in that period of church history, but, as we have seen above, not in a self-conscious and clearly defined way. When, in the course of later church history, both church leaders and church teachers began to stress the *klerikos/laikos* model in a self-conscious and clearly defined way, the de facto presence of the monks and nuns continually posed a different model, i.e. a threefold model of church, thus undermining to some degree the juridical and even ontological *klerikos/laikos* model of church.[2]

The monastic critique of the *klerikos/laikos* division of Christianity is already found in many earlier Christian writers. These writers seem to have based their description of the various groups within the church on sections from the writings of Origen, in which he uses Noah, Daniel and Job as representatives of Christian life.[3] In the west Augustine distinguished three symbolic representatives of Christian life, and his threefold division influenced almost all the monastic leaders of the middle ages.[4] An anonymous writer of the middle ages wrote: "There are three orders in the Church: Noah, Job, Daniel. Noah [represents] the teachers, Job the married, and Daniel the contemplatives."[5] And a later medieval writer expresses the same:

From both sexes of the faithful, we know that there are three orders [*ordines*], as if three classes [*gradus*], in the holy and universal Church; of which, although none is without sin, the first is nevertheless good; the second better; and the third is the best. The first order [*ordo*] exists in both sexes of married people; the second in the continent and widows; the third in the virgins and nuns. Likewise, there are three grades or orders [*gradus vel ordines*] of men: of which the first is that of the lay, the second that of the clerics and the third that of the monks.[6]

Through the influence of Origen, Augustine and Gregory the Great, it was the overwhelming view of the patristic and early medieval periods of church history that there were three major categories or orders or grades among Christians: the clerics, the religious, the lay. In practice, however, the fourth, i.e. the imperial, was clearly evident. When, in the twelfth century, the effort was made to divide Christianity into only two groups, the presence of the religious remained both an anomaly to and a critique of such a reduction.

This monastic critique of the *klerikos/laikos* model was mitigated, however, when there occurred an eventual over-clericalization and therefore under-laicization of the male monastic structures. When this process of clericalization of the male religious took place in the ninth, tenth and eleventh centuries, male monastic discipleship slowly but ineluctably began to find its own self-identity within an ideologically pre-conceived *klerikos/laikos* format.

PART TWO

Over many centuries, and particularly in the twentieth century, there have been several attempts to formulate the "essence" of religious life in a monolithic way, i.e. in a way which will apply to all manifestations of religious life within the Catholic Church. Historical studies seem to indicate that such attempts are doomed to failure, precisely because these so-called "essences" of religious life have generally been developed, from late medieval times onward, precisely on the basis of a pre-determined *klerikos/laikos* church structure. Actually, the varieties of religious-life movements, which have occurred again and again within the church, exist as a continual challenge to the very way in which both church teachers and church officials have attempted to establish an "essence" of religious life. Variety of monastic and anchoritic life is neither tangential nor secondary to these forms of discipleship, but is part of the very center of such movements, so that in spite of the fact that we speak of the anchoritic and monastic movements in a generic way, the differences in anchoritic and monastic life, which one finds even in the early data, indicate a complexity which is ignored whenever there has been an attempt to describe these religious movements on the basis of a single-essence model. Early anchoritic and monastic movements were clearly seen as a "flight" from the world. The anchoritic and monastic movements set people apart from the socio-economic structures. However, in the course of time, once a full Christianizing of the socio-economic structures had taken place, i.e. in eighth, ninth, tenth and eleventh centuries of western Europe, a "domestication" of monastic life took place. Monks and nuns were seen as "essential" to the Christian structuring of the *societas Christiana,* and no longer as a flight (*fuga*) from society. This domestication process was aided in no small measure by trying to make the various religious groups essentially similar to one another. The profoundly rich complexity of the anchoritic and monastic movements, which one finds at their inception and which continued to some degree throughout church history, radically questions both the process of domestication and the process of monolithic essentialization.

The goal of the following pages is, consequently, modest: namely, to ascertain the significance of the early stages of this anchoritic and monastic phenomenon as regards the Christian use of the *klerikos/laikos* model of church. In what ways have the ascetical movements of early anchoritic and monastic life shaped the Christian understanding of the non-ordained person in the church? In what ways have these same movements criticized the simplistic formulation inherent in a *klerikos/laikos* model? In this shaping of the non-ordained Christian's identity, were there advantages? Were there drawbacks? Naturally, by keeping this narrow focus on the non-ordained or "lay" element, many other issues will have to be either abridged or presupposed.

We will consider the issues in monasticism from 250 to 600 under the following headings:

1. **The Causes and Motives for This Movement**
2. **The Geographical Scope of This Early Movement**
3. **The Ecclesiologies of Early Monasticism**
4. **Conclusions from the Data**

1. THE CAUSES AND MOTIVES FOR THIS MOVEMENT

Even though Antony of Egypt is called the "father of Egyptian monasticism," it appears that he was not the first to begin this form of life. There were others before him, both in the Thebaid and the Nitrian Desert, as well as in the countryside around Edessa in eastern Syria, who had moved away from the centers of population to lead a hermitical life. Some of these men were strictly hermits, so it appears, living in almost complete solitude; others apparently attached themselves to a spiritual guide, even as they stayed in their solitary form of life.[7] Nonetheless, both the prestige of Athanasius, who wrote the *Vita S. Antonii,* and Antony's own charismatic personality have allowed the title of "Father of Egyptian Monasticism" to be given to this man, who in 273 left his village of Kome to live in some burial chambers near that town. This way of departure from city and village life to take up an ascetical life, either as an anchorite or as a member of a monastic community, swept across the Christian world in a phenomenal way.

What caused this powerful phenomenon to take place, and why precisely did this happen at the end of the third and the beginning of the fourth centuries? No satisfactory answers have as yet been established. Some authors try to find a relationship of this Christian movement with the Katochoi of the Egyptian god Serapis.[8] Others have looked to the religious and philosophical sides of neo-Platonism and neo-Pythagoreanism.[9] Still others have tried to trace its cause in Manichaeanism, and indirectly through Manichaeanism from early Buddhism, especially those forms of Buddhism which took root in Syrian Mesopotamia.[10] More recently, authors have turned to the Qumran communities, with particular interest in their possible relationship to the Pachomian communal form of ascetical life.[11] Still others have attempted to find in Old Testament Jewish history the basis for Christian ascetical life.[12] These several phenomena appear to be the main rootages which scholars have studied to find an aetiological pattern for this Christian movement. They all have a conjectural side, of course, and the arguments pro and con will undoubtedly continue. Some sort of ascetical movement is often found in various world religious movements, and in this Christianity is no exception. On the other hand, it is also clear that there is a specifically "Christian" aspect to this movement which disallows rootage in anything else except the Jesus movement itself. This specifically Christian aspect is the anchoritic and monastic focus on Jesus' life, death and resurrection, and secondarily on the way in which the early apostolic community at Jerusalem, namely that portrayed in Acts, tried to put this life, death and resurrection of Jesus into practice. It is a focus on discipleship.

One has also asked the question why men and women would have left the forms of life they were used to and in isolation lead such different and difficult forms of life. It is perhaps easier to ferret out these motives than it is to uncover the more generalized causes for this ascetical phenomenon. We could outline the main motives that scholars have presented as follows:

A. The desire to follow Jesus is the basic motive. Because of this connection with Jesus, the movement is clearly and decidedly a Christian movement.
B. Because of their desire to imitate Christ, the monks sought out a life of suffering; they wished to die together with Christ.
C. The monks felt that by doing this they were entering more deeply into salvation history. Thus, although their life was solitary, they were in communion with Abraham and Moses, with John the Baptist, with Jesus, with Peter and Paul, and with the many martyrs and saints who had gone before them.
D. The primitive church appeared to be some sort of a model, but the age of the martyrs was also motivating. This relationship to Christ, to the primitive church and to the martyrs helped to identify their life with a catchword: namely, the angelic life. Anchorites and monks strove to lead an angelic life (which meant a risen life) already here on earth.
E. The imminent expectation of the parousia was also part of the motivation, and this is most apparent in the early phase of the monastic movement.
F. A motive which does not seem to have been prevalent at all, at least at the beginning, was that of a protest against the organized, clerical church of the day. This anti-organized church motive does appear in some areas of later monasticism, but it does not seem to have played any role in the initial formation of monasticism.
G. Early anchorites and monks were clearly dissatisfied with a "secular" way of life. They did not want to be artisans or farmers, teachers or civil servants. Nothing in the secular forms of life, including marriage, appealed to them. Thus their life was a flight (*fuga*) from this secular form of living. This is, however, only a negative motive, and must be related to the stronger, positive motives mentioned above.[13]

To reach this perfect life—the "life in Christ" or the "angelic life"— one had to pass through the way of *apotaxis:* a renunciation of the world, or better a disordering (*apo* = from; *taxis* = order) from the worldly standards of order. This turning involved *euteleia* or frugality. Clement of Alexandria described this *euteleia* as self-simplification: namely, "simplifying the conditions of man's exterior life and thus beginning to simplify the multiform fragmentation of his psychological desires. The process was designed to bring our inner complexity into a resolution and a coherent direction; a quiescence designed to restore hegemony to the soul in man's composite anthropology."[14] Moreover, one had to be a person of *enkrateia,* that is, one in whom (*en*) power (*krateia*) resided, not one who was empowered by an outside force such as money, position, sexuality, pride, etc. This could only be accomplished through *apatheia,* a serene state of one's internal logos, which was not affected by inferior or outside conditions. *Apatheia* was a major element of the goal in this process.

This term *apatheia* had a long history and was widely discussed by the followers of Zeno and Chrysippus, by the Peripatetics and the Platonists, and by Cicero's *Cato.*[15] Some of these ideas regarding *apatheia* found their way into Clement of Alexandria and Diogenes Laertes. Even more importantly, though no doubt in a jumbled way, the notion of *apatheia* entered into normal ways of thinking in the Hellenistic world of the third and fourth centuries A.D. Some authors have stressed the fact that the early monks led a celibate life, the "white martyrdom," but the abandonment of sexuality should be seen against the views of a Zeno, who defined *pathos* as a *ptoia,* a violent fluttering. "The most common *ptoia* is sexual excitement (*eros*), and this was widely regarded from early Greek times as like a disease or as a disease itself (*nosos*)."[16] A non-sexual, solitary life led one to *apatheia,* the angelic life. With a Christianly motivated *apotaxis, euteleia,* and *enkrateia,* the "apathetic" person became a perfect person, and in short order this monastic form of life came to be described as "perfection," the "perfect life" here on earth, the foretaste of heaven itself.[17] For Pachomias and his tradition, however, this perfect life was not a replacement or displacement of the baptismal ideal of Christian living; rather, as Veilleux notes, it was seen as the goal of baptism itself.[18]

In spite of these studies of both causes and motives, it must be emphasized that there was, neither at the beginning nor throughout the history of religious life, a common denominator as regards the many forms of "religious life." Over the centuries, authors have again and again asked: What is the "essence" of religious life? Many have tried to give expression to this "essence." Even in our own day, with such writings as *Perfectae caritatis,* people have attempted to articulate that "essence," and more often than not they have attempted to define this "essence" via the three vows and on the basis of a *klerikos/laikos* church structure. In reality, the history of religious life continually eludes this attempt to find its "essence," for there have been and still are many varieties of Christian religious life, each one differing from the other. If one attempts to read the history of religious life with a pre-conceived definition of "religious life," one will clearly misinterpret the very history itself. In recent times, for instance, there have been many attempted descriptions of the "essence" of the Pachomian *koinonia,* and these descriptions are by no means essentially the same. M. Viller, K. Holl and A. Veilleux have, by way of example, each respectively presented a differing view of the "essence" of the Pachomias *koinonia.*[19] The endeavors of these quite capable scholars indicate how difficult it is, even with the best of scholarly research, to find an "essence" acceptable to the best of scholarly minds.

Accordingly, one cannot say with any exactitude that the earliest forms of monasticism focused specifically on the three vows: poverty, chastity and obedience. That the monks and nuns were poor is obvious; these men and women were not poor for poverty's sake, but because they wanted to follow the poor Christ. That they strove to be continent is clear; however, they were not continent for chastity's sake, but they wished to arrive at that stage of *apatheia* in which union with Christ could be the most radical. To accomplish this, each form of *ptoia* must be eradicated, and the most pervasive *ptoia* was sexual excitement.[20] That they were obedient in a later "religious-life" form of obedience is not clear at all.[21] However, neither poverty nor chastity was the essential element of their life, but in a much more extensive and intensive way it was the desire to follow Christ as perfectly as possible. Discipleship (the focus of an earlier chapter) lies at the center of this endeavor, but this focus on discipleship, key to anchoritic and monastic life, is common to or basic to every form of Christian life. The anchorites and monks, however, attempted to lead this Christian discipleship through such categories as *apotaxis, euteleia, enkrateia* and *apatheia.* But even with this quartet of Hellenistic ideas, one could not say that these ideas formed the "essence" of their life. Rather, one can only say that this quartet of ideas, which had in many ways permeated the *Weltanschauung* of that time, indirectly shaped the way in which these men and women attempted to follow Christ perfectly. Authors like Chadwick, McGuckin, and Baus refer to these Greek terms, and we know that early on Clement of Alexandria and Origen developed a scholarly description of the Christian ascetical life, involving these centralizing terms. But the men and women who took up this early monastic life did not first develop some rationalized ascetical ideal and then begin to put it into practice.

In the *Life of Pachomias* the term *askesis* is specifically used, but it was not defined. The use of this term indicates that the early Pachomian monks did indeed have some description of *askesis,* which they attempted to pursue, and that this desire for *askesis* did centralize their efforts. This *askesis* was closely connected to their understanding of Jesus. They were caught up both by the desire to imitate Jesus and by the way in which people of their own time described this ascetical imitation of the Lord. In later decades a more philosophical basis for monastic life was worked out, using this quartet of ideas in a quite deliberate way. What I am suggesting here is that the common anthropology of that time, particularly, the way in which Alexandrians and Egyptians, Syrians and mid-Easterners generally, understood themselves, played a role in the way in which they put together the meaning of "perfection." This anthropology, at least in general patterns, went far beyond the concepts of the Greek-speaking world; it penetrated the Coptic-speaking and Syriac-speaking worlds as well. Those who went off to the desert were by and large uneducated men, from a lower social stratum of society. These men had read neither Zeno nor Chrysippus, neither Plato nor Aristotle, neither Clement of Alexandria nor Origen. Many of these early monks neither spoke nor read Greek; a large percentage of them were illiterate. Nonetheless, there was a certain way of understanding life in this Hellenistic period, and this way of understanding life had been strongly influenced by the scholars just mentioned. This self-understanding of the Hellenistic man or woman, which permeated the sermons and spiritual direction of that period, would have been the normal way in which they would have understood both human nature itself and the perfection of that nature. The basic elements of *enkrateia* and *apatheia, euteleia* and *apotaxis,* were in the air they breathed, in the language they spoke, in the building blocks of their thought patterns.

However, almost at this very same period of history, we find still another description of Christian perfection: namely, the perfection of the cleric. One has only to read John Chrysostom's *Peri hierosynes* (*On the Priesthood*) to find an "angelic" description of the cleric.

> For it was neither an angel nor an archangel nor any other created power, but the Paraclete Himself that established that ministry, and commanded that men yet abiding in the flesh should imitate the functions of angels. Wherefore it behooves the priest to be as pure as if he stood in heaven itself amidst those Powers.[22]

Monasticism was, then, but one way in which Christianity began to find its "perfect" followers. Monasticism was not the only Christian way to lead the "angelic life." The clerical life was presented as another. These two approaches to the "perfect life" began to develop in a non-antagonistic way, at least at this early period. Later in history, these two "angelic" ways will compete in a most unangelic way.

Of importance to our present theme is the fact that the movement was almost exclusively non-clerical in its origins. The leaders of the movement were non-clerical, and the vast majority of the followers were non-clerical. Monasticism, at its origins then:

A. was *experienced* as a non-clerical movement,
B. and was, as we see in the early literature, *thought through* within non-clerical categories.

Both aspects are profoundly crucial: (a) the *experience,* and (b) the *thinking through* process. In the twentieth century, in which the clerical church is so prominent, an experience and a thinking through of church in a basically non-clerical way is almost impossible. In the section below on monastic ecclesiology, we will explore this experience and thinking through aspect in a more extended manner.

As time went on a few clerics joined the group, but the lay character of early monasticism must be stressed and kept in mind if one wishes to understand it. Only as one moves into the eighth and ninth centuries does one find the beginning of a strong clericalization of the male monastic movement. This later clericalization of religious life radically changed the male understanding of religious life. When this eventual clericalization took place, then in a gradual but ever more profoundly penetrating way, it was:

A. *experienced* in a clerical way;
B. *thought through* or intellectually articulated in a clerical way.

The lay character of early monasticism had both advantages and disadvantages. Most of the monks came at first from the lower classes, and even at the time of Augustine, the end of the fourth century, a majority of monks in North Africa were slaves, peasants and artisans.[23] For many, whose future seemed to go nowhere, entry into this monastic movement meant a "better" life—not economically better, but spiritually better. For a variety of reasons, entry to the clerical state might not have been open to them, but entry into the monastic state was indeed open. That this ascetical life was attractive can be substantiated by the large numbers who joined it. A "mass movement" might be an overstatement, but the fact that thousands of Christians moved in this direction cannot be set to one side. Toward the latter half of the fourth century, the settlement of monks in the Nitrian desert had grown so large that a new settlement was established at Kellia. At the end of the century there were six hundred monks at Kellia. Besides the Nitrian monks, there were two hundred anchorites in the immediate area. Scete also thrived. There was, indeed, an attraction to this form of life, and an attraction which overwhelmingly affected Christian lay people, and, above all, those from the lower classes of society.

On the other hand, this monastic group of lay Christians tended, although not deliberately, to make other lay Christians "second-rate." In time, in some circles at least, even the clerics, when compared with these ascetics, came to be seen as "second rate." Augustine, a champion of the monastic life but equally a champion of the clerical life, "disapproved of Catholic ascetics of no fixed abode, wanderers in the Mediterranean world," "living by mendicancy or hawking relics of doubtful credit." Augustine, moreover, disliked their long hair, worn in imitation of Samson and the Nazirites. "Augustine did not share Jerome's admiration for dirt and squalor. He thought it ostentatious."[24] The bishop of Hippo was adverse to such a demonstrative way of self-imaging as a Christian disciple of Jesus, to the detriment of the clerical disciples, to the detriment of the more "subdued" monastic disciples, and to the detriment of the discipleship of ordinary lay folk.

Still, the emergence of these movements and their astonishing success indicate that the episcopal structuring of the churches did not fully provide the length and breadth of Christian discipleship. Christian men who wanted to follow Jesus did not see in the clerically structured church either the means or the goals which they required so as to fulfill in their life, as baptized/eucharistic followers of the Lord, Jesus' call: "Come, follow me." That portion of the church which stood under the direct supervision of the *episkopos* did indeed provide some with their aspirations for discipleship, but for others that provision was found wanting. Such men and women found the kind of discipleship they were looking for within the monastic and anchoritic lifestyles.

The anchoritic and monastic movements did not begin with episcopal involvement. The directors, the leaders, and the overseers of early anchoritic and monastic movements came from the hermits and monks themselves. Men did not ask for either episcopal "permission" or episcopal "blessing" to enter into this form of discipleship. They simply went out to the desert areas, and in time they consulted not a bishop but an anchorite or a monk of known sanctity and wisdom. This raised an eventual question. What role does the bishop have as regards such anchoritic and monastic movements? Long before one can speak of "exemption" in the Cluniac sense of the term, there appears to have been a de facto exemption of these individuals and groups at their very emergence. Historical data informs us of some initial and hesitant questioning by bishops on this issue: Are monks under their supervision or not, and, if so, in what ways? We will see, later in this chapter, the emergence of these questions, the fluctuating answers that were given, and the responses thereto of the monastic communities themselves. The very fact that such questions arose at a later date in a sort of post-factum situation indicates that the issue of episcopal oversight was not part of the birthing of monasticism. Nor is there any historical data which would substantiate a claim that at the beginning of the anchoritic and monastic movements the various local *episkopoi* "allowed" these movements to take place. The movements began to take place not "with the permission" of the local bishop, nor in spite of the bishop, but simply with no reference to episcopal oversight. This rather neutral positioning of religious life within the episcopal church set the stage for an eventual confrontation.

The idea of *ordo*, which we saw above, playing a major role in the initial definition of the meaning of *klerikos/laikos* began to exert a different manner of viewing the church. In the late third and throughout the fourth century a growing process of clericalization had brought about a certain classification or ordering within the Christian community: the *ordo episcoporum*, the *ordo clericorum*, in contradistinction to the *plebs*, the Christian people. Monasticism, which was developing at this very same period of time, brought on another, though different, classification or ordering of the Christian community. Although the ascetic men and women were "non-cleric," they were considered different from the "lay" Christians who married, raised a family, engaged in business, and tried to fulfill through these vocations the Christian life. Although "set apart," the monks and nuns were not registered among the clerics, but nonetheless they were men and women who were regarded and esteemed as leaders in the Christian spiritual life, a leadership role which clerics claimed for their own. Sometimes these monks preached publicly, and such preaching was hailed by the Christian folk as important. Preaching, however, was more and more looked on by official church leadership as the preserve of the cleric, and preaching was removed not only from the ordinary lay person but from the non-ordained monk as well. More often, however, the anchorites and the monks were consulted about religious issues in the form of spiritual direction. Gradually, many of the rank-and-file Christians began to consider these hermits and monks as the *real* spiritual leaders in the church, rather than looking to the episcopal and presbyteral spiritual leadership. The ordinary Christian lay man and woman saw in the monk and in the nun, from the very start of the movement, something distinct from their own role in the church, and at the same time they saw something distinct in these same monks, nuns and hermits from the role of the cleric. This "something-distinct-from" aspect, which one finds at the very origin of monasticism, has perdured throughout Christian history and even in our day and age this ambiguity still persists.[25] This "something-distinct-from" aspect tends to center around a form of spiritual leadership, and the more spiritual leadership became ideologically centered in clerical hierarchy, anchoritic and monastic forms of such leadership were seen, at times, as antithetical, even heretical, or these monastic forms were themselves domesticated through a process of clericalization. But from the beginning this was not the case:

> Like other ascetics, Antony stayed at first in the vicinity of villages, gaining something of a reputation among the rural population along the river. Then he withdrew beyond the fertile districts to the top of the escarpment above the valley, shutting himself in a deserted fort. Even here he was visited by would-be disciples and admirers; and when he emerged, after nearly twenty years, he found an audience ready to accept his guidance and instruction.[26]

2. THE GEOGRAPHICAL SCOPE OF THIS EARLY MOVEMENT

Perhaps a clear way to approach this early movement of asceticism and monasticism is to consider it from a geographical standpoint, for in doing so we can see how thoroughly Christian people in both the east and the west were touched by this form of discipleship. It is remarkable that this movement even started; it is more remarkable that this movement in such rapid time covered a wide and diverse area of the then Christian world. We find monastic movements, some of them quite diverse, in Egypt, in Palestine and Syria, in Asia Minor, particularly in the area of Constantinople, in Italy, in Spain, in North Africa, and in Gaul. One could also include, at a slightly later date, the emergence of monastic movements in Wales, Ireland and Scotland, and then in England proper. The very extensiveness of this movement indicates its power and its attraction. Let us consider these areas, not in any in-depth way, since this has been done elsewhere,[27] but only insofar as we are tracing the meaning of "lay" within the Christian communities.

A. EGYPT

The scattered individuals of early asceticism, the anchorites, slowly moved toward a more communal form of life. The Egyptian sources for these movements remain the best we have to date. Still, we know that Novatian, the Roman presbyter, had spent some time in solitude. Narcissus, a later *episkopos* of Jerusalem, had done likewise. But in the Nitrian Desert and then in the more remote Scete, ascetics began to gather, then loosely associate with one another, especially around a person of high spiritual integrity. At this early stage, this leader is neither a "religious superior" nor a "father abbot" (in a later sense of these terms). He is rather a spiritual guide for a number of individuals. Antony's influence in this regard was indeed powerful, and his insistence on manual labor, on prayer and on the reading of scripture became standards for individual ascetics. In the struggle for the angelic life, Antony emphasized the struggle with the devil. The devil, so it was thought, had his greatest influence in the vast solitudes of the desert, and it is therefore easy to see why these ascetics continually moved away from villages and pushed ever more deeply into the desert wastelands. Indeed, only one who had lived in the desert and had there fought the devil could truly be a leader of another.[28] Antony himself had left the outskirts of his home in Kome and had moved to an abandoned fortress at the edge of the desert. For twenty years this became the arena of his spiritual struggle. During the persecution of Diocletian he had left this solitude temporarily and had gone to Alexandria to comfort the Christian prisoners, but he returned to the abandoned fort and resumed the role of a spiritual father for the many hermits who came to him for advice. In 313 Antony went even deeper into the desert, only to be sought out again by hermits, by clerics and by the faithful generally. Because of his conquering of evil and of the devil, Antony, as Athanasius described him, gained tremendous insights into the nature of the demonic and into the ways of its power. Thereby he was able to discern how others might extricate themselves from the demonic.[29] The vast majority of the people who were influenced by Antony were noncleric, just as Antony himself was non-cleric. The experience of the spiritual life with its conquering of the devil was thought through and lived within a non-clerical sphere. For Antony, only the celebration of eucharist involved the cleric, but the celebration of the eucharist, though important, was not the center of Antony's spirituality. Remarkably, when the hermit Antony, a most influential man, died in 356, the same geographical area produced still another most influential man, Pachomias.

Pachomias' monastic life and Antony's hermitical life overlap both in time and space. Pachomias was born in the Upper Thebaid around 287 and became a soldier under Maximinus Daia. As a soldier he came into contact with Christianity, and after leaving the military he was baptized and then he placed himself under the guidance of an ascetic, Palamon. After some time as a solitary ascetic, he established, between 320 and 325, a community of monks at Tabennisi. Pachomias developed a rule of life for the monks.[30] Rather than caves and other solitary dwellings, the Pachomian monastery was surrounded by a wall, with entry only through a main porter-station, with the center of the enclave at the great hall, the *synaxis,* in which the monks gathered for liturgy, prayer, and instruction. The living quarters for the monks were large buildings, each one holding thirty or forty men, and these buildings were grouped about the central area. Although the monks had tasks to perform, such as gardening, shepherding, baking, weaving, and fishing, each of the individual houses had a "house director" who supervised these occupations. These tasks brought in the necessary income to maintain the monastery.

The largeness of the community and the acquisition of properties for grazing and husbandry of all sorts already contained seeds of eventual difficulty, although at the start of the movement such difficulties were not foreseen. For Pachomias a strongly motivating ideal was the community of the primitive church at Jerusalem, in which everyone gave up his or her possessions and each shared in the community structure. In many ways, with the wall of separation from the outside world and even the outside church, and with a complete structure and infra-structure for both material and spiritual life, these enclaves can be seen as replicas of the primitive Jerusalem community, even as "small churches" in their own right. We will return to this important theme toward the end of this section, when we consider the ecclesiologies of the monastic movement.

Brotherhood and communal life were strongly stressed, for in Pachomias' view communal life had a sacred quality about it. The reading of the scriptures and meditating on the holy words became a central part of the monk's daily life, and each monk was encouraged to learn small pericopes by heart. "To all without exception applied [the Rule's] prescriptions in regard to clothing, food, furnishing of their cells, manual labor, as well as in regard to the form of religious life. There was no place here for individualism, sometimes assuming bizarre forms, of separate anchorites in their manner of life nor for their subjective attitudes of asceticism and piety."[31] Conformity, rather than individual or personal growth, was the order of the day, and the superiors themselves were under the rule and had to abide by it. This concern for a uniform community was one of the major reasons that deterred Pachomias from accepting clergy into his group, and as a result his community was overwhelmingly non-clerical. Nevertheless, Pachomias had a high regard for clergy, and he kept in close contact with the local bishop, but both bishop and clergy were outside the *koinonia*. The communal uniformity depended in a major way on the absolute poverty of each monk, that is, there was to be no monk who owned or used more than another, no monk who was special. This similarity of possession and use insured uniformity. Secondly, communal uniformity depended on absolute obedience. A monk followed the dictates of the rule in everything. Through obedience to the rule, each monk was allowed only what he needed. One should note the difference between the spiritual father of a scattered group of anchorites, on the one hand, and the superior of a Pachomian monastery, on the other. In the first place, the guidance of the spiritual father furthered the individual conscience of the follower so that he (or she) might begin to live on his own, thereby becoming less and less dependent on the spiritual father. In the Pachomian format, one never severed oneself from the superior. Self-effacement, not self-reliance, was at the heart of the matter.

Pachomias' emphasis on both poverty and obedience became highly influential in almost all subsequent religious foundations, at least in some form or another, but they were never the central issues. Discipleship of the Lord remained at the very heart of the *koinonia*. Because of this long-perduring historical influence of Pachomian ideals, one sees the genius of this man Pachomias.

At the time of Pachomias, the Egyptian monasteries multiplied beyond expectations. Nonetheless, shortly after the death of Pachomias, Horsiesios became the general superior, and during his tenure there was a major crisis in the new community. On the one hand, some of the monks were applying openly for positions within the monastic structure; on the other hand, some monasteries were involved in economic interests which contradicted the spirit of poverty. Horsiesios, together with Theodore as his vicar, managed to bring most of the communities into harmony. Their emphasis was on the strict poverty and the strict obedience which Pachomias had put in the rule, and in making this emphasis they stressed the gospel life, that is, they stressed the meaning of discipleship. Discipleship became equated with the monastic life, and monastic life became equated to gospel life. Such equations, later on, tended to make both ordinary lay life and even clerical life somewhat less than the gospel ideal. Such equations eventually raised the issue of the "perfect" life.

Neither the anchoritic life of Antony nor the Pachomian communal life focused on ministry per se. Entrance into these forms of religious life was not dominated by any particular ministerial activity. That various anchorites engaged in spiritual direction is clear; that Pachomian monasteries and other monasteries provided spiritual assistance to visitors and to the poor is also clear, but this ministerial aspect of religious life was at best tangential to the monastic way of life. Adalbert de Vogüé notes:

> Indeed, teaching held first place in Pachomias' quasi-apostolic mission. As surprising as this seems when we consider the feeble echoes and remnants of his preaching, this is what he and his sons considered his essential work. Pachomias was, before all else, a harbinger of the divine Word, a teacher, even an exegete.[32]

Vogüé goes on to note, however, that the preaching of Pachomias was primarily intra-mural, that it was to his own monks, and this was also the pattern of his successors, Horsiesios and Theodore. The preaching of these successors is presented in this same intra-mural light.[33] This lack of ministry to the outside world will not be the case in later centuries, in which religious groups were deliberately formed with clear ministerial and pastoral dimensions to the wider public, both Christian and non-Christian.

B. PALESTINE AND SYRIA

The holy places in Palestine became places of pilgrimage, attracting Christians from all over the then-known world. Sylvanus, though originally from Palestine, had become a monk in the Egyptian area of Scete. He came to Mount Sinai around 380 with a group of fellow monks and established a monastic form of communal life. Later he established a monastic *koinonia* at Gerasa, also in Palestine. The diaries of that famous Christian traveler Egeria, written about the same time as Sylvanus' arrival in Palestine, indicate that not a few anchoritic people also lived in and about Mount Sinai. A gathering of monastic people came to be called, in this area, *laura*, rather than *koinonia*, and there were differences. In a *laura*, monks lived in huts, in some sort of close vicinity to a large, common structure. This larger building was used for liturgical worship on Saturday and Sunday, for instruction, and for common prayer. Further connections to the Pachomian *koinoniai* are not all that clear, so that the *laura* seems to have had its own history, even independent of the Egyptian *koinonia*. In 405 Euthymius, who came from Lesser Armenia, arrived in Palestine, and Euthymius exerted enormous influence over Palestinian monasticism. It was he who stressed the form of life called the *cenobium*, and eventually, due to his influence, a pattern was established: a younger monk was first of all schooled in a *cenobium*, and only after testing by the abbot was he allowed to undergo the harsher form of the semi-anchoritic form of the *laura*. It is interesting to note that in the Pachomian form of *koinonia*, the goal was not an eventual anchoritic life, but a continued life in common. In the *cenobium*, however, a higher spiritual form of monasticism was seen in the rigor of the *laura*.

These initial forms of Palestinian monasticism were basically either Egyptian or eastern in origin, and they were experienced and thought through in non-clerical ways. Strange as it may seem, this basically non-ordained spiritual stratum of Christian life produced strong spiritual leadership, and many of these monastic leaders, spiritually grounded through a non-clerical formation process, were chosen to be *episkopoi* for key eastern communities, a fact which attests to the spiritual value of both the *laura* and the *cenobium*. The presence of these monks-made-bishops, in turn, assured a strong episcopal regard and protection for the various monastic movements throughout the east.

Western or Latin influence also came into play for the origin of Palestinian monasticism. Women in particular played a major role: Melania the Elder founded, with Rufinus of Aquileia, a double monastery on Mount Olivet around 380. Jerome and Paula the Elder, with her daughter Eustochium, began a double monastery near Bethlehem in 386. Pinian and Melania the Younger, husband and wife, eventually established a monastic form of life in Palestine at the beginning of the fifth century. There was, in the Latin form of Palestinian monastic asceticism, an aristocratic and intellectual tone, which contrasted notably with the more grassroots and non-intellectual approach that one sees both in early Egyptian monasticism and the eastern forms of Palestinian monasticism. The strong influence of women is more noticeable and more accepted here than one finds in other early strata of monastic life.

In the Syrian churches, the encratic movement was quite strong. One even finds in some east Syrian churches the idea that reception of baptism itself meant a life of complete poverty and total continence, that is, a life as an anchoritic or as a monk. Those not ready for such a radical step remained in the catechumenate. Although this situation is quite unique, it indicates, even in its radical resolution, the challenging seeds at the heart of the anchoritic and monastic life: Is the eremitical and cenobitic life the "real" Christian life? Or is one Christian, even if one marries, raises a family, and works at a secular task? Is one Christian if one is a cleric, and not, at the same time, a monk?

The Syrian churches' evidence of widespread monastic and anchoritic severity is not replicated elsewhere in the Christian world. Written around 444, Theodoret of Cyrus' *Historia religiosa seu ascetica vivendi ratio* describes the lives of twenty-eight men and three women ascetics who lived near Antioch and were personally known to the author. Such

men and women were called the "athletes of Christ." Their severe ascetical practices were held up as the very reasons why they were able to
overcome the devil and enter so closely into union with God. In this work
of Theodoret, we see no set pattern: one finds both solitary figures, as well
as men and women who are spiritual guides to others. We find hermits
and monks. It is in Syria that the well-known "stylites" came into such an
admired state.

Noteworthy in this area was the widespread esteem for these hermits
and monks. This esteem came not only from the rank and file Christian,
but from clerics, from bishops, and from imperial leadership. Even
though the rank and file Christian, the individual cleric, and the imperial
personage did not personally follow this pattern of life, their esteem indicated that these hermits and monks were the "heroes" of Christian faith.
They were, in many respects, considered the real spiritual leaders. In the
enthusiasm for these spiritual leaders one perceives, in hindsight, the
seeds of challenge: Are the spiritual leaders the monks? the clergy? the
imperial leadership? In the course of subsequent history, one finds many
instances when all three groups claimed spiritual leadership in opposition
to the others.

Rarely did upper class citizens join Syrian monastic movements. The
bulk of the Syrian monks were from the lower class. As a result, there were
few scholars among this group, although a few monks became copyists of
some biblical manuscripts. A few Syrian monks did oppose Arianism and
Messalianism, and Rabbula and Narsai did emerge as scholars, but these
were all rather exceptional instances, not part and parcel of this form of
monastic life.

Perhaps one could discern the beginnings of "ministry" as an ingre-
dient of the monastic movement, for in Syrian forms of the ascetical life
monks and nuns were often engaged in charitable works for the poor, the
sick, the pilgrims. Hospices and hospitals under the care of monks began
to flourish. One also finds that some of these Syrian monks moved out to
the frontiers of the empire and did so in a missionary way. John Chrysostom's writings indicate his own reliance on such missionary monks.[34] In
all of this, however, including the severe, encratic forms of life, one generally does not find any substantial tension with church leadership. The
single instance in which Meletius, the *episkopos* of Antioch, did have to
criticize some monks for excessive ascetical behavior is almost unique.[35]
Missionary activity, hospital ministry, hospice activity, extreme ascetical
practices—all these various aspects of Syrian monasticism indicate that
religious life was a very diverse and complicated kind of Christian reality.
The focus on the monk or nun as a "spiritual leader," both by the ordinary Christian and by the clerical and imperial leadership, once again

strongly suggests that we are dealing with a form of Christian life which cannot easily be characterized as either "cleric" or "lay."

C. ASIA MINOR

Monasticism seems to have begun in Asia Minor with Eustathius of Sebaste, who had established groups of monks in Armenia, Paphlagonia and Pontus.[36] Some of these monks were so opposed to marriage that they refused to attend a eucharistic liturgy if it was celebrated by married clergy. They renounced all possessions, claiming that this was the only way to be truly Christian. They fasted on Sunday, which generally was not done within the Christian community. Basil, a friend of Eustathius, attempted to moderate these extreme tendencies, and Basil, together with such men as Gregory of Nazianz [at least occasionally], formed a less rigorous monastic community. Throughout his busy life, however, Basil deeply respected the goals of monastic life, and his *asketikon* has had a varied history, and although it cannot be seen in any strict way as a "rule of an order," it has often played the role of a rule in subsequent history. In the writings of Basil, not only in the *asketikon,* but also in some of his letters, one finds an "ideal" of Christian life described in monastic terms. This description of the ideal Christian, presented by Basil in a way that would counter any excessive forms of monastic life, does raise an issue: Can Christian life find its ideal only in the monastic form of life? If so, how does one rate the "clerical" life? How does one rate the ordinary "lay" life? Basil's mingling of monastic idealism with the very meaning of a true Christian life finds a counterpart in a similar co-mingling of the two by Augustine and by Gregory the Great. The gospel appeal of the monastic life derived from the monastic efforts to be a radical disciple of the Lord. The gospel appeal of baptism/eucharist is to become a disciple of the Lord. The gospel appeal of clerical leadership in the church is to become a disciple of the Lord. The difficulty of bringing these three areas of Christian life into some sort of unity can be seen in the struggles of Basil, Augustine and Gregory. Eventually, as is well known, religious life did come to be theologically described as the life of perfection, and when this happened, ordinary "lay" life was depositioned once again, in this instance not by "clerical" life, but by "religious" life. One cannot fault Basil, Augustine or Gregory for this eventual situation, but one should note that in their writings, which were highly influential, the seeds for this eventual development were already in place.

D. ITALY

Italy, and particularly Rome, presents some special characteristics as regards monastic life. Generally, the men of Rome in the fourth century did not look favorably on monasticism. Jerome found that his own endeavors to situate monastic life in the Roman setting were unappreciated, and as a result he returned to Palestine. Damasus I (366–384) promoted asceticism for women, as did his successor, Siricius (384–399). With Innocent I and Zosimus, we even begin to find a papal oversight of monastic life, and with Sixtus III and Leo I we find the first papal establishments of monasteries, again with an ongoing papal oversight. Such episcopal governance is not found, for instance, in Egypt, Palestine, and Syria. Even in Asia Minor, Basil was a moderator, but not a strict overseer. Monks in both Constantinople and Chalcedon were well known for their, at times, riotous behavior and even anti-clerical stance. In Rome, as would be expected, there was a clear move toward episcopal control of monastic life.

Outside the city of Rome, Martin of Tours began the first island form of monasticism at Gallinara, opposite the city of Albenga. There was another island monastic settlement on Capraia, near Corsica. There was a hermitage on the island of Tinetto. On the mainland, Eusebius began a monastic settlement at Vercelli, and in 363 when he became bishop, he united his monastic group with the clergy of his cathedral. This is the first recorded instance of a clerical monastery. Shortly later, Augustine developed at Hippo a similar clerical monastic group. Ambrose favored the monks near Milan, but he was especially concerned about the women who had vowed virginity. His efforts in this regard were not all that appreciated by the Milanese. In other parts of Italy, such as Bologna, or in the communities of Melania the Younger in Sicily and the Campagnia, "domestic" monasticism seemed to find rootage. Often these "domestic" forms of monasticism were basically a product of the aristocratic and educated class, and the monks or nuns were given over to more intellectual pursuits and to a refined form of contemplative life. One does not find the rigors of Egyptian, Syrian and Cappadocian monasteries in these domestic enclaves. In the somewhat scattered but widespread appearance of monastic life throughout Italy, one sees again (a) the variety of monastic forms, (b) the seeds of struggle between clerical leadership and monastic independence, and (c) the question of the ideal form of Christian life: i.e., Is the ideal form only to be found in some monastic structuring? One sees as well that in the church there were clerics, there was an emperor, there were ordinary lay folk, and there were monks and nuns. We find no attempt to reduce these four groups to two: namely, either cleric or lay.

Gregory the Great, whose influence on medieval life was highly penetrating, was at heart a very monastic man. However, Gregory realized that human nature was the same, whether it is found in papal, episcopal or abbatial forms, whether it is found in monastic or anchoritic forms, whether it is found in the ordinary lay man or woman. Gregory calls the true follower of Jesus *vir Dei, homo Dei, famulus Dei, servus Dei, vir sanctus, vir venerabilis, sanctissimus vir.*[37] These names can be applied to a prelate, to a monk, to an ordinary Christian man or woman. Nonetheless, at the time of Gregory,

> a clerical culture had evolved that saw monastic virtues as prescriptive for the Church in general. The monk's life is a holocaust, the prelate's a sacrifice. The emphasis on sacrifice in monastic life is transferred to the Church at large, along with the essentially monastic view of life as a perpetual act of penitence.[38]

Gregory saw two models of perfection. One was, for his time, more common or more conventional: namely, the monk or nun, who left the world and spent his or her days in mortification and in contemplation. The second model of perfection was Gregory's own ideal, and it was more daring: an ascetical monk who returned (to a degree) to the world as a contemplative preacher.[39] In both models, however, the monastic element is clear. Pachomias may have created an alternative community, but the holy one in Gregory's view is one who exists within the structures both of the clerical church and of the imperial society.[40] When Gregory addressed the ordinary Christian man or woman, his examples were frequently taken from monastic literature. When Gregory addressed clerics, he placed before them once again monastic examples. "Using his divine powers, the holy man secures order in the Church and community, and he looks to the stability and harmony of monastic life as the model for all Christian experience. Consequently, Gregory shows special concern for reinforcing the patterns of monastic experience."[41] Gregory's eucharistic theology, the center of Christian liturgical life, presided over by a major cleric, is colored by monastic experience, for the eucharist is a sacrifice, and in the eucharistic sacrifice we find the model for our own life. In harmony with Faustus of Riez, Gregory's eucharistic theology focused on the words of "consecration," for here was a moment of change and radical conversion, and a moment of sacrifice. The sacrifice of Jesus, both on the cross and in the eucharist, needs to be replicated in the life of every Christian, but such a sacrifice, in Gregory's view, is exemplified by the true Christian, the holy monk. The very life of the monk is a sacrifice and therefore it is eucharistic; the conversion of the monk mirrors the conversion of bread and wine into the body and blood of Jesus, and there it is eucharistic. Gregory's eucharistic theology is reflected in his theology of monastic life.

Monastic Christianity was a major part of the legacy which Gregory left to the western church.[42] Gregory taught that the Christian world was divided into three categories: the cleric, the monk, and the lay. Loyal citizen of the empire that he was, he should have added the role of the emperor, but this was not an issue on which he concentrated. The genius of Gregory, however, certainly lies in his perception that the monk was quite special, that he could be locked neither into a clerical mold nor into a lay mold. Not only was the monk, within this ordering of the Christian world, someone special, but the monk, when found at his best, was a paradigm of Christian life. This did not mean, however, that the monks were the rulers of the church. Gregory, in this matter, is thoroughly Roman, and there is no doubt at all that the clergy, particularly the bishops and the pope, are divinely appointed to rule the church, but in both bishop and pope the spirituality should be monastic. In the holy monk Gregory saw the resolution of the dichotomous world: soul and body, spiritual and carnal, angelic and demonic. In the monastic prelate, the contemplative preacher, Gregory saw the resolution of the Christian life: the shepherd and the sheep, the leader and the led, the teacher and the taught. The monk was not the cleric; the cleric was not the monk. The two together, however, were precisely what the gospels wanted as apostle, shepherd, evangelist, and hierarch. The monk was not the lay, and the lay was not the monk. Again the two together, i.e. the monastic lay person, was, in Gregory's view, precisely what the gospels wanted when they spoke of discipleship. These Gregorian ideals of the Christian life became almost normative as the middle ages unfolded, and they remained virtually unchallenged until the eleventh and twelfth centuries, when lay groups began to assert the "laicity" of the gospel message. Even the Christian emperor and king, as we have seen, was ideally a monastic king, but once again the king was not a monk nor a monk a king.

Gregory, of course, was highly influenced by Benedict of Nursia (c. 480–550), and he wrote a *Vita S. Benedicti*, which has remained a rather single source for our knowledge of this man. To a degree, Benedict received an education at Rome, but he broke off his academic work and retired to Afide, and subsequently to Subiaco, where he lived in a cave for some three years. A neighboring monk, Romanus, provided him not only with his food but also with instruction. Soon others set up hermitages in the area, and in time Benedict organized this group of hermits into a community, later moving this community to the rugged mountain, Monte Cassino. Gregory informs us that Benedict wrote a monastic rule, but evidence indicates that Gregory had probably not read the rule.[43] Nonetheless, this rule, particularly through the manuscript sent to Charlemagne's court by Theodemar, an abbot of Monte Cassino,[44] became widespread throughout the European world in the middle ages and had powerful influence on monastic life. The rule details both the life of the monk and the goals of monastic living. That there are connections with other rules composed at the same time in Italy and southern Gaul, such as those for men and women of Caesarius of Arles, is most probable. There was also the *Rule of the Master,* which had an influence on both Caesarius and Benedict.[45] One also finds in Benedict echoes of the rules of Pachomias, Basil, Augustine, and Cassian, indicating that he had read these rules.[46] In other words, one finds in the rule of Benedict an echo of many monastic forms of life current in his day. Still, Benedict's rule has its own originality: "His thought is more refined and his argument is less cluttered with irrelevant detail . . . he reveals a more genial spirit . . . and a greater tolerance of human weakness."[47] Benedict requires that the superior, the abbot, be elected by the brothers, but the abbot reflects paternal authority, and although he listens to all the monks, including the youngest, he remains the final monastic authority, next to the rule. Benedict envisions not a single monastery, but a clustering of houses connected to the central abbey. He stabilizes the day in a strongly liturgical way. For Benedict the monastery is a family, a Roman family of course, but a family, or, as Lawrence has called it, a "villa monastery."[48] Hermits were allowed, but with utmost caution. Once a postulant had been admitted and lived through the training, he vowed stability to this single monastery and to the absolute sovereignty of the written rule, to which even the abbot must be subservient. Property was common, not individual, and this regulation included everything. Having nothing to call one's own, the monk also renounced his will, and obedience to the abbot must be prompt, willing and without murmuring. Without any doubt the personality and quality of the abbot was central and crucial for the quality of life in any given monastery. Not an autocrat, but a pastoral, shepherding father is the mirror in which an abbot should see himself.

With an abbot, a prior, a dean and other monastic officials, there arose a regulated hierarchy in the monastery, but this hierarchy was not identical to the clerical hierarchy. Indeed, there have been some recent studies on the issue of a priest and his position within the monastic framework envisioned by Benedict.[49] That priestly status did not totally agree with monastic status is clear; how the two different states might be conjoined has been handled differently at different epochs of the Benedictine monastic movement. Benedict's influence on western monasticism was enormous, as is well known, and much of his influence was due to Gregory's *Vita S. Benedicti* and Gregory's own monastic influence on the western church throughout the middle ages.

For our purposes, the distinctness of the monk's role, as also the nun's role, should be noted. A monk and a nun were neither clerics nor ordinary "lay" persons. They were in a class apart, and, even more, they were the mirrors of Christian perfection. In these "monastic" centuries of western life, discipleship was measured and judged by one's closeness or distance from monastic ideals. Monasticism and discipleship became profoundly co-identified, so much so that by the ninth and tenth centuries monastic life was called the apostolic life. The reform movements of the eleventh and twelfth centuries were called by a different name, to wit, the evangelical life, and its proponents challenged the monastic claim that the monastic way of life was the apostolic life, i.e. the true form of discipleship.

E. SPAIN

Only with the Council of Elvira (380) is there any extant data on monastic life in Spain, but even this brief notice indicates that monasticism in that part of the world was not a newly arrived reality of Christian life. The Synod of Saragossa (380) inflicted a punishment on any cleric who became a monk, and the reason for this was simply put: he (the cleric) "aspired to appear a more zealous observer of the law." Nonetheless, five years later the bishop of Rome, Siricius, in a letter to Himerius, bishop of Tarragona, advised the Spanish bishop to encourage clerics to become monks. These contradictory tendencies support the view that church authority was beginning to feel a sort of ambivalence about religious life, precisely because of the issue of discipleship. In the same letter of Siricius, one finds that monasteries for both men and women appear to be rather accepted, at least in that part of Spain.

At the end of the fourth century, a Spanish peregrine form of monastic life was both practiced by some and defended by some.[50] The furor caused by Priscillian, and his involvement with various monastic groups, occasioned an official distrust of peregrinating monks, at least on the part of some Spanish bishops, but the emergence of this vagrant form of monasticism and its defense is another indication that religious life is not monolithic.

In early Spanish monasticism, we find once again (a) a question regarding the genuine keepers of the Christian law: Are these only monks and nuns, or are clergy also genuine Christians? (b) Also, is the peregrine form of monastic life acceptable? Only a few centuries later, when Celtic monks begin to missionize continental Europe, we will see this form of peregrine monasticism take on a vigorous stride. (c) With the Priscillian situation, the question arises: What role do bishops have over monastic, even inner-monastic forms of life?

F. NORTH AFRICA

In North Africa, it is Augustine who clearly structures monasticism. After his baptism and return to North Africa, Augustine forms the community at Cassiciacum. This is a Roman villa, lent to him and to his companions by Verecundus of Milan. With Augustine were Monica, Alypius, Adeodatus, Navigius, his brother, Licentius, son of his former patron Romanianus, Trygetius of Tagaste, Rusticius and Lastidianus, Augustine's cousins, and Evodius of Tagaste. These people held disputations on a variety of subjects, relating to philosophy and to religions. Notaries were on hand to record the data.[51] To these disputations were added prayers, and on Augustine's birthday Monica provided a dinner, and for three days they held a discussion *De beata vita.*[52]

The picture of monastic life at Cassiciacum has little resemblance to a Pachomian *koinonia.* There is, rather, an urbanity and academic quality which one generally associates with the understanding of *otium* and the Roman aristocracy. When he had become the bishop of Hippo, Augustine continued this monastic way of life with a *monasterium clericorum,* as he himself called it.[53] Augustine even wrote a *Praeceptum (Regula tertia* or *Regula recepta)* as a guideline for one's daily life. Later he wrote the *De opere monachorum,* which again reveals his ideas and ideals on the monastic life. Augustine had touched base with monasticism while he was in Italy, and although he admired the asceticism of some anchorites and monks, he himself did not feel that this form of life was his own calling. Seclusion from the world was important for Augustine, as also the renunciation of marriage. Still, the view of monastic life which Augustine lived and counseled was in many ways different from other forms.

> Augustine's voice was on the side of moderation. His view of fasts was that they had become excessive and should be diminished (*De. civ. Dei,* xiv, 6). The theme that mortification is a penitential process of propitiating God for one's sins and for the indiscretions of one's youth is strikingly absent—the more so when one considers that Augustine had a number of such discretions to record.[54]

Chadwick adds that Augustine used the conventional language about the "angelic life" to describe the celibate ideal, as he writes to some nuns in Hippo.[55] On the other hand, after his clash with Pelagian ideas, he appears to shy away from the notion that there might be a possibility to attain moral perfection in this present life.[56] Augustine's monks and nuns wore a distinctive garb, and Augustine himself notes that people in Hippo, when seeing them, expressed pity for these people.[57] Action and contemplation were combined in Augustine's approach to religious life, so that there was a certain ministerial dimension at times to the Augustinian monastic way of life. For Augustine, this meant, of course, the ministry of bishop. Some of the monks who were with Augustine at Hippo became bishops, themselves, and they in turn established in their episcopal communities *monasteria clericorum*. Beyond these establishments, the monastic movements of both Caesar of Arles and Benedict owe much to the Augustinian approach.

G. GAUL

The initial missionary movement in Gaul focuses on such well known individuals as Dorotheus, who around 250 established a group of anchorites on the Ile-Barbe, near Lyon, and the founding of another group of ascetics near Clermont-Ferrand around 312. In 337 Castor established the cenobium at Cardo near Tréves, and in 341 St. Martin joined this group. In 355 St. Hilary established a monastery at Poitiers. Martin moved on to establish Liguegé (360) and Marmoutier (368). Subsequently, monastic groups began to show up in abundance throughout the Roman-Gallic area: Sens (386), Lérins (405), Marseille (415). Under the leadership of John Cassian there were the monastic developments at Ménerbes (419), and Auxerre (422). The list could go on and on.

Although this form of cenobitic life was scattered throughout the Roman-Gallic area, the Irish monks, with Columban leading the way, in the seventh century moved particularly among the Merovingian court aristocracy, from which many of the early Iro-Gallic monks came. Both the earlier community at Lérins and then the Iro-Gallic community at Luxeuil became the training ground for many bishops, at least eleven, in the course of the seventh century alone. But non-monastic bishops, such as Audoenus of Rouen and Eligius of Noyon, both of whom had been officials in the Neustrian court at Paris before entry into the clerical state, favored monks, and their personal influence at the court helped to establish several monasteries for both men and women in the Gallic area.

In this relationship of court to monastery, we see once again the special place of the kings and queens, here the Merovingian line, as well as the special place of monks and nuns. Neither of these two groups was considered a gathering of "ordinary" lay people. They were, rather, groups which represented quite special "classes" within the Christian church: the divinely graced imperial class and the divinely graced monastic class. Merovingian monasticism paved the way for Frankish monasticism, and Frankish monasticism paved the way for Ottonian monasticism, in such a way that the middle ages cannot be understood apart from these monastic movements which coursed through history during the reigns of these royal dynasties. The monasticism which dominated the middle ages, was, of course, Iro-Gallic monasticism.

H. IRELAND, WALES AND SCOTLAND

A few words on the northern isles will close this geographical survey. Although Palladius, and then Patrick, established the church in Ireland, it was a Roman church, with episcopal hierarchy quite dominant. However, a hundred years after the death of Patrick, who himself had probably been a monk or at least exposed to monastic influence, the Irish church became a monastic church, with an abbot, not a bishop, as its primary leader. One finds this same pattern of monastic church structure supplanting episcopal church structure, as this Celtic form of monasticism moved into Scotland and into Wales. From these three centers, this same monastic movement migrated to the continent. There is no other instance in the history of the church in which such a radical change of church structure occurs at such a rapid pace. The supplanting in dominance of the episcopal structure by the monastic structure, within but a hundred years, is unparalleled. In many areas this was the emergence of non-ordained dominance over the previous ordained dominance, and even here and there a feminine dominance over a previous masculine dominance.

At times the abbot was also a bishop, but in many if not the majority of situations, the abbot, at first, was not a bishop. Still, since his position resembled that of a bishop, one finds a gradual "episcopation" of the abbot, at least in externals, and to some degree in the area of jurisdiction, spiritual leadership and eventually the right to ordination itself. In the earliest church councils one finds a few, if any abbots, present at the deliberations. However, as one moves towards that grandest of all medieval councils, Lateran IV (1215), one notes the growing presence and importance of abbots, shoulder to shoulder with bishops, at local, regional, and general councils of the western church. A council, which is the gathering together of ecclesial leadership, brought together not only episcopal leadership, but abbatial leadership as well. We have already noted the substantive presence of imperial leadership at many of these councils. This union of bishop, abbot and imperial leader indicates once again the impossibility of viewing the church from a simplistic cleric/lay approach.

Irish monasticism did not have *stabilitas loci,* such as the Benedictine form of monasticism had. Thus, one finds Irish, Scottish and Welsh missionaries moving about the western world in large numbers and with powerful effect. When settled, these same monks opened their monasteries to agricultural tasks, and since many of the populace were agrarian, there was a bond set up between the lay farmer and the monk farmer, a bond which went far beyond that of similar tradesmen, and came to be seen as that of spiritual and even physical guardianship.

The first purpose of this geographical monastic journey was this: to indicate that people, *throughout the Christian world,* did not see the monk and the nun as "ordinary" lay persons, nor did they see them as "clerics." The monk and the nun were in a very special class by themselves within the Christian structure, and this appreciation of the monastic "class" lasted, historically, for many centuries. An ideological position of a lay/cleric church simply cannot muster the data of history to its side.

The second purpose of this journey was this: monasticism, both in the east and in the west, was not cut from the same cloth. The basic desire to be a disciple of Jesus was clearly present, but the way in which each family of monasticism lived out and regulated this discipleship was different. There is no "essence" to this variety of monastic ways of life.

Anchoritic and monastic life was a flight from the world, *fuga mundi,* and as such it represented a way in which Christians related to the secular world. These hermitical and monastic Christians simply "left" the world, retiring to a place of solitude, struggling against the demonic, and striving to find union with the Lord. On occasion the writings of these men and women indicate a "hatred" of the world, a disdain for the world, a rejection of the world. This disdain and rejection was not as political as a similar disdain and rejection which one finds in the Donatist movement, and therefore the episcopal church did not find the monastic movement at odds with its own basic attempt to live with the governmental structures. In fact, by and large the episcopal church favored the monastic movements. As time goes by and one enters into the middle ages, however, the monastic movement which began as a flight from the world gradually is seen as a "part" of the Christian world. Indeed, as many will write, one cannot even think of the Christian medieval world, and therefore the socio-economic medieval world, without the presence of the monasteries and convents. What began as a radical rejection of the world came to be appreciated as an essential part of the world.[58]

3. THE ECCLESIOLOGIES OF EARLY MONASTIC LIFE

In connection with this early monasticism, we have spoken of a sort of "alternative church" structure, a term used by others as well.[59] Let us explore for a moment the way in which these early ascetics both experienced church and theoretically, in their own way, described church.

First of all, "church" was not something which was a reality outside of these ascetics, which they had to incorporate into their life. When

Antony moved to the cemetery outside of Kome, he certainly believed that he was making the ecclesial dimension more specific in his life. When Pachomias moved to the anchoritic form of life and then on to the life in a *koinonia,* he was doing this because these ways of life were part and parcel of what it meant to be in the Christian church. The church was not something extrinsic to monasticism, to which monasticism continually needed to conform itself. Rather, monasticism was as much a form of church-living as the Christian life in the city with its centering around the episcopal person and the episcopal building.

Neither the anchoritic life nor the monastic life, however, was clerical. The number of presbyters who were allowed into the community was quite negligible. Although relationships with the local *episkopoi* were generally good—exceptions such as the hostility of the *episkopos,* Theophilus of Alexandria, notwithstanding—the monasteries on a day-to-day basis existed quite apart from the clerical world. Geographically, it almost appears as if there were two forms of church existing side by side in a given locale: the clerically organized church in the urban centers, and the self-enclosed monastic communities both in the less inhabited areas and in monastic enclaves on the outskirts or even within the cities themselves. Both groups professed Christianity. Both groups considered themselves as following the gospel. The clerical church stressed apostolic succession of leadership; the monastic church, for its part, stressed the primitive, apostolic, Christian, communal way of life.[60]

Both of these forms of Christian life enjoyed a leadership role. Clearly, the clerical church exerted leadership and authority, and the local *episkopos* enjoyed great prestige and obedience by the Christians in his community. Within the monastic enclave, the superior or abbot was willingly given a position of leadership and authority by the monks. However, even beyond the confines of the monastery, the superior or abbot was often held in the highest esteem. Even the rank and file of monks themselves were held in no little repute. They were the "holy" ones of God, and their prestige and influence was, at times, enormous.[61] Simeon the Stylite, for instance, was sought out by hundreds, but he kept retreating, until finally he built a hut on the top of a pillar. Although people looked to such people for spiritual leadership, the monks themselves usually tended to back away from any "full-time" ministry of this kind.

The clerically organized church was a monarchical structure, dominated by *episkopoi, presbyteroi* and *diakonoi.* As we have seen in the preceding chapter, the *laikoi,* in the fourth and fifth centuries, were continually being moved away from positions of influence and decision making as regards church life. In the monastic world, on the other hand, the *laikoi* (non-ordained) dominated. It was the leading *laikoi/monks* who held positions of influence and decision-making. The few presbyters who were part of these early monasteries rarely rose to positions of "jurisdiction,"[62] and even though they were presbyters they were counseled not to claim any superiority over other monks or live in a way that was different from the other monks.[63]

Most of the members of the monastic communities were from the lower classes. "Only rarely did members of the upper class enter a monastery."[64] Here and there, but infrequently, one hears about monks copying manuscripts,[65] and on occasion we find monks stepping forward publicly to oppose Arianism or Messalianism.[66] There were, however, no monastic schools in the early stages of this movement, and only when there was a secure economic foundation in the monasteries, that is, from the middle of the fifth century onward, do we find a few, and only a few, monastic theologians: Narsai, for instance, as also Rabula, who later became bishop of Edessa. Even the monasteries of Jerome, of Melania the Elder, of Paula the Elder, and of Pinian and Melania the Younger gave rise to only a few theologically skilled writers.[67]

The topic of the relationship between the monastic *koinonia* and the local churches has been treated by scholars in a rather frequent way.[68] In these discussions the term "ecclesiology" must be used with great caution, for a tract on the church as such, that is, a theologically articulated ecclesiology, does not appear until the late middle ages and early reformation period. Congar notes that "in the East as well as in the West, the Church was, at this period of time, a fact, not a doctrine."[69] Veilleux remarks that "it would then be better, for this period of history, to speak of an ecclesiological conscience rather than an ecclesiology properly so-called."[70] The nuns and monks, at least at the beginnings of this movement, assisted at the liturgy in the nearby local church. In the larger *koinoniai, a synaxis,* or central room for prayer and liturgy, was built. Gradually, i.e. when an ordained minister was available, the eucharistic liturgy was celebrated within the monastic enclave. When this happened, the monastic connection to the local church was radically changed. With prayer, with the sacraments, with the reading of the word of God, the nuns and monks enjoyed an ecclesial community totally within their own space. However, for the better part of their day, from morning until night, they experienced church, i.e. the daily living of their Christian life, in a non-ordained way, and on the basis of their daily experience they developed a consciousness of church, and this from a non-ordained perspective. For them, church was the routine of their daily life, and this routine was, with the exception of eucharist, totally non-clerical.

Both Veilleux[71] and Ueding[72] spend a great deal of time citing instances of harmony between local clergy, particularly the *episkopoi,* and the monks and nuns. Nonetheless, at the Council of Chalcedon (451) it was necessary to address the issue of monks and church authority. It is a truism that church councils do not take up abstract issues devoid of any practical application. Rather, church councils tend to deal with concrete, pastoral situations, provided they are of a rather extensive and pressing nature. Accordingly, one must admit, on the basis of these canons, that the actual relationship between monk and bishop was not all that smooth at that time. Since a conflictual situation here and there would not have occasioned a conciliar discussion, there must have been a rather extensive outbreak of conflicts between *episkopoi* and monks. Prior to Chalcedon, the theological stances of both Appolinarios and Eutyches provide us with the issues which brought monk and *episkopos* into conflict. Throughout the East, and to some degree in the West, Appolinarianism and Eutychianism provided the occasion for this conflict, for the archimandrite Eutyches was himself a leader of a monastic community and consequently had loyal monastic followers behind him. The history of this complicated situation of a monk, active in both the ecclesiastical and the political turmoil of the pre-Chalcedonian church, is recounted in detail elsewhere.[73] Certainly the situation of both Appolinarios and Eutyches and their relationship to monastic communities helped pave the way for eventual conciliar discussion of the monk/bishop relationship. Still, the issue behind the Chalcedonian canons seems to have been far more extensive than merely the matter of these two instances.

Ueding is careful to note that the canons of the Council of Chalcedon, which focused so strongly on the monks, involved both imperial and episcopal interventions. On the side of the clerical authority of the church, these canons, provided they were put into effect by imperial decree, safeguarded the unity of the church and the integrity of the faith. On the side of the monks themselves, these canons gave a certain official status to the monastic and convent life.[74]

Canon 4 has as its main objective the curtailing of monks who caused both civil and ecclesiastical disturbances, particularly as regards the furthering of heresy.[75] *Episkopoi,* the canon cautions, are to be on guard against this non-monastic activity. In some ways we can discover in the monastic defense of non-orthodox positions, against which the canon is directed, an indication of the reason for the antagonism between hierarchy and monk.[76] In the canon we also find that a *stabilitas loci* is demanded of monks. That there should be some movement from a monk's place was, however, part of the monastic spirituality of that time and place, since a monk might legitimately want to move for the sake of greater isolation, or for the sake of consulting another monk of known spiritual direction, or to follow in a better way the homelessness of

Christ.[77] Nonetheless, the canon stressed the *hesekia* or solitude and quietude which a monk's life demands, not a vagrancy which at times provided the occasion for a monk to be involved in civil and ecclesiastical disturbances.

Canon 3 raises the same basic issues, but as regards matters of property. What belongs to a monastery cannot be put on the market or used for personal gain. This interdiction applies to an *episkopos,* a cleric, and a monk. Without giving any specifics, the canon threatens punishments for anyone who so disposes of monastic property.

Neither of the two canons, however, implies an episcopal jurisdiction of the monks by the local bishop. That there is an episcopal care (*cura episcopalis*) and a vigilance (*vigilantia pastoralis*) is certainly implied, but one cannot find in these canons any legal jurisdiction or episcopal supremacy over monastic houses. *Ratione scandali* or *ratione peccati,* the bishop can indeed and should involve himself in the monastic structure, but only in these cases.[78] In other words, the basic independence of the monastic group was honored, and even bishops must respect this independence.

Ueding searches out the effects of these two canons in subsequent synodal and papal writings.[79] He focuses on (a) jurisdictional dependence of monasteries on the local bishop, (b) the establishment of a monastery within the jurisdiction of a bishop and whether or not there is a need to obtain his prior permission, (c) the alienation of monastic lands and assets, and (d) the episcopal oversight for monastic ideals. In the west acceptance of these canons of Chalcedon was difficult, since one of the canons of this council, namely canon 28, had to do with the recognition of the patriarchal see of Constantinople. To accept any of these canons would imply, so it seemed, an acceptance of all the canons, something which the bishops of Rome did not want to do.[80] That the canons played some role in the west is probably true, but only on one occasion is the Chalcedonian canon on the issue of monks mentioned specifically, namely in the provincial synod of Barcelona in 541. Otherwise, reference to the canons which deal with the monks is at best indirect. It would appear that the issue of episcopal jurisdiction over monasteries was not at all uniformly understood; that the issue of establishing monasteries without prior episcopal permission continued; that the alienation of monastic property and assets continued with various synods continuing to speak out against this defect; that various synods continually stressed the ideals of monastic life in a sort of generic way, which usually indicates that such ideals were not being observed, without any provision of details as regards the person[s] on whom the responsibility might lie for the rejuvenation of these ideals.

In all of this episcopal/monastic juxtaposition of authority, it is clear that two ecclesial structures were vying for existence. The episcopal or hierarchic structure had solidified around 200 and therefore was in place when the monastic movements began. Only with Chalcedon, in 451, do we have the first appearance of an attempt at some sort of "jurisdictional" rapprochement between clerical leadership and monastic leadership. At Chalcedon, monasticism, it might be said, reached an ecclesiastical acceptability. Prior to Chalcedon, the monastic movements were getting established and in a variety of ways and with a variety of relationships to local hierarchical structures. The official acknowledgement of monastic structures at Chalcedon in a real sense endorsed an alternative church structure. We find almost a chess game played out in subsequent centuries between local bishop, or even the episcopal structure as such, on the one hand, and, on the other, the monastic leadership. Exemptions and privileges, traditions and monastic rules, will again and again appear in ways which lessen any local or regional episcopal intervention into the life and structure of the monastic community. When, in the Frankish system, monasteries were placed under lay leadership (just as parish churches were also so placed), episcopal jurisdiction was for all practical purposes nullified. When, in the Cluniac reform, monasteries were placed directly under the pope and thereby exempted from local episcopal jurisdiction, we have once again a nullification of local episcopal intervention. This independence of the monasteries from the local bishop allowed in many areas the co-existence of two ecclesiastical structures, two alternative ways of being church. When this took place, however, at least in the western church, the male monasteries had been rather thoroughly clericalized, and as a result we not only have two alternative church structures, but we have two alternative clerical church structures. Moreover, as regards the internal life of the monastic church structure, at least in the case of male religious, the lay element gradually but almost universally became ineffective.

That the monastic structure became this alternative church structure can be seen in its very beginnings. Veilleux' chapter on "Baptême et vie cénobitique" (Baptism and the Cenobitic Life) is a gem of a picture and offers us some very insightful perspectives on monastic or religious life at that early period.[81] Candidates for the monastic life were accepted in the Pachomian *koinoniai*, even though they had as yet not been baptized into the Christian faith. These candidates for baptism served their time as catechumens within the monastic framework itself and were instructed for baptism by the monks themselves.[82] Their initial experience and explanation of church was by and large (a) monastic and (b) non-ordained. The role models for baptized Christians, whom these candidates would have seen and heard, were non-ordained monks.

In an even more remarkable turn of events, these candidates, at the very time of their baptism, became monks. In other words, entering the church meant, for them, entering the monastic life. The monastic life was none other than the church life. "Initiation into the Christian life and initiation into the monastic life were one and the same thing."[83] This identification of baptized life/monastic life merits our consideration, for ecclesiologically it has many ramifications. Contemporary scholars have raised the issue of monastic profession as a "second baptism."[84] Veilleux, however, concludes that such an idea of a second baptism cannot be found in the Pachomian material. Monastic profession and "first baptism" coincide for the Pachomian catechumens. Nor was the monastic *diatheke*, or promise, a "religious profession" as appears later on in church history.[85] Although Jerome used the term "second baptism" quite certainly for martyrdom, it cannot be maintained that he also used the phrase in reference to monastic life as well. The first clear occasion when "second baptism" refers to monastic profession is that found in Theodore of Canterbury (648). For Pachomias, one baptism was quite sufficient, and baptism is entry into the church. "La Koinonia pachôumienne est une véritable communauté ecclésiale, une véritable Église locale."[86] (The Pachomian *koinonia* was a true ecclesial community, a true local church.)

The eucharist also played a major role in the formation of monastic communities. It seems that in their beginnings, anchoritic and monastic men and women assisted at the liturgy in a local church. With the construction of *koinoniai* and other monasteries, a chapel for the religious gradually came to be an essential part of the enclave. In the case of the male religious, if there was no presbyter-monk, then a visiting presbyter eventually acted as a sort of eucharistic chaplain. When there was a presbyter among the monks themselves, then the monastery became self-sufficient as far as eucharist is concerned.[87] However, these early monks made no liturgical innovations to the eucharistic liturgy, which, in the Egyptian monastic structure, they most often celebrated on both Saturday and Sunday. With the eucharistic celebration within the confines of the monasteries themselves, the aspect of an "alternative" local church structure becomes even more pronounced.

The word of God was central to monastic spirituality. Although the rank-and-file monk and to some degree nun was a fairly non-educated person, efforts were continually made to make the reading of scriptural passages part of a monk's daily life. In its beginnings, communal monastic prayer could hardly be called an "office," or the "official church prayer." As yet, monks and nuns were not really acknowledged as "official" parts of the church. Nonetheless, that monks and nuns spent hours at prayer is a truism. It was part of their spiritual journey, and this prayer was based heavily on scripture. The psalms clearly played a key role. Passages from other sections of both Old and New Testaments were central to this communal prayer. Indeed, as we see in the school of Nisibis, scripture itself came to be seen by some Christians as the only source for all knowledge. Any other writings were not acceptable. The monks and nuns, for the most part, disdained pagan literature and philosophy; they focused their thinking on the one fountain of knowledge, the scriptures, God's own word. The leaders of these communities were expected to exegete scripture, a task which Pachomias and Theodore did well, and which Horsiesios did in a most mediocre way. All three of these men were non-ordained.

With this internal prayer and exegesis of scripture, we have still another element or structure for an ecclesial community. Any and every church is made up of word and sacrament, and within the walls of the *koinonia* and the *laura* we have, as time goes on, both. The pagan who became a catechumen and was baptized in the monastery and then lived his or her entire life within that structure experienced the church monastically, and for that person it was the only church experience. For those who entered as already baptized Christians, their experience of church was, from then on, a monastic church experience. These experiences of church were, with the exception of eucharist, a non-clericalized experience of church. On the basis of this non-clerical experience of church, these same men and women thought through and articulated their understanding of church. We find this articulation in the many writings of the "desert fathers," and in the many writings of early monks, including the monastic rules, and to some extent in the various lives of these early ascetics.

However, neither this monastic "lay" experience nor this monastic "thinking" on church was the same as the lay experience of ordinary Christian men and women who lived in the cities and on the farms. For this latter lay group, their experience of church was dominated by the hierarchical structures of episcopal churches. At one and the same time in church history, then, there were two differing "non-ordained" experiences of church, two differing "lay" understandings of church. The differences in these ecclesiological consciences are so strong that they call into question the ideological *laikos/klerikos* division of a later Christian church. On the basis of the data, would it not be better to consider the monk and nun as neither cleric nor lay, but as a distinct group within the Christian community?

4. CONCLUSIONS FROM THE DATA

This chapter has been fairly selective in its focus on monastic material, and yet it does not seem irresponsible to say that anchorites, monks and nuns during this early period of monastic growth were not regarded as ordinary, non-ordained Christians. Nor were they considered ordained Christians. They were in a class by themselves. It also seems quite responsible to say that the variety of monastic movements indicates an early, non-monolithic view as regards the meaning of these movements. All these ascetical men and women were attempting to lead a life of discipleship. This is a common factor, but it is also common to the hopes of clerics and the hopes of ordinary lay men and women. Nonetheless, discipleship, an issue stressed in an earlier chapter as the most important point of departure, must remain even in the issue of monastic life the basic point of departure. Such issues as poverty, chastity, obedience, expectations of the end time, etc., cannot displace this basic point of departure: discipleship. From the beginning there appears to be no "essence" of religious life, and this cautions us today to question current efforts to establish the "essence" of religious life.

From the very beginning, the issue of episcopal/monastic relationships was undefined. Only as problems arose did local and regional councils take up specific issues, and even then the edicts of such councils found little echo in subsequent history. The seeds for an ongoing struggle between the episcopal church structure and the monastic church structure were already in place, even though they remained quite unnoticed. Every century of subsequent church history might be cited for instances in which this struggle flared up in some way or another. Even today's church has many instances of such a struggle.[88] Even the fact that eventually "jurisdictional" issues continued to surface indicates that a simplistic *laikos/klerikos* model of church structure is ecclesiologically insufficient.

A final conclusion can also be drawn from the data, namely the seeds of eventual clericalization of male religious life begin to be evident even at an early stage. Clericalization of male religious life does not mean simply that more and more male religious become clerics and assume key jurisdictional roles. This indeed did happen, but clericalization is far more permeating than simply numerical and jurisdictional strength. Clericalization of religious life, directly in the case of male religious, indirectly in the case of female religious, means that religious life is (a) experienced as basically a clerical movement, and (b) thought through in basically clerical categories. In the various "ecclesiologies" of monastic life, one finds other secondary, but still quite important, factors involved in this process of clericalization. The following are some of these additional factors.

A. LITURGICAL CENTERING

Benedict structured monastic life around the liturgical horarium of the day, with the eucharistic celebration in a central position. However, since monastic life tended to involve to some degree an agrarian infrastructure, the daily life of monks had to adapt to the rhythms of animal husbandry and farming (feeding time for animals, milking time, times for plowing, seeding, reaping, etc.). These rhythms are not very moveable. Consequently, the liturgical rhythm needed to mesh with the needs of these agrarian concerns. Only at a much later date in history, when clerical monks devoted themselves to study and academic pursuits, pursuits which are not hidebound to natural, physical rhythms, could the liturgical rhythm take on a more flexible pattern.[89] Nonetheless, this convergence of monastic life to liturgical life, and most specifically eucharistic liturgical life, tended to focus monastic life around something very clerical. Gregory the Great, as we have seen, stressed the eucharist as a paradigm for the sacrificial life of the monk, and the life of the monk, in Gregory's view, was the paradigm for cleric, for ruler, and for the ordinary Christian. The intertwining of monastic life and eucharistic life makes a monastic relationship of ordained and non-ordained factors extremely close and contributes in no small measure to the process of clericalization.

B. EQUATION OF ABBOT TO BISHOP

The "episcopation" of abbots, i.e. the way in which abbots increasingly modeled their insignia of office, their liturgical function, their form of jurisdiction,[90] their presence at councils with a voice equal to that of bishops, also contributed to the process of clericalization of male religious. In a later period of the middle ages, abbots were at times far more influential than some neighboring bishops, so that an episcopal consecration of an abbot for a neighboring diocese was considered a "demotion" rather than a "promotion."

C. DOMESTICATION OF MONASTIC LIFE

The "domestication" of anchoritic and monastic life also played a role in the process of clericalization. Anchorites, monks and nuns, at an early stage, were associated with a *fuga e mundo* (a flight from the world). When European countries had been basically Christianized, which meant that Christian leaders, bishops and popes, played major roles in the socioeconomic structuring of life, monastic life was not envisioned as a flight, but as an essential and integral part of the Christian life, indeed a normal part of the *societas Christiana*. The success of the Iro-Gallic monks depended, to no small degree, on the government. Ansgar's missionary activity as well as that of Boniface, for instance, kept in tandem with Frankish economic and political activities. Earlier on, the "jurisdiction" of missionary activity in Illyricum became a matter of dispute between

Constantinople and Rome, but Illyricum was an area within the socio-political framework of the Roman empire, not outside of it. Missionary activity only on the rarest of occasions moved into areas which were not at least an inchoative part of the socio-political structures. In other words, missionary activity, which was basically monastic activity, became part of the church-empire domestication of the western world. With the domestication of monastic structures, the interconnection with episcopal structures became increasingly complex. On many occasions, the Iro-Gallic monks with their agrarian abbeys became the main pastoral centers for an entire region, while in another, even adjacent area, the episcopal structures formed an almost identical pastoral center, minus the agrarian relationships of monk and farmer. Although one was monastic and the other episcopal, these two types of religious centers tended both to imitate each other and to compete with one another.

All of these elements or seeds began to appear, here and there, in the early monastic enclaves. Not all such elements can be found in every monastic area, but when one considers the wide geographic diversity of these monastic structures, one can find the elements or seeds of eventual clericalization present in a spotty but nonetheless actual way. Historical factors, more than anything else, were the cause why some of these elements played a greater role than others. In other words, the eventual clericalization of male religious communities cannot be seen as an "essential" aspect of male monastic movements. That these male religious communities became clericalized was due to contingent factors, but the seeds of this eventual, though contingent, development can be found, here and there, in differing areas of early monasticism.

All of these particular conclusions from the data indicate that there was not a single, over-arching "ecclesiology" that pre-determined the formation of monastic life. Rather, there were many "ecclesiological consciousnesses," which molded in various ways what the western church has come to know as religious life. There will be in this same western history a series of renewals of religious life, each of which negatively critiques a given ecclesiology that at a given age appears to dominate monastic life, and which positively offers a different ecclesiology for monastic or religious life. This negative-positive renewal is most often based on a rethinking of discipleship, and the rethinking of discipleship reshapes one's ecclesiology.

7

The Lay Person in the Medieval Frankish Church: 700 to 1000 A.D. The Turning of the Tide

The beginnings of the so-called middle ages and the end of the patristic period are difficult to determine. There appears to be a quiet fading out, on the one hand, of the patristic period and, on the other, a gentle dawning of the medieval period. One might possibly think that the turning date could be 733, for it was then that Charles Martel decisively defeated the Arab invaders at the battle of Poitiers. Others might locate the turning date, as far as the east is concerned, with the death of the synthesizing theologian, John Damascene (c. 750). Still others, more focused on the west, might regard the turning date to coincide with the death of Gregory the Great (604), or the death of Isidore of Seville (636), or even the death of Bede the Venerable (735).[1]

M. Wallace-Hadrill's study, *The Frankish Church,* though not, as he states in his preface, a measured historical account of this period of ecclesiastical history, but rather an account of aspects of Frankish church history which he himself finds interesting (*scripsi quod sensi*), begins with some background material on both the Gallo-Roman period and the Merovingian church. He ends in an equally unmeasured way toward the close of the ninth century.[2] He presents, however, an exciting (in my view) portrait of many profound aspects of this Frankish church/kingdom period.

In the Fliche-Martin series on church history, the volume for this particular period, i.e. the end of the patristic period and the beginning of the middle ages, is called *L'Église au pouvoir des laïques 888–1057.*[3] This

273

is an ambiguous title, since the authors in the text itself by no means argue that the laity as such controlled the church, but only that a few, powerfully placed non-ordained people, emperors, kings and such exercised decisive control over many crucial church-related situations. Actually, from the end of the patristic period and throughout the early medieval era, the ordinary non-ordained person in the church had very little ecclesial status. Theologically and pastorally, "lay personhood" within church structures by itself provided scant basis for either ecclesial or social dignity, either position or power. The key non-ordained people, who did have dignity, position and power within the church, had these, not because they were "lay," or non-ordained, but because they were well-placed in the socio-political and economic world, which gave them entry into the ecclesial world.

The early middle ages came to an end roughly around 1000. Again the cut-off date might be a matter of dispute, for the flow from the early medieval into the high medieval period was gradual and certainly not the same in all parts of the western European world. It is safe to say, however, that from 700 to 1000 several processes took place, which had major repercussions on the positioning—or, better, repositioning—of the non-ordained person in the church.

In this chapter, we will consider the material under the following divisions:

1. **Introduction to the Four Processes**
2. **The Four Processes Which Altered the Position of Lay Christians**
   a. **The Repositioning of Royal/Imperial Persons**
   b. **The Repositioning of Educated Lay Christians**
   c. **Monasticism and the "Rediscovery" of the Lay Brother**
   d. **The Liturgical Life in the Early Middle Ages**
3. **Conclusions from the Data**
   a. **The Repositioning of Royal/Imperial Persons**
   b. **The Repositioning of the Monastic Lay Brother**
   c. **The Repositioning of the Educated Lay Christian**
   d. **The Repositioning of the Lay Person in Church Liturgy**

1. INTRODUCTION TO THE FOUR PROCESSES

A. THE REPOSITIONING OF ROYAL/IMPERIAL PERSONS

At the beginning of this period of church history, the relationship of the Frankish kings to the papacy was just beginning.

If the connection between the earliest Frankish kings and Rome was tenuous, it would be a fair guess that it was through no ill-will on the part of the kings. Communications were hazardous. The popes themselves were uneasily placed between the Ostrogothic rulers of Italy and emperors far away in Constantinople and often indifferent or even hostile to the North.[4]

Times change and circumstances with them. Merovingian kings were masters of their own church, and with strong will on the one hand, and adequate means on the other, clergy could be attracted to the court, where they could be rewarded and used. Merovingian kings could summon councils of clergy, sometimes with lay attendance, sometimes without. They could set conciliar agenda, control conciliar deliberations, and oversee the enactment of conciliar decrees.[5]

By 747, as seen from the letters of Pope Zacharias, the Roman curia was fairly well abreast of the way things were going within the Frankish world. Pippin III himself had received advice on some canonical issues from this same pope. When, a short time later, the rather famous mission of Burghard and Fulrad was sent to Zacharias on orders of Pippin with the single question "Should a ruler, enjoying no power, rightly continue to bear the title of king?"[6] it was clear that the pope was being invited to lend his prestige to the view that the Merovingians had become an anachronism.[7] The Carolingian, Pippin, then took control, and with him a new era began.

It was no great step, therefore, for men to begin to see a new and powerful king as a New David, even a New Moses. Imagery of this sort makes its appearance soon after the change of dynasty had been effected. And what would a New David lead if not the columns of a New Israel? Frankish liturgies were not slow to make the connection, which is also found in the earliest Frankish *Laudes Regiae*, the liturgical acclamations of a priest-king that invoke the martial qualities of king and Christ alike.[8]

The gradual positioning of the king (and later emperor) to a sacramental status within the Christian community led inevitably to a theological justification of this sacramental status, such as one finds in the theological writings of Alcuin, early on, and Hincmar of Rheims, toward the close of this period. At the end of this same period of church history, even with the liturgical and theological statements on such themes as priest-king, vicar of Christ, and eternal ruler with Christ, there was a concomitant, contrary process, namely, a repositioning of the imperial/regal status, which struggled to remove from the emperor/king any such liturgical, sacramental or theological positioning, and "reduced" the emperor/king to the "lay state." The success of this latter movement of course led to the eventual, ironclad dichotomy, which stated that there were only lay or cleric members within the church. The struggle of the royal and imperial parties to maintain their unique position within church and society, and the correlative struggle of the popes, particularly, but also of some bishops, to assert clerical (or at least papal) dominance over all sectors of society, including the regent sector, has been generally entitled the "lay investiture" controversy. In this controversy, the royal and imperial group (*regnum*), which was eventually reduced to "lay" status, for the most part, lost its powerful role within intra-ecclesiastical processes. However, the loss of regal ecclesiastical status served as a major step, favoring two subsequent processes, namely (a) the further and even extreme politicizing of higher clerics, but especially the pope, since the *sacerdotium* (either papally or episcopally understood) attempted to take over and sometimes actually did take over many of the prerogatives and powers of the *regnum,* and (b) the reduction of *regnum* to a lay state (*laicatus*) which provided enormous impetus to the development of the theory of Church and state, a theory that effectively removed an arena of *societas humana* from direct clerical control, and that gave an independent legitimacy to this field of lay administration.

In the early stages of the "lay investiture" struggle, one can find, both underneath and throughout the flourishes of rhetoric and the bravado of skirmishes, a deep-seated discontent, on the part of some non-ordained, with the over-arching, almost all-inclusive, clerical claim of dominance, which both some prelates, even those in the highest offices of the church, and some theologians of that era were demanding. In this early medieval struggle, however, the "lay" element both lost and gained: it lost a great deal of power within inner-church processes; it gained, at the end of the struggle, a sphere of influence, which in time became a major, often antagonistic, counter-weight to the over-clericalism of the Roman church.

B. THE REPOSITIONING OF THE MONASTIC LAY BROTHER

At the beginning of this period, i.e. 700, monastic life was still rather strongly a non-ordained preserve, but nonetheless one that was already moving toward a clericalized structure. At the end of this period, i.e. 1000, male monastic life was dominantly a clerical preserve. At the beginning, monastic life was still somewhat counter-culture; at the end of the period, monastic life had become such an integral part of the *societas Christiana* that it was often called an essential part of Christian life. In this period, religious life in the west became more and more standardized, due in no small part to the decree from the Council of Aachen, 816, making both the Benedictine rule itself and also a uniform observance of it mandatory on every religious community, either male or female. This decree and its energetic enactment by the court throughout the western world highly influenced the "theological" understanding of religious life, namely, that religious life is basically monolithic, no matter what particular founder or what particular name a group might have. The standardization of religious life in the rigid form of the Aachen decree contributed in no small measure to the domestication of religious life. At the very same time as this decree was being energetically put into practice, more and more monks were being ordained, thus clericalizing male monastic life or at least clericalizing the decision making stratum of male monastic life. At the end of this period of history, one finds a movement of reform in some male monastic communities, a reform which included within it the rediscovery of the lay brother.

Again, one notices that as the clericalization of the male monasteries began to increase, the non-ordained monk was gradually depositioned. He is gradually but systematically excluded from the decision making stratum of monastic life. The "lay" brother, however, should be carefully distinguished from the so-called "lay abbots." These latter were laymen, generally men among the higher levels of aristocratic society, who in the feudal system had received the right to govern an abbey, but without becoming a monk. Within the internal structures of the abbey itself, however, there were both cleric monks and lay monks. It is these latter who formed a major part of the renewal called the "rediscovery of the lay brother" at the turn of the millennium, and who energetically strove for a repositioning within the monastic structures. This particular lay movement, of itself, was short-lived, for the major monasteries, even after such reforms, quickly reinstated a clerical framework. Nonetheless, the failure of this lay revolt helped to bring about another religious movement, one which drastically rivaled monastic life itself, namely the *vita evangelica* movement of the eleventh to fourteenth centuries. In this latter movement, non-ordained Christians found in the various *vita evangelica* groups a way of meeting their hopes and ideals for a life of Christian discipleship, which the monastic life, i.e. the *vita apostolica,* did not seem to offer them.

C. THE REPOSITIONING OF THE EDUCATED LAY CHRISTIAN

At the beginning of this same period of church history, education of the *plebs* or ordinary layfolk was almost non-existent. Some clerics were educated, particularly in England, and from England, through the efforts of Alcuin and other reform-minded abbots and bishops, the continental clerics as well. At the beginning of this period, certain monasteries, but in a quite varied and non-uniform way, stressed the academic vocation.

Through these educational, monastic centers, a number of western monks were fairly well trained academically. At the beginning of this period, these educated monks would have included a large number of non-ordained monks. As the period under consideration progresses, however, it will be the cleric-monk who is educated, and the non-ordained monk will be systematically moved to the area of manual labor. Moreover, at the beginning of the eighth century, some, but certainly not all, royal or aristocratic children also received an education, and it was these educated kings and nobles who subsequently sponsored in magnificent ways the various monastic educational endeavors. Beyond these categories of people, education was not a priority. "The fact that the ninth century saved so much of pagan literature for the future does not imply that it was taught in the schools as it had been in the schools of Antiquity. Learning in general was elementary and spasmodic."[9] An uneducated general populace, quite naturally, kept the ordinary laity, *plebs,* from any inciteful ecclesial and socio-political role. As one moves toward the year 1000, however, the monastic (both male and female) academic centers and subsequently the cathedral schools became more and more established and endowed, with the result that there were more and more high-quality scholars/teachers. Moreover, the economic world was slowly beginning to change, so that there began to emerge a growing number of merchants, with a financial base, which allowed them, eventually in the high middle ages, to provide an education for their children. These children were not clerics, not monks or nuns, not part of the royal/imperial enclave. In other words, slowly but surely, an educated *plebs* began to develop in the western world. When an educated lay group finally emerged, the stage was set for a large and powerful group of educated lay Christians to do two things:

> Educated lay Christians began, gradually, of course, to move into the arena of "state," at the very same time in which the clerics moved exclusively into the arena of "Church." The fact that the theory of "Church-state" became an articulated one in the thirteenth century requires a pre-history, and both the "lay-investiture" struggle and the rise of an educated lay group are major parts of this pre-history.

> Educated lay Christians began to question positions, which clerics, who until this time had been the dominant group within the academic enclave, had maintained. Erasmus was not a *hapax legoumenos* in this process. There were many predecessors, and as we know from history, many successors. Men and women,

such as Erasmus, Copernicus, Keppler, Newton, etc., do not appear like comets, and the slow but steady rise of an educated group of non-clerics, non-monks, non-nuns, non-royal family, set the stage for a major lay movement in the fourteenth, fifteenth and sixteenth centuries.

D. THE REPOSITIONING OF THE LAY PERSON IN CHURCH LITURGY

In the Carolingian reformation, the liturgy of the church, and particularly the sacramental liturgies, were renewed. Basically the sacraments were more and more clericalized, a process which one sees in a striking way in marriage rites and in the rites for the anointing of the sick and the dying. However, the other sacraments also underwent changes, through which the ordinary lay person, both male and female, were positioned into a role of listener and observer (e.g. the eucharist), or into a role of ever-growing dependency on clerics for eternal life or death (e.g. penance), and a role of religious non-freedom (e.g. infant baptism). The liturgical changes grew up spasmodically and gradually, but as they became more generalized throughout the Carolingian world, theologians and canonists were quick to develop both theological and canonical justifications for such liturgical changes. Usually, the *lex orandi,* i.e. the way various churches pray, takes place first; this is then followed by the development of a *lex credendi.* Only on rare occasions does the opposite happen.[10]

It is well known that the scholastic theology, which developed from 1000 to 1500, produced a remarkable set of teachings on the seven sacraments. For several centuries thereafter this sacramental theology was viewed as the common Roman Catholic theology of the sacraments. We know today that the medieval synthesis of sacramental theology was based almost exclusively on an explanation of the liturgical *praxis* of that period of time and place. The historical development of the various sacraments, prior to the high middle ages, was for the most part unavailable to the scholastic theologians, and as a result a very narrow application of the *lex orandi, lex credendi* was utilized. The scholastic *lex credendi* regarding sacraments arose from the *praxis* which the Carolingian reformation on sacramental liturgical ritual developed, and in the Carolingian development of sacramental ritual the ordinary lay Christian was systematically moved to an ever increasing ancillary position, while the Christian cleric was systematically moved to an ever increasing centralized position.

This chapter, then, traces in particular these four processes. When these processes finally reached a stage of maturity, another process had begun to develop in a very mature way: namely that of canon law. It is canon law which formulated a stringent, even called a "divinely instituted" bi-partite division of the entire Christian world: namely, lay/cleric. In the canonical format the *ordo clericorum* becomes a divinely established caste or *ordo*, not only distinct from but superior to any lay or secular *ordo*, to which all non-clerics belong. This juridic division of the *societas Christiana* into lay/cleric was another etiological factor for the development of the theological theory that the ordained cleric is "ontologically" different from and superior to the "ontological" status of every lay Christian, even those of regal or imperial rank.

If we look just over the edge of our chapter's time period, we see a rather apical expression of this clerical superiority. Though the *Dictatus Papae Gregorii VII* (written c. 1075) was probably a private memorandum, it became, as É. Voosen notes, "a syllabus of the ideas which thenceforth were to dominate all the history of the pontificate."[11] N. 12 of this *Dictatus* states: "That it is permitted to him [the pope] to depose emperors," and in n. 27 one reads: "That he [the pope] can absolve the subjects of the unjust [lord] from their fealty."[12] The shrillness of the *Dictatus* is indeed extreme, but it provides us with some sense of the intensity of the debate in the immediately preceding period of history, in which such ideas began to be expounded, tested, and codified. The counter-arguments of the imperial scholars and theologians are, at times, no less shrill and no less indicative of the intensity of the debate. The repositioning of the king, i.e. his reduction to the lay state, was not accomplished either submissively or without great stress. Nor was the effort to make the clerical position a "class" or "caste" position accomplished either submissively or without great stress. The eventual canonical formulation of the cleric/lay church by Gratian had a lengthy and at times violent pre-history. The four areas which this chapter considers did not by themselves necessarily lead up to Gratian's formulation. The emergence and development of canon law were indispensable for that. Nonetheless, these four processes helped buttress the emergence and development of canonical law, and the eventual emergence and development of canon law was buttressed by these four movements. At the same time, however, the four movements also helped to move away from or hinder the very development of such a canonical formulation, since such extreme repositioning of the lay person could only create a situation in the church which needed to be redressed, since every imbalance demands a rebalancing situation. The development of an apodictic lay/cleric division of the church was just such an imbalance, for it has no biblical base. The word of God, which gives life to the Christian church, began to cry out for a redress.

The establishment of a dominant clerical class or *ordo* within the church, and, because of the western situation at that time, within the socio-political sphere as well, gave rise, as we mentioned in the introduction to this volume, to a series of counter-movements, which like the incoming tide gradually erodes the shoreline with an ever-increasing invasion of that same shoreline. By the year 1000 low tide for the lay Christian was reached, and the turn of the millennium coincided with the turning of the tide for a better repositioning of the lay person in the *societas Christiana*. The reassertion of the lay brother marks the first reversal of the tide. This led to the second, the *vita evangelica* movements of the eleventh to thirteenth centuries. The turning of the tide as far as lay education is concerned led to the onrush of humanistic, scientific, and artistic ideas by highly educated lay men and women of the fourteenth to sixteenth centuries. In turn, these tidal sweeps helped strengthen the way, along with other factors, for the ideas on basic human freedoms which stem from the French and American revolutions. The tidal destruction and reconstruction of western society and church which these two revolutions brought on was pervasive. More recently, the inflow of both contemporary feminist theology as well as liberation theology has continued the tidal movement, and one cannot say that high tide has, as yet, been reached. The material in this chapter, then, culminates at the point of the turning of the tide, and from this turning point one can go on to trace the slow, often painful, effort to reposition the lay person into church structures. This slow, painful process has affected not only the Roman Catholic Church, but the entire gamut of Christian churches in the western world.

2. THE FOUR PROCESSES WHICH ALTERED THE POSITION OF THE LAY CHRISTIAN

A. THE REPOSITIONING OF ROYAL/IMPERIAL PERSONS

From the coronation of Pepin down to Pope Gregory VII, 1073–1085, we find initially a powerful and almost western universal affirmation of the divine right of emperors and kings, with abundant written material, theologically justifying this imperial divine right, only to be followed in the later centuries by a clerically organized and an often bitterly waged contesting of such a divine right.

> The origin of political authority was not, for medieval publicists, primarily an historical question. . . . The question they chiefly asked was what made authority legitimate; they tried to answer it in terms of purposes assumed to be permanent and sought their premises in the nature of man and the providence of God. The problem first appeared to them as the problem of the basis of kingship rather than of "the state."[13]

The issue at stake was the origin of the "king" or "emperor," not the origin of the "state," and whenever the stability of the emperor and king turned precarious, the issue was raised to nervous heights. In the eighth century, on both the eastern and western frontiers, the position of Christendom, i.e. both church and government, was threatened by outside sources. Pope Gregory II wrote to the emperor, Leo III, that the center of gravity of the western Christian world had begun to shift to the inner west. In no way did this imply that either Gregory personally or the majority of western citizens had broken allegiance with the emperor. Rather, because of external and internal factors, the western part of the empire was more and more left to fend for itself and defend itself. Nonetheless, not only Gregory but his papal successors in the eighth century felt keenly that they belonged to the empire. However, little by little "the Popes became Italy's spokesmen [for the emperor], but at the same time they spoke for a religious and ecclesiastical group which still saw the Empire as a unity."[14] Moreover, the emperor was generally viewed, even by the highest clerics, as one whose position had been established by divine right itself, and he exercised his authority as one sent by God. This kind of "imperial theology" was, at the beginning of our period, almost universally accepted.

The emergence of Frankish rule in the west has been often described by historians as the beginning of Europe. Indeed, the very term "Europe" appears at the turn of the eighth/ninth century for the first time. Judith Herrin, however, wisely notes that "traditional approaches, which often assume that the distinct character of modern Europe was already present in embryonic form in Charles's realm [Charles the Great], are distorted by hindsight."[15] She places the rise of the Frankish church-state within a larger Mediterranean context, "where it becomes evident that it was one part of a much larger process, whose center of gravity lay in the East. . . . The correlation of all three forces, Islamic, Byzantine, and Frankish-Papal, ensured that no one military order or religious culture would again unite the world that had been Rome's."[16] The thematic focus of this present chapter is clearly on the inner-west; indeed, it is on a small detail of the *societas Christiana,* which was found in the inner-west, namely the position of the non-ordained in that society. Nonetheless, Islamic influences on western development cannot be relegated to the margin of historical judgments, and it is noteworthy that Herrin describes a key Frankish-papal document, namely the forged *Constitutum Constantini,* in a context which included the Islamic claims for the *hadith,* the so-called oral traditions pronounced by Mohammed himself. I. Goldziher notes that the systematic use (and abuse) of these sayings created "one of the greatest and most successful literary functions." One could quite similarly say that the systematic use (and abuse) of certain forged Christian documents resulted in a similar situation.[17] The presence of Islam in the west eventually affected the educational world, and it prevented the Christian world of the west to retain even a nominal unity. When one takes into account that North Africa, Spain, Sardinia, Cyprus, the coast of Provence and Crete were again and again under attack by "Saracen" pirates and some of these locales even occupied rather permanently by the Islamic forces, the alliance of Roman popes and Frankish kings begins to move beyond any mere theological interpretation, and must be seen within a context of socio-political, economic survival. The *Codex Carolinus,* i.e. the letters of Carolingian kings from 739 to 791, contains only the letters from the popes to the Carolingian kings. No codex remains of the letters from the kings to the popes. The extant written material offers Rome's view; one must go beyond this one-sided view to understand the total western view.

When the west began to turn its allegiance to the Frankish kings, kingship, particularly the source and legitimacy of kingship, remained the crucial issue. Charles the Great in 772 repudiated his Lombard wife, a step which was risky, since Desiderius, the Lombard king, held hostage the young sons of Charles' brother, Carloman. But he did this for "what he so clearly appreciated was the dependence of his rule in the eyes of Frankish churchmen on loyal implementation of solemn undertakings made to Rome by his father."[18] However, even though Charles went to Italy, and even to Rome, in order to assist Pope Hadrian, he had no intention of giving the Pope all the Italian lands which he claimed. "The pope could go on protesting at the difficulties and injustices to which his properties and agents were subjected, but the fact remained that he was simply Charlemagne's man. This was what Frankish protection entailed."[19] Such a situation indicates that the Frankish king was never a "lay" person like any other lay person within the church. He was a quite distinctive person within the *societas Christiana,* and given this distinction by God himself. He was as "ontologically" different from the ordinary non-ordained person as any pope, bishop, priest, or other cleric was "ontologically" different, even though on a different basis.

Charles the Great and his advisors carefully chose each word of his title, which was part of his coronation at Rome in 800:

Serenissimus augustus a Deo coronatus magnus pacificus imperator, Romanum imperium gubernans qui et per misericordiam Dei rex Francorum et Langobardorum.

The most serene, august, crowned by God, great and peace-loving emperor, ruling the Roman empire, who is also through the mercy of God the king of the Franks and the Lombards.[20]

In many ways there is nothing new in this Carolingian title. De facto and de iure he was already king of the Franks and of the Lombards.[21] In many ways he was already de facto the Roman emperor, and the coronation was simply one of the many de iure instances which confirmed his position.[22] Whether Byzantine emperor or Frankish king was made Roman emperor, the legitimacy of kingship was seen in the phrase *Dei gratia*. It was God himself who had chosen this person to be the august ruler. Divine right, divine institution, divine grace were the roots of kingship, not delegation by another human, even a cleric, even the most prestigious of the western clerics.

Charles was not unique in this understanding of divine destiny. His son, Louis the Pious, in 817, signed with much prayer and ceremony the *ordinatio imperii*. This document described solemnly the distribution of the empire for both the present and the future.

> It rested upon the most significant concept of the [Carolingian] Renaissance, not yet elaborated but generally felt: namely, that the empire was a Christian unity, and more than that, was itself the *Corpus Christi*, indivisible and sacred. To disturb this unity by dissension, let alone by rebellion and warfare, would be to dismember the Body of Christ.[23]

Of course, the emperor was the one who had the solemn task of preserving the unity of this *Corpus Christi*. The emperor as well as a king was clearly not a "lay" person in the sense of any other lay person. In the same period of time, Jonas, the bishop of Orléans, wrote *De institutione regia*, reminding Pippin, the king of Aquitaine, of his duties as a Christian ruler. A companion work, *De institutione laicali*, was written for a mere count. A distinction between *rex* and *laicus* is certainly evident in the titles of these two works of the eighth century.

The *Ordo of Mainz*, whose final composition dates from about 960, which coincides with the end-period of this chapter, contains an imperial coronation liturgy which is highly sacramental in tone.[24] Once again, liturgical and therefore theologically significant terms and phrases can be found which indicate that the king is clearly not a lay person. He ascends the regal throne because of his right of inheritance and *per auctoritatem Dei omnipotentis et praesentem traditionem nostram* (n. 25). The gift of kingship comes from God, and is made manifest publicly through the *officium* of the bishops. The bishops are the vicars of the apostles and the saints; the king is the vicar of Christ.[25] Schramm concludes that the *Ordo of Mainz* presents the official theory of kingship, which had been formulated by clerics themselves, and that the doctrine found in this *Ordo* is essentially the socio-political and theological understanding of kingship which Otto I as well as his successors claim as their own.[26] Thus, from the coronation of Charles the Great down through the Saxon kings, there is enough evidence to say that the emperor/king was both socio-politically and theologically considered in an *ordo* or class by himself, distinct from cleric, monk and lay. The incumbent was established in this singular position within the *societas Christiana* by God himself, not by popes, not by bishops, not by the *sacerdotium. Regnum* is God-given.

Popes and patriarchs saw themselves also established in their positions by divine right, and they too exercised their authority as men sent by God. These claims of establishment by divine right could not help but engender confrontation, since both the imperial and the ecclesial claims were not clearly divided along such lines as "church and state," or "religious and secular," or "spiritual and profane." The growing claims of papal supremacy, which one finds in the west, included political jurisdiction not only over the Roman area, but gradually and, sometimes by default of imperial protection, over many other areas as well. The dispute over the hegemony of Illyricum, for example, or over the Bulgars, contributed in no small way to the Photian schism. The patriarch of Constantinople claimed jurisdiction over Illyricum and over the Bulgar missions. The bishop of Rome also claimed such jurisdiction. The bases for these conflicting claims, made by both sides, often went beyond legitimacy, and in the course of negotiations many compromises had to be made. Illyricum and the Bulgar nations were, of course, part of the Byzantine empire, and the jurisdiction of the emperor was never in question. Rather in question was the ecclesiastical jurisdiction. This ecclesiastical jurisdiction, however, was not merely over spiritual and religious issues, for at stake were also far-reaching economic and politically strategic issues associated with Illyricum and the Bulgar region. Thus, conflicting ecclesiastical or spiritual claims [Rome-Constantinople] also involved conflicting socio-political and economic claims. As time went by, the Roman popes began to base in an increasingly global way all of their claims on a divine right, i.e. the right of papal supremacy, a right not only to the religious area, but also to political, economic and social areas as well. On the other hand, the eastern patriarchs, particularly the patriarch of Constantinople, but not only he, made their claims as well on an ecclesiastical or spiritual base, but their claims, too, had socio-political and economic ramifications. The eastern patriarchs based their claims on "apostolic" sees, and in the case of Antioch an apostolic see chronologically prior to that of Rome, with the result that the apostolic claims made by Rome and the apostolic claims made by eastern patriarchs came into conflict. If such sees were apostolic, so the argument went, they were, of course, "willed by Christ and by God." The emperor of Constantinople rather often favored the claims of the patriarch of Constantinople rather than the claims of the bishop of Rome, and this only added to the confusion. Apropos to our theme, however, is the fact that in these claims and counter-claims the role of a "non-ordained person," the emperor, carried enormous weight, both as regards the claims of the eastern patriarchs and as regards the claims of the bishops of Rome were concerned.

Another indication of the uniqueness of the emperor and the kings is the fact that church leadership, including papal leadership, during this early medieval period sought help from the emperors, and at times their assistance for a resolution of internal church affairs. It is true that some bishops of Rome were less willing to appeal either to the emperor or to other rulers, but some, such as Gregory III (731–741), were more open.[27] Caught in a desperate struggle with the Lombard king, Luitprand, Gregory III in 739 appealed to Charles Martel. His successor, Zachary (741–752), had to acknowledge the de facto conquests of Luitprand and negotiated with him.[28] In 752 Pope Stephen II concluded an armistice with the Lombard king, Aistulf, and when this armistice broke down, Stephen appealed first to the emperor at Constantinople, and then, when no help was forthcoming, to Pippin. In 754, after the pope had crossed the Alps and had come to the royal palace at Ponthion near Chalons, the pope dressed in sackcloth prostrated himself before Pippin in an act of supplication. In all of this, the popes knew that without imperial or royal support of some sort the church itself could not operate. They realized that the spiritual goals of the church could not be met without the government's help. The marriage of *regnum* and *sacerdotium* continued in the inner west much as it had formerly done in the Roman empire.

We have seen above some of the various names and titles attributed to Constantine, and these same names and titles were also attributed to the other emperors who succeeded him. The aura which was given to the Byzantine emperors provided a pattern that was eventually used for the Frankish kings. However, the Frankish kings, and even their successors, the Saxon kings, never gained the brilliance of a Roman or Byzantine emperor, although they gained a theological description of their office which outpaced that of the Byzantine ruler. In 751 Pepin was elected king of the Franks and he was anointed by Frankish bishops. With the election of Charles the Great we find, for the first time, the phrase *Dei gratia rex,* "king by the grace of God." In 794, at the synod of Frankfurt, Charles the Great could see the *Regnum Francorum* being transformed into the *Imperium Christianum.* In the same year, 794, Paulinus of Aquileia referred to Charles the Great as *gubernator omnium Christianorum,* and as *rex et sacerdos.* In the same year Alcuin referred to him as the new David and as *pontifex in praedicatione* and compared his throne at Aachen to that of Solomon. In 799, in the *Paderborn Epic,* we hear the poet calling Charles "Augustus," and Aachen is called "the second Rome." Charles the Great wrote to Pope Leo III, admonishing him to observe the sacred canons and rule the church in piety. In later centuries it would be the pope writing to a ruler admonishing him to do the same. Charles was indeed a figure of overwhelming power both in society and in the church, and his titles expressed a dignity due to no other person, lay or cleric. Indeed, he was neither lay nor cleric. He was, like kings and emperors before him, *sui generis.*

At Rome in the apse at Santa Susanna, Leo III set up a mosaic with the pope (Leo) on the right and the king (Charles the Great) on the left.[29] In the *triclinium* of the Lateran, the hall for synods, a mosaic was set up by Leo III, showing St. Peter in the middle with Leo and Charles at each side. Schramm notes that in this mosaic something new appears: the king is kneeling at one side of St. Peter, just as the pope is kneeling in a sort of mirror way at the other side of St. Peter. Such a presentation, put up at the command of Pope Leo, remained in a very public and prominent place, indicating for all to see that the ruler of the Franks held an enormously high position within the *societas Christiana,* and because of the similarity of position between pope and king, one could easily see a sort of equivalency or equi-supremacy within their own spheres of competence.[30]

In 799, Alcuin wrote to Charles:

> Until now there were three men who counted in Christendom: the Vicar of Peter, Prince of the Apostles, and you have apprised me of what has happened to him; the holder of imperial office, the temporal ruler of New Rome, and how he was toppled, not by outsiders but by his own, is in all mouths; and finally, you, the King, whom our Lord Jesus Christ has appointed head of the Christian people and who surpass the other two in power, wisdom, and dignity. See, the safety of the Church of Christ depends entirely on you alone.[31]

Alcuin summed up the belief of many contemporaries, both clerical and non-clerical: kingship comes from God ("appointed by our Lord Jesus Christ") and a king is supreme in his own sphere, and, in times of severe distress, superior to both the successor of Peter and the empty throne of a fallen Byzantine emperor. Charles could not help but be affected by such language, and he saw himself as king of the Franks, of the Lombards, and of Rome. The Roman sphere of his kingly rule had come about, however, in stages. It was in 774, that Charles the Great entered

Rome and was baptized. However, prior to his baptism, he was greeted from the thirtieth milestone, *Ad Novas,* onward with all the trappings usually accorded to the imperial exarch. In July of this same year Charles used the new title *Rex Francorum et Langobardorum* and *Patricius Romanorum.* It was on December 23, 800, that he was crowned emperor. Some sources even note that the pope, Leo III, rendered *proskynesis* to him. If so, it was the first and last time a pope so honored an emperor of the medieval west.[32]

A theocracy, which resided totally in the west, had now begun. There is no doubt that the ensuing relationship between the papacy and the western Frankish emperor was far more important than the papal relationship with any other western political leader. There is also no doubt that the relationship between western emperor and pope became a major issue regarding supremacy, for the supremacy of the pope over and over again depended in no small measure on the political and economic support of the Frankish emperors and kings, and in turn the supremacy of the Frankish rulers depended on the support of Rome and the Roman popes. Louis the Pious and his heirs continued the Carolingian hegemony down to 904. One might say it was a love/hate relationship, for there were times when the relationship of pope and emperor was warmly fostered, and there were times when the relationship was chilled. The section above on papal monism indicates one of the major reasons for this vacillating relationship.[33]

The role of the Gallic bishops also modulated the position of the emperor within the *societas Christiana.* However, even in this aspect of the relationship of *regnum et sacerdotium* it is the source of kingship and consequently the legitimacy of kingship which is central, as also the source of *sacerdotium* and the legitimacy of episcopal *sacerdotium.* In both sets of relationships, it is *not* a question of lay-cleric, *not* a question of church-state, *not* a question of spiritual-secular. In the relationship of *sacerdotium et regnum,* the emperor-king had a unique position within the *societas Christiana,* just as the pope and the bishops (*sacerdotium*) held unique positions within that same society.

With the death of the east Frankish emperor, Arnulf, in 899, the crown passed to Louis the Child in 901, who was defeated in his struggle with Berengar of Friuli. Meanwhile, Sergius of Caere marched on Rome in 904 and ended the control of the Formosan party. With Sergius in Rome the papacy became dominated by a few families of the Roman nobility. At the beginning of the tenth century, both the papacy and the imperial crown had reached a bitter low.

Politically a rebirth began with the gradual rise of the Saxon dynasty, beginning with Henry I (919–936), but especially with his son Otto I.

These kings presided over kingdom and church. Their position remained not that of a simple "lay" person, but of a unique regal/imperial person. "The ruler, from whose hands bishops, at their investiture by ring and staff, had received, not only the property and the secular rights of sovereignty, but also the ecclesiastical function, was in the view of that age not simply a layman."[34]

Clearly this was the view of that age: the highest ruler, the emperor or the king, was not simply a layman. His anointing was, at that time, considered by some theologians to be a sacrament; he was called *vicarius Christi* and, as we see in the anointing formula in a *Mainz Ordo,* a participant in the episcopal office and an intermediary between clergy and people.[35]

Schramm notes that the statement of Pope Gelasius I on the two powers disallowed, in the west, the same view of the emperor as one finds in the east. However, one should note that Gelasius' view only gradually came to be seen by subsequent popes as the standard view. The statement was neither cited nor acted on by many popes immediately following Gelasius. Moreover, outside of Rome, few took Gelasius' view into account at all. Alcuin, as we saw above, could hardly have said what he did, if he had believed in Gelasius' approach. The statement of Gelasius became more important as the clash of pope and emperor developed, but at first it played only a small and intermittent role, and even then more often than not only in the Roman circles, rather than in more global circles.

One cannot begin with the idea that at the end of the patristic period all Christians, or at least the main leadership of the Christian church, considered the Christian people to be divided into cleric/lay. This would clearly be an instance of *eisegesis.* As we saw with Gregory the Great, there was a tripartite division in the church structure: clerical leader, monk, and people. However, the position of the Byzantine emperor and then the western emperor (king) was seen in large measure in a unique and distinctive way. It would be unhistorical to say that there was unanimous agreement regarding this imperial/regal uniqueness and distinction during the several centuries of the early middle ages, but it would also be unhistorical to read history backward and find in the early medieval period a unanimous agreement on papal monism (papal supremacy) or episcopal dualism. It is only as one moves to the year 1000 that the divine right of kings is increasingly disputed, particularly as the papacy more globally asserts its own divine right over political leadership. In the course of the papal and episcopal argument against a king or emperor who is such *Dei gratia,* and who is called *vicarius Christi,* the *sacerdotium* reformulates the theological argument from *sacerdotium/regnum* to *sacerdotium/laicatus.*

The eminent position of the emperor or the king did not directly benefit the position or status of the ordinary lay person. In other words, the argument cannot be made that lay people, because "one of their own" was the emperor, could boast of their lay status. Such an argument would never have occurred at this medieval time, for the emperor was just as different and distinct from the ordinary lay person as the pope or bishop or priest was different and distinct from the ordinary lay person. The reasons for such difference and distinction might be particular to each, i.e. to *sacerdotium* and to *regnum,* but the chasm between the ordinary lay person and the divinely appointed *sacerdotium et regnum* was enormous on both counts. Indirectly, however, there were both benefits and disadvantages of this imperial status to the lay sphere. The benefits lay chiefly in the way in which both an unordained and an ordained member of the church interacted. The historical instances in which the ruler played a crucial role, even in internal church matters, indicate that an unordained person both can have and did have a major decision-making role within the *ecclesia.* Such a person did not have, however, the right to such inner-ecclesial role-playing because he was *lay,* or because he was unordained, but rather because he was *Dei gratia imperator.* The emperor's historical involvement in inner-church agenda is a major and telling critique of an ideologically presented church structure based on *klerikos/laikos.* The structure of the church is far more nuanced than the lay/cleric division would have us believe, and involvement in inner-Church agenda does not seem to be the exclusive preserve of the ordained.

The disadvantages, however, are more telling. As one nears the year 1000 the antagonism of a large and influential group of clerics gradually moved against any and every unordained, including a ruler. As theological theories were developed to defend this approach, the position begins to evolve among theologians and canonists that there are in the church, and therefore in Christendom, only two groups: cleric and lay. The further theological evolution of this argument included the idea that this separation of lay and cleric was instituted by Christ and therefore by God. Accordingly, there was an attempt to eradicate completely any privileged non-ordained person who might be or appear to be superior to an ordained Christian. The year 1000 does not bring an end to this struggle, but from that time on both in theological thought and in canon law, the issue of a lay/cleric division, instituted by God, began to be firmly established.[36]

So far, we have considered only the Frankish-papal relationship. As this was being developed, a fairly isolated area of the west moved in a different way, namely Visigothic Spain. Key to this area, at least from a theological standpoint, is Isidore of Seville, who developed a different form of royal theology. In Isidore's view, the incarnation had sounded the death knell for autocratic emperors. In the post-Jesus period of world history, many churches were allowed to form and co-exist. Indeed, the churches take over the position of the empire. The many Christian kings are made equal to the Roman emperor. Church leadership supports the kings, but does not try to dominate them. Kings, in their day-to-day activity, resemble bishops rather than autocrats, since they are to serve the people. These kings at times must intervene in the affairs of the church in order to support church discipline.[37]

Isidore's view focused on the Visigothic kingdom, and there was a strong independence of the Spanish churches vis-à-vis Rome and the popes. Isidore stressed regional and local churches, i.e. many churches, and he stressed on that basis many kingdoms. His view was not of an over-arching papal monism nor of a western imperial monism. His views, however, were not put into practice in Visigothic Spain. Kings such as Reccared (586–612), Sisebut (612–621), Suinthila (621–631), and Sisenand (631–636) did not correspond in any precise way to Isidore's idealized portrait, for they acted in most imperial and autocratic ways. Still, Isidore himself and his writings were highly regarded, for he was seen as a major leader in Visigothic Spain. He wrote as a "regional archbishop for an exclusively Spanish audience, his diocese, the Catholic population of Spain and its rulers."[38] He had an outstanding library and did not petition Gallo-Roman monasteries for books. He made no pilgrimage to Rome or any other non-Iberian locale. He was a man for his time and place and within his time and place. Even information from Merovingian councils or Carolingian and Roman councils did not seem to influence the rather isolated world of Visigothic Spain. Nonetheless, a few centuries later, when the Gallo-Roman west discovered Isidore, his comments on *regnum et sacerdotium* will be taken up by the papal writers to defend their position that the *sacerdotium* is superior to the *regnum* in all respects, a universal vision which Isidore himself had never dreamed of nor proposed. Nonetheless, Visigothic Spain with its own churches and its own kings widens our view as regards *regnum et sacerdotium*. The Frankish-papal model appears to be but one of several models of this inter-relationship of *regnum et sacerdotium*. That the Frankish form or the papal form should be seen as normative is indeed questionable. That the eventual Frankish-Saxon dispute over the sources and extent of *regnum et sacerdotium* (lay investiture) has a certain relativity to it becomes quite evident. That the outcome of a "divinely established and universally applicable lay/cleric church" shares in this relativity also becomes evident.

B. THE REPOSITIONING OF EDUCATED LAY CHRISTIANS

Political and social unrest in the early middle ages did not foster education. The patristic period had ended with a fairly strong literary and artistic expression, but invasions and wars brought this kind of an expression almost to a halt. Naturally there were instances of an educated society in the early middle ages, but the overall view seems to be that at that time educated people were few and far between.

In an almost exceptional way, the Anglo-Saxon church was a wellspring for the continuation of education in the early middle ages. From the very beginning, the Anglo-Saxon church was interrelated with monasticism, both with Irish monasticism and with Benedictine monasticism. However, to a far greater degree it was in the Benedictine form of monasticism, rather than in the Irish form, that learning was developed. Characteristic of early Anglo-Saxon monastic life was the double monastery (men and women). In particular, the monastery at Canterbury, with its school, developed the area of Roman law and even Greek law. In the eighth century, Canterbury's educational position faded, and Northumbria became the new leader, with the monastery of St. Peter at Wearmouth and St. Paul at Jarrow. From there the educational leadership moved to York. This "Anglo-Saxon renaissance" is the motherlode for the "Carolingian renaissance," since Alcuin of York was trained by the Anglo-Saxon scholars and not only took his educational training to the continent but made it the basis for continental education. Benedict Biscop had traveled to Rome, Vienna, and Lyon to consult the libraries there, but also to bring back to York books of enormous value to scholarship.

At the end of the patristic period there was a general decline in education, but also there remained, in various parts of the world (Rome, Lyon, Vienna, York, Constantinople, etc.), great libraries. Although the names of only a few men and women appear in the annals of history as the learned savants of that time, there must have been for each named and remembered individual many unnamed and unremembered teachers, tutors, and librarians who provided these named individuals with the incentives and intellectual tools for their educational triumphs. For each remembered educated person, there was some sort of intellectual infrastructure. However, it is safe to say that this educated group was found in the early middle ages almost exclusively in the monastery.

That Charles the Great was an educated individual is clear, but even more highly educated was his son, Louis the Pious, and the sons of Louis the Pious were also men of learning: Lothar I, Louis the German, and Charles the Bald. Who taught them? Monks and clerics. These regal and imperial figures did much for both church and society, and it was their education which gave them insight and perspective. They surrounded themselves with a small but highly selected group of educated advisors, who again were either clerics and monks or educated aristocratic individuals. These latter were educated by and large by monks. Numerically, however, the educated stratum of the Frankish world was thin.

In the East the traditions of classical education had never been completely abandoned, and the existence of a wealthy, leisured and literate laity must always be reckoned with. Moreover, in the East the language of scholarship and worship was the language of everyday speech. But in the West this had ceased to be so by the eighth century: by this time no one learnt Latin as his vernacular language, and no learned works and no liturgical or devotional literature existed in any other language than Latin.[39]

If one combs the archives of the early middle ages for the names of important scholars and writers, the list is not extensive. We find, for instance, such names as the following:

Walfrid	Wandalbert of Prüm
Rhabanus Maurus	Angelomus of Luxeuil
Sedulius Scotus	Hincmar of Reims
John Scotus	Anastasius the Librarian
Lupus of Ferrières	Heiric of Auxerre
Milo of Saint-Amand	Gottschalk
Otfrid	Florus
Ado	Usuard of St-Germain-des-Prés
Wulfad of Bourges	Paschasius Radbertus
Alcuin	Erchempert of Capua
Andrew of Bergamo	Abbo of St-Germain-des-Prés
Paul the Deacon	Manno
Remigius of Auxerre	Hucbald of Saint-Armand
Regino of Prüm	Bovo I
Ratpert	Tutilo of Sankt Gallen
Gerald the poet	Notker of Sankt Gallen

Almost all of these people were monks, and one might conclude that education in early medieval society was not totally but quite overwhelmingly a monastic and clerical preserve. Although Benedict of Aniane wanted monks to disengage themselves from secular education, nonetheless he promoted study as long as it remained within the cloister. In the ninth century, monastic scholarship went far beyond Benedict's intentions. There were major libraries in Lorsch, Saint Gall, and Saint-Amand, with books by Horace, Juvenal and Cicero side by side with the tomes of the fathers. Learned abbots, such as Rhabanus Maurus and Walafrid Strabo, appeared, and those two were not the only educated abbots.

> But as a whole, the monastic contribution to the Carolingian Renaissance largely lay in the transmission, collection, and preservation of the past rather than in new creation. Copies of classical authors, commentaries on the books of the Bible, mainly distilled from the Latin Fathers, and anthologies of patristic texts, were the most characteristic works that emerged from the scriptoria of the Carolingian abbeys.[40]

There were centers of learning which remained, to some degree, important during this early medieval period. In the Frankish kingdom we find such centers at Sens, Reims, Lyons, Vienne, Trier, Cologne, Mainz and Salzburg. In Rome, learning was especially important during the papal rule of Nicholas I, Hadrian II and John VIII.

> The quarter century of cultural flowering at Rome also became significant for the development of the medieval idea of the Eternal City. It was ended by the collapse of the Carolingian papacy, made visible in the discontinuation of the traditional papal *vitae* in the *Liber pontificalis*. Already there were in the *Liber pontificalis* no *vitae* of the murdered John VIII and his short-lived successors, Marinus I and Hadrian III. The last Bishop of Rome to receive a biography of the old type was Stephen V, predecessor of Formosus.[41]

In the Frankish kingdoms, with the Viking invasions of 879–891, many monastic centers of learning were affected in an adverse way. The school of Laon, however, continued to be strong, and in the area of Cologne the abbey of Werden continued its educational tradition. The *Musica enchiriadis* of Hoger (902) provided an impetus to the art of music. Music, however, remained an ecclesiastical art, developed basically by monks and for liturgical life in monasteries. The schools of Liège flourished under Bishop Stephen (901–920). The abbeys of Prüm and St. Martin at Trier were also centers of scholarship. In the East Frankish kingdom we find centers of scholarship at Bremen-Hamburg, Saxony, Franconia, Swabia, and Bavaria.

In imperial Italy there were educational centers at Ravenna, Benevento, and Monte Cassino. Connected to Benevento, under both Carolingian and Byzantine influence, there were centers of scholarship at Capua, Naples, Venice, Bergamo, Verona, Spoleto, and Pavia.

In each of these centers there were many educated people. The named people, some of whom are cited above, are simply the few who are remembered. There were many Irish and Benedictine monks in various monasteries whose names are long forgotten, but they were to some degree educated and intellectually trained. A center of learning is not created by a single individual; rather, a center of learning depends on a number of educated and trained individuals. Nonetheless, education was basically an intra-monastic enterprise, and to a strong degree it was an enterprise focused on the monasteries as well, i.e. on the church. This is a pattern one sees particularly in the Roman revival of learning. Only on the rarest of occasions does one find an interest in "secular" education, that is, in the arts. On other but still rather rare occasions, learned men and women turned their talents to history, the history of a Carolingian or a Byzantine king. Architecture is also indicative of learning, and the great architecture of this period focused on churches and regal palaces and fortresses, but the architectural monuments which survive pay lasting tribute to an educated group of engineers and artists whose names we may never know. Law was also becoming an area of research and codification, particularly as one moves toward 1000. These legal investigations, as one finds under the leadership of Hincmar of Rheims, focused on the conflicts between kings and bishops, and the conflicts on marriage regulations, which involved both the growing regulations of the church as regards marriage, and the laws of inheritance, which involved disputed church properties.[42]

In the tenth century, reforms in education began to move apace. Monasteries needed reform, and a key component of this reform was in the area of learning.

> The time when the scholars from all parts of the Carolingian *Imperium* made their way to the imperial court to work on great themes in common belonged to the past. More than ever, scholarship withdrew into monastic and cathedral schools. It was they that, in a silent work of reconstruction, were preparing the future development of Western scholarship.[43]

Almost every monastery had developed at least a small school which was generally intended for young monks, but at times included a few outsiders as well. Three notable monks who clearly influenced the reform in learning were Notker the Stammerer, Remigius of Auxerre, and Hucbald of Saint-Amand, all of them living at the beginning of the tenth century. The new monasteries which arose in the tenth century, particularly Cluny and Fleury-sur-Loire, favored learning but each had differing views on scholarship, with the monastery of Fleury-sur-Loire by far the academic leader.

Cathedral schools developed as well, especially under Gerbert of Aurillac and the school at Rheims, and Fulbert, his student, at that of Chartres. But one finds as well strong cathedral centers at Pavia, Milan, Vercelli, Parma, Verona, and Ravenna. From these centers, both monastic and cathedral, come, slowly at first, but then in an impressive way, the various universities of the thirteenth century. The cathedral schools, more so than the monastic schools, contributed to the open approach to an educated group of lay persons.

Stress began to be placed on the *artes liberales* with the revival of the *trivium* and *quadrivium*. Interest arose in such authors as Porphyry, Aristotle, Cicero, Virgil, Maritanus Capella, Horace, Persius, Juvenal, Boethius, Statius Terence, Lucan, and Sallust. Mathematics in this tenth century reform, however, did not advance very much, whereas music, particularly in the school of Reichenau, did move ahead. The invaluable work of Guido of Arezzo remains important down to our own times. To these more secular authors, one must add the names of the fathers of the church, particularly those of Augustine, Jerome, Gregory the Great, Isidore of Seville, and Bede, who were highly regarded. The *Florilegia*, that is, sayings of the fathers of the church on a given theme, compiled by the monks of this period, became tremendous theological sources for high scholasticism.[44] Unfortunately, they also came to be seen as *regulae fidei*, i.e. norms beyond which one should not stray.

At the conclusion of our time period, theological studies were not yet at their best, and theological writings basically repeated what had been written in the heyday of the Carolingian age. The theology of the eucharist became a center of focus with the writings of Paschasius Radbertus, a monk of Corbie, who wrote the first theological treatise on the eucharist, *De corpore et sanguine domini* (c. 831–833). Ratramnus, another monk at Corbie, was asked by the emperor Charles the Bald in 833/834 to respond to certain doctrinal questions on the eucharist. His work is also entitled *De corpore et sanguine domini*. G. Macy, in his excellent study on this theme, *The Theologies of the Eucharist in the Early Scholastic Period*, has indicated that the appearance of these two works did not occasion any eucharistic conflict.[45] Some initial work on canon law also developed in the tenth century, but this initial work was surpassed with the writings of Burchard of Worms in the twelfth century. History became a rather strong intellectual pursuit, which included many biographical works. Even the epistulary art was pursued with vigor.[46] A certain Vilgardus of Ravenna, a grammarian, preferred the pagan views of the ancients to the Christian dogma, but he appears to be quite alone in this preference of the pagan over the Christian sources. Actually, it was the dialecticians who were the more "dangerous" scholars, and this danger reached a certain plateau with Peter Abelard in the twelfth century. Dialectics appeared to be the root of a later problem: the problem of faith and reason.

As education developed during the tenth century and into the eleventh century, and as the scope of learning moved out of its theological focus into such areas as law, history, rhetoric, and dialectics, more and more lay men and women began to receive an education. The rise of the burger or merchant class also allowed more lay men and women access to education. Learning was no longer the preserve of either the monks and the clergy, on the one hand, or the upper aristocracy on the other. One cannot speak as yet of a general education or of mass education, but one can surely speak of a growing number of educated *laici*, and of an educated sector in the *plebs*. With education comes, however, a demand for position, status, and involvement in decision making. Thus, this lengthy review of western education moves directly into our theme: the role of the lay person in the church. With educated lay men and women, their role in the church became more and more an issue. By itself, this educational growth did not result directly in any raised hopes as regards positioning within the ecclesial structures, for the lay person gained status in the church primarily through a spiritual reform, and this began with the reform of religious life in the tenth and eleventh centuries. Nonetheless, the rise of an educated lay stratum of society became, as the middle ages moved into the reformation period, a challenge to clerical authority, particularly an authority which tried to claim either omnicompetence in educational matters or at least final judgment in educational matters.

C. MONASTICISM AND THE "REDISCOVERY" OF THE LAY BROTHER

Picasso notes that from the seventh century onward throughout the early middle ages, Gregory the Great's words from the *Moralia in Job* stand as a guideline for western early medieval thought:

> In tribus ordinibus sancta Ecclesia constat, coniugatorum, videlicet, continentium et rectorum. Unde Ezechiel tres viros liberatos vidit, videlicet, Noè, Daniel et Job.[47]

> Holy Church exists in three orders: namely [the orders] of the married, the continent and the leaders. For this reason, Ezekiel sees three men, namely, Noah, Daniel and Job.

Add to these three groups the singular position of the king, and one has all the Christian classes or strata of the Christian medieval society. It is the interplay of these four groups—cleric, king, monk and ordinary lay person—which gives rise to our theme: the turning of the tide. The uniqueness of the monk and nun within the *societas Christiana* was a given. They were neither lay nor cleric.

Monasticism, as we have seen earlier, began as a movement of unordained folk, but here and there clerics, particularly presbyters, were accepted as monks. However, in this situation the presbyter-monk had no prestige over other monks, with the usual exception of the eucharistic liturgy. Cassian wrote: "The monk ought to flee women and bishops."[48] For Cassian, monks who sought clerical office did so due to diabolical temptation under the guise of helping others spiritually. In the *Life of St. Romanus,* we read that monks who got ordained did so out of rabid ambition:

> They are straightway inflated with pride and exalt themselves, not only over their worthier contemporaries, but even over their elders; mere youths, who for their juvenile vanity ought to be put in their place and whipped.[49]

One of the things which monks renounced was ecclesiastical office. Gregory the Great regarded clerical office as incompatible with the monastic life. In one of his many letters he wrote:

> No man can both serve under ecclesiastical obedience and also continue under a monastic rule, observing the strict regime of a monastery when he is obliged to remain in the daily service of the Church.[50]

As one moves into the eighth century, this begins to change. More and more monks, both in the east and in the west, were ordained. By the time one arrives at the eleventh century, a very high proportion of monks were ordained.[51] The earlier and simpler liturgies of the Benedictine tradition had become, as one moves toward the year 1000, quite elaborate, and instead of a weekly eucharistic liturgy, a daily communal liturgy, sometimes twice daily, had become fairly common, and in addition the practice of many priest-monks saying private votive masses became more and more common, again as one moves nearer to the year 1000.[52]

> Gregory III, Alcuin, Benedict of Aniane, Adalhard of Corbie and Angilbert of Centula would have all been familiar with the multiplication of daily Masses in the monasteries of the eighth and ninth centuries. Certainly by the time of the Carolingian

and Cluniac reforms, the Eucharist played a key note in the spiritual orientation of Benedictine communities.[53]

The gradual clericalization of religious life, at least in the sense that those who were in positions of leadership within a monastery were clerics, eliminated the non-ordained or lay monk from any leadership status. In the sixth and seventh centuries there had been double monasteries in Gaul, such as those at Chelles and Jouarre.[54] Actually, the basis for this arrangement can be found in Pachomias and Basil, both of whom had organized communities of nuns in close proximity to communities of monks. The foundations in Gaul of these double monasteries arose rather often from aristocratic foundations, particularly in northeast Gaul, many of them appearing within thirty years after the death of Columban. The nuns needed the liturgical ministrations of the priest-monks, and perhaps also the manual skills of the unordained monks. Noteworthy is the fact that the head of these joint communities was generally the abbess, a non-ordained Christian. The *Rule of a Father for Virgins,* perhaps the work of Walbert of Luxeuil, a successor to Columban, gave the abbess "much the same role as a male abbot—including the power to hear the confessions of her nuns and absolve them."[55]

At Nivelles in Brabant, Itta, the wife of Pippin the Elder, after his death in 640, had a monastery constructed and endowed. Itta appointed as its first abbess her own daughter Gertrude, who organized a double monastery, sending to Ireland a request for monks who might instruct the nuns in charge. She also began to build up a library and wrote to several monasteries, requesting books. She was the abbess, in charge of both the men and the women, in this double monastery and was a most capable woman. The Carolingian family of Austrasia found in Gertrude their own family saint, which gave no small measure of prestige to this aristocratic lady and to her family, as well as to the monastery. In the beginning centuries of the early middle ages, the position of unordained monastic men and monastic women was indeed prestigious. In seventh century Spain we find many double monasteries, with a *Regula Communis,* attributed to Fructuoso of Braga.

At the beginning of the ninth century, the difference between the monks and the canons was quite ambiguous. In many monasteries the monks lived in a way similar to the canons; in a few cathedrals the canons followed a monastic lifestyle. The reforms of religious life, as we find in the Frankish church, attempted to purify both monasticism and the canonical life. A decree from the Synod of Aachen (816) clearly distinguished the *ordo saecularis* (canons) and the *ordo regularis* (monks).[56] This distinction of the two orders, with their concomitant regulations and lifestyles, received further impetus from the *Institutio Canonicorum*, Chordegang's rule for the clergy at Metz. Convents of canonesses, which had developed in the west prior to the ninth century, were also affected, and rather radically, for from the ninth until the twelfth centuries all women religious in the west gradually came under the Benedictine rule. Thus we have an instance of the "monasticizing" of all community life.

Religious life, in the earliest parts of the middle ages, might be considered, from our standpoint reading back into history, a dominantly "lay" movement, although during these early middle ages the dictum of Gregory I dominated, namely that the church was divided into three distinct groups: clerics, monks and lay. In this period of time, however, male religious life gradually lost its distinctiveness and its individualized and unique character, and as it became more and more dominantly clerical, the division and even distinction between cleric/monk, which Gregory had so emphasized, became blurred. Male monks, especially those with position and power, came to be equated to clerics; the other monks, as well as the nuns, were slowly equated to the ordinary "lay" Christian.

Early on, however, the non-ordained person, both male and female, had found a spiritual status by his or her entry into *religious life,* a status which did not depend on ordination. Even when clerics had taken over the leadership of the male monastic movement, there were still lay men who joined the monastic ranks and remained unordained for their entire monastic life. They rose to no leadership positions, and rarely developed any educational skills. The dominance of the cleric monk over the lay monk was a further step toward the full clericalization of the church. Monasticism, it is true, remained open to the "layman," but in a way quite different from the dominantly non-ordained character of monasticism's origin.

The clericalization and domestication of monasticism also produced a similarity between bishops and abbots. Many an early medieval abbot was a major religious person in a region, not only economically, but also politically and spiritually. Many medieval abbots, indeed, had more power than the bishops within their own region. The successes of the Carolingian reform depended strongly on the monastic movement, and above all on the quality and prestige of the monastic leaders, the abbots.[57] From the beginning, particularly with Pachomias, we saw that in a given region a sort of "alternative church structure" had begun to develop. There was the episcopal church structure, and there was a monastic, or *koinonia,* structure. The relationship between a group of monks or nuns, on the one hand, and the bishop, on the other, was generally not antagonistic but rather undefined. In some instances this relationship did become antagonistic, or at least an irritant. A canon of the Second Council of

Nicaea attempted to bring monks and nuns under episcopal supervision, but in reality and for the most part this canon proved meaningless. In the early medieval church monks either tended to be independent of the bishop, or at times found refuge under royal control rather than episcopal control. Many bishops, however, represented not only the episcopal or spiritual center of a region, but also the socio-political and even royal center, and not a few proprietary monasteries became indebted to their patrons, and in such instances the patrons, whether episcopal or royal, could claim a percentage of the economic base of the monastery and a right to determine, at least to some degree, the election process of the abbot. Because of these claims, rulers and bishops, who were at odds with each other, could use the economic base and the election base of monasteries as pawns in their moves and counter-moves with each other.

At the end of the medieval period, religious life needed a major reform. One of the major aspects of the various reforms in the eleventh century was the restoration of the lay brother. Four causes are often attributed to the decline of monastic life in the latter part of the early middle ages:

1. The secularizing of the monasteries by various rulers;
2. The squandering of property by abbots;
3. The weakness of royal power and consequently the lack of protection for monasteries;
4. The devastation caused by Vikings, Muslims and Magyars.[58]

Reforms began in Lower Lotharingia under Gerard of Brogne (d. 959), and his efforts were noticed by Marquis Arnulf of Flanders (918–965) who asked Gerard to renew the monasteries of Flanders as well. This renewal involved, to a marked degree, the rebuilding and restaffing of devastated monasteries. At the same time in Upper Lotharingia a few families of the nobility provided the impetus for monastic revival. The policies of the Ottos and the early Salians played a major role in these renewals. Rather quickly, Gorze, Toul, Verdun, Trier, and Liège became centers of renewal. At times the success was more dependent on economic factors than on religious factors, but there was a clear renewal of monastic life during the tenth century throughout the German lands, and the influence of this Germanic reform was felt at Monte Cassino under the German reform abbot, Richer of Niederaltaich (d. 1055). These reformed Germanic monasteries were loosely connected with one another, but not in the organized way which the Cluniac group eventually developed. Nor did the German reformed monasteries seek out a form of papal exemption. The protection of the Germanic rulers was adequate for their needs.

This is important to notice, because reform of religious life in the middle ages did not follow a single pattern, i.e. the Cluniac style of reform. Secondly, papal exemption was not necessarily an essential role for monastic reform. In fact, the development of papal exemption by monastic communities gave rise to further abuses which then needed further reform.[59]

In the eleventh century the relationship between monks and lay people began to change. Monasteries were often like great manors, with servants, maids, serfs, and renters. There was a special group of people who lived on the monastery lands, who had renounced some aspects of their ownership rights, and who led to some degree a monastic life. These were the *conversi*. These lay members of a religious community received strong impetus from the reform movement of St. Romuald at Vallombrosa, who became a monk in 972, the very end of our present consideration.

> These [*conversi*] were not monks in the proper sense. Even if they, for the most part, made the monastic renunciations, they did not make monastic vows until the fourteenth century.[60]

The rediscovery of the lay brother, which flowers so strongly in the century beyond this chapter at such centers as Hirsau under Abbot William (1069–1091), with the Florentine John Gualbert and his establishment at Vallombrosa, with Eudes, the *scholasticus* of Tournai, and his hermits, with the monastery at Afflighem in Brabant under Fulgentius with both male and female lay members, and with Stephen of Thiers, who founded the Order of Grandmont which had, early on, a decidedly lay character. Some of these reform movements succeeded; some were ephemeral; some were gradually changed from a strong lay dominance to a clerical dominance, not only because of episcopal pressure but also because of the pressure of new recruits.[61] One of the major reasons, perhaps, why this "lay brother" reform movement did not last was the success of the reform at Cîteaux. This latter reform movement far surpassed that of Cluny and indeed of almost every other reform movement of its time. Nonetheless, the issues of simony, clerical incontinence, monastic greed, and political machinations clamored for reform; the rise, even though short-lived, of the lay brother was a major part of the turning of the tide. The revival of the lay brother must be seen in the broader context of the need for monastic renewal as such. This clamor for monastic renewal in all its facets clearly gave rise to the many *vita evangelica* movements which followed in rapid succession. The emergence and visibility of the "lay brother" in these reform movements provided a strong example for the emergence of the non-monastic lay man and woman in the *vita evangelica* movements.

D. THE LITURGICAL LIFE OF THE EARLY MIDDLE AGES

One of the major efforts of the Carolingian reform was a renewal of liturgical and sacramental life. Presbyteral ministry was, at the beginning of the middle ages, in need of a reform. The substantial development in the liturgy took place between the eighth and the tenth centuries. The various rituals—e.g. the Roman liturgy, the Old Spanish, the diverse Gallican, the Ambrosian, the Irish-Scottish—gradually moved to the edges or were pushed to the edges and brought into conformity through the Carolingian reform.[62] The *Sacramentarium Gelasinum* was revised in the middle of the eighth century into the *Gelasianum.* A monk at Sankt Alban in Mainz, around 950, compiled the *Pontificale,* which included the *Ordo Romanus Antiquus.* This *Pontificale* was the basis for the later *Pontificale Romanum.* The forced baptisms among the Saxons proved to be a disaster, and under pressure from Alcuin a form of pre-baptismal preparation was gradually formed for adults. Augustine's *De catechizandis rudibus* was used as an instructional exemplar. Penance vacillated between the Roman public penance, still visible particularly in cathedral churches in the eleventh century, and the Celtic form of penance, which was private and frequent, though to some degree still unauthorized. One finds here and there a prescription that confession should take place at least once a year.[63] The anointing of the sick, which had been administered by lay person and cleric alike at the beginning of the middle ages, became the preserve of the clergy by the beginning of the eleventh century. Marriage which had been either a personal or familial event at the beginning of the middle ages also came under clerical control by the beginning of the twelfth century. However, it was the eucharistic liturgy which affected the life of the lay person most. In the west, contrary to the eastern practice, only the three languages, Hebrew, Greek and Latin, were allowed.[64] The populace gradually was unable to understand the liturgy. The synod of Frankfurt in 794 reminded people that one could pray in any language, even though the eucharist, as well as other liturgical rites, were in Latin. The altar was gradually placed to the rear of the church building, far away from the people. Singing parts, such as the *Gloria Patri* at the Introit, the *Kyrie* and the *Sanctus,* were more and more sung by clergy and monks. The eucharistic bread also emphasized "the distance from the daily life of the people,"[65] for a uniform pure white form of unleavened bread became rather standard in the ninth century. The host was no longer given to the people in their hands, but placed on their tongues. Explanations of the mass, such as those of Walafrid Strabo and Amalarius of Metz, which were meant for the people generally, concerned themselves only with the parts of the mass which were said out loud, thus excluding the eucharistic canon, or else the parts of the mass were described in a very allegorical manner. Amalarius saw in the early part of the mass a similarity to the beginning of salvation history with the call to the Old Testament prophets and the final dismissal as the final blessing of Jesus at the ascension. This became very popular in spite of the protestations of Florus of Lyon and the Synod of Quierzy in 838. "Thus in the details of its development did the Mass become exclusively the priest's business."[66] It is at this point in time that private, devotional prayers of the priest begin to insert themselves into the liturgy: prayers of unworthiness at the beginning of the mass, the *confessio* and Psalm 42. These became part of the Rhine *ordo missae* and from there became standard in the west. Private masses, particularly in monasteries, even without servers, became rampant. The Synod of Seligenstadt (1023) specified that a priest could only say three masses per day.[67] The clericalization of liturgy was but another stage in the depositioning of the laity.

By the year 1000 the church was certainly not under the control of the laity, *au pouvoir des laïques*. Parts of the church, and indeed significant aspects of church structure, were indeed under the control, more or less, of emperors, kings, rulers, and nobles. Such aristocratic and powerful people even invested bishops and abbots with the symbols of their office. However, it was not because they were *lay* that they acted in this manner; rather, it was because they held prestigious roles in the socio-political and economic structures of that time. In the case of the emperor, there was even a stated theological position: namely, that he acted as the vicar of Christ himself. Economics too often overrode all other issues, with the result that simony became a major issue demanding reform. The papal reform, only slightly begun by the first two German popes, Clement II (1046–1047) and Damasus II (1048), was moved into high gear by Bruno of Toul, who became Leo IX (1049–1054). From 1000 onward an official reform clearly began to take place, sponsored by a number of popes, by some bishops, and even by some of the emperors. There was also an unofficial reform which emerged from below. This was a call for reform in the sense of a call for the restoration of lay status in the church. At times these two reform movements, one official and the other unofficial, did not reinforce each other.[68] Both reforms, however, stand at the threshold of the later middle ages, and both remain active throughout the entire late medieval period.

3. CONCLUSIONS FROM THE DATA

We have considered some of the movements which took place as regards the lay person in the medieval Frankish church during the time period 700–1000. These movements pushed the ordinary lay person farther to the margins not only of the ecclesiastical world, but also of the socio-political world. The *societas Christiana* was a very structured and hierarchical society. At its center was *regnum et sacerdotium*. The focus of both king and his entourage, namely the *regnum*, and bishop and his entourage as well as pope and his entourage, the *sacerdotium*, was on the source of both kingship and priesthood (i.e. episcopacy/papacy). Both were seen as divinely instituted, but as the period under consideration progressed, the *sacerdotium* began to question the divine institution of the *regnum*, and, even more, the *sacerdotium* began to see itself, at least in its highest echelon, as the source of *regnum*, at least mediately. This struggle between *regnum et sacerdotium* gradually so focused the energies and skills of both sides that the ordinary lay person became further moved to the margin of society.

If we use the same grid which we have used in some of the previous chapters to gauge the role of the ordinary lay person, man or woman, in this early medieval period, we could formulate our results as follows.

A. LITURGY

From 741 onward the lay person—distinct from the monk and the cleric—was gradually excluded from active participation in the liturgical rituals of the church. Baptismal catechesis was taken over by clerics; anointing was taken over by clerics; marriage *in facie ecclesiae*, i.e. under the ministration of a cleric, became mandatory; even the antiphonal parts of the eucharist were taken over by monks and clerics. Liturgy tended to become a clerical and monastic preserve, to which the lay man or woman came as an observer and listener. Moreover, with the decrease of Latin as a common language, the liturgies became more and more unintelligible for the ordinary lay person. Unfortunately, the vernacular languages had not as yet produced a devotional literature, and this lack further created a spiritual impoverishment of the ordinary lay Christian.

B. DISCIPLINE

The role of a lay person, as far as influencing the discipline of the church, became almost non-existent. Unordained monks had often played a major role in church discipline at the beginning of the early middle ages, but with the steady and progressive clericalization of monasticism, the clerical monk took over all the major disciplinary aspects of monastic and ecclesiastically connected life. Decision making, as far as church discipline was concerned, became a clerical matter, which included in no small measure the clerical monk. Only a handful of non-ordained (and these were generally the royal or noble elements of society) continued to share in any substantive way in the ecclesiastical decision making processes, but they did so not because of *laicità*, but because of their societal positions. The very term "church" was gradually coming to mean the clerical/monastic aspect of the Christian community, while the remainder, the *laici*, the *plebs*, were reduced to learners and listeners, obeyers and followers. Ordinary lay Christians were not to have such roles as leaders and teachers, as speakers and directors.

C. CHURCH LEADERSHIP

In the socio-political world, however, the emperor, king, ruler, and noble continued to play a major role in the leadership of the church, not because they were lay, but because of their political position within the social/ecclesial structure. The progressive removal, however, of the ordinary lay person from church leadership structures could not help but contain the seeds for an eventual reaction, even revolution, by these same lay people to regain a rightful, structural voice within the church. However, in the early middle ages, the very channels through which a lay person might voice his or her concern, thus regaining some structural voice, became non-existent. Leadership in the church closed its doors to lay interference, and even the non-ordained, regal/imperial influence was gradually questioned and then, in the eleventh and twelfth centuries, moved beyond the closed doors as well.

D. CHURCH MAINTENANCE

The entire feudal system provided for the maintenance of the church, whether the proprietary church or the episcopal church. The tax exemption of various church properties, together with the enormous endowment of church properties by noble families, created a wealthy monastic and clerical class. The ordinary lay person, however, even though a "church person," was neither tax exempt nor fiscally endowed. Feudal society included a way of life in which the lower classes, who were "church people," provided a large portion of their work to the benefit of the upper classes, who were also "church people." As one sees, there were privileged church people and non-privileged church people.

E. PROFESSIONAL TEACHING

An educated laity slowly became non-existent in the west, a situation which was not paralleled in the east. In the west, education, teaching, and learning became the preserve of monks, nuns and clergy. Only a few noble and aristocratic children gained an education, and in many instances, it must be said, the education given to these noble children was, for its time, first-rate. However, the mass of people progressively became more and more illiterate, thus closing to them a means of participating in both political and ecclesiastical structures. Part of the situation lay in the separation between an ecclesiastical and royal group, who had mastered Latin, and a populace who spoke various forms of early European dialects, but had no knowledge of Latin, the language of the educated folk.

When all is told, the status of the ordinary lay person in the west, at the end of the early middle ages, i.e. 1000, was not very promising, nor did the ordinary lay person at that time have the means to reassert himself or herself. Both the socio-political and the ecclesiastical structures tended to exclude ordinary lay participation. The glories of the early medieval period were monastic and clerical, on the one hand, and aristocratic and imperial, on the other. The margination of the ordinary lay person could have progressed even further, but historical circumstances prevented this. The steady process of marginalization and disenfranchising of the ordinary lay person within the *societas Christiana* had within itself the seeds of redress. When the tide finally turned, the inward surge of the changing tide became a power which the clerical levees could not restrain.

8

The First Millennium of the Christian Community and the Role of the Lay Person: An Evaluation

In the preceding pages we have considered some of the major first millennium situations in church history, particularly western church history, which have affected the role of the lay person in the Christian community. As we move out of the first millennium and enter the second thousand years of Christian existence, it is both fair and necessary to ask the following question:

Is the ecclesial role of the ordinary lay Christian, at the end of the first millennium, theologically acceptable?

The question is, of course, focused on the theme of this present volume, and it attempts to center on certain major theological issues connected to the issue of the lay person and the church. Since the question and its answer are both theological, and not merely historical or factual, the answer can only be expressed in systematic or theological terms. A theological answer, however, involves grave implications, implications which affect ecclesiology at all its levels.

There can be, perhaps, several answers to this question, but each answer rests on the basis of certain criteria. If the criterion is that of a divinely instituted cleric/lay church, the theological answer will be expressed in one way. However, as we noted in part one of this study, such a criterion has fragile foundations. If the criterion is canon law, namely, the closer a church community reflects canon law, the more perfect it is, then the theological answer will be expressed in another way. However, as we also saw in part one, canon law itself is based on and stems from statements of Christian faith and from theological perspectives. Canon law does not shape theology; theology shapes canon law. To put the cart before the horse is an odd procedure. Moreover, as we also noted in that first section, the present canon law sees the terms "cleric/lay" as juridical only, and offers a typological, not a theological description of both cleric and lay.

The criterion which I believe is the basis for every other criterion is that of discipleship, as found in the word of God itself, the New Testament. Discipleship is the basis which gives meaning to church community. Discipleship is the basis which gives meaning to any and every form of church ministry: papal, episcopal, presbyteral, etc. Discipleship is the basis which gives meaning to Christian ethical life. In other words, the church community is not the basis for discipleship; hierarchy does not determine discipleship; a code of ethical behavior does not tell us what discipleship is. In all of these cases—and there are many more—the opposite is true.

Because Jesus has called us to be his disciples, therefore, we have a church.

Not vice versa: because we have a church, therefore, we must be disciples.

Because Jesus has called us to be his disciples, therefore, we also have service leadership.

Not vice versa: because we have service leadership, therefore, we have disciples.

Because Jesus has called us to be his disciples, we have an ethical dimension in our life.

Not vice versa: because we have an ethical dimension in our lives, therefore we are disciples.

On the basis of Christian discipleship as the basic theological criterion which one must use to evaluate the lay person's ecclesial role in the church at the end of the first Christian millennium, the theological answer to the above question can only be negative. An understanding of discipleship, based on data from the New Testament, has already been presented at great length in an earlier chapter of this volume, so that it is unnecessary at this time to repeat the description of discipleship here.

At this millennium juncture of church history one finds little that can be used to justify the depositioned state of the ordinary lay person in the church. Since the ordinary Christian disciple, however, had not always been in such an ecclesial position of non-importance during those first thousand years, the positioning of the lay person at the end of the first millennium cannot be seen as normative. One finds, for example, in the first Jesus communities after the resurrection event, that discipleship as such was much more valued as an official status than it was in the year 1000. One finds, for example, in the first three hundred years of Christian existence, that the heroes of the church, the martyrs, were more often than not Christian men and women who had no official church leadership position. One finds, for example, within the Christian community even down to the sixth century, that many lay men and women were still prominent in church leadership. Given all of this, one can rightfully call the situation of the lay person at the turn of the millennium a "repositioned" and "depositioned" situation. One can rightfully call it an insufferable situation. One can legitimately criticize all those elements which led to such a repositioning and depositioning.

The repositioning and depositioning, which we have outlined throughout the course of this present volume, occurred through a steady process of both deterioration and marginalization of the ordinary Christian. The process was clearly not a programmatic one, in the sense that the respective leaders of both the church and the governments, individually or collectively, had agreed on this kind of development. Nowhere in the annals of history for this period of time do we find any pre-determined pattern to marginate the lay Christian, with the two exceptions as mentioned previously, namely:

1. Gregory the Great's deliberate replacement of lay people in the papal curia by monks and priests;
2. the deliberate pressure by the hierarchy, i.e. popes, patriarchs, and bishops, to clericalize male monastic communities, a pressure which began around the eighth century.

One of the questions which has energized me throughout this lengthy study of church history has been the following:

What were the reasons why the ordinary lay Christian progressively became so powerless within the church structures in this period of time?

Both the question and the answer are important on this matter, for if one could articulate in detail the reasons for this process of inferiorization, one would more clearly understand both the operative positive factors, and, at the same time, the operative errors. That the ordinary lay Christian became marginated within the *societas Christiana* is historically verifiable; that the ordinary lay Christian should be in such a marginated position within the *societas Christiana* is theologically indefensible. There is then, in this matter, both a de facto issue and a de iure issue. De facto, the ordinary lay Christian was repositioned and depositioned; de iure, such a depositioning and repositioning of the ordinary lay Christian runs counter to the teaching of the New Testament on discipleship.

The judgment that the repositioning and depositioning of the ordinary lay person is de iure counter to the gospel is, of course, a theological judgment, not simply an historical one. Such a theological judgment requires a criterion, but the criterion cannot be discerned from a study of the early Christian use of the terms *klerikos/laikos,* nor can it be discerned from the early Christian use of the term *ordo* as applied to *klerikos/laikos.* The very terms *klerikos/laikos* are generally interpreted through the term *ordo,* so that *ordo* becomes the hermeneutical tool to understand *klerikos/laikos.* The Christian use of the term *ordo,* however, in its early historical context, rather quickly received its own non-theological, hermeneutical tool, for the Christian *ordo* began to be interpreted in a socio-political way. When the Graeco-Roman *societas* within the first millennium of Christian history became the *societas Christiana,* socio-political and economic factors entered into the very meaning of the term *ordo* as used by the Christian world. However, one can legitimately ask: Is such a situation consonant with the message of the gospel or not? Does the gospel itself move one into the direction of a *societas Christiana?* Does the gospel even speak about various orders (*ordines*) within discipleship? Does the gospel even provide a basis for such orders of discipleship, and, stated more sharply, does the gospel provide a basis for the socio-politicizing of such orders, if such orders might exist?

The churches, of course, do not exist in a spiritual vacuum; they exist within a variety of historical contexts which involve socio-political and economic dimensions. Nor have the churches existed in some ideal, socio-political, economic, historical situation. Ecclesial communities, over the centuries, have necessarily had to co-exist with the many complex factors which make up the continually changing and multi-structured *societas humana.* The issue of the relationship of church to society is, accordingly, focused not on an effort to create an asocial or apolitical ecclesial situation, but rather on an effort to create Christian communities, at any and every given historical time, which have as their primary and most overriding goal the fostering of gospel discipleship among their members. Everything else, including the structure of church leadership and the structures in which this church leadership relates to the socio-political and economic world, is secondary and subservient to this primary goal. Discipleship, not preservation of some leadership structure, is the basic criterion for church communities.

Let us reflect, retrospectively, on some key aspects of Christian life which shaped the way in which the issue of Christian discipleship became articulated during the first Christian millennium, and which caused the insufferable ecclesial situation of the ordinary lay person. The following two topics help us manage this material:

1. The issue of *regnum et sacerdotium*
2. The slow process of the lay depositioning

1. THE ISSUE OF REGNUM ET SACERDOTIUM

In the first millennium of Christian existence, deliberately after Constantine, and in the west, from its particularly nuanced situation, after the emergence of the Frankish hegemony, church leadership moved to make the *societas politica* of the European world a *societas Christiana*. As this movement developed, a major issue arose which in many ways captivated, focused, even in a sense dominated the western world. This fundamental issue was the origin of kingship. From Constantine onward, both in the east and in the west, the origin of the emperor/king was considered to be divine. This was acknowledged by the people, by church leadership, by political leadership, by theologians and by other scholars of the period. In this view, it was God himself who gave kingship to the social world. Emperors and kings had their authority from God alone, not from the people, not from the senate, not from the *sacerdotium*. Almost at the very same time, particularly in the west, a monistic view of the papacy began to develop, and in a haphazard, non-orthogenetic way, a theory of papal power began to develop. At the end of the first Christian millennium there had arisen a view that the pope's power, which also came directly from God, was the *only* power which came directly from God. A collision course between these two "divinely instituted" powers was, in many ways, inevitable. The focus, however, was not on *potestas papalis* and *potestas regalis,* although at a later date this dichotomy became more prominent. Nor was there a contrast between the spiritual and the temporal, much less between church and state. Both of these contrasting issues emerge at a much later date as well. During the early decades and centuries of this question on the twofold divine institution, both the *regnum,* i.e. the emperor/king, and the *sacerdotium*, i.e. popes, patriarchs and bishops, were considered spiritual. After all, the major western kingdom was called the *Holy* Roman Empire. The formal or thematized idea of a non-spiritual or secular "state" began to emerge, inchoatively, only in the late middle ages. Thus the issue was not between the spiritual and the temporal. Moreover, since the idea of a "secular state" had not yet been thematized, the issue was also not that of church/state. The issue was clearly the origin of *regnum*.

This focus on *regnum et sacerdotium* was by no means the only theo-political, and certainly not the only theological, theme during these centuries, but as one moves from 500 to 1000 this particular theme became more and more operative throughout western theology. One finds it influential in the manner in which christological issues were formulated, in the manner in which liturgy and sacramental theology was developed, in the manner in which an ecclesial consciousness (not yet an ecclesiology) was assimilated. This issue became so central that it permeated every aspect of western Christian thought between 500 and 1000, and it is one of the major reasons why the lay person was depositioned and repositioned within the ecclesial community.

A major church situation, which was not, however, directly centered on the lay person in the church, took place with the so-called "Photian schism." This was a schism whose name became attached to the patriarch Photius, but which had a lengthy pre-history to the actual patriarchal career of Photius. He was simply one of several major foci which eventually gave rise to the division of the Christian church. Many complex factors entered into the causes of this division. The western issue of *regnum et sacerdotium* as such, however, was not specifically one of these major causes, but the way in which *sacerdotium* was interpreted by the west, particularly in its papal interpretation and, dependently thereon, in its episcopal interpretation, was indeed a major cause. This long-lasting schism, which only in the twentieth century showed major signs of healing, was and is a strong indication that the interpretation of *sacerdotium*, as developed by the west from 500 to 1000, was not and is not acceptable within the wider Christian *oekumene*. One might present western church history in a manner in which one presupposes that the western view of *sacerdotium* is correct and unassailable. The Photian schism certainly calls such a position into question, but so too does the western situation, namely the western depositioning of the lay person in the church. If the position of the lay person in the year 1000 is theologically unacceptable, then one must look at the theological acceptability of the opposite of lay person in that same time period, namely the position of *sacerdotium*. Both the Photian schism and the western depositioning of the ordinary lay

Christian stand in criticism of the western positioning of *sacerdotium.* The Photian schism consequently reinforces the critique which the western church leadership and scholarship must face as regards *sacerdotium/laicatus.*

During the first millennium, a comparable schism did not occur in the west. Rather, two major things did occur. First, the papacy so pursued the issue of *regnum et sacerdotium* with its own goal of papal monism that eventually the divine origin of kingship was eliminated. When this occurred, only the *sacerdotium* remained as a dimension within human society which enjoyed the status of divine origin. The momentum, however, did not stop simply with the elimination of a divine origin of an emperor/king and the establishment of a divine origin of *sacerdotium;* a certain sector of influential medieval theology pressed on to develop, besides the divine origin of the highest *sacerdos,* the pope, a theory of an almost omni-competent papacy. Once the king was reduced to the lay state, the issue was no longer *regnum et sacerdotium,* but it became the issue of *laicatus et sacerdotium,* a situation which is centrally germane to our theme. When this happened, and it happened gradually, the stage was clearly set both for the emergence of a man like Gratian and for an almost immediate acceptance by the leadership of the western church of Gratian's views that the entire church is divided into cleric and lay. The next step, which soon followed, was that such a division was itself considered *ex institutione divina.* This particular development from *regnum et sacerdotium* to *sacerdotium et laicatus* theologically and canonically sealed the fate of the repositioning and depositioning of the lay person in the church for almost all of the second millennium of Christian existence. Gratian's position—and if Gratian had not formulated it, another person would have done so, since all the issues were present in the medieval air—came about only on the basis that the emperor/king had no "special" status of his own, no special status of divine origin, and that the emperor/king did not present an exception to the cleric/lay structure. Likewise, Gratian's bifurcation of the Christian world rested on the basis that religious men and women had no special status beyond the cleric/lay structure. The laicization of the emperor/king and the clericalization of male religious provided a scholar like Gratian with the groundwork on which to build the ecclesiastical construct: a *klerikos/laikos* church.

Indirectly from the entire event called the "Photian schism," but directly from the ever-increasing rejection of the repositioning/depositioning of the lay person in the church by many western Christian groups, one can only conclude that major elements in the medieval resolution to the issue of *regnum et sacerdotium* were not acceptable. The repositioning and the depositioning of the lay person in the western Roman Catholic

Church was indeed insufferable. The various western movements after the first millennium which strove to improve the status of the lay person in the church have been mentioned previously:

1. the rediscovery of the lay brother;
2. the emergence of a church/state dichotomy;
3. the rise of educated lay Christians;
4. the theological emphasis on the priesthood of all believers in the reformation period;
5. the breakthrough of *liberté, fraternité* and *égalité* of each human being as championed by the French and American revolutions;
6. the theological emergence within Roman Catholicism of a theology of the laity;
7. the contemporary rise of various women's movements, even within the Roman Catholic Church;
8. the contemporary demand for social justice, particularly for the marginated, by Roman Catholic liberation theologians.

All of these movements have one thing in common: a call for a repositioning and better positioning of the ordinary lay person within the church. The fact that such demands for the ecclesial status of the lay person have occurred again and again and again indicates that the medieval interpretation of *sacerdotium,* even though it has many positive qualities, has as well seriously erroneous dimensions. To express it bluntly: if there were not something essentially and insufferably wrong with the way in which the medieval view of *sacerdotium* was developed—and developed at the expense of *laicatus*—why has there been such a continuous and unabated effort to reinstate in a better way the lay person within the church?

The New Testament does not indicate in any way the precise sociopolitical form for human life. It does not advocate that human society must be a *societas Christiana* along the lines of the Justinian or Carolingian structures. The New Testament provides no indication at all that a monarchical government, an aristocratic government, a democratic government, a republican government, a socialist government, or any other defined form of government must occur in human society. The sociopolitical form, which the *societas Christiana,* particularly in the west, gradually became, was conditioned by historical factors, not by revelation, and consequently medieval social structure has no normative value in itself. Because of its historicity and relativity, both its weaknesses and its failures must be assessed and interpreted precisely as weaknesses and as failures, not only on the basis of erroneous political theory, but also, whenever valid, on the basis of erroneous theology. The theological aspect cannot be set to one side, since during this medieval period theology was co-opted by every faction, papal and imperial, to provide a substantiation for the existence and validity of such a society.

In the theological discussions of that period of time, the ordinary lay person was repositioned and depositioned, but such a repositioning and depositioning took place only on the basis that there was a concomitant repositioning and better positioning of another group, namely the *regnum et sacerdotium*. If, then, there is legitimate theological judgment against the repositioning and depositioning of the ordinary lay Christian, there will of necessity be a legitimate theological judgment against the repositioning and better positioning of the *sacerdotium,* the clergy, which took place during this same period of time. One cannot make a case for a better status of the lay Christian within the Christian community as such, without at the same time altering the status of the clerical Christian. One cannot maintain that the clerical position is sacrosanct and untouchable, and at the same time maintain that the ordinary lay Christian's role must be improved. The two sides, because of historical factors more than theological factors, interface, and any alteration of one side will affect the other side as well. This interfacing and mutual reshaping of *sacerdotium et laicatus* affects the entire gamut of *sacerdotium.* No sacerdotal position remains untouchable. If the ordinary lay Christian's position is to be changed in accordance with the demands of New Testament discipleship, then not only does the presbyter's position change, but also the episcopal and papal positions will also be modified.

In today's late twentieth century Roman Catholic theology, there is an enormous amount of discussion on the issue of the lay person within the church. This has taken place, and is taking place, primarily due to two major factors:

A. A number of major Roman Catholic theological scholars have raised the issue of the lay person and his or her ministry in the church in a way which has brought this entire subject into center-stage.

B. Vatican II itself made the issue of the *christifidelis* central to its presentation on the meaning of church.

The contemporary discussion on the lay person in the church, and more pointedly on the issue of lay ministry, did not arise in reaction to an anti-clerical stance, but rather from a pro-church stance, namely the resurfacing of the question: What precisely is the theological understanding of church, i.e. of the community of Christian disciples? In raising the issue of the lay person or the *christifidelis,* one cannot help, however, but reevaluate the status of the "cleric," and the "cleric" at every level. One reaction to this discussion of the non-ordained with its concomitant discussion of the ordained was predictable, for some clerics, from popes to deacons, find any and every criticism of their status as "destructive," "counter-productive," even "heretical" and "schismatic." Nonetheless, the current reassessment of the non-ordained Christian does involve a concomitant reassessment of the ordained Christian, a reassessment of the ordained Christian at every level: papal, patriarchal, episcopal, presbyteral, and diaconal. If at the present time a repositioning and better positioning of the ordinary non-ordained Christian is beginning to take place, there exists concomitantly and inevitably a repositioning—but perhaps not a better positioning—of the ordained Christian within church structures, and this is taking place again at all levels: papal, patriarchal, episcopal, presbyteral, and diaconal. Any repositioning of the lay person will involve a repositioning of each and every level of the ordained persons as well.

At times one hears a catch-word or a phrase which is meant to sum up all the reasons for the historical depositioning of the ordinary lay Christian. For instance, one hears today the catch-words "clericalism," or "patriarchal bias," or even "power." Care needs to be taken with such simplistic or all-explanatory terms. Historically there might have been a form of clerical structure within the church, and thus a "clericalism," which would have resulted in a different configuration. What if, for instance, the clerical structure from the beginning had been open to both men and women? Would this have changed the critical understanding of the term "clericalism" as it is sometimes bantered about today? Let us take another related term: *ordo.* What if the term *ordo* had never been associated with the clerical element in the church? Would not this have changed the meaning of "clericalism"? What if the phrase *ordo laicorum* had found an acceptable usage within the church and socio-political structures? Would this not have changed the meaning of the term "clericalism"?

Even in the case of *ordo,* however, what if the major leaders of the early patristic church had not become so cozy with the governmental structures, first of the Roman empire and then of the Frankish empire? What if the trend had resembled to a greater degree the stance of the Donatists, who wanted little or nothing to do with the Roman government? Or what if the official church stance had resembled the non-antagonistic but still quite separate position of the church toward government which the early ascetics and monks had displayed? In such instances, *ordo* would not have taken on the socio-political overtones it did, and the clerics in that *ordo* would not have become the form of a societal caste which they did become.

What if, we might further ask, the leaders of the Christian church had not officially adopted the form of intolerance for other religious practices, an intolerance which one finds with the decree by Theodosius? After all, when the edict of toleration had first appeared with Constantine, it gave a governmental tolerance to *all religions,* but this was rapidly changed, primarily due to Christian influence (which means an influence placed on the government through the Christian leadership of that day), to an edict of a state religion, i.e. Christianity, intolerant of any rival religious group. In a religiously pluralistic world which was involved in the earlier edict of toleration by Constantine, no single given religion was supposed to receive a special socio-political status or even economic favor. In the religiously intolerant edict of Theodosius, only the Christian faith was legally acceptable within society. Our study of church history indicates that Christianity took a quite intolerant position vis-à-vis other religions during the Constantinian, Justinian, and Carolingian periods.

These are all hypothetical situations, of course. They all begin with the phrase: "What if . . . ?" Historical scholarship is not established by a variety of "what if" situations. Rather, historical scholarship focuses on what actually happened, on hard data, on factual evidence. However, one of the results from this study of hard data as regards church history, and from the factual evidence of the early Christian communities, is the clear evidence that at each stage of history when terms such as *klerikos, laikos,* and *ordo* came to be common currency, at each stage of history when Christian leadership was called on to take a stance vis-à-vis the various governmental structures, **legitimate alternative positions were available to the church leadership of the time.** That one position was selected over another indicates that the actual historical forms which were eventually taken cannot be seen as absolute. Decisions were made at each period of church history, but these decisions were time-conditioned and socially-conditioned. No period of church history, therefore, offers us an absolutely normative position. In each period of church history we find good things and we find unfortunate things; we find correct judgments and we find erroneous judgments.

The criterion which was suggested at the beginning of this volume was that of discipleship, more precisely the discipleship of Jesus. Throughout the first millennium this criterion was never lost sight of, but it manifested itself differently in the differing periods of church history which we have studied. Each church community attempted in its own way to develop disciples of the Lord, but each church community in its own way never attained an ideal situation. In fact, each church community created situations quite opposed to such discipleship. Each church community attempted to create and often did create an ecclesial situation which would strengthen discipleship, and at the very same time that these attempts were being made, the same Christian communities with its own leadership developed situations which ran counter-productive to the formation of Christian discipleship. Even our own present-day Christian communities reflect this same *pro/con* situation.

We find, for example, in the time immediately after the resurrection event, that is, in the apostolic and sub-apostolic communities, enormous struggles on the part of local communities and their leadership to make Christian discipleship meaningful, but at the very same time there were issues which caused not only disunity in this endeavor, but also disunity of practice, disunity of theological substantiation, disunity of leadership. Among the Christians of the apostolic and sub-apostolic communities, we find that there were some who maintained in quite apodictic ways the retention of many aspects of Jewish law, and at the same time there were some early Christians who in quite apodictic ways advocated that such laws had been abrogated. The clash of these views created division within the early communities, fundamentally a division on the very meaning of Christian discipleship. The *Hellenistai* and the *Hebraeoi* wrangled over many issues on the living out of discipleship, a wrangling which one finds in the Pauline letters, in the Acts of the Apostles, and even in the Johannine writings.

In the second and third centuries, discipleship found a major paradigm in the martyrs. Indeed, martyrdom was viewed as the very acme of discipleship, and this acme of discipleship was found in both men and women, in "unordained" and "ordained." The extant literature provides us with many *encomia* for those men and women who gave up their lives for the faith. All of this indicates that in the time of the persecutions and the martyrs, the criterion of discipleship was quite strong and animating for many communities. At the very same time, persecutions created a counter-productive situation: apostasy. Disorganization and disunity arose in many communities in which those who had once denied the faith later clamored for reinstatement. Crises in leadership arose precisely because of this issue of apostasy. The North African church under Cyprian offers us a solidly documented case-study of this critical situation. Various church leaders in the North African communities were taking diverse stances on the matter of the readmission of apostates. The *libelli* from martyr-confessors of that period of time only complicated the matter. Cyprian's instructions were often not followed and at times were ineffective because of the resurgence of persecution and Cyprian's own flight from the persecutors. People looked to their leaders for guidance, and leadership was not unified in its answers. Did discipleship of the Lord allow for the reintegration of an apostate or not? The issue troubled not only the North African church, but all the churches of the Christian world at that time, and a resolution to this vexing question came only slowly and sporadically. No sooner had this question been to a degree resolved than the question of the reintegration of publicly known adulterers came to the fore. Once again, the issue of true discipleship arose, and conflicting positions clamored for acceptance.

These conflicts on the issue of discipleship were fought out at a time when church leadership was still in a rather undeveloped stage of existence. The very naming and the tasks of the leaders of the Christian communities were at this particular period still in flux, and only gradually did both the names and the functions of central Christian leaders come to be more unified throughout the various Christian communities as one moves through the third century. It is at this time that the first ordination ritual appears. It is at this time that the connection of *ordo* and *klerikos* becomes stronger. The *episkopoi*—and Cyprian is certainly a major figure in this situation—begin to equate themselves more and more to the apostles. Cyprian's writings offer us the first extant instance in which the apostles themselves are called *episkopoi*. In making this rather gratuitous statement, Cyprian further integrated *episkopos* and apostle, and further involved the *episkopoi* as the successors of the apostles. Since the apostles were presented as the major paradigms of discipleship, their successors, the *episkopoi*, were also presented as the major paradigms of discipleship. At the same time, however, the martyrs were seen as the paradigms of discipleship. This dual listing of paradigms indicates that conflicting criteria for Christian discipleship vied for recognition: namely apostolicity, on the one hand, and martyrdom, on the other. In the Donatist struggle, both sides venerated Cyprian, but often for different reasons. One side stressed his role as *episkopos* and successor to the true "apostolic" teaching; the other side stressed his martyrdom and therefore his truly apostolic succession.

When the age of the martyrs subsided, ascetics and monks often became the paradigm of discipleship. Extant literature indicates that many bishops of the patristic period praised these ascetics in glowing terms precisely as true disciples of Jesus, and the non-ordained person of that same patristic period perceived them as marvelously holy leaders and renowned disciples of the Lord. Bishops such as Basil of Cappadocia, Eusebius of Vercelli, Augustine of Hippo, and Gregory of Rome tried to combine clerical life and monastic life in a way which would draw the best from both. Gregory, it may be recalled, presented monastic life as the ideal of discipleship. However, in all of this, ascetics, monks, and nuns never displaced the leadership role of the cleric. They may have been presented as great paradigms of discipleship; they were not, in the official episcopal church world, the paradigms of official leadership. The non-antagonistic approach of early ascetic and monastic Christians allowed for a peaceful co-existence of the two groups: the clerical leadership and the monastic movement. In time, struggles between the two, even here and there antagonistic struggles, took place, but the denouement did not take place in a violent confrontation, but rather in the clerical leadership's progressive domestication and clericalization of male monasticism and the ramifications of this process in the domestication of religious women within a clerically-led church structure.

The volume by C. Volz, *Pastoral Life and Practice in the Early Church,* draws together many facets of the patristic period, indicating how the spiritual leaders, *episkopoi* in particular, were concerned about the people of God.[1] Their pastoring, their preaching, their care of souls, their efforts at reconciliation, their urging of ethical lives which were deeply Christian, their continual efforts to promote prayer—all these clearly show that discipleship was indeed a centralizing issue. One cannot but be deeply touched by the sermons of so many of these early bishops, sermons which urged the Christians to follow Jesus more honestly and thoroughly. Preachers such as John Chrysostom, Basil, Ambrose and Augustine attracted large groups of ordinary Christians, and their words undoubtedly deepened the spiritual lives of many.

On the other hand, however, in all of this, certain issues tended to shape and reshape the understanding of discipleship. The decision of the church leaders to move into a strongly positive relationship to the Roman government led to the positioning of these same leaders as an *ordo* within the Roman society.

> Dramatic changes for the clergy came with the Peace of the Church. They were immune from municipal levies and adminis-tration. . . . These financial exemptions led many city council-lors (*curiales*) to apply for clergy status. Further privileges were granted to the clergy by placing the public post at their disposal to attend the Council of Arles in the year 314. In the year 318 bishops' jurisdiction was given the same validity as that of mag-istrates and the jurisdiction of the church courts was extended.[2]

We realize as well that the role of women within the Christian com-munity, which at first tended to be somewhat open and accepted, became in time quite restricted. A patriarchal framework developed which incul-cated a degree of acceptable discipleship that was far more open to men than to women. As time went on, with the introduction of clerical *ordo,* particularly as a definite socio-political *ordo,* not men generally but only certain men were gradually viewed as having an acceptable degree of discipleship which was "superior" to that of other men, and to all women. In all of this, we see that discipleship, though it remained somewhat key, found its meaning modified, nuanced, differentiated.

The causes for this major reshaping of discipleship, however, took place more indirectly than directly, i.e. church leaders did not focus deliberately on a reshaping of Christian discipleship which would downplay women or downplay non-ordained men, but rather these leaders focused on a secondary issue which became in the course of time the primary issue: namely the relationship of church leadership to governmental leadership. The results were devastating. Once the focusing of this leadership-to-leadership relationship began to take center stage, the jockeying for a correct relationship between church leadership and governmental leadership began to dominate all other concerns. The issue of *regnum et sacerdotium* became not merely a major theme, but the dominant theme. This issue, more than any other, galvanized the way in which the so-called *societas Christiana* progressed. We have seen that eventually three major forms of this relationship gradually took root and vied for acceptance: imperial monism, papal monism, and episcopal/imperial dualism. What I wish to stress here is this: the focusing on this issue of *regnum et sacerdotium* so dominated the way in which church and government leadership interacted that all other concerns were colored by this struggle. The issue of discipleship was no exception. Only that form of Christian discipleship which furthered one of the forms in this struggle was considered acceptable.

A similar example, found in our own day, might make the situation clear. In a typical North American diocese today there is great concern, and therefore a great expenditure of human resources, time, and money, on the matter of religious education. Not only schools but also religious education classes for children, for teens and for adults are indeed *foci* of this concern. There is also the great expenditure of personnel and time on the RCIA, and, to some degree, on the retreat movement and on such programs as Renew, the charismatic movement, and the cursillo movement. In all of these, the clear intent of Christian leadership is to deepen one's Christian life, that is, to make those who are already disciples of Jesus even better disciples than before. In all of this one sees that discipleship plays a major role in the way a diocese, through its leadership, sets its pace. Discipleship is without any doubt a major criterion for the way personnel, time and other resources are used.

However, can one say that this rather broad and strong interest and actual effort in religious education is the top priority of the main spiritual leader, the bishop? As long as the various educational leaders and teachers are "doing their job," a bishop tends to stay apart from such efforts. Actual, hands-on religious education is not his primary personal task; his task is oversight and animation. If the diocese has a viable and strong religious educational component, a bishop can generally believe that his leadership is going well, and that the criterion of discipleship is strongly present. One might ask, however, a different question: What issue almost immediately involves the bishop's personal and hands-on attention? The answer can be well documented: namely, any challenge to episcopal authority. When such authority is questioned, an abundance of activity begins to take place. The questioning of episcopal authority might come from below, i.e. by certain groups of lay people, by non-Christians, by theologians, or it might come from the bishop's peers, i.e. a questioning of one bishop's decisions by the National Conference of Bishops, or it might come from the Vatican itself, either from the pope or from one of the sacred congregations. No matter what its source, the notoriety of such questioning and even challenging makes the matter of episcopal authority central. With all the ensuing attention, even by the secular media, on the issue of episcopal authority, the issue of discipleship is not abandoned, but it ceases to be center-stage. The question, when it is restated by church leaders, is generally not formulated as follows: Is episcopal authority being used to develop discipleship? Rather, the question is generally set in a different formula: Can a true disciple of Jesus question episcopal or papal authority? In other words, does the criterion of discipleship determine episcopal/papal authority, or, rather, is not discipleship itself subjected to the criterion of episcopal/papal authority? If one looks at all the major issues which the Roman Catholic Church has engaged in from the time of the Second Vatican Council down to the present, one finds many things which focus rather directly on discipleship, for example, the entire renewal of the sacramental rituals, the openness to the role of the laity within the church, the stress on prayer and spiritual renewal. Nonetheless, no issue has caused more concern and heated discussion than that of authority in the church. The issue of "authority in the church" for us today in the twentieth century has as its counterpart the issue of *regnum et sacerdotium* in the period of church history we have reviewed. For us today, the issue of authority in the church often totally dominates the discussion, as we see on various occasions, such as in the discussions on the role of the laity in the church, in the discussions on the collegiality of bishops with its wrangling over papal/episcopal claims to authority and over an individual bishop's claims to authority and national/regional claims to episcopal authority, and in the many ecumenical discussions, particularly with the eastern religions, but also in the discussions with Anglicans and Lutherans, in which papal/patriarchal claims to authority, Roman/non-Roman claims to authority, more often than not are the real issues on the agenda.

The struggle of *regnum et sacerdotium* involved a heated and at times even violent clash on two fundamental issues: (a) the God-given source of kingship (*regnum*), and (b) the God-given role of the cleric (*sacerdotium*). What affected the positioning of the lay Christian most of all was the concentration in this debate on *sacerdotium*. Notice that the alternative term to *regnum* is not *ecclesia*. The struggle was not between church and state, nor between church and government, but between a governmental leader (*regnum,* i.e. the source of kingship) and a numerically small part of *ecclesia*, namely the clerical part, the *sacerdotium*, and even here only the highest echelon of the *sacerdotium*, the bishops and/or the pope. This focusing on the clerical section of the *ecclesia* alone, and even in this focusing on the clerical section, the focusing on episcopal and papal *sacerdotium*, not presbyteral, diaconal or other parts of the *sacerdotium*, made the episcopal and papal *sacerdotium* the central criterion by which *regnum* was evaluated, by which *ecclesia* was evaluated, and by which the *societas Christiana* was evaluated. Only that form of discipleship which supported *sacerdotium* (either episcopal dualism or papal monism) appeared to be acceptable to one side of the argument, while only that form of discipleship which supported imperial monism appeared to be acceptable by the other side of the argument. In all of this, papal and episcopal *sacerdotium* became the criterion to evaluate discipleship, not vice versa. The fall-out in this *regnum et sacerdotium* included the depositioning of the lay person.

At the end of the millennium just studied, however, the issue of episcopal and above all papal *sacerdotium* had not yet run its course. We have yet to reach the positions of such leaders as Innocent III, Gregory IX, and Boniface VIII, and the theory of *plenitudo potestatis.* When the theory of the *plenitudo potestatis* of the papacy began to be placed before the *societas Christiana,* the only viable opposition appeared to be a defense of the governmental power. The disintegration of *regnum,* however, helped tip the scales toward the theory of papal monism. In turn this favored the theory that only those forms of discipleship which accepted a *plenitudo potestatis* of the pope were truly one, holy, catholic and apostolic.

It would be simplistic to think that the dominance of the *regnum et sacerdotium* issue alone brought about the repositioning and depositioning of the ordinary lay Christian. One might legitimately ask: Why did the majority of the ordinary lay Christians not reject such a depositioning? As one lists the other major factors for this lack of resistance, one realizes the complexity of the issue.

2. THE SLOW PROCESS OF LAY DEPOSITIONING

Were one to chart the process of this depositioning of the lay person, one would see that its movement was incrementally slow, and often indirect. Questions which might arise in the tenth and eleventh century regarding the status of the "non-ordained" (to use an anachronistic term) would have been meaningless in the apostolic and post-apostolic churches, in the churches of the martyrs, in the *koinoniai* of Pachomias and the *laurae* of Palestine. Even in the sixth century there were still many influential lay Christians within the church structures, lay Christians who were not part of the imperial family or entourage. The fact that one is not dealing with a programmatic process of historical change spelled out by some detailed form of long-range planning disallows a programmatic cataloguing of each step toward lay depositioning. When one recalls the various views which authors of no mean repute offer as regards the so-called "fall of the Roman empire," one sees that civilizations, cultures, governments often find themselves in a given historical situation, which oddly enough *seems* to have occurred out of nowhere.

A. THE DEPRIVATION OF EDUCATION

In the west more than in the east, educational opportunities were removed from the environment of the ordinary lay Christian. In both the west and the east, education under Christian influence tended to disassociate itself from classical studies and to focus on Christian elements alone. At times not only was classical literature denigrated, but libraries were destroyed and teachers of such classical disciplines were deprived of their positions, and occasionally deprived of citizenship and even life. In the west, the gradual restriction of education only to certain clergy or certain monks and nuns, and to a few well-positioned imperial, regal, and aristocratic individuals, created an illiterate lay majority. In the west, but not in the east, the formation of vernacular languages without an educational base, and the retention of Latin as the educational language, further deprived the ordinary lay Christian of literacy. An uneducated group of people becomes a powerless group, while an educated group of people becomes a powerful group. Instances of such situations go far beyond western Europe in the early middle ages. A "pedagogy of the oppressed" has a validity at almost every stage of human history. The illiteracy of a majority of Christians in the early middle ages of western Europe meant that such a group had no leaders who could argue pro or con on such topics as imperial monism, papal monism, and episcopal/imperial dualism. They could not argue on the basis of scripture, which they could not read, what discipleship truly means. An illiterate majority of Christians had become "hearers" and "observers."

This issue of illiteracy cannot be taken lightly, for once lay men and women began to be educated, as we shall see in the high middle ages and in the reformation period, a revolt by lay people began to take place, and it was a revolt that had its own educated lay leaders. The fact that education appears as a major reason for the repositioning of the lay person in the church at a later date indicates that the lack of education was actually one of the major reasons why at an earlier date the ordinary lay Christian was not only repositioned but depositioned.

B. THE LACK OF LAY SPIRITUALITY

When one compares the spiritual experience of a monk who entered the *koinonia* of Pachomias and the spiritual experience of a monk who entered a monastery in the tenth century, the differences are enormous. For the Pachomian monk the entire monastic experience, with the one exception of perhaps weekly eucharist, was lay. Such an experience was profoundly Christian. It was spiritually nourishing. It produced holy people, even heroic holy people, the saints. On the other hand, in the tenth century the entering monk experienced a form of life centered around daily eucharist, often several times daily, and a monastic structure dominated by clerical members. The spirituality he received was refined and well formulated, but in Latin, the language of education, and if he were to truly grasp its depth, this monk needed to be educated in Latin, and thereby enter himself into the small group of educated medieval people. The direction of his life was provided by clerical monks, particularly his abbot, who resembled a bishop, and he considered himself to be an integral part of the episcopal and papal church. If he proved himself an able student and a pious monk, he too probably became a cleric.

Outside the monastery, what kind of spirituality was given to the ordinary farmer, the ordinary artisan, the ordinary merchant, the ordinary person who belonged to the military? Such people perhaps attended mass on Sunday and heard a reading (homily) from Gregory the Great. There were perhaps places of pilgrimage where miracles had supposedly taken place, and therefore places of holiness. By and large, however, western church leadership, whether monastic or episcopal, did not provide the ordinary lay Christian with very many facets of spirituality. The liturgy, especially the eucharistic liturgy, had by the tenth century been clericalized and monasticized. The ordinary Christian attended as an observer and a listener.

The fact that in the eleventh and twelfth centuries there was a reaction to this in the various *vita evangelica* movements must be seen as a reaction to a deprivation. To those who took up this *vita evangelica*, neither the episcopal form of church structure nor the monastic form of church structure appeared to be gospel-oriented. These people did not consider either the episcopal or the monastic forms of church structure truly adequate to their legitimate spiritual needs. The fact that such movements became so popular and in many ways so threatening to the established church—consider the reaction of Innocent III—indicates that there was a deep-seated longing by ordinary lay Christians for discipleship, which is precisely the reason why these movements were deliberately called *vita evangelica* movements, and not *vita apostolica*, which was a term used by monastic groups of that time.

C. THE MISINTERPRETATION OF DISCIPLESHIP

If we return to the chapter on discipleship, we might make note that in Mark's gospel we have a description of a disciple of Jesus who is neither a "cleric" nor a "religious." Yet it was precisely in this period of time, the first thousand years of Christianity, that we see the status of monk/nun referred to as the "more perfect way" of discipleship, and that we find that the very term "church" is used, even by major writers, to mean the leadership of the church, thereby indicating that "true" discipleship can be found primarily in church leadership.

In Luke's gospel we found that faith in Jesus, repentance and conversion, and baptism were major Lucan hallmarks of a disciple. But we also found that a disciple of Jesus should be a person who is inclusive, seeking out the lost and the sinners, that the disciple of Jesus should be a person who has a message for both men and women and who shatters the boundaries of the clean and the unclean, and that the eucharist in Luke was a picture of an inclusive community, not an exclusive community. And yet we find in this first thousand years of Christianity a depositioning of Christian lay women in particular, as also Christian lay men, and a setting of many boundaries between cleric and non-cleric, monk and non-monk, bishop and non-bishop, pope and non-pope.

If we reconsider the material from Matthew's gospel and the Matthaean picture of a disciple, we find a warning about leadership people preferring special clothing and symbols, seeking primacy of position, craving special titles and names. We saw that Jesus was a model not only for leadership, but also for every Christian, and that Matthew nowhere presents a double standard of discipleship. And yet it is during this first thousand years of Christianity that the church leadership in particular began to assume titles and ranks, symbolic dress and seating arrangements, and in many ways these leaders did not see themselves on a par, as disciples of Jesus, with every other baptized person.

In the reflections on John's gospel we saw, once again, the significant positioning of women within the community of disciples. We noted that belief and conversion were fundamental aspects of discipleship, and that this conversion was open to all without exception, including those who might appear on the outside: ethnic individuals such as the Samaritans, and the powerful profession of faith in Jesus by the woman Martha. And yet in the first millennium of Christianity we find that church leadership was systematically opposed to women in ministry, at least from the time of the demise of deaconesses onward, and that uneducated lay people were viewed as "children" in the faith, and as the "rudes" who needed to be trained by those who "knew better."

In the Pauline letters, the centrality of Jesus is put before the various churches again and again, and although at times Paul refers to his own leadership role, the real leader is always seen as Jesus. For Paul, the church is not co-terminous with church leadership (*sacerdotium*), but with the various communities to which he sends his letters. Paul emphasizes the call to discipleship, a call which comes to men and women, regardless of position, status, gender, and ethnicity. And yet in the first thousand years of Christianity, church leadership did not follow Paul's example as far as openness to women in ministry and to the presentation of Jesus as the center of discipleship. Rather, women were excluded, and obedience to church authority, not Jesus, was the criterion of true discipleship.

In the deutero-Pauline letters and the other New Testament writings, one finds that there is no basis for a *klerikos/laikos* division in the Jesus community, and that leadership roles in these writings are described again and again as service-leadership, not as power-leadership. And yet during the first millennium of Christianity, one is faced with the amassing of the power of clerical *ordo,* from about 300 onward, a power which leads in the west to the theory of *plenitudo potestatis* of the pope, not a *plenitudo servitii.*

Were one to judge the way in which these first thousand years of Christian leadership moved the Jesus community, there would clearly be a number of issues for which these leaders deserved commendation. But when the first millennium comes to a close, and their stewardship as regards the issue of discipleship is raised, the evaluation does not rate high, and the primary reason why there is not a high rating lies in the way in which the ordinary lay Christian, male and female, was processively both repositioned and depositioned within the Jesus community. Secondly, it does not rate high, since the issue of *sacerdotium,* and its demand that its sacred authority be respected, increasingly became the criterion for true

THE FIRST MILLENNIUM AND THE LAY PERSON   329

discipleship, rather than discipleship being the criterion for true *sacerdotium.*

It is interesting to read an author such as Walter Ullmann, who in his volume *The Growth of Papal Government in the Middle Ages* will move from page to page to page, outlining his thesis on the validity of a monarchical papacy, and yet page after page the name "Jesus" is never mentioned. The term "church" occurs again and again, of course, but is not the church the community of Jesus, with the "of" a possessive genitive? Not to raise the Jesus-criterion, on this matter of church, appears unacceptable, and the critique of the very church structure of leadership, which Ullmann carefully documents by the rising voices of lay men and women during the second millennium of Christianity, is a critique which does not talk about *potestas,* monarchy, jurisdiction, keys, as though these were the most fundamental issues, but rather it is a critique which raises the question of discipleship, the meaning of *christifidelis,* the Christian meaning of being human, of being male, of being female, of being Greek, of being Jew, of being slave, of being free. The disciple of Jesus is called the *christifidelis,* not the *papaefidelis,* not the *episcopifidelis,* not the *presbyterifidelis.* He or she is the one faithful to Jesus, who hears that being male or female, Greek or Jew, slave or free, plays absolutely no role at all.

A Jesus-criterion presents its own problematic issues as well. There are many christologies within the Christian communities, and there will continue to be many christologies. Officially, church leadership in ecumenical councils has spoken out only rarely on christological issues, and these solemn statements are quite circumspect and narrowly focused. On the basis of official church documents, it would be impossible to develop a total christology. One, therefore, looks elsewhere for christological criteria. To some degree, the *lex orandi* provides us with the meaning of Jesus, although not every prayer nor every prescribed ritual is christologically sound or sufficient. Another area, which goes far beyond official church documents, far beyond systematic theology, far beyond liturgical celebrations, is found in the mystical life of the church. Men and women who reached profound stages of Christian mysticism provide more pedestrian Christians with an insight into the meaning of Jesus. When one asks the question "Who determines the 'correct' interpretation of Jesus for the Christian community?" the answer is certainly not simplistic. It is not simply the authority of church leadership. Church authority had indeed a role to play in this matter, but it is not omni-competent. In the *lex orandi* of the Christian communities, there are many areas of prayer which are not given an *imprimatur* or *nihil obstat.* Christians simply pray under the guidance of the Spirit. Mystics do not ask for official endorsement prior to mystical experiences. The *sensus ecclesiae* has a validity in this matter of

Jesus, which can never be programmed by church leadership structures. New Testament scholars provide us with sharper insights into the meaning of the text and context, but even these insights do not provide us with all the necessary criteria for understanding discipleship. Discipleship is first and foremost a lived reality, not a cogitated reality, and it is a lived reality not only at leadership levels, but at all levels of Christian existence. Christian leadership has as its primary role to serve discipleship within the *ecclesia* of God. Christian leadership does not have as its primary role the imposition of only one form of discipleship.

Jesus was an individual at a given time and a given place in history. In many ways Jesus is both time-conditioned and place-conditioned. Each generation and each group of Christians and each individual Christian is called on to reflect on the message, mission and person of Jesus, and to involve into his or her life as much as possible the Spirit of Jesus. In other words, the task is not to replicate Jesus, but to make my or our time and space as open to God's presence as Jesus in his time and space was open to the presence of the Father. It is in this sense alone that each Christian generation can be seen as disciples of the Lord, as *christifideles*.

In today's Roman Catholic Church, one still hears leaders demanding obedience and making obedience the touchstone or criterion for orthodoxy and orthopraxis. One also hears highly educated and deeply spiritual women and men calling on Christians to look to discipleship as the basic criterion, and calling on, if not demanding of, church leaders to verify their own authoritarian demands not on the basis of position, but on the basis of discipleship. As we consider the second millennium, the critique of ordinary lay men and ordinary lay women will become extraordinarily sharp. It will also become extraordinarily well rooted in the New Testament, God's own revelation. It will, in a slow but steady way, become extraordinarily opposed to any system, even an ecclesiastical one, which substantially depositions the inherent dignity and freedom of human beings.

The saga, of course, moves beyond the first millennium of Christian life. In the second millennium major and at times tumultuous situations arose which attempted to correct the unbalanced situation, affecting the ordinary lay person in the church. This period of the account, however, will be considered in part two, addressing the second millennium of the Christian community with the identical theme in mind—the non-ordained ministry in the Roman Catholic Church: its history and theology.

PART TWO

The Rise of the Lay Movement within the Western Church and the Decline of Clerical Dominance: 1000–2000 A.D.

9

The Later Medieval Period

INTRODUCTION

The year 1000 marked a low-tide level as far as the role of the ordinary lay person within the Christian church was concerned. That same year, however, also showed signs of a noticeable turning of the tide, a turning toward a better repositioning of the ordinary lay person in the church. This repositioning did not take place dramatically all at once; rather, events, extending over several centuries, increasingly brought about this heightened respect for the ordinary non-ordained Christian, a respect which involved a rethinking of that central meaning of discipleship which the New Testament places before us on every page of its various writings.

In this second part we will concentrate on those areas of western church history which significantly moved the lay person into a more central position within the Christian church. In doing so, we must necessarily omit altogether or merely allude to other issues and events which were shaping western Christian thought. History is a complex interweaving of numerous issues, ideas, events and lives, and as a result it is almost impossible to arrange such a kaleidoscopic fusion of historical elements into a cohesively written unity which remains true to the historical reality. No person can ever pen the "final word" on any given historical subject. This is particularly evident when one focuses on a single issue, in our case the issue of the ordinary lay person in the church. In the presentation of such a particularized theme, only those factors immediately germane to the topic at hand can receive any consideration at all, whereas other factors, to a lesser degree perhaps, but nonetheless to a real degree, might also have played some role in the historical shaping of the given theme. Sweeping areas of historical background material are also of necessity left to one side, and can only be presumed as known to the reader.

The aim of this book is certainly not an anti-clerical one. That there has been an in-service ministry to the community of faith from the post-resurrection times onward is a given. The community called church was never, not even in its incipient stages, a totally democratic, congregational church. From the beginning there were servant-leaders of the community. Such service-leadership has continued to be in evidence during each Christian generation and is evident as well in today's churches, no matter what denomination. Nonetheless, it is also correct to say that this leadership, which eventually came to be called "clerical" leadership, has itself a history. At various times and places in the history of the church, this leadership has been structured differently and has been named in sundry ways. Moreover, such leadership has not always measured up to the fundamental criterion of discipleship which the New Testament describes, nor has such leadership always fostered, through its structural behavior, the priority issue of "making disciples" of all nations. In these areas of non-discipleship, there is room for an "anti-clerical" stance.

One of the main issues which rendered the western Christian community, as it moved into the later Carolingian period, unfocused on the meaning of discipleship was, as we saw above, the almost single-minded concern over the *regnum et sacerdotium* struggle. Although this struggle involved more than a conflict between a pope and an emperor, the issue often degenerated into the two-person struggle: the western world, it seems, was not large enough to have two individuals who were both leaders *ex institutione divina.* At the end of the first millennium, prior to the renewal of the papacy by Henry III, popes were not very influential outside of Italy. Still, the papacy, often more in theory than in practice, did exert some influence in the west. B. Hamilton attempts to draw a composite picture of a pope as the second millennium begins.

> All popes had some degree of influence in the western church, because certain powers belonged to the pope alone. He was the final court of appeal in ecclesiastical cases; his permission was needed to set up a new province in the church; he alone could remove an archbishop from office, or exempt clergy from the jurisdiction of their bishop. The pope could make written rulings, known as decretals, which were binding on the whole church, appoint legates to represent him in any part of the church, and summon a General Council. Because the pope possessed these prerogatives his power was felt throughout the western church, but it was exercised only occasionally, not routinely.[1]

This generalized picture of a pope at the year 1000 is both reality to some degree and wish to some degree. The picture, however, moves in a definite direction, abetted by the *regnum et sacerdotium* struggle, for it indicates a "papal view" of the way in which the western Christian world should exist, namely a world in which the pope is supreme in many key areas. Emperors of that same period, however, also had grandiose ideas about their own role in the western world, and imperial theologians developed a quite differing approach to the question: How has God determined the fundamental way in which the Christian empire, the *societas Christiana,* should be directed? In the imperial view, the emperor or king played a role which at times overshadowed that of the pope. These two views of societal leadership became increasingly antithetical, with the result that this struggle, *regnum et sacerdotium,* continued to galvanize the thinking of both leader and theologian as one moves into the second millennium. Indeed, in the first four hundred years of this new period, it continued to hold sway in a most powerful way, even after the emperor's position *ex institutione divina* had been theoretically, though often not quite practically, removed. However, while this over-focusing struggle was going on, there occurred several attempts to enhance the position of the ordinary lay person in the church.

In the nine hundred years of this period of western church history, namely, from 1000 to 1900, powerful, change-inducing movements took place, spiritually, intellectually, economically, socially and politically. These major changes took place, east and west, north and south, in new discoveries on earth and in new discoveries in space. This period was a time of discovery and rediscovery, of brutal wars and tenuous truces, of intellectual revolutions, of inner-church revolutions, and of ethnic revolutions. Old western orders and structures, whether political, economic, social or ecclesiastical, were challenged, not in superficial ways, but in massive and radical ways. Changes took place, but not without enormous struggles and deep resentments.

Steven Ozment begins his study of *The Age of Reform, 1250-1550* with an introductory survey on the various interpretations of medieval intellectual history, starting with E. Gilson's approach which "measured the whole of medieval thought by the work of Thomas Aquinas."[2] "After Aquinas and the so-called golden age of scholasticism, Gilson saw a steady decline into confusion in the intellectual history of the fourteenth and fifteenth centuries."[3] On the other hand, there are scholars today who find William of Ockham more on the cutting edge than on the waning edge of medieval thought.[4] In contemporary scholarship new interest by scholars has developed around the writings of Meister Eckhart, Jean Gerson, Nicholas of Cusa and Gabriel Biel. Damasus Trapp, for example, has portrayed "the fourteenth century as the most intellectually fertile period of the Middle Ages."[5]

In all of these varying intellectual views of the middle ages, the question which surfaces and resurfaces again and again is the relationship of the spiritual or religious dimension of life to the earthly or "secular" dimension of life. Anselm of Canterbury (1033–1109) had attempted to reason to the existence of God and the necessity of the incarnation, thus attempting to combine logic and faith in an intimate way. Bernard of Clairvaux (1091–1153) and Hugh of St. Victor (d. ca. 1141) saw the earthly world as a faint mirror of the divine. Peter Damian (1007–1072) as well as Lanfranc of Bec (1010–1089) feared that theology was becoming the servant of philosophy, due to the wide-scale importation of the thought of Aristotle and Averroes into Christian ways of reasoning. Thomas Aquinas attempted to bridge revelation and reason, but always kept revelation superior to reason. In all of this intellectual turmoil, church leadership tended both vehemently and consistently to oppose any form of non-ecclesiastical autonomy. Non-ecclesiastical autonomy, however, cannot be understood as non-ecclesial autonomy. In the first instance, church officials, i.e. clergy, strive to be independent of the social, political and economic powers, but this does not mean that the social, political and economic powers are not part of the church structure. In other words, this defense of ecclesiastical autonomy cannot be seen as a struggle between the church and the secular, for at this period of time the social, political, and economic powers were essential parts of the *societas Christiana,* the western church.

On the other hand, a lawyer at Bologna, Irnerius (ca. 1050–1130) strongly defended the sovereignty of rulers, and this defense not only allowed supreme rulers, namely the emperor, to rise above tribal laws, but also in a religious way, not a "secular" way, this defense allowed them to remain independent from ecclesiastical and above all papal interference. Duns Scotus (1265–1308) and William of Ockham (ca. 1285–1347) stressed the otherness of God, which to some appeared as a "secularizing" of the here-and-now. The non-necessity of creation, of the incarnation itself, of the church, and of most other aspects of the Catholic faith, which this Scotistic approach seemed to imply, raised serious, even (to some) abhorrent, questions, in the mind of many contemporaries, for such a view questioned the need for sacramental and priestly activity.[6]

How does our earthly, bodily, sometimes sinful life relate to the divine, spiritual, and heavenly life? As this question began to surface in new ways during this period of time, many answers began to arise, and some of these varying answers had wide social effects. As we have already seen, the papal answer was indeed a spiritual one, but with a specific understanding of "spiritual": namely, in the western world and sometimes by extension in the entire world there was a spiritual domain which was solely under the jurisdiction of the pope and the bishops. This spiritual domain even began to claim in an increasingly universal way jurisdiction over every other domain as well. The imperial answer was also clear: the ecclesiastics were commissioned by God to provide for the sacramental and spiritual needs of the church, but the emperor was commissioned by God to provide a world in which people, including all clerics, could be at peace with one another and thus lead spiritual lives, and in which, under imperial supervision, the church leadership could provide the sacramental and religious means of grace to Christian people.

New factors, however, complicated this struggle between *regnum et sacerdotium*. The rise of the merchant class gave a new position to certain influential lay people. The rise of the universities also enhanced the position of influential medieval lay persons. A division between a strictly "lay" or "secular" area, as opposed to a strictly "religious" or "church" area, developed in a slow way. It is incorrect to envision medieval emperors and kings as "secular," for they were described and viewed in almost every apposite theological treatise as divinely commissioned. In the medieval worldview, the non-ecclesiastic or non-cleric was also not viewed as "secular"; rather he or she was viewed as an integral part of the church. The issue was not "lay and/or religious," which is a much more modern construction, but the question was: Who had ultimate power? In the medieval period only a few people denied in any overbearing way the power of the ecclesiastical leader, i.e. the pope, the bishops, the priests, etc. What was controverted by many, however, was the area in which these church leadership people had dominant power. Only a few people as yet denied the power of the emperor. What was controverted was the area in which he had dominant power. In many instances, the gradual political power-demise of the western emperor and the rise of national states simply transferred to the various kings a spiritual power, even over the ecclesiastical realm, which they continued to use. Only a few people, moreover, denied that the ordinary lay person was not part of the church. What was controverted by many was the power *in spiritualibus* which lay people had in the church.

Reason and revelation, the divine and the human, the church and the empire, *regnum et sacerdotium*, all of these "spheres" of influence or even spheres of "being" pushed against each other not only in academic argument but also in the daily political, social, economic and cultural give-and-take of life. One finds throughout this period of time that church leadership constantly moved into political, social, economic and cultural areas in a variety of ways, some of which movements often lasted only a short time and some of which often were not universal but only regional in scope. One sees as well that emperors and then kings moved piecemeal into the very same areas. One finds, moreover, that lay people moved into the very same areas as well, opposing both ecclesiastic and noble leadership. Just as the water's edge on the shoreline undulates and changes with each new surge of wave and breaker, so, too, the line which appeared to divide the "cleric/lay," the "secular/ecclesiastical" and the "imperial/papal" continually shifts throughout this period of time. Economically, or politically, or socially, or culturally, the boundaries of "cleric/lay," etc. evidenced great variety. At one time, for instance, the church leadership might make enormous claims on the political boundary, but economically, at the very same time, the imperial claims stretched deeply into the ecclesiastical world. On other occasions, the imperial claims reached deeply into ecclesiastical venues, while at the same time church leadership moved increasingly into the cultural worlds of the empire. The high and late medieval struggles of *regnum et sacerdotium,* which increasingly became struggles of *regna et sacerdotium,* resemble a chess game with many incursions at one area and simultaneous retreats and vulnerabilities in other areas.

Not to see the question of the lay person in the church within this economic, political, social, cultural and religious surging of these medieval times would be a fatal flaw. The question of the lay person in the church is a small question within a much larger question: namely, the question of reason/revelation, ecclesiastic/secular, spiritual/earthly. Not to see the question of the lay person in the church against the background of a complicated and intense western and medieval upheaval of ideas and structures would be to miss the very import of the question. In the pages which follow, we will focus on the rather narrow question: the role of the lay person in the church. In doing so, we will necessarily leave to one side or at best only allude to the wider framework within which this very question finds its meaning. An attempt to discuss the role of the lay person within the encyclopedic breadth of this total background would require a political, social, economic, intellectual, and religious history of the period. Not to see the question of the lay person against this background, however, would mean that one does not understand the question at all. The same is true, for instance, of the question of papal or episcopal power at this same period of time. When such an issue is removed from the social, political, economic and cultural aspects and viewed only from the "spiritual" or theological framework, the very question loses its meaning.

To illustrate this issue of the "larger question," let us consider, for a moment, one or the other indicator of this larger question. In the intellectual scene, the rediscovery and creative use of Aristotle's thought at the beginning of this period threatened centuries-old positions, and although we today look back on the era of scholasticism and note its successes, we cannot help but see how such successes arrived on the medieval scene only after years of suspicion and resentment. Another indicator is evident in the scientific revolution which men like Galileo, Copernicus, Keppler and Newton began to energize. An old order never passes away quietly. Today we might also look back on the rise of medieval universities and science and note their story of success as well, but once more these new universities spawned, in their time, many unheard-of ideas, which in turn created hostility and fear among those who felt at home in the status quo. Mind-sets do change, but never overnight and never without a struggle. The political and economic activity of this lengthy period of history has transformed the entire social structure of our globe. East met west, at least in a beginning sort of way. The West Indies met European looters and landlords, some of whom stayed on and changed the very face of that area. In an odd blending of elements, sometimes pathetic, sometimes therapeutic, both North and South America were colonized, Christianized and cannibalized by western Europeans. The trampling and trekking of conquistador and missionary clearly changed the western hemisphere. In the year 1000 the Christian churches of western Europe were regionally strong, vibrant and dominant. These regional churches were unified, one with the other, to some degree but not yet in any monolithic way by the patriarch of the west, the pope. Although up to the year 1000 several popes had struggled to become the focus of Catholic unity throughout the west, this central role remained more a papal theory than a papal reality. "So long as papal authority remained weak, real power in the church rested with the bishops."[7] In a far more decisive way, outside of the papal territory in Italy, the Christian churches were, at the turn of the millennium, united by the emperors and their massive influence from Spain and England to the Danube and the Adriatic. One faith, one God, one Christ, one baptism were clearly unifying elements throughout the churches of christendom, but even with a single faith and even with a single emperor, and even with a single bishop of Rome, ethnic separatism, tribal provincialism, and regional clannishness made both churches and social structures more a patchwork than a cohesive unity. This is particularly noticeable in the area of law.

> One extremely important aspect of early medieval law was the doctrine of the personality of the law, that is, the rule that a free person could be judged only by the law of the people into which he was born, regardless of where or among whom he was charged with an offense. In many cases, early Germanic kings

created particular legal codes for their Roman subjects, not because they admired or understood Roman law, but because Roman law was regarded as the personal law of those born Roman.[8]

Clerics, in most early medieval legislation, fell under the rubric *ecclesia vivit lege Romana,* which means that a church person was expected to live according to Roman personal law, and he was to be judged accordingly. What precisely this Roman law involved, however, was regionally not always clear in the early period of medieval life and was interpreted differently in different regions of Christendom. The lay person, for his or her part, was judged by the personal law, which had validity in the region of his or her birth. At least this was the rule of thumb, which does not mean it was observed uniformly. Only at the end of the tenth century and into the eleventh and twelfth centuries was there a concerted effort to unite Roman law and Germanic laws. Complex marriage issues among high-ranking aristocratic families were a major stimulus to this endeavor, and Hincmar of Rheims helped move the development of a unified law both for the western political society and for the western ecclesiastical society. The 1087 collection of information gathered in the *Domesday Book* under William the Conqueror in England was another major step in this tendency toward a more universal codification. The collection of laws drawn up by Regino of Prüm or those drawn up by Burchard of Worms, Anselm of Lucca and Ivo of Chartres moved in the same direction. The *Concordia discordantium canonum* of Gratian of Bologna, which came to be known as the *Decretum,* was an unofficial document at first, and only in the course of time came to be regarded as official legal teaching of the church. The rise of the universities in the high medieval period, several of which had prestigious faculties of law, only increased this preoccupation throughout western Europe with a unified form of law.

It is clear that those who are the lawgivers have considerable power once such law has been established in any given area. In the struggle between *regnum et sacerdotium* it was imperative and inescapable that both the papacy and the regency would struggle to be the more dominant law-giving element in medieval society. When, ultimately, the king/emperor had been "reduced to the lay state," that is, he was no longer considered *rex/imperator ex institutione divina,* and only the pope in Rome could claim divine institution for his office, then and then only was the pope, at least theoretically, the focus of unity for the churches of the western world. This combination of a more-or-less unified law throughout Christendom with a single, divinely instituted law-giver and therefore law-interpreter gave the pope, at least for a while, the focal point which papal policy had in varying ways but certainly not in any orthogenetic way been advocating for several centuries. Such a centering of power in the pope, the major *sacerdos* of the west, inevitably enhanced to some degree the entire *sacerdotium* of the Christian world, but in a marked way the episcopal and abbatial *sacerdotium*. Such a centering of power in the clerical area, however, also left the *sacerdotium*, at all levels, but particularly at its higher levels, open to major criticism. The adage "Power corrupts and absolute power corrupts absolutely" cannot be shunted to one side merely because the realm of power is ecclesiastical and religious. Criticisms were raised again and again throughout the period, 1000 to 1900, by voices representing every stratum of society, but in an increasingly shrill way by the lay voice. In the pages which follow, we will concentrate on these lay voices, although in doing so we may appear to be overlooking factors which were highly influential for the changes of this period. These other factors were intellectual, political, geographical, economic, and structural. Our focus on the lay voices in no way wishes to disclaim the influence of these other factors, nor to claim more value for the emerging lay voice than is justified by historical research.

This chapter begins with the dawn of the second millennium of the Christian church and traces the vicissitudes of the lay person in the church from the so-called Gregorian reform down to the eve of the Protestant reform. The structure of this chapter is as follows:

1. **The So-Called Gregorian Reform Movement and the *Vita Evangelica* Movements**
2. **The Lay Person and the Crusades**
3. **The Lay Person in High Scholasticism**
4. **The Lay Person in the Fourteenth and Fifteenth Centuries**
5. **General Overview**
6. **Conclusions from the Data**

1. THE SO-CALLED GREGORIAN REFORM MOVEMENT AND THE VITA EVANGELICA MOVEMENTS

In a most remarkable way, the period from roughly 1000 to 1300 witnessed the appearance of a number of disparate movements by a variety of Christians from all walks of medieval life. One cannot speak of a single reform movement at this time, but rather of many reform movements, with varying degrees of interconnection and interdependency.[9] Within monasticism, the Cluniac reform and the Cistercian reform, begun by Robert of Molesme (ca. 1028–1112), gave evidence of this urgency for renewal. These monastic reforms, however, were but two of many monastic reform movements: there was, for instance, the reform by Robert of Arbrissel (d. 1117), a diocesan priest, who was also a hermit and a wandering preacher. He founded at Fontévrault a monastery which attracted large numbers of both men and women. Eventually he had a double monastery constructed, and all members, male and female, were placed under the leadership of the abbess-general, in memory of the dying Jesus who had entrusted his disciples to his mother Mary.[10] His influence also stimulated the monastic reforms of Vitalis of Savigny (d. 1122), Bernard of Tiron (d. 1120), and Gerald of Salles (d. 1120).[11] In all of these monastic reform movements, both a solitary form of life and gospel poverty and simplicity, rather than preaching and apostolic ministry, appear to be major motivational factors.

A solitary life clearly marks the reform efforts of the diocesan priest Bruno of Cologne (d. 1101), who was the founder of La Grande Chartreuse and also of the hermitage of Santa Maria dell'Eremo in the diocese of Squillace.[12] One could also think of Stephen of Thiers (d. 1124) and the establishment of the Order of Grandmont. Stephen, who had been highly influenced by the society of Calabrian hermits, rejected many of the elements found in western monasticism. He rejected landed property and proprietary churches. For him, the basis of monasticism was the gospel.[13] Still another reform-minded cleric was Norbert of Xanten (ca. 1082–1134), the founder of Prémontré, who renewed the canons regular. Norbert, however, was simply one of the more important canons who during this same period of time began rejuvenating in one form or another the *ordo canonicorum*.[14]

Still other groups, basically lay, established hospices, such as *La maison du Grand-Saint Bernard* and the hospice of Mont-Joux. There was also the lay society of St. Anthony which staffed the hospital at Saint-Didier de la Mothe. At first this latter group led a communal life, dedicated to health care, but without vows. In time they were urged to take vows and thus move from lay to religious status. There was also the brotherhood of Bénézet of Avignon (1171–1199), a lay society whose main purpose was the rebuilding of bridges.[15] One could also include the Beguines, a society of women living by their own handiwork, who were organized by Jacques de Vitry with the approval of Honorius III. Under the direction of Mary of Oingies these women accepted mendicant poverty. Their male counterpart were the Beghards. "Since the Beguines were technically neither religious nor seculars, they were often suspected of heresy, and in 1274, the Second Council of Lyons attempted to suppress them; they generally then became associated with the various third orders in the Church."[16] The listing of similar reform movements could be further developed, but it is clear that in both the monastic or religious world and in the lay world a series of reform groups sprang up during this period of time.

Two major strands of these reform movements have received enormous attention:

A. GEOGRAPHICALLY DISPARATE REFORM MOVEMENTS

This reform movement was actually a series of disparate reform movements which tended to circle around a focal theme, namely the gospel life, *vita evangelica*.[17] These reform movements include the so-called "heretical movements" of the eleventh and twelfth centuries, as well as the more acceptable reform movements of the twelfth and thirteenth centuries.

B. THE GREGORIAN REFORM MOVEMENT

This reform movement had both imperial and papal backing, and is often called simply the "Gregorian reform," but which more accurately is the reform movement begun by the emperor, Henry III, with the installation of the German popes, Clement II (1046–1047) and Damasus II (1048), and ending with the papacy of Callistus II (1119–1124).[18] In that period of time, Leo IX (1049–1054), Gregory VII (1073–1085), and Urban II (1088–1099) were the three key prelates who shaped the reform from the papal position of influence. At times, but not always in the same way nor for the same reasons, this reform movement had the endorsement, sometimes more and sometimes less, of both emperors/kings and popes.

Let us consider the geographically disparate reform movements first, and then turn to the so-called Gregorian reform.

A. GEOGRAPHICALLY DISPARATE REFORMS

1. The Scope of Their Appearance

To date no scholar has satisfactorily established the causes which occasioned the quite widespread appearance of these various regional movements, movements which first appeared at Mainz in 1012, at Orléans in 1022, at Arras in 1025, and then at Monteforte and in Burgundy from 1042 to 1048 and at Goslar in 1051.[19] Did these geographically scattered movements find their source of inspiration from a desire to return to simple gospel living, as R. Morghen among others has proposed?[20] Or did they arise from the influence of Bulgarian Bogomiles as A. Dondaine and his supporters emphasize?[21] More recent scholarship, as one finds in the writings of A. Borst[22] and H. Grundmann,[23] has moved away from the exclusivity of either of these positions. Other scholars have even proposed that the movements were social in origin and that they evidenced a class struggle, a position which, however, has not had many followers.[24] The contemporary chronicles of these early middle ages, which mentioned the various movements, labeled them rather often "Manichaean," but this attribute appears to reflect more the imagination and judgment of the chroniclers themselves rather than the realities to which they were alluding. Manichaeism does not seem to be one of the causes for the emergence of these movements.

The initial appearances of these disparate reform groups, which occurred from about 1000 on, are often called by church historians "heretical reform movements." At the beginning, however, they were not necessarily heretical,[25] and only in time did a few of them come to be branded as "heretical," while even fewer of the groups became "heretical" in actuality. It is clear that one must move with caution both on the matter of the origin of these movements and on the "heretical" status of these movements, since the initial historical data on them is rather meager.

> Between 1000 and 1051 there are eight passages in chroniclers and the like [referring to the movements], and a few slighter references which have formed the base for a very substantial literature, ringing the changes, refining, but rarely adding anything new in the way of evidence; a sort of Enigma variations. For fifty years after 1051 we have total silence. Even this has not silenced the pens of the modern scholars; there has been fervent discussion whether it is due to the disappearance of heresy underground or to the chronicler's attention being claimed by rival excitements. . . . But heresy as such only reappears after 1100; and its rise must be reckoned one of the most dramatic aspects of the twelfth century.[26]

In the twelfth century one finds, of course, the two groups, Cathars or Albigensians on the one hand, and the Waldensians on the other.[27] In many ways these two specific movements have claimed the lion's share of historical research, and therefore, to some degree, have shaped the way in which the many movements of the early period of these reforms have also been considered.

In the thirteenth century one finds some very significant movements of reform, in particular the Franciscans, the Dominicans, the Servites, the Carmelites, the Hermits of St. Augustine, the Williamites, and the Mercedarians.[28] These varying groups of reform and renewal movements involved both clerical elements and lay elements, and represented diverse geographical areas of the western world, and the influence of these thirteenth century groups on the subsequent life of the Roman Catholic Church was both extensive and intensive. On the part of many of these groups there was a freedom of movement which gained for them an "international" arena of ministry, and as a consequence an "international" sphere of influence. The Friars Minor, in a special way, had pastoral contacts with almost every stratum of the then social world and pursued among these varying strata a ministry of intense religious fervor. At the early stages of these movements, not only members of church leadership, both episcopal and papal, saw in these mendicant orders a unique and timely resource—many bishops and even some popes came from the mendicant ranks—but also the ordinary Christian man and woman found in the message and lifestyle of these mendicants a form of discipleship which energized their own Christian life. On the other hand, the thirteenth century debate between diocesan clergy and the Dominicans and Franciscans over the issue of evangelical poverty at times created hostility between bishop and mendicant. Moreover, the ministry of preaching regardless of diocese, which was a privilege that the Franciscans enjoyed in the early phase of their development, also caused some strain between bishop and friar. Many of these preachers were not clerics, and at times their preaching was done without episcopal authorization, even though they had papal approbation. Again one sees an element of change within the status quo of the church which occasioned both enthusiasm and rancor.

As time went on, the development of theology at the major universities became the domain of the mendicants, and medieval theology was shaped by Dominican and Franciscan scholars, especially the two Dominicans, Albert the Great and Thomas Aquinas, and the trio of Franciscans, Alexander of Hales, Bonaventure and John Duns Scotus.[29]

The Franciscans and Servites, in a special way, provide a landmark for lay ministry in the church. The Servites originally were a lay brotherhood of various merchants and urban patricians. Only in time did the clerical element enter the community and then almost dominate the community. In the Franciscan communities there were both lay and cleric friars almost from the start, with little privilege given to the cleric as far as the brotherhood's internal life was concerned. The priests were, of course, respected in a special way because of the sacramental life.[30] The Mercedarians were also originally a lay group of men which became a military religious order in 1235. In 1318 it was ranked as a mendicant order, but only on the condition that a priest would be the superior general.

Women became very influential at this time of reform as well. The Beguines were pace-setters for many women's groups.[31] They were lay women who looked to the gospels as a focus for one's spiritual life. Often, as time went by, they were accused of heretical influences, with no small emphasis placed on the fact that they were not "canonical." Some of them associated themselves to the various third orders which were quite popular in the thirteenth and fourteenth centuries, and by doing so they attained an ecclesiastical respectability. The rise of the Poor Clares and the cloistered Dominican Nuns had enormous influence on the religious life of the church, for these groups deliberately modeled their life on the gospels, particularly on gospel poverty. Once again we find gospel discipleship central to these reform movements, movements which involved both men and women.

The formation of new religious communities, both male and female, produced a great desire on the part of many lay persons of that time for some sort of association, and various third order groups began to appear. The popularity of these groups became widespread, and third order lay men and women prominently affected the life of the church. The *Montes pietatis,* funds for the poor, not only became large in cash value, but also played a role in the banking world of the middle ages. As such, the lay people who directed these funds had not only a strictly religious influence on society, but also a powerful monetary influence. At the very same time as the third orders were expanding, hospital ministry also expanded. Prior to this time, hospitals had generally been connected to monasteries and cathedral chapters. The early Premonstratensians were especially influential in the reshaping and renewing of hospital ministry. In time, however, hospital ministry separated itself from both the monks and the canon regulars, and became an independent and specialized pastoral church ministry. Many lay confraternities began to assume the sponsorship of such hospitals, with the result that many lay men and women themselves took up this ministry. This interest in the care of the sick and the dying, viewed from a spiritual and theological standpoint, arose because there was a renewed interest in Jesus the healer, an image of Jesus which is found so intensely in the gospels and which consequently provided the base for this new ministerial involvement. Confraternities, which were inspired by the poverty of Jesus and the service of Jesus to the poor, made this gospel ideal of healing central to their active lives. This period of time, the twelfth, thirteenth and fourteenth centuries, witnessed a change in religious life. Whereas the *vita contemplativa* had been the primary *raison d'être* of monastic life, with its *opus Dei,* i.e. liturgical prayer, at the center, and the pastoral care of the poor and the sick only a secondary, though still important, goal of religious life, in the newly formed communities the *vita apostolica* began to move into greater prominence. The so-called "mixed" religious communities, i.e. those with both contemplative and apostolic facets of religious life, became very popular. Even more ministerially or pastorally focused were the confraternities of lay men and women who, without disregarding prayer, dedicated themselves to the apostolic life in a primary way. All of this brought the lay person, male and female, far more closely into the structuring of church life within the *societas Christiana.* Such ministries as the care of the sick and care of pilgrims cannot be seen as a "secular" pursuit, nor as an extra-ecclesial vocation. Rather, the foundation for such work was gospel-centered, i.e. gospel discipleship, and the ministry was clearly seen as "church" ministry. However, nowhere was it described as "church" ministry because it was organized and controlled by the clergy, nor was it described as the lay person's cooperating or participating in the work of the clergy. Such a view of the lay apostolate became commonplace in the late nineteenth and early twentieth centuries, but the surge in apostolic ministry at this medieval juncture of church history cannot be read in twentieth century terms. There was not at this time a "work of the clergy" to which lay people associated themselves and in which they participated. The basis for this medieval ministerial activity was not the desire or need of lay people to be involved in the clergy's ministry. Such an interpretation would be grossly anachronistic. Rather, the basis for this enthusiasm for pastoral ministry arose from the repossession of the scriptured word by lay man and lay woman, by monk and nun, and by clerics of all ranks. It was the reading and the rereading of the gospel message which inspired the medieval man and woman to follow in the footsteps of the poor Christ.

Moreover, the wide geographical scope of these early reform movements must be appreciated in order to understand the lengthy temporal scope such reform movements and trends also enjoyed. The repercussions of these early reform movements continued down to the cataclysmic Protestant reformation movements of the sixteenth century. Since one can include in this strand of reform movements both the mendicants of the thirteenth century and the third order confraternities which they developed, one might also say that these disparate reform initiatives of the eleventh and twelfth centuries have had an effect on the Roman Catholic Church quite beyond the sixteenth century reformations, namely down to the present day, in which these same mendicant groups and third orders continue to press for gospel discipleship.

2. Descriptive Guiding Ideas of These Reform Movements

On the basis of recent scholarship regarding these reform movements from the year 1000 onward, some descriptive guiding ideas are in order as we study this period of church history:

a. From 1000 to 1300 there were many reform movements in the church, and although their interconnection, if any, is not clear, nonetheless one can say that at this period of church history, a strong felt-need for a return to gospel life was widespread.

b. All levels of society were involved in these various reform movements, and in a majority of these reform movements one finds that all levels of society are generally represented: cleric and non-cleric, aristocrat and serf, artisan and merchant. This indicates that in all levels of western society there was a dissatisfaction with the way in which Christian life was presented, and there was a strong endeavor to regain the gospel ideal of Christian life.

c. This clamor for reform, in many ways, can only be seen as an indictment of the contemporary church leadership and its lack of presentation and fostering of gospel ideals. This leadership included the leadership in western monastic structures, in societies of canons regular, as well as the leadership of popes and bishops. This clamor for reform was a widespread statement: church leadership had failed to understand the meaning of gospel discipleship.

d. These reform movements, particularly those which involved the lay people, i.e. the non-ordained and the non-monastic, were generally not initially motivated by an anti-clerical stance nor by an heretical position. Nonetheless, as mentioned above in n. 3, there was a strong criticism of church leadership, which one finds in all forms of the reform movements. Deeper than such criticism, however, is the desire for a gospel form of discipleship.

The spiritual goals of these reform movements, however, cannot be seen, as was noted above, in isolation. Hans Wolter rightly notes: "From the beginning of the twelfth century the layman became much more prominent than before, alongside the cleric, in the life of the Church."[32] This prominence, Wolter goes on to say, stems from the development of medieval urban culture, from the crusades, from the integration of feudal and agrarian elements into an organized form, from the growing international relations among armies, merchants and scholars, and above all from the families of ministerial rank. All of this made the lay person, even to some degree the ordinary lay person, more prominent within society, but it was the entry of the lay person into public advocacy of the spiritual life, that is, *vita evangelica,* which brought the lay man and lay woman more intimately into church leadership structures. The lay voices, in public ways and in ways which won a public, called for a more genuine example of Christian discipleship.[33]

3. The Logic of Discipleship in These Reform Movements

These geographically disparate reform movements, as well as the so-called Gregorian reform movement, raised complaints about identical failures in the church of their time: namely, the greed of simoniacal bishops and abbots, and the rather common sexual immorality particularly of the common parish priest, but also at times of the abbot and bishop. Both positions in these reform groups yearned for a far more pure church than the actual church of the day. However, rather than start with either simony or sexual immorality, one must, it seems to me, start any research and discussion of these reform movements with the historical data, which indicates that all these reform movements had a deeper common thrust:

namely, the yearning for a clearer and truer form of Christian discipleship.

Because of this basic yearning for gospel discipleship, these movements, secondarily, were in mutual agreement, to some degree at least, that simony and clerical sexual license were the "fundamental evils" which needed to be removed from Christian life. These movements, therefore, were not primarily crusades to remove abuses, at least at their genesis. The initial motivation of the many and various reformers was something far more positive: the reformers wanted to put into practice their profound yearnings for *vita evangelica.*

Discipleship, consequently, again becomes the major criterion. The Christian west would not have had such an endemic appearance of reforms if medieval Christians, at all levels, had not felt that gospel discipleship was central to their lives. Many monks and nuns found that their own monasteries were not offering them the gospel discipleship they craved, and consequently one finds the multiple monastic reform movements of this period. Many lay men and women found neither monastic life nor clerical life appealing to them as means of becoming "disciples" of the Lord. As a result, they began lay reform movements, and these new movements attracted numerous Christians. In the eyes of many the papacy itself was not providing adequate leadership for Christian discipleship, and a reform of the papacy was increasingly demanded. The installation of German popes with a reform mentality began to meet this particular aspect of the reform movement: namely the aspect that papal leadership had failed and needed to be reestablished. However, not even in all of the above was there agreement between the geographically disparate reform movements on the one hand, and the so-called Gregorian reform movement on the other. It should be noted that long before Henry III put into motion the establishment in the papacy of reform-minded popes, i.e. the German popes, there was already in the air a current of reform which was geographically widespread and disparate. The various geographically disparate reform movements which had sprung up rather spontaneously throughout Europe both predated and to some degree influenced the imperial/papal desire for reform, even at the papal level. In this call for reform the most fundamental criterion was not the removal of abuse but the desire for gospel discipleship.

Many bishops and abbots, clearly leaders of the medieval church, were so involved in simony that they often offered no example to the Christians in their churches of what gospel discipleship should be. The outcry against the simoniacal bishops and abbots was based on the criterion: discipleship. The ordinary parish priest, who more often than not lacked both academic training and spiritual formation, provided a local religious leadership which only minimally at times reflected gospel discipleship. This minimal reflection can be found in the ways in which eucharistic and other sacramental liturgies were celebrated at a parish level and in the ways in which homilies at the parish level were preached. Nonetheless, it was the sexual immorality among the parish clergy which became the strident issue, rather than better priestly training and formation. The final result, unfortunately, was perhaps a more sexually moral clergy, but certainly not one which was better educated and spiritually trained.[34]

The commonality which all these geographically disparate reform movements shared is highly significant, since it indicates that among fiefs and servants, among merchants and artisans, among nobles and aristocrats, among priests and monks, among abbots and bishops, among emperors and popes there arose in the eleventh and twelfth centuries a widespread desire for a more spiritual Christian life. The reform movements were against simony and clerical immorality, but one is only against something if there is an ideal, a hope, a dream, a yearning which is positive and acts as a criterion. In all of these reform movements, the negative side has received enormous attention: scathing descriptions of simonistic behavior and immoral clerical behavior can be found both in medieval literature and in contemporary literature. But once the simony and the immoral clerical behavior have been removed, what was the hope and dream that should emerge? The answer is clear: a Christian church which resembled the gospels—in other words, *vita evangelica.* An understanding of and a yearning for true Christian discipleship prompted and motivated these several reform movements.[35]

The fact that those movements, which are often dubbed "heretical," as well as those "non-heretical" movements, which are specifically called "*vita evangelica* movements," had followers from all walks of life indicates that there was a widespread dissatisfaction with the ways in which discipleship was presented at that time. If the monasteries had been offering a form of discipleship which was attractive to the spiritual aspirations of Christian men and women, then many of these reform movements, which even included monks and abbots, would never have taken place. Evidently religious life, both male and female, was at this period of Church history insufficient to meet the aspirations of discipleship. If clerical life had offered a form of discipleship which was attractive to many Christian men, then these reform movements would not have included so many clerics. Evidently, at this period of church history, clerical life was insufficient to meet the spiritual aspirations of discipleship. One might also consider the liturgical life of the church, especially the sacramental life, and arrive at the same conclusion. If the liturgy and the sacramental life of the church had at this period of church history been encouraging a form of discipleship which met the aspirations of discipleship, then there would have been little need for reform. Evidently neither the liturgical nor the sacramental life of the church at this time fed Christians adequately in their desire to lead a life of discipleship.

For many of these geographically disparate reformers and their followers the logic of discipleship lay in the realization of the gospel way of life. Again and again it was the gospel which provided the initial impetus for the appearance of lay men and women as well as religious men and women who wanted to live more closely *vita evangelica*. Popes and emperors, bishops and abbots, monks and clerics of all grades, Christian lay men and lay women, all were judged by the logic of the gospel.

The main issues in all of this, consequently, seem to be:

There was a spiritual vacuum in the church of the eleventh and twelfth centuries which gave rise to a variety of reform movements.

This spiritual vacuum was not fundamentally caused by a negative factor, i.e. an opposition to simony and clerical immorality, but basically by a positive though unfulfilled factor, i.e. a profound desire to lead a life of discipleship, a gospel life, *vita evangelica*.

Discipleship is the fundamental criterion by which one can evaluate both the reform movements as such and the reasons why these reform movements appeared in such numbers during this period of time.

Discipleship was judged against the statements of the gospels. This was the basic logic of discipleship which these movements, in various ways, tended to use.

These characteristics must be carefully weighed, for they are quite general and apply in a quite discriminating way to each of the various reform movements and even apply differently to the same movement, as a given movement developed, changed, and came to be somewhat refocused. Nonetheless, at least in the initial stages of almost every one of these geographically disparate reform movements, these descriptive guidelines provide a solid orientation for the movements and the motivations of the reformers who envisioned such reforms.

4. The Significance of These Geographically Disparate Reform Movements for an Appreciation of the Lay Person in the Church

Among those who joined these various reform movements there were many non-ordained—indeed, perhaps the majority were non-ordained. Many a lay person in the church of the eleventh and twelfth centuries took part in these movements of reform precisely because the clerical, monastic and liturgical forms of church life did not offer him or her the ways and means to lead a Christian life of discipleship. Most of the lay folk who took part in these movements of reform did so not from greed or a desire for power, nor from an anti-clerical or anti-monastic motive. Such lay people took part in these movements for a profoundly spiritual reason. The same motivation can, of course, be attributed to the clerics and monks who also took part in the movements of reform.

In many ways these various reform movements provided the ordinary lay person in the church with a way to follow Christ which did not entail some form of clericalization. The fact that these movements continued to arise and that they included the mendicant movements of the thirteenth century and the brothers and sisters of the Common Life movement of the fifteenth century as well attests strongly to their appeal. Often the reading of the gospels or of the New Testament itself by these reform groups was limited to some sort of *florilegium* or concatenation of various texts; often the gospel texts were simply excerpts. One cannot think of any critical study of the New Testament by these reform-minded people, such as one might find in the various Protestant reformations of a later period.

It is not surprising that at the very same time that these reform movements, as well as the Gregorian reform movement, were taking place, there was a springtime of mysticism. "The great monastic revivals of the tenth and eleventh centuries, out of which came the Cluniac, the Cistercian and Carthusian orders, produced a setting in which mysticism was fostered."[36] Peter Damian, Anselm of Bec, above all Bernard of Clairvaux, but also Hugh, Richard and Adam of St. Victor gave expression to this monastic mysticism. Yet even more striking in many ways are the writings of Hildegard of Bingen, Mechtild of Magdeburg and Elizabeth of Schönau. These women wrote a number of mystical tracts which found their inspiration in biblical writings such as the Song of Songs and the book of Revelation.

Basic to all of this was the fact that the lay people had rediscovered a fundamental source of spirituality and had made, to some degree, the repossession of the scriptured word the *vade mecum* for their journey of prayer. From these movements onward, one can see in the history of the western church a continued and growing pattern: not only are lay men and women fed with the eucharistic word, but they are fed again and again by the scriptured word. The eucharistic word of God depended on the ministration of a priest; the scriptured word of God was open to all. Because of this, we will also see an effort by the clerical part of the church, especially its leadership, to curtail the use of scripture by the ordinary lay man and woman, and, if this is not possible, to make sure that it is interpreted only in those ways approved by the clerical or hierarchical magisterium. The repositioning of the lay person in the church in virtue of these geographical reform movements began a process of repositioning of the clerical person in the church, and this clerical repositioning was quite often repulsed by the clerics themselves. A repositioning of the cleric was a major repositioning of the status quo.

B. THE SO-CALLED GREGORIAN REFORM

1. The Scope of This Reform

Hildebrand, who became Gregory VII, spent most of his adult life working in the papal curia. It was in many ways the only world that he knew and the only world that he loved. For him the service to St. Peter and to his vicars was the highest task that anyone could have, next to being pope. Faced with the evils in the church, such as simony and clerical immorality, a pope, in Gregory's logic, should first of all remove any non-cleric from provisioning an ecclesiastical office, particularly the episcopal office. The interference of non-clerics in the work of the church was deemed the root of the problem, and any imperial claim of divine right to such a provisioning was, for Gregory, theologically impossible. In other words, for a man like Gregory, the solution to the evil of simony within the church was to resolve the struggle between *regnum et sacerdotium,* of course on the side of *sacerdotium.*[37] Not only for Gregory, but also for some of the popes who preceded him (though faintly) and for several of the popes who came after him (some of whom quite vehemently) the scope of such a reform should lead to every episcopal see in the western world and throughout the entire world. Intellectually, then, the scope was church-wide, although, practically, such a divesting of imperial and regal claims to provision the church with bishops and other clergy became impossible.

Let us consider some of the history of this reform movement prior to Hildebrand. In 1046 Pope Gregory VI died. He had been a respected Roman, but he had accepted the papacy under the cloud of simony, and as a result, even before his death, he had been deposed by a synod at Sutri, held under the leadership of the emperor, Henry III, and Clement II had been elected and enthroned. Clement II then conferred imperial anointing and coronation on Henry III and Queen Agnes.[38] Clement II died in 1047, and Henry III participated as emperor in the election of Damasus II who died in 1048, twenty-three days after his papal enthronement. Finally, again under Henry's aegis, the Alsatian, Bruno of Toul, who became Leo IX, was elected by the Roman people in accord with the law of that period and was enthroned as pope. It is with Leo IX that one can truly speak of the beginning of a papal reform, although with his two predecessors the reform movement was already at the door. But it should also be noted that in all of these papal elections—attempts to bring into the papacy a man who might engender a reform of the church from on top—was Henry III. Without his influence this so-called Gregorian reform would not have taken place. It was the presence and activity of a "lay" person in these papal elections which played a key role in the so-called Gregorian reform. Leo eventually brought Hildebrand back to Rome and made him a key person in his inner circle, although Hildebrand, who had once supported Gregory VI, had been removed from his curial position at Rome.

Leo IX's rule as pope ended, however, with a military failure, for Leo had led the troops against the kingdom of Naples and had lost. With his death Victor II was elected and ruled briefly (1055–1057); his successor, Stephen IX, was in office only a year (1057–1058). Two successive disputed papal elections followed: the first involved Benedict X (1058–1059) vs. Nicholas II (1059–1061); the second involved Alexander II (1061–1073) vs. Honorius II (1061–1071/72). In the first, the Roman choice,

Nicholas, was chosen over the hastily-elected and enthroned Benedict. In the second, the imperial choice, Alexander, was selected over Honorius, although Honorius lived on for a while as a claimant of the papal throne. During all of this, Hildebrand, who was active with Nicholas II and then most closely with Alexander II, formed his vision of papacy even more stringently. The decree on papal elections, which Nicholas II issued at the Roman Synod of 1059, included a new twist: a pope would *grant* to each succeeding German ruler the right to assent to papal elections, a right which until then had been the tradition for the Saxon rulers since Otto I. With this decree it was no longer a right inherent in the office of the emperor, but a privilege granted *seriatim* to the reigning emperor. It is obvious that this part of the decree indicated anew a basic thrust of papal policy: namely, the papacy alone rules the church, and, in a most special way, everything which has to do with papal elections. This law of Nicholas II, however, remained a law in the papal curia alone. It certainly did not affect the way the emperors continued to view their role in papal elections.

The decrees of several successive Roman synods, in 1059, 1060 and 1061, had forbidden the acquisition of ecclesiastical office through simony, but the wording of the decrees left open the issue of the validity or non-validity of such offices in those instances when in actuality the offices had been obtained through simony. Humbert of Silva Candida considered such ordinations invalid and subsequently all sacramental acts were also invalid. Peter Damian took an opposite view, which saw such acts as illicit, thus preserving valid sacramental life within the churches. On the issue of married or concubinate clergy, Humbert railed against this situation, without calling such priests or bishops invalid ministers; Peter Damian, horrified by the thought of a married clergy, considered any sacramental actions by such clergy as invalid. Both sides, with papal statements as support, urged lay people to boycott masses and other sacramental rites performed by such clergy. Thus, the whole thorny issue of invalid clergy and invalid sacraments once again arose, and theological thought at that time became stridently divided. One of the laws from the synod of 1059, which Hildebrand had urged, was the regulation that priests should live a *vita communis et apostolica.* This style of life, of course, dissuaded a married or concubinate state of life and at the same time fostered the notion of canons regular, who eventually became strong components of the Gregorian reform.

The reform movement stressed that noble lay people of any rank were legally ineligible to confer ecclesiastical office, and that only ecclesiastics, but especially in this instance bishops, were able to do this.[39] Still, this curial position must be read against a wider background. At this time the appointment of bishops was being more and more removed from regional decisions and elections, and more and more focused on the appointment by the pope.[40] In disputed elections, the pope alone claimed the power to resolve the issue. In doing this, the very meaning of episcopacy was being radically changed, and this change, though gradually brought about in the western church, has had from that time down to the present day enormous implications in the relationship between the churches of the east and the west. Is the bishop the major *sacerdos* in his area—a view which sees episcopacy as the crowning point of the sacrament of holy order, and which stresses the regional positioning of a bishop as well as his regional collegiality? Or is the bishop a delegate of the pope —a view which sees the presbyter as the highest stage of holy order and the bishop as a major position in the juridical framework of the mystical body and therefore as a regional spokesman for the pope? Small steps toward this latter view were taken throughout this so-called Gregorian reform of the church, which eventually led to the theological position, common among the major theologians of high scholasticism, that excluded episcopacy from the sacrament of holy order.[41]

The decree of Nicholas II at the Synod of Rome in 1059 carried a further innovation. This innovation involved the role of the people of Rome in a papal election. In this decree the right of papal election was given to the cardinal bishops, called significantly "quasi-metropolitans." In the event of any encroachment on the freedom of election by the Roman people, these cardinal bishops could legally arrange for a papal election outside of Rome, with recourse only to a few religious and a few lay people. Someone so elected was already pope, even though he had not yet entered Rome itself and been enthroned and even though he had not been elected by the people of Rome. This new law "broke away in principle from its connection to the people of the city of Rome."[42] This law is indicative of the wider trend by some major clerics of that period, namely to reject any and all lay involvement in the area of ecclesiastical decision making.

Hildebrand had lived in Rome for over twenty years as a dedicated servant to Peter and to his vicars. This career was his life and his view of life, and without any doubt Hildebrand was a dedicated reformer with a deep spiritual vision, but one profoundly colored by his Roman, curial career. On April 22, 1073 he became Gregory VII, and a quite revolutionary person with a revolutionary view of the papacy began to lead the western church. This man, who saw that the authority of Peter was the one thing in the world that was totally real, brought a new step to the *regnum et sacerdotium* struggle, and he did this particularly in his struggles with the emperor, Henry IV.

2. Descriptive Guidelines of This Reform Movement

Although every age has its purists who find the existing church in need of drastic reform, the reform that these Germans had in mind focused on the "secular" elements, which in their view had taken over the very heart of the church: "sacred offices bought and sold for money, clergy melting into the crowd and sharing the way of life and the vices of the ordinary layfolk, including under this head the vice (as some of the reformers undoubtedly saw it) of marriage."[43] In this view, many of the reformers felt that church offices should be independent of any lay or "secular" influence. Since many of the reformers were monks, they also believed that clerics should lead quasi-monastic lives. Hildebrand, a monk, shared these views.[44]

The historical vicissitudes of one reform group, the Patarenes in Milan, in the second half of the eleventh century, is almost an exemplar or typological presentation of the so-called Gregorian reform movement, and in many ways an historical arena in which one can see quite clearly the difference between the Gregorian reform movement on the one hand and the geographically disparate reform movements on the other.[45] In this Patarene reform, not quite from the start but very close to its initial stages, both the pope played a role and the emperor played a role, with the result that the reform movement of the Patarenes became an instance of the struggle between *regnum et sacerdotium*. Moreover, in this Patarene reform, several bishops played a role and several popes played a role, with the result that one sees as well the struggle between local episcopal autonomy and an episcopal position defined by and dependent on the pope. In this Patarene reform, one sees the use of religious endeavors toward reform, but one also sees the use of force to bring about the reform particularly for certain desired goals. In this Patarene reform, one sees an involvement of all classes of society, but in the end it is the papal understanding of reform which wins the day. In this Patarene reform, one sees that fundamentally the criterion was gospel discipleship, but one also sees a conflict of logic on the issue of discipleship: on the one hand, the logic of discipleship, held by Gregory VII, which viewed all true discipleship as necessarily that which is directed totally by the pope and the bishops loyal to the pope, and, on the other hand, the logic of some reformers who saw that true discipleship is based on the gospels and that even the pope is held accountable to the gospels.

3. The Logic of Discipleship in This Reform Movement

Gregory VII clearly wanted to be a disciple of the Lord, and he wanted the church to be filled with Christian disciples. This cannot be gainsaid. Still, the logic of his discipleship was not as scripture-rooted as one finds in the various disparate reform movements. We find this in various statements of the *Dictatus Papae Gregorii VII,* such as:

> n. 22   That the Roman Church has never erred nor will ever err, as the scripture bears witness.
> n. 18   That his decision ought to be reviewed by no one, and that he alone can review the decisions of everyone.
> n. 19   That he ought to be judged by no one.[46]

The centrality of the pope throughout this *Dictatus,* and echoed in such later writings as the *De ecclesiastica potestate* of Aegidius Romanus, written ca. 1301, and the *Summa de potestate ecclesiastica* of Augustinus Triumphus, dated either 1320 or 1324–1328, clearly attests to a certain logic of discipleship: namely, only if one is a disciple of the pope is one a disciple of the Lord. In this view, the criterion might ultimately be the gospels, but gospel discipleship must have the *imprimatur* of papal interpretation.[47]

4. The Significance of This Reform Movement for an Appreciation of the Lay Person in the Church

Contemporary historians, however, too often present one of the key aspects of the Gregorian reform, i.e., the provisioning of all church offices by ecclesiastics alone, in a way that makes a theologian shudder. The following are simply random statements, but statements which are, in their very sampling, representative of an odd ecclesiology that finds expression in books of church history:

> Ireland found itself in a first irresolute change, after the Synods of Cashel in 1101 and Rath Breasail in 1111 had begun to free the Church from its entanglement with lay powers.[48]

> The dependence of the secular sphere of law was then so extensive that royal decrees which contradicted canon law in important matters could be declared null by the Church.[49]

In this way of writing, the "church" equals the cleric, especially the pope. The non-clerical world is at times termed the secular world and at other times the lay powers. Logically, those who belong to the secular world or to the lay powers were "not church." One must recall that at this precise time of western history there was in the west a Christian society, and even more specifically stated, because of the east/west split of the Christian world, a Roman Catholic Christian society. Nonetheless, church historians at times speak too glibly about the church being free of the secular, about the struggle for the freedom of the church,[50] about the ways in which the church must be independent. Whenever the term "church" is restricted simply to the hierarchical leadership or to clerics as such, one can only say that such statements are all theologically inept ways of describing the situation. In this same period of time there was no developed theory of church and state, as we have noted, but clearly many contemporary church history books present us with such a dichotomized picture when their authors use the term "church" to refer to pope, bishop and cleric, with the enemy referred to by the term "secular." In such a view the church is equated almost totally with clergy; the secular area is equated with the enemy of such a church. The ecclesiology for this approach is not only odd, it is doctrinally incorrect, for the church is the total people of God, not simply the hierarchy, and not to see "church" in the reality of emperor, king, lay person, i.e., in the so-called "secular" area, is untenable. Within the total church there were diverse and competing struggles, often for power, often for an ideological stance, but theologically one cannot describe these struggles in terms of church and non-church.[51] Already, however, through such language, one can see a different "scope" of reform than that envisioned by the geographically disparate reform movements, namely a reform which clericalized the very meaning of church.

It must be admitted that Gregory VII, to a great degree, thought in this direction, namely that the church was primarily, even exclusively, clerical, indeed, papal, and any secular influence or interference was inimical, since such an influence was not truly the "church." This was his logic, but from the standpoint of an ecclesiology, based on solid theological foundations, what is the meaning of "church" when the word only applies to the clergy? When one says, as later during the time of Boniface VIII it was said: *Ubi Petrus, ibi ecclesia,* what does such a statement say about the people of God? Is the status of "secular" outside the church? If so, are lay people, the *saeculares,* outside the church? Although Gregory's logic of discipleship moves in this direction, the direction itself, which tends to make papacy or *sacerdotium* "church" and all else "non-church" or only secondarily and derivatively from the *sacerdotium* "church," should be faulted as doctrinally inept and not presented as an "ideal."

Since this Gregorian reform had in its day and continues to have repercussions in the modern church as well—for the papal positioning in the world which the reform advocated can be found in Leo XIII, Pius XII and even John Paul II—one must admit that it has also had enormous significance as regards the role of the lay person in the church. This significance is, of course, negative, for the term "church" continues to be interpreted in papal, episcopal and clerical ways, with the secular and the lay aspects of Christian life interpreted, to some degree, as "inimical" to the real core of "church." It is no wonder, then, that this Gregorian reform never truly "reformed" the church, but only led, in one way or another, to further reformations of the church.

Both the geographically disparate reform movements and the so-called Gregorian reform movement, although in differing ways, affected the repositioning of the lay person in the church. The disparate reform movements, by and large, opened many lay men and women to the reading of the scriptures, thereby making the prayerful reading of the gospel message the model and measure of their yearning for Christian discipleship. These disparate movements were open to men and women of every social strata, and at times were not immediately directed by ecclesiastical leadership. Moreover, many ordinary Christians, who were themselves not part of these disparate reforms, admired the men and women who were so central to them. The disparate reform movements had both many adherents and many listeners. The movements themselves continued on through the well-known mendicant communities of the thirteenth century and through the Brothers and Sisters of the Common Life in the fifteenth and sixteenth centuries.

The so-called Gregorian reform also affected the repositioning of the lay person. This reform clearly helped to marginalize some of the major abuses which affected church life: simony and concubinate clergy. In theory and often in practice, it also tended to marginalize the lay person in the church, including lay political leaders. However, this marginalization had as its effect a counter-movement: the assertion of the role of the lay person within the *societas Christiana.* The element of overbearing clericalization involved in this Gregorian reform movement eventually denied the movement of its genuine reform value. This reform movement never truly reformed the church, but only led to further reformations of the church—reformations which eventually splintered the western Christian world.

2. THE LAY PERSON AND THE CRUSADES

An anonymous knight who in 1095 personally heard the stirring words of Pope Urban II at Clermont—words which to some degree can be called the beginning of the first crusade—returned home and wrote the following:

When that time had already come, of which the Lord Jesus warns his faithful people every day, especially in the Gospel where he says, "If any man will come after me, let him deny himself, and take up his cross and follow me," there was a great stirring of heart throughout all the Frankish lands, so that if any man, with all his heart and all his mind, really wanted to follow God and faithfully to bear the cross after him, he could make no delay in taking the road to the Holy Sepulchre as quickly as possible.[52]

The writer-knight remains nameless, but Cowdrey notes: "He was a highly sophisticated and articulate man—a skilled, professional warrior with a developed sense of feudal loyalty and social obligation."[53] He was a man who went out to fight with high ideals: to suffer for the name of Christ and free the road to the Holy Sepulchre.[54] Over the years since this man's warring journey, writers and scholars have traced and retraced the crusading paths, so that the literature on this subject of the crusades is rich and abundant.

Because of its vastness, any attempt to reassemble the fruit of all this research would be counter-productive for this relatively slender volume on the lay person in the church. Rather, one question alone focuses our inquiry:

What precise significance did the crusades have for the role of the lay person in the church?

Even this centralizing question, however, has its own wide range of presupposition and implication. Presupposed is the position that the crusades were not caused by any immediate threat from the Muslim world on the western world. Historians cannot find an incident or situation which sparked the first crusade. Neither the Muslim world nor the emperor in Byzantium, Alexius Comnenos, had made a move which invited the crusading hordes into the eastern territories. Nor have historians found an issue within the western European boundaries which provoked the crusades. There was indeed an increase in population within western Europe which placed stretching demands on familial inheritance, i.e. how many sons can divide and live on a small inheritance (*frérèche*)? There were the many instances of a "Peace of God" or a "Truce of God" through which church leadership and political leadership curtailed fighting, at least during certain seasons of the year. The Council of Narbonne in 1054 had felt emboldened enough to state: "No Christian should kill another Christian, for whoever kills another Christian undoubtedly sheds the blood of

Christ."[55] Although some historians have argued that the reduction of warfare in the west, together with the rise in western European population, created a situation in which a number of war-ready men were looking for an arena, and that the call for a crusade in 1095 was issued at a fortuitous time, their conclusion seems to be an overstatement.

A second position, held by some scholars, is that the knight's standing in the eleventh century had changed for the better. Church leadership had contributed in no small measure to this enhancement of the warrior, for we find, from 950 on, liturgical formulas for the blessing of knightly banners, for the blessing of swords and other weapons, and for the blessing of the knights themselves, *Oratio super militantes*.[56] The investiture of a knight was a religious rite. In all of this, the blessing and consecrating of the knight and his weapons, there was a churchly blessing on warriors and warfare.

The *Life of Gerald of Aurillac* by Odo of Cluny[57] became a widely known book, for it presented an ideal for knighthood, namely a person who defended the poor and stood for justice. So also the *Chanson de Roland* portrayed a religiously Christian warrior, for in this volume there is a churchly encouragement for knights to fight the Muslims for the reconquest of Spain.[58] Nor are these the only instances in which church leadership is seen as abetting warfare, since there is also the urging of Popes Leo IV and John VIII, who promised the martyr's crown to those who fought in the Ottonian wars, and Leo IX's spiritual promises to those who took part in the campaign against the Normans in southern Italy.

On the one hand, church leadership fostered and blessed the knight and the war he engaged in. On the other hand, church leadership appeared to teach that killing in warfare was gravely sinful. Cowdrey notes that in 1066 the Norman army at the battle of Hastings fought under a papal banner, a sort of blessing and justification of this war of conquest. But after this battle, the Norman bishops, together with the papal legate, imposed a penance on those very same warriors: "for the killing of a man, a year's penance; for wounding, forty days."[59] This theoretical and practical religious ambivalence toward warfare can be found throughout church documents, from Augustine with his very tentative positioning on a "just war," to the influential writings of Peter Damian and Humberto, the cardinal bishop of Silva Candida. One man, however, turned the tide as regards this ambivalence, and it was none other than Hildebrand himself. In his struggle with Henry IV, he called on knights of all lands to dedicate their swords to the service of Christ and of St. Peter. The *militia Christi* was no longer something spiritual, i.e. the martyr and the monk; the *militia Christi* was with Gregory the warring knight. The soldier Erlembald of Milan in the Patarene struggle was virtually called by Gregory VII a saint.

> It was only after Gregory had so drastically revised the official attitude of the West to warfare, and after his ideas had been disseminated by such publicists as Bishop Anselm II of Lucca— only, therefore, at the very end of the eleventh century—that the preaching of a Crusade became feasible. Only then could a man like the author of the *Gesta Francorum* have heard and answered a papal summons to go eastward, traveling with words from the Gospel upon his lips, and fortified by the assurance that, far from being sinful, his warfare would avail for the remission of sins and the winning of salvation.[60]

In 1095 at Clermont the crusade became the knight's way of gaining remission of sins. Guibert of Nogent had written: "In our own time, God has instituted a holy manner of warfare, so that knights and the common people, who, after the ancient manner of paganism, were aforetime immersed in internecine slaughter, have found a new way of winning salvation."[61] Bernard of Clairvaux similarly wrote his blessing of warfare in the *De laude novae militiae*. Another step was taken with the formation of the Knights Templars, the fusion of monk and knight. "A Christian warfare for ideas had now indelibly registered itself in the consciousness of the Catholic West."[62] "When the Gregorian papacy accepted warfare without reservation as a meritorious activity, and the profession of arms as a Christian vocation so long as it was directed toward the extirpation of what is alien to Christianity both inside and outside Christian society," we have a reversal of a thousand years of a Christian tradition.[63] The logic of Gregory VII was continued with more finesse by Urban II. Gregory had failed to develop a "first crusade" in 1074, but Urban had done so in 1095. Gregory had tried to develop a crusade which would enhance his own hierarchical political goals at the expense of the socio-political rulers of his time, and his words were unheeded. Urban had the insight to include the socio-political rulers of his time, and his words were heeded. Still, Urban's call required the turnabout in policy, which Gregory had done. In this we find the significance of the crusades for the lay person. The knight and, even more than he, the leader of the knight, i.e. the socio-political leaders of chivalry, were given a spiritual status which they had not had before. Their swords may have been blessed; their armor may have been blessed; their investiture into knighthood itself might have been a ritualized blessing. Now, however, their very status as knight and as leader of knights was blessed. This blessed status was, even more, a part of Christian salvation history, and their wars were part of this salvation history as well. Knights became the new martyrs, and like the martyrs of old they were proclaimed as the new and fearless disciples of the Lord. When Urban II—in contrast to Gregory VII—indicated that crusaders were the followers of the gospel, and therefore disciples of the Lord—not merely warriors to maintain the papal states—the criterion which has threaded our chapters so far emerges once again, and, even with all its misapplication in the crusades, provides once more the basis for the repositioning of the lay person in the church.

We see this, however, reach even a deeper level with the fusion of monk and knight in the various orders which developed: the Knights Templars under Hugh of Payens (d. 1136) and the Knights Hospitallers, which had their beginnings with the merchants of Amalfi, but rose in significance after the first crusade under Gerard (d. 1120) and Raymond du Puy (1120–1160). The backing of Bernard of Clairvaux and Stephen, patriarch of Jerusalem, clearly aided the Templars, and eventually they became an international society, with enormous financial strength and independence both from the kings of Jerusalem and from episcopal hierarchies. A *Fratres militiae Christi* was founded in Riga at the beginning of the thirteenth century. The Teutonic Knights stem from the hospital erected by citizens of Bremen and Lübeck, and when these Teutonic Knights were recalled to the west, they developed a health-care system which was of superior quality for its time. The Order of Lazarus began in a leper colony at Jerusalem in 1120, and when it was expelled from Syria in 1253, it founded settlements at Boigny, as well as in England, Scotland, Switzerland, Italy, Hungary and Germany. Other groups could be mentioned as well: The Hospital Order of St. Anthony at La Motte-des-Bois; the Hospital Order of the Holy Spirit from Montpelier; the Order of the Bearers of the Cross; the Order of the Brothers of the Holy Sepulchre at Jerusalem.

The rise of such military and hospital groups—with some of these hospital groups military as well—indicates once again that there was some sort of vacuum, into which the spiritual hopes and dreams of many a lay man and lay woman of that age found a place of life and growth. The attraction at first was religious and spiritual, and focused on the issue of discipleship. In time, as some of these groups became power-brokers, less spiritual motives certainly entered into the picture.

These kinds of religious communities were engendered, for the most part, by the crusades. They were not reforms "against" such issues as simoniacal clergy or concubinate clergy. They were new movements responding to situations which directly arose from the crusades. The attractiveness and meteoric growth of some of these groups can only be understood on the basis of two issues:

(a) these new orders presented a form of gospel discipleship which had great appeal;

(b) the then-contemporary forms of mainstream monastic and clerical life did not offer such an appeal.

These military and hospital groups were for the most part made up of three groups: the knights, the serving brothers and the chaplains. The last, of course, were clerics. The knights and the serving brothers were most often non-cleric, and it was these two groups which gave meaning and value to the community, rather than the chaplain. As the prestige and significance of the knights and therefore the community itself with its serving brothers became more and more involved in major church policy-making, merely belonging to such a group was a powerful enhancement of the lay state. Eventually, as is well known, the military orders, which had become highly influential power-brokers both in church structures and in socio-political structures, were dismantled, but during the long centuries of their existence, lay status grew in a powerful way. Prestige came from two sources: the prestige of the newly blessed knighthood, and the prestige of the long-standing position of monk. The union of monk and knight (even on occasion canon-regular and knight) moved the ordinary lay person into a more central position within the church structure. In all of this, one sees that the crusades, or, more specifically, the ramifications of the crusades, strongly brought about a repositioning of a large segment of the lay population within the *societas Christiana* and within the structures of the medieval church.

3. THE LAY PERSON IN HIGH SCHOLASTICISM

Up until now we have discussed various socio-political and religious movements in the church which have, in sundry ways, brought the ordinary lay person more prominently into church life. When we turn, as we must do at this juncture, to the theoretical positioning of the lay person in the church, we find an enormous body of theological and canonical material. From 1000 to the middle of the fourteenth century, theological writings in general multiply in an ever increasing way. The rise of the *studium generale,* the term first given to what later was called a university, certainly helps account for this intellectual foment. The meeting of the Latin west with the learning of the Muslims began in the tenth century, with the earliest translations dating from the eleventh century.[64] Slowly the works of Aristotle were translated and impacted the thought of the Latin west. When Alexander of Hales began to use the *Book of Sentences* by Peter Lombard as a text, he began a pattern which lasted well into the reformation period, namely a unified way of presenting theology which closely followed the structure of this *Book of Sentences.* Numerous commentaries on Lombard's material are written from Alexander's time onward. Simultaneously, a different format began to appear, namely that of a *Summa,* of which the *Summa Theologiae* of Thomas Aquinas is the most renowned. Again, however, there is a general format to most all of these various *Summae,* a format which both helped the theological presentation and which limited the same.

In all of these theological writings, however, there was no section which dealt specifically with the church, i.e. ecclesiology. Treatises, which we today could call *Tractatus de Ecclesia,* start to appear only at the beginning of the sixteenth century, as we shall see. In the various commentaries on the *Book of Sentences* and the various *Summae* written before 1300, discussion about clerics and laity tended to appear most often, but only in a fairly piecemeal way, in the discussion on the sacraments. Because of this particular localization of this theme, a discussion of the cleric was far more organized and far more carefully explained than a discussion of the lay person. Nonetheless, both discussions remained somewhat fragmentary and occasional, due in no small measure to the lack of a theological analysis on the meaning of church. In the major scholastic theologians of the thirteenth century, Alexander of Hales, Albert the Great, Thomas Aquinas, Bonaventure and John Duns Scotus, one is able to gather the main theological positions regarding church from each of these respective authors, but such a resume of their respective ecclesial thoughts is only derivative. Even in the political writings of Thomas Aquinas, there is no ecclesiology as such, and the distillation of his "ecclesiology" from both his theological and his political writings remains generic in tone.

Still, in the scattered discussions of these major scholastic theologians on the theological meaning of church, both an ecclesial and an ecclesiological framework was in an inchoative way presented, out of which, and to some degree against which, the subsequent fourteenth and fifteenth century studies, dealing more specifically with the theology of church, began to develop. In this manner, the later-appearing discussions on ecclesiology relate orthogenetically to the quasi-ecclesial/ecclesiastical presentations of the major scholastic theologians of the thirteenth century.

It must be stated, however, that Melanchthon's *Loci theologici* (1535–1541) and book four of Calvin's *Institutes of the Christian Religion* (1559) represent in many ways the first embryonic ecclesiologies, and that those treatises on the church which appeared from 1300 to the middle of the sixteenth century, and antedated Melanchthon and Calvin, were only transitional in character, even though some of them had clear thematic presentations on one or the other major ecclesial and ecclesiastical issue.[65] The late medieval treatises on certain aspects of church were at best intermediary and cannot be seen as full-blown ecclesiologies.

Both this relationship to the major scholastics and this disrelationship to them, which later ecclesiologies will manifest, is crucial for an understanding of the theological development on the theology of the lay man and lay woman in the church. It is precisely this late medieval focus on ecclesiology which is a major theoretical turning point on the issue of the lay person in the church. Once a thematized theology of the church emerges, the theologizing of both cleric and lay person takes on various new emphases and counter-emphases. For this reason, it is absolutely necessary to study, in some detail, the issue of "ecclesiology" in the high middle ages, since from 1200 onward it will increasingly be the clash of ecclesiologies which accounts for the clash in various theologies of the cleric as also in various theologies of the lay person in the church.

This high and late medieval theologizing on the lay person in the church within the framework of its unthematized and then inchoatively thematized ecclesiologies is, of course, not the only reason why theoretical divergence on the role of the lay person in the church begins to appear in a clashing and often strident way. The various reform movements, with their repossession of the scriptures, and in them the issue of discipleship as a criterion for *vita evangelica*, and the crusades with their religious enhancement of knighthood and warfare, together with a religious enhancement of all those who assisted knights in these holy wars, surely played significant roles in the development of diverse ecclesiologies. Moreover, the continued struggle over the issue of *regnum et sacerdotium*, particularly in the way it developed between Gregory VII and Henry IV, between Innocent III and Frederick II, and then between Boniface VIII and Philip the Fair, played a major role as well in the development of theological treatises on the church. When one joins the theoretical-theological with the socio-political, and includes as well the many economic factors of that period of time including the steady rise of the middle class, one has the seed bed from which and through which diverse and clashing ecclesiologies arise, and with these diverse ecclesiologies diverse views on the roles of both clerics and lay men and women ineluctably began to appear. From 1100 to 1500, one might conclude, it is evident that:

1. The many and continuing reform movements throughout the western church contributed to a repositioning of the lay person in the church.
2. The crusades blessed the knight in a special way, but also blessed those who assisted these holy warriors, which again enhanced the position of the lay person.
3. The continued struggles of *regnum et sacerdotium* engendered a number of treatises on both sides which attempted to spell out the positioning of a hierarchical person, namely the pope, and the positioning of a non-hierarchical person, namely, the emperor/king. In this literature the wider issues of hierarchy and laity appear and reappear.
4. The infusion of Aristotle's understanding of *polis* into medieval thought, as one sees for instance in the writings of Dante, raised the question of natural ends of government as well as the meaning of *polis* for both the rising national kingdoms and the lingering idea of empire. In this discussion, the role of both lay person and ecclesiastic came to the fore.
5. The new studies, occasioned by the injection of Muslim thought into the Latin world, particularly as regards astrology, astronomy, mathematics, physics, and medicine, provided the necessary seed bed from which the revolutionary concepts and methods, dating from 1500 onward, arose. This "secularization" of science influenced the world in which a secular, "lay person," lived.[66]
6. The political growth of kingdoms throughout the west raised the issue of independence, both from the pope and from the emperor. Not only did lay people raise this issue of independence, but also regional bishops and regional governments.

The repositioning of the lay person in the western church was influenced by all of the above factors (and more as well), which indicates to us that a "dogmatic" position on the issue of cleric/lay is insufficient. If one were to bypass the rise of the theory of church, i.e. an ecclesiology as a separate study, with all of its theoretical and non-theoretical genealogy, one would never appreciate the issue of the lay person in the church. Dogmatic stances alone are insufficient for this task, and even the various dogmatic treatises which appeared in the high and late middle ages must be seen as historically conditioned by the socio-political and economic factors of that same period.

Although one could delve into each of the main theologians of the high scholastic period, we will consider only three: Thomas Aquinas, Bonaventure and John Duns Scotus, since in many ways they represent the main approach to the issue of church as found in all the theologians of the high middle ages, and each of them offers a very specific aspect of thought which contributed to the way in which the thematized ecclesiologies of subsequent generations began to take shape.

A. THOMAS AQUINAS

Many contemporary authors have discussed the issue why there is no ecclesiology per se in the writings of St. Thomas.[67] M. Grabmann explains this absence of an ecclesiology in St. Thomas (and by implication in the other scholastic theologians of that same period) by the "fact" that the theme of the church was not acute at that time: "in its essence and authority, the Church was not so openly and directly attacked and denied as was later to be the case."[68] Instead, Grabmann notes that the theme of church seems to pervade the writings of Thomas in a way that resembles some sort of architectonic law.[69] Y. Congar, for his part, sides with Grabmann, but moves the issue one step further, stating that Thomas deliberately did not draw up a separate treatise on the church, since the issue of church pervades all of his writings. Congar states that Thomas Aquinas acted in a deliberate way, and the omission of a separate study on the church was not simply due to some presupposition.[70]

R. Busa, in the *Index Thomisticus: Sancti Thomae Aquinatis Operum Omnium Indices et Concordantiae,* lists all of those passages in the writings of St. Thomas in which the term *laicus* or one of its cognates appears.[71] There are not as many instances in which this term is used as might be expected. *Clericus* and its cognates are used far more frequently. In many ways, then, a study of the use of *clericus/laicus* in the writings of St. Thomas, or in the writings of any of the other major scholastics of the thirteenth century, will not provide a far-reaching insight into the issues involved in the question of the role of the lay person in the church.

Of far greater importance is an analysis of terms by which Thomas describes the church. Sabra has done such an analysis, and leaving to one side very occasional symbols and similes,[72] which Thomas used to describe the church, he arrives at the following main words and phrases:[73]

1. *Civitas:* a city, namely the city of God;
2. *Domus:* a house or domicile of God;
3. *Populus:* a people of God;

4. *Congregatio fidelium:* a gathering of the faithful;
5. *Corpus Christi mysticum:* the mystical body of Christ.

Thomas employs these terms because they are biblical, and through-out his writings he tends to stay with a biblical term or phrase rather than a non-biblical one. These are also descriptive terms, not defining terms. *Civitas,* however, is used only three times.[74] This term describes the life of a community of human beings sharing in God's grace. *Domus* is used more often as *domus Dei* or *domus Christi,* and at times simply as *domus.*[75] He uses this term because it is found both in 1 Timothy 3:15 and in traditional Christian literature. Accordingly, Thomas adds nothing to this term. *Populus,* on the other hand, is used often throughout Thomas' writings. Sabra arranges Thomas' use of this term into three categories: (1) instances in which *populus* is used in a Christian political context; (2) instances in which *populus* designates the church as a totality; (3) in-stances in which *populus* designates the non-religious, non-clerical com-munity within the total church. This last designation is of interest to our theme.

> Whoever is not of the hierarchy, whoever is not ordained for
> some function in the church, and whoever is thus the field of
> work for the apostles, bishops, popes, priests, friars and doctors
> is signified by the term Christian or faithful people. . . . The
> aforementioned dispense the sacraments to the people; they are
> mediators between God and the people; they represent and pray
> on behalf of the people; they prepare, direct, fructify, and work
> for the salvation of the Christian people; they teach and preach
> to the people; and they rule, pasture and decide for the faithful
> people.[76]

Each phrase indicating a task of the hierarchy, in this citation, has a footnote which catalogues the places in Thomas' writings to substantiate the respective task. Thomas' use of *populus,* in this third sense, has little affinity with the use of "people of God" in the Vatican II document *Lumen gentium.* Thomas sees this non-hierarchical people of God basi-cally from a juridical and sacramental stance, in which *populus* is called on to support the clergy, propagate Christian children, be obedient and attend the worship services conducted by the hierarchy. Even though there is a clear negative and passive stance of the *populus* in the use of this term, the passages throughout Thomas' writings in which this term is used indicate a common theological understanding of the non-hierarchical, non-monastic group of Christians at the beginning of the thirteenth century.

The term *congregatio fidelium* should be linked with similar descriptive titles: *aggregatio, collectio, collegium, adunatio,* which are also found in Thomas' writings. There is a certain vagueness in the connotation of these terms within the Thomistic corpus. At times these terms are used to indicate the social structuring of the church, which A. Darquennes stresses.[77] At other times the gathering (*ecclesia*) refers to all who have been called by grace to share in God's love, and as such includes those before Christ and those after Christ, those on earth and those in heaven. One can also make a point that in the many instances in which this term is used throughout the Thomistic writings, there is, cumulatively considered, an emphasis on two aspects: (1) the unity of this group, but a unity which arises from God and not from the group itself; (2) a group which is unified on the basis of faith, but again not a faith which the group itself has developed, but a faith which has been given to it by God.[78]

An analysis of Thomas' use of the term *corpus Christi mysticum* enjoyed a heyday of emphasis in the middle part of this present century.[79] Thomas generally referred to the eucharist as *corpus Christi verum* or *corpus Domini,* and to the church as *corpus Christi mysterium* or *corpus ecclesiae mysticum.* This distinction had already become part of the theological vocabulary of the time.[80] By this term, Thomas emphasizes the basic christological aspect of the church, and therefore the unity of the church. But the term also indicates for Thomas the variety of function within an ordered unity, i.e. the many parts of one body. Through this term Thomas can describe the role of pope, bishops, priests, etc. He can speak of spiritual and sacramental powers, given to some but not to others. He can speak of the power of jurisdiction. In all of this, the juridical (*corpus*) elements are secondary; the theological (*mysticum*) elements are primary.

In all of this descriptive presentation of the church, Thomas consistently saw the church as a gift of grace established by Christ.[81] Because of this central presence of the incarnate Christ within the church, the Holy Spirit, the Spirit of Jesus, also plays an effective role. Thomas does not focus on the juridical, legal, institutional church, although these elements appear in his descriptions of the church; rather, he presents a theological portrait of the church, one that is seen *sub ratione Dei.* In this view, God's grace in Christ, the unity of the church which consequently includes all who have been touched by God's grace, and the church's continuation of the work of Christ are the centralizing ideas. Because of this somewhat amorphous use of the term "Church," one finds in Thomas a church which now refers to all graced people, to angels and saints as well as the

Christians on earth, to those in purgatory as well, and to old and new covenant people.

> **All these possible significations create an undeniable ambivalence in his ecclesiology, and these various notions sometimes stand in a certain unresolved tension in relation to each other, e.g., in the questions of membership and the necessity of the Church for salvation.**[82]

Clearly, Thomas Aquinas provides us with many profound theological insights into the meaning of church, but the ambivalence of his presentation cannot be discounted. We will see that this theological ambivalence on the issue of church provided a major part of the background against which the question about the lay person in the church began to be raised so strongly in the fourteenth, fifteenth and sixteenth centuries. It was the unravelling of the ambivalent character which spurred the theological clarification of a lay person in the church.

If one considers the political writings of Thomas, one finds another major contribution to the development of a theology of the lay person in the church, though again more indirect than direct, more remote than immediate. For Thomas, the Aristotelian notion of *polis* was central, for the philosopher had seen the goal of the city-state to be one which brought peace and sufficiency to those who lived within it. Thomas began to apply this notion to the political situation of his own day, and although he did not succeed in applying it to the empire as such, he nevertheless stressed a temporal goal for local governments, which eventually helped to base the rise of kingdoms vis-à-vis an empire. This temporal aspect of a localized political area provided a philosophical *raison d'être* for lay leadership.

B. BONAVENTURE

When we turn to the issue of the church in the writings of Bonaventure, we find a situation similar to that we found in Thomas, namely that there is no specific "treatise" on the church and that the issue of church underlies almost all of Bonaventure's thought. Moreover, the literature on this subject is quite substantial.[83]

Bonaventure alludes to the people of Israel as a *populus peculiaris*,[84] and he does not use the term *populus* for the church, which he designates primarily as *ecclesia*, a *congregatio fidelium*.[85] It is *convocatio* and *unio* of the faithful.[86] It is the body of Christ who is the head of the church.[87] The same descriptive titles for church, which were mentioned above, are found in Bonaventure, for these are all scriptural, and as such common to all the theologians of the middle ages.

For Bonaventure, the description of the church as a body, which was found in the writings of Paul, provided a continual source of his meditation on the church. Bonaventure had no problem with the hierarchical church as it was structured in the west of his time. For him this was a given. However, in his reflections on this hierarchical church, he spoke often on the role of *caritas* as the bond of union within a hierarchical church. A. Blasucci notes, however, that there is no opposition in Bonaventure between a "Chiesa guiuridica" and a "Chiesa della carità."[88] Bonaventure himself writes: "In hierarchicis eloquiis optime sonat nomen dilectionis."[89] The very purpose and the perfection of hierarchy, for the seraphic doctor, is *unitiva dilectio.*[90]

P. Caporale, in his study of Bonaventure's ecclesial thought, summarizes his observations as follows:

> Bisogna ammettere che nel Serafico Dottore l'aspetto istituzionale della Chiesa viene accentuato. Era una mentalità ed una esigenze di ordine che gli Scolastici perseguivano nell'insegnamento e nella vita. Però anima dell'ecclesiologia bonaventuriana è la visione spirituale della Chiesa, che per lui è un'entità soprannaturale, in quanto formata de Cristo de dai fedeli per una communità di vita il cui apice sta nella carità que unisce insieme le membra al capo et tra loro.[91]

Bonaventure clearly came more and more to consider the church from a deeply religious standpoint, and it is within many of his mystical writings that one finds references to this profoundly spiritual approach to the meaning of church. Bonaventure respected the juridical and institutional church, but his mind again and again moved to the foundations of this juridical and institutional church, namely the *unitiva dilectio,* which comes from God through Christ to the people of God. As regards the theme of this present volume, namely the role of the lay person in the church, this notion of unitive love from the writings of Bonaventure is perhaps the most significant. One could argue that only when this unitive love becomes evident in the hierarchy's pronouncements and example can the hierarchy in the church be considered credible. *Unitiva caritas* is the basis not simply for church, but for discipleship, and this unitive love must be found in every disciple, at every level of church structure. Discipleship, under the rubric of unitive love, is Bonaventure's key to the very meaning of church, and therefore—by extension in a thematized ecclesiology—to the very meaning of both the hierarchical and lay structures of the church. Whenever this key is lacking or at least diminished, the very meaning of Church, as well as the very meaning of cleric and lay, is likewise lacking or diminished. Bonaventure's spiritual and mystical emphases continued to play a role in the centuries following his death, and he has seriously influenced many areas of the mystical tradition in the western church from the beginning of the fourteenth century down to the present century.

C. JOHN DUNS SCOTUS

The relevance of John Duns Scotus for a theology of the lay person in the church does not lie primarily with the descriptions of church scattered throughout his writings, as is the case with Thomas and Bonaventure. Rather, Scotus gave to both the philosophy and the theology of his time a somewhat new direction. From the viewpoint of Scotus, Thomas had tied God too closely to the church's sacramental system, and by extension, as one finds in a post-Scotistic framework, to the church's hierarchical system. For Scotus, God was and remains absolutely free, and God's ordinations in reference to anything created were utterly contingent and played only a secondary role in salvation history.[92]

The contingency of all creation, which includes the created nature of Jesus, the course of salvation history, the Church and its sacraments, etc., is taken seriously by Scotus. But if this contingency is so pervasive throughout all creation, then "we must assume that he does not create, conserve, or cooperate with the causes he creates in any necessary way."[93] Is God, in Scotus' view, free to deal with his creatures in a purely arbitrary and whimsical way? Scotus pursues his thought by a profound analysis of free will in God.[94]

> I say that God is no debtor in any unqualified sense save with respect to his own goodness, namely, that he loves it. But where creatures are concerned, he is debtor rather to his generosity, in the sense that he gives creatures what their nature demands, which exigency in them is set down as something just, a kind of secondary object of this justice, as it were. But in truth nothing outside of God can be said to be definitely just without this added qualification. In an unqualified sense where a creature is concerned, God is just only in relation to his first justice, namely, because such a creature has been actually willed by the divine will.[95]

Both the discussion on natural goodness and the discussion on moral goodness followed this line of reasoning. Many of Scotus' contemporaries had come to a conclusion, based on Augustine (which Augustine had derived from Stoic ideas), that the decalogue was a sort of impersonal eternal law, written into nature and binding on God just as it is binding on a rational creature. Scotus rejected such a view. For him, any moral law is based on a fundamental principle stemming from the very justice of God: God should be loved.[96]

From this perspective, Scotus will teach that sacraments are efficacious media of grace, but quite subordinate to the divine will. In all of this the phrases *potentia Dei absoluta* and *potentia Dei ordinata* play a fundamental role. The absolute power of God is "subject only to the law of non-contradiction, which leaves the actually chosen order out of consideration." The ordained power of God "is the order established by God and the way in which God has chosen to act in his *opera ad extra*, i.e., over against the contingent order outside him."[97] This description of *potentia Dei absoluta* is expressed negatively; positively it is an expression of divine *justitia.* The description of the *potentia Dei ordinata* clearly emphasizes the contingent factor, but without stating the reasons for such contingency. Out of this way of thinking, eventually a sort of covenant theology will be elaborated by later thinkers, and, more for our point, the contingent factors which Scotus uses in his discussion on sacraments will be transferred to a discussion on the power of the hierarchy, and eventually to the church itself, which then radically alters the way in which a lay person in the church is viewed.

> For Scotus and his followers, there was nothing necessary and absolute this side of eternity. That is the upshot of these discussions about secondary causes. . . . Scotus' intention had been not to denigrate created things, but to define their nature more accurately. To some, however, Scotist "divine psychology" seemed a very unnatural perspective with mischievous consequences for the church and its media of salvation. Most people, both simple and learned, found priests and sacraments primary in the actual course of salvation; the church was the point at which believers consciously dealt with God—there, where he revealed and executed his will in time, not while he was formulating it in eternity.[98]

What occurs in subsequent decades is a questioning on what among all the issues of our contingent world, even those revealed by God in Christ, are more primary and what are more secondary. This questioning occurred precisely at the time when, at Avignon, the Roman curia as we know it today was being established. The number of people employed by the papal curia during this time increased astronomically. The primary reason for this increase in bureaucracy was economic, and this economic thrust by the papacy, which in many places was experienced by the ordinary person through the local bishops, created a major questioning of Christian structure. The "contingency" factor, which Scotus made rather central, and which was then taken up by many others such as Ockham, helped raise the critique of the hierarchy in general, and caused them to look for a better criterion than *plenitudo potestatis*. In such a discussion, the role of discipleship again focused with major force, and the role of the lay person in the church became much more a central issue.

Scotus never envisioned the myriad and innovative applications his views might and did eventually take. By themselves, Scotus' ideas would not have moved in these directions as far as some later "covenant" theologies were concerned nor as far as the "contingent factor" of his theology would be applied. These derivations and reconstructions of Scotistic thought occurred only when the issue of individualism came to the forefront within an understanding of church, a position which Marsiglio of Padua clearly promoted.

Thomas, Bonaventure and Scotus, three key theologians of the thirteenth century, have strongly influenced subsequent western Christian theology. All three of these men did not formulate a precise ecclesiology, but all three developed their ideas within an ecclesial framework. The mystical element, which Thomas stressed in his use of the term "mystical body of Christ," and which Bonaventure stressed in his development of the *dilectio unitiva*, moved some of the subsequent theological endeavor away from an institutional and predominantly clerical approach to the church. In doing this, these two theologians provided a speculative foundation for the repositioning of the lay person. Scotus, with his speculative basis for the relativization of the entire contingent world, including the church, the hierarchy and the sacramental life, provided a different base for the subsequent repositioning of the lay person—as well as the subsequent repositioning of the clerical person—in the church.

The theological work of these three men, along with other less influential theologians of that period, must be joined to the many reform movements which were concomitantly taking place, and with the effects of the crusades on the life of the church. The union of these factors, plus others to which I have only alluded, sets the stage for the portrait of the lay person in the western church on the eve of the sixteenth century. That a process of repositioning and depositioning of both lay and cleric in the western church was already taking place prior to the major reformation movements of the sixteenth century can hardly be denied. Let us consider this immediate "pre-reformation" situation in more detail.

4. THE LAY PERSON IN THE FOURTEENTH AND FIFTEENTH CENTURIES

In the fourteenth and fifteenth centuries a number of pamphlets, treatises, even books on various aspects of a theology of church appeared. A few similar volumes had already been written in the thirteenth century. Although these works cannot be considered complete "ecclesiologies," they did, both individually and collectively, focus attention on the theological meaning of church, and a result of this literary production, though most often not an intended result, was the further clarification of a theology of the lay person. However, certain fairly general issues should be noted by way of introduction, since at times one might be tempted to read more contemporary ideas back into these medieval discussions. The galvanizing issue during this time was once again *regnum et sacerdotium.*

> The relation between kingship and priesthood was the dominant problem of medieval political thought. The political speculation of the Middle Ages was not, of course, entirely focused on this one continuing and complex issue. . . . But those who write the history of medieval political thought in terms of the conflict between secular and spiritual authority do not greatly destroy the historical picture. Of all conflicts, this was by far the most enduring and the more comprehensive.[99]

This umbrella *regnum et sacerdotium,* from a co-temporary medieval framework, has, however, the following caveats:

1. *Regnum et Sacerdotium* Were of One Piece.

The *respublica christiana* was comprised of both. There was never any view of an empire without a hierarchical church, nor of a hierarchical church without an empire. *Regnum et sacerdotium* was never *aut regnum aut sacerdotium.* More contemporary ideas about church and state are not applicable during this medieval period.

2. *Regnum et Sacerdotium* Were Seeking a Balance of Power.

Each side of this equation had for centuries struggled to find its weight and counterweight. Gregory VII and Henry IV, Innocent III and Frederick II, Boniface VIII and Philip the Fair, to name only the personages involved in the most dramatic moments of this conflict, all made grandstanding claims which at times far surpassed either de iure or de facto situations. The mere fact that a pope or an emperor (king) made some respective claim to power over the other cannot be cited by itself as proof that such a claim is true. Thus we have on the papal side: the claims made for the so-called donation of Constantine, the claims made regarding the coronation of Charlemagne, the claims made regarding papal intervention in sustaining the empire under Otto the Great, and the claims made (from the time of Gregory IX and Innocent IV) that Frederick II's defying the pope was a revolt against both the spiritual and the temporal lordship of the pope. The imperial side also grandstanded a number of claims: the claim that Charlemagne had given the empire to the Germans, that the empire was of divine origin, that the emperor had no temporal superior, not even the pope, and that the emperor was the lord over all kings, an issue which became acute in 1312 when Henry VII summoned Robert of Naples to appear before him on the charge of lèse majesté. These and other claims were made, but the mere act of claiming, as history has shown, often proved nothing.

3. The Terms "in Spiritual Matters" and "in Temporal Matters" Are Part of One *Societas Christiana.*

Over and over again, in the writings of these centuries, the terms "in spiritual matters" and "in temporal matters" play a major role, but only in the most extreme other-worldly spiritualities of some reform groups of the period were they seen as oppositional. Rather, the issue was one of final control. Was the emperor the final arbiter in temporal matters? Was the pope the final arbiter in spiritual matters? Did the emperor have at least indirect decisive power over a heretical pope? Did a pope have at least an indirect, or even, as some popes claimed, a direct claim over both the spiritual and temporal aspects of the *societas Christiana?* In this struggle to determine the "ultimate limits" of power, whether papal or imperial, a vision of a unified Christian society was never abandoned. At times imperial leaders, royal leaders, even leaders in the commune, claimed total power over temporal matters, leaving popes, bishops and priests with only spiritual matters. Pierre Dubois, for instance, in *De Recuperatione Terre Sancte,*[100] urged that the papal states should be given to the king of France, and the pope, stripped of all temporal power and supported financially by the French treasury, should devote himself to his spiritual ministry, which included a full spiritual reform of the church. This interplay of temporal matters and spiritual matters appears again and again, but they are never pitted one against the other in the same way that "church and state" are pitted against each other in our contemporary framework.

4. The Role of King Vis-à-Vis Emperor Slowly Became a Major Issue

The collapse of the Hohenstaufen empire marked a major moment in medieval history, for the interregnum together with the papal residency at Avignon as well as indecisive papal policies occasioned the rise of the French monarchy as a rival to the German emperor. "The [French] king has no sovereign in temporal things nor does he hold from anyone but from God and himself, nor is there any appeal from his judgment save to God."[101] This contemporary statement indicates that something new was appearing on the scene, and in a massive way: the royal power of the French king, not only as a rival to the emperor, but also as another "temporal" ruler by divine right, and in temporal matters subject to no one, not even the pope. When canonists and theologians began to discuss the role of "kings" vis-à-vis the role of "emperors" and "popes," some new terminology began to appear: namely the emperor was universal, but the king was *sibi princeps; rex est imperator in regno suo* and the emperor was the far-off but still important symbol of unity. This way of thinking led, in some writers, to a presentation of the emperor as the emperor of the universal world, not merely of the western world. One finds as well a presentation of the pope as the spiritual leader, and even for some writers the de jure temporal leader of the universal world as well, and not merely of the Latin, western world. This appearance of such terms as "universal" emperor/pope, i.e. worldwide, began to appear, it should be noted, at the very same time that new discoveries of lands and peoples in the east were taking place.

In all these discussions, focused so strongly on the issue of *regnum et sacerdotium,* a defining and redefining of terms such as temporal, spiritual, *populus,* state, empire, papal power, imperial power, individual conscience, church/government, etc., began to take place. At the close of the fifteenth century, one still does not have a complete "ecclesiology," but many major terms, which will appear so centrally in the later elaboration of a theology of church, had already been established. In this issue of clarified terminology, more than in any other issue, we have the theoretical importance of these two centuries, fourteenth and fifteenth, as regards the theology of the lay person in the church. Georges de Lagarde, in his *La naissance de l'esprit laïque au déclin du moyen âge,*[102] undoubtedly overstresses the rise of the lay spirit during these medieval times, but it must be stated that major steps were indeed taken by late medieval theologians, canonists and philosophers which clarified, particularly through terminology, but also through history, the meaning and the limits of both ecclesial and societal elements.

The beginning of the fourteenth century saw a number of books written which in some way or another were occasioned by the dispute between Boniface VIII and Philip the Fair—a struggle which was only one among many regarding the issue of *regnum et sacerdotium*. In these works, the focus, however, was on neither the kingdom nor the priesthood as such, but on the extent of papal and imperial powers. For instance, there are such works as Henry of Cremona's *De potestate papae,* his *Non ponant laici,* and also *Quaestio de utraque potestate;* James of Viterbo's *De regimine christiano;* Augustinus Triumphus' *Tractatus brevis de duplici potestate prelatorum et laicorum;* Giles of Rome's *De ecclesiastica potestate;* Angelus Nigri's *De potestate papae;* Herve Nédelac's *De potestate papae;* Aegidius of Rome's *De regimine principum.* On the side of the imperial crown, there were such works as *De prerogativa romani imperii,* attributed in part, perhaps chapter 1, to Jordan of Osnabrück but revised and enlarged by Alexander of Roes;[103] the quite popular *Disputatio inter clericum et militem* by an anonymous writer, as also another anonymous writing, *Rex pacificus.* John of Paris wrote a more formidable work, *De potestate regia et papali,* and Englebert of Admont wrote a quite philosophical text: *De ortu et fine romani imperii.* Certainly Dante Alighieri's *De monarchia* should be mentioned as an answer to the papal position of Tholommeo of Lucca's *De regimine principum.* William of Ockham's *Dialogus,* Lupold of Beneburg's *De iuribus regni et imperii romani,* and Marsiglio of Padua's *Defensor pacis,* as well as his *Tractatus de iurisdictione imperatoris in causis matrimonialibus* and *Tractatus de translatione imperii,* also belong to this genre of writings. Many others works could also be cited for both sides, and the above listing is not meant to be a bibliographical bravura, but a powerful indication of how concentrated the theological, philosophical and canonical thought of these centuries was on the specifically church-related issues, even if these writings cannot be considered genuine "ecclesiologies." In each of these works, so sensitive to the issue of the positioning, repositioning, and depositioning of either a lay person or a cleric, the theme of *regnum et sacerdotium* in one or other of its forms claimed center-stage.

The titles of these volumes alone indicate how the "church" question focused on the papal question, and how the papal question could not be addressed unless one focused on the "imperial" question. In the thirteenth century "medieval theologians and canonists tended to be content with a world of many distinct and limited lordships; they had no craving for unity that could not be satisfied by a vision of an orderly society in which separate authorities functioned cooperatively and harmoniously each in its own divinely-established sphere."[104] The idea of a separate "state" in contrast to a separate "church" had not yet been fully developed. *Ecclesia* and *respublica* were used in a way which suggested inter-penetration of one to the other. Even during the papacy of Innocent III, there was an ambiguous bond between pope and emperor, a bond as yet unformulated by legal terms. For Innocent, papal policy was not centered on a worldwide papal political *imperium,* for the *civitates et regna* which made up the fabric of the western world were continually acknowledged in his writings.[105] Only here and there, in the glosses of some lawyers or in the grandstanding of some emperors and even popes, the hint of a universal empire began to make its appearance.[106]

Boniface VIII's papal bull *Clericis laicos,* issued February 24, 1296, played a major role in the continuing battle between this pope and the French king, Philip the Fair. In this bull Boniface was addressing the issue of the king's taxation on the clergy, but his introductory statements merit consideration as regards our theme. He writes:

> Antiquity teaches us, and the experience of the present time make clear, that the laity are hostile to the clergy; inasmuch as, not content with their own bounds, they aim at what is forbidden them. . . . Nor do they reflect that power over ecclesiastical persons and goods has been denied them.[107]

The placing of hostility on the shoulders of the laity vis-à-vis the clergy reflects an attitude which will perdure in one way or another, on the part of the Roman Catholic Church's leadership, down to the present day. This attitude was not new by any means, and had been fostered by many popes prior to Boniface VIII. Even more indicative of this papal power over all other powers is Boniface's teaching on the two swords, spelled out in the bull *Unam sanctam* in 1302.

> In this his power we are instructed by evangelical statements (Lk. 22, 38; Mt. 26, 52) that there are two swords, namely the spiritual and the temporal. Both, therefore, are in the power of the church, namely the material and the spiritual sword. But the first is to be exercised indeed for the church, the second is to be exercised by the church; the latter is that of the priest, the former is in the hand of kings and knights, but at the pleasure and patience of the priest.[108]

The *plenitudo potestatis* is clear, and it is a matter of complete power of clergy over laity. This document *Unam sanctam* became one of the most controversial medieval documents, but *Clericis laicos* was itself invoked often enough during the entire struggle between Boniface and

Philip. In this struggle, it might be noted, the French king called for a meeting of the Estates General at Paris, and in this meeting of 1302 for the first time, besides the nobility and prelates, the cities were invited. One sees in this step a clear involvement of ordinary lay people, not merely the royal and aristocratic lay people, in an area which affected the structuring of the church. The same could be noted in the case of England, for the bull *Clericis laicos* occasioned a constitutional difficulty which reached a conclusion in 1297 with the submission of Edward I to lay, albeit aristocratic, power, and a confirmation by Edward of the *Magna Carta.* In other words, *Clericis laicos* effected precisely what Boniface did not intend: the involvement of even a wider sphere of the laity in determining issues regarding the church. However, the view of the church, evidenced in both of these bulls of Boniface VIII, continued to dominate papal policy during the next two centuries, although it cannot be said that it dominated the way political governments viewed the church during the same period of time.

Meanwhile, a different view of church had also been developing within the western church world. Marsiglio of Padua defined the church as the "whole body of the faith, who believe in and invoke the name of Christ, and all the parts of this whole body in every community, even the family."[109] In this definition we hear the typical understanding of church as the *congregatio fidelium* and *corpus Christi mysticum.* Marsiglio's contemporaries, William of Ockham[110] and John of Paris,[111] both advocated a church with a monarchic form of government, but at the same time both advocated a major role for the people of God. However, two things should be noted as regards Marsiglio of Padua, for when Marsiglio writes *universitas fidelium,* in what sense is the genitive, "of the faithful," to be taken? For him, the "of" means that the faithful are no longer subjects of a ruling hierarchy. Rather, the church exists for the faithful and is controlled by the faithful. In his analysis the hierarchical structure of the church is turned on its head, and the relationship of priesthood to God is weakened. Lay people are superior to priests, and all priests, whether papal, episcopal or presbyteral, are equalized.

Secondly, in his view of church membership the faithful are indeed involved with an institution, and there are legitimate corporate, public acts and powers which must be respected, but more important than these is the individual privatized conduct and belief of the single Christian, with its focus on a direct relationship of the believer to God.

Marsiglio finds a place for sacraments, for priesthood, even for the papacy, with the true historical successor of Peter in the bishop of Antioch, not the bishop of Rome. For Marsiglio a monarchical papacy is as contingent as a monarchical civil leader, that is, contingent on the needs of the people who constitute each and every governmental or societal structure. Erwin Iserloh is cautious but quite on target when he writes: "In summary, it can be stated that the *Defensor pacis* was too radical to exert an immediate influence, but indirectly it had a great and far-reaching effect."[112]

Reform was surely necessary within the church. After Avignon, Martin V issued the first reform bull and Pius II in 1464 issued the first significant reform legislation. In this latter three items were presented as key:

    a. a strong papal position;
    b. a plea for peace;
    c. a reform of the curia.

J. D'Amico, however, comments: "Although Pius expressed a theological preference for reform on the individual level, his procedure was essentially the administrative-mechanistic one that characterized all curial reform programs."[113] Somewhat later, Sixtus IV also drew up a fairly comprehensive reform program, but it was very Roman-oriented in scope. Oddly enough, Sixtus never issued this bull, but it did provide the plan for a bull issued by Alexander IV, another papal bull which remained unimplemented. Julius II was too occupied with political and cultural issues to spend much time on church reform, and immediately prior to the reformation Leo X, in 1513 and again in 1514, issued two bulls on reform, again more administrative and mechanistic than profoundly ecclesial.

Of interest are the writings of the humanist B. Maffei (1429–1474). In his program for reform, Maffei centers and bases the reform movement on the role of the pope and the Roman curia; second, he focuses on the lifestyle of the clergy which should evidence apostolic simplicity; third, he urges the religious orders, particularly the Franciscans and the Dominicans, to return to the charism of their founders; fourth, he proposes that all religious writings be overseen by papal and curial guidance; next he calls on civil rulers to act on the principles of the gospel; finally, there could be no church reform without peace among the various kingdoms of the then known world. Maffei was both a humanist and a papalist, but his sketch of a reformed *societas Christiana*, drawn together on the eve of the reformation, covers all facets of society and does stress discipleship, but a discipleship which has the pope as final approver and endorser.[114] Many persons at this point of history were seeking reform, but not all in the same way, and not all with the same focus on the very heart of the matter: gospel discipleship.

5. GENERAL OVERVIEW

The first four hundred years of the second millennium were filled with momentous events, and the above material has only touched on a few of them. "The last four mediaeval centuries, the twelfth through the fifteenth, witnessed a great increase in the power and wealth of the middle class, the rapid growth and then the slow decline of papal power, the beginnings of representative government in the towns and in the national assemblies of England, France, Germany and the Spanish States."[115] From the twelfth century on we have the steady appearances of a translated Aristotle with Arabic commentators. Medicine, law, art, music, literature and architecture found new meaning and new imaginative configurations. The mendicant friars, from the thirteenth century onward, played a major role in developing the spirituality of the ordinary people and offered a new sense of discipleship and gospel living. Currents, however, of nationalism and skepticism began to appear. New names of critical individuals appear: Dante, Marsiglio of Padua, William of Ockham, Wycklif and Hus. Critical corners were turned in other areas of western life beyond theology, philosophy and politics. Giotto changed the world of art; Landino changed the world of music; Petrarch and Boccacio in Italy, Chaucer in England changed the world of literature.[116] In the midst of this foment of culture, the Black Death stalked through Europe and devastated the population.

In the last of the medieval centuries, the Hundred Years' War came to an end. England became a limited monarchy and France an absolute one, with the Germanic form of a western empire in major disarray. Creativity continued apace with Brunelleschi, Donatello, and Leonardo da Vinci. Slowly the agricultural world of the west, with its feudal and ecclesiastical forms, turned into more urban and nationalistic forms. A state-controlled economy, often called mercantalism, began to appear, and strong efforts to have a state-controlled religion, not an empire-controlled religion, also began to take shape.

Who were the creators and formators of these new shapes to history? By and large they were lay men and lay women with new visions, new possibilities, new life goals. The *societas Christiana* remained a guiding form, of course, but both the structure—better, structures—of the *societas Christiana* were radically beginning to change, and these new forms of the Christian societies were on the cutting edge of change as well. New forms, however, were most often the result of reforms. Again and again, throughout this period of church history, the call had gone out: reform. The popes, as we saw, had staged a major reform movement, but in the end the movement had been too often channeled into the enhancement of the papacy. The history of two simple words, *plenitudo potestatis,* evidences this absolutistic drive of papal theology. There was, however, a geographically scattered appearance of various reform movements, some of which ended in a decree of heresy lodged against them, while others faded away, with their leader becoming a monk, or with their leadership itself not replicated. A few of these reform movements reactivated in a long-lasting way the *societas Christiana* of late medieval times. All of these reform movements had, each in its own way, spoken eloquently about discipleship and had stirred many a lay person to rethink his or her Christian life. This stress on personal discipleship had engendered a certain repositioning of the lay person within the *societas Christiana,* a repositioning not always appreciated by the clerical leadership since every repositioning involves a depositioning factor as well. Nonetheless, when one adds to this spiritual repositioning of the lay person an educated repositioning of the same spiritually attuned lay person, as also a monetarily improved status of this same spiritually attuned lay person, powerful energies were let loose within that *societas Christiana* which the clerical leadership was unable to restrain.

In an almost overwhelming way, it was the lay sector of the medieval *societas Christiana* which occasioned and fostered these changes. Only if one equates church to papacy and clergy would one say that the "secular" element brought on these changes. As we have seen above, this is an intolerable view of the church. Even though it is primarily lay men and lay women who engineered and steered so many of these changes in culture, they were men and women who belonged both spiritually and culturally to the *societas Christiana,* who belonged to the *congregatio fidelium,* who were, therefore, "church."

The repositioning of the lay person during this time was a repositioning toward strength within the *societas Christiana.* The theological and philosophical theorizing of this new role of lay person appears only at a later period, in a non-medieval period. At best, in the late medieval period we have only the start of this theorizing, as one finds in the writers who focused on the interplay of royal and papal power, or as one finds in the writings of Marsiglio of Padua, William of Ockham, and John Hus. But none of these efforts can be called a full-blown ecclesiology, nor were these efforts seen as the development of a totally secularized state over against a religious church. At the end of this period, the issue is no longer *regnum et sacerdotium,* but rather *regna et sacerdotium,* with a new emphasis on an emergent theoretical issue: *laicatus et sacerdotium,* i.e. a socially repositioned lay person within a restructured *societas Christiana*. The repositioning of the lay person, as mentioned above, necessarily involved a depositioning, in some degree, of the cleric. This presented the second major issue: a rethinking of *ordo* within the *societas Christiana*. Both of these issues will play major roles as the reform movements continue into that period of history which has been called "the reformation," but which is better described as a time of several major reformations, all of which stood in continuity with the reform movements that had been buffeting the *societas Christiana* since the turn of the millennium.

6. CONCLUSIONS FROM THE DATA

The following conclusions are not meant to be a summary of the material we have considered in this chapter. Rather, these conclusions are meant to indicate the significance of this important period in Christian church history as regards the changing role of the lay person in the church.

1. The geographically disparate reform movements indicate a deep desire on the part of many men and women for a form of discipleship that closely resembled that portrayed in the gospels. In spite of some eventual deviant and even heretical aspects in a few of these reform movements, these widespread reform movements gave enormous impetus to lay preaching, lay teaching, and lay spirituality.

2. The impetus for these movements of reform, which included all strata of society and included clerics and non-clerics, monks and nuns, and non-religious as well, continued into the fourteenth and fifteenth centuries. The Franciscan movement in particular, even with its splintering into various groups including the spirituals, the followers of Angelo of Clareno, the *Fraticelli* from Ancona and Tuscany under Henry of Ceva (*Fraticelli de paupere vita*) and the followers of Michael of Cesena and Bonagratia of Bergamo (*Fraticelli de opinione*), continually focused on the meaning of discipleship, *vita evangelica, vita apostolica*. Mainstream Franciscans were compelled to define their form of discipleship in contrast to these various other, sometimes extreme, forms of discipleship. With scholars such as Peter John Olivi and William of Ockham, the very issue of the poverty of Christ and the theological meaning of Christian discipleship came before popes such as Celestine V, Boniface VIII, Benedict XI, Clement V and above all John XXII. Papal responses occasioned at times an anti-papal reaction, which responded that the popes themselves were proposing a heretical view on discipleship. Once again, however, one finds this theme of discipleship at the very center of these reform movements in the church. Large numbers of lay men and lay women were

involved in this struggle to lead the simple gospel life, in spite of what certain popes, certain bishops and certain other religious leaders might say.

3. The German reform movement, the so-called Gregorian reform, which became so enmeshed in Gregory VII's agenda for the papacy and papal centrality, and which was continued so strongly by Innocent III, Innocent IV and Boniface VIII, in its struggle against simony, lay investiture and concubinate clergy both succeeded and failed. The ongoing condemnations of simony, lay investiture and a concubinate clergy, all of which from Gregory onward came to be called "heresies," which they most often were not, did, though quite eventually, create a hierarchy free in many ways from governmental interference and an eventually unmarried clergy, which, from Innocent III's time onward, was bound in law to an unmarried state. However, these gains did not really come to grips with the root reason for church reform. Discipleship, in the development of this particular reform movement, was a discipleship to papal determinations, with a pope accountable to no one. The Avignon papacy with its meteoric expansion of bureaucracy and its demands for money, the eventual division of the papacy into three separate claimants, each of whom had a right to the papacy and each of whom had a colored title to the papacy,[117] the resistance of Martin V and Eugene IV, even after the Council of Constance, to seeing the problems of the church except through a narrow papal view—all of these issues made the Gregorian reform less than successful.

4. The crusades gave a new position to knights and to the leaders of knights, as well as to those who assisted these warriors of God. The radical alteration by official church leadership on the position of war within the Christian view made such knights and their leaders and assistants key players in the history of salvation. This enhancement of the warrior was a powerful repositioning for the better of many a lay man and lay woman in the structures of church life.

5. The activity of scholars, defending either the imperial position or the papal position of power within the *societas Christiana*, brought an enormous amount of thought to the issue of church, church structure, the role of the cleric, especially the pope and to some degree the bishops, and by contrast the role of the imperial or regal leader and to some degree the role of the ordinary lay person within this *societas Christiana*. In this intellectual ferment, words, phrases, concepts and ideas were all being formulated, which in the period after 1500 gave rise to what we today could call a "theology of the church" or an "ecclesiology." When one realizes that under the influence of Alexander of Hales, particularly, a definition of priest was developed, which centered the priest on the power

to celebrate the eucharist and in a secondary degree on the power to forgive sins, and that Alexander's position eventually became the common position among the theologians and canonists of the time, one finds that another central piece of intellectual moment was set in place: namely, a commonly-accepted definition of priest *against which* an eventual description of lay person came to be seen, i.e. one who does not have the power to celebrate the eucharist nor have the power to forgive sins.

6. Marsiglio of Padua, more than any other writer of this period, dramatically called into question seemingly central aspects of church structure. In doing this, Marsiglio gave great impetus, not immediately because of his condemnation, but in the course of time to a rethinking of the fundamental meaning of church and the role that the ordinary lay man and lay woman play in this church, as also the role of priest and sacrament.

7. Not since the first four centuries of church life do the names of influential women appear with such frequency. In many ways the growth in a strong western mystical tradition accounts for this, as we have seen with Hildegard of Bingen, Mechtild of Magdeburg and Elizabeth of Schönau, but also with a Clare of Assisi, a Catherine of Siena, a Bridgit of Sweden, an Agnes of Prague. Moreover, the geographically scattered reform movements at times consisted predominantly of women. There can be no doubt that the Beguines presented a "women's issue" in its own day. Berengaria Donas, Amoda of Limoge, Maria de Serra and Astruga Renundaria were apocalyptic in their writings; they expressed strong anti-John XXII statements, who in their view was the mystic antichrist, and they were ideologically caught up with the expectation of an "angelic pope," whom, they predicted, would soon be elected to the chair of Peter. The large numbers of "ordinary" non-apocalyptic Beguines and Beghards, with their stress on the simple and prayerful life, cannot be dismissed as a quirk of history. Rather, these women and men were witnesses to a strong current among the laity for a gospel spirituality, a gospel form of discipleship, which they did not find in either the clerical church structures or in the monastic structures of their time.

8. The rise of the universities, with an ever-growing number of lay people in attendance, provided a small but strong base of educated lay men, and to a smaller degree of lay women, who began to question positions taken by the clerical leadership of the church. This was a questioning, not out of frustration or anger, but out of knowledge and research. There is no doubt that the rise of an influential educated lay stratum within the *societas Christiana* was a major impetus for the repositioning of the lay person in the church. The culture of the renaissance, even in its extremes, witnesses to the intellectual and artistic creativity of the lay

person. With this meteoric change in culture, the lay-creator, that is, the artist, the writer, the musician, the architect, etc., as also the lay persons who supported these creative people, found new and powerful positions within the *societas Christiana.*

9. The rise of a merchant class, both politically and economically, eventually affected the ways in which the church structures of power were conceived. The Christian church is indeed a spiritual entity, animated by the Holy Spirit, but this spiritual entity is as well an historical entity and as such has a history. This history is not some meta-historical sphere of salvation, but it is an incarnated history within socio-political and economic structures. These various aspects of human history mutually affect each other in each era of history. Thus the rise of merchants in this era clearly affected the way the spiritual Church of Christ could exist within human history, and, it should be noted with great emphasis, the merchants by and large were lay men and to some degree lay women.

10. At the turn of the fifteenth century, the European world had begun to develop a new sense of *polis* and of citizenship in this *polis.* In the socio-political and economic framework, more and more people saw themselves as citizens who should have a say in the way their lives were governed. We might not find democracies rampant at this juncture of history, with freedom and equality for all involved, but there was an incipient democratic spirit. The term "republic" seems to correspond more to the actual political structure of these times, but with diverse nuances both in meaning and in practice. In the theological world, the scholars and ecclesiastics never came to grips with this changing reality. *Polis* and *civis* were strange bedfellows for the ecclesiastical structures. The clergy's lack of understanding and of study as regards the changing social world of both the city and the citizen mentality, which clearly affected the identity of a very influential sector of the lay person of that time, had serious consequences in the period 1500 to 1900 and beyond. The new self-identity of the human person within a socio-political world will time after time confront an ecclesiastically paternalistic position, an ecclesiastically monarchical position, which envisions children and subjects, not mature human beings who have an innate freedom and dignity. We will see that this lack of understanding, which exhibited itself on the part of church leadership in a continual attitude of father to child, monarch to subject, became as the decades went by not only increasingly anachronistic, but also increasingly antagonistic, and on the basis of gospel discipleship theologically indefensible.

11. The papacy continued to be rather galvanized around the theme of *regnum et sacerdotium.* The rights and prerogatives of the popes, the rights and prerogatives of the Roman curia, over against the rights and

prerogatives of the emperor, the various kingdoms and even the emerging city-states, remained a most sensitive issue. This focus on *regnum et sacerdotium,* however, was not merely on the pope and an emperor or a king. It was not and could not be a struggle between two personages. Rather, the role of the papacy could only be maintained if there were concomitantly a strong *sacerdotium,* both episcopal and presbyteral. In other words, the positioning of the pope in this interplay of *regnum et sacerdotium* was only possible by a continued positioning of the entire *sacerdotium.* Such a positioning of both pope and *sacerdotium,* of course, required that the non-ordained sector remain more or less in its counter-position. If the non-ordained part of the Church were to be repositioned into a more strengthened lay structure, the ordained part of the church, both pope and *sacerdotium,* would be to some degree depositioned and destrengthened. The papal struggle to prevent any dimunition of power and position included a struggle to prevent any dimunition of sacerdotal power and position, and, as a consequence, this included a struggle to prevent any growth in non-ordained power and position. It is unfortunate that the issue of *regnum et sacerdotium* continued to play such a centralizing role, for this emphasis prevented church leadership from attending to its real focus: gospel discipleship.

10

The Reformation
and Tridentine Churches
and Their Aftermath: 1500 to 1800 A.D.

Rather than a single Protestant reformation, there were in the sixteenth century several reformations, each of which had historical links with the various reform movements of the preceding centuries, and each of which had differing characteristics as well. It is painfully clear today that this sixteenth century climate of reform created a situation in the Christian church which down to the present day remains a major Christian scandal. In the Vatican II decree on ecumenism, *Unitatis redintegratio,* we read:

> Certainly, such division openly contradicts the will of Christ, scandalizes the world, and damages that most holy cause, the preaching of the gospel, to every creature (n. 1).

How much this fragmented Christianity is truly considered de facto a scandal is however debatable, since most western churches today de facto do not consider ecumenical endeavors a very high priority, much less the highest priority, on their respective agenda. One would think that a scandal which damages the preaching of the gospel would energize all the various Christian churches and that the deep desire for unity of the gospel would urge the various factions to overcome this scandalous situation. Once in a while—for example, during the immediate aftermath of Vatican II—ecumenical issues have received high priority, even at the highest levels of ecclesial structures, such as the Secretariat for the Promotion of the Unity of Christians on the part of the Roman Catholic Church and the

Lambeth Conference on the part of the Anglican Church. Efforts by the World Council of Churches, particularly in the formation and publication of the document *Baptism, Eucharist and Ministry,* should be noted. Here and there, in less international and more localized ways, other moments might also be mentioned. Still, for the most part, western Christian churches today continue to operate with a "business as usual" attitude in spite of the "scandal."

These sixteenth century reformations which fractured the Christian community in such a major way were highly complex and can be understood only when one takes into account not simply religious and theological issues, but also the socio-political, economic and nationalistic aspects of the western world at that time, as well as the foment in education and culture generally. One must also candidly admit that the reform movements of the prior centuries had met with only measured success. Even the so-called Gregorian reform, sponsored so strongly by the papacy, avoided the issue of reform *in capite,* stressing rather reform *in membris,* and more often than not certain groups of members received greater stress as regards reform than other groups. The leadership and at times the misdirected leadership of the Roman Catholic Church in the thirteenth to fifteenth centuries, then, must be reckoned as a partial cause for the multiple reform movements of the sixteenth century. Many other factors were also causative in nature, but it certainly cannot be said that the sixteenth century reform movements simply arose from within the Roman Catholic Church in a totally unexpected and unexplainable way.

Nor can it be said, apropos to the theme of this volume, that the issue of the lay person in the church was the key issue that sparked these various sixteenth century reformations. Deeper issues were at stake, but these deeper issues did indeed have repercussions on the theology of the lay person within the Christian church. In the study on the lay person in Christian history, sponsored by the World Council of Churches, several of the authors make a strong opening statement to their respective contributions as regards the reformation and the lay person.

E. Gordon Rupp:	That the layman has no mere walk-on part in the drama of the Reformation is self evident.[1]
Martin Schmidt:	[The age of orthodoxy] maintained the new positions which Luther and Calvin and their colleagues had won for cleric and layman, for office-bearer and for voluntary worker alike.[2]

Peter Meinold: The emancipation of the layman began
                       in the period of the Reformation.[3]
Stephen Neill: It has become a commonplace of histo-
                       rians that the Reformation was in large
                       measure the layman's reformation.[4]

These are all generous statements on the issue of the lay person in the church and its historical connection to the reformation and indicate that the theme of the lay person in the church was indeed a factor within the reformation foment of the sixteenth century. This theme, nonetheless, was not the central theme or issue of the reformation debate. In the following pages let us consider this theme of the lay person in the church at the time of the reformation in more depth, and we do so with all the caveats previously mentioned: namely, that the sixteenth century reformations occurred because of a complex interconnection of spiritual, political, cultural and intellectual forces, that the causality for these reformations was multiplex in nature, and that this multiple-sourced causality included the insufficiency of the previous reform movements.

In this chapter, then, our search for the theological meaning of the lay person and lay ministry in the Christian church will cover the following issues:

1. **The Lay Person in the Writings of Martin Luther**
2. **The Lay Person in the Writings of John Calvin**
3. **The Lay Person in the Writings of the Anglican Communion**
4. **The Lay Person in the Writings of the Radical Reformers**
5. **The Lay Person in the Documents of the Council of Trent**
6. **The Lay Person in the Roman Catholic Theology and Ministry in Tridentinism**
7. **The Lay Person from 1700 to the Eve of the French Revolution**
8. **General Overview**
9. **Conclusions from the Data**

The metaphor of the seashore and the tides is highly evident during this period of church history, for these sixteenth century reform movements were like an inward tidal flow, causing an enormous battering to the status quo, the seashore. The contour of the western Christian church was radically changed, just as the inward tides at times radically alter the contour of the strand. These radical changes included an altered structuring of the cleric and, above all, an altered structuring of the lay person within the Christian community.

Discipleship, the major criterion which we have used throughout this study, played a central role. The various Protestant reformers critiqued the Roman Catholic leadership precisely on the issue of discipleship. The strong indictment of the Roman Catholic leadership over such issues as the absolute gratuity of God's grace, the process of justification, and the complete adequacy of the work of Christ, to name only a few of the major themes of this indictment, created a situation among these early reformers which was both personally and theologically of profound import. These early reformers had all belonged to the Roman Catholic Church. It was in this Roman Catholic Church structure that they had developed spiritually and intellectually. These reformers, however, came to the conclusion that it was impossible to be a disciple of the Lord and *at the same time* remain within the Roman Catholic structure. They came to realize that there was indeed true discipleship, not outside the Christian church, but outside the Roman Catholic Church structure. They did not come to the conclusion that there were two ways of being a true disciple of the Lord: one within the Roman Catholic community and one without it. True discipleship, for them, could only be found in taking fundamental issue with the way in which the Roman Catholic leadership at that time propounded discipleship. In taking issue, these reformers categorically stated that under Roman Catholic leadership true discipleship of the Lord had been vitiated.

In response, the Roman Catholic leadership in the sixteenth century had to defend its propounding of discipleship, and they did so not by stating that the reform communities were also a form of true Christian discipleship, but rather in stating that the reform communities were themselves false forms of Christian discipleship.

In the ecumenical spirit of the present century, one speaks of the "wider Christian church," and of "ecclesial communities," in which one does not find heretics, schismatics, and such like, but rather in which one finds Christian brothers and sisters. In today's Christian world, one can more readily (though not in every instance) speak of Christian discipleship outside of one's own denomination. This was not the situation in reformation times. True discipleship was an either-or situation: either with one of the reform groups or with the Roman Catholic group. It was not a both-and situation: both in one of the reform groups and in the Roman Catholic group. Even in the various reform groups, not all were of one mind on the issue of discipleship, so that certain Protestant reform groups condemned other Protestant reform groups as advocating a false form of discipleship.

In the sixteenth century, both the reform groups and the Roman Catholic groups defended their positions on discipleship on the basis of:

a. a true reading of the scriptures;

b. a true living out of the sacramental life of the church.

The scriptured word played a decisive role in the reformers' program, while the magisterial word played a decisive role in the Roman Catholic program. In both programs, however, the meaning of discipleship was at the heart of their respective *apologiae pro vita nostra.*

1. THE LAY PERSON IN THE WRITINGS OF MARTIN LUTHER

Martin Luther did not initiate his call for reform on the issue of the lay person's theological position in the church. Rather, Luther's primary and originative concern appears to have been his theological concern regarding the process of reconciliation or, as he called it, more often than not, the process of justification. However, if this is his reform basis, it is difficult to accept the fundamental issue in Erik Erikson's thesis that Luther's primary personal motivation came from an oppressive childhood.[5] Rather, it seems, both religious (not merely theological) and cultural issues present a more secure historical basis for Luther's initial searchings and positionings than any psychologizing on Luther's youth and early development.[6]

These few pages on Luther and the issue of the theological and pastoral role of the lay person in the church are divided as follows:

a. Luther's Basic Theological Direction

b. Luther's Challenge to the Issue of *Ordo*

c. Luther's Challenge to the Issue of *Plenitudo Potestatis*

d. Luther's Position on the Issue of *Regna et Sacerdotium*

e. Luther's Position on Christian Discipleship: The Priesthood of All Believers

As one readily sees, each of these issues takes up the key threads which have been woven through this volume on the theological and pastoral role of the lay person in the Church.

A. LUTHER'S BASIC THEOLOGICAL DIRECTION

A study of Luther's 1517 *Disputation Against Scholastic Theology,* which was his last work prior to the ninety-five theses, deserves special consideration, since it indicates in so many ways the foundational theological issues which Luther had at this precise period of his life found questionable in scholastic theology, namely, those theological issues which had been influencing in a profound though varied way both the practical and pastoral life of the late medieval church as well as the theological discussions of the late fifteenth century.[7] The issue of the relationship between grace and forgiveness of sin was a major theme in this disputation of Luther, and in his probings he challenged some of the positions which late medieval theology had formulated.

Luther made these challenges to the theological issues on grace and reconciliation on the basis of an even deeper issue: the theological presentation of God, which they attempted to clarify.

> The center of Luther's understanding of Christianity is the proclamation of a God who is both hidden and revealed. . . . Luther's view of the hiddenness of God is intimately connected with his view of faith. The fundamental human predicament is unbelief. Men and women will not put their ultimate trust in God, will not receive their lives as a gift from God, but place their ultimate trust in themselves, in their world.[8]

This view by David Steinmetz that the theological center of Luther's understanding of the Christian life was the proclamation of a hidden but revealed God is certainly true as far as it goes. There is more to God than hiddenness, however, for in and behind this hiddenness of God, Luther was expressing an absolute freedom on the part of God. The hidden God is a God who is not only hidden, but a God whom humans cannot manipulate through works, through rituals, through theological disputations. To say that God is hidden is, accordingly, not quite adequate. On the other hand, to say that God is the fullness of freedom, and that God is infinitely free, relativizes all theological speculation about God and relativizes all ritualistic worship of God. The absolute gratuity of God's grace is based on the absolute freedom of God, and it is precisely this issue which caused Luther to react so strongly against many of the Roman Catholic positions, both theological and pastoral, which in his view placed the church above the freedom of God. God is indeed hidden, but his hiddenness is due to the unfathomable and infinite freedom of God, and in Luther's mind this needs to be spelled out and maintained in both theory and practice.

In a quite similar vein, J. Pelikan begins his volume on Luther in the following way:

> The institutions of medieval Christendom were in trouble, and everyone knew it. Intended as windows through which men

might catch a glimpse of the Eternal, they had become opaque, so that the faithful looked at them rather than through them. The structures of the Church were supposed to act as vehicles for the spirit—both for the Spirit of God and for the spirit of man. . . . Instead what he [man] found was a distortion of the faith. . . . Captive in ecclesiastical structures that no longer served as channels of divine life and means of divine grace, the spiritual power of the Christian gospel pressed to be released. The pressure exploded in the Reformation.[9]

When Pelikan speaks of the Spirit of God, he is clearly speaking about a Spirit which is ultimately hidden, by nature infinite and absolutely free. On the other hand, Pelikan argues, five ecclesial structures of the historical church were, in some ways, "integral elements of the one holy catholic and apostolic Church" as Christians "had known it and believed in it for more than a millennium."[10] On the basis of Luther's key volume, *The Babylonian Captivity of the Church,* published in 1520, Pelikan traces the fate of each of these structures in the reforming foment which Luther's leadership created. In this treatise, Luther had pressed for the elevation of spirit over structure, so basic to his reform movement. As we are painfully aware, this reform movement, as also several others in the sixteenth century, became not simply movements of reform, but churches in their own right. Because of this transformation from reform movement to self-standing church, one must honestly ask, as Pelikan honestly does:

Did the elevation of spirit over structure in this treatise contain within itself the institution-building power necessary for the establishment and maintenance of a proper ministry? Or could these new churches perhaps dispense with institutional life and become communities of the Holy Spirit in which the only structure was the free exercise of the universal priesthood of all believers?[11]

Pelikan's questions are acutely apropos, for they raise the question about certain forms of the institutionality of the church. In his work *On the Papacy in Rome* (1520), Luther refers to "two Churches," the spiritual church and the physical or external church.[12] Luther, like most of his contemporaries, realized that the church existed and could exist only in an external and institutional form. Part of this institutional church included ministry, but there is ministry only if there are some who minister to others. The ecclesial structure of the "ministers" and the "ministered to" involves the same dynamics in Luther's works as the *klerikos/laikos* issue had done for centuries. The fact that Pelikan ends his questions with the phrase "priesthood of all believers" indicates that the elevation of spirit over structure, the defense of the hidden and absolutely free God vis-à-vis the historical forms of God's revelation, has fundamental ramifications as regards all basic ecclesial structures of the Christian church, one of which was the theological and pastoral role of the lay person. Luther's starting point is clearly not the theological and pastoral role of the lay person, but it is also quite obvious that the theological and pastoral role of the lay person eventually becomes a major derivative issue in Luther's description of church.

As Luther's career moved beyond 1517, beyond the *Disputation Against Scholastic Theology,* and even beyond *The Babylonian Captivity of the Church,* these foundational issues of the hiddenness and freedom of God and the elevation of Spirit over structure quite naturally raised major questions regarding the theological meaning of church, particularly the theological meaning of the sacraments as the ecclesial means of grace par excellence and the sacramental meaning of the priest as the "mediator" of reconciling grace. In the sacramental system, in both its theological and its liturgical formulation at the time of Luther, various as these actually were, the dominant role of the priest was continually evident, and the passive role of the recipient of the sacraments, most often the non-cleric, was also continually evident. For Luther, the ways in which priests were presented as "ministers," even "mediators" of God's grace, and the ways in which the sacramental actions themselves were presented as "means" of grace *ex opere operato* raised serious questions in his mind as regards the absolute freedom of God and therefore the absolute gratuity of God's grace, on the one hand, and, on the other hand, the absolute sufficiency of Christ's work, as one finds in the revealed word of God. The usual, late medieval, although by no means uniform, theological presentations on the role of the priest in the sacramental action and the usual, late medieval, but again by no means uniform, presentations on the role of the sacramental action itself appeared to Luther as compromising some basic New Testament truths. In other terms, the very word of God was being compromised by theological and liturgical words of men. Structure was elevated above Spirit.

In Luther's rejection of these Pelagian and non-scriptural approaches to grace and the forgiveness of sin, he could not help but challenge the then common understandings of the priestly role. This challenge to the priestly role, however, led necessarily to a similar challenge of the then common theological understanding of the lay person's role in the church. The interconnection of these ideas, it seems to me, is vitally important if one wishes to understand Luther's statements on the lay person in the church. Perhaps, the following outline might clarify this interrelationship:

1. Luther radically questioned the late medieval, theological and liturgical formulations on God and the Spirit of God, which in his view compromised the very hiddenness, i.e. absolute freedom of God; he took an adamant stance on the superiority of God's revelation, found in the scriptured word of God; and as a consequence he demanded a relativizing of the role of the church, whose existence should be that of a window for this gracious, but absolutely free and hidden God. These issues posed fundamental questions on the structures of the *societas Christiana* of his day.

2. These basic issues formed the basis to his questions on the relationship between the gratuity of God's grace and the absolute sufficiency of the salvific revelation of Christ, on the one hand, and the forgiveness of sin and the sanctification of the human person, on the other. These issues informed his quest for ecclesial reform.

3. This radical questioning led to a radical challenge of the then-contemporary theological positions regarding the role of the priest and the role of the sacramental action itself in this process of reconciliation.

4. The challenge to the meaning of priest in this process occasioned a rethinking of the theological role of the lay person in the church.

As one readily sees, the issue of the lay person in Luther's writings, at least in the first half of his reform career, was not the center of his focus, but it was not peripheral either. As he struggled to integrate the absolute gratutity of God's grace and the complete satisfactory value of Christ's life and death into each area of theological thought, both the theological and the pastoral role of the lay person in the church of necessity came under scrutiny.

B. LUTHER'S CHALLENGE TO THE ISSUE OF ORDO

Two fundamental themes regarding the clerical world appear in the writings of Luther, but they do not appear with approbation. The first theme is *ordo*. The second theme is the *plenitudo potestatis*. As regards the issue of *ordo*, once again Dionysius the Areopagite enters the arena. When Luther published *An den christlichen Adel deutscher Nation von des christlichen Standes Besserung* (1520), the theme of the universal priesthood came to the fore. Luther had mentioned the priesthood of all believers in earlier writings, but with this treatise it became an ecclesio-political weapon, "showing that the spiritual estate was neither above the temporal estate—nor above being reformed by it."[13] In a central way, both Dionysius' *De ecclesiastica hierarchia* and his *De coelesti hierarchia* were used in an almost canonical way by the first wave of Roman Catholic scholars who challenged this early position of Luther: namely by Jodocus Clichtoveus, Johannes Cochlaeus, Marcello Cervini, John Fisher, Johannes Dietenberger, Lambertus Campester, Thomas Rhadinus, Edward Powell and Johannes Fabri. All of these men, identifying this Dionysius with St. Paul's Athenian disciple, accepted the authority of Dionysius as untouchable, first-hand evidence that from the very beginning of the church there was a threefold ministry, based on the order of creation.[14] The same view of *ordo,* as an ontological given, was also to be found in the *Peri hierosynes* of John Chrysostom, and Hieronymus Emser, who likewise was among the first to be called on to refute Luther's claims, cited passage after passage from Chrysostom's work.

> As the soul excels the body, so does the priesthood excel the lay estate.[15]

> The priest has no equal on earth for he who brings salvation to princes is greater than princes.[16]

> The role of the laity is subordinate: to provide for the physical needs of priests and to defend and protect them.[17]

> Priests are superior even to heavenly powers.[18]

Emser concludes: In short, the superiority of priests to people is not just permitted by Christianity, it is its very soul and foundation.[19] In John Chrysostom's view, he argues, there is an order or ranking which is not only in the moral order but in the very order of creation itself. To this ontological order belong priests and bishops.

Ministry, in Luther's approach, was not an *ordo* (*Stand*) but a service (*Amt*). Nowhere in the scriptures did he find a basis for any ontologizing of ministry; nowhere in scripture did he find that the ministers are a separate caste, a higher form of disciple, an *ordo.* Luther expressed his views as follows:

> We neither can nor ought to give the name priest to those who are in charge of Word and sacrament among the people. The reasons they have been called priests is either because of the

custom of the heathen people or as a vestige of the Jewish nation. The result is greatly injurious to the church. According to the New Testament Scriptures better names would be ministers, deacons, bishops, stewards, presbyters. . . . Paul's frequent use of the word "stewardship" or "household," "ministry," "minister" "servant," "one serving with the gospel," etc. emphasizes that it is not the estate, or order, or any authority or dignity that he wants to uphold, but only the office and the function.[20]

Using the comprehensive study of Hellmut Lieberg on Luther's position regarding ministry, *Amt und Ordination bei Luther und Melanchthon,* Robert Kolb notes that Luther himself found three major distortions in the medieval concepts of priesthood, all of which, one might add, derived basically from the concept of *ordo:*

1. priests are agents, rendering satisfaction to God and thereby controlling God's grace;
2. priests are agents of a justification through good works;
3. priests are placed in a hierarchy (*ordo*) making them superior to the laity.[21]

Often, however, it is easier to state what Luther opposed than to state what Luther proposed. This is particularly true as regards Luther's view of priest (minister) and consequently as regards his view of the lay person's role in the church. During his long career as theologian and writer, his theological and pastoral views on the relationship of priest and lay person changed, so that it is difficult to obtain from the corpus of his abundant writings a uniform understanding of the lay/cleric issue. Bernhard Lohse attempts to outline these fluctuations as follows:

From 1517 to 1520 Luther was in conflict with the authorities of the church and developed his concept of the universal priesthood of the baptized.

The period 1520 to 1523 began with the breaking off of relationships between Luther and Rome and is characterized by Luther's polemic against the priesthood and the sacrifice of the Mass.

Beginning in 1524 Luther was constantly in opposition to the enthusiasts.

After 1530 the Reformation developed under less-conflicted conditions. In this context, Luther developed a comprehensive structure of Protestant church and was increasingly able to realize it in practice. He now emphasized the coordination of the office of the ministry, ordination and the church.[22]

Ordo, as we saw previously, had become for both later patristic and medieval theology the hermeneutic through which the term "cleric" was interpreted. It is precisely this hermeneutical use of *ordo* which Luther challenges. For Luther the hermeneutic to understand both the "cleric" and the "lay" person remained the New Testament, in which the Greek word *kleros* never applied to a ministry or minister, and the Greek word *laikos* never even appeared at all. On the other hand, Luther does not in any way promote a congregational form of Christianity in which there are no ministers. The scriptured word of God speaks otherwise, and this was enough for him. It was not precisely the issue of a "clerical ministry" which brought about Luther's challenge, but it was the establishment of a priestly and episcopal *ordo,* with its power structures, not merely over the people of God, but above all else over the Spirit of God, which grieved Luther. Remove the notion of *ordo* (*Stand*), and one has left a notion of ministry (*Amt*). From the medieval standpoint, however, such a view was clearly a depositioning of the clergy, and with every depositioning of one side of the *klerikos/laikos* equation, the other side, here the lay side, was of necessity repositioned and in this case for the better. This is precisely what Luther intended to bring about.

C. LUTHER'S CHALLENGE TO THE ISSUE OF *PLENITUDO POTESTATIS*

In Luther's treatise, *An den Adel,* he condemned the "three walls" which popes had used to keep the *societas Christiana* subject to the papacy.

The **first wall** was the claim of the pope to temporal power over earthly rulers. This claim, as we have seen, is first enunciated by Innocent IV, but its roots go back to earlier popes. In other words, such a claim was a mid-medieval claim at best and was never accepted by the imperialist theologians. Nonetheless, Boniface VIII was certainly ready to assert such a claim and he did so on several occasions, but with disastrous results.

The **second wall** was the claim that the pope, ultimately, enjoyed the sole right to interpret scripture. This claim had arisen, as we have seen, when some of the geographically scattered reform groups began to read scriptural passages, either in Latin or in the vernacular, and expound on these passages in a faith-sharing way. Little by little, the Roman Catholic leadership tried to make all scriptural interpretation its own prerogative, and thereby control "misinterpretations" of scripture.

The third wall was the claim of the pope to be the sole person who could call a council. This claim, too, had a long history, but, particularly in medieval times, several councils had been called by non-popes in times of crisis. After the Council of Constance popes had been quite unwilling to call councils, even though Constance had required councils on a regular basis. This conflict was and is, in part, the conflict between pope and bishops, and agitates the Roman Church even today in the papacy's nervousness over episcopal collegiality.

Luther's descriptions of the "three walls" focus on issues of power, issues which were neither original to Luther, nor confined to Luther's times. From history we are well aware that there had been an ongoing confrontation between papal power and regal or imperial power. That the *plenitudo potestatis* doctrine expressed by some popes was challenged was nothing new. In the relationship between Luther and the leadership of the Roman Catholic Church, however, Luther's challenge, and the tone of the challenge, affected the lines of communication between the two sides: Rome and Luther.

1. In making his case on basic theological and liturgical positions, Luther inevitably challenged the authority of both the pope and the bishops, and he did so, on many occasions, in a rather strident way. As a result of these challenges to authority and the stridency in which they were clothed, the pope and many bishops responded more often than not in a highly defensive way. On many occasions it became not a defense of the basic theological issues which Luther was promoting, but rather a defense of the rightfulness of church authority, i.e. papal and episcopal authority. This is one of the many tragedies which occurred at this time, namely that on several key occasions the focus was turned away from the theological issues and turned almost exclusively to the issue of ecclesiastical authority and power, including the issue of *plenitudo potestatis*. One sees this translation of focus in a marked way during the debates at the Council of Trent, when such fundamental theological issues as the meaning of the term "faith," a meaning which separated Luther's view from the Augustinian-scholastic view, were never directly confronted. One sees this also in the

way the bishops at Trent constructed both the chapters, but particularly the canons, of their decrees, as is evident in the chapter and canons on the sacrament of penance.[23] This pattern of refocusing the issue on the question of authority rather than on the precise theological question was also operative in the discussions held by key Roman Catholic figures with either Luther himself or with one of Luther's followers. Whenever one took up a defense of church authority, which was in practice the authority of the cleric or more specifically the authority of the priest/bishop/pope, the role of the lay person in the church could not help but be left to one side or even to a certain degree downgraded by those who were defending clerical authority.

2. The defense of ecclesiastical authority, made by the church leadership of Luther's time, resulted in an over-focus on authority, on an overly defensive stress of the clerical role within the church, and consequently on an overly defensive stress against any lay erosion of this clerical role. The history of the opening of the Council of Trent makes this quite clear. H. Jedin notes:

> The fact that the Pope [Paul III] was filled with anxiety lest his authority should be tampered with at Trent, is abundantly proved by the frequent directives to the legates not to tolerate any narrowing of the papal authority, even in small matters, such as the granting of indulgences.[24]

Instead of facing the long-disputed issue regarding the limits of papal authority, Paul III took the opposite approach: no limitation to papal authority at all, even in small matters. Through this maneuvering, *reformatio in capite* was radically circumvented.

Besides the papal defense of authority, one can also find at Trent a defense of episcopal authority, e.g. when the bishops at Trent were faced with a "reformation position" which called into question previous episcopal determinations, such as a determination of a particular sacramental rite. Many Tridentine bishops bristled at the very thought that episcopal authority would be rejected, even though historical study at a later date has indicated that the previous bishops could have only determined such an issue, as for instance the use of oil in confirmation, or the establishment of certain sacramental formulae, *iure humano,* and if bishops had acted only in virtue of human law, then these laws can be called into question.

All of these various defensive positionings by the then contemporary church clerical leadership gave rise to a counter-emphasis regarding the theological and pastoral role of the lay person in the church. This counter-emphasis was formulated not only by Luther but by almost every reform voice of the time. The overly defensive, pro-clerical stance of church leadership elicited a challenging pro-lay stance on the part of all reformers. In other words, the Roman Catholic defense of clerical authority abetted the very issue it was trying to counter, namely the issue of lay authority in the church.

3. Neither theologically nor pastorally did Luther at first reject either the role of the papacy or the role of episcopacy. In other words, he had no initial rejection per se of a clerical role within the church.[25] Throughout the fifteenth century there had already been many voices against popes, but not against the papacy itself. The Joachimite-inspired dream of the apocalyptic appearance of "angel popes," among whom Celestine V was considered by many to be the first, indicates that historically criticism of the pope was part of the medieval air, but this did not necessarily mean criticism of the papacy as such. The criticism of simoniacal bishops had been endemic since 1000, without at the same time a radical criticism of episcopacy as such. Even the criticism of concubinate priests did not include an outright rejection of priesthood. The clerical criticism which Luther voiced simply followed this rather common pattern. On the other hand, as we have noted above, there was no extant theology of the church, i.e. no ecclesiology, available either to Luther or to those he challenged.[26] As we have seen, there were only snippets of such a thematized theology of the church, some of them tending on the one hand to defend the *plenitudo potestatis* of the pope, and some of them tending on the other hand to defend the role of the emperor/king within the *societas Christiana*. Only in the course of the continuing challenge of ecclesiastical authority, both from the side of the imperial theologians, which had been going on prior to the sixteenth century, and from the sixteenth century on from the side of the emerging reform theologians, did various articulated and thematized theologies of the Church (ecclesiologies) begin to take formal shape, and the later shaping of these various theologies reflected, of course, the differing positions: i.e. the papal/episcopal position, the imperial/regal position, and, as a new element, the emergent reform positions. Luther's views were incorporated in only some of these later ecclesiologies, and one cannot say that Luther's views were the most dominant ones among Protestant ecclesiologies. The papal claim to *plenitudo potestatis,* not accepted by the imperialist theologians of late medieval and early reformation times, and not accepted by the eastern churches, was also not accepted by the ecclesiologies which developed from the various Protestant reforms.[27] God alone has the *plenitudo potestatis,* and a share in this fullness of power is given first of all to God's church. A claim for *plenitudo potestatis* which has within it the possibility of subjugating Spirit to structure, of

manipulating the absolutely free God, of making the freedom of grace depend on the finite will of a "minister," of making the work of Christ inadequate for the salvation of the world—such a claim, Luther would say, has no Christian value at all.

D. LUTHER'S POSITION ON THE ISSUE OF *REGNA ET SACERDOTIUM*

The social teaching of Luther has been widely debated over the last one hundred years. W. Dilthey, E. Troeltsch and M. Weber all delved into Luther's writings and argued their respective positions, but with differing conclusions. Was Luther merely a late medieval person or was he truly a modern pioneer? The answer to this question may never be established in a totally satisfactory way, but Luther's approach did give rise to some currents which, in the course of time at least, bolstered a modern approach to social life. One can, it seems, agree with Troeltsch that four areas in Luther's thinking abetted the modern approach to western life.

1. First of all, Luther's attack on the idealization of celibacy and monasticism did enhance the role of marriage and the family, and this enhancement changed the theology of the lay person. However, Luther continued to envision marriage in a paternalistic way, so that the role of wife remained well within the medieval pattern.
2. Secondly, Luther's opposition to many church laws did enhance the role of civil law. However, the notion of an authoritarian political ruler finds a deep rootage in Luther's approach.
3. Luther's evaluation of secular life and secular work enhanced the theological role of the lay person. However, Luther remained focused on the agrarian forms of work, whereas Calvin moved into more urbanized forms of labor. It is also noteworthy that the picturing of Luther surrounded by peasants, such as one sees in Sebastian Beham's drawings, began to disappear after the Peasants' Revolt, against which Luther had taken a strong stand.
4. Lastly, humanistic education was to some degree fostered by Luther, an education which eventually developed a strong nonclerical educated lay group, but in other ways Luther was as opposed to humanism as he was opposed to scholasticism.

To these four, one could add that Luther did not advocate a clean-cut division between the church and the state. "Neither is sufficient in the world without the other," Luther wrote in *Temporal Authority: To What Extent It Should Be Obeyed.*[28] In Luther's writings there are indeed the two kingdoms: that of God and that of Satan, but these two kingdoms struggle for dominance both in the church and in government. At one and the same time the devil wants to be both pope and emperor, and at one and the same time both pope and emperor should be striving to be filled with the grace of God. Just as in the writings of Augustine the city of God and the city of man do not correspond to the Christian church and the Roman empire, so, too, in Luther's writings the doctrine of the two kingdoms does not correspond to the actual historical church and the actual historical government. Similarly, lay/cleric, in Luther's writings, cannot be seen along the same divide as kingdom of God/kingdom of the devil. God's kingdom is both lay and cleric, and the devil's kingdom is also both lay and cleric.[29]

The various controversies which rocked the German lands at the time of Luther created not only a theological foment but a political foment as well. Certain rulers sided with Rome; others sided with the evangelicals, the name which Luther's followers first used. In this clash, both sides had recourse to political power on many occasions. Just as the western church, from the time of Pepin onward, had experienced an ambiguity in its relationship to the emperor, and then to various kings, so, too, the same dynamics of ambiguity beset both the Roman side and the Lutheran side in the sixteenth century. Nonetheless, whether one, either from the Roman side or from the Lutheran side, is reading the complicated history of this relationship of *regna et sacerdotium* in the sixteenth century, one must keep in mind that the term "church" cannot theologically be used exclusively for the *sacerdotium*, leaving the *regna* as non-church. A totally non-Christian or totally secularized state did not exist in the west at this period of history. For both Luther and for his Roman protagonists, the *societas Christiana* was of one piece. We have seen above several occasions when the governments were treated, especially by church historians, as though they were the enemies of the church, i.e. the non-church. Even the bull of Boniface VIII, *Clericis laicos,* implied this kind of antagonism. Nonetheless, both spheres, *regna et sacerdotium,* were integral parts of the one church, and both had a rightful place in any and every ecclesiology which was developing at that time. The Lutheran side as well as the Roman side, however, fluctuated in the way these two spheres of the single *societas Christiana* ought to relate to one another. Luther's denial that the *sacerdotium* formed an *ordo,* with ontological superiority, did allow for a better positioning of the non-ordained than the Roman position had done. This is especially true as regards the pope, who, in some overly papal theologies of that time, viewed the pope in an *ordo* which surpassed *in toto* every emperor and king. In this respect, there was in Luther's position more latitude given to the non-ordained or lay element in the *societas Christiana* than one finds in this kind of papal view regarding *sacerdotium* and above all regarding the major *sacerdos,* the pope.

E. LUTHER'S POSITION ON CHRISTIAN DISCIPLESHIP:
THE PRIESTHOOD OF ALL BELIEVERS

When it comes to the theological role of the lay person within the Christian church, no phrase in Luther's writings has engendered more Roman Catholic discussion than the term "the priesthood of all believers." In the *Dictionnaire de la Bible,* published in 1908, the author of the entry on *Ordre* referred to the phrase as metaphorical, unapplicable in any strict sense to the Roman Catholic theology of priesthood.[30] However, in the 1969 edition of the *Lexikon für Theologie und Kirche,* there are four columns dedicated to this theme, in which the value of this notion for Roman Catholic theology of priesthood is expressed in very laudatory terms.[31] There is a major misunderstanding of this phrase if it is called "priesthood of the laity," for in actuality there is no such thing as a priesthood specifically for the laity. There is a universal Christian priesthood or, more carefully stated, a priesthood of all believers. The phrase "priesthood of all believers" is, consequently, not in opposition to a ministerial priesthood. All belong to the priesthood of all believers; a few are called to ministry.

Some Roman Catholic theologians today remain quite uneasy with this term "the priesthood of all believers." J. Galot is surely one of these uneasy people. Indicative of this uneasy stance is his description:

> The universal priesthood has a role to play in the Church, namely, the worship in spirit and in truth, with the offering of spiritual sacrifices. This role too takes on a fundamental importance in Christian existence, but it is not accompanied by an authority comparable to the authority conferred upon the Twelve, nor does it entail a pastoral mission.

> By calling on them [the Twelve] to relinquish their families, their worldly possessions, and the pursuit of a profession, he established a mode of consecrated life not required of those who are called *only to believe in him* and *cling to the Church.* This mode of life is not exclusive to the Twelve. It is required of all those who are called "disciples" in the gospels and are invited to devote all their energies to the promotion of the kingdom. It is lived even by women who follow Jesus.[32]

Not only Luther, but the most reputable Roman Catholic exegetes today, would find this description of the difference between the priesthood of all believers and the ministerial priesthood totally unacceptable. When one reads that the "universal priest," i.e. the baptized Christian, is called "only to believe in him," only to "cling to the church," the response can only be one of theological shock. Luther's biblical view of faith would not tolerate such a phrase: "only to believe," since time and again throughout the New Testament one hears a much different understanding of faith: "Your faith has saved you!" "Your faith has made you whole." "I have not seen such faith in all of Israel." And the list of gospel passages could go on. The faith of one who belongs to the priesthood of all believers and the faith of one who is in ministry are not different kinds of faith, one of lesser value and the other of greater value. There is no such "lesser" task, which can be described as "only to believe in Jesus and cling to the church."

The same theological shock arises over the term "disciple." A lengthy section earlier in this volume carefully combed the various writings of the New Testament for the meaning of "disciple." Nowhere is discipleship in the New Testament presented as a calling for a separate group or caste with a different standard of discipleship, a different "consecration," as Galot wishes to have it. The New Testament is not and never has been a "manual for priests." Unfortunately, Galot is not alone in this demeaning approach to the "priesthood of all believers." There are other Roman Catholic writers today who agree with Galot, and the basic reason they do so is to maintain an understanding of ordained priesthood in which *ordo* is the foundational hermeneutic.[33] A theory of some two-track form of discipleship, based on an "ontological" positioning, remains as much today an unhealthy form of Christian life as it was when Luther challenged such a view in the sixteenth century.[34]

Luther's own views on the relationship between the universal priesthood and the ministerial priest have been reviewed time and time again.[35] Some scholars, such as Lieberg, find two different lines of thought in Luther. The first sees the ministry (*Amt*) deriving from the call from the community, the priesthood of all believers.[36] The second approach in Luther emphasizes "das auf göttlicher Stiftung beruhende konkrete Amt."[37] In this approach the minister is not the delegate of the community, but is a messenger (*Legat*) from God, even though there is a call from the church, which provides a certain orderliness to the ministry in a given community. In situations of emergency, Lieberg interprets the texts of Luther as maintaining that there is a sort of linkage which allows political leaders, *Fürsten und Magistraten,* to intervene, acting in some ways as a bishop.

Wolfgang Stein has taken a different stance to the Luther material. For Stein, the priestly people of God as a group, not as individuals, have received the power of ministry (*Amt*), which in a collective way (i.e. through an ordination) they give to an individual. Only in a state of emergency could a Christian not so designated, i.e. a non-ordained person, take upon himself or herself such a ministry (*Amt*).[38]

In both of these presentations of Luther's views, the priesthood of all believers plays a major role. That Vatican II officially included this theme into mainstream Roman Catholic theology was certainly a major step, and it has helped the better repositioning of the lay person in the Roman Catholic Church in a profound way. The documents of Vatican II, however, do not provide one with a clear theological understanding of the relationship between the priesthood of all believers and the ordained priesthood. Certainly, within the Lutheran tradition, the teaching on the priesthood of all believers has established a strong precedent for the theological and pastoral role of the lay person, i.e. the non-ordained person, the person not entrusted with a ministerial *Amt*, not only for Lutherans but for all the Christian traditions, and, with the statements from Vatican II, for Roman Catholics as well.

In conclusion, we might ask: Did Luther help or hinder the theological and pastoral role of the lay person in the church? The answer is both a yes and a no. One can answer in the affirmative because of his stress on the priesthood of all believers, because of his rejection of *ordo* as a theological hermeneutic for the understanding of ecclesial ministry, because of his denial of a papal *plenitudo potestatis,* because of his elevation of Spirit over structure, because of his teaching of the absolute gratutity of God's grace, because of his emphasis on the full gratutity of the work of Christ which called into question the way in which the sacramental system and the priestly system was then portrayed, because of his stress on the inviolability of the human conscience in the presence of God's Spirit.

On the other hand, a negative answer is also required because of his lack of clarity on ecclesial structures, because of his lack of clarity on the source of ministerial *Amt,* because of his lack of clarity on the role of socio-political power within the *societas Christiana,* because of his lack of a thematized ecclesiology.

The Lutheran tradition has maintained the affirmative aspects of this picture and has struggled with many in-house divergencies on the negative aspects of this picture. In all of this, the Lutheran tradition has been, to some extent, more open to the theological and pastoral role of the lay person in the church than has the Roman Catholic tradition or the traditions of the eastern churches. Other Protestant groups, however, have been even more open than the Lutheran Church to the lay person's theological and pastoral roles.

2. THE LAY PERSON IN THE WRITINGS OF JOHN CALVIN

John Calvin's description of the theological and pastoral role of the lay person in the church is not that easy to systematize. As with the teaching of Luther, one must first establish a theological basis on which the teaching of Calvin can be established and therefore understood. The next few pages will attempt to draw this basis for and presentation of the lay person in Calvinist thought through the following stages:

a. Calvin's teaching on the church;
b. Calvin's teaching on church ministry;
c. Calvin's teaching on the lay person in the church.

In assembling the material in this way, we will touch on those same themes which structured the presentation of Luther, namely, the themes of *ordo, plenitudo potestatis, regna et sacerdotium,* and discipleship.

A. CALVIN'S TEACHING ON THE CHURCH

In his captivating portraiture of John Calvin, the historian W. Bouwsma has rightly stated:

> Because, for Calvin, the improvement of society and government depended finally on the improvement of human beings, the crucial arena for the reformation was the Church.[39]

John Calvin was very much a church person, and although he distinguished between a visible and an invisible church, his concern more often than not centered on the visible church, and even more specifically a local church, that of Geneva. Book IV of the *Institutes of the Christian Religion* is entitled: "The external means or aims by which God invites us into the society of Christ and holds us therein."[40] Still, it "mainly treats ecclesiastical organization and practice rather than ecclesiology."[41] Although the author of the introduction to the English translation of the *Institutes* does not make as forthright a judgment as Bouwsma on the presence or nonpresence of a thematic ecclesiology in this work, it is still evident from this introductory material to the *Institutes* that the practical side of church issues tends to dominate the material of Book IV.[42]

With high self-assurance, however, B.C. Milner's dissertation *Calvin's Doctrine of the Church* argues that Calvin indeed had a thematized ecclesiology:

> The unity of Calvin's thought becomes apparent in his doctrine
> of the Church, because the Church is just that order which appears in the correlation of the efficacious work of the Holy Spirit
> and the diverse manifestations of the Word.[43]

Milner argues his entire case from the principle of order, which he finds throughout Calvin's writings, but particularly in the *Institutes*. In contrast to E.A. Dowey, who divided the *Institutes* on the basis of the *duplex cognitio Domini*,[44] Milner unifies the *Institutes* on the basis of "Calvin's conception of order as that is structured in the correlation of the Spirit and the Word."[45]

Still another scholar, Alexandre Ganoczy, maintains that Calvin formulated a strongly thematic ecclesiology:

> While individual elements of christology, soteriology and sacramental theology are spread through the *Institutes* and the other
> works of Calvin, his ecclesiology is found totally in the *Institutes*. . . . It appears in the *Institutes* as a closed system.[46]

After analyzing the way in which Calvin developed his thoughts on the church in the various editions of the *Institutes,* namely those of 1536, 1539, 1543, and the final edition of 1559, Ganoczy concludes that in 1559 Calvin had developed a treatise (*Traktat*) on "Ministry in the Church."[47] This is a phrase which Calvin himself used on several occasions to describe the material of Book IV. Ganoczy remarks that there are many important ramifications to the fact that the ecclesiological legacy of Calvin was finally presented in this way, i.e. a ministerial way. Ganoczy also maintains that it is the understanding of the church as "mother" which provided Calvin with his final point of departure for this ecclesiological synthesis.[48]

That there has been and still is considerable discussion on the issue of ecclesiology in Calvin is evident, but even with this continued discussion by Calvinist scholars, there can be no doubt that for Calvin the church was a central focus. The church, however, has both a visible and an invisible aspect to it, for the church is at one and the same time both a mystery and an historical community. It is impossible to formulate an ecclesiology on an invisible church, and Calvin's many descriptions of the unity of the church all imply a visible or perceptible situation. We read, for instance:

The basis on which we believe the Church is that we are fully convinced we are members of it. In this way our salvation rests upon sure and firm supports, so that, even if the whole fabric of the world were overthrown, the Church could neither totter nor fall.[49]

The sureness of faith in the church, Calvin adds, is based on God's election and the steadfastness of Christ. Nonetheless, he also states:

Yet, to embrace the unity of the church in this way, we need not . . . see the church with the eyes or touch it with the hands. Rather, the fact that it belongs to the realm of faith should warn us to regard it no less since it passes our understanding than if it were clearly visible. And our faith is no worse because it recognizes a church beyond our ken.[50]

Calvin realizes that an understanding of an invisible church makes it difficult to judge the visible church. "Just as we must believe, therefore, that the former Church, invisible to us, is visible to the eyes of God alone, we are commanded to revere and keep communion with the latter, which is called 'Church' in respect to men."[51] Calvin finds the criteria in certain marks and tokens which the Lord has given to us, through which we can know about the church.[52] These marks are the preaching of the word and the observance of the sacraments.[53] This is, of course, the "pure ministry of the Word and the pure mode of celebrating the sacraments."[54] Whatever is meant by this term "pure," it implies criteria, and the ultimate criteria, which Calvin tends to use rather often, focus on the absolute gratuity of God's grace, on the one hand, and the complete adequacy of Christ's sacrifice, on the other. The church, in Calvin's thought, must be thematically explained on the basis of christology and on the basis of an absolutely free God. Scholastic Calvinism, unfortunately, did not remain loyal to this Calvinist base as G. Yule has duly noted.[55] Scholastic Calvinism was much more centered on the divine truths and propositions in the Bible, of which Christ was simply one, though a major one, among several.

A true disciple of the Lord is, for Calvin, one who believes in the absolute gratuity of God's grace, and who believes that Jesus alone, not one's good works, effects salvation. If the preaching of the word and the celebration of the sacraments reflect this basic position, then the preaching of the word and the sacramental actions are "pure." This is the logic of Calvin: logic that begins with God, then moves to Christ, then to church, and then to disciple, but each of these four must be carefully presented in a way in which the freedom of God is meticulously maintained, the full gratuity of God's grace is not compromised, and the complete adequacy of the work of Christ is honored.

In his lengthy reply to Cardinal James Sadolet, who had pleaded with the people of Geneva, on the occasion of Calvin's exile, to return to the Church of Rome, Calvin, with a great deal of respect for the highly esteemed and intellectually well-trained man, Sadolet, nonetheless makes it very clear that word and Spirit are central to the church: to its doctrine, to its discipline, to its sacraments and to its rites.[56] Calvin adroitly uses the very basis of Sadolet's argument as his own argument. Sadolet had said: "There is nothing more perilous to our salvation than a distorted and perverse worship of God,"[57] and Calvin used this to show that the introduction of so many ceremonies into the worship of the Roman Church with the demand to consider them as though they were part of both word and Spirit is precisely a distortion and a perverse worship of God. Calvin insisted on the gratuitous grace of God, not one which was obtained by works: "Assuredly we do deny that for justifying a man they [good works] are worth a single straw. . . . If by faith, then not by works; on the other hand: if by works, then not by faith."[58] In all of this, Calvin tried to emphasize again and again that the church must exhibit word and Spirit, and do so precisely in the way the scriptures indicate. "When the preaching of the gospel is reverently heard and the sacraments are not neglected, there for the time being no deceitful or ambiguous form of the Church is seen."[59]

With christology as the foundation for Calvin's understanding of the church, and with Jesus as the primary head of the church, there is no room for any Christian to claim *plenitudo potestatis.* Calvin rejected the papacy sharply and definitively.[60] The papacy with its claims was a tyranny that was essentially counter to the gospels. That a pope might be acceptable was something, however, which Calvin noted on a few occasions. In 1549, he wrote:

Wollte Gott, daß diese Folge, mit der sie sich fälscherweise rühmen, bis auf den heutigen Tag reichte. Gern würden wir die verdiente Ehre geben. Mag der Papst doch der Nachfolger Petri sein, wenn er nur die Aufgabe des Apostels wahrnähme. Worin aber besteht die Nachfolgerschaft, wenn nicht im Fortdauern der Lehre?[61]

Four years later he wrote in the same way:

Er also will als der Nachfolger gelten: wäre es doch! Niemand hindert ihn daran, Christus zu lieben, sich zu mühen und sein Herde zu weiden.[62]

Notice that the criterion for true papal ministry is discipleship, which is, of course, the criterion par excellence for any and every Christian, cleric or lay. The *plenitudo potestatis* is ruled out by Calvin on the primary criterion of all Christians, namely discipleship. The claim for a fullness of power cannot be squared with gospel discipleship.

B. CALVIN'S TEACHING ON CHURCH MINISTRY

It is on the basis of church that Calvin then takes up the issue of ministry, and again there are distinctions to be made as regards the visible forms of ministry within the visible forms of regional churches. It is on the basis of church that he also views the distinction between a clerical ministry and the ministered people.

> Calvin's clericalism was based above all on God's appointment. Pastors have been "called," as he had been, by a God whose calling they cannot reject "without being rebels against him."[63]

In Calvin's presentation, the visible church is clearly marked by a cleric/lay structure. Calvin indeed used the terms cleric/clergy, but he preferred the term minister/ministry, and this meant that there were Christians to whom and for whom these people ministered. In the first edition of the *Institutes,* Calvin named two orders of ministry: pastors and deacons, whereas in the *Ecclesiastical Ordinance* of 1541, there are four orders: pastors, teachers, elders and deacons.[64] When one considers all of Calvin's writings, one might tend to agree with Yule, who mentions that Calvin "seems to have been indifferent as to whether the diaconate and also the eldership was a lay or clerical office."[65]

Basic to Calvin's thought on ministry is the belief that it is God who calls one to ministry, and this call is the hidden call. But there are also, according to Calvin, four external signs, which indicate that God has indeed called a person to ministry. By asking four questions, Calvin indicates those areas in which one can find the external signs:

a. What sort of ministers should they be?
b. How are they appointed?
c. By whom are they appointed?
d. By what rite or ceremony should they be installed?[66]

These four questions concern themselves with the outward and solemn call to ministry and with the public order of the church. He answers the first question with references to the qualities of a minister found in Titus 1:7 and 1 Timothy 3:1–7. The second question is not concerned with a ritual, but rather with "religious awe," with prayer and fasting by the entire community. The third question is far more difficult to answer. After all, a community is trying to discern God's will and not impose its own will on God. The consent and approval of the community is, for Calvin, an essential part of this process, but the pastors should preside over the election process to avoid human mishaps.[67] The final question receives the answer: the laying on of hands. Ultimately, however, it is God who calls one to ministry, not the community. These four external areas are merely signs through which a community discerns the action of God.

The Roman Catholic scholar Heribert Schützeichel comments that Calvin's passionate stress on that which he calls the *apostolicum ac pastorale munus* in the church is extremely inspiring and imposing. For Calvin this apostolic and pastoral ministry in the church is more important to life than the light and warmth of the sun, or more important than food and drink are for health.[68] The true gospel minister together with his ministry is deeply revered by Calvin, and calling from God of such a minister is never in doubt. Where, then, does this place the people of God?

Is there an *ordo* in Calvin's presentation of ministry? The answer to this is yes and no. Throughout Calvin's writings there is a fundamental appeal to the notion of an order of creation, and in the revelation of Christ in the gospels there is equally an order to the church which Calvin maintains.[69] What is rejected is the notion that the minister is placed in a different created *ordo,* on the one hand (i.e. an ontologically different order), and, on the other hand, that the minister is placed in a "higher" *ordo* within the church, in the sense that this *ordo* has the right to interpret the very word of God. *Ordo* is not Calvin's hermeneutic to interpret cleric/lay; the word of God is the only hermeneutic he wishes to use, and the same word of God is the hermeneutic which interprets the concept of the order of creation and the order within the church. Sometimes, however, the absolutism of Calvin's judgment, his stance that he has the true interpretation of the scriptures, raises questions on whether he has totally escaped the understanding of *ordo* which he himself has rejected.

C. CALVIN'S TEACHING ON THE LAY PERSON IN THE CHURCH

In *Confession de la foi,* Calvin states that the lay person must "listen to them [the clergy] as to God himself."[70]

> If the clergy are authorized to command, the laity are obligated to obey lest they be "bears" rather than sheep. Calvin was incensed by lay resistance to a clerical control so benign and well

intentioned, so different from the tyranny of the Roman priest-hood. It was scarcely to be endured, he felt, that those who had "calmly endured the harsh tyranny of the pope" and "calmly swallowed the most cruel insults of the monks" now tended "to fly into a passion against the paternal and wholesome rebukes of their pastors."[71]

For Calvin the true church remained a church with clerics and lay people, and in this Calvin continued the patristic and medieval form of church life. But, one might ask, has he not substituted one form of clerical-ism for another, even though this new form is more benign and whole-some? Is there not a lingering but dominant paternalism throughout his writings which continues the male dominance within fundamental church structures? If all of these questions merit an affirmative answer, in what ways, then, can Calvin be said to have advanced the role of the lay person in the church? I would offer the following:

1. Although Calvin was not the first to use an historical method in his criticism of the late medieval church structures, he certainly used what historical data he had at hand to indicate how fragile many of the argu-ments for papal, episcopal and presbyteral power truly were.

> Calvin's very considerable knowledge of church history is used in an animated polemic against Roman assertions of Peter's au-thority in Rome and the rising claims and exercise of papal power in the Middle Ages. If the too abundant invective were removed from these chapters, there would remain a rather im-pressive body of historical data germane to the issue; but he views historical changes with too little sense of the complexity of the forces involved.[72]

This judgment by the editors of the English edition of the *Institutes* is quite fair. Calvin's polemic too often becomes harsh, even vindictive, and this tended to divert his critics into a defense of authority, as happened with the criticism of Luther as well. But if one can lay aside the polemic, Calvin's historical critique of many papal and clerical claims to positions which were only of human origin remain, by and large, quite valid. That Calvin did not appreciate the historical complexity of some of these is-sues, as the editors above note, is also a fair assessment of his historical passages. Even with these provisos, however, one can say that Calvin's use of historical criticism as regards key issues of church structure, particu-larly clerical church structure, has proven to be a major factor in the repositioning of the lay person within the Church. More often than not, the official Roman Catholic Church, that is, its highest leadership, has from the reformation down to the twentieth century struggled against this intrusion of historical data. As late as 1918, U. Stutz was able to analyze the first code of canon law as follows: "The Catholic Church is the Church of the clergy. . . . Lay people simply form the flock which is to be led and instructed."[73] Stutz could say this under the claim of a divine institution. Such an interpretation of the authority of the Roman Catholic cleric was continually defended by beleaguered church leadership, by some theologians of high repute as well as by many canonists, in spite of the massive amount of historical data, which has indicated and at times has clearly proved that certain claims are only a human institution and not a divine institution. Calvin wrote precisely at a time when not a few scholars, many of them lay, were reviewing the historical data regarding many key clerical claims. The popularity of the *Institutes* helped make this historical critique of clerical claims an even more widespread issue, and as clerical claims, whether papal, episcopal or presbyteral, were being challenged throughout the church catholic, a repositioning of the lay person within church structures began to gain momentum.

2. Calvin also influenced the repositioning of the lay person in church structures by his emphasis on the local church and the role he gave to local leaders in the church. Although it is necessary to note that Calvin never ceded clerical power to political power, he did make strong efforts to incorporate the political and the clerical into a highly-bonded format.[74] Calvin's efforts in this regard moved in differing directions at differing stages of his life, and as a consequence the precise direction, which this bonding should assume, remained ambiguous. One does not find a unified approach to the church/city government relationship in his writings. Many of the complex issues which were involved in the *regna et sacerdotium* struggle reemerge, although in a less universal way, in the *ecclesia et civis* struggle, so fiercely fought at Geneva, but which one finds also at Neuchâtel, Lausanne and Zurich. The Palatinate reformation of the mid-sixteenth century also evidences this struggle between the clerical ministry and the governmental laity.[75] The struggles of Calvinist Protestantism in France, from Saint-Barthélemy down to the Edict of Nantes, are both religious and political ones, so intimately combined with each other that one is unintelligible without the other. The role of lay people, both of Catholic France and of Protestant France, was central, not only to the political issues involved, but also to the ecclesiastical issues involved.[76]

It is clearly safe to say that in those church groups which have remained enriched by the Calvinist tradition, the highly visible and central role of lay people in church structuring has almost always been evident. Historically speaking, one could say that it would be impossible for a

Calvinistic writer ever to state: "The church is a church of the clergy. . . . Lay people simply form the flock to be led and instructed." Roman Catholics have written this way, even in the twentieth century, but Calvinist writers have not, and they could not do so. Even though Calvin himself did not express a clear-cut principle on this issue of lay-cleric relationship, and even though Theodore Beza, Calvin's successor, was far more diplomatic and moderate in his approach to the lay-cleric relationship, the affirmation of a major theological role for lay people within church structuring has remained a hallmark of Calvinist thought, and from the sixteenth century on this affirmation has been a major operative criticism of every Christian church, including the Roman Catholic, which has disallowed a lay voice in ecclesial decision-making processes. It would be foolish, however, to think that Calvinist thought on this matter has always been of one piece. "The Reformed system in France bore the bitter fruit of that clericalism so stoutly denounced by Milton and the English Independents. The latter had tried, but in vain, to bring back French Protestants to Congregationalism, particularly those on the Atlantic seaboard—for that was, after all, the doctrine of the early Reformation."[77]

To this "congregational" and "independent" invasion, Léonard describes the response as a Calvinist clerical panic which worried about the "contagion of this poison," which feared "that such a plague would put disorder and confusion among us," which opened "the door to all sorts of singularities, irregularities and extravaganzas," which could only lead to "as many religions taking shape as there are parishes and particular assemblies."[78] It was even held "to be inadvisable for a layman to feel entitled to interpret the Bible for the benefit of his family, at family prayers."[79] Such phrases are similar to the responses of the clerical leadership in the Roman Catholic Church when confronted with lay involvement. These fears of Calvinist clerics, and of some lay Calvinists as well, did not come true. Nonetheless, there was a clear laicization of French Protestantism in the latter part of the sixteenth century, but a laicization that did not mimic the English independent-church program.

3. Calvin himself was a figure of transition. Is he, for instance, essentially medieval, the "last of the schoolmen"? Certainly the neatness of his *Institutes* would lean in this direction, but in today's research, late medieval thought was anything but unified and neatly put together. Still, Calvin was very much a traditionalist and wanted passionately to revitalize the true church of the gospels, and in this he has many ties to the complex goals of the medieval church. Calvin was also, from early years onward, attracted to the humanist movement, with its skepticism, relativism, and pragmatism. This would make Calvin a spokesperson for the "modern" world. This factor only stresses the ambiguity which one finds in Calvin's

writings themselves. There developed a "dogmatic" Calvinism, on the one hand, but also a Calvinism which found a nesting place in Scottish Presbyterianism as well as in Anglican establishmentarianism and in English disestablishmentarianism. It is true that each and every form of dogmatic unchangeableness, religious, theological, political, and philosophical, provides human beings with a sense of stability and well-being. It is also true that the world these same human beings live in is not rigidly put together, but rather quite fluid. Out of this precarious fluidity, however, human creativity and human wisdom reach new goals and new plateaus. Clericalism, once it has been established in some form within a church structure, has generally tended to remain dogmatic; only when clericalism is itself going through a process of restructuring has it been creative. The clerical medieval church had become dogmatic, although in a complex way, at the time of Calvin. Humanism at that same time was challenging the clerical dominance in church structures, in education, in the arts, in politics, in social structures generally. This humanism was spearheaded, not by clergy, although some were involved, and involved in a leadership way, such as Erasmus. Rather, by and large, this humanism was spearheaded by lay men and to some degree by lay women. The humanistic world was clearly giving birth to a repositioned role of the lay person within the world, and the western church had only one place to exist, and that was in the very same world. Calvin was a major figure in this transitional moment of history. If Luther's death brought about a momentary but rather momentous check on Lutheranism, Calvin's death did not have the same result. The spread of Calvinism throughout Europe moved with a rapidity that is hard to explain with full satisfaction. This spread of Calvinistic thought and practice continued Calvin's own retention of the past, the dogmatic side, and the openness to the future, the ambiguous humanistic side. This spread of Calvinism continued a clericalism of its own stamp, but it opened one church group after another to a repositioning of the lay person within the very decision-making chambers of church leadership. It advocated in principle a laicization of the church which was not in any way a secularization of the church.

4. Charmarie Blaisdell has written an interesting essay, "Calvin's and Loyola's Letters to Women: Politics and Spiritual Counsel in the Sixteenth Century,"[80] and Willis P. De Boer has also focused on the issue of "Calvin on the Role of Women."[81] Others have also written on this subject.[82] One of the important aspects of sixteenth century life which comes to the fore in these studies is the educated and influential position of many women at this time. This is a given, not a *desideratum*. Marguerite de Valois, a member of French royalty, corresponded with Calvin. In her *Discours docte et subtil,* she argued that women were higher and

more perfect than men, since the order of creation is an order of ascendancy—the last the best—and woman was created later than man.[83] Katherine Zell, who was married to a priest, wrote quite bluntly to the bishop:

> You have reminded me that the Apostle Paul told women to be silent in the church. I would remind you of the word of the same apostle that in Christ there is no longer male nor female.[84]

Calvin's views on women, however, were very conservative. Women were, because of the order of creation, subject to men, and they had no official role to play in the ministry of the church. Again and again, Calvin based his position on the ordering of creation, and on the words of Paul regarding women.[85] In the spiritual order, men and women share an equality, but not in the historical order. In the historical situation, men are superior to women.[86]

All of this sounds harsh for today's world. The same can be said when Calvin emphasizes the term "propriety" as the reason for the exclusion of women from ministry, even with its cushioning as something "cultural." The same can be said as regards his letter to William Cecil, which was an effort to distance himself from John Knox and to indicate his acceptance of Elizabeth I as the supreme governor of the church. In this letter he sees Elizabeth's position as an extraordinary exception to the gospel's counsel.

Still, three things stand out, as regards Calvinism, which clearly indicate a process of repositioning of the theological and pastoral role of the lay person, and more pointedly of the lay woman, in the church.

A. The reform movement, which Calvin initiated, was strongly propagated by well-educated and politically influential women. Without the activity of these women, one could ask whether Calvin's influence would have succeeded.

B. The historical appearance of these women in the *societas Christiana* indicates that prior to the sixteenth century reform movements, women had already been established in key positions within that society. In other words, the times had already repositioned women upwardly within society.

C. The historical data on the role of women in the Roman Catholic counter-reformation substantiates this upward repositioning of women within the *societas Christiana*. In the Roman Catholic counter-reform, women, to some degree, but not as strongly as in Calvinistic reform, played a major role.

Although Calvin remained basically conservative, many of his ideas on Christian life, such as the role of the Spirit within the church, the role of conscience, and the supremacy of the word over ecclesial structure, not only helped reposition the lay person in the church, but in a marked way helped reposition the lay woman in the church.

If we ask whether Calvin advanced the theological and pastoral role of the lay person in the church, the answer is again both yes and no. Calvin was very conservative on the issue of ministry in the church, and for him this was a male ministry. It was also a ministry dependent on God, and the community played a secondary and quite controlled, not truly controlling, role. Although Calvin was not that concerned about the term "cleric" and "clergy," he was quite concerned about proper ministry and properly established ministers. He had no use for the congregational structures, such as those the Anabaptists were advocating; in fact, he rejected them as fiercely as he rejected the papal forms of ministry.

Nonetheless, his affirmation of the gratuity of God's grace, the rejection of a good-work approach to sacraments and spiritual life generally, and his advocacy of reading the scriptures to find God's plan for the church and for society clearly enhanced the lay person's role. Outside of specific areas in Germany, which were Lutheran, and outside of the initial reform movement in England, the Protestant reform movement throughout the remainder of Europe was strongly, and in some areas almost exclusively, that of Calvin. This movement, however, was not a movement simply of clerics. Rather, it was a movement of large groups of people, only a few of whom were ministers. This means that this geographically most influential reform movement, formulated by Calvin, was by and large a movement which spoke to the ordinary lay man and woman, and which was fostered by the ordinary lay man and woman. In this sense, Calvinism provided a major repositioning of the theological and pastoral role of the lay person within the Christian community.

3. THE LAY PERSON IN THE WRITINGS OF THE ANGLICAN COMMUNION

The sixteenth century reform movement in England had deep roots, going back in a special way to the fourteenth century and the emergence of the Lollards. In 1395 a group of such Lollards submitted to the lords and commons in parliament a manifesto, the *Twelve Conclusions,* in which the clerical priesthood was denounced as misuse, and in which a call to gospel simplicity was urged. "The dissemination of Lollardy in the reign of Richard II, the first large-scale outbreak of heresy in England, marks an important stage in the emergence of an articulate laity."[87] In the

England of the late middle ages, one finds wealthy bishops who were never in residence because of their duties as servants of the king. Many powerful monastic abbeys had been given numerous rectories and vicarages, but the abbots provisioned these parish churches with a mere pittance, leaving a local priest too often on the threshold of poverty. Both of these factors discredited the English clergy. At the very same time, literacy of the lay society of England increased rapidly from the fourteenth century onward. English lay men even wrote books on the spiritual life, books which were read and reread by many.

Such an English world provided the *mise-en-scène* for John Wyclif, who spent almost his entire adult life at the University of Oxford. The death of Edward III and the succession of the child Richard II in 1377 helped the notoriety of Wyclif, for John of Gaunt, Richard's uncle, needed a theologian who spoke out against the wealth of the church. Things changed, however, when Wyclif also began speaking out against other theological positions, such as that of transubstantiation. He was subsequently forced into obscurity at Lutterworth, but he continued to write, advocating, among other issues, the use of scripture by the lay person, which meant translation of scripture into English. A disciple of Wyclif, Purvey, together with a few others, began such a translation, and their English versions of 1382 and 1395 were the only English versions until that of Tyndale's New Testament in 1526.

In this English reform movement, we see, as we have seen on the continent, a reform which has at its heart a return to the gospel, a return to discipleship. The English lay people, who read parts of the scriptures in English and let this word of God nourish their spiritual life, gave evidence of yet another stage common to the many reform movements of the late middle ages, namely a religious personalism, even a religious individualism. Claire Cross notes:

> Had Lollardy not stimulated a mood which was already present, had there not been a body of laymen determined to seek God for themselves without waiting on priestly guidance, it would be difficult otherwise to account for its power to create a continuing lay tradition once the impact of its initial protest had passed.[88]

By 1460 some of the laity in England had strongly supported a movement to reform the church, but this had failed. The clergy, for its part, had urged a movement of orthodox subservience, but this, too, had failed. From 1460 to 1520, educated lay people continued to make demands on the structures of the church in England. Some of this demand came from people influenced by Lollardy and by Wyclif, but some of this demand came from English men and women who were quite orthodox. Reform was certainly in the English air at the beginning of the sixteenth century, and this sentiment for reform did not depend on either a Luther or a Calvin. This sentiment of reform in England had a widespread base among educated and articulate lay men and women. All of this helps one see that the English reformation was, in many ways, very distinct from the reformation on the continent. It had its own pre-history, which was quite English, and its own lay base, which again grew out of English soil. Although there was a deep-seated criticism of the clergy, a call for gospel simplicity, a rebuke of episcopal involvement in the affairs of government —all of which can be found in similar reform movements of the continent —the rootage of the English reform was not an implantation. The English reform had developed in its own way in English soil. Probably not until the reign of Mary did the ordinary English person begin to resent the church as an implant, for it was Mary's ties to Rome and to Spain that made her form of Catholicism alien to the ordinary English individual. Henry VIII, her father, may have severed the ties with Rome, but it was Mary and her policies, including indiscriminate persecution of dissenters, which turned many ordinary lay men and women away from Roman Catholic ways of thought.[89]

Henry VIII had been an outspoken opponent of Luther as well as an outspoken proponent of the Roman Catholic Church. In the course of time, however, he became disillusioned with the papacy and eventually, as is well known, rejected the papacy, but not the Christian faith. In England such a change could not be dictated by the monarch alone; the king required parliament to recognize the role of the king over the church. Because of this need for parliamentary action, there is no one moment when the English church "broke" from Rome, or as Cross describes it: "There was no one instance when England remained in full communion with the see of Rome and another when the tie could be seen to have been cut irretrievably."[90] Both the desire for reform of the church and the desire for an annulment of Henry's marriage to Catherine of Aragon were motives enough for several parliamentary actions from 1529 to 1534. Each of the steps which the king and parliament took appeared to be reversible. Only with the act of supremacy in 1534 was the crown considered the supreme head of the English church on earth. But the notion that the authority of the king extended to the church—at least in certain areas —had been a part of the English climate from the time of the conversion of England to the Christian faith. Similarly, the Greek emperors from Constantine on, and the western emperors from Charlemagne on, had claimed authority over the church in a number of ways.

That the request for and the refusal of an annulment of marriage created ill-feeling between Henry VIII and the popes cannot be denied, but it must also be seen that the issues in the pope's refusal were not purely religious. Politics played a major role, with the emperor, Charles V, exerting strong political influence over Clement VII not to grant the annulment, and the emperor urged this for political reasons, not theological reasons. Just as the papacy, as depicted both in Luther's *Babylonian Captivity* and in Calvin's *Institutes,* was an historical papacy which not only needed reform, but which had betrayed itself by political intrigue and the lust for power, so, too, Henry's rejection of papacy was not simply a rejection of a "theological papacy," but a politically, power-driven papacy.[91]

In England, isolated geographically as it was, the papacy was not an institution which affected the daily life of the ordinary English person. There does not seem to have been a major protest by the English people when Henry was made the supreme authority over the church. Only a few protested with their life against this matter, such as Thomas More and a few Cistercian monks. Although Henry, a lay person himself, had become the ruler of the church, "he had no intention of sharing his newly acquired power with the laity in general."[92] It is not in the act of supremacy itself that one can see a major step in the repositioning of the lay person.

When Henry began to dissolve the monasteries, there were a number of English lay people who felt that the moneys gained thereby would be used to benefit the commonwealth. When this did not happen, with the money going to the crown alone, these lay people began to be disillusioned with Henry's supremacy. Indeed, Henry began to levy taxes on church-related benefices in a higher degree than any pope had ever done. This action of the supreme monarch over church-related benefices caused much more alarm to the ordinary lay person in England than the secession from Rome had done, because it affected their life in a much more concrete way. One should notice, however, that it was not the actual dissolution of religious life in England which caused a stir. When Mary attempted to reinstate religious life, the majority of English people remained quite indifferent. Religious life, it seems, was at the time of the Tudors a form of church life which the ordinary English person found superfluous.

When Edward VI at a minor age succeeded to the throne, a number of regents actually governed England. During Edward's reign the policy of taking over and taxing church-related benefices increased rapidly, and the question of dissolving all chantries and guilds in favor of the government appeared as well. Under Edward, however, much of the money did not end up with the crown but with the noble families who were part of the regency. In doing this, the Edwardian government was again touching the daily life of the ordinary English people, and not to their advantage. Those who felt that such moneys should go to aid the country at large became even more alarmed at this enrichment of a few noble families, but even more intense was their alarm since much of the social care for needy and poor people were provided by the chantries, as well as by church-related entities, and to dissolve such socially charitable institutions would leave an unalleviated and unallieviable poverty in many neighborhoods of England.

Even more than with the issue either of papacy or of taxation, the ordinary lay person in England, who was quite Christian and fairly conservative, began to feel the religious change through the various liturgical changes, especially through the several editions of the *Prayer Book*. When Mary ascended the throne and attempted a Catholic restoration, the rejection by the people in many parishes of the vernacular mass, of a table for an altar, of a disdain for vestments, etc., occurred almost immediately. The people in many instances reverted to the former liturgical ways of prayer, especially the eucharist. This data is indicative that the religious change in England was not simply an intellectual change. The changing of religious rituals, which had deep symbolic and personal meaning, was paramount. In many ways, for the ordinary English lay person, the papacy, far away in another land, was at best an intellectual issue. Taxation, for its part, was an immediate economic issue. Ritual change, particularly in the mass, was an immediate, theological and spiritual issue. It is perhaps easy today to consider the break with the papacy the "major" issue in Tudor times, but this would be reading a more contemporary positioning of the pope into these same Tudor times. Papal supremacy was an issue, but not the most decisive for the English people in the sixteenth century.[93]

The English reformation, in spite of the Lutheran and Calvin scholars whom Cranmer had invited to Cambridge and Oxford as professors, and in spite of the many Calvinistic advisors of Elizabeth I, remained a distinct form of sixteenth century reform. Episcopacy continued on, even with avowed Protestants as bishops, such as John Hooper, bishop of Gloucester. Priests continued on in their pastoral activity, with most of them remaining quite conservative in religious matters, and not, for that day and age, "liberally Protestant."

Mary's efforts to restore Catholicism met with little popular opposition as far as the renewal of relationship with Rome was concerned. Once lay Catholics had restored the mass to the way it was, they did not exert much further activity. Mary's restoration of a few monasteries created no great enthusiasm for a monastic revival. In the ordinary English mind, it seems that monastic life had become an anachronism, not a vital aspect of Christian life. As long as Mary did not try to give the monastic lands and income back to the church, the monastery issue was dead. Rather, it was her program, abetted by Pole, to punish the Protestant heretics which created a major backlash.

> In the four years between the revival of the heresy laws and Mary's death in November 1558, almost three hundred people are known to have been burnt for heresy in England in addition to a considerable number more who died in prison awaiting trial or before their sentences could be carried out.[94]

Not only did Mary's actions provide the Protestants with a number of martyrs, but the extremes of her ferocity repulsed the lay people. Although counseled again and again not to pursue her marriage with Philip of Spain, she went ahead with her plans, thus making Catholicism appear to many an English man and woman a foreign religion. In Mary and her advisors we see the tragic flaw in many Roman Catholic revisionists: a renewal of the Catholic faith meant a restoration to the "way it was." No appreciation of the changed situation was comprehended by Mary and her advisors. Just as the theologians, canonists and church leaders of the late medieval period had not understood the newly appearing *civis,* so, too, Mary and her advisors did not grasp what the English reform movement had been attempting to do again and again from the first appearance of the Lollards down to the middle of the sixteenth century.

Elizabeth I solidified the non-Roman aspect of the English church, but not without a host of problems. That she was a woman raised serious questions on her ability to be considered head of the church. As a consequence, Elizabeth assumed the title "Supreme Governor" rather than "Supreme Head." She maintained the medieval form of two provinces, Canterbury and York, and in actuality no major change in diocesan organization took place in England until the nineteenth century. Elizabeth continually faced the issue of lay involvement, particularly in parliament, especially in the House of Commons. Presbyterianism and Separatism continued to harass Elizabeth's religious plans down to her death. Uniformity of religion in Elizabethan England proved illusive. Indeed, only after the Laudian ascendancy in the English church, and only after the subsequent lay supremacy struggle of 1640 to 1660, and, to be more specific, only in the year 1714 could one say that the laity had "made good their superiority in the national Church; some laymen, more precariously but as it proved permanently, had also established their right to live outside its bounds; an age of religious pluralism had begun."[95]

Through its influence in the United States and in Canada, the English forms of church did affect the repositioning of the lay person, both theologically and pastorally, far beyond the British Isles. We find this influence echoing in the present ecumenical discussions in which there is a distinct Anglican/Roman Catholic format of dialogue, making these dialogues very different from the present Lutheran/Roman Catholic and Presbyterian/Roman Catholic dialogues. There are ecumenical issues today which are specifically Anglican, and many of these specific issues involve the role of the lay person, and above all today the role of women. The excommunication of Elizabeth (1570) may have been "an answer" by the Roman Catholic leadership in the sixteenth century, but it was certainly not "the answer" to the issues posed by the English reform movement. The distinctive issues of the English reform must clearly be appreciated, and, in its own special way, the role of the lay person and the role of a woman in the English church, and consequently for the church catholic, must be evaluated. Both the lay and the women's issues, as regards church life, stem from the English reform movements of the sixteenth century.

4. THE LAY PERSON IN THE WRITINGS OF THE RADICAL REFORMERS

The various people and movements of the sixteenth century radical reform group deserve more attention than can be given to them in this volume. Nonetheless, the repositioning of the lay person within these movements more often than not far outran the repositioning of the lay person, which the more mainstream reform movements advocated. Indeed, mainstream reformers often opposed the radical reformers as much as they opposed the papists, as we noted above in the section on Calvin.

Franklin Litell indicates that contemporary scholarship includes a wide range of sixteenth century people under the umbrella of the term "radical reformers." He mentions:

1. Religious revolutionaries, such as Thomas Müntzer, Bernt Rothmann, the Fifth Monarchy men.
2. Anti-Trinitarians, such as Michael Servetus, Adam Pastor, the Polish Minor Church.
3. *Spiritualisten,* such as Caspar Schwenckfeld, Sebastian Franck, Johannes Bünderlin.
4. Biblical restitutionists such as the Swiss Brethren, the Southern

German Brethren, Hutterites, Mennonites, Congregationalists, Baptists, Quakers.[96]

Such a wide variety of sixteenth century movements and people is not easily brought into a unified topical discussion, since their variety often outruns their unity. Litell attempts to link these diverse people together by stating that for some the key word was *reformatio,* while for others it was *restitutio.*

1. *Restitutio* involved a new periodization of church history: namely, (a) the early church or golden age; (b) fall, often dated from the era of Constantine; (c) the new age or their own time.
2. *Reformatio* involved many of the same issues and struggles which the mainstream reform movements of the sixteenth century advocated.

The idyllic view of the early church, which the restitutionists held, viewed the earliest Jesus community as a group in which all were equal. In this sense there were neither clerics nor lay in this portraiture. In some groups, such as those which eventually developed under John Wise (1652–1725) and John Owen, the minister or theologian did indeed have a trusted position in the church community, but it had been given to him by the community itself. Menno Simons (1496–1561) advocated a decision making process which involved the entire community, not simply a clerical overlordship. Many free churches have found his approach a support for their own convictions.

In the course of history since the sixteenth century, those who advocated either a restitution or a reform format of this so-called radical reform group have developed strong missionary activity, while some of the free churches developed an anti-missionary stance. In the former group, the missionaries were the Christian individuals (laity), not a special ministerial or clerical group. In some instances, as in the restitutionist government of England (1640–1660), the lay person became co-terminous with the citizen. A good government resembled a good Christian church: all members were heard and all shared in decision making. "For the restitutionists' cause was not only the enlivenment of the total believing membership; it led inevitably and logically to the appearance of a new type of man in civil affairs as well, a man who was not a subject but a citizen."[97]

Did the radical reform reposition the lay person in the church? The answer is again both affirmative and negative. The stress in most of the radical reform groups was on a community of believers who were to be in large measure a grouping of equals. This involved a radical dismantling of clerical and even, to some degree, ministerial structures. The success of some of these radical reform movements in the socio-political structures of various countries, such as England and the United States, brought about a temporary equation of Christian and citizen. When this occurred, the lay person was repositioned not only in the church but in the socio-political structures as well.

This repositioning was based on a guiding principle: namely, that the early church was a "golden age," and as a result normative. This view of an idyllic and normative early church has been shattered by modern and contemporary biblical research, and as a result raises serious questions about the major premise of these radical reform movements. The first question is that of historicity itself. There is no way of moving from a later age to the primitive church without moving through history, and this means an appreciation not only of the historicity of the earliest period and an appreciation of the historicity of the contemporary period, but an appreciation of the historicity of the in-between period as well. The church of the sixteenth century radical reformers was not only the primitive church, but it was also the patristic church, the early medieval church and the late medieval church. The simplistic dismissal of the "middle-section" of church history as a "fall," and thereby ignoring it, is a simplistic approach and one which cannot be maintained. In today's church many fundamentalist groups attempt to maintain such a position, but the more they do this the less convincing is their case. Secondly, the primitive church was neither uniform in structure nor uniform in doctrine, as the advocates of the radical reform groups believed. J.A. Möhler's *Die Einheit in der Kirche* was a seminal work in the Catholic field of early church history, and the Protestant author W. Bauer, in *Rechtgläubigkeit und Ketzerei in ältesten Christentum,* draws together much of the best of historical research up to 1934. Contemporary biblical scholarship, both Catholic and Protestant, continue to indicate the diversity of New Testament thought. As a result, no single age of the church is a "golden age." No single age of the church is normative. Because of this sensitivity to historicity, and particularly the historicity of the New Testament, one of the major bases for the repositioning of the Christian lay person which the radical reformers advocated has become untenable and needs to be reconsidered.

5. THE LAY PERSON IN THE DOCUMENTS OF THE COUNCIL OF TRENT: 1545–1563

The Council of Trent (1545–1563) did not center its deliberations on the issue of the role of the lay person in the church. Nonetheless, the summoning of this council had, as one of its major goals, the strengthening of the Roman Catholic people of God. The major portion of this people of God was, of course, the lay man and woman. That other motives were also at work for the calling of the council cannot be denied, but that a foundational desire for the council was the betterment of the church in its entirety, namely, cleric, religious, and lay, cannot be ignored. In many of the reform decrees, but also in the doctrinal decrees, the lay person was clearly on the minds of those who prepared, revised and voted on the individual issues.

The Council of Trent, as a major event in the Roman Catholic Church, was and remains an enormously complex event, involving not only the time of the council sessions themselves, but also the subsequent effects of this council on the Catholic world. These effects have been felt down to the twentieth century. However, a number of caveats and observations must be made, so that the theological value of this council may be correctly gauged. The gathering of primary source material by the Görresgesellschaft, and then the critical evaluation of the primary material by such scholars as H. Jedin and G. Alberigo, as well as others, have reoriented the interpretation of Council of Trent. In many ways, this scholarly reinterpretation of Trent has drastically reinterpreted the post-Tridentine positions, and above all this new evaluation has affected the ways in which the doctrinal positions both of Trent itself and of the post-Tridentine interpreters (the counter-reformation theologians) are currently presented.[98] The following observations are, in my view, key to a theological interpretation of this council.

WHAT THE COUNCIL OF TRENT DID NOT DO

A. The Council of Trent did not formulate any explicit ecclesiology, i.e. a concept of the church, which one might consider the "Tridentine church" model, nor did it formulate fundamental positions for such an ecclesiology or model of the church. One looks in vain through the entire corpus of Tridentine documents for any coherent teaching on the church.

B. The Council of Trent did not develop any momentous prestige for the papacy. "While unquestionably deferential to papal authority, it left open important questions about authority in the Church. Thus, the ensuing age was not one of unfettered papal control, particularly after 1600. (It was, for example, commonly taught in French seminaries until 1870 that a council was superior to the pope)."[99]

C. **The Council of Trent did not address certain key issues which were divisive even at the time of Trent**—issues such as the difference between the theological understanding of faith held by the reformers, and the theological understanding of faith held by the Roman Catholic theologians. "As regards the theologically central question of Luther—the question of faith—Trent . . . did not address it."[100]

D. **The Council of Trent formulated its decree on justification far too late to prevent a split in the western church,** even though the decree basically agreed with the conclusions of the reformers. Moreover, the bishops at Trent did not make any attempt to integrate the conclusions of this decree on justification with the decrees on the sacrifice of the mass and on the sacrament of reconciliation, leaving the theology of these two sacraments thereby vulnerable to continued criticism by the reformation theologians.[101]

E. **The canons of the Council of Trent cannot be read *prima facie* as statements of heresy.** Each canon must be considered separately, and the mere appendage of *anathema sit* does not per se indicate that the holding of such an opinion as stated in the canon is heretical.[102] Indeed, it is incorrect to state that: "It is precisely through the unequivocal doctrinal propositions, which defined the dogmatic substance and not the opinions of the schools, that the catholic faith was saved, and one might say, explicated the most important and most threatened points."[103] The doctrinal propositions, by themselves, cannot be interpreted as the historian H. Tüchle, in this citation, presupposes.

F. **The Council of Trent did not define anything implicitly.** Some systematic theologians, in their manuals of dogmatic theology, have made the claim that certain ideas were implicitly defined by this council, but there is not a shred of evidence in the acts of the council to indicate that the bishops had any intention of defining certain issues implicitly. Rather, they were at pains to determine as precisely as possible the focus of each respective canon. There are indeed definitions in the documents of Trent, but the issues which are defined were carefully circumscribed, both in the final wording of each statement, as well as in the clear intention of the voters on these statements. To go beyond either the intent of the wording or the intent of the bishops, i.e. to make a claim that some additional issues were implicitly contained in the defined statement of Trent, is theologically reprehensible.

WHAT THE COUNCIL OF TRENT DID DO

A. **The Tridentine decrees dealt with certain specific doctrinal issues, namely:**
  1. Decree on the sacred books and the traditions of the apostles (1546);
  2. Decree on the vulgate edition of the Bible and the correct manner of interpreting scripture (1546);
  3. Decree on original sin (1546);
  4. Decree on the reading [of scripture] and preaching (1546);
  5. Decree and canons on justification (1547);
  6. Decree and canons on the sacraments in general, on baptism, and on confirmation (1547);
  7. Decree and canons on the sacrament of the eucharist (1551);
  8. Doctrine and canons on the sacraments of penance and of extreme unction (1551);
  9. Decree and canons on communion under both forms and on communion of children (1562);
  10. Doctrine and canons on the sacrifice of the mass (1562);
  11. Decree on communicating the chalice to the laity (1562);
  12. True and catholic doctrine and canons on holy order (1563);
  13. Doctrine and canons on matrimony (1563);
  14. Decree on purgatory and on the invocation and veneration of relics and images (1563);
  15. Decrees on indulgences; on various penances and on the celebration of holy days; on the censure of books, on catechisms and liturgical volumes, and on the arrangement of processions and seating at liturgical rituals (1563).

In all of these decrees, there were specific issues addressed and at various levels of authoritative statement. The statements in each of these doctrinal decrees, not only depending on whether they are only an introductory chapter or a listing of canons, but also depending on the particular issue in the respective canons, do not all have the same magisterial import. Some of the material in these decrees is explanatory background only; some of the material is disciplinary; a very small part of this material can be called "defined doctrine." Even in the material which can be considered defined doctrine, care must be taken to specify precisely what is "defined."

B. Concomitant with these doctrinal decrees, there were pastoral reform decrees, namely:
1. Decree on episcopal residency and the residency of other clerics (1547);
2. Decree on benefices, perpetual unions, annual episcopal visitation of parishes, and various ecclesiastical faculties (1547);
3. On episcopal visitation of parishes and on various crimes, censures and absolutions (1551);
4. On the pastoral care of souls and on the life of clerics entrusted with pastoral ministry (1551);
5. Decree on abuses in parish life and in monastic life, and the duty of local bishops to remove such abuses (1562);
6. Decree on the moral and intellectual aptitude of the clergy (1562);
7. Decree on the education of seminarians and on the proper manner of ordination (1563);
8. Decree on the reform of marriage (1563);
9. Decree on diocesan organization, and on various crimes and punishments (1563);
10. Decree on religious men and women (1563);
11. Decree on various abuses and their correction by local bishops (1563).

In doctrinal matters, the lion's share of conciliar concern, as is evident, was the doctrine and practice of the sacraments. In pastoral matters, the lion's share of conciliar concern was the residency and pastoral care of the local bishop and the moral, spiritual and educational adequacy of the parish priest. With the bishop and the priest receiving such attention, where does this leave the non-ordained person? In its pastoral concern was Trent really concerned about the laity? The answer is, of course, affirmative, but only in an indirect way. It would seem that the bishops' reasoning was as follows: if the spiritual leadership of local churches was doctrinally correct and morally exemplary, the lay person would benefit enormously, and not only would the clergy be better disciples of the Lord but the ordinary lay man and woman would also become better disciples of Christ.

As far as the internal structures of the Roman Catholic Church were concerned, the direct goal of the council bishops was clearly to upgrade the clerical leadership, both episcopal and presbyteral, while the indirect goal was, therefore, the resultant improvement of Christian life among the non-clerical people of God. This was a typical methodology of the Catholic leadership at that time. Whereas in some of the reform movements of the Cinquecento the goal was to reform the people of God so that from such a reformed group new leadership might arise, the Roman Catholic approach at Trent was clearly the opposite, believing that a reformed leadership, particularly episcopal and presbyteral, would produce a reformed people.

We see a Tridentine interest in the lay person in the initial decree for the opening of the council. Those in attendance were asked whether the council should be formally inaugurated and be done so for the following reasons:

A. for the praise and glory of the Trinity;
B. for the increase and exaltation of the faith and the Christian religion;
C. for the reform of the clergy and *the people of God.*[104]

Even though the wording of this question makes a distinction between "clergy" and "people of God," "ad reformationem cleri et populi Christiani"—an inept ecclesiological description—it is clear that both the non-ordained and the ordained were part of the focus of the Tridentine bishops. However, with both the doctrinal and the reform decrees of Trent focusing so consciously on the clergy and only indirectly on the laity, one must go beyond the actual decrees listed above in order to discover what effect the Tridentine decrees had on the status of the non-ordained person in the church. To accomplish this, I would like to consider three major areas of the Tridentine event:

1. the socio-political influences on the ecclesial structures;
2. certain aspects of the doctrinal focus of the council;
3. certain aspects of the reform focus of the council.

1. The Socio-Political Influences on the Ecclesial Structures

Long before the council was formally summoned by the pope, the emperor Charles V played a major role as regards the time and place of the council. The diet at Ratisbon and the estates of the empire were also key socio-political players in the calling and structuring of a council. The kings of France and Spain and various other kings, dukes, and other nobles were all key to the success of this council. Popes and papal legates worked with this socio-political group with no bias that such non-clerics had absolutely no place in the planning and sustaining of the council. There were frequent differences of opinions and differences of immediate goals, but the presence of these lay people at the very center of the conciliar event was never questioned. A council with the involvement of such lay people—in this instance the Catholic nobility of Europe—was taken for granted. This involvement was not seen by the major prelates of that time as an encroachment of the "state" into the "church" domain, of the "secular" into the "sacred," of the "lay" into the "cleric." Rather, it was seen as an integral part of the total Roman Catholic Church, the *societas Christiana,* meeting in a general, ecumenical council.

When we compare the involvement of the non-ordained sector of the *societas Christiana* at Trent with the involvement of the non-ordained at the next general council, Vatican I, we find a different understanding of the clerical/lay relationship. At Vatican I the question of inviting Catholic lay political leaders of the nineteenth century was a major preliminary issue, but discussed only by the pope and his clerical advisors. Neither the pope, Pius IX, nor his clerical advisors felt any absolute obligation to involve the Catholic lay leadership in Vatican I; it was simply a matter of propriety. When we compare the Council of Trent and Vatican II on the same issue of the conciliar involvement of the non-ordained, the theme played no central role at all. In fact, John XXIII, without any consultation even with some of his ecclesiastical advisors, single-handedly called for the convocation of the council. The approach of either Pius IX (Vatican I) or John XXIII (Vatican II) was unthinkable at the middle of the sixteenth century. At that time, the pope was, by himself, impotent to call a council if the lay leadership of the *societas Christiana* had not only not been in agreement but also had not personally and structurally been supportive of a council. The Council of Trent became an historical reality only on the basis that together the *regna et sacerdotium* willed it. Neither the *regna* nor the *sacerdotium,* i.e. the emperor/kings on the one hand, and the papacy on the other, could, without the help of the other, have called or convoked an effective council in the sixteenth century.

Jedin throughout his history of the council indicates again and again the delicate but essential balancing between pope and bishop on the one hand and emperor, kings, and nobility on the other. As a force at the council itself, however, Jedin notes:

> The influence of the secular powers was surprisingly feeble at the Council. Their representatives or oratores did not bear an exclusively diplomatic character—even in the eyes of Cervini—but were considered as the representation of a part of Christendom.[105]

Alberigo, for his part, considers the influence on Trent by the various governments far more incisive and telling than Jedin does. Without any doubt the Council of Trent would have been a non-entity—in fact it would never have taken place—if this union of cleric and non-cleric (i.e. the governments) had not been an historical reality. This substantive role of the lay person in the church at the time of Trent cannot be overlooked, for it indicates that in the sixteenth century there remained in Europe, at least in the Roman Catholic mind, a single *societas Christiana,* frayed and tattered, but not yet divided into a religious church and a secularized state. It indicates that the non-ordained sector of the one church was structurally essential to the total well-being of the Christian community.

J. Grootaers makes special mention that Paul III had appointed a whole group of laymen as cardinals and made them agents of his reform endeavors.[106] One of them, Gasparo Contarini, became Paul III's right-hand as papal legate of the council. Reginald Pole also served as papal legate for the council in 1546. Only ten years later did he become a priest, two days before becoming archbishop of Canterbury. Marcello Cervini was a layman when appointed cardinal in 1539. Angelo Massarelli was officially appointed secretary to the council, and it appears that only eleven years later was he ordained to the priesthood. Count Ludovico Nogarola, another layman, drew up the reports of the theological discussion, and, while still a layman, he preached on St. Stephen's Day to the entire assembly of council members. All of this happened in the first period of the council, which came to an end with the death of Paul III in 1549.

Even though the imperial power and the various royal powers did not have a vote in the council itself, their presence, either directly or indirectly, at the council was an accepted situation; this is especially evident as regards the emperor.[107] Nonetheless, it is clear that Trent was by no means a mirror of Lateran IV. At Trent the political nationalization of Europe was already in evidence, and the consequent separation of the *societas Christiana* into national societies, which also had, to some degree or another, ties with a "national church," was also beginning to show. The rootage of an eventual form of a Europe, divided into various secularized societies, was beginning to take place, even though the reality of secularized states had not yet formally occurred.

Nonetheless, from 1300 onward canonists in particular, and through them most of the major church leaders, i.e. popes and bishops, had failed to adjust their teachings to the serious economic and social changes which had been taking place. "This left the Church unprepared for the emergence of the concept of the *civis,* or citizen, which replaced the term *laicus.* It signified a diminution in the social functions of the Church and called for a realignment of traditional distinctions."[108] The interrelationship of *regnum et sacerdotium* had changed not only through the introduction of *regna* instead of *regnum,* but also through a different structuring of the socio-political and economic world. In this new structuring of the socio-political and economic world which was slowly emerging at the time of Trent, the role of the *civis,* the citizen, was becoming more and more dominant in the area of social welfare, education, and government. A sphere of influence was slowly forming which was autonomous, that is, a sphere shaped and governed exclusively by the non-ordained sector. As this autonomous lay sphere of influence grew, the Roman Catholic clerical world, in a defensive reaction, began to turn in on itself, forming its own autonomous sphere of influence, the ecclesiastical sphere. In time the lay sphere became totally laicized, while the religious sphere became totally ecclesiasticalized. When this finally happened, the modern/contemporary church/state situation arose.

Although at the time of Trent the pope and the bishops still courted and worked with the lay leaders of the age, the over-riding focus on the clerical enclave of the church's structure and not on the nature and mystery of the entire church only hastened the process of secularization. Secularization did not only arise because of anti-clericalism; it also was caused by the clerics themselves, retreating from the *societas Christiana* into a *societas clericalis.*

> Culpability for the dramatically long delay in calling the Council weighs heavily upon almost all the leaders of Europe, but it weighs most of all upon the papacy and the Roman Curia, victims trapped in their own political designs. The papacy feared from the Council an attack on its prerogatives, and the Curia feared that a real reform "in head and members" would reduce the powers that had accrued to Rome in recent centuries.[109]

This comment by Alberigo indicates once again how controlling the issue of *regna et sacerdotium* was in the minds of the popes and the curial officials. The political, power-oriented machinations of the governmental leaders of the time, but even more so the political and power-oriented machinations of the papacy and the curia of the time cannot help but raise the question: Was Trent really interested in the people of God as such or was Trent really interested in the maintenance of clerical power?

Congar, in discussing the Tridentine period and its aftermath, makes the following observation:

> While Protestantism was making the Church a people without a priesthood and Catholic apologists were replying by establishing the rightfulness of priesthood and institution, the Church in more than one place was finding herself reduced to the state of a priestly system without a Christian people.[110]

This is a simplification of the Protestant position, as we have seen above, and to some degree it overstates the concern of the Roman Catholic world as well. The aftermath of the Council of Trent did, however, stress the cleric over the lay. During the council "the most consistent concern" was, as J. Weiss notes, "to reinstate the authority of bishops over their sees and to cut away the undergrowth of dispensations which had exempted from their authority such groups as cathedral chapters, lay patrons, and religious orders. Trent's crowning glory was the mandate for seminaries to educate the hitherto haphazardly trained diocesan priests."[111] The language which Weiss uses should be noted: if this was Trent's *most consistent concern* and its *crowning glory,* then clearly there was an overwhelming emphasis by the Council of Trent on the clerical world, almost to the exclusion of the lay world. The ecclesiastical church had still not found a way to rethink the ecclesial church. It had not yet found a way to describe the role of the lay person within the *societas Christiana,* a role which from the fourteenth century onward might more aptly be called *civis,* not *laicus.*

2. Certain Aspects of the Doctrinal Focus of the Council

In the above listing of the doctrinal decrees we noted that there was no decree either on the theology of the church or on christology. It is precisely on the basis of christology and a theology of the church, however, that the theology of the lay person finds its rootage. Nonetheless, neither christology nor a theology of the church can be formulated without a solid scriptural base, and because of this scriptural base certain doctrinal decrees of Trent and their relationship to the lay person in the church might be seen in the following way.

A. THE BIBLICAL EMPHASIS

The Tridentine insistence, which had in the council a rather stormy trail, that the Bible should be given a privileged position in the teaching of theology, had as its first effect a stress that biblical studies be promoted both in the training of the diocesan clergy and in the monastic and mendicant houses of study. As its second effect, it influenced in many ways the various catechisms which developed after the Tridentine council. As a third effect, it made the study of the Bible, including the return to Hebrew and Greek texts, a part of the Catholic emphasis. Trent clearly made the Bible more central to Roman Catholic life, and eventually this biblical emphasis affected the repositioning of the lay person in the Roman Catholic Church, in ways similar to the repositioning of the lay person in the various Protestant Churches.[112]

The theological emphasis on scripture in the Roman Catholic Church, however, received a severe setback within Roman Catholic circles with the negative injunctions of Paul IV, Pius IV and Sixtus V, with the condemnations of Quesnel in 1713 and of the synod of Pistoia in 1794, and with the advent of nineteenth century modernism. It was argued, especially by certain bishops at Trent, that the lay person, who had little education for biblical matters, could not understand the true meaning of the scriptures. That one must not cast pearls before the swine was a frequent description of allowing lay people to read and thereby interpret the Bible. Vernacular versions of the scriptures had already been going on at the time of Trent, and a growing number of lay men and women throughout the *societas Christiana* were indeed reading the scriptures. This pattern continued in spite of papal injunctions. The biblical renewal, though slow in maturation, provided Roman Catholic systematic theologians with the impetus to reinvestigate both christology and the meaning of church. When this occurred, the role of the lay person came to be seen as central to the mystery of the church, not as an appendage.

To a certain degree, the bishops at Trent faced certain issues on biblical matters. In doing so they gave a prominence to the word of God, which had not been the case in previous centuries. As the history of this newly-found emphasis on the word of God within the Roman Catholic Church structure indicates, however, the serious question arose again and again: Does the clerical world control the word of God, or does the word of God control the clerical world itself? From 1000 to Trent, the reading of scripture, at least certain sections of it, can be found in almost every one of the geographically scattered reform movements, and from Trent to the present the reading of scripture, by ordained and non-ordained alike, can be found in almost every reform movement. This freedom of the word of God to move the hearts of men and women cannot be controlled by clerics. Moreover, it is not only the reading of scripture itself which is noteworthy; it is even more the effect of this reading of scripture by each and every Christian which is important, an effect that centers on discipleship, the primary criterion which we have used throughout this present work. The reading of the word of God again and again enthused the Christian person to become a more perfect disciple of the Lord and to help others become more perfect disciples as well.

B. THE SACRAMENTAL EMPHASIS

The various doctrinal decrees on the sacraments, together with their respective reform decrees, did make sacramental life more central to the spiritual life of the church than it had been even in the middle ages. After Trent, baptism, penance, eucharist, marriage, and anointing not only became the major spiritual moments in the life of a Christian community, but they also became the major indicators both of one's personal spiritual life and of the parish or diocesan spiritual life as well.

This focus on the sacraments was especially clear in the sacrament of the eucharist. "Through the controversy with the Reformers, the whole stress of thought on the Eucharist was directed to and bound down to the Real Presence, almost to the neglect of other aspects."[113] The eventual Tridentine mass did remove many of the gross abuses found at times in the liturgies of the middle ages, "but still the Mass remains a service in which only the priest and his assistants have an active role. The faithful follow the divine action only from a distance."[114]

Clerical control in the administration of all sacraments was enhanced by the Council of Trent, while frequent or regular non-clerical reception of the sacraments was made more mandatory. The spirituality of Roman Catholic Christian life became in a centralized way sacramental spirituality, and eventually a triadic configuration of Roman Catholic spirituality became standard:

a. Clerical celebrational control of the sacraments;
b. Requisite non-clerical reception of sacraments, but for the most part as passive recipients;
c. A Christian spirituality, centralized in the proper clerical celebration of each sacrament and the proper lay reception of each sacrament.

This triadic spirituality, with its focus on the sacraments, especially the eucharist, eventually paved the way for a different triadic form of spirituality which one associates with Vatican II theology:

a. The sacraments are a celebration by the entire people of God (i.e. a Christian community), not simply the celebration by a priestly cleric;
b. The sacraments are fundamentally a christocentric, and only secondarily an ecclesial ritual;
c. The sacramental celebration is ritualized through a multiple ministry, including clerical and non-clerical ministries.

This linkage between the sacramental system of Trent and that of Vatican II can be stated in the following way:

The Tridentine focus of Christian spirituality, primarily in the celebration of the sacraments by duly ordained priests and in the

correct reception of sacraments by the non-ordained, made sacramental life the center of Roman Catholic spirituality. Sacraments became the criteria of genuine catholicity.

When the theology of sacraments began to change, the very positioning and repositioning of the cleric and the non-cleric substantially changed as well. Trent made sacramental life central, but only on the basis of a particular theology of the sacraments. When that theology of the sacraments changed, sacramental life still remained central, but the celebration of the sacraments was no longer exclusively that of the ordained. The sacraments, instead, were the celebration of the gathered church, the community of faith, the people of God. The lay person moved directly into the center of sacramental life.

The restructuring of the word of God into each and every sacramental celebration, something which rarely happened in the aftermath of Trent but did take place both before and after Vatican II, also transformed the positioning of the ordained and the non-ordained in the celebration of sacramental life.

3. Certain Aspects of the Reform Decrees of the Council of Trent

Although the reform decrees of Trent centered on bishops and parish priests, and to some extent on abbeys and monasteries, it should be noted that this emphasis was clearly meant to build up the local church. As mentioned above, the Council of Trent did not in any major way enhance the papacy. Rather, bishops were enhanced, and they were told in no uncertain terms to "stay home."[115] Parish priests, who were at the time of Trent both too many and too poorly educated, were enhanced and they were told to "be educated," "be holy," and "be pastoral." Bishop and parish priest alone, however, do not constitute a local church. Why should a bishop stay home? Why should a parish priest be educated, holy and pastoral? The answer is obvious: to serve the local community of faith, to serve the *local* people of God. The reform decrees of Trent did not primarily advocate a loyalty to a "universal church," a "papal church." They did not advocate a loyalty to a "national church." They stressed the local church.

Unfortunately, in the course of the counter-reformation, the stress was on apologetics: namely, the Roman Catholic Church is distinct and "better" than the Protestant churches because Roman Catholics have an allegiance to the pope and to a unified belief and a standardized liturgy, thus stressing the universal church over the local church. When the counter-reformation had finally run its course, the local church was somehow buried under the banners of a universal church. It is true that in the counter-reformation period Roman Catholic bishops observed residency more dutifully than in the period prior to Trent, and it is also true that parish priests in the counter-reformation period gradually became more educated, more pastoral, and to some degree more holy. Nonetheless, in that same period of time, the counter-reformation, other factors took place which made the local church at times less important than the reform decrees of Trent had envisioned. From 1848 onward, the obsession of the papacy with spiritual and political power almost obliterated the value and meaning of the local church. This nineteenth and twentieth century papal positioning moved in counter-productive ways to the intent of the reform decrees of Trent.

In conclusion, what can one say about the Council of Trent and the theological and pastoral role of the lay person in the church? Did the Council of Trent bring about a repositioning of the lay person in the church? In some ways the answer is yes, but always in an indirect way. Directly the Council of Trent focused on the clergy, indirectly on the laity. The times in which this council lived were so characterized by division that the bishops, few in number as they generally were, often seemed bewildered by the complexity of issues, overwhelmed by the divisions in the *societas Christiana,* and unsure of their own authority because of the often conflicting papal directives. These bishops focused on a few certain specific issues, both as regards doctrine and as regards discipline. On these issues they made specific statements. Some of these issues did have or at least promised to have an effect on the lay person in the church. Circumstances after the council, however, either officially moved the effects of the council in a direction not advocated by the council, e.g. the focus on the universal church rather than on the local church, or placed some of these directions virtually on hold, e.g. the role of scripture in the life of the individual Christian. The Council of Trent, as a result, exhibits a "polyhedral quality" (Alberigo). Tridentinism, if that is the label we can use, strongly moved the effects of this council into a clerical and Roman conformism.

After one considers the long history of reform in the church from 1000 to 1563, the closing of the Tridentine council, a period of various reforms which includes the many Protestant reforms as well as Roman Catholic reforms, one might ask: Did the notion of discipleship play a key role in any or all of these movements? The answer is clearly affirmative. Most reforms, and particularly the several Protestant reforms, reacted against a situation in the church, but it was not the reality against which the reformers reacted that can be considered the root cause of the reaction. Rather, the reformers acted *for* some issue, and on the basis of this pro-action they took a contra-action. In the earlier reforms, from 1000 onward, we found that men and women again and again wanted to live a life based on the gospels. This was the fundamental pro-action. That they opposed a simoniacal episcopacy, a concubinate priesthood, a wealthy monasticism was a consequence, a contra-action, of their basic pro-action.

Luther, Calvin, and other reformers of the sixteenth century reacted against an overbearing papacy and papal church. They did so, however, because of a deeper pro-action. In the writings of both Luther and Calvin it is evident that they were deeply concerned about living the gospel life, i.e. discipleship. Because of their basic desire to lead a life as the gospels, the word of God, indicated, they reacted, and strongly, against ecclesiastical areas which tended to place structure over Spirit. The bishops and prelates at Trent followed this same pattern, although in their own way. The following diagrams might help clarify this.

Diagram One.

On the basis of discipleship the Tridentine bishops asked: What is the meaning of:	Scripture?
	 Justification?
	 The sacraments, but above all:
	   Baptism?
	   Eucharist?
	   Priesthood?
	 Residency of bishops?
	 Formation of Priests?

They Did Not Ask:

On the basis of the issues involved in *regnum et sacerdotium*, i.e. on the basis of the role of the pope, what is the meaning of:	Scripture?
	 Justification?
	 The sacraments, but above all:
	   Baptism?
	   Eucharist?
	   Priesthood?
	 Residency of bishops?
	 Formation of Priests?

In this diagram, we see that the Tridentine bishops placed to one side the issue which had almost dominated papal policy and structure for several centuries: the issue of *regnum et sacerdotium*. Trent did not have as its main agenda the enhancement of the papacy. Indeed, as we mentioned above, the Council of Trent did not develop any momentous prestige for the papacy. Defense of the pope was not the primary issue through which the bishops considered the individual agenda topics. Rather, and the data bears this out, the bishops, who were quite pastorally concerned, were asking: How can we help bring about a better community of faith, i.e. a group of disciples, in the churches of our various lands?

On the other hand, the Tridentine bishops did not follow through as completely as one might wish, since once they had issued their doctrinal statement, they did not pursue as fully as they should its implications. The following diagram might help clarify on this:

Diagram Two.

On the basis of: 　Scripture 　Justification 　Sacraments 　Residency of bishops 　Formation of priests　　　　　What is the meaning of discipleship?

The Protestant reformers, for their part, had asked the primary question: How can one be a disciple of Jesus on the basis of the word of God? This was the pro-action. The contra-action was the rejection of ecclesiastical structures which stood in the way of this scriptured discipleship, which placed structure above Spirit. In the formulation of their own approach to justification, the sacraments, ministry, etc., they asked in a more pointed way than their Roman Catholic counterparts: What are the implications for discipleship, given this scriptured response to these fundamental themes? After making their reform decrees, which in some ways attempted to bring about the implications of the doctrinal decrees, the Tridentine bishops went home, leaving the promulgation of the decrees, reform and doctrinal, to the pope. When this happened, the pope together with the curia once again let the issue of *regnum et sacerdotium,* not discipleship, control, perhaps not in an exclusive but certainly in a major way, the promulgation and therefore the activation of the Tridentine measures. Whenever discipleship ceases to be the primary criterion and the basic motivational factor, whether at a personal level, a local church level, a diocesan level, a national level, or a universal church level, the theological and ministerial role of the lay person in the church suffers. Tridentinism, for lack of a better term, disallowed discipleship to serve in this primary way. Instead, Tridentinism was a form of church leadership, motivated by a desire for church uniformity under clerical control, a uniformity throughout the *societas Christiana* which could only be realized by a deemphasis on the local church and a pro-emphasis on the papal church. Let us consider this aftermath of the Council of Trent in some detail.

6. THE LAY PERSON IN THE ROMAN CATHOLIC THEOLOGY AND MINISTRY IN TRIDENTINISM

There is a dispute on the very term which one uses for the period in Roman Catholicism immediately following Trent. Counter-reformation was the term of preference since the late eighteenth century. Is it, however, a serious misnomer? Should not the immediate, post-Tridentine period in the Roman Catholic Church be primarily called "the Catholic reform," with the term "counter-reformation" applicable only to the endeavors during that same period to thwart the advance of Protestantism? This is, at least, the view of J. Weiss.[116] On the other hand, the term "counter-reformation" continues to be used by major scholars who deal with the period of post-Tridentine Roman Catholic history and theology. When precisely the counter-reformation came to an end is also debated, and as yet remains an open question. This section deals with a period of church life that comes to an end with the French and American revolutions, roughly 1800. That there were a number of significant efforts at Catholic reform from 1570 down to 1800 can be well documented: e.g. the formation of new religious orders such as the Jesuits, the Theatines, the Ursulines, and the Oratory of Divine Love; the renewal of older religious communities, e.g. Capuchins and Carmelites. There was also a renewal in Christian spirituality, e.g. the Spanish mysticism of Teresa of Avila and John of the Cross, and the French mysticism of Berulle and Olier. Even the spirituality of Jansenism cannot be set aside as irrelevant, since it clearly caught on in a widespread way. There were advances in humanism and education generally, as well as in the arts, which incorporated new ways of living the Christian ideal. On the other hand, there was a clear apologetic strain of thought and action throughout this same period: a defense of the Roman Catholic approach against Protestant and Anglican forms of Christian life. There was a clinging to the past, rather than a moving into the future, a desire for restoration rather than reformation.

There was a clear retention of clerical dominance and a suspicion of non-clerical intervention.

To help us understand the actuation of Tridentinism, let us consider one of the major effects of the council: the publication of the Roman catechism. On April 5, 1546, mention was first made at Trent of such a catechism. Twenty years later this catechism was published. The various authors and editors of this catechism intended the volume to be a summary of doctrine, based on the teaching of the Tridentine council.[117] Like many catechisms of the time, it used the creed as the framework for its presentation, and this indicates at once that the catechism goes far beyond the discussions at Trent, for the Tridentine bishops did not issue any statements on God, the Trinity, Jesus, the Holy Spirit, the church, the resurrection of the body, and the last things. The authors of the catechism had to go elsewhere to establish the basis for their presentation on the creed. In the text itself the citations are basically biblical and to a very slight degree patristic. Only once, in this exposition of the creed, is there a direct reference to the decrees of Trent. Still in 1566 the work appeared with the title: *Catechismus ex decreto Concilii Tridentini ad Parochos, Pii V. Pont. Max. iussu editus.*

What is of singular interest for our theme on the lay person is its presentation of the church.[118] Although this section is not a full ecclesiology by any means, it does shed light on the way the term "church" was used at that time by the *periti* who authored this catechism. The church is first of all seen as "those who are called by faith to the light of truth and the knowledge of God." The church is the "faithful dispersed throughout the world." It is the "Christian people" who are called by God. This people is divided into two parts: the church triumphant and the church militant. This latter is the "society of all faithful still dwelling on earth." In this earthly society there are two classes of people: the good and the bad. There are three groups which are outside the church: infidels, who have never known the church; heretics and schismatics, who have separated themselves from the church and are "deserters"; and excommunicated persons, who have been cut off from the church.

Only after all of this does the catechism consider other uses of the word "church"—a remarkable turn of phrase. The first "other" use is the use of the term "church" for a local church, which is a main Tridentine focus, when one considers the council's reform decrees. The second "other" use of the term "church" is to "signify prelates and pastors of the church." The third "other" use of the term "church" is for the building.[119]

This section of the catechism is of singular interest because it indicates the way in which a group of theologians attempted to formulate a theology of the church on the basis of the Council of Trent, i.e. in the spirit of Trent. The stress is on God's call (*ecclesia*) or a community of faithful. In the text itself the stress is not on a "church of the clerics." Unfortunately, this way of viewing the church, found in the Tridentine catechism, was not continued as the counter-reformation theology developed. "The catechetical instruction, which had been planned in well-balanced form by the *Roman Catechism* of 1566, became disjointed and 'off-center' in the very influential *Catechism* of Robert Bellarmine (1598) which to far too great an extent was taken up with the controversies against the Protestants."[120]

What was called in the Tridentine catechism an "other" use of the term "church," namely when the term "church" was used to refer to clergy, became central in the counter-reformation presentations of the church, especially through the influence of Robert Bellarmine and Peter Canisius. If, however, the Tridentine catechism reflected the spirit of Trent, then one must say that any ecclesiology which tends to see the church primarily as a "church of the clerics" goes against the spirit of Trent. Far more fundamental than this, however, is that such a clerical form of ecclesiology goes against the biblical presentation of church. A clerical church may not correspond to a Tridentine Church, but even more blameworthy is the fact that it does not correspond to a biblical church. One must, then, be quite cautious when Trent is invoked as the basis for an understanding of the church as primarily a church of clerics. Tridentinism, not Trent itself, is being invoked on such an occasion.

Alberigo notes that, when the council ended, there were two tendencies regarding the interpretation of the Council of Trent. The first was papal, based on the principle of a centralized and uniform direction by Rome for the renewal of the entire church. This view stems clearly from the *regnum et sacerdotium* mentality of the papacy. The second view placed its emphasis on the local church and its local energies. Charles Borromeo, the archbishop of Milan, advocated this position.[121] Rome, however, deliberately obstructed Borromeo's activity in this regard. When Borromeo died on November 3, 1584, his reputation of holiness created an even more difficult obstacle to this Roman opposition to Borromeo's approach. Now one had to oppose a "holy man." His biography, written by C. Bascapè, was immediately challenged by Rome, but the process of Borromeo's canonization continued apace. Eventually, when Charles Borromeo was canonized, a Roman interpretation of him was drawn up by Robert Bellarmine, with the result that not only was he canonized for the Catholic world, but his image was Romanized for that same Catholic world. As Alberigo notes, Borromeo is painted wearing the robes of a cardinal, not the robes of a bishop. In many ways this Romanization of Trent and of the issues connected with Trent continued to develop, and a "Tridentinism" with papal overtones took over. Only recent scholarship has begun to dismantle this seemingly "orthodox" view of the Tridentine council.

Even in the Lutheran world a clericalization of the church was, in some ways, evident.

> The effect of both Reformation and Counter-Reformation was in different ways to strengthen the idea that the clergy formed a separate estate. Protestant reformers following Luther may have argued that all men were priests, but this did not mean that all men were equal.[122]

This congealing of structures fits in well with J. Delumeau's analysis that seven qualities affected both Roman Catholic and Protestant positions during this period of time:

1. The elaboration of clearly stated theological positions;
2. Their promulgation and distribution through institutional structures;
3. Their internalization through education and catechesis, at the parish level and at a seminary level;
4. Their distribution through the press together with a censoring of opposite views;
5. Disciplinary measures to insure orthodox acceptance;
6. Clerical control of ritual;
7. The development of a preferred confessional and liturgical language.[123]

The churches continued to focus on both word and sacrament. In the Protestant churches, the word of God played a more liturgical role; in the Roman Catholic churches, catechesis became paramount. The sacramental life of the churches was no less important.

> Although Protestant theologians had a different view of the sacraments [from that of the Roman Catholics], it would be wrong to think that they downgraded them or those who performed

them. Correct performance of the sacraments was, like preaching, one of the marks of the true Church.[124]

Indeed, mainstream Protestant churches emphasized the true administration of the sacraments, in contrast to the "untrue" administration in Roman Catholic sacramental life, and Roman Catholic churches emphasized "seven sacraments" with its sacramental system as opposed to "only two" in the Protestant churches. This sacramental emphasis by both sides of the reformation divide finds a strong echo in the ecumenical discussions today, in which the issue of sacraments, more often than not, becomes the focus of so many other underlying issues, such as ecclesiology, authority in the church, the role of the word of God, the meaning of ministry, etc. Sacramental issues would not have this focusing effect today from both Protestant and Roman Catholic participants, if in the many preceding centuries a certain sacramental approach had not been developed respectively in both sets of churches, a sacramental approach which in so many ways summarized the meaning of church and discipleship. In the Roman Catholic approach, the separateness of the priest, because of his powers over the sacraments, but especially the eucharist, played a major role, but one which included a quite defensive aspect as well.

> As for the Counter-Reformation, it responded to the challenges thrown down by late medieval heretics, sixteenth-century reformers, and an increasingly literate and critical laity by trying to accentuate the separateness of the priesthood.[125]

Although this is true of the Roman Catholic world, it should be noted that in the period 1520–1780, in both the various Protestant and Roman Catholic parishes, many clerical similarities can be seen:

1. Clergy were not uniformly educated.
2. Clergy remained involved in a number of both religious and political situations.
3. Clergy became to some degree a professional group of people.
4. Protestant and Roman Catholic clergy tended to resemble one another in task and life-style rather than move in separate ways.
5. Perhaps the changes in the clergy from 600 to 1100 were greater than the changes in the clergy from 1520 to 1780, whether one considers either Protestant or Roman Catholic clergy.

On the part of the lay person, one notes in both Protestant and Roman Catholic communities the following characteristics:

1. As the defensiveness of both Protestant and Catholic abated, the lay person simply accepted the social situation in his or her area without much anxiety. Pluralism gradually became acceptable.
2. The lay people did not really make any concerted efforts to displace clerical power, whether Protestant or Catholic. Only a few exceptions can be found in several radical reformation movements.
3. The lay person became complacent to the religious situation of the country. Religious issues were increasingly not seen as the main issues of one's life. Secularization slowly infiltrated the lives of both Protestant and Roman Catholic.
4. Some studies on "popular piety," or, perhaps better stated, on the ordinary people's piety, have indicated a continuing enthusiasm among Catholics for various confraternities, a continued veneration of saints, and catechesis through drama.[126] Pietism in Lutheran circles and Methodism, Quakerism and other spiritual-minded groups mushroomed in various Protestant sectors of the western world. In all of these there was a "popular" piety, i.e. a piety, by which lay people, most often without clerical leadership, grew in their Christian spirituality.

What one finds throughout this lengthy period of Roman Catholic Church history, with the founding of many new religious communities, especially of women, with the development of Jansenism and its influence on the piety of Europe and eventually the western world generally, with the development of a doctrinally fixated theology and the overflow of this fixated theological approach into catechisms and various other religious writings, is an ever-present and an ever-increasing group of lay men and women who are key to the life of the local churches. Madame Acarie, Madame Guyon, Jeanne-Françoise de Chantal, Marie de l'Incarnation, Maria Maddelena dei Pazzi, and Pascal are names which come to mind, but unremembered names of men and women, all lay, must be taken into account, for Catholic parishes continued to exist only because there were people who frequented the parishes. These lay men and women increasingly moved upward in the areas of education, political and economic positions, and spiritual sensitivity. They listened to their clerical leaders and performed their ecclesiastical duties, but they also were reading theological works and discussing theological issues.

Kathryn Norberg, in her essay on "The Counter Reformation and Women: Religious and Lay," is one of the first Catholic authors to investigate the role of women in the church during this period of time. She is, however, not totally alone, but a Roman Catholic investigation of this topic is, in the scholarly world, only of very recent vintage. Prior to these investigations, the prevailing view was:

> Protestantism enhanced the position of women by sanctifying the family, instituting divorce and admitting women to the priesthood of all believers. In contrast, Catholicism in the sixteenth and seventeenth centuries meant "business as usual." Catholic women were still excluded from the priesthood and their roles as mothers and wives were depreciated by a Church that still preferred celibacy to the family.[127]

One of the major indications of the accomplishment of women in the Protestant churches was the fact that during this period of time many Catholic women joined the Protestant churches. Nonetheless, recent research has indicated that such an either/or description of Protestant women/Catholic women is not all that accurate. Trent's rule of strict claustration for women's orders, which was supposed to affect all religious communities of women, was more often than not disregarded, with the result that more and more religious women moved into educational, pastoral, and health-care apostolates. In doing this, religious women resisted the attempt on the part of the hierarchy to diminish their independence. Many of the communities of women, founded after Trent, were specifically exempted from such claustration, as we find at least in the original intent of Angela Merici and Francis de Sales for the Ursulines and Visitations, and which we find in the actual accomplishment of the Daughters of Charity.

The sacramental spirituality which Trent developed tended to make the lay people, and in rather distinct ways women religious, dependent on the sacramental ministration of the cleric. However, religious women moved in a different direction of spirituality quite out of the control of clerics: namely, into the direction of mysticism, and Teresa of Avila is in this regard only the stellar personality. Michel De Certeau has argued quite conclusively that mysticism in France during this period of time was structurally feminine, and at the same time was generally opposed or denigrated by the clerical church.[128] It is becoming evident, though slowly, that many of these religious women also opened their convents to lay women, so that activities, which today one might call support groups, spiritual direction, and faith-sharing, were already taking place in the sixteenth, seventeenth and eighteenth centuries. A major rootage for the contemporary woman's movement as regards the church must be traced back to the post-Tridentine era.

Our knowledge of non-religious women during this same period of time is limited. Research has often been focused on the "heterodox" woman. More research is needed on the presence of women in various confraternities and spiritual associations, as Norberg argues:

> Post-Tridentine Catholicism, like its Protestant rival, attracted women and retained their loyalties long after their husbands had gone over to disbelief. The strongest case for Protestant superiority when it comes to women—the support of women for the Reformation—no longer seems so convincing.[129]

The contemporary disdain for the various women's movements in the church, which some church leaders have mislabeled as an "American phenomenon," has rather deep roots within the church's history, and particularly its European history. These contemporary women's movements have not appeared all of a sudden. Indeed, foundations for the role of women in the contemporary church can be found in the ways in which the Council of Trent tried to address the role of the lay person in the church, but above all in the ways in which post-Tridentine women themselves creatively addressed the theme of discipleship through mysticism, apostolic religious communities, and the feminine formation of spiritualities for women who were not members of a religious community.

7. THE LAY PERSON FROM 1700 TO THE EVE OF THE FRENCH REVOLUTION

The French Revolution was a turning point in western civilization. Congar notes this change as western culture ended the eighteenth century and moved into the nineteenth century.

> It is quite another thing when we come to the nineteenth century and are face to face with a society born of the Enlightenment, rising industrialism, the French Revolution and (eventually) its Napoleonic prolongation, aggressive and widespread unbelief, and the disappearance of the props of the faith provided by political powers. Christians were shaken. The world's structure had changed: it was now deeply divided, separated from Christ by hostility or indifference, full of new forces at work, enthusiastic for values unknown to classical theology, heedless, often ignorant, of the traditional Catholic set-up.[130]

In the eighteenth century, the rise of the *Aufklärung,* the rise of the industrial state, the rise of revulsion for the high-handedness of royalty and the aloofness of the upper-clergy came to a major confrontation with the French Revolution and the various other revolutions which stemmed from it. This is, however, the theme of the next chapter.

8. GENERAL OVERVIEW

In chapter nine of this volume we began a review of the history of the western church from roughly 1000, i.e. the end of the first millennium and the beginning of the second millennium, down to the beginning of the sixteenth century. Our focus was on the theological and pastoral role of the lay person in the church during this period of time. In this chapter we have continued this review, from the appearance of the major Protestant reforms at the beginning of the sixteenth century down to the end of the so-called Roman Catholic counter-reformation, i.e. somewhere in the middle of the seventeenth century, followed by a very brief consideration of the Catholic Church during the eighteenth century. Our focus throughout has remained constant: the theological and pastoral role of the lay person in the church during this period of time. If there is one term which appeared unceasingly in western church history from 1000 to roughly 1800, it is the word "reform." There were, as we saw, the geographically scattered reform movements from 1000 to 1400, as well as the more official reform begun by the Germans, more often than not called the Gregorian reform. There was, as well, the clarion call for a reform in head and members, which is well documented from the period of the Avignon papacy through the Council of Trent. At Trent there was the demand of many governmental leaders as well as ecclesiastical leaders to include not only doctrinal issues but also reform issues in the agenda of the Tridentine council, a demand which the pope initially was not willing to support, wanting only doctrinal issues, not reform issues on the agenda. His reluctance did not win out, and the bishops and others met at Trent with both a doctrinal and a reform agenda. The Protestant movements of the sixteenth century were each in their own respective ways a reform movement, but these particular reform movements were of such a magnitude and importance that they alone have subsequently been called quite simply "the reformation." Is it not interesting that one never thinks of either the Gregorian or the Tridentine reform when one says "the reformation." Rather, one thinks only of the non-Roman Catholic reforms of the sixteenth century. In the various historical writings, these and these alone have merited the title "the reformation." After the Council of Trent, reform movements, both Protestant and Catholic, continued. Nonetheless it is well known that it was a few German scholars in the nineteenth century who began to call the Roman Catholic efforts of this Tridentine and post-Tridentine period the "counter-reform." The term is an odd one, since it means "against reform," whereas in essence the movements they were discussing were Roman Catholic and quite deliberate movements of reform.

Reform, reform, reform—both the word and the effort occurred over and over again from 1000 to 1700, a period of seven hundred years! How could such diverse calls for reform last for so long a time and not reach some resolution? The very frequency of these reform movements and the length of time during which they occurred with such intensity is certainly a major issue which needs analysis. I offer the following:

1. The Presence of Serious Anti-Christian Life in the Roman Catholic Church

First of all, there would not have been such a stirring for reform over seven hundred years if there had not been something of overwhelming and perduring magnitude which seriously needed to be reformed. In a Christian church, serious and substantive reform takes place only when there are serious and substantive anti-Christian elements within the community of faith itself. The reform movements from 1000 to 1700 did not focus on people outside the Christian community. In nature, these seven-centuries-long reforms were not missionary and conversionary of the non-Christian. Rather, these reform movements were centered inwardly on Christians within the church community itself. In other words, there were serious and substantive anti-Christian elements within the Christian community itself which called forth this barrage of reform movements. Movements of reform would not have continued to arise throughout these seven hundred years if there had not been something in the church itself, and more specifically in the Roman Catholic Church itself, which was both chronic and pathological.[131] Something was seriously amiss in the Roman Catholic Church which needed serious and substantive rectification. In order to understand this, let us continue to use the medical metaphor: from the data of history, one could state that besides an original diagnosis, namely, that which one finds in the first emergence of various localized reform movements, there were as well "second," "third," "fourth," "fifth," etc., opinions regarding the malady, as one begins to review reform movement after reform movement after reform movement from 1000 to 1700. One reform movement after another emerged, and each reform movement in its own way reached a similar though not identical diagnosis: there was something seriously and substantively wrong *within* the Christian church. The diagnosis was not that the western church was surrounded by external evil forces, that something external was threatening the health of the Christian community. This prolonged series of reform movements did not blame any outside, "pagan," "secularizing," elements. Rather, these movements found fault with something internal to the church structure itself. However, there is only something wrong *within* a Christian church, that is, not something wrong because of external factors, when the internal "wrong" factor is itself anti-Christian. That is the reason one must say that there was something anti-Christian *within* the Christian church during these centuries which occasioned time after time reform movements of diverse dimensions and emphases.

One might counter that the long period of reform simply indicates that in each and every generation the church is in need of reform. Theologically speaking, one might advance the Protestant principle of reformation, or the theological statement which one finds in some of the post-Vatican II official documents: *ecclesia semper reformanda.*[132] In such a theological view, each Christian generation should necessarily find something which needs reform in the church community. This position might certainly be verified if the focal issue of reform during the seven centuries we have just considered had tended to change from generation to generation. If the focus of the reform varied over a wide range of inner-church problems, then one would be correct to invoke a principle of reformation as a constant and native factor of church life. However, when one begins to see that the issue of the various reforms remained quite constant, then one no longer is faced with a church which always needs reform, but a church which has a chronic and pathological situation. From the historical data, it would appear that this latter is the case, not the former. The historical data, in my judgment, indicates that again and again and again the issue remained constant, and that this specific issue can be summarily described as "discipleship."

2. The Continued Presence of the Call for Reform and Actual Movements of Reform

The geographically scattered reform movements of the middle ages were all movements in which cleric and non-cleric, religious and non-religious, attempted to put into practice gospel discipleship. We have seen how these men and women continually went to the New Testament, particularly the gospels, in their struggle to lead a life of discipleship, which they did not find adequately in the church communities to which they belonged, including the clerical and monastic communities.

In the Germanic reform movement, the Gregorian reform, the goal of discipleship was clearly foundational, but this movement became skewed through the narrowly papal vision of Gregory VII. Gregory's vision of papacy, not the gospels, became the hermeneutic for the meaning of discipleship. Even the gospels were interpreted from the standpoint of his vision of papacy. This papal vision of Gregory was a major continuation of the *regnum et sacerdotium* tension, but it paved the way for the exaggerated claims of Innocent III and Boniface VIII, and above all the unheard-of claim of Innocent IV.

It was this exaggeration and hermeneutic which in many ways brought on the powerful reaction of the early Protestant reformers, and these men raised their voice on the issue of gospel discipleship. The *Babylonian Captivity* of Luther was fundamentally a criticism of the papal understanding and advocacy of discipleship. The *Institutes* of Calvin, more often than not, raise the same criticism against the papal presentation of discipleship. Other factors entered into the causes of the sixteenth century reformation, but the inner-church problem was basically a question of gospel discipleship.

Trent, as we have seen, was a major effort on the part of the Roman Catholic Church leadership of that time to regain a credible discipleship. The pastoral concern at Trent is undeniable, but pastoral for what purpose and for whom? The answer is clear: to help Catholics be better disciples of the Lord. This same pastoral intent is found, in its own way, in the reform efforts which have been called "counter-reformation" or "Tridentinism."

It was mentioned above that there was something chronic and pathological within the Christian community of faith which occasioned the barrage of reform movements from 1000 to 1700. It was mentioned that this was basically a perduring and constant situation. It was also mentioned that an inner-church issue of this nature had to be something serious and substantive and as such can only be described as "anti-Christian." In other words, there was a perduring, chronic, and pathological issue, which was serious and substantive, of an anti-Christian nature within the community of faith itself. It is my judgment that this cancer was a falsified form of discipleship. The very nature of the church, which theologically can only be seen in terms of genuine gospel discipleship, was struggling throughout this entire period to rid itself of an anti-body, a falsification of gospel discipleship, which had cancerously grown within it.

Roman Catholic apologetic theology, which became so dominant in the counter-reformation period, tended to downplay the seriousness of the problem within the Roman Catholic Church. Rather, these apologetic attempts blamed the Protestant groups for the ills and evils, and placed the best light possible on the Roman Catholic position, especially as regards doctrine.

Protestant apologetic theology, which developed with equal strides in the post-Tridentine period, stressed the reformed aspects of the various

Protestant churches and the continued decadence of the Roman Catholic Church. It is ironic, however, that many of these Protestant churches were called the reformed church, as if they had already been reformed and were thereby healed and healthy. In many instances of various Protestant churches, the principle of reformation at times ceased to exist or continued to exist but only in a most feeble way, as if the true "reformed" church had finally been reached.

3. The Demise of the Term "Reform" and Its Replacement with "Renewal"

The unceasing reform movements of these seven hundred years, 1000 to 1700, left the western church in disarray, splintered and scattered across the nations of Europe and from there splintered and scattered across the remainder of the world. Denominational lines became rigidly maintained; communication between the vying groups was, more often than not, strident and shrill, negative and pejorative. Oddly enough, in the Roman Catholic Church the word "reform" gradually faded as new movements arose. In the Protestant churches an established "reform" church group retained the name, of course, but new church movements slowly but surely shunned the name "reform." In Roman Catholicism, the term "counter-reformation" was a nineteenth century retrospective appellation. In the twentieth century the various calls were never couched in the term "reform." Rather, the favored terms were and are "renewal" and "aggiornamento." As one moves from 1700 onward, the phrase "reform in head and members" quietly becomes inoperative. This phenomenon is "odd," since for seven hundred years the term "reform," or the phrase "reform in head and members," had been so intensely operative, and these very terms were used with gusto even by the highest church leadership, popes and councils. In the twentieth century, were a charismatic group of Roman Catholics or a Roman Catholic group of *cursillistas* to call themselves a reform group, or to advocate a reform in head and members, enormous suspicion would be directed their way by church leadership and by other church members as well. On the other hand, were these same groups to use the term "renewal," little suspicion would be engendered. A few books which have advocated a renewal of "head and members" have emerged, but the call for a renewal of both the papacy and the episcopacy (head) has generally met with negativity.[133]

4. The Repositioning of the Lay Person into a Gospel Role of Discipleship

Nonetheless, in all these reform movements, even the more wrenching movements of the sixteenth century, the lay person in the church, male and female, became more and more prominent. There was a clear and expanding repositioning of the lay person in the structures of church life during these centuries. This is not to say that the reform movements alone occasioned such a repositioning of the lay person. As noted many times, other fundamental factors of a cultural nature were also involved, including social, economic and political factors. Still, it is obvious that as one enters into the seventeenth century, lay men and lay women are far more prominent throughout the scattered and splintered *societas Christiana*. This progressive repositioning of the lay person within the church structure did not take place without simultaneously affecting the positioning of the cleric. The position of the cleric at all levels within the *societas Christiana*—papal, episcopal, presbyteral, diaconal—was also repositioned. If one concludes that the lay person's position in the church became more prominent from 1000 to 1700, it is impossible to say in the same breath that the position of the cleric nonetheless remained unchanged. Indeed, the position of the cleric did change, and if the lay person began to have more prominence, the cleric in many ways began to lose prominence. The repositioning of the lay person into a stronger role within the church *ipso facto* brought on a depositioning of the cleric within the same church. This depositioning was, in the Roman Church, often disavowed by many of its leaders and theologians, as though such a repositioning, much less a depositioning, did not and could not exist. It was also, in certain areas of church life, factually ignored, as one notices in the clerically-oriented liturgical developments throughout the seventeenth and eighteenth centuries. But in spite of such denials and inadvertence, the role of the lay person within the Roman Church continued to edge its way into ever more influential positions.

Throughout the sixteenth century there were not only a call for reform, but major movements of reform. Since the anti-Christian life had become so endemic and widespread, various attempts at systemic reform took place. Whenever a system or structure is overhauled, major displacement and major changes take place. These changes, though major, do not mean of necessity "new" situations, for the major restructuring of all these reforms was focused on making the church at all levels as scripturally genuine as possible. Every true reform effort attempted, in some way or another, to make disciples of all nations. Again we notice that the reforms fundamentally were neither "anti" issues (anti-simony or anti-concubinate-clergy) nor "anti" elements (anti-clerical, anti-monastic). Deeper than the anti-aspects of each true reform movement was the "pro" factor: namely, each reform wanted desperately to bring about gospel discipleship. This was the genuine and religiously sound basis which one finds in almost every instance of reform from 1000 to 1700.

The ways in which this profound positive desire worked itself out in the historical time-space continuum of that period of church life were diverse, since gospel discipleship was considered from diverse hermeneutical frameworks. One can, for instance, perceive differing, even if not totally consistent, hermeneutics in operation as regards reforms which stressed Spirit over structure as opposed to those which seemed to stress structure over Spirit. We find as well differing, even if not totally consistent, hermeneutics in operation as regards reforms which stressed papal supremacy and control over those which stressed more localized, even non-sacerdotally controlled movements. We find differing, even if not totally consistent hermeneutics in operation as regards reforms which were mechanistic and administrative in nature—more often than not the pre-Tridentine reform packages of various popes—over those reform movements which were more mystical, charismatic and spiritual in nature.

Although some reforms seemed to be disruptive or mechanistic, in this present analysis they should not be discounted. All reforms, in one way or another, aimed at gospel discipleship, and this fact alone should provide us with a clue as to the greatest need of the church at that time: namely, a reinvigoration of evangelical life, not merely for a few elite, such as monks or clergy, but a reinvigoration which in its length and depth, its height and breadth, is accessible to all who have been called to Christ and who want to respond as fully as possible to this graced call. This means a form of discipleship to which non-ordained and ordained, non-religious and religious, women and men, people of all nations, races and cultures, can with God's help and the loving support of fellow Christians reach. Any other form of discipleship and any presentation of gospel discipleship which is class-stratified into lesser and better has, *ab ovo*, ceased to be evangelical. The repositioning of the lay person in the church, which clearly emerged more and more as these church reforms took root, was a repositioning into gospel discipleship.

9. CONCLUSIONS FROM THE DATA

From the material in this chapter, we can bring together the following conclusions. These conclusions, as in previous chapters, are not meant to be a summary of the material. Rather, they are meant to indicate the salient issues which contribute in no small measure to the repositioning of the role of the lay person in the western Christian church.

1. Martin Luther together with the subsequent Lutheran movement did not have as his central theological issue of contention the role of the

lay person in the church. However, Luther's central theological issues, such as justification, grace, good works, and the role of word and sacrament within the church, were important for Luther, since they were key to the true meaning of gospel discipleship as he understood it. Luther's insistence on a gospel form of discipleship of necessity enhanced, as time went by, the role of the lay person in the Christian community. However, in making his case on these theological matters, Luther did not operate theologically from a clearly enunciated ecclesiology nor, as a consequence, from a clearly presented position on church ministry. This is evident in his own writings from the many areas of ambiguity as regards his views on the ordained person and the lay person within the church. Nonetheless, Luther's insistence on a gospel discipleship which did not countenance a Babylonian captivity of Spirit by structures enhanced the role of the baptized/eucharistic Christian in a very keen way.

2. John Calvin, in turn, attempted to present the Christian faith in a theologically systematized way. Still, the *Institutes,* with all their clarity and logical structures, do not offer the reader an organized ecclesiology, as one finds in theological discussion from about 1700 onward. As a result the role of the lay person within a church structure often remains unclear in the writings of Calvin. Moreover, both Calvin's views on ordained ministry and his views on women did not allow him to pursue the issue of disciple equality in a way which contemporary scholars might find adequate. Nonetheless, in the period immediately following Calvin's death, Calvinism to a remarkable degree spread rapidly throughout Europe, and Calvin's views on discipleship helped Christian lay people, and especially Christian women, to move into more significant positions within Calvinistic church communities, and then within Protestant church communities generally, and finally within Roman Catholic communities as well.

3. The English reformation had a lengthy pre-history which did have as a central issue the role of the lay person in church structures. One finds this in early Lollardism. In a way which was quite different from the reformations on the continent, the English reformation, when considered in its own characteristics, separated from the importation of either extrinsic Lutheran or extrinsic Calvinistic ideas, tended to be quite concerned about a stronger repositioning of the lay person in the church, while at the same time, concerned about the retaining of the episcopal and presbyteral structures. This marriage has produced a particular, often subtly differentiated understanding of various ministerial church positions, both lay and clerical.

4. The role of the lay person in the church was clearly advanced by the radical reform movements. However, those radical reform movements which were restitutional of an early church era tended to be some-

what unable to unite the cultural movements among the citizens of Europe of the sixteenth century with the theological insights of a restitutional radical reform. It remained an impossibility to replicate in a sort of literal way the apostolic times in a later century. Each century, each generation, must make the gospel message its own. Restitutionalism has proven again and again to be a chimera. The non-restitutional movements of the radical reform groups emphasized the role of laity at times in an almost exclusive way, to the virtual reduction of clergy. This has raised enormous questions about their ecclesiology.

5. The Council of Trent did not focus on the lay person in the church in any direct way. Indirectly the lay person was very central to the deliberations of this council. However, the manner in which gospel discipleship was approached and the ways in which it might be furthered within the Roman Catholic community were seen by the bishops at Trent primarily on the basis of an educated and spiritual clergy. If the clerical leaders were well trained and deeply spiritual, the people of God would be enhanced in their efforts toward discipleship. This method, so reminiscent of Gregory VII's approach, had only a mixed effectiveness. In the aftermath of Trent, clergy did become better educated, at least some of them, although this academic formation, i.e. seminary training, did not take place either quickly or monolithically. Nor did the spiritual formation of priests occur at a rapid pace. The defensive attitude of church leadership during this post-Tridentine period of time also prevented an open discussion regarding certain issues of gospel discipleship which the entire series of reform movements from 1000 to 1600 had raised. In many instances, the taint of a "Protestant" interpretation was attached to such discussions, silencing thereby any deliberation of such themes, and this *non placet, non decet* factor kept both Roman Catholic theology and practice within a fairly set status quo. One finds, of course, examples in practice which did not follow such strictures, such as the efforts of the Oratory and the efforts of St. Philip Neri, to mention only two.

6. The ecclesiology which one finds in the catechism which Trent had mandated never became the standard Roman Catholic view. Instead, other catechisms, with more apologetic and hierarichical views of the church, such as those of Robert Bellarmine and Peter Canisius, became the standard forms of catechetical training. These catechisms, on the one hand, both developed out of a markedly hierarchical form of ecclesiology, and, on the other hand, influenced the further development of theological thought in the Roman Catholic Church. In the study and teaching of theology in the post-Tridentine era, ecclesiology, for the first time in the history of the Christian community, began to appear in a systematic way. Since a theologically systematized way of viewing both the role of the

cleric and the role of the lay person in the church is based on an ecclesiology, the post-Tridentine formation of an ecclesiology affected in no small measure the way in which the Roman Catholic Church viewed the *klerikos/laikos* issue. The more common form of post-Tridentine ecclesiology, which often defensively presented the dominant role of clergy, to some degree raised the question: Were the terms "church" and "clergy" synonymous?

7. The leadership of the Roman Catholic Church, both hierarchical and theological, did not understand the cultural changes which were taking place with rapidity throughout the western world. Of particular significance were the rise of the "citizen" and the increasing role of women within society. To these issues, which were fairly central to the issue of the role of the lay person in the church, one could immediately add the repositioning of many Roman Catholic lay people in almost all aspects of western culture with the exception of Roman Catholic theology. Lay men and women were key to the vast cultural and educational changes which were taking place throughout Europe. However, these same powerful lay men and women were excluded from decision making areas of the church. This lack of understanding by Roman Catholic leadership could not help but spell disaster once the American and French revolutions took place.

8. Throughout all of this time period, however, there took place one of the most remarkable reform processes that the western church has ever experienced, namely the rediscovery of the scriptured word. More and more Christians were reading parts of the New Testament and finding spiritual nourishment in so doing. This reading, unlike the sacramental rituals of the church, was not presided over by a cleric. This reading of the word of God was done privately or in a small faith-sharing group, and the presider was the Spirit of God. The rediscovery of the scriptured word increased on the part of thousands the desire for gospel discipleship, a discipleship which they did not find in the then-current structures of the clerical and monastic world. Throughout the sixteenth century reformations and the Roman Catholic reaction at Trent and in the post-Tridentine period, the reading of scripture and the yearning for gospel discipleship as outlined in scripture remained apace. In this rediscovery of the scriptured word, one finds an example of Spirit over structure, and no church structure, Roman Catholic, Anglican, Protestant or Orthodox, can corral the Spirit.

11

The French and American Revolutions and Their Influence on the Role of the Laity in the Roman Catholic Church

In this chapter we will consider two revolutions, the American and the French, from the standpoint of their impact on the Roman Catholic Church, and more precisely their impact on the theological and pastoral role of the lay person in the church. This period of revolution narrowly extends from the American Revolution in 1776, through the various phases of the tumultuous French Revolution from 1789 to the establishment of the Consulate in 1799. However, there is a larger extent of time involving these revolutions, which includes many decades prior to 1776, during which ideas concerning society and the role of citizens coalesced, and also many decades after 1799, including the many European revolutions which took place in 1848, in which these newly activated social ideas became part of western civilization. During all of these times, slowly but inevitably, radical changes in western society began to become dominant.

When faced with these radical changes, the responses of the then contemporary Roman Catholic leadership was for the most part either negative or defensive. However, when one asks the question "Why did this church leadership reject or stonewall these new movements, many of which included major elements of social justice and personal freedom?" various answers have been presented by historians. Among these answers is the recurring theme that the church leadership of that age was reacting against the strong and at times bitter anti-clericalism which accompanied the European forms of these revolutions. Certainly the anti-clericalism found in some of these revolutionary movements formed a basis for this leadership's reaction, but the fact that the such terms as "laity," "laicism," etc., rather swiftly came to be used by certain radical groups, and therefore seen by the church leadership as anti-clerical terms, indicates in a very telling way why the anti-clericalism attributed to many revolutionary-minded people was met by a corresponding anti-laicism of many church-minded people. In their heated and often defensive confrontation with the anti-clerical factions of society, not a few church leaders reacted to the questionable and reprehensible anti-clerical stance of these factions with an equally questionable and reprehensible anti-lay position.

Over the centuries of Christian life, only a very few movements in society have ever elicited major negative responses from church leadership, and the response by church leadership to these revolutions was certainly one of these instances. We will consider this church leadership response, with its anti-lay element, under the following themes:

1. **The New Elements to the Meaning of "Lay" Found in These Revolutions**
2. **The Response of the Roman Catholic Church Leadership to These Revolutions**
3. **The Growing Pressure on the Church Leadership by the Laity During the Nineteenth and Early Twentieth Centuries**
4. **General Overview**
5. **Conclusions from the Data**

1. THE NEW ELEMENTS TO THE MEANING OF "LAY" FOUND IN THESE REVOLUTIONS

The contemporary, late twentieth century concern for the lay person's theological and pastoral role in the Roman Catholic Church takes on its particularized form from the thought patterns of both the French and American revolutions and their implementation throughout western society. Neither of these revolutions, however, simply happened. There were many strands of thought already in the air by 1776 and 1789 which were shaping the social realms of the west in quite radical ways. The revolutions were major catalysts that made such issues unavoidably present to all areas of western society, including the area of religion. In line with this inter-relationship, I would like to consider three issues which these revolutions in one way or another brought into focus and which in turn impacted strongly on the role of the lay person in the Roman Catholic Church.

A. The Inalienable Rights of an Individual
B. The Relationship of Church Leadership and Governmental Leadership: A New Chapter in *Regnum et Sacerdotium*
C. The Issue of Discipleship

Let us consider each of these themes in some detail.

A. THE INALIENABLE RIGHTS OF AN INDIVIDUAL

Much of the revolutionary pattern of thought focused around the role of the individual citizen and his or her inalienable dignity and privileges. Such ideas were voiced, for instance, in the natural rights philosophy of the age, and the ideas found one of its strongest forms of expression in the Declaration of Independence of the United States of America:

> All men are created equal . . . they are endowed by their Creator with certain unalienable rights . . . among these are life, liberty and the pursuit of happiness.

The complex series of events in the United States of America in the late 1700s led to something much more than merely a decree of secession from England or a statement of independence. The events led to a quite revolutionary situation, with their most important effects taking place not merely in the political area but throughout the wider areas of society itself. Locke and Montesquieu, the English Puritan revolt of 1640, and the aspirations of early English Levellers who stressed a vote for every citizen, were, each in its own way, antecedents of this American revolt. In their argumentation with both the English parliament and the king, the leaders of the American revolt were championing many historic positions of the English people themselves, and, in many ways, they were championing the timeless rights of every human person. All thirteen of the new states almost immediately formed written constitutions of their own, each with its own bill of rights, stating the natural rights of each citizen, rights which no government might justly override.

It would be naive to think that this exaltation of human dignity by the leaders of the American Revolution was stainless. In the area of religion, many prejudices remained. There were also the major denials of equal human dignity to large human segments of the colonial society: slaves, women, and even children. The altruism of the various writings of this American Revolution did indeed present noble causes, but it has taken decades, indeed two centuries, to begin to apply, though only inchoatively in many instances, social equality to all sectors of the American people. At the end of the second millennium, as one prepares to enter the twenty-first century, there are in the United States of America glaring inequalities in spite of the Bill of Rights. Nonetheless, such ideas as voiced in the Bill of Rights (and elsewhere) have energized the western world from the time of this revolution down to the present.

The French Revolution exhibited many such ideas. France in the 1700s was already an established and in many ways a strong nation, and the revolution did not need to create a new nation. The revolutionaries simply had to gain control of the pre-existent nation. At the very beginning of the revolutionary change people already greeted each other with the term: *Citoyen*. They already could shout: *Vive la nation!* On August 26, 1789 the *Declaration of the Rights of Man and Citizen* was issued by the National Assembly, in which the rule of law was affirmed, together with an equality for every individual citizen and with an affirmation of the collective sovereignty of the people. Article I of this declaration states: "Men are born and remain free and equal in rights." In many ways this declaration, which was reprinted a thousand times over and distributed widely throughout France, became the most-quoted and best-known statement of the principles behind much of the French Revolution.

That there was anti-Catholicism at the time of the beginnings of the American nation cannot be denied,[1] and this anti-Catholicism stands in opposition to the very basis of the Bill of Rights. That there was anti-clericalism at the time of the beginnings of the French Revolution cannot be denied, and this anti-clericalism often denied to clerics basic human rights. Faced with this anti-Catholicism and anti-clericalism, Roman Catholic leadership was at times understandably defensive. However, it was not always a defense against anti-Catholicism per se which inspired the reaction of the highest Roman Catholic leadership; it was rather this leadership's deep suspicion and even hostility to such ideas as religious tolerance, the rights and privileges of "citizens" and their relationship to internal church matters, and the lack of a preferential position for the "one true church" within a kind of pluralistic society. All of this filled some Catholic Church leaders, ecclesiastical and theological, with serious apprehension. Each of these issues—namely, religious tolerance, the rights of citizens, and the lack of preferential status for the Roman Catholic Church—involved, and again each in its own way, major roles for the lay person which did not appear compatible with a hierarchically established church. Each of these issues consequently provided a grounding for the church leadership's anti-lay reaction.

Equality of all people, based on their humanness, and the people as the fundamental source of government were ideas which did not sit well with a social structure based on kingship and on an aristocracy. Nor did it sit well with a church leadership which in many ways had modeled itself after a monarchical ordering of society. Even from a practical standpoint, the church leadership at this period of history found these ideas questionable. During the reign of Louis XVI every bishop in France was a nobleman. This had never happened prior to the eighteenth century, since many French monks, not of noble origins, had been made bishops. What this new situation of nobility-episcopacy indicates is this: the highest church leadership in France, at the time of the revolution, had to a large degree lost its connection with the ordinary people, and consequently as a leadership group it no longer expressed the ideas of the Christian populace but rather voiced the ideas of the nobility.[2]

With the changes wrought in society by these two revolutions—and they were followed by other less dramatic but no less important revolutions throughout the European world—one sees that the dynamics of the ancient struggle of *regnum et sacerdotium,* which had become from the fourteenth century onward the struggle of the *regna et sacerdotium,* now was becoming a differently constituted struggle: namely that of *laicatus et sacerdotium.* Citizenry as such, which was at least the theoretical basis of the new socio-political governments, became the correlative power which church leadership now faced. Nonetheless, even the *Civil Constitution of the Clergy,* adopted by the Constituent Assembly in 1790, was not an instance of a "secularized state" vis-à-vis the church, since the document in actuality established a national church, much as had occurred in England under Henry VIII and Elizabeth I, or under several of the German states. Quite different from the American approach, the Constituent Assembly of France did not operate on the basis of a profound separation of church and state. Rather, the church was seen as one form of public authority, subordinate, of course, to the sovereign power. In principle, many of the items in the *Civil Constitution of the Clergy* were not new at all. The French kings had rather regularly designated French bishops and had rather regularly determined which papal documents could be promulgated in France and which could not. At the time of the revolution, the government had indeed changed from a monarchy to an assembly, but the procedures as regards the selection of bishops remained fairly much the same, with, however, a new component: it was no longer the king but rather the assembly which had a say in the determination of episcopal assignment. Moreover, in a way quite different from the English form of a national church, the French assembly did not sever its relationship to the papacy. Odd as this may seem, there was not an establishment of a "secular" state over against a "church." The French citizens were, in their own way, not only religious but also Christian, the majority Catholic but a sizable minority non-Catholic yet nonetheless Christian. This situation cannot be interpreted as a denial of the anti-clericalism which one finds throughout this period, but it is an affirmation that a pro-laicism is not equivalent ipso facto to an anti-Catholicism. To describe the situation as an instance of "the secular versus the religious" or of "the lay versus the church" is to miss something quite basic, not only in this *Civil Constitution of the Clergy,* but also in many of the writings of the French Revolution.

In the *Civil Constitution of the Clergy,* some things were of course new: parish priests and bishops were elected by the citizenry just as other important social officials were elected. A reduction of dioceses was mandated, so that departments and dioceses became co-terminous. The state henceforth began paying the salaries for the clergy, but this situation was not all that bad, when one considers the then-average clerical reimbursement. With this new arrangement parish priests began receiving a slightly higher stipend than before, and bishops began receiving a slightly lower stipend than before. In all of these instances, however, one sees that it is no longer a single lay voice, e.g. that of a king or of an emperor, which has entered into the decision making processes of the church. From this period of western history onward, there is a much wider non-ordained voice evident in these church structures, namely that of the citizenry as such, which claims a voice in the decision making processes of the church. This is the reason why one is able to say that the new situation, created by the two revolutions, radically rearranged the older rubric: *regnum [regna] et sacerdotium* into a new rubric: *laicatus et sacerdotium* or, perhaps more accurately stated, *cives et sacerdotium.* Under this new rubric, the lay person is repositioned in a radical or revolutionary way.

Even though this citizen-voice in actuality came only from a few elected individuals, or from a "senate," or from an "assembly," or from a "congress," more representative of only a portion of a nation's citizenry, nonetheless a major change had taken place. From the king and emperor "by divine right," one moves to a group of people who have been endowed by their creator with inalienable rights, which is another way of saying "by divine right."

This was the first issue which created severe difficulties for the leadership of the Roman Catholic Church, not only the ecclesiastical leadership but the theological leadership as well. A diagrammatic juxtaposition of certain ideas might illustrate this tension.

Hierarchical Structure	All Humans Equal
Divinely Instituted Authority	Religious Tolerance, Personal Integrity
Ontological Superiority of Priests and Bishops	Human Equality for All Men and Women
Only One True Church, i.e. the Roman Catholic Church	Tolerance for an Individual's Faith and Other Forms of Christian Church
By Divine Law a Juridically Clerical and Monarchically Governed Church	All People, Lay Included, Source of Government and Law, Even Ecclesial Government and Law

These two sides are not meant to be opposite, one to the other, in the sense of an either/or. Rather, the first side indicates positions which had been maintained, and the second side indicates positions which raised substantial theoretical questions and profound practical consequences. Nor were the two revolutions the origin of these conflictual issues, but they moved such ideas into center stage as far as the western world was concerned. Ecclesiastical leadership in the Roman Catholic Church was not equipped at the time of the revolutions to respond in any adequate way, for we find in the course of the nineteenth and twentieth centuries church leadership, both theological and juridical, slowly making some of these ideas part of an operative ecclesiology, and at the same time stonewalling many of these ideas, if not rejecting them absolutely.

We will see that in many of the statements of the official church which began to appear during and after Vatican II an emphasis on the dignity and freedom of every human person, men and women, gradually becoming a major and fundamental theme of church expression. Among such statements are the Declaration on Religious Liberty, *Dignitatis humanae,* issued by Vatican II on December 7, 1965; the Pastoral Constitution on the Church in the Modern World, *Gaudium et Spes,* issued by Vatican II on the same date; the two statements on liberation theologies, *Instruction on Certain Aspects of the "Theology of Liberation"* (September 3, 1984),[3] and *Instruction of Christian Freedom and Liberation* (April 5, 1986);[4] the *Instrumentum laboris, De Vocatione et missione laicorum in ecclesia et in mundo viginti annis a concilio Vaticano II elapsis* for the Synod of Bishops on the Laity of 1988;[5] and the encyclical of John Paul II, *Mulieris dignitatem*.[6] In each of these documents we find fundamental statements on the equality, dignity and freedom of every human being. We will return to these kinds of statements in a subsequent chapter. What is important to notice at this juncture is the following: at the end of the eighteenth and the beginning of the nineteenth centuries, the issue of inalienable human rights, the equality of all men and women, and the dignity of each individual, which both the American and French revolutions had stressed, confronted in an enormous way a clerically dominated church and caused, in turn, enormous confusion for the leadership of that church. At first a major response by many key church leaders was an inwardly-focused defense of hierarchy against any form of anti-clericalism, together with an outwardly-focused defense against any lay intrusion into major areas of church leadership. Movements external to church leadership which were in fact or at least perceived as anti-clerical were met by movements internal to church leadership itself which were in fact or at least perceived as anti-laical.

When one speaks of "inalienable rights of an individual," these are rights which are given by the creator, not by any other authority, church authority included. Indeed they are rights which all authority, church authority, even the highest, must respect. These rights are more than simply a "matter of individual conscience," since the human person is never simply an individual but always a social being as well. The individual dimension of human rights was slowly and at times painfully incorporated into Roman Catholic thought through its teaching of human conscience—a conscience whenever possible "formed" by church teaching. The social dimension of human rights was an extremely difficult theme for the leadership of the Roman Catholic Church to incorporate into its ordinary theological, juridical and structural positions, for the recognition of social rights often included a recognition of social bodies and institutions, some of which were not Roman Catholic, and some of which were not Christian. Indeed, some of these social bodies and institutions were not even religious.

Another major difficulty for the Catholic leadership regarding these rights was that of interpretation. Since these rights, both individual and social, are fundamental to every human person, a position which the documents cited above openly acknowledge, the interpretation of these rights cannot be seen as the exclusive task of the hierarchical magisterium of the Roman Catholic Church. Human experience, diverse as it is, provides a major area through which the interpretation of human rights, individually and socially, takes place. This situation as well, namely the hermeneutical factor involved with these rights, has proved to be very difficult to integrate into the theological, juridical and structural positions of the Roman Catholic Church, as one sees in the various attempts by the Catholic leadership to be the final arbiter as far as "natural law" is concerned. In other words, simply to state that the rights are a matter of one's individual conscience or to say that the hierarchical magisterium of the Roman Catholic Church has the God-given right to be the ultimate interpreter of the meaning and scope of such rights has not been an accepted position, even though the church magisterium has continued to make such statements. Neither lay people themselves, including Roman Catholic lay people, nor theologians, including Roman Catholic theologians, nor governments, nor other Christian churches, nor other religions acknowledge such claims. It is precisely in this issue of inalienable rights of every human being that one sees the contemporary struggle in the Roman Church as regards the repositioning of the lay person and the depositioning of the cleric. The two revolutions and their aftermath hurled this already pre-revolutionary notion of inalienable rights into the central arena of western society. One major effect of this new central focus was and is the contemporary lay-cleric struggle in the Roman Church.

B. THE RELATIONSHIP OF CHURCH LEADERSHIP AND GOVERNMENTAL LEADERSHIP: A NEW CHAPTER IN *REGNUM ET SACERDOTIUM*

The United States of America seceded from the parliamentary monarchy of England and established a government of the people, by the people and for the people. The French nation moved, though with many ups and downs, from a monarchy to a constitutional government. In both instances there was a radical change in the very form of government. How did the wider church leadership react to this changing governmental situation? What response did they give to these particular revolutions of governmental life? In order to answer this we must move, for a moment, from the end of the eighteenth century to the middle of the twentieth century, a span of one hundred and fifty years. Around 1950 we see the end of a process:

   a. an **end,** since shortly thereafter the renewal of Vatican II began to take place;
   b. but also a **process,** since in 1950 one could look back and see what historical issues had taken place and what steps the church leader-

ship during that time had taken to preserve the nature and mission of the church.

Fortunately, there is a document, written in 1951 by Pope Pius XII, which presents a brief though interpreted summary of this struggle, namely his address to the World Congress of the Lay Apostolate, given on October 14, 1951.[7] In this document we find not only the ideas of Pius XII himself, but ideas which were shared by many ecclesiastical and theological leaders of that time.

Every historical presentation is, of course, an interpretation, followed in time by a reinterpretation, followed in turn by a reinterpretation of the reinterpretation, and this is precisely what has happened as regards the period from Trent down to Vatican II on the issue of the role of the lay person in the church. The views of Pius XII present one stage in this historical process of interpretation and reinterpretation. In this well publicized and frequently cited address of Pius XII, he praises the role of the lay person in the then contemporary, mid-twentieth-century church, and affirms that the lay person has actually never been absent from such a role throughout church history. He states clearly that his intent is to define the place and role of the lay person at mid-twentieth-century "in the light of the past history of the church" (n. 4). By saying this, Pius XII alerts his listeners and readers, from the very opening of his address, that he will present an interpretation of history. He writes:

It is often said that during the past four centuries the church has been exclusively "clerical" as a reaction against the crisis, which in the sixteenth century had tried to achieve the abolition, pure and simple, of the hierarchy. In this regard it is insinuated that it is time for the church to enlarge its framework (n. 5).

With all due respect to Pius XII, the sixteenth century reformers did not try to abolish the hierarchy "purely and simply." Such a reading of reformation times is historically incorrect. When Pius XII rejects such terms as "exclusively clerical," he is indeed correct, since the church has never been exclusively clerical, except theoretically in those few instances in which a few authors had spoken of an *ecclesia clericorum*.[8] To my knowledge, however, such a theological view has never been the official teaching of the Roman Catholic Church. From Trent onward the church was never, either theoretically or practically, "exclusively clerical." Nonetheless, there was at Trent, as we have already seen, a strong tendency and firm intent to strengthen and enhance the role of the cleric within the church. This clerical emphasis became quite apparent in the so-called Tridentinism immediately following the council, but it can also be found in the many theological treatises on the church developed by theologians during the seventeenth and eighteenth centuries.[9] "Exclusively clerical" may be an inappropriate and undocumentable term, but "dominantly clerical" and at times "overbearingly clerical" are documentable descriptions of given church structures. Thus, although the Tridentine and post-Tridentine church was never "exclusively clerical," it was certainly and quite overwhelmingly presented both in catechisms and in works of a theological nature, such as the various *Tractatus de Ecclesia,* as predominantly clerical and hierarchical.

Pius XII continues his survey of church history:

> Such a judgment is so far from the reality that it is precisely since the sacred Council of Trent that the laity has taken rank and progressed in apostolic activity. The issue is easily documented. It here suffices to recall two patent historic facts from among so many others: the Marian congregations of men actively exercising the apostolate of the laity in all the domains of public life and the progressive introduction of women in the modern apostolate (n. 6).

There is no doubt that lay men and women within the Roman Church have become much more active since the Council of Trent; however, as we have seen above, Trent did not directly address the issue of the lay person in the church, but did so only indirectly through its doctrinal and reform decrees which *directly* centered on clerical roles. Was it then really the Council of Trent which occasioned the increased participation of lay people in the church, or was it not rather the ideas and example of Protestant churches which in part brought this about in the Roman Church? Did not the fact that in the period after Trent, but not because of Trent, more and more lay men and women became highly educated, entering into key roles within society, which consequently brought them into higher profile as regards the church? Did not the rise of the middle class, with its centering of wealth and therefore socio-political power—an occurrence which was assuredly not caused by the Council of Trent—also bring about a repositioning of the lay person within the *societas Christiana* of post-Tridentine times? The conclusion, which Pius XII appears to make—namely, that the Council of Trent itself contributed in a major way to the involvement of lay people in the church—is not as documentable as he suggests. In fact, the documentary evidence appears to go against his conclusion, particularly if one includes the historical data developed in the so-called period of Tridentinism.

Associations and congregations, even those dedicated to Mary, were of medieval origin, not Tridentine origin. The Council of Trent made no official, direct approbation of such associations. It is true that in the aftermath of Trent the people continued to enroll in such associations, but at times this was done without clerical control, and consequently was not favored by church officials. Studies by G. Le Bras, M. Agulhon, J.F. Soulet, and P. Burke, to name only a few, have come to quite different conclusions regarding these associations and confraternities from those which Pius XII affirms. One citation can be presented here as a summary voice of the many scholars who today would disagree with the pope's view:

> The confraternity was a kind of parish within the parish (as Le Bras once put it), and it is not surprising to find that the Council of Trent expressed unease about this independence. The bishops were ordered to visit them and check their accounts. There was a move to centralize them and place them more firmly under clerical control by grouping them into "archconfraternities," like the one of Santa Maria sopra Minerva, founded in Rome in 1539.[10]

At times the religious practices which were such a central part of these associations were espoused by the lay people, precisely because the official liturgy was not an affective liturgy and therefore not an effective liturgy. In the various rituals of these confraternities and associations, the lay people took active and leading roles, which made such rituals very important for their spiritual life. Fortunately we have lay people of that period who kept journals, describing the rituals and their sentiments about the rituals, such as those of Gianbattista Casali, a carpenter at Milan in the late sixteenth century, of Bastiano Arditi, a tailor at Florence around the same time, and of Pierre Ignace Chavatte, a serge-maker in Lille in the late seventeenth century.[11] It is difficult, historically, to say that a renewed interest in the religious associations and confraternities was a direct effect of the Council of Trent.[12]

The role of women in the church developed in spite of Trent. The Tridentine rule of claustration would have systematically removed religious women from the apostolate, and it was precisely people like Vincent de Paul, who disregarded the Tridentine regulation, which spurred religious women such as the Daughters of Charity to be so active in the apostolate. Moreover, it was precisely the role of women in the Protestant churches which provided major incentives and examples to local Catholic

Church leadership and to Catholic women themselves to claim a more active role in parish and diocesan life.

In the two instances which the pope mentions as specifically Tridentine enhancements of the role of the lay person, it is difficult today to conclude that historical data support his positions.[13]

Pius XII then makes a pointed reference, not only to the French Revolution, but also to the American Revolution:

> At the end of the eighteenth century, a new factor came into play. On the one hand the Constitution of the United States of America—a country which had an extraordinarily rapid development and where the church soon began to grow considerably in life and vigor—and on the other hand the French Revolution, with its consequences in Europe as well as overseas, led to the detachment of the church from the state (n. 9).

This paragraph is quite telling, since it reveals not only the view of Pius XII, but also of a number of other church leaders influential in 1951, for the pope was not alone in his way of thinking. The two instances which apparently caused most trouble to the church were the issuance of the Constitution of the United States and the changes effected by the many phases of the French Revolution. Indeed, in the preceding paragraph of his address, Pius XII had clearly stated:

> Nor can one let pass unnoticed or without recognition the beneficent influence of that close union which, until the French Revolution, marked the mutual relations, in the Catholic world, of the two divinely established authorities: the church and the state (n. 8).

Prior to the French Revolution, and, as he mentions in the subsequent paragraph, prior to the Constitution of the United States, a "beneficent" situation had existed in the Catholic parts of the western world: a beneficence based on a union of church and government. The implication of these words is clear: after the American and French revolutions, a situation began to develop which was less "beneficent." Church leadership in particular was either separated from the socio-political world and left "to assure by its own means freedom of action, accomplishment of its mission and defense of its rights and liberty" (n. 9), or the church leadership had to interact with a sovereign citizenry, rather than a sovereign king, which often proved to be confrontational. These situations, when compared to the pre-revolution period, were precisely what Pius XII considered less "beneficent." In many ways the role of the Roman Catholic laity, working in the lay apostolate of the mid-twentieth century, was viewed by the pope as a major way to regain once again that more beneficial, pre-revolutionary mode of existence.

Pius XII's discussion on the role of the lay person in the church, and particularly on the way this role had developed since the Council of Trent, avoided in many ways the hard glare of historical research. It also, and perhaps more tellingly, skirted the fundamental issue regarding church leadership and governmental leadership, which, from the two revolutions onward, church leaders such as Pius XII found extremely difficult both to comprehend and to accept. As regards this relationship of church leadership and governmental leadership, Pius XII in this same address states in n. 8 that there are "two divinely established authorities: the church and the state." The belief that these two elements of society, church and state, were divinely instituted had become a part of Christian tradition since the era of Constantine. Leo XIII in his encyclical *Immortale Dei* on the Christian constitution of the state issued on November 1, 1885, had said the same thing. Leo XIII writes:

> Everything, without exception, must be subject to him [God], and must serve him, so that whoever holds the right to govern, holds it from one sole and single source, namely God, the sovereign ruler of all. There is no power but from God (n. 5).

> In like manner, in civil society, God has always willed that there should be a ruling authority, and that they who are invested with it should reflect the divine power and providence in some measure over the human race (n. 6).

When the ruler of a nation was an emperor, as we have seen, there was considerable religious ritual at his investiture, a ritual which attempted to capture symbolically, even sacramentally, this "divine institution," just as a ritual ordination attempts to portray symbolically and sacramentally the "divine institution" of a bishop or priest. It is true that already in medieval times debates began to appear in the west regarding this imperial investiture, with papal theologians arguing that it was the pope himself who conferred imperial authority on the emperor-to-be, while imperial theologians maintained that the authority came directly from God to the emperor, not through any papal mediation. When the various national kingdoms began to appear in western Europe, an investiture ritual for kings continued in imitation of the investiture of an emperor, but the debate over the mediate or immediate source of regal power did not abate. As noted above, it was Innocent IV who made, for the first time, the pretentious claim that the pope alone received all power, ecclesial and political, but delegated the political power to others, if he so willed. This affirmation was the theoretical basis why Innocent IV himself claimed that a pope was above all kings and that he had, consequently, both the power and the right to depose kings.

The American and French revolutions changed this debate in an irreparable way, and the fundamental idea of government to which these revolutions subscribed gradually became the common currency among almost all western European states, namely government by the people, for the people and from the people. From this time onward it was increasingly the citizenry which was the foundation of socio-political government, not an emperor, not a king. When we consider, for instance, the various successions of presidents, senators, and congressional leaders, some of whom are elected for a single term only, one can legitimately ask: Are these men and women "divinely instituted" for a term only? Or should one not argue that the citizenry itself has been "divinely instituted" as the source of government, deputing its "divinely instituted" power for a limited time to the administration of a few? This latter is a view which has roots, as we have seen already, in the writings of Marsiglio of Padua, and which surfaced again and again in other writers such as Locke and Montesquieu. In this latter situation, how does a "divinely instituted papacy and episcopacy" relate to a "divinely instituted citizenry" without thereby opening itself to laity in a much more comprehensive way than ever before? Even if it is the elected rulers who temporarily enjoy "divine institution," the parade of such elected rulers makes the relationship of the church to the laity far more extensive and comprehensive. No longer does a pope or a bishop deal with a single lay person: an emperor or a king. Now it is a question of a senate or other group in which decisions are arrived at by vote, at times a vote which requires ratification by the populace itself.

The entire theoretical approach of the Roman Catholic Church over the centuries to the issue of socio-political government had been based on the *regnum et sacerdotium* premise, which in reality meant emperor and pope, or king and pope. The radical change in government which was based on a populace, on elected representatives of the people, on decisions arrived at by votation, could not be met by the theoretical basis of church/

government which ecclesiastical and theological leaders had formulated in their traditions, one which had envisioned only a *regnum et sacerdotium* reality. We see both Leo XIII and Pius XII pining for that former approach which Pius XII even called "beneficent." Nineteenth and twentieth century western reality, however, disallowed this Camelot-quest for the "beneficent" pre-revolutionary situation, and many Catholic lay people were not and are not open to using lay apostolate movements to bring about this return to an antiquated status quo.

Again we might present this distressing situation in the form of a diagram:

REGNUM ET SACERDOTIUM		LAICATUS ET SACERDOTIUM	
EMPEROR	POPE	CITIZENRY	POPE
KING	BISHOP	PEOPLE	BISHOP

When one views the situation from the second standpoint of the above diagram, wide vistas for the meaning of such theological phrases as *sensus fidelium,* or the priesthood of all believers, or even the sharing in the *tria munera* of Jesus through the sacrament of initiation, namely, baptism/eucharist, begin to open up. This extensive and intensive emergence of the lay person into the governmental structures of society at large repositioned the role of the lay person in the relationship of both church leadership and governmental leadership. Such a repositioning on the part of the lay person, however, did not occur nor could it occur without a corresponding repositioning of the cleric. Herein was the problem, for the clerical repositioning in this relationship clearly involved a depositioning of clerical control to some degree, and a consequent repositioning of lay involvement *ad meliorem,* also to some degree. All of these ideas and struggles are found in abundance in statements and writings connected to Vatican II and post-Vatican II, a time when these issues dramatically erupted into ecclesial prominence. We will consider these Vatican II statements in a subsequent chapter. What is important to notice at this juncture is this: a government of the people, by the people and for the people necessarily brought about a new and different kind of relationship between church leadership, i.e. the papacy and the episcopacy, on the one hand, and governmental leadership, i.e. a wider lay group, the entire citizenry, the entire people, on the other. It is impossible for one side of the relationship—here the lay side—to be repositioned without the other side —here the hierarchy—being repositioned as well. In this process of lay/ cleric repositioning it is the cleric who is likewise repositioned, although this is at times a depositioning, and the lay person who is repositioned, at times *ad meliorem.*

C. THE ISSUE OF DISCIPLESHIP

There is one further aspect of this address by Pius XII which should be emphasized, for it addresses the issue of discipleship. Even though this address was delivered in 1951 by one person, it is, in so many ways, a summation of the response by a large portion of church leadership, both ecclesiastical and theological, to the elements in the two revolutions which caused major repercussions on the theology and role of the lay person in the Roman Catholic Church. This address not only is indicative of the positions which were dominant in 1951, but it is indicative of the process which, spanning the period from 1776 to 1951, led to the ideas proposed in the mid-twentieth century address.

From the opening pages of this present study on the role of the lay person in the church, the issue of discipleship has been selected as the major criterion through which one might appreciate and evaluate various historical stages of the church's stand on lay people. Since gospel discipleship means, of course, that one is a disciple of Jesus, the role of Jesus himself, both in his message and in his life, is paramount whenever one assesses a presentation of gospel discipleship. To express it in other terms, christology is the basis of ecclesiology, not vice versa. Serious questions, however, immediately arise when one begins to present a description of gospel discipleship: In what way does Jesus center such a presentation? In what specific way is Jesus presented? Does the presentation of Jesus which is offered in a given presentation have a solid New Testament base?

With these kinds of questions in mind, let us consider the same papal address considered above. Remarkably, there are only eight references which Pius XII makes to Jesus.

1. The pope mentions that the lay people have come to Rome to renew their "fidelity to the vicar of *Jesus Christ* and to beg him to make fruitful by his blessings" the resolutions and activity of this lay assembly (n. 2).
2. Later on he mentions that all the faithful are members of the

mystical body of *Christ,* and that all must give good example because of the law of *Christ,* "for we are the fragrance of *Christ* for God" (2 Cor 2:15) (n. 18—Jesus Christ is mentioned three times in this paragraph).

3. All must be concerned about the reign of God "according to the spirit of the Our Father, which *Jesus Christ* himself has taught us" (n. 18).

4. Lay groups should rejoice when they see non-members of such lay groups winning "their brethren to *Christ*" (n. 25).

5. The apostolate of the laity is subordinate to the hierarchy; "to think otherwise would be to undermine the very wall on which *Christ* himself has built his church" (n. 26).

6. Finally, in his conclusion he prays with 2 Corinthians 13:13: "The grace of our Lord *Jesus Christ* . . . be with you all" (n. 41).

In this address Pius XII is certainly exhorting the gathered lay people to be disciples, but it is very evident that discipleship is not focused on Jesus. Rather, the stress is on being "disciples of the church" much more than on being "disciples of Jesus." My precise criticism at this juncture is not only that there is the lack of presenting Jesus as the focal point for lay apostolate which causes serious questions; rather, my precise criticism is that the pope's clear emphasis on the church, not Jesus, raises serious theological questions. The response to the American and French revolutions, as seen in this 1951 summary by Pius XII, is clearly: remain loyal to the church. But the "church" means church leadership. Ecclesiology, far more than christology, is operative in such a presentation and interpretation. That Pius XII is urging a form of discipleship cannot be denied. That this form of discipleship is expressed in terms more ecclesiological than christological is also undeniable. It is precisely in this subtle *norma normans* of ecclesiology over the *norma normans* of christology which makes one pause. If ecclesiology is *norma normans,* then christology becomes *norma normata,* whereas Jesus should be the *norma normans* with the church *norma normata.* One often finds, in post-revolutionary papal, curial and episcopal statements, only a token reference to Jesus, such as is evident in the above address of Pius XII, but simultaneously one finds in these same documents a deliberate, abundant and heavy reference to church and to church loyalty, more often than not centered on loyalty to church leadership. Jesus is not presented as the touchstone of discipleship; loyalty to church leadership is presented as the touchstone. The reason why one should be loyal to church leadership lies only if and when that church leadership reflects Jesus. Loyalty to church leadership is secondary to loyalty to Jesus. The criterion why church leaders can ask for loyalty lies in the way this same leadership reflects and sacramentalizes Jesus. At Vatican II the major document *Lumen gentium* speaks precisely in these terms: the light of the world is Jesus, and only when all aspects of the church, including church leadership, reflect Jesus, the light, can we even speak of church.

Given the strong emphasis on ecclesiology and only a slight referencing to christology which one finds in the document cited above, one legitimately asks: Is the Roman Catholic Church leadership, in the wake of the American and French revolutions and all the changes which these revolutions brought about, emphasizing once again structure over spirit in a way that is reminiscent of that same emphasis on structure over spirit found in the pre-reformation period of church history? If so, that leadership is once again in serious trouble.

In summary form let us consider both the positive and the negative which became critical in the wake of these two revolutions. The "positive" element, in this summary, is that aspect of church and society which church leadership considered "beneficent" prior to the two revolutions, while the "negative" element is that aspect of church and society which was found by church leadership to be "less than beneficent" after the two revolutions. By doing this we are able to see those revolution-caused aspects which Roman Catholic Church leadership, by and large, found controversial or even unacceptable.

FIRST ELEMENT:

Negative: The disunion of a traditional form of union between church and state

Positive: The maintenance or, better, the reestablishment of the traditional form of union between church and state

SECOND ELEMENT:

Negative: The disintegration of a Catholic Christian-inspired society and the development of a secularized or at least a religiously pluralistic society

Positive: The integration of a society inspired by Christian values, and the development of a religiously-based society, in particular a Roman Catholic Christian society

THIRD ELEMENT:

Negative: The development of a society which did not provide a proper preferential safeguard for the true Christian faith nor assure the infusion of a faith-oriented standard into the practical life of society, i.e. Roman Catholic faith and standards

Positive: The social safeguards provided by the Christian state to the church, and the consequent facility by church leadership to bring Roman Catholic standards into the practical life of society

One sees in the above diagrammatic form that the basic issues in the dynamics of *regna et sacerdotium* continued to make their appearance throughout all of these revolutionary times, even though kingdoms and empires may have disappeared and in their place one found presidents and other elected official leaders. Pius XII, in the citation above, still indicated that the state is divinely established, a position which one also finds in his encyclical *Mystici corporis.* One might legitimately ask: Is the government of the United States divinely established, even though the government itself is based on the position of a separation of church—any church—and state? Is the government of France, at the mid-twentieth century mark, of divine origin, even though it continues to be negative in its approach to church leadership? Is the government of Mexico, another offspring of the two revolutions, of divine origin, even though it is avowedly anti-Catholic? Is it as easy to say today that the state is of "divine origin" and then indicate such a divinely established state in the concrete realities of state governments? Even more to the point, after so much contemporary literature on the issue of the origin of a state government, is the divine establishment of a state government direct, as was the view for kings and emperors, or indirect, namely, through the election and will of the people? Is it not therefore more correct to see in the people themselves the "divinely instituted" power of state, if one wishes to continue to use the theme of divine institution?

Can one see a *societas Christiana* as a society which is not only pluralistic socially, but also Christianly, i.e. the Christianity of the society which can at one and the same time be justifiably Roman Catholic, Anglican, Protestant, Eastern Orthodox? Or is the meaning of a contemporary *societas Christiana,* which one might call "beneficent," only that particular society which has an exclusively Roman Catholic Christian base? When one considers the turmoil which at Vatican II preceded the Declaration on Religious Freedom, *Dignitatis humanae,* one realizes how divergent the leadership of the Roman Catholic Church was and is, even today, on this issue of religious pluralism. The *societas Christiana,* prior to the two revolutions mentioned above, was in many areas dominantly Roman Catholic, but Europe even prior to the revolutions evidenced a Christianly pluralistic pattern. With the separation of church and state, a movement set in throughout the bi-Atlantic world to secularize the government of an individual state, at least to some degree, as well as a movement, again quite varied, which tended to leave the various religious spheres of the respective citizenry to the private sector. In reality, this privatization of religion has never taken place, since religion is of its nature not a purely private issue but has of its nature a social dimension as well. The ideal form in a contemporary society is not a total separation of "church and state," even though this is advocated by many as the "ideal form." Rather, one finds in all contemporary governmental structures some co-existence of "church and state," of "religion and state," and at the same time one finds within these same governmental structures some specific anti-religious bias, e.g. anti-Catholicism, anti-Protestantism, anti-Buddhism, etc.

Roman Catholic lay people today exist as an integral part of this turmoil. They are an integral part of various governments, and they are an integral part of the church. Mixed signals tend to arise from all sides involved. In this rather muddled situation, the lay person himself and herself has a voice, both for the governmental leadership and for the church leadership. The lay people, more often than not, do not see themselves as puppets speaking either for the governmental leadership or for the ecclesiastical leadership. As part of the source of civil government, they have a voice of their own, based on their experience and their expertise. As part of the church they have a voice of their own based on their experience and their expertise. All of this is clearly bringing about a strong repositioning of the lay person, both in church and in governmental structures.

2. THE RESPONSE OF THE ROMAN CATHOLIC CHURCH LEADERSHIP TO THESE REVOLUTIONS

When one surveys the response of the leadership of the Roman Catholic Church to these revolutions during the nineteenth and early twentieth centuries, one finds a wide range of approaches. In the early part of the nineteenth century, one finds, for instance, situations in which leadership was at a loss as regards the correct procedure. In the newly formed United States of America, when the final peace treaty with Great Britain was signed and awaiting ratification in early 1783, steps were necessary to organize the Catholic Church in this new nation. J. Hennesey, in his volume *American Catholicism,* documents the faltering steps which were taken by the Roman Church leadership on this issue.[14] From the start, when John Carroll had to face the problem in New York regarding the two Irish Capuchins, Charles M. Whelan and Andrew Nugent, and also the first instance of "trusteeism." Hennesey notes:

The problem was how to conciliate historic Catholic polity, with its bias for hierarchical and clerical control, with a legal system and popular feeling strongly influenced by prevailing American democratic winds as well as by even older English antipathy—long antedating the Reformation of the 16th century—to the claims of Roman and canon law.[15]

One is only at 1786, and already it is clear that the ideas so prevalent in the American Revolution were confronting the quite dissimilar ideas of the Roman Church. It would take a volume of its own to trace in detail each and every response of the Roman Catholic leadership during the nineteenth and early twentieth centuries to the new currents which the two revolutions stirred up. We will consider merely a few illustrative but quite typical responses of this leadership. Each of these responses can be seen in both a positive and a negative light: positive, since each response did make some room for lay involvement in the church; negative, since each response limited this lay involvement by a hierarchical or sacerdotal framework. Indeed, the final judgment on these leadership responses must be seen as far more negative than positive, that is, an openness to the lay person was tolerated rather grudgingly, while the hierarchical or sacerdotal oversight was described in most favorable detail.

The respected historian Carlton Hayes cautions us to tread carefully through the various factions of nineteenth century, post-revolutionary western history. To speak easily or even simplistically of "liberals" and "conservatives" during this period is to miss the complexity of these societies. He writes:

> There was a political, an economic, and an intellectual liberalism. There was a radical, an atheistic, a moderate, a conservative, a Christian liberalism. Wherefore such diverse groups as English Tories and French Radical Republicans, Italian followers of Mazzini or of Cavour, German admirers of Bismark and German disciples of Karl Marx were all somewhere in the liberal tradition.[16]

It is true that economic liberals "acquired a virtual monopoly over the term," but they were the sectarian liberals who were responsible for giving liberalism an ugly connotation, such as one finds among liberal industrialists, bankers, railroad tycoons, etc.[17] In the Roman Catholic Church of this period, one finds theologians who are liberal in certain areas, conservative in other areas; one finds popes and bishops who are liberal in certain areas and at the same time very conservative in other areas. It would be incorrect, then, to review this period of church history with the bias that all pro-lay movements were liberal and all pro-clerical movements were conservative. Certain lay movements were pro-lay but quite conservative, while certain clerical movements were pro-cleric but quite liberal. Even more complex is the focus of a liberal or conservative bent, since one and the same church leader, whether theological or ecclesiastical, more often than not evidences at one and the same time but with different *foci* liberal and conservative stances. I wish to highlight certain illustrative and to some degree typical responses to the emergence of new situations in the post-revolutionary western world, but I hope that they will not be construed as moments of an either/or: either a liberal or a conservative approach. In almost all of these responses, both liberal and conservative aspects, but from different standpoints, can be found.

Let us consider these illustrative and rather typical responses by Roman Catholic leadership from the standpoint of various popes. However, the papal response found an echo within the episcopate generally, although individual bishops here and there were at times not in total agreement with the papal leadership on these issues. Through the pope's leadership and its echo in various dioceses, the ordinary lay person tried to lead a gospel life. However, in daily relationship with cultural and sociopolitical situations, many Catholic lay people moved into a peripheralism, as far as their religious living was concerned. Other lay men and women, however, tried to bridge Christian ideals with post-revolutionary ideas. Time and time again, this lay activity met with a church leadership which found no value in such lay movements. Canonists became almost exclusively focused on the eventual and imminent codification of church law and, once promulgated, its explication. Throughout this same period of time many Roman Catholic theologians and biblical scholars remained quite gun-shy because of the continuing threat of a modernism label. Such a constellation of these various elements tended in a general way to make Catholic life and Catholic thought, more often than not, incapable of sorting out the valuable qualities of nineteenth and twentieth century western culture from the nonvaluable ones. Polarizations easily occurred, and adversarial sides began to arise. From mid-century onward the papacy began to reassert itself. In the first half of the nineteenth century, the prestige of the papacy had sunk to fairly low levels throughout the western world. From about 1850 onward, the popes and his advisors made a concerted effort to regain prestige for the pope. In many ways, this objective of pope and papal advisor unfortunately became *the major operative factor* for the ways in which each pope and his advisors developed their leadership. In such a major focus on recouping papal prestige, however, other key church issues were either given a secondary rank of importance, or they were reshaped in ways by which they, too, would advance papal prestige. Unfortunately, this orientation prevented papal leadership from seeing the valuable issues which the revolutions had fostered, with the result that lay persons, in the eyes of church leadership, tended to be seen only as co-adjutors of clerically controlled apostolates.[18] Let us consider some of the key popes during this time period and their leadership as it affected the laity of the Roman Catholic Church.

A. PIUS IX

R. Aubert, in *The Church in a Secularized Society,* notes that Pius IX "was incapable of judging fairly between the principles of 1789 that were of positive value, and indeed in the long run prepared the way for a greater spiritualization of the church's apostolate, and those which represented a transposition into political terms of a rationalist ideology inherited from the Enlightenment."[19] On the other hand, Pius IX made great efforts to develop popular devotion. Even the readiness of local churches to turn to Rome, a centralization process which Pius encouraged, was done not simply because of his mind-set and that of his nunciatures as well as that of the leadership in the Society of Jesus at that time, but also because the Catholic people had developed a genuine love for this man. Even the papal misfortunes, Aubert remarks, won Catholic sympathy for him.[20] At his death in 1878 there was a strength to the Roman Catholic Church which had not been there during the papacy of his predecessor, Gregory XVI. Still, in many ways at the death of Pius IX the situation of the Roman Church was worse off than it was at the time of Gregory's death and Pius' election.

> It was no longer in relation to the population of the Roman state and enlightened circles in Italy, but in the eyes of a large body of opinion, in the old world as in the new, that the papacy appeared isolated and exposed to the growing hostility of all who were determined not to turn their backs on modern civilization.[21]

The encyclical *Quanta cura* and the *Syllabus errorum* created an enormous burst of activity, pro and con. Particularly those parts which dealt with the relationship of church leadership and the various governments raised enormous issues. Certain Roman Catholic leaders were delighted with these documents; others, however, both in Europe and in the western hemisphere, were less than enthusiastic. Dupanloup wrote a pamphlet, explaining and even, to some degree, altering the *Syllabus,* and his efforts tended to quell the antagonistic elements.

Pius IX held as one of his most cherished goals the spiritual and educational development of priests. In doing this he was following the pattern set by Trent. Through priestly ministry, which should be at once deeply spiritual and profoundly loyal to the church, as Pius envisioned it, the pope attempted to affect the lives of the Catholic laity. Given the activity of many liberal, social, and political groups in Europe at that particular time, and given his own inability to sort out what was good among the new movements in the western world, it is easy to see that Pius IX was not someone who championed lay movements in the church unless they were strongly under clerical direction. In France particularly, but also in other parts of Europe, a war of words developed between the "liberal Catholics," on the one hand, who had little sympathy with economic liberalism, but a great deal of sympathy for adapting the strong points of the emerging society with the gospel message, and, on the other hand, the "integralist Catholics," who saw little value in the French Revolution. This confrontation of the traditional church structures with developing societal structures appeared not only in France, but in every western country, each, however, in slightly different patterns. Pius IX progressively allied himself ever more strongly with the integralists. Ultramontanism was rejected and intellectual, liberal Catholics were put down. Ordinary Catholics became more pious, with devotions to Mary and the Sacred Heart and with frequent—for its time—reception of the sacraments. A spirituality focused on Jesus slowly became important, and in many ways this spirituality was affective in nature, and not merely formal and rationalistic. Vowed religious life became quite strong, with increased enrollment in male groups, such as the Dominicans, Franciscans, Jesuits, Sulpicians, Passionists and Christian Brothers. Numerous new groups were founded and encouraged: the Fathers of the Blessed Sacrament, the White Fathers, the Society of the Divine Word and the Salesians. The number of vowed religious women also increased, and more new communities of women were approved by Rome than new communities of men. In many ways, however, this growth in a sense of church, this deepening of christocentric and Marian spirituality, and this burgeoning of religious life, both male and female, did not offset the inner disequilibrium of the Roman Church. Catholicism in so many ways and in so many areas of the western world was inching more and more into a peripheral phenomenon of the contemporary world, and there is no doubt at all that Pius IX contributed enormously to this peripheralization of the Catholic community. Thus a strange situation arose during the time of Pius IX. Slowly but surely, Catholics worldwide began to sense a certain pride in belonging to this "international" church. The pope, and in many ways because of him the local bishops, were seen as spiritual leaders of this internationally large and significant church. Belonging to the church became something important. This was, in the United States, for instance, strengthened by the growth of ghetto-parochial units, through which Catholics were reinforced in their Catholicism by church, school and social activities. On the other hand, the peripheral way in which Catholics found themselves generally vis-à-vis society tended to create a sense of isolationism from the socio-political and even cultural mainstream. In the United States, the question even arose: Could one be a Roman Catholic and a United States citizen?

The growth-phenomenon of Catholic life helped make the ordinary lay Catholic much more spiritual, particularly through devotional activities, but also through the sacraments. This spirituality was, deep down, very ecclesiastical, with its emphasis on church. Belonging to the church, loyalty to church leadership, observing church regulations—these were all very important indications that one was spiritual, saintly, religious.

Sacerdotal oversight was, for the most part, an accepted aspect of Catholic life, but there were a number of lay men and women during this period of time who found this sacerdotal authority quite constraining. Gatherings of various Catholic labor unions and even of Catholic political parties, the calling of national conferences of lay people and even of international convocations, took place which were neither sponsored nor countenanced by the clergy, and which evidenced an outspoken lay independence.

All of this indicates a rather mixed situation. During the pontificate of Pius IX, Catholic life generally began to show signs of a renewal, and the leadership of Pius cannot be discounted as a major cause for this renewal. Nonetheless, the renewal was flawed because the leadership, including that of Pius and therefore that of most bishops, could not and did not provide a satisfactory bridge between the church life of the ordinary lay person and his or her socio-political and cultural life.

B. LEO XIII

There is a section in the quite respected volume *Handbuch der Kirchengeschichte: Die Kirche in der Gegenwart: die Kirche zwischen Anpassung und Widerstand*[22] which brings together material regarding Leo XIII, and which at the same time raises a formidable question on the church-state issue, and in consequence on the role of the laity in the church. The opening section of this study, written by Oskar Köhler, is called "The World Plan of Leo XIII: Goals and Methods."[23] Köhler notes that the papacy, to which Gioacchino Pecci was finally elected, had always been a source of great study for him, but especially the papacies of Gregory VII, Innocent III, Alexander III, and Pius V—all popes who held the view that a pope was the supreme moderator of the entire world, all popes, therefore, who had a papal worldview which in many ways Leo XIII unabashedly endorsed. Innocent III in particular was a role model for Pecci. After all, Innocent III was buried in Perugia where Pecci had been bishop, and after Pecci became pope, he transferred the remains of Innocent III to an elaborate mausoleum in St. John Lateran, and then began to construct his own mausoleum on the opposite wall of the same basilica.

With Leo's papal worldview theme in mind, let us consider in some detail the following statements by Köhler which in many ways provide an assessment of Leo XIII's basic ideas on papal power:

> It was the goal of Leo XIII to present the Catholic Church and the papacy to all of mankind as the great world power with an intellectual and spiritual mission.[24]

In other words, Leo XIII clearly had a world plan in which the Roman Catholic Church, and in a special way the pope, were viewed as world powers. This worldview has an order of being which God has authored, and is consequently "ontological" and "essential."

> In 1881, Leo XIII began his formation of a papacy which would, in the revolution-ridden world of that time, resume the universal task from which it had profited during the Middle Ages.[25]

The world plan of Leo XIII was modeled on the grand plans of an earlier papacy—namely the papacies of Gregory VII and Innocent III. In this worldview the pope is central.

> From this background it is understandable that, in an age of imperialism, against all political reality, Leo XIII highly valued the prospects of an international office for arbitration. Such an office he claimed principally for the papacy.[26]

In no way did Leo XIII see himself as simply a mediator for international disputes; rather he saw himself as an arbitrator, and this view of a papal arbitrator occurs in his writings time and time again. A mediator simply attempts to bring various factions together and to facilitate a consensus, arrived at by those involved. An arbitrator, however, is one who hears the case and ultimately decides the issue. Although Leo XIII did not see himself as the possessor of all authority, whether governmental or ecclesiastical, as Innocent IV had stated, he did push for an international position in which the pope would be accepted as the final arbitrator in moral issues that affect world politics and the social situation generally. A pope would be consequently the ultimate moral spokesman for the entire world. An example of this is found in the following observation by Köhler.

> Queen Wilhelmina of Holland had asked Leo XIII if he would be willing to be part of the peace negotiations in the Hague. She had asked him for "moral support." In his reply, Leo noted that it was the duty of the papal office not only to provide the confer-

ence with moral support, but also to "play an effective and active part in it." This, he wrote, was in keeping with the tradition of the papacy, whose authority transcended all national borders.[27]

Leo XIII's request for such a role was discreetly rejected by the queen. Political leadership at that time of history did not wish a pope to have such an effective and active role as Leo sought.

In his public writings Leo XIII sought to make his influence both effective and active. Of all these writings *Rerum novarum* (1891) is perhaps his best known. The significance of the encyclical *Rerum novarum* is correctly evaluated and not in the least diminished if placed in the context of Leo XIII's world design. Indeed, this Leonine world plan is the key both to understand and to evaluate not only this encyclical but almost all the writings of Leo XIII. Individual issues pertaining to Leo's papacy have to be seen against the background of his world plan. For Leo the remedy for the social and political disruptions in the modern world, that is, the world after the American and French revolutions, could only be realized in the recognition of the moral authority of the *vicarius Christi*.[28]

Leo XIII expected that his papal nuncios, placed in key positions throughout the political world, would be recognized as executive representatives of his authority, "through which he ruled the world Church in a centralized manner."[29] There is no doubt that Leo XIII saw himself as a world ruler, not simply as an inner-church leader, and that he expected, because of the divine right of the papacy, to be so considered by world leaders, even though such leaders might not be Christian or even though they might not be Roman Catholic. Papacy, in his view, was not simply a ministry within the church; papacy had a position of authority within the entire world, whether that world was professedly Christian or not.

Given this background of Leo's worldview of the papacy, let us consider some major issues which undergird *Rerum novarum,* realizing at the same time that they are the same major issues which undergrid the goals of his entire pontificate. These issues, since they touch on the church and its relationship to the social dimension of life, had major repercussions on the issue of the lay person in the church, and are therefore most apropos to the theme of this present study.

A. THE ROLE OF ROMAN CATHOLICISM WITHIN THE SOCIAL STRATUM

After the French Revolution, Catholicism throughout the west slowly but surely lost its social station, that is, it lost a privileged positioning of influence within society. Catholic leadership, immediately after the revolution, was, however, at a loss as regards the specific ways in which the church should act/react to this new situation. Certain sociological and political configurations of the post-revolutionary world were for the most part accepted by Catholic Church leadership, but often only in an external way, not in an internalized way. When, in the post-revolutionary period of the nineteenth century, Catholic lay leadership began to move more directly into the new social strata, the higher clergy particularly became very uneasy, since many of these movements did not have clerics in control. Indeed, the entire rise of the lay movements is fraught with an ongoing struggle between lay leadership, on the one hand, and clerical dominance, on the other. In other words, the value of Christian discipleship, whether lay or cleric, was not made the fundamental criterion; rather, the fundamental criterion was, again and again, the preservation of clerical control. The hermeneutic of discipleship in this struggle was not the New Testament view of discipleship; rather the hermeneutic was the dominant role of ordained ministry, most especially bishops and popes, over every major aspect of the lay movements.

Catholic lay movements during the nineteenth century moved increasingly beyond the parish and diocese; indeed, they moved at times beyond the national boundaries and attempted to become international in membership and purpose. By the mid-nineteenth century, associations of lay people had formed in Belgium, Ireland, and France. Parisis, the bishop of Langres, had written a pamphlet which gained a wide readership, entitled: "The Role That Lay People Must Play Today in Questions Pertaining to the Freedom of the Church." In 1848 there was a lay congress at Mainz, a multi-national gathering of Catholic lay men and women, with some clergy. The expressed views of many at this congress differed considerably from the view of Pius IX. Likewise, in 1863, a gathering of Catholic scholars took place in Munich without any hierarchical permission. One of the main leaders of this congress was Josef Ignaz von Döllinger. The internationalism of Roman Catholicism, even quite beyond the lay movements, was intentionally fostered in his time by Leo XIII, and in doing this he placed a strong and deliberate stress on the unique sovereign leader of this international Roman Catholic society, a leader common to all, namely the pope, who was to be seen as the one figure who united these internationally disparate national groups of Catholics. The role of Roman Catholicism within the social stratum of the late nineteenth century can be characterized by two elements: the first is the strong emergence of various lay movements, some of which tended to be international in character and at times independent of hierarchical dominance; the second is the strong insistence by Leo XIII on international papal sovereignty.

B. THE ISSUE OF SOCIAL REVISION OR SOCIAL REFORM

During the papacy of Leo XIII, individual social questions were analyzed time and time again by leading Roman Catholic scholars, but more often than not they did so only from the perspective of a total or comprehensive view of society. In other words, various social questions could not be resolved unless one had a comprehensive and universal social view. The labor question, for instance, which is the theme of *Rerum novarum,* was simply a part of a total social view. To address the labor issue by itself, in this Roman Catholic perspective, would have had no lasting value; only a full-scale revision of society itself would allow the particularities of the labor issue to reach a resolution. However, proposals of fundamental and universal structural change in nineteenth century western, post-revolutionary society were seen either as something utopian, and therefore idealistic and not practical, or as something revolutionary. The term "revolutionary," however, was not an acceptable term in papal thinking, since it had vivid connections with both the American and French revolutions. The role of the church, therefore, should not be one of revolution, but—and this was the favored term—one of revision.

How deeply official Catholicism was affected by the idea of developing a concept that would embrace all of society and put it in competition with a liberal bourgeois ideology is documented by the encyclical *Rerum novarum.* This encyclical continually revolves around a few central ideas which form the basis of a total social reform, but these centralizing ideas were enough to help revitalize many Catholics of that period.[30] Because of *Rerum novarum,* Catholics in many countries developed ever more deeply an alienated relationship to the secular bourgeois society which surrounded them. Through the influence of *Rerum novarum,* Catholics began to develop a different set of social ideals from those which dominated their immediate world, and they began to develop hostile sentiments toward the economic systems within which they lived.

Tolerance, for instance, was a word which Leo XIII rejected without further ado.[31] For Leo, a Catholic cannot be tolerant of a pluralistic society. Tolerance for Leo XIII meant untruth and amorality. When tolerance is applied to religious freedom, it indiscriminantly (*promiscue*) granted freedom even to atheists. Leo preferred the term "patience," *patientia,* which for him indicated that the church leadership was waiting patiently until the time when society discovers the one and only truth, the Catholic truth.[32]

Leo XIII sought to have governments provide the Catholic Church with the favor of the law and the privileged protection of the state, a position which placed American Catholics in an intolerable situation: on the one hand they wanted to adhere to the Constitution of the United States, but on the other hand they were asked to accept Leo's program, which involved a favored if not an established religion.[33] For the American Catholic this was a task of reconciling the irreconcilable. This disfunctional effort created no little problem both for the ordinary American Catholic lay person and for the Catholic episcopal leadership in the United States.

When one looks back today on the hundred years, stretching from 1890 to 1990 or thereabouts, one notes that a fair amount of scholarly research has been focused on the theme of the relationship of church and society during the reign of Leo XIII. Distance in time has also provided scholars with a sense of academic, disinterested judgment, so to speak. At the time of Leo XIII and shortly after his death, to criticize the pope was not considered helpful to the church, especially if this was done by qualified scholars. The then enemies of the Roman Catholic Church, particularly those who were Freemasons, would only have reveled in such criticism. Early scholarly appraisal of church and state during the pontificate of Leo XIII tended to be adulatory. At a later period of time this has not been the case, and, as a consequence, the scholarly appraisal of Leo XIII, his times and his goals, has more sharply identified both his positive and his negative achievements.[34]

It is the judgment of such later scholars that a universal or worldwide vision clearly lies behind Leo XIII's program. In other words, his statements on labor, on political parties, on national churches, on a pluralistic society, etc., are fully understandable only against his perspective of a total social theory, a universal, worldwide plan. This plan, as mentioned above, had, for Leo, its roots in the vision of Gregory VII and Innocent III. Since this worldview or world plan plays such a major role in Leo's thought and action, a major issue arises in evaluating the life and accomplishments of this man. If such a vision is itself unacceptable, then the validity, correctness and viability of its details must be more carefully scrutinized, since they might be totally unacceptable as well.

The vision of the papacy which Gregory, Innocent and then Leo pursued can, in my view, be criticized on the basis of gospel discipleship, because in this view the honor, the positioning and the maintenance of the pope are too often placed above the honor, the positioning and the maintenance of discipleship generally. In this view a disciple of the Lord is fundamentally one who accepts the pope. This appears to be the disciple's first and basic step. However, from a more profound theological and christological standpoint, one should say that the first and fundamental step in gospel discipleship is the acceptance of Jesus Christ. Christology determines ecclesiology, not vice versa, and a christologically determined ecclesiology places the papacy in a deliberately relativized role, relativized not only in its relationship to God and Christ, but also in its relationship to the people of God, the community called "church," *ecclesia*, as well.

Since many social issues and situations are so vital to the question of the lay person, both in society and in the church, one might ask the following question as regards Leo XIII: What precisely is of value in *Rerum novarum*, his mostly widely acclaimed social encyclical, and by extension in his other writings on the social issues of the late nineteenth century? Are there issues in these writings which we should not and cannot endorse? Are there aspects of Leo's entire social program which in retrospect appear myopic and narrow?

Put in another way we might consider the following themes, using the term *Rerum novarum* to indicate not only the encyclical itself but the entire social program which Leo XIII embraced.

1. The Inalienable Dignity and Freedom of the Human Person

Does today's Catholic concern for the dignity and freedom of each and every human being have its roots in *Rerum novarum*? Or has this particular concern in today's church originated from other sources, including those basic human issues which surfaced so strongly in the American and French revolutions? It is difficult to find in the worldview of Leo XIII a fundamental concern for the dignity, equality, and freedom of each and every human being. Indeed, the problems which Leo attempted to confront were far more complex than he perceived them to be, and they were also not confined to Catholicism, but were endemic to western European society as such. The complexity of the social situation included such issues as private property, socio-political theories, marriage and family, public and private education, freedom of the press, the free association of individuals, and the particularized social movements of industrial workers, of farmers, of the middle class itself. In all of these the issue of an individual's human dignity, his and her human freedom, and his and her human equality appeared again and again. The complexity of the issues just enumerated became more intensified in the twentieth century, and have moved far beyond a European vision and version of the civilized world. The worldview which Leo XIII attempted to give to these issues seems today to offer little value. The contours of a quite different worldview have begun to emerge, one that is multi-cultural, multi-religious, multi-lingual, multi-philosophical. Respect for individuals and the social groupings of individuals cannot be determined by a claim for papal oversight. Long before one might ever accept the pope as a spiritual leader, one must be respected for who he or she truly is. The creator, not the pope or the church, has endowed each human being with inalienable rights. A foundational non-recognition of such innate rights and freedoms can only undermine any further claim.

2. The Issue of Racism

Does twentieth century Catholic concern for the abolition of racism stem from *Rerum novarum* and the other writings of Leo XIII, or does this concern have other rootage? It is impossible to trace the twentieth century cry of outrage against racism, both in society and in the church, back to the writings of Leo XIII. But if *Rerum novarum* and his other publications are not the source of today's outrage against racism in the contemporary church, why has this encyclical been celebrated by still other encyclicals marking various anniversaries of its appearance? These subsequent encyclicals tend to give the impression that *Rerum novarum,* and by connection the entire social concern which Leo XIII developed for church leadership, marked the beginning of the contemporary church vision on the social needs of the world. However, since racism, in its many forms, is central to the social problems and the social answers in today's world, its absence in the Leonine writings raises enormous questions on the very validity of Leo's social analysis.

3. The Role of Women in Society and in the Church

Does today's Roman Catholic concern for the dignity, equality and freedom for women both in society and in the church arise from *Rerum novarum* and the other writings of Leo XIII, or does this particular contemporary concern stem from other sources? Again, it would be most difficult to find in Leo XIII's writings the basis for the liberation of women, either in the church or in society generally. Leo XIII clearly saw the woman's role in the home, and his paternalism, evident in all of his writings, militates against any attempt to make his writings a turning point in the liberation of women. For Leo, the woman's position is in motherhood and home-making, not in roles of social leadership, much less in roles of church leadership. But if, in the western world at the end of the second millennium, when the issue of women in society is seen as central and essential, how can a social vision, which does not respect the full humanity of women, be touted as the source of a Roman Catholic social stance? Since all women, in the canonical world of Roman Catholicism, are lay, their positioning and repositioning plays a major role in the issue of the lay person within the church.

4. Liberation Theologies

Do the various liberation theologies, both the black liberation theologies of the United States, and the liberation theologies of Latin America, with their preferential option for the poor, find their base in *Rerum novarum* and in Leo's other writings, or do these theologies of liberation stem from other sources? Once again it would be more than difficult to document the rise of these liberation theologies on the basis of the social vision of Leo XIII. In many ways, at least as far as Catholicism is concerned, it is precisely that kind of church leadership which Leo XIII included in his vision of a worldwide church that the theologians of liberation theology tend to criticize. The Leonine view of church leadership in their view has indirectly and even at times directly allowed the continuance in power of governments which have systemically oppressed the poor. Church leaders within oppressive governments have not been noted for their critical stances against these oppressive governments of Latin America, nor have these church leaders made any strong efforts to uproot the causes of widespread poverty in their dioceses. The very singularity of such church leaders as Romero and Arns indicates that the rank and file of episcopal leadership did not raise voices against such oppressive leadership, and that a papal view of church and state, based on the Leonine material, in many ways prevented such bishops from voicing outrage.

5. The Ecumenical Movement

Did the ecumenical movement with its advocacy of tolerance grow out of *Rerum novarum* and the other writings of Leo XIII, or has the ecumenical movement emerged out of other soil? The very notion of tolerance and religious freedom was quite alien to the vision of Leo XIII, as was noted above, and in his dealings with the issue of Anglican orders he allowed himself to be more politically than religiously motivated. For Leo the Roman Catholic Church was waiting patiently, not tolerantly, for the other Christian communities to "return" to mother-church. Such a view is categorically opposite from that of the ecumenical movement, and at Vatican II, with the promulgation of the Decree on Ecumenism, *Unitatis redintegratio,* the Roman Catholic Church officially entered into this contemporary ecumenical movement, but not on the basis of a "return to mother-church." Leo XIII would not have understood the thinking behind *Unitatis redintegratio.* In the Christian church community at the end of the second millennium, Christians within all the churches are disciples of Jesus, the majority of whom would be considered "lay." Because of this situation, the role of the lay person in the church today cannot be adequately dealt with unless the ecumenical issues are taken into consideration. This ecumenical aspect has serious repercussions within the socio-political vision of a multi-religious world. Leo XIII's non-openness to an ecumenical worldview cannot help but raise questions about the adequacy of his social vision for the late twentieth and early twenty-first centuries.

6. Vatican II Theology

Did Vatican II and its theology stem from *Rerum novarum* and the insights and programs proposed by Leo XIII in his many writings, or did it arise from factors quite distinct from those advocated by Leo XIII? It would be quite difficult to say that the calling of Vatican II was brought about because of *Rerum novarum* or because of the world plan of Leo XIII. In many ways the aims of Leo and the aims of Vatican II are not only distinct but diverse. Leo XIII clearly advocated a form of neo-Thomism, and there was a renewal of Thomistic thought during and shortly after his reign as pope. Nonetheless, much of the theology behind Vatican II was based on the scholarship which arose from the *Nouvelle Théologie* of the mid-twentieth century, a theology based in strong ways on the patristic era. The liturgical movement, which was also based on patristic and post-patristic scholarship, influenced the thinking of Vatican II as well, and indicated a major departure from scholastic categories. In scriptural studies the acceptance of historico-critical methods has profoundly altered Roman Catholic views of both Old and New Testaments. In philosophy, phenomenology and existentialism have been very influential in the latter half of the twentieth century, and to some degree have influenced the way in which Vatican II considered many vital issues.[35] The theology of Vatican II, as is well known, presented the theology of the lay person in the church in a very positive and strong way. If, however, this theology was not an outgrowth of the world and church vision of Leo XIII, but came from quite other sources, then one must conclude that the role of the lay person in Leo's view, when contrasted with the role of the lay person in Vatican II's approach, is radically different. Indeed, Leo's approach in such a contrast appears repressive of lay people, and not expressive of lay people in the church, whereas the documents of Vatican II tend to be expressive of the lay person and not repressive.

If the answer to these various questions is predominantly negative, and if the issues involved, such as the fundamental dignity, freedom and equality of each and every human being, the issue of racism, the issue of the role and position of women in society and in the church, the issues which liberation theologies strive to present, the issues of ecumenism, and the issues behind the basic theological forces of Vatican II, are not grounded in the writings of Leo XIII, one can legitimately give a negative response to the question: Did Leo XIII really advance the role of the lay person in the church? Most of the issues just mentioned are fundamental to the positioning of the lay person, e.g. his or her dignity and freedom, the question of racism and sexism, the issues in ecumenism, and the systemic roots of widespread poverty. A gospel-based repositioning of the lay person in the church will, of necessity, begin to eliminate the blight of racism, sexism, systemic poverty, and Christian disunity.

When one reviews the writings of Leo XIII, using the fundamental criterion of gospel discipleship, that is, a theological understanding of discipleship which places christology as the basis of ecclesiology, one sees that it is precisely the lack of such criterion as fundamental which mars the world vision of Leo. When the fundamental issue of gospel discipleship is applied to the social issues regarding the poor of the world as well as the causes for such poverty, when gospel discipleship is applied to the social issues involved in the position and role of women both in society generally and in the church specifically, when the fundamental elements of gospel discipleship are applied by Roman Catholics to the non-Roman Catholic Christians of the world and then even further to the Christian way of relating to non-Christian religions and even to those who hold no religious belief at all, and when the fundamental elements of gospel discipleship are applied to the social concerns regarding racial inequality throughout the world, then the efforts of Leo XIII, in spite of many positive values, must be seen in the final analysis as inadequate. Key to the limitation and inadequacy of the Leonine position is his world plan. This world plan, through which and against which he viewed every social issue, was the major issue which prevented his way of thinking to come to grips with the social issues of the contemporary world and which prevented him from making gospel discipleship the criterion by which he might view his world. A world plan, which has as its center the role of the papacy and not Jesus, cannot be seen as the major criterion for Christian social thought. Only gospel discipleship, which has as its center the message of Jesus Christ as one finds it in the New Testament, fulfills that central role. Christology, not ecclesiology, must be the *norma normans*. Leo, unfortunately, made ecclesiology the *norma normans* and christology became *norma normata*.

This rather long digression on Leo XIII is key to the theme of this study: the role of the lay person in the church, since through such a digressive study one sees that the issue of discipleship and the issue of *regnum et sacerdotium*, even in its modern dress, affect one another. Leo's worldview was a continuation of this centuries-old fascination by popes as regards *regnum et sacerdotium*. Time and time again, as we have seen, a papal understanding of *regnum et sacerdotium* has controlled the manner in which other issues are judged. The church, however, was not sent by

Christ and his Spirit to settle a *regnum and sacerdotium* issue. The church was sent to make disciples. Thus, the theme of gospel discipleship once more becomes key, and it is gospel discipleship, which should be the fundamental governing issue. The *regnum et sacerdotium* issue finds its base in gospel discipleship, not vice versa.[36]

C. PIUS X

Pius X (1903–1914) has been described as a fairly reactionary pope. In his encyclical *Pascendi gregis* (1907) he writes:

> Note here, Venerable Brothers, the appearance already of that pernicious doctrine which would make the laity a factor in the progress of the church.[37]

In the encyclical letter *Il fermo proposito*, Pius X explains the relation which all the works of Catholic action should bear to ecclesiastical authority.

> Whence it is manifest how ill-advised were those, few indeed, who, here in Italy and before our very eyes, sought to take upon themselves a mission which they had received neither from Us, nor from any of our brethren in the episcopate and set out to act upon it not only without the respect which is due to authority but even by going openly against her wishes, seeking to render their disobedience lawful by futile distinctions. They said they were raising aloft a banner in the name of Christ.[38]

Pius X goes on to say that such a banner could not be that of Christ, since it did not have on its fold the teaching of Jesus: "He that heareth you heareth me; and he that despiseth you despiseth me" (Lk 10:16), as also the gospel passage: "He that is not with me is against me; and he that gathereth not with me, scattereth" (Lk 11:23). The pope then adds that these scriptural texts offer us "a doctrine, therefore, of humility, submission and filial respect."[39] Pius X had just dissolved the *Opera dei Congressi* and replaced it with a federation of various parochial Catholic Action groups under the tight control of the Italian bishops, and it is this situation to which he alludes. But he places it in a much wider context, stating very clearly that lay Catholic Action is only acceptable if it is sanctioned by hierarchical approval. "He who hears me" is interpreted not simply as "he who hears Jesus," but "he who hears Jesus and pope/

bishop." Biblical scholars might justifiably find such an interpretation neither textually nor contextually acceptable, but, even more, it is clear that for Pius X the lay person is "subject" to hierarchy.

In this same encyclical, Pius X describes the priest as a person "raised higher than other men to fulfill the mission he has received from God"; he is an "ambassador of God" (n. 60). Even more telling than his views on *sacerdotium*, it is the entire first section of this letter which has as its topic the theme of church and state (*regnum et sacerdotium* in contemporary format). He cites with approval *Rerum novarum* of Leo XIII, and even more pointedly he refers to his own *motu proprio* of December 18, 1903 "which comprises the whole Catholic social movement, a fundamental constitution to be the practical rule of the common work, and the bond of union and charity."[40] Once again we find ourselves face to face with three profoundly interdependent elements which affect the theological and pastoral positioning of the laity in the church:

1. the issue of gospel discipleship;
2. the issue, even in its modern form, of *regnum et sacerdotium;*
3. the meaning and understanding of *sacerdotium,* including papacy, but also episcopacy and the presbyterate.

The role of the *Opera dei Congressi e dei comitati cattolici,* begun in 1874 and restructured in 1884, had become one of the leading forces in the Catholic movement in Italy. It had influence in Catholic Action generally, in education, in the press, and in Christian art. Some Catholic Italian labor unions were also invigorated by the *Opera dei Congressi* movement. Its history, however, encompasses personalities of strong mind, of extensive education, and, consequently, of conflicting opinions. "Most of all, they [the key members within the *Opera*] fought over merging the Catholic movement into the socio-political reality of the Italian state under the regime of the *Non expedit*."[41] Pius X forcefully reorganized the *Opera dei Congressi,* making it an instrument of a clerically controlled activity. Pius X also made *Le Sillon,* the movement founded by Marc Sangnier in France, into a quasi-heretical movement through his letter to the French episcopate.[42] In condemning *Le Sillon,* Pius clearly sided with and improved the situation of *Action française,* which was a royalist group of quite conservative bent, led by Charles Maurras. Aubert, in describing this move against *Le Sillon* by Pius X, expresses the issue in precisely that kind of ecclesiology which represents the position of Pius X: "For the pope, any plan aiming at a modification of society was a matter of the moral order for which the church alone was responsible."[43] In this view,

the "church alone" means *sacerdotium,* but especially the papal and episcopal leadership; the lay person is viewed in a position which has no
leadership role, and is evidently not part of the "church alone." One
wonders, of course: If the lay person is not part of the church, what, then,
is either he or she?

A third serious conflict between lay Catholics and Pius X could be
also cited—namely, the pope's positioning vis-à-vis the Christian trade
unions of Germany. "Foreign influence, mainly German, was blamed for
the progressive ideas that had infected French and Italian Catholicism.
Pius X's condemnations of political activism among Catholics were really
made only against progressive political movements and people."[44]

Pius X was concerned about a renewal of the church. He spearheaded
the codification of canon law; he fostered eucharistic devotion, and took
the bold step of advocating frequent, even daily communion.[45] Through
the international eucharistic congresses, not only was the eucharist venerated, but devotion for Christ the King was fostered and the internationalism of the church was visibly presented through the presence of foreign
delegations and other political figures at such congresses. Liturgy was a
major part of the pope's renewal as well, but a liturgical renewal which
was strictly traditional in character and unswervingly monolithic in tone.
The seminary system for clergy education was forcibly promoted, and
solid catechetical activity was urged on both priests and bishops. Did all of
this help renew the Catholic Church? The answer is mixed. A renewal in
the areas mentioned above did take place, and the spiritual life of the
ordinary Catholic lay person was indeed furthered. Nonetheless, the Roman Catholic leadership, under Pius X, still remained unable to bridge
Catholic life and the cultural socio-political realities of the post-
revolutionary western world, much less the socio-political realities of the
international scene beyond the western world.

> Replacing Leo's progressive secretary of state, Cardinal Ram-
> polla del Tindaro, with the arch-conservative Cardinal Rafaele
> Merry del Val, Pius X encouraged the development of "integral-
> ism." . . . Progressive Catholics were reprimanded for not ac-
> cepting the divinely ordained distinctions of social classes. "So-
> dalitium Pianum," the sacred inquisitorial society founded and
> directed by Msgr. Umberto Benigni . . . operated freely as a
> Vatican-sponsored doctrinal and political spying agency. Anti-
> modernist purges took their toll among laity and clergy. This
> reactionary period of the early part of the twentieth century was
> to have lasting effects on the development of contemporary
> Catholicism.[46]

Under Pius X, spiritual, ecclesiastical, and theological isolationism remained entrenched. For Pius X ecclesiology in too many basic areas determined christology, not vice versa. This, of course, skews not only the meaning of Christian life generally, but in a particular way, for our theme of the lay person in the church, the very meaning of discipleship.

3. THE GROWING PRESSURE ON THE CHURCH LEADERSHIP BY THE LAITY DURING THE NINETEENTH AND EARLY TWENTIETH CENTURIES

Hennesey, in *American Catholicism,* describes an event at the end of the nineteenth century which in many ways recapitulates the contemporary *klerikos/laikos* situation. Some influential lay people, Henry Brownson, Daniel Rudd and Henry Spaunhorst, together with William Onahan and Peter Foy, called for a congress of lay people to be held in Baltimore in 1889. When Onahan gave in to the bishops' insistence for some control of the conference, Brownson and Foy were indignant. Nonetheless, the conference took place, and John Ireland, the archbishop of St. Paul, even went so far as to say in a public address to those gathered at the conference:

> Go back and say to your fellow Catholics that there is a departure among the Catholics of the United States. Tell them that heretofore, so to speak, you have done but little, but that henceforth you are going to do great things. Tell them that there is a mission open to laymen.[47]

Ireland even apologized for his own lack of recognition of this lay potential in the church, and "with God's help," he said, "I shall do all I can to bring out this power."[48]

When a second congress for Chicago in 1893 was in the planning stage, James Gibbons, the bishop of Baltimore, penned a private letter to Ireland:

> With regard to the Congress, we must act with caution. Any overt attempt on your or my part to suppress it would raise a hue and cry, and the worst motives would be ascribed to us. The best plan is to enjoin on Onahan and our friends a passive attitude that little or nothing should be done to advance the Congress till our meeting in October, and then we would try to kill it, or failing that, to determine that this should be the last Congress.[49]

At this second congress, which did take place in Chicago, there were in attendance a large number of Catholic women, and Rose Hawthorne Lathrop called on them: "Oh, woman, the hour has struck when you are to arise and defend your rights, your abilities for competition with men in intellectual and professional endurance."[50] To think that the Catholic feminist movement is a late twentieth century phenomenon is a misreading of history, or to think that it is a purely North American phenomenon is equally a misreading of history.[51]

In this same congress there was an appeal to church leadership, clerical and lay, for the recognition and respect of the rights of native Americans. There was as well an appeal to church leadership, clerical and lay, for the recognition and respect of black Catholics and colored people generally. C.H. Butler, speaking on behalf of the Colored Catholic Congress, said:

> I here appeal to you, first as American citizens, second as loyal sons of our Holy Mother the Church, to assist us to strike down that hybrid monster, color prejudice, which is unworthy of this glorious republic.[52]

Between 1889 and 1894 five Catholic congresses of African-Americans were held in the United States. Issues of discrimination in labor unions, in work, and in housing were discussed, and these same issues remain with the multi-racial world of America today. One can legitimately ask if and to what degree the Roman Catholic Church leadership has extended its influence and power to eradicate these forms of racial discrimination.

The congress in Chicago in 1896 also dealt with the arms race, and sent a "Peace Memorial," translated into various languages to national governments. But, as Hennesey remarks:

> After that there were no more congresses. American black Catholic congresses and lay Catholic congresses fell victim to the same conservative reaction which spelled the end of the series of international Catholic scholarly congresses held in Europe from 1888 to 1890.[53]

This incident, with all its ramifications, is typical of the two issues: (a) the pressure which Catholic lay people, well educated and well trained, brought to bear on Catholic life, and (b) the slow-but-sure negative response of most of the higher clergy. Setbacks for the leadership of lay Catholic men and women, such as the one described above, can be joined to the *Opera dei Congressi* in Italy, *Le Sillon* in France, the labor unions in Germany, the lay congress at Mainz in 1848 and a similar congress in Munich in 1863, and the formation in 1867 of the *Società della Gioventù Cattolica*. Benedict XV (1914–1922) may, as pope, have been open to lay movements, just as he had been while bishop of Bologna. But his leadership was hampered due to the First World War and its aftermath.[54] In 1922 Pius XI (1922–1939) was elected, and there was a reversion to a more conservative papal leadership.

Another incident, highly indicative of the church leadership's uneasiness with lay people in this last part of the nineteenth and first part of the twentieth centuries, involved Isaac Hecker. Hecker was defended by Felix Klein, professor at the *Institut catholique* in Paris, calling him the "priest of the future," and in his presentation of Hecker to the French public, Klein referred to the "American way" of Catholicism as a model for the French people. In turn, Denis O'Connell lectured at the Congress for Catholic Scholars in Fribourg, extolling Hecker in particular and the advantages of American democracy in general. Hecker, however, was criticized strongly in France when Charles Maignen wrote a series of articles in *Vérité Française* on *Américanisme mystique*, and then in 1898 published *Études sur l'américanisme, Le Père Hecker: Est-il un saint?* This was followed by still another even fiercer critique of the "American" way, written by the Jesuit, A.-J. Delattre, *Un Catholicisme américain.*[55] Delattre, however, also condemned the biblical work of Lagrange, as well as the work of the Louvain scholar L. Janssens. In many ways, it was this criticism of Hecker and his ideas on democracy and lay involvement in the church that prompted Leo XIII to issue *Testem benevolentiae*, which was a condemnation of an Americanist vision of church and society.[56] Among the many issues which Leo condemned, one finds the following:

> Ecclesiastical office is to refrain from authoritative statements to ensure the freedom of the individual through whom the Holy Spirit speaks more distinctly today than ever.

> The apostolate has to relinquish the old methods, if operating among non-Catholics.

These views of Leo were echoed by Pius X in *E supremi* in 1903 and by Pius XI in *Ubi arcano* of 1922 and in *Quas primas* of 1925. "This papal vision of a unified social and spiritual renewal functioned as an illusive but attractive ideal for the Church in the United States."[57] But it also served as an illusive though attractive ideal for many Roman Catholics throughout western Europe. The dreams of Brownson, Hecker, and

Keane in the United States, and the hopes of a Lammenais in France, in which the lay person played a more significant role than that envisioned in the papal statements, mentioned above, ran headlong into the authoritarian and clerical attitude of papal and episcopal leadership.

History, and above all patristic history, created a critical situation in the Roman Church through the publications of such men in France as A. Duchesne, J. Tixeront, P. Batiffol, and J. Turmel. Roman Catholic biblical studies began to change with such scholars as E. Lenomant and Salvatore de Bartolo, followed by A. Loisy and M. d'Hulst, only to be met by the encyclical *Providentissimus Deus*. A. Lagrange met strong opposition with his treatment of the Pentateuch, and A. van Hoonacker's volume *Le sacerdoce lévitique dans la loi et dans l'histoire,* published in 1889, gained international acclaim, but his work on the *Hexateuch* remained, by orders, unpublished until after *Divino afflante Spiritu* in 1943.

In much of this intellectual ferment, traditional positions, though not positions declared in an official or solemn way, held by the Catholic Church leadership were called into question. Many of the reasons for such questioning arose not because of some theologically disputed issue, but because of the historical, philological, anthropological and philosophical background, supplied more often than not by the scholarly areas of lay expertise. A calling into question of church clerical authority was and has remained one of the difficult repositioning elements in the current *klerikos/laikos* tug-of-war. The calling into question has generally not included a calling into question of clerical authority per se. However, it has been a calling into question of a clerical claim to omni-competence, particularly when historical research, technology, psychology, and sociology stand in stark opposition to certain specific claims made by clerical authority.

These vignettes of historical moments during this period of time are meant to be indicative, not taxative. Each of them offers an example of how some Catholics attempted to be open to the post-revolutionary world, an openness which involved a more active and pro-active role of the lay person. In case after case such forms of lay activity in the structuring of the church were met by church leadership with negativity, and even at times with reprisals. Nonetheless, such movements and forms of thought continued to grow apace throughout the first part of the twentieth century. Two world wars and a number of lesser wars may have focused national and international attention on issues other than the church and its relationship to the modern world, but in spite of such wars and even more importantly because of such wars, the issue and relevance of gospel discipleship in the present age has become increasingly more acute. Church isolationism and privatized or ghettoized spiritualities appear more and more unable to resolve the question: How can gospel disciple-ship be relevant in the multi-cultural and multi-religious world of the twentieth century. It took more than Vatican I with its declaration of papal infallibility to meet this challenge. It took more than papal and episcopal encouragement of Catholic Action, as the participation of the laity in the apostolate of the hierarchy, to meet this challenge. It took more than expanding the college of cardinals to include members from an international world to meet this challenge. Vatican II itself did not fully meet this challenge either, but it did serve as a catalyst. Several major ecclesiastical stonewalling positions were removed at this council, but it will be, as we shall note in the next chapter, the post-Vatican II Church which has the possibility to meet the challenge of gospel discipleship and the contemporary world.

4. GENERAL OVERVIEW

There is no doubt that the American and French revolutions brought into sharp focus the critical elements of a lingering dilemma within the Roman Catholic Church. Vaillancourt describes the situation as follows:

> The crisis of Catholicism started with disintegration of the re-ligious legitimation of medieval society, and reached a first breaking point during the period that extended between Luther's Reformation and the French Revolution.[58]

The two revolutions, American and French, gave a sharp and power-ful voice to issues which had been fomenting within western culture since the fifteenth century, and among those issues was that of the "citizen." Church leadership in the fifteenth century simply ignored this aspect of western culture and continued to think in more medieval categories. Al-though the role of the lay person, both in the church and in western culture generally, was undergoing a radical change, Roman Catholic Church leadership failed to understand some of the basic issues behind these changes. A few of the major reasons why this leadership failed to comprehend the issues of such change are precisely those issues which form the major themes of this present study.

1. The Understanding of *Ordo*

The highest levels of *sacerdotium* had become an order not only within an ecclesiastical framework, but also within a social framework. Theological reflection on this religio-political situation utilized the views of Dionysius the Areopagite, founding such an *ordo* within creation itself, that is, within the very structure of being. This line of thought formed the basis for an "ontological" difference between the *sacerdotium* or priesthood and the rest of the Christian community. Since such an *ordo* arose from creation or being itself as also from divine institution, it was seen as untouchable. Moreover, this view of *ordo* continued, through these critical centuries, to be the hermeneutic through and by which the clerical world was seen and understood. The basic and fundamental flaw in this line of thinking can be stated as follows: a theologically based view of *ordo,* not a New Testament view of gospel discipleship, became the hermeneutic by which the servant-leadership of ordained ministry came to be described and lived. With this "cart before the horse" situation, the leadership of the Roman Catholic Church found itself overwhelmed by the cataclysmic events which led up to these two revolutions and which continued on in the wake of these revolutions. A world in which all men and women are created equal raises serious questions about an *ordo* within that same human world.

2. Regnum et Sacerdotium

With such an approach to priestly *ordo,* the leadership of the church also found it difficult to come to grips with the changing relationship of governmental structures to society generally and to the church specifically. In the programs of Pius IX, Leo XIII and also the later approach of Pius XII, a pre-revolutionary form of such a relationship was considered an optimal situation. Such a dream for a former set of relationships, expressed overtly in their writings, indicates a viewpoint which was basically unrealistic. The western world had moved far beyond the medieval *regnum et sacerdotium* relationship which had developed, with many vicissitudes, from Constantine to the Ottonian emperors. This clinging to a past and irretrievable form of relationship influenced the way in which this same church leadership, which was completely a priestly leadership, both viewed and dealt with the non-priestly segment of the church. However, since the non-priestly segment of the church did not unanimously by any means share this view of *regnum et sacerdotium,* many areas of this non-priestly segment of the church pressed for quite different roles and quite different structures. A conflictual situation could not help but take place, and the two revolutions abetted the depth and strength of this smoldering conflict.

One could say that the flaw in all of this lay in not making gospel discipleship the basic criterion and hermeneutic. In struggling to come to grips with a different form of socio-political structures and their relationship to an ecclesial structure, the church leadership's retention of one form of the various medieval forms of *regnum et sacerdotium* seriously clouded all other issues, for in this precise medieval form, which the leadership defensively maintained, it was papal prestige and episcopal prestige rather than gospel prestige which more often than not was being maintained. During this same period, the lay side, as well, cannot be seen as totally exonerated, for quite often gospel discipleship did not serve the lay Catholic as a basic criterion and hermeneutic, but rather an anti-clerical struggle ensued. Gospel discipleship did not serve the lay person as the hermeneutic through which he or she viewed the servant-leadership of ordained ministry.

3. Gospel Discipleship

Two elements, which find deep roots in any analysis of gospel discipleship, became quite powerful in the nineteenth and early twentieth centuries: namely, the dignity and freedom of each and every human individual, and the social dimension of life with its demands for justice not only to all individuals involved in such social groupings but a justice which needed to be extended to the social group *qua tale* itself. However, the individualistic aspect of basic human rights and the social aspect of communal justice did not always mesh together well. This precise period of time saw rampant individualism in economics and politics, but this same period of time witnessed the rise of socialism, not simply Marxism, and various voices were raised on social justice. Among these voices, as we have noted, was that of Leo XIII. The incorporation of each individual's freedom and dignity into church structures proved very difficult to a leadership, both theological and ecclesiastical, which had strong rootage in an ecclesiology based on *ordo* and a papal form of *regnum et sacerdotium*. Social justice likewise proved difficult to integrate, since the ecclesiology just mentioned maintained a hierarchical paternalism and dominance, as well as a religious intolerance toward non-Christian religions and toward the breakaway forms of Christian religion itself. Time and time again the leadership segment of the church did not bring forward gospel discipleship either as the basic criterion for a self-criticism, or as the fundamental hermeneutic and criterion through which it interpreted everything else. Other criteria and other hermeneutical issues time and again supplanted this role of gospel discipleship. As a result, the place and position of the lay person in the church was seen on the one hand as a means whereby the papacy and the *sacerdotium* could maintain its traditional positions, not only from a theological and faith standpoint, but from a social and political standpoint as well. This is one of the main positions in the study by Vaillancourt.[59]

In spite of aspects of ecclesial disintegration, the lay person in the church found a repositioning of his or her role. Many lay men and women, throughout the nineteenth and early twentieth century, continued to develop significant roles as members of the community called church, sometimes within the traditional church structures and sometimes in spite of the traditional church structures.

That there was a major repositioning of the lay person in the nineteenth and early twentieth century cannot be denied on the basis of historical data.

That this repositioning of the lay person brought on a concomitant repositioning of the ordained person is also a matter of historical data.

That much of the clergy resented this repositioning and fought it is also clear from history.

That this conflictual situation remained unresolved throughout that time period, and that the conflictual situation erupted at Vatican II and in the post-Vatican II period, is equally evident. This eruption, however, carries us into the next chapter of this study.

5. CONCLUSIONS FROM THE DATA

In this section of our review, we have seen the following major issues, which affected the role of the lay person in the church.

a. Catholic Lay Movements and Catholic Action

Catholic lay movements and Catholic Action developed during this period of time in a very strong way. The phrase "Catholic lay movements," however, refers to those movements within the lay sector of the Roman Catholic Church which took place primarily under the impetus of lay men and women and which more often than not had neither the blessing nor the leadership of the hierarchy. Such movements were both local and international and cannot be interpreted simply as splinter groups or as dissident groups. They were an essential part of the church. They gave an historic expression to the desires and goals of large segments of educated and qualified lay men and women within the Roman Church. The men and women who participated in these movements of lay people did so again and again on the basis of gospel discipleship. Here and there some anti-hierarchical feelings were in evidence, but these movements did not arise on the basis of an anti-sentiment of any kind, but a pro-sentiment, namely, a sentiment pro-gospel, pro-discipleship. This positive element deepened the spiritual life of many participants.

On the other hand, and at the same time, there was a growth in what has come to be known as Catholic Action, i.e. the sharing of the laity in the apostolate of the hierarchy.[60] The development of these lay movements involved, in its earlier stages, a struggle between lay leadership, on the one hand, and hierarchical leadership, on the other. In the end, particularly through the intervention of the pope and certain bishops, the hierarchical leadership prevailed. In various national episcopal meetings one hears an echoing of this hierarchical control for those lay activities which could be officially considered "Catholic Action." Any other lay activity was outside the pale of Catholic Action and was not endorsed by episcopal groups, much less by the pope.

These movements of Catholic Action were local, regional and international, and did much to enhance the role of the lay person within the church. The involvement in such Catholic Action movements was encouraged by both pope and bishops, and this encouragement gave a profound sense of identity to the lay person and provided the lay person with a spirituality which could only enhance his or her personal life.

b. Papal Leadership from Pius IX to Pius XII

The papal leadership during this same period of time presented many mixed signals. That the various popes, each in his own way, encouraged lay men and women to become more active in the church cannot be denied. Nonetheless, these very same popes clearly maintained both the superiority of the hierarchy and the hierarchical control of lay movements. In this latter, they were not always as successful as they wished, and in pressing the superiority of the hierarchy they pursued an ecclesiology which had serious *lacunae.* Vatican II attempted to realign the official ecclesiology of the Roman Catholic Church in ways that might address and remedy such *lacunae.*

Still, even with such limitations, it is quite evident that these various popes provided a leadership for lay identity in the church. They heightened the role and the expectations of the lay person in the church. They encouraged and blessed both a respectability and an identity to various lay movements. The impetus toward a fuller appreciation of the people of God, the *christifideles,* and the priesthood of all believers, which the bishops at Vatican II voiced so eloquently, went in directions quite unforeseen by these earlier popes. Still, the bishops at Vatican II would not have felt qualified to make their own assertions, had not a part of the past history of this role for the baptized been encouraged, to some degree, by the popes from Pius IX to Pius XII.

c. The Role of Women in the Church

During this period of time, Roman Catholic women, both those in vowed religious life and those who were married or unmarried but in secular life, gained an enormous voice, both in society and in the church. The rise of secular institutes, many of them primarily institutes of women, also provided a prestige for the Christian woman. Religious women moved out into a variety of ministries which required a high professional level. In the field of education such women were college presidents and deans, tenured faculty in all departments including theology, and respected research scholars in a wide range of fields. In the area of health ministries, such women became administrators of large hospitals, financial overseers of such institutions, and professionally trained nurses and technicians and at times medical doctors. In the field of social welfare such women became the leaders in the promotion of groups who were anti-poverty, anti-racism, anti-feminism, but more importantly pro-gospel and pro-human dignity, equality and freedom.

At the very same time, Catholic women along with women generally began to find a stronger voice in politics, in law, in education, in the social sciences, in journalism, in almost every facet of the contemporary scene. Their voice was not as respected nor as sought after as that of the male counterpart, and the struggle of women's groups for equality was often misunderstood and belittled by the dominant male society. Even today, genuine equality is still unattained in many sectors of the socio-political and cultural life, but enormous steps have been taken. Catholic women engaged in this move for equality and dignity have also reflected on the message of the gospel and on the current church. They have brought their critique, both positive and negative, to bear on church structures, gingerly at first but in an ever more vocal way. The women's movements in the church antedated Vatican II. The silence of the documents of Vatican II on the issue of women in the church and in society at large remains one of the major weaknesses of these documents. If the bishops at Vatican II intended—and they expressly did so intend—to give an accounting of the church in today's world, the silence on women's issues can only be seen as a major weakness in such an accounting.

d. The Role of Religious Communities, Both Those of Men and of Women

During this period of time new religious communities of both men and women were founded and they flourished. In the aftermath of the

French Revolution, Europe particularly experienced a major decline in the number of religious vocations. However, from almost the middle of the nineteenth century onward, there was a rebirth in many older religious groups, but especially a new birth of many religious communities. Ministry appears to have been the focus for most of these new religious establishments: ministry to the growing number of poor children in the larger cities and their need for both housing and education; a ministry to the working class of people, but especially housing for young men and young women who found themselves in large industrialized cities, but with sparse means for human life; a ministry to the missionary life of the Catholic Church, with many religious men and women leaving Europe for those areas of the world which were "unevangelized."

All of this provided a strong incentive for Christian life and Christian idealism. For the most part, older religious communities continued to set the tone of religious life. There was a monastic *horarium,* traditional in such religious communities, which formed the basis for religious life. Grafted into this were the new forms of ministry, most of which did not have a temporal flow in harmony with a monastic *horarium.* In many of these newly founded religious communities a time bomb was present from the start: ministries to people in various needs on the one hand with its *horarium* that was as erratic as poverty and sickness, missionary needs and pastoral concerns, and, on the other hand, a monastic framework which had an *horarium* or pace of its own and which disallowed the erratic element of such ministries. A major conflict of these two *horaria* could not help but take place, and this conflict clearly erupted in the Vatican II and post-Vatican II periods. It was, however, not the *horaria*-conflict as such which created disarray; it was, rather, the disparate world-views and the disparate church views undergirding these *horaria* which created the tensions in religious life. Religious life needed to be reevaluated from top to bottom, and those who were hanging on to the "traditional" and the "tried" found themselves often hanging on to a form of religious life which had no contemporary meaning. The criterion should not have been what had always been traditional in a given community, but rather what is the very meaning of gospel discipleship.

Even contemplative groups had to rethink their *raison d'être,* and eventually the example of Charles de Foucauld became a major impetus in this contemplative rethinking as also the writings of Thomas Merton. It is important, however, to see that this reevaluation of religious life came about because of a desire to follow the gospel, to be true to discipleship itself.

e. Church and State

The issue of *regnum et sacerdotium* has been a major theme throughout this volume, since the way in which popes and bishops in particular see their role in society, i.e. in the various "regna," has shaped the way they see the role of the lay person. If this relationship is seen as one in which the pope and by concomitance the bishops (and only then the priests) have a *plenitudo potestatis* over both the spiritual and the temporal, the role of a lay person, even an emperor, will be viewed accordingly. After the American and French revolutions, the relationship of a governmental structure (the *regna*) with the papacy and the episcopacy (the *sacerdotium*) entered a totally new phase. The popes, however, found this very difficult to understand. Leo XIII's worldview clearly evidenced this papal desire for the approach of Gregory VII, Innocent III and Innocent IV. Leo XIII, and with him all the other popes of this period of time as well, could not come to terms with an independent state, with a non-Christian state, with a state which had little to no relationship to the pope and therefore to the bishops and therefore to the *sacerdotium*. In the endeavor to hang on to a former way of understanding the *regnum et sacerdotium* issue, these same popes continued to see all lay people in an inferior and secondary way. This colored their approach to Catholic Action, their approach to women in the church, and their approach to the non-clerical world as such.

f. The Dignity, Freedom and Equality of All Human Beings

The aspiration of the two revolutions, American and French, for the dignity, freedom and equality of all human beings did not find a welcoming home in the church leadership of the Roman Catholic Church. This leadership had come to see itself within a monarchical and paternalistic framework. Anything which might contradict such a pyramidical approach to church life could only be viewed as anti-church. *Ordo* was based on creation and being, and on the will of God. There was no attempt on the part of church leadership to reevaluate their understanding of church ministry by the criterion of gospel discipleship. Time and again discipleship was presented in the terms which Gregory VII had so strongly articulated: loyalty to the pope and to the hierarchy in union with the pope. This was the only criterion for genuine discipleship. To raise the issue that the gospels, i.e. the New Testament, should be the primary criterion was seen as "Protestant." The pope, in this view, was presented as "higher than" the scriptures, not in so many words, of course, but in the demand that loyalty to the pope served as the fundamental criterion for true discipleship. The view that all men and women are created equal, that all have an innate dignity and freedom, was treated very delicately by church leadership, both ecclesiastical and theological. That the New Testament only speaks of one class of discipleship, which gives to each person an enhancement of his or her human dignity, equality and freedom, was not an issue which found a home in a monarchical and paternalistic church structure, and which might, if let in to this home, become a critique of the ecclesial structure. Greater stress was placed on the passage from Matthew: "Thou art Peter and upon this rock I will build my church." This section of Matthew's gospel came to be seen as the hermeneutic through which all other passages of the New Testament should be interpreted, rather than allowing the New Testament teaching on gospel discipleship as such to be the hermeneutic through which and by which that particular section of Matthew's gospel might be interpreted. The demand for a new hermeneutic, namely that of gospel discipleship, was not part of the mainline nineteenth century Roman Catholic Church. It became a major building block in the documents of Vatican II, but even there not in a way which pleased everyone.

g. Ecclesiology

From a theological standpoint, the various ecclesiologies, particularly those which are found expressed in the manuals of theology and in the official documents of the church, were basically hierarchical, not ecclesiologies which stressed the people of God, the *christifidelis,* the priesthood of all believers. When the bishops at Vatican II rejected the prepared document on the church, a document which mirrored such a hierarchical approach, and developed the approach now found in *Lumen gentium,* a new form of ecclesiology became the official teaching of the church. Such an ecclesiology did not receive any blessing from the nineteenth century church leadership. As a result, the structuring of the nineteenth century church downplayed the lay person, even at the same time as it attempted to upgrade the lay person through Catholic Action. As a result, one finds major conflictual elements at work in the Roman Catholic Church, particularly in the latter part of the nineteenth century and the beginning of the twentieth century.

h. Missionary Movements

Still another area in which the nineteenth and early twentieth century Roman Catholic Church leadership found uneasiness was the relationship between various world religions, of which Christianity was but one. Such a view of Christianity, which made the Christian religion in a sense equal to other major religious movements, was considered heresy.

Even within Christianity, the Roman Catholic Church in the nineteenth and early twentieth century did not enter into the inter-church ecumenical movement. Ecumenical positions were not fostered. The Roman Catholic Church was seen as the one and only true church founded by Jesus Christ. The major criterion for this one and only status was, more often than not, seen in the acceptance of the pope. The hierarchical and papal factor played the key operative role. This hierarchical and papal factor also affected the way in which the lay person in the church was viewed.

12

Vatican II and Post-Vatican II
Theology of the Lay Person

In the period between the First and Second Vatican Councils, the entire world, east and west, north and south, was involved in monumental changes and situations. There were not only two world wars, but also the devastating wars in Korea and in Vietnam; there were wars which continued to batter the continent of Africa, there were wars in the mideast, and there were wars both in China and in Tibet. The massiveness of these wars and of the resultant destruction affected human life in disastrous ways. Economic bedlam took over and ravaged many peoples. Early on in the twentieth century a revolution broke out in Russia, and a communist form of government swept across eastern Europe and deep into the northern parts of Asia. Many other issues, economic, political, and social, might also be cited.

During this same period of time the Roman Catholic Church leadership, not only in Rome itself, but in the various countries of the globe, tried to offer some sort of meaning to an increasingly so-called absurd world. Technology moved to dizzy heights, both for good and for evil purposes. Poverty increased geometrically as wars and social unrest took their toll. Men and women struggled to find daily bread and a modicum of meaning in an otherwise relentless downswing of human life. During this time, the leadership of the Roman Church was not of one voice, a sort of monolithic chorus. Some church leaders were moving as best they could to reestablish the church from the ashes of war into its former structures. Others were trying to make the church viable and meaningful in a post-modern world and trying not to reestablish a past structure and ethos. Other church leaders found intriguing challenges from and opportunities in various non-European cultures which had a validity and vitality all their own.

518

The ecclesiastical word "council" was mentioned here and there by these leaders, but certainly not often, and the sudden proroguing of Vatican I had made many church leaders in the first half of the twentieth century wary of yet another council which also might end in a tattered way. Still, that some form of world meeting was needed became more and more obvious, and the calling of the Second Vatican Council by Pope John XXIII was in itself not a totally unexpected event. The sudden timing and the lack of preparatory episcopal discussion on the viability of a council were the unexpected elements. Eventually, this council, Vatican II, formed for the Roman Catholic communion the major event of this church during the entire twentieth century. This council not only attempted to but in many ways did gather together many strands of the immediately preceding period of church life, and it also did steer the church into definite, though at times somewhat generalized, directions during the period immediately succeeding the council, namely the period called "post-Vatican II."

For the sake of organization, in this present chapter we will consider the contemporary period of the lay person in the church through an overview and an analysis of the following topical headings:

1. **Aspects of the Immediate Pre-History of the Second Vatican Council Which Focused on the Role of the Lay Person in the Church**
2. **The Documents of Vatican II as Regards Lay Ministry and Their Effect on the Meaning of Priesthood, Both Episcopal and Presbyteral**
3. **Post-Vatican II Documents and Movements Which Involve the Role of the Laity**
4. **The Role of Women in the Vatican II and the post-Vatican II Church**
5. **Ecumenical Aspects of Both Ordained and Non-Ordained Ministry and Their Influence on the Theology of the Non-Ordained Person in the Church**
6. **Conclusions from the Data**

1. ASPECTS OF THE IMMEDIATE PRE-HISTORY OF THE SECOND VATICAN COUNCIL WHICH FOCUSED ON THE ROLE OF THE LAY PERSON IN THE CHURCH

As far as the role of the lay person in the church is concerned, the immediate pre-history of the Second Vatican Council was key. World events had radically reshaped people's lives, and a sense of direction was dearly needed. That there was also a pressing need for a clearer theological presentation of priesthood, both episcopal and presbyteral, was indeed an additional factor for the calling of a council, but far greater than the clarification of ordained leadership was the need to face the more fundamental issue of the self-identity of the Roman Catholic Church in the world of the twentieth century. Too many question marks had been raised about the relevancy of the church in a technological and post-world war society. Too many questions which had been so dramatically posed by both the American and French revolutions, as was mentioned above, remained unanswered or answered only in a negative way. Catholic lay men and women throughout the world, and these of course were the majority of the Church, were experiencing on a daily basis a major dichotomy in their lives. The area of their technological and post-modern world was moving in one direction, and the area of their church seemed to move in a different direction, so much so that the church life appeared to have less and less to say to the world of their daily life. The church became increasingly a haven of other-worldliness, while the major part of a person's life dealt with a this-worldliness. Time and again, church leadership spoke out, but on too many occasions their message was of little avail to the day-to-day activities of human life, even though the message may have comforted the privatized, spiritual sector of one's being. The split between day-to-day human life and the life of the church, oriented toward one's interior holiness, was becoming broader, to such a degree that the very relevancy of the church itself was called into question.[1]

Factors external to the church, however, are not enough to explain the apparent irrelevancy of the church in the first part of the twentieth century.[2] There were also factors quite internal to the church. Pius XII, for instance, had a style of leadership which tended to over-centralize the church. Personally, he did not want to have collaborators, but only executors, as Martina notes, and deliberately, throughout fourteen years of his papacy, he refused to appoint a secretary of state for the Vatican, thereby retaining a personal control over all international matters. Moreover, during the papacy of Pius XII, contact between the pope and the bishops of dioceses became quite reduced, and this brought about a stagnation in the Roman curia, since ideas and issues from the outside did not easily find access into the Vatican world.[3] With Pius himself thereby cut off from the bishops of the world and even from the cardinals, "he ended up in splendid isolation."[4]

Because the Pope [Piux XII] did not have any effective, living contact with the base and was assisted only by a group of specialists, whose competence was undeniable but who were declared exponents of a very specific orientation, he ended up in splendid isolation. For this reason, his attitudes were not always as effective as he had hoped, and some of them were sooner or later seen as outmoded. This tendency was also influenced by his innate awareness of the deep crisis in contemporary society, which seemed to him to be dominated by opposing ideologies; this led him to an immobility.[5]

Under this kind of papal leadership, episcopal leadership throughout the Catholic world likewise found itself, as it tried to carry out some of these papal directives, isolated and immobilized. Bishops, who were continually looking over their shoulders to see whether Rome was in favor of their positions or not, never felt free to move beyond certain "official" perimeters. Moreover, the leadership provided by theologians remained, for the most part, wary, and seminaries tended generally to be conservative in their approach to either doctrinal or moral issues.

Nonetheless, some Catholic scholars did indeed move in more creative directions as they analyzed the present and restudied the past. R. Aubert, in his volume *La théologie catholique au milieu du XXe siècle,* speaks of four factors which in the first part of the twentieth century called for an internal reassessment of the Church, namely:

1. the biblical renewal;
2. the liturgical and patristic renewal;
3. the openness to the modern world;
4. the encounter with ecumenism and with existentialism.[6]

Pius XII was interested in the first two, but only in a moderate and quite cautious way. The encyclical *Divino afflante spiritu* opened Catholic biblical scholars of the Old Testament to the various historical methods, but did not extend this same methodological openness to the New Testament scholars. The encyclical *Humani generis,* while affirming patristic and liturgical scholarship, nevertheless strongly attempted to limit patristic and liturgical scholars. The last two elements in Aubert's list were perceived by Pius XII in a most cautious way, and at times almost in an adversarial way.

O. Rousseau adds a fifth issue of major importance to Aubert's list: namely, ecclesiology, concluding that with such an addition one has all the renewal movements, both theological and pastoral, which were present at the time of Vatican II.[7] In the ecclesiological renewal the lay movements which preceded Vatican II had given the ordinary Christian a collective self-identity, not merely an individualistic self-identity, as far as his or her belonging to the church was concerned.[8] There was a growing sense of ownership of the church on the part of the lay person, but an ownership and sense of responsibility which was communal, not privatistic. This did not always harmonize with the more privatized spirituality which nourished the lay people. The emphasis was on personal holiness, which then would be a great example to others in the home, in the marketplace, and in the workplace. This form of spirituality generally reinforced the basic premise of Catholic Action, namely that lay people participated in the apostolate of the hierarchy. Dorothy Day and Peter Maurin were atypical, rather than typical, of approved models of lay Christian life.

The formation and development of "La Mission de France" in 1941 was enormously popular and creative, but it was also short-lived, for in 1952 a letter from the Congregation for Religious demanded that all religious withdraw from this "worker-priest" movement, and in the same year Cardinal Pizzardo's letter forbade seminarians to take on secular jobs. The sober picture of H. Godin and Y. Daniel's book, *France, pays de mission,* which was a rather clear though startling and forthright study of the actual situation of the lay person in France, was shunted to one side, to make sure that religious would stay "religious," clerics would stay "clerical," and seminarians would remain as untainted as possible by the secular world.

The case involving R. Aubert's volume *Le Pontificat de Pie IX,* which called into question the value of Pius IX's positions, on the one hand, and, on the other hand, the case which aroused the antagonism of the Vatican to the activity for social justice and to the call for a Christian's individual responsibility, advocated rather fiercely by the two parish priests, Mazzolari and Milano, were, each in its own way, indicative of a basically conservative church leadership at mid-century. Criticism of a pope and advocacy of social justice were not seen as conducive of genuine piety. Add to these two issues the somewhat puzzling approach of the Vatican to the writings of Jacques Maritain, a celebrated and respected scholar, and the negative response of *Humani generis* by Pius XII to *La nouvelle théologie,* a movement filled with profound scholarship, and one sees still other indications that an entrenched and conservative positioning was being advocated by the highest church leadership in the Roman communion—not only by the pope and his selected advisors from the Gregorianum, but also by many entrenched theologians at the Angelicum and Lateran universities in Rome. For whatever reasons, the highest major superiors of various orders of men felt obligated to abide by the directives of the pope as regards the priest-worker movement and by his rejection of *La nouvelle théologie.* Religious were recalled from any worker-priest position, and scholars were in varying ways muted, such as the Jesuits de Lubac, Bouillard, Daniélou, Teilhard de Chardin and le Blond and the Dominicans Chenu, Congar, Boisselot and Féret.

Aubert summed up the situation rather succinctly, noting that since World War II it was the French church which had been setting the pace, much more than the church in Germany or in Belgium. In this urge to come to grips with the trends of the twentieth century, many leaders of French Catholic life had sought to respond to the whole of tradition—scriptural and patristic, theological and liturgical. They had also sought to come to grips with the contemporary, technological, scientific, and philosophical approach to the world.[9] This two-pronged approach to the contemporary world, led by a few ecclesiastical and theological French church leaders, was followed by a few similar church leaders in Germany, Belgium, Holland, and even elsewhere. At the very same time, and in the very same countries, other church leaders opposed both such an openness to the contemporary world and such a questioning of the "traditional" church positions.

Although in the above paragraphs, popes, bishops, and clerics appeared at the center of the debate, this entire clash of thinking did not arise because of clerics or specifically clerical issues, but rather because of world issues whose primary significance was predominantly lay. The world of the twentieth century was the world that surrounded the ordinary man and woman, husband and wife, mother and father, son and daughter. Some theologians of that time—and at that time theology was still very much an enclave of the clerical world—attempted to form bridges between a Christian's ordinary life and the gospel message. These attempts, however, were met by another group of church people, once again basically cleric, who reacted negatively and defensively to this bridge-building effort. That there was the possibility, even probability of an eventual major collision between the official self-stated meaning of the Roman Catholic Church itself and the world in which Roman Catholics, especially the non-ordained, lived cannot be denied. That is why something drastic, such as the calling of a council, was sorely needed.

One must balance this theoretical and theological side, which focuses basically on intellectual issues within the small world of theological studies, with other issues, no less theological and no less theoretical, which one finds outside seminary education and inner-church soirees. These issues involved the rise of various lay movements during the first half of the twentieth century, at times called Catholic Action, and at times outside the pale of Catholic Action. In the latter group one should include the resurgence of Catholic novelists and poets, almost all of whom were lay men and women. Names like Bernanos, Leon Blois, François Mauriac,

Georges Peguy, Graham Greene, Flannery O'Connor, and Carol House-lander come readily to mind. In their novels and poems one finds the struggles of the non-clerical person who attempts to find day-to-day meaning with God, with religion, with church, with faith, with sin, with forgiveness, and in doing so one discovers how the authors of these novels and poems raised fundamental questions about the contemporary clerical church structures and their inadequacy at times to make the gospel message relevant to life in the trenches.

One should also consider the development of women religious during this same period of time, particularly the theological, scientific and professional education these women gained within the American-European society. The development of professionally trained teachers and educators, college administrators, hospital administrators and skilled medical technicians created a form of ministry which the spiritual structures of religious life had never envisioned. The traditional, spiritual structures of religious life were based on certain theological premises and found a home in a fairly rigid, even monastic time-space continuum. The ministerial demands of a more contemporary religious life, with its high degree of professionalism, on the one hand, and, on the other, with its pastoral involvement in the very rhythms of lay life, raised serious questions about the meaning of religious life, about the meaning of a rigid monastic spiritual formation, and about the meaning of authority within a religious life structure. A professionally trained religious at times had, in the area of his or her competence, far more authority than a duly constituted religious superior. The theological premises of an older style of religious life and their concrete manifestations in the spirituality of more ministerial and professional religious life were increasingly called into question. Two conclusions became quite acute: first, the monastic spiritual structures of contemporary religious life, particularly among communities of women, appeared to be more and more incompatible with the twentieth century ministerial work of these same communities; second, religious women were becoming more and more theologically trained and sophisticated, so much so that not only did a clarification of the role of women in the church become increasingly more requisite, but also the demand for a feminist view of church history and church structure became unstoppable. The continued reading of church history only from a male standpoint, and, even more, only from a dominantly male hierarchical standpoint, was seen as a biased misreading of church history. To continue exegeting the scriptures only from a male standpoint, and even more only from a male hierarchical standpoint, was seen as a mis-exegeting of scripture. To continue to encode church life in rules and regulations which were enacted only from a male magisterium was seen as a discoding, not decoding, of church life. These kinds of judgments on twentieth century church life were based not on psychology or history, not on philosophy or anthropology. They were based primarily on the meaning of gospel discipleship. This was the criterion *par excellence.* Gospel discipleship was not and is not a male enclave, nor could the meaning of gospel discipleship be interpreted only by male authorities. Discipleship is both male and female and must be lived, interpreted and magisterially structured by both masculine and feminine elements. The rise of women in society and in the church, both of vowed, religious women and of married and single-but-in-the-secular-world women, antedated Vatican II. As such, the very status of women in church and society must be seen as an integral part of the "world" to which the twentieth century "church" needed to relate.

Still another ecclesially internal aspect which called for renewal gradually emerged. When Pius XII in 1946 had included in the company of cardinals men from various countries, there was a great stir. Moreover, he had personally consecrated native bishops in 1939 and in 1951. With *Evangelii praecones,* he had moved to establish native hierarchies in mission territories. This internationalizing of the episcopacy and college of cardinals was dramatic. The impact of non-Anglo-American and non-European bishops on the church became most evident, however, only with Vatican II, for the bishops from these non-European, non Anglo-American areas, were key to the emergence and shape of the Vatican II understanding of church.

Two major issues were intimately connected with this internationalization of church leaderships.

A. MULTI-CULTURAL FORMS OF CHURCH LIFE

The first issue focused on the multi-cultural form of church. The internationalizing of the church, which Pius IX and Leo XIII had already fostered but with a very papal interpretation, eventually became something which those two popes had certainly not fostered: namely, the formation of culturally distinct forms of church, based on distinct cultural approaches to life, to the world, to government, to family, to authority, etc. A multi-cultural form of church is not simply a church which has its liturgy in various languages and with various systems of symbolization. A multi-cultural form of church is a regional or even local church community which expresses in its prayer and liturgy, in its outlook on life and interpersonal relationships, the very deep cultural hopes and dreams of that same regional or local group. A multi-cultural church is not simply a Roman Church in linguistically varied clothing. Indeed, just as the Roman Church is "Romanly" cultured, so, too, sister churches need to be "non-Romanly" but indigenously cultured. The European model of church-state relationships, exemplified so strongly in the concordat signed by Pius XII and the government of Spain on August 27, 1953, was almost totally inoperative for these situations involving an inter-faith or inter-religious situation. In the concordat of 1953 one finds echoes of the thinking of Pius IX and Leo XIII, and even echoes of the *regnum et sacerdotium* of still earlier periods of western life. One finds in these very concordats an antiquated form of church and society.

B. A MULTI-CULTURED CHURCH AND RELIGIOUS FREEDOM

With such multi-cultural worldviews, however, a concomitant consideration had to be taken into account: namely, that of religious freedom in those areas in which non-Roman Catholic and non-Christian religions were dominant. The theme of religious freedom, however, had major implications for the very meaning of the Roman Catholic Church, not only in the area of church-state relationships, i.e. the Roman Church's relationship to a governmental structure which was religiously neutral or secularized, or even to a governmental structure which was clearly religious, but not in any Christian way. Acknowledgement of religious freedom by the leadership of the Roman Catholic Church for non-Catholic and non-Christian forms of religion seemed to imply, in the minds of many of these same Roman Catholic leaders, a parity among various religions and as a consequence a relativization of the Christian faith.

These are but some of the key areas which had brought about a questioning of the relevance of church, particularly the Roman Catholic Church, in the twentieth century. Mere discussion of issues in the hallowed walls of theological seminaries could not resolve the question of church relevancy/irrelevancy. Mere encyclicals from a pope who had isolated himself from so much of the world, including the Catholic world, could not resolve the issue of relevancy/irrelevancy either. Something more on the part of the Roman Catholic Church leadership was necessary, and it was the decision to hold a council which finally created an arena large enough to face the fundamental Roman Catholic Church issue of the twentieth century: namely, is the Roman Catholic Church relevant today, and, if so, in what ways? Certainly Vatican II did not provide a total or perhaps even a satisfactory response to this question. What it did provide, however, was a major arena large enough and open enough to surface the various aspects of the question. This council clearly changed the face of the Roman Catholic Church, although not all the changes were either clearly envisioned or clearly thought out, nor were their implications clearly presented. It must also be candidly admitted that not all the changes set forward by Vatican II have been wholeheartedly appreciated, or even wholeheartedly accepted, by subsequent Church leadership.

2. THE DOCUMENTS OF VATICAN II ON LAY MINISTRY AND THEIR EFFECT ON THE MEANING OF PRIESTHOOD, BOTH EPISCOPAL AND PRESBYTERAL

The theme of this council was aptly stated by Paul VI: What does the church say about itself? *Quid dicis de te ipso?*[10] When this issue on the meaning of the church became more clearly focused during the sessions of the council, the deep divisions of thinking by the bishops also became evident.[11] The very fact that the prepared text on the church, which the bishops had received in a pre-packaged form, was ultimately rejected, and the second fact that an entirely new document, *Lumen gentium,* was then prepared, are in themselves indicative of the need for a new statement on the meaning of church and not simply a restatement.[12]

With these introductory remarks in mind, let us consider our theme of the role of the lay person in the church in light of the documents of Vatican II,[13] but particularly of *Lumen gentium,* under the following headings:

A. The Christological Base of Vatican II
B. The Naming of Disciple
C. The *Tria Munera*
D. The Secular Character of "Lay" Ministry.

A. THE CHRISTOLOGICAL BASE OF VATICAN II

Lumen gentium, which begins with a chapter entitled *De ecclesiae mysterio* (On the Mystery of the Church), and in which the church is presented as a reflection of Jesus who alone is the light of the world, indicates that the church is fundamentally christological. The affirmation that christology is the primary basis on which and from which not only the text of *Lumen gentium* but also all the documents of Vatican II establish the meaning of church is common to all the major commentators.[14] In other words, the christological base is a given. To say that Jesus is the primary basis for the church is, however, a very generalized statement. The statement itself involves major implications which have a serious bearing on the role of the lay person in the church. Most of these major implications are also mentioned by the various commentators, yet it must be kept in mind that generally implications are never the focus of a given text or context in an official document. Nonetheless, implications derive from the textual content and context, and are, whether one likes it or not, consequential to positions taken by the bishops at Vatican II. Statements such as the documents of Vatican II, and *Lumen gentium* in particular, have serious implications for the role of the non-ordained, and these serious implications cannot be brushed to one side.

One such serious implication of the fundamental christological base is this: christology determines ecclesiology, not vice versa. The title *Lumen gentium,* the light of the world, refers to Jesus, not the church. Whatever light the church may have is only a reflection of Jesus. Kloppenburg aptly describes this light metaphor as the mystery of the moon.

> The Council begins its Dogmatic Constitution on the Church with the words, *Lumen gentium.* But this "light of the nations" is not the Church: Christ is the light of all nations" (LG 1/14). From its very opening words, therefore, Vatican II seeks to give a completely Christocentric and thus relativized idea of the Church.[15]

Further on, Kloppenburg writes:

> Only Christ is the light of the world. He is the Sun, sole source of light. At the side of this Sun, which is Christ, stands the Church like the moon which receives all its light, brilliance and warmth from the Sun.[16]

The church, by its very nature, is itself relativized—relativized over again Jesus, i.e. over against the word of God, not only enfleshed, but also enscriptured. This "subsidiary relationship" of church to Jesus also means that church leadership is relativized, since church leadership is itself under judgment by the same christological base. This same "subsidiary relationship" of the church to Jesus means that all Church ministry, whether ordained or non-ordained, is relativized by the identical christological base. Kloppenburg expresses it well:

> If the Church is absolutized, separated from Christ, considered only in its structures, viewed only in its history, and studied only under its visible, human and phenomenological aspects, it ceases to be a "mystery" and becomes simply one of countless other religious societies or organizations.[17]

This christological base opens the church structures, from papacy to parish, to a continual christocentric accountability. The gospel message of

Jesus and of a Jesus-discipleship, which is precisely what is intended by this christocentric base, becomes the primary criterion for each and every church structure, since the disciple of Jesus, at any and every level of church, must reflect the one light, Jesus. Only insofar as the church, at each and every level of its existence, reflects Jesus is it church at all. Only insofar as the church leadership, at each and every level, reflects Jesus is it church leadership. Whenever something or someone ecclesiastical does not reflect Jesus, it is not and cannot be "church." Rather, in that non-reflecting situation, such a person and such an activity are anti-church, since they are anti-Jesus.

> While the sun remains always glorious, the moon constantly passes through its various phases, now waxing, now waning, both in its external measurable size and in its inner lightsomeness. . . . These darker phases of the moon show us that the Church is in continuous distress in this world and that it renews itself when it draws close to Christ.[18]

That Vatican II, through its documents, is unabashedly christological is crystal-clear. However, it is also crystal-clear that nowhere do these same documents present even a basic outline of christology. Ecclesiology, not christology, was the theme of Vatican II. This lack of any christological presentation accounts for a certain ambiguity throughout the documents themselves, since one can read these documents from various christological standpoints. When one addresses the issue of ecclesial authority in the Vatican II documents, christological presuppositions become acute.[19] Since the documents of Vatican II present no christology, nor even a christological framework, many passages from these documents can be read differently. As a result, a basic ambiguity can be found throughout the various documents of Vatican II. This ambiguity does not mean hopeless unclarity, but rather the term "ambiguity," as used here, should be interpreted in the sense of the French, *ambiguité*, i.e. polyvalence. Certain texts from the documents of Vatican II can be interpreted in differing ways, not because of the text itself, not because of the context itself, but because of the kind of christology which the interpreter of the text and the context might be using. More often than not, arguments over the exact meaning of certain sections of the Vatican II documents are not specifically based either on the text itself or on the context itself, but rather on underlying and even opposing christologies in the minds of those who differ. In other words, the discussion or argument should not remain within the field of discourse, which attempts to certify the precise meaning of a given Vatican II text or context, but rather the discussion or argument should inquire about the christological presuppositions which the various proponents of the disputed area are bringing to the discourse. This same questioning of the christological base applies to the "official interpretations" of certain passages of the documents of Vatican II which have been presented by various Vatican congregations and even by papal statements as well. Too often these official statements, both papal and congregational, reflect the unthematized christological presuppositions of the authors, and the specific Vatican II text or context of itself cannot account for the official interpretation given to such texts and contexts.[20]

In the area of the lay person in the church, the relationship of discipleship and christology is acute, since a fundamental question, which affects the way the role of lay person is understood, can be expressed as follows: How does one's christology find expression in the way one describes the disciple of Christ? To answer this question requires a reading and rereading of the entire New Testament. From all that we said above on the New Testament theme of discipleship, the only acceptable meaning of discipleship in the church is a single form of gospel discipleship, in which and through which Jesus is manifested. The title *Lumen gentium* itself implies that there is only one discipleship, namely a discipleship which reflects Jesus. No other discipleship is allowable, and to the extent that one's discipleship does not reflect Jesus, it can only be seen as antidiscipleship.[21] Once again we are confronted with the fundamental criterion used throughout this study: gospel discipleship.

B. THE NAMING OF DISCIPLE

Of fundamental importance to the basic ecclesiology of Vatican II is the fact that the second chapter of *Lumen gentium,* entitled *De populo Dei* (On the People of God) was deliberately placed before the chapters on the hierarchy, on "lay" ministry, and on vowed religious. In doing this, the bishops at Vatican II want to describe the common matrix for all Christians.[22]

Immediately, however, a problem arises. How can one name this common matrix? Three names for this common matrix were officially and preferentially used: namely, the people of God, *christifidelis,* and priesthood of all believers. All three names continue to be used in post-Vatican II material as a description for this common matrix of gospel discipleship, but at the same time all three names have also been used both in the Vatican II documents and in post-Vatican II literature to indicate the non-ordained sector in the church as distinct from the ordained sector. In other words, not only have these three names been used to indicate a common matrix, but the same names continue to be used to indicate a non-common situation. In the Roman Catholic Church today there is no agreed upon name for this basic discipleship, and the very use of these three terms continues to be ambiguous. Nonetheless, let us consider each of these names in some detail.

1. People of God

This name became the very title of chapter two of *Lumen gentium.* It is abundantly clear that in this entire second chapter the word "people" (Greek: *laos*) does not mean a group of people *over and against a hierarchical or clerical leadership.* As we saw earlier, such an over-and-against understanding of the term *laos,* people, formed the core of de la Potterie's position against that of Congar. Clearly, the bishops at Vatican II did not have such a view of *laos*/people in mind. For them, people, *laos,* meant everyone in the church, as yet undifferentiated by such terms as cleric/non-cleric. The bishops were focusing on the common matrix, the fundamental equality and dignity of each and every follower of Jesus, not on a sector of such followers who were the "people," as distinct from a different sector of followers who were the leaders.

However, since writings found both in church history and in church theology use the same designation, "people of God," as the counterweight of hierarchy, there was and there is even today an ambiguity to this term. People of God is often used in this balance-counterbalance way, as we see in such phrases as the following:

In his Christmas allocution, the pope addressed the people of God, urging them to obey their bishops and priests.

In his sermon, the bishop admonished the people of his diocese to honor their priests and support them.

The pastor of the local church works tirelessly for the people of his parish.

In all of these rather typical instances of the ways in which the name "people" often appears in church writings, the very term "people" means those who are not the clerics, i.e. not pope, not bishop, not priest. However, this use of the term "people" is precisely opposite to that intended by the bishops of Vatican II when they dedicated an entire chapter to the people of God. This second chapter of *Lumen gentium* is describing the common matrix of each and every member of the church, whether that member is a husband or a pope, a wife or a nun, a child or a bishop. This second chapter is attempting to describe the very basis of gospel discipleship. There is no ambiguity whatever, either in the text or in the context of the second chapter of *Lumen gentium,* when this term "people of God" (*laos Theou*) is used.

In the post-Vatican II period, this term "people of God" is often not used for the common matrix, but rather it is used in the way it had been so often employed prior to Vatican II: namely, as a referent to that sector of Christians who are the followers, distinct from another sector of Christians, the clergy, who are the leaders. In the *Lineamenta: The Formation of Priests in Circumstances of the Present Day,* which was prepared in Rome for the 1990 synod of bishops, and therefore an official document, but a document written some twenty-five years after the council, one reads in n. 7:

> The ministry of the priest makes him the "witness to the Gospel of God's grace," and the "dispenser of the mysteries." This element of mystery in no way diminishes the humanity of the priest, who close to all and in solidarity with his people, must be capable of bearing his responsibility as pastor.[23]

In this phrase we hear about a "priest" and "his people." His people are one group; the priest is their minister with many related responsibilities.

In Paul VI's *Sacrum diaconatus ordinem* of June 18, 1967, in which the pope established norms for the restoration of the permanent diaconate, one finds that deacons are:

> To read the scriptures to the faithful and to teach and preach to the people (22/7).[24]

The same pope, in the same year, 1967, addressed the third world congress of the lay apostolate, and said:

> Certainly the People of God, filled with graces and gifts, marching toward salvation, presents a magnificent spectacle. But does it follow that the People of God are their own interpreters of God's word and ministers of His grace? That they can evolve religious teachings and directives, making abstraction of the faith which the Church professes with authority? Or that they can boldly turn aside from tradition and emancipate themselves from the magisterium?[25]

In both of these documents, the term "people" is used by Paul VI in counterbalance to (a) the deacon and (b) the hierarchical magisterium. In both of these documents the term "people" is not used as the common matrix of gospel discipleship, such as one finds in the second chapter of *Lumen gentium.*

In another document, specifically focused on the lay person, namely, in the conclusion of the NCCB pastoral statement *Called and Gifted: The American Catholic Laity,* issued in November 1980, again, many years after Vatican II, we read:

> We bishops wish simply to take our place and exercise our role among the People of God. We now await the next word.[26]

The term "people of God" in this sentence places an emphasis on the distinction of bishop and people, not on the common matrix.

Other instances could easily be cited, but it is clear that in the post-Vatican II church the term "people of God" is used:

1. at times to indicate the common matrix of every follower of Jesus;
2. at other times, however, to indicate and name those followers of Jesus who are not part of the clerical leadership.

That **there is a common matrix for all the followers of Jesus, for which** *Lumen gentium* **in chapter two used a term "people of God," is clearly taught by the Roman Catholic Church in the documents of Vatican II.**

That, **after Vatican II,** *a distinct name,* **such as "people of God," has been used exclusively for this common matrix of all disciples cannot be maintained.**

People of God is often used even after Vatican II to name that sector of disciples who are non-clerical, indicating that the term "people of God" has not been accepted by the Roman Catholic community as *the name* for the common matrix of all disciples. We will search out the reasons for this wavering use of the term "people of God" later, but we should first consider the two other names which official church documents have used to indicate the common matrix.

2. *Christifidelis*—The Faithful or the Christian Faithful

This term *christifidelis* is also used to name the common matrix of all Christian discipleship. Not only do we find this in the documents of Vatican II, but this precise term has become the preferred term in the revised code of canon law to indicate the common discipleship of all believers, whether ordained or non-ordained. Canon 204, a major canon in this regard, reads:

The Christian faithful (*Christifideles*) are those who, inasmuch as they have been incorporated in Christ through baptism, have been constituted as the people of God; for this reason, since they have become sharers in Christ's priestly, prophetic and royal office in their own manner, they are called to exercise the mission which God has entrusted to the Church to fulfill in the world, in accord with the condition proper to each one.

It is obvious that in this canon the name *christifidelis* attempts to describe the common matrix, the discipleship to which all baptized (also confirmed and eucharistic) people are called. *Christifidelis* in this section of the code means all baptized, none excluded. All baptized share in Christ's *tria munera*, and all exercise this task in and through the specific graces God gives to each one.[27] *Christifidelis* was selected by the framers of the code to describe the discipleship of each and every Christian, i.e. the common matrix for all baptized.

However, it has been more than commonplace to hear such phrases as: the pope, the bishops or the priests "have addressed the faithful," "have called on the faithful to lead better lives," "have prayed for the faithful." In all of these utterances, "faithful" (*christifidelis*) does not mean all baptized, but rather it means those who are not the pope, not the bishops, not the priest.

The *Circular Letter Concerning the Preparation and Celebration of the Easter Feasts,* published on January 16, 1988 by the Congregation for Divine Worship, uses the term "faithful" again and again to indicate those who are not ordained. For instance, the lack of enthusiasm in certain areas of the world for the Easter triduum is due in good part to "the inadequate formation given to the clergy and the faithful regarding the paschal mystery as the center of the liturgical year and of Christian life" (n. 3). The distinction clergy/faithful should not be readily overlooked. Again in another paragraph of the same document we read: "Pastors should draw the attention of the faithful to those moments of significant importance in their spiritual life" (n. 8). The distinction pastor/faithful should not be quickly disregarded. Still another paragraph in the same document reads: "In this procession [Palm Sunday] the faithful carry palms or other branches. The priest and the ministers, also carrying branches, precede the people" (n. 29).[28] Once again we have a distinction: priests and ministers on the one hand, the faithful on the other hand.

In such examples, and the above are cited as merely indicative of many, many more, we see that since Vatican II, and since the promulgation of the revised code, there has been and remains down to the present time an ambiguity or polyvalency to the very name *christifidelis*. Neither the documents of Vatican II nor the code designedly wants to continue such ambiguity, but historical inertia often works against their intent. The framers of the code, in particular, went to great pains to use a term to express the common matrix of all believers, but if such a term as *christifidelis* should only be used when the common matrix of all Christians is emphasized, what name, in the practical, day-to-day situation, should be used when one wishes to refer to the non-ordained, as distinct from the ordained?

When John Paul II used the term *Christifideles laici,* it seems he was attempting to straddle an almost unsurmountable ravine.[29] On the one hand, there are not two kinds of *christifideles:* one lay, *christifideles laici,* and the other cleric, *christifideles clerici,* if by the term *christifidelis* itself one wants to specify the common dignity and equality which belongs to each and every Christian in virtue of the sacrament of initiation. At the level of *christifidelis,* the distinction "lay/cleric" is theologically not applicable. However, putting them together as John Paul did seems to make the issue even more muddled than ever. There are indeed lay/cleric individuals, or ordained/non-ordained individuals, in the church, but this precise combination of the two, *christifideles laici,* does not appear to be theologically helpful.

In a way quite similar to that of the name "people of God," the name *christifidelis,* though used deliberately in very official documents of the church to specify the common matrix, the common discipleship of all baptized Christians, continues to be used even in official church documents to name those who are the non-ordained.

That there is a common matrix, a common discipleship for all the baptized is official church teaching.

That the name *christifidelis* has been accepted after Vatican II, as the exclusive name for this common discipleship, has not yet occurred.

Before we address the reasons for this continued wavering as regards such names as "people of God" and *christifidelis,* let us consider the third and last main name which the documents of Vatican II used to indicate the common matrix, the common discipleship of all the baptized-eucharistic Christians.

3. Priesthood of All Believers

A third name, applied to all baptized-eucharistic Christians as the common matrix of one's gospel discipleship, is "priesthood of all believers." This designation has engendered an extensive amount of literature, for if all Christians are priests, what is the meaning of the ordained or ministerial priesthood?[30] Even at the council itself, a number of explanations for the difference between the priesthood of all believers and the ordained priesthood were presented to the bishops. None of them, however, were officially adopted. At Vatican II the bishops were presented with the following distinctions between the priesthood of all believers and the priesthood of the ordained ministry.

PRIESTHOOD OF ALL BELIEVERS	ORDAINED PRIESTHOOD
1. A figurative priesthood	a real priesthood
2. A spiritual priesthood	a real priesthood
3. An interior priesthood	an exterior priesthood
4. A non-sacramental priesthood	a sacramental priesthood
5. A lay priesthood	a hierarchical priesthood
6. A private priesthood	a public priesthood
7. An incomplete priesthood	a full priesthood
8. A royal priesthood	a service priesthood
9. A feminine priesthood	a masculine priesthood[31]

The bishops at Vatican II did not endorse any of the above; nevertheless, they officially used the term "priesthood of all believers," to denote the common matrix of gospel discipleship. Once they did this, a major questioning of self-identity swept over many parts of the Roman Catholic Church, both as regards the identity of one who is baptized-eucharistic, and as regards the identity of one who is ordained. If all Christians are indeed priests, and essentially so, then what is the very meaning of *sacerdotium*, i.e. the ordained priesthood. Basic questions regarding the meaning of the name "priest" remain down to the present time, but the main question is quite clear: If all disciples in virtue of their baptism-confirmation-eucharist are priests, then why do we have ordained priests and what is their specific identity?[32]

> *That* there is a common matrix of gospel discipleship, which the documents of Vatican II call "priesthood of all believers," is an official teaching of the Roman Catholic Church.

> *That* since Vatican II the name "priesthood of all believers" has been accepted as the exclusive name for such a matrix has not occurred.

We will consider the fundamental difficulties involved in this particular name for discipleship when we consider below the role, function, and mission of each and every disciple, i.e. their participation in the *tria munera,* the threefold mission of Jesus. We will see that it is not simply the name "priesthood of all believers" which has caused the abundant and often heated discussion, although some bishops at the council were quite opposed even to the name itself. It is rather the precise theological meaning of "priest," and the use of *tria munera* to describe both the priesthood of all believers and the ordained priesthood, which is at the heart of the debate.

These three names or designations—"people of God," *christifidelis,* and "priesthood of all believers"—have been proposed by the official church leadership as the preferred terms to express the common matrix of gospel discipleship. Other names have also been used, but not with the intensity of these three, namely the "baptized," or "member of the mystical body," or even "member of the kingdom of God." These latter names are never centrally used in the documents of Vatican II when the bishops deliberately wished to specify the common matrix of gospel discipleship. The three names are, however, centrally used in the documents.

One specific issue which is vitally important to note, as far as our study on the role of lay ministry is concerned, is this:

The documents of Vatican II, and *Lumen gentium* in particular, never used the term *laicus,* "lay," to designate the common matrix of gospel discipleship.

Chapter 4 of *Lumen gentium* takes up this term *De laicis,* but only after the chapters on the people of God (chapter 2) and the hierarchy (chapter 3). To read backward and use the term *laicus* to interpret chapter 2 of *Lumen gentium* would be a misreading of both text and context. Through the very structure of the document, the bishops of Vatican II were attempting to make a clear distinction between:

People of God
Christifidelis   and   Lay person
Priesthood of all believers

This distancing of the term "lay" from the common matrix indicates that as one enters into the Jesus community through the sacrament of initiation [baptism-confirmation-eucharist] a person is not thereby a lay person. Baptism-eucharist is not the sacramental initiation into lay status in the church. Rather, some new name needs to be developed, one which does not have any of the implications of *klerikos/laikos,* but rather a name through which the fundamental reality of Christian discipleship can be expressed. In a former theological terminology, for instance, there was an equation between basic Christian and lay person, but this way of speaking is no longer viable. A recalcitrant cleric, for example, used to be, but now no longer can be, said to be "reduced to the lay state." However, one might note that there remains anachronistically a process called the "laicization" of priests.[33] Such a name, theologically, is today incorrect and is indicative of the current ambiguity in the Roman Catholic Church, even at the level of its highest leadership, as regards this naming process. Moreover, the retention of this name "laicization" for such a process is also indicative of the inertia of tradition. It is very difficult simply to change a name and expect a change in mentality.

Another instance in which one can see this name-changing but not reality-changing factor is the renaming of the sacrament of "extreme unction" to "anointing of the sick." The name was officially changed, but the reality in pastoral practice and even in theology itself has not yet been completely altered to correspond to the new name.

Still another example of this disparity between a name-change and the reality-change is the following: theologically speaking, one cannot say, on the basis of Vatican II, that a person is "chosen from the lay state" and "elevated to the clerical state."[34] Such language, used in many texts prior to Vatican II, equated "lay" with a sort of "common matrix." The documents of Vatican II, however, disallow such an equation. Nonetheless, one finds from time to time a continued use of the pre-Vatican II terminology as regards this issue of priestly "elevation," even though such terminology and the theological intent beneath the terms run counter to the documents of Vatican II. A name-change has indeed taken place, together with a change in theological meaning beneath the name, but both the older linguistic phrases and the older theologies perdure.

Having described the common matrix of gospel discipleship in terms of "people of God," *christifidelis,* and "priesthood of all believers," the bishops at Vatican II subsequently found the term "lay" problematical. In the discussions on the text for chapter 4 of *Lumen gentium,* in which they focused specifically on the lay person, it became necessary for the bishops to formulate a working description of the term "lay." They did this as follows:

Lay is to be understood as all the faithful except those in holy orders and those who belong to a religious state approved by the church (n. 31).

Even allowing that this description was not meant to be a definition, but only a working explanation, one realizes that at this juncture of *Lu-*

men gentium (chapter 4) the focus of the bishops' discussion has clearly shifted. The focus is no longer on the common matrix of all believers, but on specific "lay" situations within the church which are distinct both from those of the ordained and from those of vowed religious. In making this kind of distinction, and in doing it so deliberately, the bishops were attempting once again to separate the term "lay" from their previous discussion of the common matrix of gospel discipleship.

This textual and contextual separation of "lay" from such designations as "people of God," *christifidelis,* and "priesthood of all believers" does not negate the theme of this present study: namely, the role of the "lay person" in the church.[35] What had in former centuries of church life been called the "role of the lay person in the church" is now, in a Vatican II and post-Vatican II period of church history, considered under a series of new names, namely, the role of the "people of God," the role of the *christifidelis,* the role of the "priesthood of all believers."[36] The name may have been altered, with the term "lay" becoming in a post-Vatican II church a description of a special form or vocation of ministry in the church, but the issue of the role of the baptized-eucharistic Christian, whether ordained or unordained, within the church retains its full intensity.

Indeed, the role of the baptized-eucharistic Christian has now attained an intensity far stronger than before, due to the fact that the official church leadership at Vatican II has itself deliberately and officially repositioned the baptized-eucharistic Christian within the church structures. This repositioning is not merely titular. This repositioning is also structural. One cannot say in the same breath that all baptized/eucharistic Christians are indeed people of God, *christifideles,* and members of the priesthood of all believers—the titular aspect—but that they have no specific role thereby *in the church*—the structural aspect. Nor can one say that the specific role of each and every Christian is to be exercised only in the world, *in saeculo,* since such Christians are secular, but they are not to exercise their role in the church, *in ecclesia,* since this ecclesial sector is reserved exclusively to the ordained. The sacrament of initiation, baptism-confirmation-eucharist, is an initiation primarily into the church, *in ecclesiam,* not into the secular world, *in saeculum.* The sacrament of initiation gives each one a positioning in the church itself, not in the secular world. This positioning in the church is a positioning which involves the exercise of the *tria munera* of Jesus, which is to be exercised by each Christian primarily within the church, and only secondarily within the wider secular society. To be a teacher/preacher (prophet), to be a sanctifier (priest), to be a leader (king) is primarily an ecclesial reality, and participation in the *tria munera* of Jesus has *ipso facto* basic structural ramifications within the church. Attempts, either by theologians or by some officials in the church, to relegate the role of the *tria munera,* given to all through baptism-eucharist, to the secular arena alone is theologically impossible after Vatican II. Such attempts are against the ordinary magisterium of the church.

By stressing the common matrix of gospel discipleship, the documents of Vatican II, especially *Lumen gentium,* and also the revised code of canon law raise, in a very strong and heightened way, the same issue which has emerged in church history century after century regarding the role of the Christian, whether ordained or not, and these same documents clearly state the kind of role each Christian has, namely, an active ecclesial role in the very *tria munera* of Jesus. Therefore, every Christian has both the right and the obligation to fulfill these *tria munera* primarily within the community called church and secondarily within the socio-political society in which he or she lives. It is, however, precisely this relationship between the *tria munera* of Jesus and the names—people of God, *christifidelis,* priesthood of all believers—which has, since Vatican II, created the major theological tension and source of quarreling as regards the very meaning of the common matrix of gospel discipleship.

C. THE *TRIA MUNERA*

Each of the names referred to above clearly speaks of a basic Christian discipleship, not merely common to each and every follower of Jesus, but also fundamental to the very meaning of any further naming-process and any further structural-process. In other words, only on the basis of gospel discipleship, whether this is preferably called "people of God," *christifidelis,* or "priesthood of all believers," is a "clerical or hierarchical person" in the church meaningful. Only on the basis of discipleship, employing any of the same names, is "religious life" meaningful. Only on the basis of discipleship, however it be designated, is "lay ministry" itself meaningful.[37] No longer can the term "cleric" be defined over against the term "lay"; rather, the meaning of "cleric" is one who is not only or also a disciple, but one who is primarily a disciple, and only secondarily a "cleric." In the very structuring of the document *Lumen gentium,* and in the theology behind this structuring, the bishops at Vatican II not only relativized the hierarchy vis-à-vis Jesus (the christological dimension), but also relativized the hierarchy vis-à-vis gospel discipleship (the ecclesiological dimension). A relativized hierarchy—and relativized in these two dimensions—is the theological base of *Lumen gentium,* a document which represents a solemn moment of church magisterium as regards the very meaning of "cleric," "lay," and "religious."

This position deserves to be stressed, since the basic criterion of this present volume on the role of the lay person (i.e. *christifidelis*) in the church has been, chapter after chapter, the same, namely the meaning of gospel discipleship. It is evident that the bishops at Vatican II were reshaping the very language used by the Roman Catholic Church, since in the second chapter of *Lumen gentium,* on the people of God, the focus is not on *laity,* but on something more basic than laity. This second chapter is talking about a common matrix, a foundational and primordial basis, prior to any subsequent distinction of cleric/lay or cleric/religious/lay. This second chapter is talking about gospel discipleship.

All Christians are equal at this foundational and most sacred level of discipleship, but this equality and communality must be seen in a context far wider than simply the context of a *klerikos/laikos* situation. This communality and equality must be seen along gender lines: there is no privileged position to male disciples over female disciples, nor vice versa. This communality and equality must be seen along ethnic lines: there is no privileged position to European or Anglo-American disciples over non-European and non-Anglo-American disciples. Nor is there *qua* disciple any privileged position of ordained over non-ordained.

Such statements can remain simply rhetorical unless one immediately adds that such equality and communality has major theoretical and practical implications: e.g. the understanding and meaning of discipleship is one-sided and insufficient if it is interpreted, described and lived only from a male position, only from a male-oriented theology, only from a male-magisterium. When the feminine insight into discipleship is disregarded both in theory and in practice as regards the interpretation of scripture, as regards the interpretation of church history, as regards the interpretations formulated by the hierarchical magisterium, as regards the liturgical life of the church, as regards the pastoral life of the church, then gospel discipleship itself in such limited interpretations is more than likely open to grave distortions. When the insights from various African, various Asian, various South American, various Central American, etc., cultures are disregarded in theory and practice as regards the interpretation of scripture, as regards the interpretation of church history, as regards the interpretations formulated by the hierarchical magisterium, as regards the interpretation of church law, as regards the liturgical and pastoral life of the church, then the very meaning of gospel discipleship in such limited interpretations is more than likely open to grave distortions. When the various insights of married Christians, non-clerical Christians, single but in-the-world Christians, and Christians who are not part of religious communities are disregarded in any or all of the above instances, then the very meaning of gospel discipleship in such limited interpretations is once again more than likely open to grave distortions. A celibate view of discipleship, or an interpretation of discipleship which is formulated only by celibate Christians, without comparable input from married Christians, distorts the essential meaning of gospel discipleship.

Such a judgment on all these various possible distortions can and must be made on the basis of gospel discipleship itself. In the analysis at the beginning of this study on gospel discipleship, it was apparent that none of the New Testament material indicated a two-level form of gospel discipleship:

one level for lay people	another for clerics;
one level for men	another for women;
one level for a given culture	another for differing cultures;
one level for celibates	another for married people.

The scriptural position, which rejects any two-level approach to gospel discipleship, finds echo and confirmation in the revised code of canon law. In canon 208 one reads:

> In virtue of their rebirth in Christ there exists among all the Christian faithful a true equality with regard to dignity and the activity whereby all cooperate in the building up of the Body of Christ in accord with each one's condition and function.

One could summarize this theological understanding of gospel discipleship as follows:

The New Testament indicates that there is a common matrix to gospel discipleship and that this discipleship is:

COMMON and EQUAL to ALL

Official church documents indicate that there is a common matrix to gospel discipleship and that this discipleship is:

COMMON and EQUAL to ALL

Such a position, so starkly stated in the above format, is indeed the official teaching of Vatican II and of the revised code. Even more importantly, however, it is the very teaching of the New Testament. Nonethe-

less, such a view regarding Christian equality has neither totally nor overwhelmingly been accepted by the Roman Catholic world today, not because certain people deliberately disagree either with the New Testament
or with Vatican II or with the code of canon law, but because such a view
of common and equal discipleship does not, in their approach, clearly do
justice to the theology of ordained priesthood and hierarchy which they
have previously heard and which they have previously accepted.

An example of this uneasiness as regards a common and equal positioning of the baptized-eucharistic person in the church appears in the
positioning of women in the church. In sometimes subtle and sometimes
not so subtle ways, the opposition or uneasiness of church leadership,
both hierarchical and theological, to the role of women in the church has
become documented in ways which clearly undermine a common and
equal discipleship. *Inaestimabile donum,* an instruction of the Congregation for Sacraments and Divine Worship, issued in 1980, makes its own a
previous instruction issued by the Congregation for Divine Worship, *Liturgicae instaurationes,* (1970), when it states: "There are various roles
which a woman may fulfill in the liturgical assembly. Among these are
reading from the word of God and proclaiming the intentions at the
prayers of the faithful. However, women are not permitted to undertake
the functions of acolyte or minister at the altar."[38] The 1970 document is
referred to in the relevant footnote, to indicate that it is the basis for the
1980 rejection of women in such ministerial roles. These two documents
place unordained male Christians above unordained female Christians as
regards certain non-ordained ministries in the church. Both documents
are indicative of a non-acceptance of the fundamental common equality
of all Christians.

Yet another indication of this non-acceptance of common equality
of all Christians can be found in canon 230, ¶ 1, which states that "Lay
men [*viri laici*] . . . can be installed in the ministries of lector and acolyte."
In the same canon women can be deputed, temporarily, as lectors; no
mention is made in the canon, however, that even temporarily women
might be designated as acolytes. The preferential treatment and positioning of non-ordained men over non-ordained women in non-ordained
ministries raises a serious question: Has the teaching of Vatican II and the
teaching of the New Testament itself on the common equality of gospel
discipleship been fully appreciated and accepted or not?

If we look more deeply into the 1970 instruction of the Congregation
for Divine Worship, *Liturgicae instaurationes,* mentioned above, we find:

> In conformity with norms traditional in the church, women
> (single, married, religious), whether in churches, homes, con-

vents, schools or institutions for women, are barred from serving the priest at the altar.[39]

This, of course, raises the issue of female acolytes or servers. Such a ministry does not require ordination. Nonetheless, in an official church statement, a non-ordained ministry is reserved to men only and forbidden (barred) to women. In this instance, the question again arises: Has the common equality of gospel discipleship taught by Vatican II and by the New Testament itself been accepted or not?

In the *Roman Missal* itself one finds: "Women may be appointed to ministries that are performed outside the sanctuary."[40] On the other hand, men can be appointed to ministries which require no ordination and which are performed within the sanctuary. This distinction between male baptized-eucharistic Christians and female baptized-eucharistic Christians indicates that the teaching of the New Testament on gospel discipleship and the teaching of Vatican II on the people of God, *christifidelis,* and the priesthood of all believers, as well as the position of canon law, mentioned above, have not yet been fully integrated into the life of the Church.[41]

On the other hand, in 1971 the United States bishops' Committee on the Liturgy noted:

> It is certain that in the liturgical celebration, as in other facets of the church's life, there should be no discrimination or apparent discrimination against women. . . . The basic or radical equality of the baptized members of Christ takes priority over, and is more significant than, distinctions of order and ministry.[42]

Similar views were repeated by bishops at the synod on the laity in 1987. But how can one speak of a "priority" which is more significant than distinctions of order and ministry, when flagrant dispriorities are maintained?

One can legitimately ask: Are all baptized and eucharistic Christians equal? Or are baptized and eucharistic men superior to baptized and eucharistic women?[43] Some of the documents cited above indicate a superiority; the major documents, however, indicate an equality. The lack of terminological unanimity and the presence of mixed signals indicate a theological uneasiness which is far more serious than merely the ambiguity as regards the difficulty in naming this common gospel discipleship which was mentioned earlier. The lack of unanimity indicates that the acceptance of a basic gospel discipleship, with its inherent equality for all, and not the acceptance of a particular name for it, is truly at stake, and this should be of major concern to church leadership at any and every level, since the lack of accepting fundamental gospel discipleship calls into question their own credibility.

All of this leads us to the crux of the problem, namely, the *tria munera.*[44] Through baptism/eucharist all Christians share in this threefold ministry and mission of Jesus. Such is the clear teaching of Vatican II.

> All baptized and eucharistic Christians "share a true equality with regard to the dignity and to the activity common to all the faithful for the building up of the body of Christ" (*LG* 32).

> All share "in the mission of the whole Christian people with respect to the church and to the world" (*LG* 31).

> All "have an active part to play in the life and activity of the church" (*AA* 10).

> All are called upon by the Lord "to expend all their energy for the growth of the church and its continuous sanctification" (*LG* 32; *AA* 2).

> All "are commissioned to the apostolate by the Lord himself" (*LG* 33).

> All are "made sharers in the priestly, prophetic and kingly functions of Christ" (*LG* 31; *AA* 2).

> "The supreme and eternal priest, Christ Jesus, wills to continue his witness and serve through the laity too." He "gives them a share in his priestly function" (*LG* 34).

> "The great prophet . . . fulfills his prophetic office . . . not only through the hierarchy who teach in his name and with his authority, but also through the laity" (*LG* 35).

> "He made them his witnesses and gave them understanding of the faith and grace of speech" (*LG* 35).[45]

Lumen gentium in article 33 speaks of the vocation of all Christians, "given to all without exception; it is given with one's incorporation in the People of God, in the one body of Christ, under one Head, Christ. Here, then [in article 33], we are dealing with a general Christian vocation,

rather than a specifically lay one, but it concerns the secular layman because he is a Christian."[46] The source of this vocation is clearly stated by
Lumen gentium: baptism and confirmation, with the eucharist mentioned as nourishing such a vocation.[47] It is, therefore, Christ in and
through the sacraments, not a pope, not a bishop, not a priest, who both
calls and commissions a person, whether male or female, to such a Christian vocation. The call and the commission to the *tria munera* of Jesus are
not, therefore, deputed or delegated tasks given to Christians by church
hierarchy; they are given *vi sacramenti*, not *vi delegationis*.

Klostermann mentions:

> As the following three articles (34, 35, 36) show, the Council is
> aware that baptism and confirmation do not merely confer a
> share in Christ's priesthood but also a share in Christ's office as
> prophet and king. . . . Baptism and confirmation each provide
> the foundation for a general Christian apostolate, an apostolate
> of all Christians.[48]

Lumen gentium in article 34 states that all such Christians share in
the *priestly* function of Jesus, the first of the *tria munera.* Article 35 describes the Christian's share in Christ's prophetical office, the second of
the *tria munera.* Article 36 presents the Christian's share in Christ's kingly
office, the third and last of the *tria munera.*[49] The Christian's mission and
ministry, a sharing in Jesus' own *tria munera*, arise from the sacramental
initiation of baptism–confirmation–eucharist. The sharing in these *tria
munera* is present in each and every Christian in virtue of the call and
commissioning by the Lord himself, not by a clerical delegation or depu-
tation. The sharing in the *tria munera* is present *vi sacramenti*, not *vi
delegationis.*

**It is this sacramental connection of every Christian to the *tria
munera* of Jesus which has become the crucial issue of dispute.**

Neither the attempts at naming the common matrix of gospel discipleship nor even the doctrine of a common gospel discipleship has occasioned the current theological uproar. Rather, it is the conflict between
the way in which all baptized-eucharistic Christians share in the mission
and ministry of Jesus, the *tria munera*, and the way in which ordained
clergy share in the same mission and ministry of Jesus, the *tria munera*,
that has caused the current theologically strident problems.

Two things need to be noted:

1. First of all, all baptized-confirmed-eucharistic Christians share in the *tria munera* of Jesus.
2. Secondly, the mission and ministry which stem from this, the "apostolate" of all Christians, can no longer be presented in accordance with the teaching of Vatican II as a sharing by the faithful in the apostolate of the hierarchy.

Let us consider each of these issues in some detail.

1. The Baptized-Eucharistic Christian as a Sharer in the *Tria Munera* of Jesus

The commissioning of all Christians to the threefold mission and ministry of Jesus takes place, as was noted above, in a sacramental way, not a delegational way, namely, through baptism–confirmation–eucharist. Such a participation is a direct effect of the sacraments of initiation themselves. If, on the one hand, we say that all Christians share in these *tria munera* of Jesus, can we say, on the other hand, that with ordination priests share in the same three offices but in an *essentially* different form from that of all Christians? This is the core-problem, the theological crux of the issue, which the documents of Vatican II—and post-Vatican II documents as well—have raised and continue to raise.[50]

Prior to these documents, the office of teaching, sanctifying and leadership, the *tria munera,* was presented by many theologians and canonists in a quite different way. In 1961, for instance, Udalricus Beste, a professor of canon law at the Anselmianum in Rome, a consultor of the Sacred Congregation of the Holy Office, and a member of the pontifical preparatory commission on the sacraments for Vatican II, described the order of clerics specifically in terms of the *tria munera.* I cite Beste here only as typical. Many other canonists as well as theologians wrote in quite similar ways. Beste described the specifically clerical situation as follows:

> Ordini clericorum cui ex voluntate divina commissum est officium docendi, regendi et sanctificandi fideles, Christus Dominus pariter contulit.[51]

> Christ the Lord likewise established the order of clerics, to whom the office of teaching, ruling and sanctifying the faithful was commissioned by divine will.

He goes on to say that the hierarchy, objectively considered, has received its specific character precisely through this faculty of sanctifying, teaching and directing the society of Christians, which Christ entrusted to the apostles and to their successors.

> Itaque, **hierarchia** *obiective spectata* denotat universam faculta-tem, quam Christus apostolis eorumque successoribus legitimis tribuit in ordine ad sanctificandam, docendam et dirigendam societatem christifidelium seu ecclesiam ab Ipso conditam, quamque distribuimus in potestatem ordinis et iurisdictionis.[52]

> Therefore, **hierarchy,** *objectively considered,* denotes the univer-sal faculty, which Christ has given to the apostles and their legiti-mate successors, in the order of sanctifying, teaching and leading the society of the Christian faithful or the church, which he him-self founded, and which we distribute into the power of order and the power of jurisdiction.

In other words, the *tria munera* were the specific hallmark of the ordained clergy. Sharing in the priestly, prophetic and kingly mission and ministry of Jesus provided the precise identity to that person, who was through ordination part of the hierarchy of the church.

Vatican II has, however, widened this view of the *tria munera.*[53] Sharing in the threefold office of Jesus is now a hallmark of the baptized-confirmed and eucharistic Christian, not simply of the ordained or hierar-chical Christian. When the bishops at Vatican II built their doctrine of Christian identity on this threefold office of Jesus, they clearly altered the older theological position that sharing in the *tria munera* of Jesus pro-vided the specific identity for priests.

On several occasions, the documents of Vatican II indicate that there is an essential difference between the ordained and the non-ordained pre-cisely in this matter of the *tria munera.*[54] If the ordained, however, "share" in the *tria munera* in an essentially different way from the "shar-ing" in the *tria munera* which is part and parcel of all Christian life, then at least one of the following two situations must be verified:

A. The Share Itself Is Different
The "share" itself which the ordained have is essentially different from the "share" itself which not only the unordained have, but which the ordained also continue to have, since they continue to "share" in this common matrix along with every Christian. In this sense, the essentially different "share" is something "more" than the "share" which all Christians in common have.

B. The Way of Sharing Is Different

In this view it is only the "way" in which the ordained share, which is essentially different from the "way" in which all Christians, the unordained and the ordained, share in the *tria munera* of Jesus.

A. THE FIRST APPROACH: THE SHARE ITSELF IS DIFFERENT

In the first instance, the office of teaching, sanctifying and leading is itself viewed as a divisible reality. In this view, only certain aspects of the *tria munera* are given to all Christians; certain additional aspects of these same *tria munera* are given only to the ordained.

In such an approach one can clearly speak of an "essential" difference between unordained and ordained. As regards the mission and ministry of Jesus, called the *tria munera,* certain missions and certain ministries of Jesus are not given to all Christians, but only to the ordained Christian. In such an approach, every Christian indeed shares in the prophetic, priestly and kingly mission and ministry of Jesus, but only in a limited form of this mission and ministry. There are certain prophetic, priestly and kingly tasks which baptized-eucharistic Christians do not and perhaps cannot perform. Only those Christians who are not only baptized and eucharistic Christians but also ordained Christians can perform the full scope of the prophetic, priestly and kingly missions and ministries of Jesus. That there is a divisible reality in the *tria munera* of Jesus is the import of the first position. The "share" itself is "essentially" different. Consequently, the phrase *tria munera,* when used for all Christians, means one thing, while the same phrase *tria munera,* when used for the ordained, means something quite different. By making this kind of distinction in the *tria munera* of Jesus himself, one can theologically maintain an "essential" difference between the ordained and the unordained.

Theological questions, however, immediately begin to arise when one moves in this direction of the *tria munera* of Jesus as an intrinsically divisible reality. Neither the sharing in the *tria munera* which all Christians have, nor the sharing in the *tria munera* which only the ordained have, when they are respectively considered apart from each other, corresponds completely to the full scope and meaning of the *tria munera* of Jesus himself. First of all, the sharing in the *tria munera* of Jesus, which each and every Christian has, does not mirror the full range of the *tria munera* of Jesus, since such Christians share only in a part of the *tria munera* of Jesus. Secondly, the sharing in the *tria munera* of Jesus, which ordained Christians specifically have, does not mirror the full range of the *tria munera* of Jesus, since this particular and specific "share" in the *tria munera* of Jesus is again only a part of the *tria munera* themselves.

The ordained Christian mirrors or shares in the *fullness* of the *tria munera*, not because of the sacrament of ordination by itself nor because of the sacrament of initiation, baptism-eucharist, by itself, but only because he "shares" in both sacramental realities. Does such a view, however, correspond to the teaching of Vatican II? Is this divisibility of the *tria munera* of Jesus consonant with the texts and contexts of the Vatican II documents?

First of all, we must begin with Jesus. The fullness of the *tria munera*, which one finds in Jesus himself, includes both "shares." One without the other can only be seen as a partial sharing in Jesus' *tria munera*. The documents of Vatican II do not appear to move in the direction that the *tria munera* of Jesus himself can be so "essentially" divided. Nowhere do we find in those documents that only "part" of the *tria munera* is given to the baptized-confirmed. Nor do we find in the documents that only "part" of the same *tria munera* of Jesus have been entrusted to the ordained.

Secondly, the documents of Vatican II indicate that Christians fulfill their baptism–confirmation–[eucharist] vocation precisely in living out the *tria munera*, i.e. in living out the mission and ministry of Jesus to which they have been called by the sacrament of initiation, and which they nourish through eucharist, through meditation on the scriptured word, and through prayer and works of brotherly and sisterly love. According to the approach of a divided "share" in the *tria munera*, they would and could accomplish this fulfilling of the gospel, even though they, as baptized/eucharistic Christians, do not have a part in certain aspects of the *tria munera* themselves, aspects which they are "essentially" lacking. If there is, however, something essentially lacking to the baptized Christian's teaching, sanctifying, and leading mission and ministry, then the further question immediately arises: In what way can this "something lacking" be considered either "essential" or "non-essential," if each and every Christian can find his or her holiness without it? To what does the term "essential" refer? If baptized and eucharistic Christians can essentially fulfill their gospel discipleship without sharing in certain aspects of the *tria munera* of Jesus, then does the term "essential" have its reference and meaning only to something that is not "essential" to gospel discipleship itself? If a baptized-eucharistic Christian can truly become an ideal disciple of Jesus, i.e. a saint, without those aspects or shares of the *tria munera*, which some theologians would see as constituting the "essential" difference between the baptized and the ordained, what does the term "essential" mean and to what does it refer? One can indeed be a model disciple of Jesus and not be ordained. Since possession of or non-possession of that "share" in the *tria munera*, reserved for clerics, is not necessary for or "essentially" a part of true gospel discipleship, what meaning does the term "essential" really have? Is that "share" in the *tria munera* of Jesus, which only the ordained have, simply peripheral and secondary to the meaning of gospel discipleship? Such a "share" might make the ordained "essentially" distinct from the non-ordained, but is that ordained "share," considered in and by itself, something "non-essential" to gospel discipleship and therefore "peripheral" to the most important dimension of Christian life, namely gospel discipleship?

Bishops and theologians are generally not anxious to say that the ordained "sharing" in the *tria munera* is merely peripheral or only a secondary aspect of the fundamental *tria munera* of Jesus. Nor are many bishops and theologians generally anxious to endorse both of the following two statements at one and the same time:

1. There are "essential" *munera* which the ordained have and which the unordained do not have, as far as teaching, sanctifying and leading in the church are concerned.
2. These "essential" *munera* make the ordained "fuller" or "better" or "more complete" disciples of Jesus.

Some bishops and theologians might want to accept the first statement, but not the last. Nonetheless, it is difficult to give theologically convincing reasons why one might be able to select the first without implicitly selecting the second, since a person who has received "essentially" different and important *munera* of the mission and ministry of Jesus would accordingly reflect Jesus more perfectly or more fully. If there is not a more "perfect" or "fuller" imaging of Jesus through the reception of these essentially different *munera,* then the additional "share" in the *tria munera* of the ordained would appear to be only secondary or peripheral to the very mission and ministry of Jesus and, consequently, peripheral to the essential meaning of gospel discipleship. An ordained minister, like all Christians, already has that "share" in the *tria munera,* which is common to all baptized, and by living out the mission and ministry of this particular "share" in the *tria munera* he could be a saintly follower of Jesus, i.e. he could be a "full" disciple of Jesus. However, he also has a "share" in the *tria munera* of Jesus, "essentially" different from the "share" of the baptized-eucharistic Christian. This implies that such a person shares in the mission and ministry of Jesus in an "essentially" different format, namely with an "essentially" different claim on the mission and ministry of Jesus. It is precisely this distinction which has created the theological problem. What does this ordained "share" add to the call and commission to gospel discipleship which a person already has in virtue of baptism and eucharist? It is, as we believe, precisely our resemblance to Jesus that makes us gospel disciples. If a Christian can resemble Jesus in the "ordinary" way, and this means without that essentially "different" way given to the ordained, i.e. without that particular "share" in the *tria munera* which only the ordained receive, what significance can be assigned to the essentially different share in the *tria munera* which the ordained alone possess? Can one say that the Christian who has both "shares" in the *tria munera* of Jesus is more fully like Jesus? Can one say that such a person is a better disciple of Jesus? An affirmative answer does not seem to be the magisterial teaching of Vatican II. Indeed, on the basis of *Lumen gentium,* particularly in chapter 2 (on the people of God) and chapter 5 (on the universal call to holiness in the church), the bishops at Vatican II clearly denied a "fuller" or "better" discipleship to the hierarchy simply on the basis of an essentially different sharing in the *tria munera* of Jesus.

It is this "better disciple" implication, this "more perfect disciple of Jesus" implication, which bishops and theologians generally do not want to allow, but which logically follows when one begins to divide the *tria munera* of Jesus himself into a "common" share and a "share" essentially different and given only to a "few." The person who has both "shares" reflects the *tria munera* of Jesus in a more complete way, and consequently must be considered a "fuller" or "better disciple" of Jesus. This, however, not only contradicts Vatican II, but more importantly it contradicts the meaning of disciple as found throughout the New Testament. Nowhere does the New Testament indicate that the servant-leaders of the Jesus community are "better" than the others, simply because they have been chosen to be servant-leaders.

This line of thought is not simply a tour de force in semantics. The belaboring of this issue of an "essential" difference is central to the problem of inequality in the church. Nowhere has the meaning of "essential" been defined. Every view which offers some explanation of the meaning of the "essential" difference is merely a theological opinion, a *sententia theologica.* When one inquires why certain theologians and bishops are so tenacious in their defense of this "essential" difference, one sees that the main issue, and therefore the priority issue, is the maintenance of hierarchical superiority. This is the fundamental criterion. In their presentations and their defense, gospel discipleship is never the fundamental criterion.

B. THE SECOND APPROACH: THE MANNER OF SHARING IS DIFFERENT

The second approach to this "essential difference" does not affect the share itself, but only the manner or way in which all Christians share in the *tria munera* and the manner or way in which ordained Christians share in the same *tria munera*. There are, in this view, not different missions and ministries, but only a difference in the precise manner or way of sharing in one and the same mission and ministry of Jesus. All Christians share in the teaching or preaching ministry of Jesus, but only the hierarchy possess a way of teaching and preaching which is ultimately authoritative. All Christians share in the priestly ministry of Jesus, but only the hierarchy possess a way of priestly ministry which is eucharistically effective and penitentially effective, i.e. those specific sacraments which involve forgiveness of sin and valid administration of the eucharist. All Christians share in the leadership or kingly ministry of Jesus, but only the hierarchy can be seen as the duly appointed and official leaders in the church. This particular approach, however, seems to imply a quantitative difference rather than a qualitative difference, and as such does not seem to comply with the texts and contexts of the documents of Vatican II. These documents nowhere indicate that there is only a qualitative difference between the ordained and the unordained. Simply a degree or difference in the manner of prophetic, priestly and kingly ministry does not appear to do justice to the teaching of Vatican II.

One might use scholastic terminology to bring the problems connected to this second position to the fore: namely, in order to express an "essential" difference, is a modal distinction adequate? Is a formal distinction adequate? Is a virtual distinction adequate? In the mission and ministry of Jesus, which the church in part continues through the celebration of the sacraments, the ordained person in this approach would indeed share in the celebrations of baptism, of eucharist, of reconciliation, etc., but only in a different "way" from the way in which all the baptized Christians celebrate baptism, eucharist and reconciliation, etc. Sacramentally, the role of the priest in these liturgies is simply qualitatively different from that of the non-ordained. Many bishops and theologians would be uneasy with this modal approach. For them the hierarchy is not simply qualitatively different from each and every baptized-eucharistic Christian when it comes to the issue of the ecclesial priestly office (*munus sacerdotale*).

Let us consider, secondly, the prophetic office of Jesus, as this is manifested in the church. In the ministry and mission of the Lord's magisterium, which the church in part continues through its own hierarchical magisterium, the ordained person would indeed share in such a magisterium-ministry, but only in a qualitatively different "way" from that "way" in which all baptized Christians share in the basic magisterium-ministry. The magisterial role of the hierarchy, in this approach, would only be qualitatively different from the teaching/preaching role of each and every baptized-eucharistic Christian. Many bishops and theologians would, it seems to me, be somewhat uneasy with this "modal" but "essential" difference, separating the ordained from the unordained as far as magisterium is concerned. For them the hierarchy is not simply qualitatively different from all baptized and eucharistic Christians when it comes to the issue of the ecclesial teaching office (*munus propheticum*).

Thirdly, one should consider the kingly role of Jesus and its manifestation in and through the church. All baptized-eucharistic Christians share in this kingly *munus* of Jesus. Through ordination, some Christians modally manifest this same kingly *munus* in a different way, but the manner in which the hierarchy exercises this kingly office is only qualitatively different from that of each and every Christian. Once more, many bishops and theologians would find this approach to the regal *munus* of Jesus not acceptable. For them, the hierarchy are not simply qualitatively different from all baptized and eucharistic Christians when it comes to the issue of ecclesial leadership (*munus regale*).

There seems to be no doubt that since the publication of the documents of Vatican II the crux of the problem on this issue of ordained/nonordained, theologically and pastorally, does not lie:

a. with the way in which the common matrix or gospel discipleship is named;
b. with the teaching of the New Testament and that of many official documents—though not all—that gospel discipleship brings about a true equality and dignity for each and every baptized and eucharistic Christian.

The crux of the problem lies in the theological and pastoral way in which one explains how the *tria munera* of Jesus himself can be shared by all baptized-eucharistic Christians, on the one hand, and, on the other hand, how the very same *tria munera* of Jesus himself can be shared in an "essentially" different format by the ordained Christian. It is precisely the teaching on the *tria munera* of Jesus, as formulated officially and magisterially by the documents of Vatican II, which has engendered the innumerable theological discussions and, at times, strident theological arguments.

Mention might also be made, at this point of our discussion, that the *tria munera* approach to ministry, put forth by the bishops at Vatican II, has itself been criticized.[55] This criticism does not focus on the *tria munera* doctrine as incorrect, but rather as insufficient. Perhaps one should jettison the entire *tria munera* doctrine with its role as the basis for gospel discipleship and for ordained ministry. Since such a move would be so radically contrary to the teaching of Vatican II, it does not seem proper to follow such a route at this time. At this juncture of our discourse on the role of the baptized-eucharistic person in the church, however, it is only necessary to indicate that:

> a. the official teaching of Vatican II attributes the sharing in the *tria munera* of Jesus himself to all baptized-confirmed and eucharistic Christians;
> b. the same official teaching of Vatican II then attributes the sharing in the *tria munera* of Jesus himself to the ordained ministers;
> c. the same official teaching of Vatican II then states, without any explanation, that there is an "essential" difference between the ordained and the non-ordained precisely in this matter of the *tria munera.*

It is the juxtaposition of these three positions which has raised major theological questions, questions which to date have not been satisfactorily resolved. We will return to this very complex issue later on in this section as we consider the unfinished agenda of Vatican II, but hopefully it is clear that it is precisely this issue, the various forms of sharing in the *tria munera* of Jesus, and the basic criterion which is used to differentiate these various forms of sharing, which is at the heart of the problem. On occasion, other issues appear to be the center of focus, but these other issues will never be resolved unless there is some resolution to the problems raised by the juxtaposition of the three aspects of the *tria munera* doctrine stated above.

2. Catholic Action: The Participation of the Laity in the Apostolate of the Hierarchy

The second major issue, pointed out above, is also related to the current difficulty in understanding the role of the non-ordained in the church. From Leo XIII onward "Catholic Action" was increasingly seen as the participation of the laity in the apostolate of the hierarchy.[56] However, since Vatican II this commissioning to the *tria munera* comes to all who have been baptized, confirmed, and eucharistized, and therefore such a definition of Catholic Action, as it was understood prior to Vatican II, is no longer viable. There is not, first of all, an apostolate of the hierarchy, and then, secondarily, a participation in that basic apostolate by the non-ordained. Rather, with a doctrine of a common discipleship, there is, first and foremost, a common apostolate arising from one's sharing in the *tria munera,* an apostolate which does not originate, as we have insisted many times above, *vi delegationis* but *vi sacramenti*. In the first half of this century, however, the exact contrary was presented by the official church leadership: namely, there is a basic apostolate of the hierarchy in which lay people were allowed to share. Such a view, after Vatican II, is no longer theologically tenable.[57]

There is, rather, an apostolate, in which all Christians, whether unordained or ordained, share and share equally. There is also an apostolate, or a ministry, which the ordained, and they alone, administer.[58] These two "apostolates" are not co-extensive, nor is the "apostolate" of the hierarchy, taken by itself, inclusive of the "apostolate" of the baptized. Kloppenburg expresses this Vatican II doctrine very clearly:

> Before someone is looked upon as either layman or deacon or priest or bishop or even pope, he should be considered first of all as a Christian or member of God's people. These terms express the basic condition, the primal state, the common element, the most important aspect, indeed the very reason why there exists a divine plan for the human creature. It is in this common foundation on which all else rests, that the greatness, dignity, and newness brought by Christ properly reside. Without it we would be nothing, whether we happened to be pope, bishop, priest, deacon or layman.[59]

The focus of this common matrix, this fundamental discipleship, highlights the fact that there really is only one basic "apostolate" in the church, namely that of Jesus himself. The church, as the people of God, as the fundamental sacrament of Jesus, shares in this "apostolate" of Jesus, just as the moon shares in the light of the sun. Each baptized Christian, consequently, *qua* Christian shares in this mission and ministry of Jesus, and each ordained person likewise *qua* Christian, not *qua* cleric, shares in this fundamental mission and ministry of Jesus. This "apostolate" or fundamental mission and ministry of Jesus has been officially described by Vatican II as the *tria munera*. Wonderful and opening as the doctrine of the *tria munera* was meant to be when it was developed by the bishops at Vatican II, it has clearly opened a Pandora's box and has caused no little theological uncertainty.

Catholic action is the participation of the laity in the apostolate of the hierarchy—such was the former way of understanding this mission and ministry of the church. Throughout the documents of Vatican II the bishops made a deliberate effort to indicate the change, and they did this through terminology:

a. *Apostolate:* from baptism–confirmation–eucharist, all Christians have an "apostolate."

b. *Ministry:* from ordination, some Christians have a "ministry."

In the documents there is a scrupulous attempt to differentiate the two forms of sharing in the *tria munera* of Jesus by using two distinct terms: apostolate for the unordained and ministry for the ordained. This usage of terms in itself indicates that the former description of Catholic Action has become obsolete and inoperative. To cite Kloppenburg once again:

> Both groups—"laymen" and "hierarchs"—are equally "believers," equally "Christians," equally members of God's people, temples of the Spirit, configured to Christ, and living with, through and in him. Only after this common foundation has been laid do differences begin.[60]

There is an implication to this change: namely, insofar as the baptized-eucharistic Christian shares in the *tria munera* of Jesus, not in virtue of any participation in a "ministry" or "apostolate" of the hierarchy, but in virtue of one's own sacramental initiation into the church, then that "apostolate" or "ministry" arising from the sacramental sharing in Jesus' *tria munera* must have a different way of relating to the hierarchy than was presented in the past decades by the term "Catholic Action." If baptized-eucharistic Christians have a mission and ministry given to them by Jesus himself, then there is a certain as yet theologically undefined *autonomy* to their exercise of this mission and ministry. When the description of a Christian in a former age was said to participate through "Catholic Action" in the hierarchy's apostolate, the autonomy of the participating Christian laity was severely limited, for it was, in this view, the hierarchy, and only the hierarchy, who commissioned, endorsed, directed and organized such "Catholic Action." However, in the magisterial teaching of Vatican II documents, the basic sharing in Jesus' *tria munera* is fundamentally not hierarchical; as a consequence, a different base for the relationship between (a) the sharing in the *tria munera* by all baptized and (b) the sharing in the *tria munera* by the ordained needs to be developed. To date, this has not yet been satisfactorily worked out in either a theological or a pastoral framework, and as a result there is significant tension within the Roman Catholic Church precisely on this issue.

There is as well a major christological issue present in this tension which has not yet been resolved. The documents of Vatican II center the entire mission and ministry of the church itself and of each and every specific mission and ministry in the church in the mission and ministry of Jesus. In this sense Jesus is the primordial sacrament of all and every mission and ministry within the church community. It is true that the documents of Vatican II nowhere state that Jesus in his humanity is the primordial sacrament. Rather, the documents of Vatican II state only that the church is a fundamental sacrament. However, the theology which involves the church as a sacrament is essentially connected with the same sacramental theology which presents Jesus as the primordial sacrament. The sacramentality of church is unintelligible unless there is a more fundamental sacramentality of Jesus as well. The documents of Vatican II clearly go beyond the church as the basis of mission and ministry, for these documents deliberately base all and every mission and ministry within the Christian church on the very mission and ministry of Jesus himself. How christology relates to ecclesiology remains unclear in the documents, and it is this christological/ecclesiological issue which has not yet been resolved. The node of the issue can be stated as follows:

The christocentric center of all ecclesial mission and ministry provides the basis for both non-ordained and ordained mission and ministry in the church. This is found in Vatican II's teaching on the *tria munera* of Jesus.

This position, however, leads to the following conclusions:

A. Jesus himself is neither cleric nor lay.
B. Jesus' mission is itself neither clerical nor lay.
C. Jesus' ministry is itself neither clerical nor lay.

Let us consider each of these conclusions more carefully and in some detail.[61] For those who have generally considered Jesus as "high priest" and, therefore, to a certain extent clerical, this conclusion may sound strange. But if Jesus himself is a "cleric," then in what way can the documents of Vatican II base the mission on and ministry of the *lay* Christian in Jesus himself? If the baptized-eucharistic Christian shares in the very *tria munera* of Jesus and if Jesus himself is a high priest, then all baptized-eucharistic Christians are sharing in the high priesthood of Jesus. If Jesus' ministry is "clerical," then how is it possible for the documents of Vatican II to consider the ministry and mission of all the baptized a part of Jesus' own *tria munera* and not state that the baptized are sharing in his "clerical" priestly ministry?

If Jesus' mission is a "clerical" mission, how can the documents of Vatican II describe the mission of the baptized-eucharistic Christians as a sharing in Jesus' own "clerical" mission and at the same time not consider the baptized "clerical"?

The opposite is equally valid: If Jesus is lay only, then in what way can the documents of Vatican II base the mission and ministry of the clerics, specifically, *qua* ordained, in the "lay" Jesus? How can the ordained mission be a participation in the very "lay" mission of the "lay Jesus"? How can the "clerical ministry" be a sharing in the "lay ministry" of Jesus?

If Jesus' very mission and ministry, the *tria munera,* are the basis of all ecclesial mission and ministry, then both the non-ordained and the ordained mission and ministry must find their basis, their root, in this christocentric origin.

However, one does not go directly from a given ordained or non-ordained mission and ministry to Jesus himself. One goes to Jesus, the christocentric origin, through the mission and ministry of the church itself. Once again, however, the question arises: Is the church's mission clerical or lay? Is the church's ministry clerical or lay? If the church's own mission and ministry are the mother lode (with Jesus as the primordial foundation) of all ecclesial mission and ministry, then how can they give birth to both an ordained and a non-ordained mission and ministry at one and the same time, while at the same time this ecclesial mother lode would be considered either "lay" or "clerical"?

The conclusion is clear. Jesus transcends both ordained and non-ordained; the church transcends both ordained and non-ordained. When we use the term "priest" for Jesus, his priesthood is totally different from the "priesthood" of the ordained. When we call gospel discipleship "the priesthood of all believers," we are speaking about a "priesthood" which is totally different from the "priesthood" of the ordained. There is, in this view, a closer resemblance between a baptized-eucharistic Christian, a disciple of the Lord, and the priestly Jesus than there is between an "ordained priest" and the priestly Jesus. There is, in this view, a closer resemblance between a priestly church and the priestly Jesus than there is between an individual ordained priest and the priestly Jesus. It is not the priestliness of the ordained Christian which is the paradigm against which either the priestliness of Jesus or the priestliness of the church is measured. Rather, the priestliness of Jesus is the paradigm against which the priestliness of the church itself, the priesthood of all believers, is measured, and only then—that is, only against the priesthood of Jesus and the mirrored priesthood of all believers—does the priestliness of an ordained person begin to find its meaning. There is no direct passage between "ordained priest" and Jesus as high priest. The passage is through the priesthood of all believers.

When we speak of Jesus as high priest, as the letter to Hebrews clearly does, we see a priestliness which is unique. Only Jesus is, in this New Testament writing, truly "priest." It is in him alone that one sees the real meaning of the *tria munera sacerdotalia.* Sacramentally, these *tria munera* are reflected in the church *qua* church. In a tertiary way, these *tria munera* are then reflected in an ordained Christian. In viewing priestliness in this way, one can only conclude that the very foundation of all church mission and all church ministry, that is, Jesus as fundamental priest and the church as the priesthood of all believers, is neither lay nor cleric. The specification "lay-cleric," ordained and non-ordained, finds its meaning in a quite different context and at a quite different stratum.

Unfortunately, since Vatican II has presented us with no clear christology, but has simply used a major christological framework, i.e. the *tria munera* framework, a theological synthesizing of all the elements has become a priority post-Vatican II task. In this synthesizing task, a repositioning of the clerical world has necessarily been taking place, due precisely to the fact that a major repositioning of the non-ordained did take place at Vatican II. A repositioning of the non-ordained cannot take place unless there is a concomitant repositioning of the ordained. Since the segment of ordained Christians have had and still do have major positions of power in the church, this repositioning has been seen as a threat to their position of power, and, even more deeply, has been seen as a threat to their self-identity. The tendency to cling to the past hierarchical forms of either structure or identity, as though these cannot be repositioned in any way, has only led to further disintegration rather than to a possible synthesizing.

The Vatican II document on the lay person, *Apostolicam actuositatem,* offers many encouraging and positive statements on the role of the non-ordained, but the text itself does not clearly sort out the personal dignity and freedom, the sharing in the *tria munera,* and consequently a fundamental mission and ministry, which belong to all the disciples of the gospel, from the specific tasks of a "lay" ministry. Indeed, the focus of this document is on the "lay" ministry which comes from a specific call, and not on the ministry of gospel discipleship which comes from the sacrament of initiation.[62]

One way, which some theologians and even some church officials have selected as a possible approach to resolving the tension, is to consider the ministry or apostolate of the baptized-eucharistic Christian as a ministry or apostolate *to* the secular world and *within* the secular world, while the ministry or apostolate of the ordained is *to* the ecclesial world and *within* the ecclesial world. This way of considering the situation has, however, become quite controversial and merits more than a mere mention.

D. THE SECULAR CHARACTER OF "LAY" MINISTRY

For some theologians who base themselves on the documents of Vatican II, the specific task of the "lay" person is the sanctification of the secular sphere.

> Certain authors, such as Klostermann, speak of a definition and even discern in number 31 a *genus proximum* (the link to the *christifidelis*) and a specific difference (31a: in general in the expression *pro parte sua;* 31b: with the precise indication in *indoles saecularis*).[63]

Magnani, a few pages later, provides this description of the "lay person":

> The lay person is the *christifidelis* (or "member of Christ's faithful") who fully recognizes the *ratio* itself of the *christifidelis* in relation to the world (*distinctio nominalis*).[64]

Magnani cites a number of theologians who want to minimize, even eliminate the notion of "lay," in favor of the common matrix of all discipleship which has been described above. For these people, "lay person" and *christifidelis* are identical, and the retention of the term "lay" might be of value, but only to prevent a reclericalization of the church. He cites such authors as L. Sartori, P. Colombo, S. Dianich, and B. Forte.[65] In this view, all Christians through baptism, confirmation and eucharist share in the ministry and mission of Jesus to the "secular" world. The reaction to this view is strong, for by making all Christians responsible for the evangelization of the secular area, the precise character of the "lay" person is lost. This is the reason why there is such theological discussion regarding 31b of *Lumen gentium*. In this text we read:

> Their secular character is proper and peculiar to the laity. . . . By reason of their special vocation it belongs to the laity to seek the kingdom of God by engaging in temporal affairs and directing them according to God's will. They live in the world, that is, they are engaged in each and every work and business of the earth

and in the ordinary circumstance of social and family life which, as it were, constitutes their very existence (*LG* 31b).

By stressing this secular dimension of "lay" life, some theologians emphasize the contrast between cleric and lay.[66] The cleric has a ministry and mission within the church; the lay person has a ministry and mission outside the church. In this approach, the lay person is "excluded" from the inner or centripetal life of the church and is directed specifically to the outer or centrifugal life of the church.

Two statements from the same council modify any either/or position on this matter, since in these statements there appears to be a rather fluid boundary between the ecclesiastical and the secular.

> Although those in holy orders may sometimes be engaged in secular activities, or even practice a secular profession, yet by reason of their particular vocation, they are principally and expressly ordained to the sacred ministry (*LG* 31b).

> It is to the laity, though not exclusively to them, that secular duties and activity properly belong (*GS* 43).

Words such as "principally" and "not exclusively" cannot be set to one side. They were chosen deliberately by the bishops to indicate that such a boundary as "inner-Church/secular world" has great fluidity. Moreover, in *Gaudium et spes,* which presents a deliberate picture of the mutual roles for the church and for the secular world, the term "lay" is used only six times, indicating by its very non-use that in this document the spotlight is more often than not on a Christian *qua* Christian, whether lay or cleric, rather than specifically on a Christian *qua* lay.

In chapter 4 of *Lumen gentium,* the terms "lay" and "Christian" often seem to coincide, since the "naming" process of the common matrix was still in flux. G. Philips, in his lengthy commentary on this exact section of *Lumen gentium,* 31 a/b, notes: "The day-to-day use of language sees in the lay person the ordinary Christian who lives in the world. . . . In our context the lay person is the believing Christian."[67] The bishops had no intention of formulating a definition of the "lay" person; they used rather a typological, not an ontological, description of the lay person, one which contrasts the cleric and the vowed religious with a Christian who is neither cleric nor vowed religious. They describe typologically the situation in which a Christian, often married and with a family, generally working in some secular job, finds himself or herself. Such a Christian today brings the gospel message to bear in a basically non-ecclesiastical, but not consequently non-ecclesial, secular situation.

To deduce from this typological description an ontological one goes beyond both text and context. To deduce that the *proper* sphere of mission and ministry for a non-ordained, non-vowed-religious Christian is primarily or exclusively to the secular arena is again a reading beyond the text and context of the Vatican documents.[68] In fact, *Lumen gentium* (12, 2) speaks of *opera vel officia* for all Christians, and *Apostolicam actuositatem* (3, 4) speaks of *ius et officium* given to baptized Christians through various charisms.[69] This kind of language was chosen carefully and has strong theological overtones as regards one's role in the church.

When all the theological dust begins to settle, it is clear that the documents of Vatican II hardly provide us with a clear-cut specific difference on cleric/lay, namely that the lay person's specific difference is the secular character of his mission and ministry.[70] These same documents deliberately mention a non-exclusivity of a mission and ministry to the secular area. Cleric, religious and lay at times move outward to this secular area. Cleric, religious and lay at times move inward to the ecclesiastical area. In the wake of Vatican II, many lay ministries in the church's liturgy itself are seen as the proper role of the baptized-eucharistic Christian.

There has been, however, a strong move to keep the "lay" person in the secular area, and this secularity has been proposed as his or her specific difference, as his or her form of spirituality, i.e. a secular spirituality, as his or her specific mission and ministry within the people of God. When one reviews the reasons for such a stress, one sees that the issue once again is the role of the *tria munera*. This might be even more precisely stated: in order to safeguard the clerical role in the *tria munera*, the prophetic, priestly and royal role of the non-cleric is kept as far as possible away from the inner-ecclesiastical arena of operation. It is generally on the basis of maintaining some "essential" difference vis-à-vis the sharing in the *tria munera* of Jesus by both baptized Christian and by ordained Christian that this secular stress has been developed, but it is an "essential difference" which uses hierarchical superiority as the fundamental criterion, not gospel discipleship as the fundamental criterion. Gospel discipleship, however, is the fundamental criterion by which the proper form of servant-leadership can be interpreted; hierarchical servant-leadership is not and should never be the fundamental criterion which serves as the hermeneutic to determine the meaning and scope of gospel discipleship.

The bishops at Vatican II clearly enhanced the theological positioning of the baptized-eucharistic Christian. The inward tide, which had been encroaching on the clerical shore for the past five hundred years, crashed through many poorly constructed theological barriers in virtue of Vatican II. This inward rush of the tide, with its dramatic changing of the shoreline, could not help but cause a repositioning of the cleric. The subsequent feverish attempts to interpret the doctrine on the *tria munera* of Jesus, in which all Christians share and in which clergy too share, provide clear evidence at times of a theological scrambling to shore up the clerical repositioning. Time and again throughout Christian history, we have seen that whenever one sector of the people of God takes on a new positioning, all other sectors experience some repositioning. Until the end of the first millennium, the continual repositioning of the cleric and the religious continually depositioned the ordinary Christian. From the turn of the first millennium into the second millennium, the tide began to turn. Slowly, but inexorably, the ordinary Christian's positioning in the church became ever more pervasive, and especially from the Protestant reformation and then from the American and French revolutions onward, this inward surge of the tide has become geometrically more apparent. The theological positioning of the *christifidelis* at Vatican II was one more powerful surge in this turning of the tide, and the surge has affected the placement of the clergy.

Some, perhaps, had hoped that this repositioning of the *christifidelis* would leave the positioning of the cleric untouched, that the theology of priesthood, both episcopal and presbyteral, would remain unchanged. That was a vain hope. The theology of priesthood in all its dimensions has been significantly changed, and this change has occurred precisely in that area in which the greatest theological stress has taken place, namely in the sharing of the *tria munera,* both by the Christian and by the cleric. In the wake of almost every church council, there has been a concerted effort to bring the church back to where it was prior to the respective council. On the issue of priesthood, this same tendency is clear in the post-Vatican II church, in which some theologians and some church leaders tenaciously hang on to the priestly status quo and tenaciously attempt to restrain the non-priestly sector of the church.

3. POST-VATICAN II DOCUMENTS AND MOVEMENTS WHICH INVOLVE THE ROLE OF THE LAITY

Although some mention has already been made of certain post-Vatican II documents, I would like to consider certain documents and movements which relate to certain major themes in this study of the role of the baptized-eucharistic Christian in the church. These themes are the following:

A. The post-Vatican II understanding of *regnum et sacerdotium* and its influence on the meaning of discipleship.

B. The post-Vatican II discussion on priestly *ordo* or order and its influence on the meaning of discipleship.

A. THE POST-VATICAN II UNDERSTANDING OF *REGNUM ET SACERDOTIUM* AND ITS INFLUENCE ON THE MEANING OF DISCIPLESHIP

To speak of kings and priesthood in the Vatican II church may sound like an anachronism, but there is a major issue which relates *sacerdotium* or priesthood to *regnum* or political and social structures, and which seriously impacts on the way in which the non-ordained are viewed. This issue can be stated as follows:

The way in which church leadership understands and expresses its own relationship to the social and political structures is the framework within which these same church leaders will interpret the role of the people of God, the *christifidelis*, the priesthood of all believers.

A baptized-eucharistic Christian lives today, more often than not, in a religiously pluralistic milieu within a morally pluralistic horizon, and in a politically non-religious structure. Such an overarching cultural framework cannot help but define his or her life both in its human dimensions and in its Christian dimensions.

As we saw above, Leo XIII, and through him much of the church leadership of his time, interpreted the cultural milieu or world for the rank-and-file of the Catholic Church within a "world vision." Every culture has its particular dominant "world vision" and a number of subdominant, counter-culture "world visions," and the members of each respective culture or social group live in both the dominant and the subdominant forms of human life. They live in a world of several world visions. In the case of Christians this is equally true. However, besides the respective, indigenous, cultural "world visions," time and time again another "world vision," which stems from its highest ecclesiastical leadership, is urged on the rank-and-file Christian. Trying to live within these two major arenas of world visions has made the life of the rank-and-file Christian at times somewhat schizophrenic. The "world vision" of Leo XIII, as we have seen, was not primarily a gospel world vision, but a politico-papal world vision. The same can be said of the politico-papal world visions of Gregory VII, Innocent III, and Boniface VIII.

Since Leo XIII, there has been a series of papal encyclicals on the social, political world. Through these various encyclicals one can see that there remains, even under John Paul II, a politico-papal "world vision."

> As supreme pastor of a flock still in disarray from the shock waves of Vatican II and the birth-control crisis, Karol Wojtyla, it seems, has dedicated himself to a strategy of "restoration"—a concerted effort to recuperate those parts of the great Catholic tradition which he and his colleagues feel have been neglected and almost lost in the aftermath of the Council.[71]

This strategy of restoration is basically inner-church, but John Paul also has his own world vision. Consecrated pope at a fairly young age, John Paul II rightfully planned on a fairly extended papacy. During this length of time, he could slowly but surely attain the goals he had in mind. When he was shot by Mehmer Ali Agça on May 13, 1981, he realized that his time in the papacy might not be as long as he wished. His devotion to Mary, the mother of Jesus, played a role in his thinking as well, for, cognizant of the "letter of Fatima," he has dreamed of a united world: united politically primarily through Eastern Europe and Russia and united religiously through himself as pope. One speaks today of "super-powers," and in John Paul's view, there would be a union of two super-powers, one basically political and the other basically religious. These two interacting super-powers, of which John Paul would be one, would have as their primary goal the further unification of the world.[72]

Such a politico-papal vision reminds one of Leo XIII, Innocent III and many other popes. Not only does such a vision make the pope not a servant-minister of the church, but a servant-minister of the world, which in itself raises innumerable theological difficulties, but such a vision has repercussions on the way in which such a politico-papal pope relates to the baptized-eucharistic Christian. The more a super-power mentality for *sacerdotium* prevails, reminiscent of the medieval theory of *plenitudo potestatis,* the more questionable is the place of gospel discipleship as the fundamental criterion for all mission and ministry within the Christian church. If the pope is viewed in this world-vision theory with a sort of "super-power" status, this "super-power" status will have a trickle-down effect on the entire *sacerdotium,* since a pope could never make such a claim to super-power status by himself alone, but only in virtue of his status within the *sacerdotium.* Accordingly, the entire *sacerdotium* will be affected by such a world-vision positioning of the pope, and this can only mean, in turn, a major effort to reposition the non-ordained once again toward the margins of the church.

B. THE POST-VATICAN II DISCUSSION ON PRIESTLY *ORDO* OR ORDER AND ITS INFLUENCE ON THE MEANING OF DISCIPLESHIP

Throughout the historical part of this study on the role of the lay person in the church, we have considered in a tangential way the rise of the theological view of priesthood as an *ordo,* the way in which this gradually took on further significance, and the impact this has had on the way in which the non-priesthood sector of the church is consequently viewed.

R.M. Schwartz, in his analysis of priestly spirituality in the United States today, writes:

> This correlation of Christ, the twelve and ordained ministry is essential to an authentic understanding of the sacrament of orders. In restating the traditional teaching, Vatican II affirms that although ordained ministry is rooted in the sacraments of initiation, it derives from a special sacramental celebration. In doing so, it highlights the distinctive ontological foundation of the ministry of the apostles and insists that this ontologically distinct ministry continues in the sacrament of orders.[73]

Schwartz accurately presents the traditional theological key to this "ontologically distinct" ministry of ordained priesthood: namely the imprinting of a special character through the sacrament of order. Not only does the metaphysical language present "its own difficulties in articulating the faith of the church in a community no longer accustomed to think in these categories,"[74] but the theological connection between some ontological element through ordination to a theology of sacramental character has its own problematic arena as well.[75] The official teaching by the church on the issue of sacramental character is this:

> *that* three sacraments, baptism, confirmation and order, confer a character is defined;

> *what* this character is theologically is not defined.

Every theological description of the meaning of sacramental character, consequently, must be considered a theological opinion or view and no more than this. Even the Vatican II document *Presbyterorum ordinis* does not present us with a theological position on the matter of "sacramental character." Neither in the text itself nor in the context is there any indication that the bishops at Vatican II wanted to make an official statement on the meaning of sacramental character beyond the official statement found in the Tridentine documents.

Let us pursue this "ontological distinctness" of the ordained priest, using the language found in Schwartz' book, only because he sums up in his statements the usual theological position presented by many other scholars.[76] Priests, he says, are called on to deepen their spiritual life "in response to the permanent ontological grace conferred in ordination."[77] Moreover, he says, the bishops at Vatican II used the phrase *in persona Christi* only in connection with the ordained priesthood in their effort to indicate a distinct identity in the very meaning of priesthood.[78]

> While affirming the significance of the sacraments of initiation in priestly life, *Presbyterorum ordinis* uses the phrase "in the person of Christ" to make an ontological statement attesting to the importance of the sacrament of orders in conferring a distinctive identity on priests in the mission of the church.[79]

In stressing this Vatican II connection of priestly ordination with the phrase *in persona Christi,* Schwartz concludes:

> Thus the council affirms that there is a change in being in those receiving these sacraments, an ontological change, which is rooted in the activity of God, relating the recipients to Christ and the church in a new way.[80]

This new way is described by Schwartz as a "change in identity," an "ontological change," and as an "essential change in the way priests are related to Christ the head and through the head to the church."[81] One can even speak of this, he adds, as an "ontological foundation of their ministry."

Presbyterorum ordinis speaks of Christ the head and the ordained priest:

> Priests through the anointing of the Holy Spirit are signed with a special character and thus they are configured to Christ the priest, so that they are able to act in the person of Christ the head [*in persona Christi Capitis agere valent*] (n. 2).

Apostolicam actuositatem, however, says the same thing about the laity and Christ the head:

The lay person obtains the office and right [*officium et ius*] to the apostolate from the very same union with Christ the Head [*ex ipsa sua cum Christo capite unione*] (n. 3).

Through baptism . . . through confirmation they are deputed [*deputantur*] to the apostolate by the Lord himself (n. 3).

In this text of *Apostolicam actuositatem,* the Lord (*Dominus*) is clearly Christ the head (*Christus caput*). It is Christ the head who deputes the baptized-confirmed man and woman to a mission and ministry, called at this juncture "the apostolate." The use of the term *laici* in this paragraph, however, muddles the water. *Lumen gentium* in chapter 2 had spoken of the common matrix of all gospel disciples, not simply the *laici,* whom *Lumen gentium* focused on in chapter 4. Not even the documents of Vatican II present us with a clear distinction between ordained and non-ordained on the basis of Christ the head.

However, there are other major theological problems in this entire approach of an ontological difference between ordained and non-ordained. If the very meaning, function, ministry, and role of both presbyter and bishop over the centuries has undergone major variations, then there is no permanent element or dimension in the ordained priest, whether presbyteral or episcopal, which through the centuries has remained constant. When one argues that A is ontologically, i.e. in the order of being, different from B, one would expect that there is "something" in A which remains ontologically constant, i.e. in the order of being, against which B can be described as "ontologically distinct," i.e. in the order of being. But if the very identity or meaning of A shifts radically and in major ways during the course of history, one can legitimately ask: What is there in the "order of being," in the "ontological structure," which gives rise in A to such an essential difference from B? What is the presbyteral or episcopal constant, the A or priestly factor, which forms the very basis for its essential difference from B, the non-priestly factor? The answers to this have been varied, but they are not theologically convincing.

A. Sacramental Character

Sacramental character is not the answer, since each meaning given to sacramental character is only a theological position, which can be supplanted tomorrow by another, better theological position.

B. Power To Consecrate Bread and Wine

Power to consecrate bread and wine is not the answer, since this theological position, developed in the thirteenth century, has been supplanted by the teaching of Vatican II on the *tria munera,* and it is not mentioned in the first extant ordination ritual, found in the *Traditio apostolica.*

C. In Persona Christi Capitis

In persona Christi capitis is not the answer, since every sharing in the *tria munera,* with its call and commissioning to ministry and mission, is possible only if each baptized-eucharistic Christian images Christ, the head, in the mission and ministry of teaching/preaching, sanctifying and leading. The power of their ministry and mission lies in the power of Christ, the head, of whom they are a sacrament.

In order to make this clearer, let us review those moments in the history of priesthood, both episcopal and presbyteral, which indicate that there has never been a "constant" dimension.

A. DATA WHICH QUESTIONS THE PRESENCE OF AN EPISCOPAL "CONSTANT"

The various commentaries on Vatican II, particularly those on *Lumen gentium,* such as Philips, Kloppenburg, and the *Herder Commentary,* written especially by Vorgrimler and Rahner, all indicate that in the theological presentation of the bishops at Vatican II, the presbyterate can only be "defined" or "described" in and through its relationship to episcopacy. This means that the self-identity of the post-Vatican II priest must include as part of this self-identity a relationship to the bishop, and vice versa. A bishop's self-identity is essentially related to the presbyterium. There is then an intrinsic relationship between the theological understanding of what a presbyter is and what a bishop or *episkopos* is, so that one cannot be understood except in the light of the other.

The question, however, arises: What is a bishop? What is an *episkopos?* From the historical research which has been done in recent times, it appears that the following conclusion must be drawn:

From an historical analysis there has never been an immutable definition of "episkopos" within the Christian tradition.

The following items substantiate this statement.

1. The term *episkopos* is used only once in the Pauline letters, and there is absolutely no indication either as regards the identity of such an *episkopos* or as regards the role of such an *episkopos* in the Christian community at Philippi. All efforts to give this name some identifiable content remain conjectural.

2. In Acts the term *episkopos* is used, but not frequently. In fact, *presbyteros* is used far more often than *episkopos*. Even more to the point, in Acts the two terms *episkopos/presbyteros* appear to be interchangeable. Secondly, in Acts there is absolutely no indication that either an *episkopos* or a *presbyteros* is a "successor of the apostles" or a "successor of the twelve." Quite the contrary, for Luke, the twelve apostles are presented in a unique though ephemeral way. Only on a single occasion is someone chosen to be a part of this group of twelve. No data, even outside of Acts, indicates that an election to the group of twelve ever again occurred. The apostles simply fade away as Acts continues. *Episkopos/presbyteros* in Acts appear to have a leadership role and a teaching role, but they are presented only in generalized terms. Liturgical roles for the *episkopos/ presbyteros* are not mentioned.

3. The deutero-Pauline letters do not widen our vision on this matter in any substantial degree. *Presbyteros* and *episkopos* continue to be interchangeable. There is a leadership role of a local community, with teaching and preaching mentioned as part of this leadership role. Stress is placed on the moral or Christian character of such leaders. Again, there is in these letters no indication whatsoever that such leaders can be called "successors of the apostles," nor are such leaders described in a collegial way. Specific preaching, teaching and leadership activities are not described.

4. The New Testament nowhere equates *episkopos* with the twelve. Nowhere does it equate *episkopos* with the apostles. Consequently, a defining of *episkopos* through a connection with either the twelve or the apostles has taken place in an arena and time-frame outside of and beyond the New Testament communities.

5. In such writings as the *Letter of Clement to the Corinthians,* recent scholarship has indicated that in late first century Rome a joint leadership of several *presbyteroi-episkopoi* seems to be the more accurate picture of the Christian community's leadership. Clement was one of this group. Catholic authors tend to say—but perhaps more from a dogmatic standpoint than from an historically justified standpoint—that Clement was the leader of this group. In actuality, he might only have been the one who was asked by the leadership group to write the letter on behalf of the

leadership of the Christian community at Rome. This, of course, raises serious questions on the issue of the "bishop of Rome." However, when this indication of a *presbyteroi-episkopoi* group leadership in Clement is joined with other data from other areas of the then Christian world, which had similar local leadership, namely a group of *presbtyeroi-episkopoi*, we find it very difficult to see in the sub-apostolic world, and indeed throughout the first three quarters of the second century, any historical data which indicates that *episkopoi* were essentially or ontologically considered as:

A. individually, the main leaders of a given Christian community;
B. either as an individual *episkopos* or as a group of *episkopoi*, the successors of the apostles or of the twelve;
C. as an episcopal *college* of church leaders.

6. A major change for an understanding of *episkopos* took place at the end of the second century: gradually but eventually in a fairly geographically comprehensive way, the title *episkopos* came to be used for the main leader of a given Christian community. This leader was the highest local Christian administrator and also the main teacher and preacher of a localized Christian community. Because he was such a leader, he was also the presider at the various Christian liturgies, including the eucharist. This positioning came not on the basis of any theological foundation, such as: *episkopos* is the "successor of the apostles." Nor was there any clear view, at the end of the second century, of a collegial nature of such *episkopoi*.

7. With the appearance at the end of the second century and the subsequent widespread practice of ordination, the role of the *episkopos* gradually came to be portrayed in Old Testament terms, particularly terms which described the Aaronite or Levitical priesthoods. These ordination rituals, of which that of Hippolytus can claim a major influence, hastened the connection of the two terms *episkopos* and *hiereus*, imbuing the episcopal role with a sacerdotal or hieratic aura, which is not found in the data prior to this period of time.

8. At the beginning of the third century, Cyprian, as we know, made a move which was subsequently taken up by a number of Christian authors. He described Peter and, by connection, the other apostles as the first *episkopoi*. This clear linkage of *episkopos* to apostle provided a major rational—though clearly unhistorical—for the view that the *episkopoi* were the "successors of the apostles" and as such were "collegially" united one to the other. Cyprian was reading back into history, *eisegesis*, rather than reading from history, *exegesis*. Nonetheless, his theological position changed the meaning of *episkopos*.

9. The next step in the changing view of *episkopos* took place from

400 onward, when satellite churches, surrounding the episcopal church, began to be staffed by a presbyter. This form of presbyteral, not episcopal, local leadership was further developed by the Frankish structuring of ministry, with Frankish proprietary churches which were not under episcopal supervision, and which were administered by a presbyter. In this new circumstance the new aspect for *episkopos* was this: the *episkopos*, who had been the main leader of a localized Christian community, was for now rarely seen by a local Christian community, with the result that the presbyter, not the *episkopos*, was practically and then theoretically considered the main leader of the Christian community.

10. At the same time as this presbyteral restructuring of local Christian leadership began to occur, the papacy in the west also added its form of restructuring: namely, the mutual ties between regional *episkopoi*, one with another, were slowly but surely replaced by ties of each individual *episkopos* to the pope, and not to his *co-episkopoi*. This papal restructuring brought about two major changes in the meaning of bishop which are apropos to our theme:

A. first, it weakened in great measure the reality of episcopal collegiality;

B. second, it made the *episkopos* more and more a deputy or delegate of the pope.

All of this occasioned a major change in the very meaning of *episkopos*/bishop.

11. In the middle ages, because of all of the above, it was the presbyterate, not the episcopate, which was theologically considered the highest grade of order in the sacrament of *ordo*. Neither the medieval canonists nor the Council of Trent altered this theological presentation, that is, Trent did not officially endorse it, nor did it officially reject it. In fact, the Council of Trent, for all practical purposes, used the then-current understanding of the sacrament of *ordo*, with its view that the priest is at the highest stage of such a sacrament. In this theological presentation of the sacrament of order, the power to celebrate the eucharist and the power to forgive sins controlled the meaning of holy order and gave the rationale why the priest, and he alone, should be considered the highest stage in this *ordo*. The "definition" of bishop came to be viewed much more as a church dignity and an office. Even as regards the issue of power, so central to the Tridentine position of holy orders, presbyters could confirm, when given special faculties, and it appears from historical data, which would have been known by some of the bishops at Trent, that presbyters, namely abbots, had also been allowed to ordain, even to presbyteral ordination.

The theological explanations of how priests could use these powers to confirm and to ordain, normally exercised only by bishops, varied. That priests did validly and licitly confirm and, on limited occasions, ordain is historically certain. In all of this, the "definition" of bishop was changed.

12. The next major change in an understanding of bishop developed at Vatican II, when the bishops asserted that episcopacy was the fullest rank in the sacrament of holy order. Many theologians prior to the council had urged this, but it is only with Vatican II that we have—at least from the high patristic period onward—a western magisterial statement which linked episcopacy with the sacrament of order in any integral or essential way. No longer can the "definition" of bishop be simply one of dignity and office, one which involves the *corpus Christi mysticum* but not the *corpus Christi eucharisticum*, one which involves only *potestas iurisdictionis* but not *potestas ordinis*, or one which describes the local bishop as a deputy or delegate of the pope.

There has been a definite purpose behind this listing of such historical data: namely, when the bishops of Vatican II inform us that the only way to understand the meaning of priest-presbyter is through its connection to bishop-presbyter, the issue immediately arises: What precisely is a bishop? If, however, there appears to be no unchangeable portrait or definition of bishop in our past history, then what can we say today as regards the "ontological" definition or distinctness of the ordained minister? If during a long period of church history the bishop/*episkopos* was not, *qua* bishop, part of this ontologically distinct positioning of ordained priesthood but only *qua* priest, and if from Vatican II onward the official teaching is that only in virtue of a relationship to *episkopos*/bishop precisely *qua* bishop can the ontological distinctness be understood, is there not some temporalizing and therefore relativizing of the very meaning of "ontological"? Given the historical vicissitudes of the very meaning of bishop and consequently the varied historical theologizing of the meaning of bishop, can one speak about something "ontological," i.e. something in the very "essence" of episcopacy? The "ontological" difference appears to have changed radically as the very meaning of *episkopos*/bishop has radically changed. This episcopal "essence" has apparently changed in the course of history in several ways, which can only mean that the "ontological" factor has changed as well. The meaning of the "ontological difference" depends, it seems, on the period of history under discussion.

I. First of all, history has a way of questioning which engenders crises, and in this study of the "ontological" distinctness of the ordained, we find history doing the same thing. T. Bokenkotter writes as regards the historical method, particularly in reference to scripture, but also in reference to the entire framework of an historical worldview:

Catholic officials, however, saw the historical method as a lethal threat to the Church's whole system of supposedly immutable doctrines and they fought desperately to shield the faithful from the dangers of history. They fell back especially on scholastic philosophy with its façade of immutability.[82]

The reality that even today there might be a changed situation as regards the meaning of episcopacy is not to be brushed aside. For instance, theologians and canonists ask some questions which indicate that the meaning of episcopacy is not that clear:

What is episcopal collegiality?

Does episcopal collegiality require a rethinking of papal authority?

Who belongs to the college of bishops?

As regards this latter point of membership, why are the orthodox, non-uniate bishops considered by the Roman Catholic Church leadership as true and valid bishops, but denied a place at the collegial table?

Is collegiality something "extra" to episcopacy or is it an integral part of episcopacy? If it is integral or essential, then it is part of the "ontological" difference and it should be officially acknowledged that all the orthodox bishops and patriarchs belong ipso facto to the collegial structure of the church and that a gathering of only part of this collegial group, namely the Roman Catholic part, does not represent fully the true meaning of episcopal collegiality.

If collegiality is, however, not ontologically essential to the very meaning of episcopacy, but only a "second" step, added on to episcopacy, then aspects of the teaching of the bishops at Vatican II are rendered quite ambiguous.

This latter approach de facto seems to be the Vatican position, since that leadership acknowledges the sacramental validity of orthodox episcopacy but disallows a collegial role to such bishops. In this exclusion of valid bishops from the "college of bishops," collegiality appears to be merely an accidental appendage to the "essence" of bishop and an issue only of jurisdiction.[83]

II. Secondly, a changing view of the very meaning of *episkopos* is seen today in the questioning of the theological significance of an auxiliary bishop who is not in charge of a diocese or local church. Is this person truly a bishop, even though he is not the main leader of a local, diocesan community, or is he rather a presbyter elevated to a certain jurisdictional level?

III. Thirdly, national conferences of bishops are today quite vital for church leadership, but such conferences require that bishops be absent from their dioceses over long periods of time. They have necessary tasks at the central headquarters which encroach on the time they are able to give to their local dioceses. What does this de facto situation say about local episcopal leadership, when a diocese de facto is being run by non-bishops or at least non-ordinaries?

Since Vatican II has indicated to us that a theology of priesthood cannot be developed without an understanding of bishop, the question "What is the very meaning of a bishop?" becomes acute. If episcopacy is the fullness of priesthood, then the fullness of any "ontological" distinctness should be found par excellence in the episcopacy. On the other hand, if the very meaning and understanding of *episkopos* has changed, and at times in quite theologically significant ways, even to the degree that episcopacy was not even considered part of the theology of *ordo,* and when even at this present time episcopacy itself cannot be "defined" clearly, then where can one find the unchanging "ontological" element in the various historical "definitions," "descriptions," and even "functions" of the *episkopos?*

To say today, in the face of historical data, that there is an ontological difference in the ordained priesthood, episcopal and presbyteral, is a questionable statement at best. One must also note that any alteration in the understanding of such an "ontological difference" on the part of the ordained will ipso facto affect the way one views the role of the non-ordained person in the church.

B. DATA WHICH QUESTIONS THE PRESENCE OF A PRESBYTERAL "CONSTANT"

Let us consider briefly some of the historical data regarding the essence of the presbyteral ministry. As in the case of the *episkopos,* one can, on the basis of the historical data, conclude:

History indicates no unchangeable definition of a presbyter. Rather, it indicates several major changes in the theological meaning of the presbyter.

It is no secret that the bishops at Vatican II presented the Catholic world with a view of the presbyterate which departed quite deliberately from the rather narrow understanding of priesthood which both scholastic and Tridentine theologies had followed. The introduction of an understanding of priesthood, based on the *tria munera* of Jesus, clearly moved away from the eucharistically controlled priestly definition which had dominated Roman Catholic theology since the thirteenth century.

When one looks back on those seven hundred years, namely 1200 to 1900, one sees that the dominant approach to priesthood, with its centralizing focus on the power to celebrate the eucharist and the power to forgive sins, was theologically developed and rationalized time and time again. This occurred at the very time in which a seminary system was also being developed in the west. When one juxtaposes these two elements, namely a dominant definition of priesthood, which is the theological element, and an emergent but gradually uniform structure of priestly education and formation, which is the institutional element, one sees that the two elements, theology and seminary life, mutually reinforced each other. As the institution called "seminary" became more acceptable as also more sophisticated and professional, the scholastic/Tridentine definition of priesthood became more rooted in Roman Catholic life and doctrine. Vice versa, as theologians and canonists utilized this priestly definition more centrally in their own research and studies, in their own teaching and publications, the more this particular definition of priesthood shaped both the seminary curriculum and the seminary forms of spirituality. Eventually the eucharistic theology of priesthood became the center of the eucharistic spirituality of priesthood. The "ontological difference" was described as the power to consecrate the bread and wine into the body and blood of Jesus, a power which belonged exclusively to the priest in virtue of his ordination, more specifically in virtue of the indelible character one received at ordination. Neither this theological description of priesthood nor its related priestly spirituality has ever been defined officially by church leadership. Even though it was only a theological view, it did, however, enjoy a long period of acceptance, but longevity alone does not make issues immutable.

The rethinking of the meaning of priesthood, which Vatican II undertook, has had major repercussions on such a theology of priesthood. When at Vatican II a wider and more pastoral understanding of priesthood was presented, the issue of the "ontological" distinctness also became a matter of revision. Can a teaching of priestly "ontological" distinctness be maintained, however, on the basis of historical data which indicates that there is no immutable "essence" of the priest? A few of the salient historical moments in this priestly variation are as follows:

1. In the New Testament we do not find the term *presbyteros* either in the Pauline letters or in the four gospels. Neither the letter to the Colossians nor the letter to the Ephesians uses the term *presbyteros*. These sections of the New Testament are not a small or unimportant segment of the revealed word. The absence of such usage prompts the question: If *presbyteros* was an essential ministry in the church from the foundation onward, why is this term never used in these basic writings, even when these writings discuss church ministry?

2. In the various Johannine writings, excluding the fourth gospel, *presbyteros* is used, while the term *episkopos* is totally lacking. Is this exclusive use of *presbyteros* indicative of a specific view regarding Christian ministry not shared by other writers of the New Testament? Can one simply bypass the issue by relegating the non-use of *episkopos* and the exclusive use of *presbyteros* as cultural? Does not this exclusive use of *presbyteros* in these Johannine writings indicate that this ministerial term describes the main leadership in the respective Johannine communities? The *presbyteros* in these writings is portrayed as the main leader. There is no mention, even with the dissentions in the community, of an appeal to a higher church leader, i.e. *episkopos*. It may be impossible to unravel all the difficulties which stem from this exclusive use of *presbyteros*, but there can be no solution if one equates the Johannine *presbyteros* with a presbyter of a later date.

3. How does one explain the role of the *presbyteros* in Acts? One finds indications that such ministers enjoyed a leadership role of some kind, as also a teaching and preaching role of some kind. Nothing, however, is clearly spelled out and there is no indication of a liturgical role for the *presbyteros*. A similar situation is found in the deutero-Pauline literature. Dogmatically, one might say that these *presbyteroi* naturally played a liturgical role, but such an assertion is made gratuitously, and even were it accepted, the scope of such liturgical ministry is purely conjectural. Dogmatically, once again, one might say that this scope included the celebration of eucharist, but this, too, is gratuitous, and even more so, since it makes assertions not in some general way, i.e. liturgical ministry, but in specific ways, i.e. eucharistic presidency.

4. In the letters of Ignatius of Antioch, the *presbyteros* is clearly presented as the "successor of the apostles." Along with the *Didache*, this is the first extant statement we have on this matter of who might be the successors of the apostles, and in both documents it is the *presbyteros*, not the *episkopos*. Hermas, for his part, appears to make the *presbyteros* far more significant to the local community than the *episkopos*. Irenaeus in no way makes the *episkopos* a successor of the apostles; indeed, he clearly states that the *presbyteros* succeeds to the apostles.

5. In our first extant ordination ritual, that of Hippolytus, the *presbyteroi* are selected and ordained, not for liturgical worship, nor does it seem for teaching and preaching, but rather they are ordained primarily to be advisors to the *episkopos*. One can say, on the basis of the data, that from mid-second century until the fifth century, *presbyteroi* apparently did not celebrate eucharist and did not preside at a liturgy of reconciliation. These two issues are, as is evident, the basis for the scholastic/Tridentine definition of presbyter. Yet if history indicates that many were ordained without either this intention of the ordaining person or this ministry conferred on the ordained, then the scholastic/Tridentine definition is called into question if one wishes to see in it something "essential" or something "ontological." One must also conclude that the description of priest, as presented by the *tria munera* view of Vatican II, is also called into question by this data, if one wants to make the mission and ministry in the *tria munera* of Jesus, even *in persona Christi*, as the essence of priesthood, and through this "essence" to deduce an "ontological" difference. In other words, there appears to be no clearly agreed upon "eternal" definition of presbyter which undergirds this ministry from New Testament times onward.

6. When we realize that in the period after 400, when presbyters were indeed placed over small communities and became the main ministers of a community, either in virtue of the satellite communities surrounding an episcopal church, or in the Frankish form in virtue of proprietary churches, it was not a definition of priesthood which occasioned the change of presbyteral ministry in this regard, but pastoral need. Pastorally, the *episkopos* was unable to attend to all the churches in his area; pastorally, the lord of the manor wanted someone to staff his proprietary church.

7. The scholastic definition of priest, based on eucharist and forgiveness of sin, was an instance in which a later theory substantiated an ongoing *praxis*. The medievalists did not question the presbyteral ministry, which they experienced. They did, however, provide a theological basis for this ministry or pastoral situation. The presbyter, at that medieval time, was almost universally throughout the western world the main leader of a local community, with his centralizing tasks those of celebrating eucharist and of forgiving serious sin. This pastoral practice became legitimated by the scholastic definition of priesthood: namely, a baptized male Christian who through ordination to the priesthood received the exclusive power to consecrate the bread and wine into the body and blood of Jesus and to forgive sins in the sacrament of reconciliation. The scholastic legitimation came to be viewed, at least until it was replaced at Vatican II, as almost an "eternal verity."

8. The renewed view of priestly ordination which one finds in the documents of Vatican II has raised even further questions on this issue of "ontological" distinctness. If all Christians, in virtue of their baptism–confirmation–eucharist, share in the mission and ministry of Jesus, i.e. the *tria munera,* and they do this because they have been called and commissioned by Jesus himself for this very mission and ministry, they must, in fulfilling this mission and ministry, be acting *in persona Christi.* If this is not the case, then in whose *persona* are they acting? The statement on the ordained as found in *Lumen gentium* and *Presbyterorum ordinis,* in no way negates this kind of question, for the many other passages in the same document refer explicitly to the baptized Christian's sharing in these *tria munera,* which clearly involve a mission and ministry in Jesus' name and person.

9. If Jesus is presented, through the *tria munera,* as the basis for all ministry, whether ordained or non-ordained, and if through baptism/eucharist all Christians play a role in this ministry and mission of the *tria munera,* what is the difference between the ordained and the non-ordained? What is an "ontological" difference between the ordained and the non-ordained?

10. If Jesus is presented through the *tria munera* as the basis for imaging Christian ministry, then on the basis of image what is the distinction between ordained and non-ordained? In *Lumen gentium,* n. 31, we read that all baptized/eucharistic people "Christum aliis manifestant." Is this not imaging Jesus? Is this not both men and women imaging Jesus? The entire issue of the ministry of all Christians, based on the *tria munera,* and the entire issue of the lay minister in the church, which ministry is also based on the *tria munera,* raise serious questions on the issue of an "ontological difference" between ordained and non-ordained.

All of these issues raise the question: If the "essence" of presbyteral priesthood has fluctuated over the centuries, can one even speak of an "ontological difference"? The fluctuations in the essential meaning of both episcopal and presbyteral ministry present one with the problem:

A. If there is an "ontological difference" between an ordained priest and a non-ordained Christian, something must constitute this "ontological" difference.

B. If, however, there is no constant element in the identity of an ordained Christian, but rather a history of variants, then the phrase "ontological difference" has little theological meaning.

Every time that the meaning of "priest" changes, the so-called "ontological difference" also changes, with the result that what was once described as "ontological," "essential," "metaphysical," actually rests on what one might describe as "existential," "practical," or "historically current" as regards the description of presbyteral or episcopal ministry.

For our present purpose, namely an understanding of the role of the baptized-eucharistic Christian in the church, the basic inconsistencies of the theological opinions regarding "ontological difference" prevent a teaching on "ontological difference" to be the vital or fundamental key in distinguishing ordained baptized Christians from non-ordained baptized Christians. "Ontological difference" appears to be no longer a viable theological approach to determine the difference between *klerikos/laikos*.

4. THE ROLE OF WOMEN IN THE VATICAN II AND THE POST-VATICAN II CHURCH

The role of women in the Roman Catholic Church has vastly changed within the last half of the twentieth century. Never, in the course of church history, have there been so many competent women scholars in the field of theology. Never before has there been so strong a rereading of both scripture and church history from the standpoint of women. The very newness and strength of this feminine influence in theology and church literature must be seen as a major factor in the repositioning of the baptized-eucharistic person in the church, with its concomitant depositioning of the clerical person.[84]

The role of women in the church, and above all in theological studies, must nonetheless be understood within the social, political and economic framework of the modern and contemporary world. In almost all areas in these periods of history, women have found, to some degree at least, a new positioning in the socio-political culture. A major impetus for this cultural repositioning stems from the American and French revolutions, which, as we saw above, summed up dramatically many philosophical and religious strands of the immediately preceding centuries. In the very structure of these two revolutions was the notion that all people are created equal and possess a fundamental human dignity. This was the theory. In practice, sexism, racism, and elitism continued apace both in France and in the United States, and indeed in all the countries which were affected by these two revolutions. Only in the course of time, and with major struggles, even on occasion wars, have major steps been taken to eradicate male chauvinism and patriarchy, ethnic and racial bias, economic and cultural elitism. As one enters into the twenty-first century, it is clear that there are still large numbers of human beings, both male and female, whose innate freedom and equality are systemically denied.

The leadership both of the Roman Catholic Church and of many other Christian churches as well has tended to move quite cautiously on the issue of women and their role within a church structure. In the Roman Catholic Church, the role of women and church structure has become a very brittle theme. Roman Catholic Church leadership, however, has perhaps unwittingly at times abetted the stronger role of women in the church. Beginning with *Lumen gentium* and *Gaudium et spes*, a whole series of official statements have increasingly centered on the dignity and equality of each and every human being. Because of this often repeated official stance regarding the dignity and equality of every man and woman, it has become increasingly more difficult for the leadership of the church, both theological and ecclesiastical, to make a case which denies full equality and full dignity for women at all levels of the church structures. The official statements leave little room to quibble about basic human freedom, equality and dignity.

A. LUMEN GENTIUM

We have alluded to the many areas in *Lumen gentium* which speak of the common matrix of all baptized-eucharistic Christians. It would be fruitless to repeat such material once again. Let one citation from this document suffice for all:

> There is, therefore, one chosen people of God: "one Lord, one faith, one baptism" (Eph 4:50); there is a common dignity of members, deriving from their rebirth in Christ, a common grace as sons and daughters, a common vocation to perfection, one salvation, one hope and undivided charity. Hence there is in Christ and in the church no inequality on the basis of race or nationality, social condition or sex, because "there is neither Jew nor Greek; there is neither slave nor freeman; there is neither male nor female. For you are all 'one' in Christ Jesus" (Gal 3:28; cf. Col 3:11) (n. 31).

B. INSTRUMENTUM LABORIS: DE VOCATIONE ET MISSIONE LAICORUM IN ECCLESIA ET IN MUNDO VIGINTI ANNIS A CONCILIO VATICANO II ELAPSIS

> Once the existence of God is acknowledged, the person is ushered into a life of interpersonal relationships and immersed in a basic awareness that the other person is entitled to an equal dignity.

The affirmation of the dignity and freedom of each person, the basis for the dynamic of participation, characterizes the life of a great many people in our day. However, in spite of this, many different forms of oppression against the dignity of the human person and whole peoples are increasing, demonstrating the urgent need for total liberation for all people (n. 8).

The movement for the advancement and liberation of women is certainly one of the more significant manifestations of the general tendency toward participation. The just struggle in favor of recognizing the equality of rights between women and men at all levels, founded upon the assertion of their equal dignity, has not failed to bear fruit. . . . The full recognition of the dignity of women—closely aligned to the question of the acceptance and affirmation of her feminine identity—is still a goal to be reached. In fact, when equality of dignity and rights between men and women was pursued in a purely formal way, resulting in the rejection of women's femininity, women found themselves faced with new experiences of oppression. A one-dimensional emancipation, almost exclusively bound to the access of women to the economic world of production, has risked causing them to fall into a new state of alienation. When women are not part of the economic production system because they devote themselves to the family, they have had to face new denials to their dignity and their rights (n. 9).

C. DIGNITATEM MULIERIS

Every individual is made in the image of God, insofar as he or she is a rational and free creature capable of knowing God and loving him. The foundation of the whole human "ethos" is rooted in the image and likeness of God which the human being bears within himself from the beginning (n. 7).

D. INSTRUCTION ON CERTAIN ASPECTS OF THE "THEOLOGY OF LIBERATION"

This yearning [for liberation] shows the authentic, if obscure, perception of the dignity of the human person, created "in the image and likeness of God" (Gen 1:26–27) [I/1]. . . . The yearning for justice and for the effective recognition of the dignity of every human being needs, like every deep aspiration, to be clarified and guided [II/1].

E. INSTRUCTION ON CHRISTIAN FREEDOM AND LIBERATION

Awareness of man's freedom and dignity, together with the affirmation of the inalienable rights of individuals and peoples, is one of the major characteristics of our time.... The church of Christ makes these aspirations her own (n. 1).

When the cumulative import of these official statements—and there are others as well—is evaluated, the implications which they involve are clear. A fundamental equality and dignity, inherent in each and every human life, must find expression in Christian life and in church structure as well if both Christian life and church structure are meant to reflect the dignity of human life given to each individual by God.

A second theme, therefore, which church leadership has officially emphasized in the present moment of history, and which has abetted the repositioning of women within the structures and roles of the church, is the emphasis on the common matrix of gospel discipleship. As we have seen above, a major move to establish this fundamental Christian equality and Christian dignity is found in *Lumen gentium,* not only in chapter 2, but in the arrangement of the various chapters of this document. The effort of the bishops at Vatican II to name the common matrix of gospel discipleship, i.e. "people of God," *christifidelis,* and "priesthood of all believers," further enhances this basic Christian equality. In the bishops' endeavor both to emphasize the reality of this common matrix and to name it, the theological teaching on the *tria munera* of Jesus himself was applied to all baptized and eucharistic Christians, male or female. When this same theological teaching on the *tria munera* was used to "define" the role of the ordained Christian, a major doctrinal ambiguity began to emerge. Nonetheless, the official church leadership has presented the Roman Catholic world with major statements on the common matrix of gospel discipleship, a view of discipleship through which and in which all other aspects of church must be seen. This applies in a special way to the teaching of the *tria munera* and the relationship between the "priesthood of all believers" and the "ordained priesthood." Friedrich Wulf expresses this inadequacy as he comments on article 2 of *Presbyterorum ordinis:*

The tracing back of the general and the special priesthood to their deeper theological basis of unity has not been entirely successful. . . . It is never made sufficiently clear [in the documents] that the fundamental priesthood is that of the Church, the community of those who believe in Christ, and hence that the special priesthood essentially grows out of the mystery of the priestly Church, without simply being under the control of the Church.[85]

In article 3 of *Presbyterorum ordinis,* Wulf notes that the text does not consistently maintain the view of priest favored by the bishops at Vatican II, and that "traditional theology of the priesthood was never quite authentically integrated into the new view of the Council." Article 3 "proceeds one-sidedly from the traditional folk-Church, a Church of leaders and those who are led. Other conciliar statements—even in this same decree—go much further in correcting this inadequate concept."[86]

This precise issue, the relationship of the two priesthoods, was to some degree addressed in the *Declaration on the Question of the Admission of Women to the Ministerial Priesthood:*

Jesus Christ did not call any woman to become part of the twelve.

This rather blunt statement is presented as a breakwater beyond which the incoming tide should not go. However, as we have seen above, there is no New Testament linkage of the twelve or the apostles either to *episkopos* or to *presbyteros.* In other words, from the standpoint of the New Testament, what Jesus might actually have done in the calling of the twelve or in the sending of the apostles would have, at best, only an indirect bearing on the New Testament statements as regards *episkopos* and *presbyteros,* an indirect bearing which continually is open to the criticism of *eisegesis* rather than *exegesis.* In an exegetically correct though indirect way, one could argue only this: from the beginning of the Jesus community there existed a servant-leadership ministry. The Jesus community was never, even at its origins, an egalitarian or totally democratic community. From the earliest evidence there was both a community and a servant-leadership structure. The precise naming, the precise allocation of distinct functions for such ministry or servant leadership, and the theological positioning of such leadership in apostolicity, however, developed only in the course of time.

The "apostolic" argument mentioned by the *Declaration* reflects a very complex theological issue which cannot be dismissed in a single apodictic sentence. From quite early patristic times the church community has expressed in an official way its belief in one, holy, catholic and apostolic church. The various creeds read:

We believe in one, holy, catholic and apostolic church.

The official creeds do not read:

We believe in one, holy, catholic and apostolic church ministry.

The difference in these two statements—the one official, the other arbitrary—can be stated as follows:

Because the church itself is one, holy, catholic and apostolic, one can say that its ministry is apostolic.

On the basis of the credal statements of the church, it would be incorrect to state the situation as follows:

Because the ministry, i.e. bishop, presbyter and deacon, is apostolic, therefore the church itself is apostolic.

The apostolicity of the ministry depends on the more fundamental apostolicity of the church community itself, not vice versa. The apostolicity of the church community does not depend on the apostolicity of the episcopal, presbyteral and diaconal ministry.

This becomes clear when we consider the way in which the other "marks" of the church have been traditionally taught. We do not say that the unity of the church depends on the unity of the ministry. We do not say that the holiness of the church depends on the holiness of the ministry. We do not say that the catholicity of the church depends on the catholicity of the ministry.

A. UNITY OF THE CHURCH

The Roman Catholic Church recognizes non-uniate eastern churches to such a degree that a full *communicatio in sacris* has been officially endorsed for the sacraments of eucharist, reconciliation and anointing of the sick. If church unity depended on a unity of church ministry, in this case the recognition of the pope and an acknowledgement that appointment to episcopacy can be made by the pope alone, then such a *communicatio in sacris* would be impossible. Rather, the unity of the church, expressed officially by the Roman Catholic Church leadership in its documents, which allow such a full sharing of sacramental life, rises from far different roots than the "unity of ministry." It rises from a unity of church community. We believe in one church.

B. HOLINESS OF THE CHURCH

That the holiness of the church does not depend on the holiness of the ministry has been a debated issue from earliest ecclesiastical times onward. Again and again, after extensive deliberation and after heated argument and even after fluctuations in practice, the official response of church leadership, both ecclesiastical and theological, has come back to the repeated conclusion that the holiness of the church *does not depend* on the holiness of the minister. Rather, the holiness of the church rises from far different roots than that of the holiness of the minister. This holiness is the very holiness of God, a holiness revealed in the incarnation, and a holiness continued in the holy church, the sacrament and icon of Christ, who in his human nature is the sacrament and icon of God. We believe in one, holy church.

C. CATHOLICITY OF THE CHURCH

The catholicity of the church cannot, in turn, be seen simply in a "Roman form" of catholicity. If acknowledgement of the "Roman element" were necessary for catholicity, then acknowledgement of baptism in other Christian communities would be impossible; the full sacramental *communicatio in sacris* with the eastern non-uniate churches would be impossible; the special occasions when Anglicans and Protestants can licitly receive the eucharist at a Roman Catholic liturgy would be impossible. In all of these cases, the recipients and ministers of such sacramental action do not accept a "Roman form" of catholicity. The catholicity of the church rises from different roots than that of its Roman character. The catholicity is found in the basic sacramental structure and word structure of the church. We believe in one, holy catholic church.

D. APOSTOLICITY OF THE CHURCH

If such theology for the marks one, holy, and catholic has any validity, then the same line of argumentation applies to apostolicity. It is the church itself which is apostolic, and consequently:

because the people of God, the community of baptized-eucharistic *christifideles,* and the gathering of the priesthood of all believers are apostolic,

therefore the ministry of the church is also apostolic, various sees are apostolic, the teaching office is apostolic, etc.

The ecclesial and theological approach on the call and commissioning of the apostles themselves, and on a call and commissioning of episcopal or presbyteral ministry, rests on the New Testament data, as we have seen above, and on the official profession of faith found in the ancient creeds. We believe in one, holy, catholic and apostolic church.

On these two bases, i.e. the New Testament data which makes no connection of apostle-twelve and episkopos-presbyter, and on the credal profession of faith, the stark statement of the *Declaration,* "Jesus Christ did not call any woman to be part of the twelve," must be seriously reexamined. By itself this statement alone cannot serve as an immutable breakwater, thrusting to one side all incoming tides.

The second fundamental argument in the *Declaration* which disallows women to the ordained ministry is the argument of history:

> This practice of the church, therefore, has normative character:
> in the fact of conferring priestly ordination only on men, it is a
> question of an unbroken tradition throughout the history of the
> church, universal in the east and in the west.

Such an historical statement, if directed exclusively to either presbyteral or episcopal ordination, might be verified on data from the patristic church period, beginning with the first ordination ritual in the *Traditio apostolica* and ending in a post-Tridentine period. Prior to the *Traditio apostolica,* any position on the ordination or non-ordination of church ministers is conjectural for either side; in the post-Tridentine period, several Protestant church communities began to ordain women. In the intervening period of these two eras, there seems to be to date no compelling historical evidence for the presbyteral or episcopal ordination of women in the Christian church.

In the case of the diaconate, which is an integral part of the sacrament of order, however, it is clear today that such an "ordo" was conferred on women, at least in the Byzantine rites, and that this conferral took place through an ordination ritual.[87] If women have been ordained to the diaconate, which is an integral part of the sacrament of *ordo* as it has been understood in the west from 1000 onward, some new reasoning needs to be presented to disallow presbyteral ordination to them than simply the unguarded statement above. In the diaconal ordination of women the sacred *ordo* barrier has been breached by women. What theological reasons could be given to validate the position that such a breaching of the ordination barrier must necessarily stop at diaconate? If the sacrament of *ordo* includes bishop, priest and deacon, then a universal and unbroken tradition against "ordaining" women cannot be maintained. On the other hand, if one in counter-argument would suggest that diaconate itself be disengaged from the sacrament of *ordo,* then one immediately confronts yet another "universal and unbroken tradition," one with even more historical documentation in its favor, namely that diaconate is an integral part of the sacrament of *ordo*.

Besides the rereading of scripture from a feminist standpoint, besides the rereading of church history from a feminist standpoint, besides the arguments against patriarchal societies, the above issues make the rethinking of the role of women even more acute, namely:

1. The official teaching of the bishops on the dignity, equality, and freedom of all human beings, women and men, based on creation itself.
2. The official teaching of the bishops on the common matrix of gospel discipleship, male or female, and the relationship of this fundamental discipleship to every other reality of church life and structure.
3. The lack of New Testament data, relating either the twelve or the apostles to *episkopos* and *presbyteros,* and the historical data which indicates that this relationship of bishop to the twelve and to the apostles was only gradually formulated by church leaders, both ecclesiastical and theological, particularly during the third century. Jesus' own historical relationship to the twelve and to the apostles has only an indirect relationship, therefore, to episcopal and presbyteral ministry.
4. The creeds of the church which express a belief in an apostolic church, in the very same way in which these creeds express a belief in the unity, holiness and catholicity of the church: namely, the church is one, holy, catholic and apostolic. Only on the basis of the church as one, holy, catholic and apostolic can one move to other segments of the church and call them apostolic, catholic, holy or one.

The bishops at Vatican II did not address the issue of women in the church, and this is clearly a serious hiatus in their agenda, for by their silence they ignored a major church issue which was already existent within the Roman Catholic Church. To attempt to answer the basic question "What does the church say of itself in today's age?" without discussing the role of women makes the resultant answer, the ecclesiology of Vatican II, a very unfinished product. However, post-Vatican II documents have made several claims, as we have seen above, which, whether intended or not, have furthered the integration of women, at least theologically, into the structuring of the Church.

5. ECUMENICAL ASPECTS OF BOTH ORDAINED AND NON-ORDAINED MINISTRY AND THEIR INFLUENCE ON THE THEOLOGY OF THE NON-ORDAINED PERSON IN THE CHURCH

When the leadership of the Roman Catholic Church at Vatican II deliberately moved into the ecumenical movement, the theological issues regarding church ministry could not be avoided. To date, no satisfactory agreement on all the issues of ministry has been reached. The full acknowledgement by the leadership of the Roman Catholic Church of the ministry in the non-uniate eastern churches raises serious theological questions, not for the non-uniate eastern churches, but for the "traditional" teaching of ministry in the Roman Catholic Church itself. Bishops in particular are the focus of such questions, since a connection to Rome is not an essential element in episcopacy, and the exclusion of non-uniate bishops from the "college of bishops," accepted by the leadership of the Roman church, raises questions about its own "collegial" validity.

The married presbyterate in the eastern churches has, since the time of the Lateran Councils, never been fully accepted by the leadership of the Roman Church. Although disavowals are again and again made that celibacy has absolutely no essential connection to priesthood, this same leadership, when speaking of priestly spirituality, continually asserts that the celibate priest images the priestly Jesus in a better way.[88] It is impossible, however, to have it both ways, and the incongruity of this manner of speaking should be once and for all eradicated in all discussion on priesthood.

When it comes to the ministry of the Anglican and Protestant churches in comparison with the Roman Catholic/Orthodox discussions, the Roman Catholic leadership takes several steps backward. Lack of acknowledgement by Rome of Anglican and Protestant ordinations appears immediately at the center of discussion. The possibility of presbyteral ordination to priesthood, of which there are several papal documents from the fifteenth century, is shunted to one side. The lack of any mention of "consecrating" bread and wine or "celebrating the sacrifice of the Mass" in a priestly ordination ritual appeared to be a way of illegitimating such ordinations, as was done in the case of Anglican ordinations by Leo XIII in *Apostolicae curae*, even though the first extant ordination ritual for presbyters, *Traditio apostolica*, itself lacks such references.

The fundamental issue, however, which causes hesitation by the Roman Catholic leadership, is basically not a theology of ministry, but a theology of the "true" church. Were there to be an official acknowledgement of a valid ministry in the Anglican and Protestant churches by the leadership of the Roman Catholic Church, then the position that the Roman Catholic Church is, by itself, the one, true church of Jesus would be severely compromised. At this writing there is a major effort to interpret officially the term *subsistit* found in article 8 of *Lumen gentium,* in a way which understands church as exclusively the Roman Catholic Church and holds that outside this one church, only elements of church can be found. These voices, including major prelates, press their interpretation, in spite of the opposing position of such eminent commentators on the documents of Vatican II as G. Philips,[89] A. Grillmeier,[90] and F. Sullivan.[91] Grillmeier writes:

> There are two points here, which stand out all the more clearly when one compares the draft of 1963 and the various *vota* of the Fathers with the definitive text.
>
> 1. The true and unique Church of Christ exists as a concrete fact of history. As such, it must be recognizable and definable in spirit of all the character of mystery which attaches to it.
>
> 2. The concrete form of existence of this Church founded by Christ is the Catholic Church.
>
> a) It is no longer said that it "is" the "Roman" Church. This means that the Roman Church, as a local Church, is only part of the whole Church, though its bishop is head of all the bishops of the Catholic Church . . . .
>
> b) No absolute, exclusive judgment of identity is uttered, such as for instance, that the Church of Christ "is" the Catholic Church.[92]

Generally theologians—and Grillmeier himself is not an exception —make mention of ecclesial elements found outside the Roman Catholic Church. To some this means that the "full" reality of church is found only in the Roman Catholic Church, and that outside this Roman Church only elements, i.e. partial aspects, of church are found. If we examine this kind of statement and argumentation in reference to the non-uniate eastern churches, it is remarkable what theologically we find. Among the ecclesial "elements" which one finds in the non-uniate eastern churches one could list the following:

True sacramental baptism and confirmation
True sacramental eucharist
True sacramental bishops, presbyters and deacons
True sacramental reconciliation
True sacramental marriages
True sacramental anointing of the sick
True acknowledgement of the word of God
True prayer
True belief in the creeds
True acceptance of the first four solemn councils of the church
True means of salvation
True belief in God, Christ, the Virgin Mary and the saints

This list could go on. When one asks, in face of this, what "elements" are lacking, the answer is much smaller:

Non-acceptance of the pope
Non-Roman or western theology

The major question which such a listing raises is this: If it cannot be established that the term *subsistit* meant precisely acceptance of the pope and acceptance of a Roman or western theology, then how can such a superabundance of ecclesial elements found in other churches not indicate that these ecclesial groups are indeed church? In fact, the majority of commentators, including those cited above, indicate that an "openness to Church" was precisely the intent of the bishops, and not a rejection of "Church" to such groups on the basis of Roman Catholic exclusivity. "The theological commission which reviewed the *vota* of the bishops on this matter did not accept the desire of 25 bishops who pressed for the term: *Iure divino subsistit;* nor that of 19 bishops: *Subsistit integro modo in ecclesia catholica;* nor the desire of 13 bishops who wanted the term, *est,* instead of *subsistit.* The Theological Commission decided in favour of the simple 'subsistit in', thereby deliberately leaving open the question of the relation of the One Church to the many Churches."[93]

Debates by Roman Catholic leadership on the validity/non-validity of Anglican and Protestant ministry focuses too often on issues not central to the problem. The problematic area is clearly not one of ministry, but one concerning the theological meaning of church. One church/many churches—only when this theme is better resolved will the issue of ministry be itself better resolved.

However, in the effort to reach some resolution, it is precisely the role of baptized-eucharistic discipleship which will be central, since the church is fundamentally a community of disciples, a people of God, a priesthood of all believers. Ecumenical discussion has already enhanced and will continue to enhance the role of the baptized and eucharistic Christian. Each Christian group will help the other Christian groups understand the very meaning of church, as the topic of ecumenical discussion centers more and more on the meaning of gospel discipleship. Once again we have returned to the basic criterion used throughout this study: gospel discipleship.

6. CONCLUSIONS FROM THE DATA

We can highlight the main conclusions derived from the data in this chapter in the following way:

1. The discussion at Vatican II on the self-identity of the church had a rootage in the many unanswered issues which Roman Catholic Church leadership, during the past century and a half, had either not dealt with directly or dealt with only by negative dismissal. These issues included both inner-church issues and socio-political and technological issues.

2. The presentation of church by the bishops of Vatican II was clearly based on christology. The documents state unequivocally that Christ, the light of the world, is the only basis for the meaning of church. Likewise, church ministry, in all its forms, is based on Jesus, particularly in the teaching of the *tria munera.* All baptized-confirmed and eucharistic Christians share *vi sacramenti* in the *tria munera* of Jesus.

3. The bishops developed at great length a portrait of the baptized-confirmed and eucharistic Christian, and used the names "people of God," *christifidelis,* and "priesthood of all believers" to describe this common matrix. The bishops did not use the term "lay" or "laity" to name this common matrix of gospel discipleship. In the post-Vatican II period, these names have been used not only for the common matrix of all gospel discipleship, but also for that specific segment of disciples called "lay." This crossing-over of names has given many mixed signals and has led to no little theological and pastoral confusion.

4. The crux of the problem, which the documents of Vatican II created, was not in the precise name for the baptized-eucharistic disciple, but in the use of the *tria munera* teaching to describe each and every form of ministry and mission in the church, namely, from that which comes from the sacrament of initiation, to that which comes from the sacrament of ordination, to that which comes through the new specific ministries for the non-ordained. Even though the documents state that there is an "essential" difference between the ordained and the non-ordained, the bish-

ops nowhere indicated what this "essential" difference might be, and there are serious theological difficulties to all the subsequent proposals made by scholars.

5. Behind this discussion on the essential difference lies the intent of some authors to maintain an "ontological difference" between ordained and non-ordained. It is the preservation of this "ontological difference," rather than gospel discipleship, which more often than not has been used as the primary hermeneutic for an understanding of ecclesial mission and ministry. *Ordo* remains the hermeneutic through which words like cleric, lay, ordained and non-ordained are interpreted. It is argued that such an "ontological difference" makes no theological sense whatsoever and should be eliminated from the field of discourse. In its place, gospel discipleship should be maintained as the fundamental hermeneutic in which and through which all mission and ministry in the church would be evaluated.

6. A further step to maintain the status quo of the ordained ministry is the proposal to limit the ministry and mission of the *tria munera,* as far as the "lay" person is concerned, to the secular realm. In spite of post-Vatican II documents, which at times tend to move in this direction, the official documents of the council do not allow such an apodictic approach. That some passages of the Vatican II documents lend themselves to such a conclusion cannot be denied; but that some passages in the same documents lend themselves to an inner-church mission for the "lay" person is also undeniable. The data from the documents of Vatican II must be judged as data which leaves the question an open one, since the *tria munera* of Jesus are not exclusively secular-oriented. Everyone, therefore, who shares in these *tria munera* of Jesus shares also in the direction to which Jesus himself oriented his mission and ministry: both internally to his community and externally to the socio-political world in which he lived.

7. The issue of *regnum et sacerdotium* continues even at the end of the second millennium to influence the way the papacy acts. The leadership of the papacy has, of course, an effect on the way episcopacy and to some degree presbyteral ministry acts as well. One can say clearly that the stance of the *sacerdotium* to the socio-political and cultural world influences the way in which that same *sacerdotium* views the "lay" person. If this stance is one of "world-vision" and "world-power," then the baptized-eucharistic Christian will fundamentally be a "subject," not a co-worker or a co-disciple.

8. The issue of gospel discipleship has been enhanced in no small measure by the bishops at Vatican II and by much of the post-Vatican II reality as well. Nonetheless, when it comes to the issue of ordained min-

istry, too often gospel discipleship still does not serve as the fundamental hermeneutic to understand the ordained servant-leadership of the church. Too often, status quo positions on the ontological difference between ordained and non-ordained, and on the hierarchical exclusivity or finality in all church structures and procedures, are used as the basic hermeneutic. This stance by church leadership is being called into question today by competent scholars, and at the same time many statements and decisions of the church leaders are simply being ignored by the baptized-eucharistic people, who see such statements as out of touch with reality.

9. The role of women in the church is the strongest it has ever been in the past two thousand years. Nonetheless, male church leadership, in many sectors, continues to raise hurdles against a full Christian equality for women in the church. This resistance goes far beyond the ordination issue, although the ordination issue remains one of the key issues which need further clarification on the basis of New Testament data and on the basis of historical data. In many ways the credibility of the leadership of the Roman Catholic Church today will depend on the way in which it will handle the issue of the equality and dignity for all Christians, women and men, not merely in the external social world, but in the internal church world as well.

10. The stance of the leadership of the Roman Catholic Church in the post-Vatican II period has sent out mixed signals. The current attempt to equate the term *subsistit in,* as found in *Lumen gentium,* to mean that the Roman Catholic Church is the only one, holy, catholic and apostolic church, goes beyond either the text or context of the document, and given the recognition of full *communicatio in sacris* with the non-uniate eastern churches, and a limited *communicatio in sacris* with Anglicans and Protestants, serious theological positions have been raised which both reject and refute this equation of *subsistit in* to the Roman Catholic Church in an exclusive way. The question of ministry within an ecumenical dimension is fundamentally not a ministerial question, but an ecclesiological one, and needs to be treated as such.

13

Looking to the Future

No one can predict the future, but on the basis of the past one can certainly obtain some insight into the immediate future at least, since the key issues which are with us today will not disappear by tomorrow. The configuration of the issues may be different, and therefore conducive to a better resolution, but nonetheless content-wise they will remain. In this final chapter, I would like to consider the role of the lay person in the Roman Catholic Church from the following three standpoints:

1. **Non-Ordained Ministry in the Twenty-First Century: A "Lay" Vocation, Open to Some Baptized-Eucharistic Christians.**
2. **The Spirituality of Non-Ordained Christians and Its Significance for Ministry in the Twenty-First Century:**
   a. The Centering in God
   b. The Centering in Jesus
   c. The Centering in the Enscriptured Word
3. **A Tentative Profile of the Baptized-Eucharistic Catholic Christian at the Beginning of the Third Millennium**

1. NON-ORDAINED MINISTRY IN THE TWENTY-FIRST CENTURY

It was theologically exciting to study the structuring of the *Lineamenta* for the Synod of Bishops on the Lay Person in the Church Today. After a few prefatory remarks, the text itself began with the theme of human identity, both personally and socially, and then moved to the identity of the same person as a baptized-eucharistic Christian. From there the text entered into a lengthy discussion of the vocation and mission of the "lay" person in the church today. The structure exhibited the following pattern:

Human Identity
    Christian Identity
        Vocation and Mission as "Lay"

In traditional Roman Catholic documents, one often heard the term "vocation," e.g., a vocation to marriage or a vocation to the priesthood or a vocation to religious life. The phrase "a vocation to lay life" was not used, although there were surely occasions when one spoke of a vocation to a specific lay ministry, such as youth ministry or religious education.

With the emphasis on the common matrix of Christian life arising from one's baptism–confirmation–eucharist, there has been a post-Vatican II tendency, not always adhered to but nonetheless quite evident, to separate any discussion of "lay" from this common matrix of gospel discipleship.

With this move of separation away from the common matrix, the very meaning of "lay" and "laity" has become somewhat unclear. The *Lineamenta,* however, points us in a new and, it seems, better direction. It points us in the direction of vocation. An infant is not said to have a vocation to marriage, or to priesthood or to religious life. We do not say about a newborn that he has a vocation to be a priest or that she has a vocation to be a nun. The very term "vocation" at that beginning level of development makes no sense whatever. Even in the seminary training of the past, when teenagers were "in the seminary," they were there basically to find out whether or not they might be called. In religious life, the time spent in candidacy, in novitiate, or even in temporary vows was intended as a trial-time, to discern whether or not one had a vocation to religious life. Only in the course of one's development did a Christian begin to think about such vocations, and many eventually selected one of these vocations. Some Christians, however, did not select any of them. Such Christians were not married, were not ordained, and were not vowed in a religious community. They were left in a sort of netherworld.

With the discussion in the *Lineamenta* on the vocation to the lay state, a new direction has opened up. The three vocations, priesthood, marriage, and religious life, do not totally divide the Catholic Christian community. Now we are presented with a "fourth" option: to enter into a "lay vocation."

The *Lineamenta* forms a sort of working definition of "vocation":

Vocation is broader than mission because it is composed of both a call to *communio* and a call to mission. *Communio* is the fundamental aspect destined to endure forever. Mission, on the other hand, is a consequence of this call and is limited to an earthly existence (n. 15).

With this generalized description, one could say that baptized-eucharistic Christians themselves have a "vocation." This is a vocation to the Christian way of life, with its sharing, its *communio* in the people of God, and with its mission in the *tria munera* of Jesus. This is the vocation to gospel discipleship, to the common matrix for all Christians. This vocation is not a vocation to "lay" status, and the separation of chapter 2 from chapter 4 in *Lumen gentium* makes this quite clear. It is one thing to be a baptized-eucharistic Christian. It is a different thing to be a "lay" person.

Lay status, then, is a positioning in the church which only an adult or mature Christian selects. He or she decides as an adult to take an active and specific role in the church as a servant-leader, a role which, though traditionally not involving an ordination, needs some form of credentialing or ritual of institution. The reason for this credentialing lies in a vocation as *communio.* The community has a say in the accepting of a given member into a specific mission and ministry, and after the community's discernment process, this is celebrated in a ritual of institution. Lay status, as a result, is not a private issue, but rather a choice made, under the guidance of the Holy Spirit, by an individual, but also a choice made, under the guidance of the same Spirit, by that community in which the lay person will serve. Like priestly vocation, lay vocation is a two-way street, requiring both an individual's assent and the assent of the community.

In this perspective of vocation, a change from Gratian's approach to the structure of the church has clearly been made. For Gratian, the church was divided into cleric/lay. In this post-Vatican II approach, the church is primarily the earthly *communio sanctorum,* an undivided people of God, an undivided community of *christifideles,* a casteless priesthood of all believers. At this fundamental level, terms such as lay and cleric have absolutely no meaning. Some *christifideles* may eventually find their God-given vocation as ordained ministers. Some *christifideles* may eventually find their God-given vocation as non-ordained ministers. Some *christifideles* may eventually find their God-given vocation in neither of these. Thus, ordained/non-ordained, *klerikoi/laikoi,* represent only a small segment of the people of God. Instead of dividing the church community into two distinct groups, the cleric and the lay, ministries are in this view only two smaller groups in a much wider and more complex framework. The following two diagrams indicate the difference between Gratian's view and the vocation view:

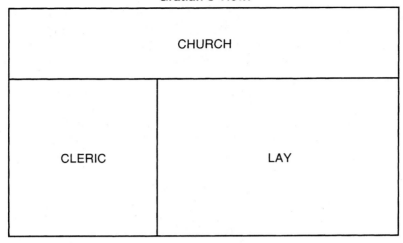

In this view the entire church is divided into only two groups: the leadership group of clergy, which is small, and the majority group of lay, who are to follow the line of leadership determined by the clergy.

Vocation View.

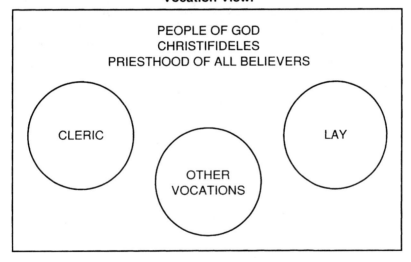

In this view, the church is basically the people of God, in which there are many small segments: the servant-leadership of the ordained, the servant-leadership of the non-ordained, and other segments with a vocation, a communion, and a mission. Even the sum of these smaller groups, however, does not add up to the total people of God.

From an earlier canonical standpoint and from an earlier theological standpoint, this move, namely to see the lay person as one who has a distinct "vocation" in the church, marks a major shift or repositioning in the church, and it is clearly one which does justice to gospel discipleship, the common matrix of all believers. The shift also indicates that a taxative lay/cleric view of the church is not an adequate format so as to grasp the full nature and mystery of the church itself (chapter 1 of *Lumen gentium*). The shift removes the constricting either/or aspect of the lay/cleric perspective, and emphasizes that the common matrix—people of God, *christifideles*, priesthood of all believers—is the essential and fundamental element behind any and every subsequent and derivative description or working definition of a "lay" person or a "clerical" person.

Lay ministry, in this approach, is an ecclesial entity, with its own grace-given vocation, with its own role within a *communio*, and with its own mission, which is ecclesial, even though it involves an extra ecclesial mission and ministry as well. It is a "vocation *in ecclesia*" and must be honored as such. As with every vocation, every ministry and every mission *in ecclesia* (in the church), it has its roots in the call and commission to the *tria munera* by the Lord himself; it also has its communal role within the Christian community, a role which includes the discernment process by the community and a validation by the community through some liturgical service. This vocation to the "lay state" has both a mission within the ecclesial community and from the ecclesial community to the larger world community as well. In many respects it runs parallel, not competitively, with the vocation to ordained servant-leadership ministry, which has, in its own way, all the same characteristics of a vocation just enumerated.

2. A SPIRITUALITY OF THE NON-ORDAINED MINISTRY IN THE TWENTY-FIRST CENTURY

Called by the Lord (*vocatio*), called by and for the community (*communio*), and called to sacramentalize anew the *tria munera* of Jesus himself (*missio* and *ministerium*), the non-ordained person in his or her role either as a gospel disciple or in a specific role as a "lay minister" will be in both cases nourished by the Spirit of Jesus. This nourishment has been traditionally called a spirituality. Some subtle but distinctive changes in this spirituality seem to be already taking place, and they center around one's belief in God, one's belief in Jesus, and one's belief in the enscriptured word of God.

A. THE CENTERING IN GOD

The facile question Do you believe in God or not? is today far too simplistic, and although various church people continue to preach a view of God simply on the basis of belief or disbelief, such a presentation of God in this day and age is rapidly losing credibility. An unreflected view of God, which continues to bolster paternalistic and patriarchal elements of a given church community, has become suspect. An unreflected view of God, which continues to present God favoring a "chosen elite" or a "covenanted few," even though this might have strong overtones in the covenant-theology of the Old Testament, has become suspect. An unreflected view of God, which self-assuredly explains God's plans and intentions for creation and redemption in intricate detail, has become suspect. An unreflected view of God, which includes a God allowing the many holocausts of various peoples, not only those during the Third Reich but other holocausts, such as those in Cambodia and Armenia, in Ethiopia and in Kurdistan, has become suspect. An unreflected view of God, which does not reach out in love and even in preference to the dispossessed and the poor of the world, to the racially others and to the culturally marginated peoples of the created universe, has become suspect. In other words, a domesticated understanding of God, an ecclesiastical understanding of God, a covenanted-nationalistic understanding of God, is, today, less and less acceptable.

The question is not: Does one believe in God or not? Rather, the question has become: What kind of understanding of God is, for the contemporary man or woman, not a rationalized God, but a credible God, i.e. a God in which one can genuinely believe?

A spirituality which takes into critical account the view of God presented in traditional Catholic Christian spiritualities has not yet been fully explicated, but there is a pressing need to "liberate" God from the human-made constraints which disallow God from being sovereignly free. Humans do not tell God how God can be God. Human beings, Christians included, listen, both in the sounds of creation and in the sounds of revelation, for God's own voice telling us what the sovereignty and freedom of God is all about. God is not a Roman Catholic. God is not even a Christian. God is not Jewish. God is not Islamic. Rather, God is the God of all. God is a God in whom women as well as men can believe. God is a God in whom the marginated and poor, as well as the comfortable citizens, can believe. Indeed, only that understanding of God which sees God as preferentially the God of the poor, the God of the marginated, the God of the second-rate, will stir up any embers of human faith.

This approach to a credible God who loves the entire world and who loves each and every part of creation, above all human creation, is revealed throughout this wide canvas of creation. When a given religious leadership attempts to speak *in persona Dei,* such statements will be tested against a creation which also speaks *in persona Dei.* Such statements will be tested against the voice of the Spirit which enters into the very heart and conscience of each and every human person, a voice that also speaks *in persona Dei.* Women as well as men can speak *in persona Dei,* and sometimes more clearly as well. The marginated and poor speak *in persona Dei,* and most of the time in a very loud and powerful way. Only a spirituality which honors the Spirit of God in all will be a spirituality of the third millennium.

B. A CENTERING IN JESUS

For a Christian the Jesus-event is central, and as Vatican II tells us, it is in the humanness of Jesus that we begin to see the divineness of God. Jesus alone is *lumen gentium,* the light in which we begin to see the very meaning of God and the meaning of God's created world. There is, for a Christian, no other fundamental *lumen mundi* or *lumen gentium* outside of Jesus. For this reason, a spirituality of the twenty-first century will be much more focused on the humanness of Jesus; it will study and restudy the ways in which Jesus led a human life, and it will find in Jesus' own human responses models for the human responses of the twenty-first century. Various forms of liberation theology have tended to locate their point of departure precisely in the historical Jesus: in his message, in his mission, in his ministry, in his self-identity. Rather than a one-sided christology from above, there has developed a christology from below which dialectically relates to a christology from above.

This christological centering takes seriously the official and solemn teaching of Chalcedon, in which one finds the parallel passages of belief in Jesus:

Truly God	Truly human
Homoousios with God	*Homoousios* with us
Perfect in godliness	Perfect in humanness
Born of the Father	Born of Mary

That Jesus was fully human is as much a dogma of Christian faith as the dogma that Jesus was fully divine. The human aspect of Jesus should not be passed over quickly as one rushes to assert that Jesus was truly God. It is this humanness of the christological dogma which will energize a twenty-first century spirituality, in ways which have at times been forgotten in the rather one-sided christology-from-above models of the past few centuries. Jesus' message, especially that of the kingdom of God, will become a major nourishing factor for such a spirituality. The kingdom of God, however, is not co-extensive with the church, and this will make this third millennium spirituality, perhaps, less ecclesiastical and more universal. Jesus' message which centers so much on the good news preached to the anawim, the dispossessed, the poor, the marginated, those without power and clout, whether in the tidy areas of proper society or the tidy areas of proper churchness, will also be a major nourishing element of this spirituality. The socio-political structures of government as well as the inner-church structures of one's denomination will be judged on the basis of their openness to the presence of God's kingdom throughout such structures, and on the basis of their compassion and concern for the marginated. A church leadership which arrogates to itself the defining of the limits of the kingdom will be seen as a church leadership which has not heard the length and depth, the height and breadth of the message of Jesus. A church leadership, whose very structures give rise to a dispossessed and a marginated group, will be seen as a church leadership which has not heard the total range of the message of Jesus. "Church, what do you say of yourself?"—the very question behind the deliberations of Vatican II—will be viewed critically in the very light which the bishops at Vatican II emphasized, namely Jesus, the *lumen gentium.* Under the light of Jesus, *sub lumine gentium,* will the third millennium Christian continue to interpret church and world, *regnum et sacerdotium.* Christology in an ever increasing way will be seen as the basis and substance of ecclesiology. Spirituality will, as a consequence, become more and more christological and less narrowly ecclesiastical.

In this light of christology, one will hopefully find a credible God, a God in whom one might believe: namely, the God whom Jesus called "Father," "Abba." This dim and mysterious view of a credible God will be seen ever more clearly as one studies the compassion of a human Jesus, as he healed, as he proclaimed salvation to sinners, as he spoke in parables to struggling husbands and wives, mothers and fathers. This dim and mysterious view of a credible God will be seen ever more clearly as one meditates on the dying of the human Jesus and all that such dying means for the life of a human being. This dim and mysterious view of a credible God will be seen ever more clearly as one ponders on the meaning of risen life, with its promise and hope, its joy and peace, not simply for oneself but for the world at large. For a Christian and for his or her spirituality, only the kind of God that one sees at work in the human Jesus will be a credible God.

C. CENTERING IN THE ENSCRIPTURED WORD

In the post-Vatican II era, Roman Catholic Christians have begun to rediscover the enscriptured word. This is certainly one of the more dramatic aspects of post-Vatican II Catholic Christianity. In small *communidades de base* and in neighborhood groups of men and women who gather to read the enscriptured word, to pray the enscriptured word, and to let the enscriptured word activate their daily lives, Catholic Christians continue to discover a major source of nourishment for their spiritual lives. More and more, these sharing the word sessions take place not with clerical leadership, but with the leadership of God's own Holy Spirit.

In the many reform movements from 1000 to 1600, it was the reading and rereading of the enscriptured word which nourished the longing for gospel discipleship. Such a reality is taking place today in many new forms, and there results a new reformation both of life and of person. Gospel discipleship has become, once again, a powerful spiritual magnet, and as one attempts to put into personal and social practice the words of the gospels, one is putting into personal and social practice the word of the gospel. This enfleshing anew of the enscriptured word is a major form of today's Pentecost. Pentecost was the sending of the Spirit, the enspiritualizing of the primitive Jesus community, and such a divine activity is taking place today as Christians prayerfully read and prayerfully hear the enscriptured word of God.

There is an attraction to this communal reading of scripture, for it begins to meet a need which Christianity itself, but in strong ways Roman Catholic Christianity in particular, has tended to disallow: namely, the formation of home liturgy. In the structuring of the church, liturgy has generally been placed in the domain of the clergy and in the milieu of the church building. All the official sacraments, except in emergency situations, were channeled into clerically regulated church moments. Church leadership approved only certain forms of para-liturgical prayer, and although these were fostered and encouraged, such encouragement was extended to them only in secondary ways. Primary encouragement was directed to the liturgical celebrations held in the church and under the aegis of clerical leadership. The contemporary reading of the word of God in small communities, in faith-sharing groups, has become a form of home liturgy. In many ways it has become the "rosary" of the present era. Such prayerful and communal readings play and will continue to play a major role in the spirituality of the people of God, the *christifidelis,* the priesthood of all believers.

These are but three of the main strands of contemporary spirituality. These three issues, however, seem to be at the very roots not only of a vocational "lay" spirituality, but of a spirituality for the entire people of God. Spirituality is rooted in one's identity, and there are three root-dimensions in one's personal identity. The first stems from one's humanity itself. What does it mean to be alive in the world as a human person?

Alive with others in a co-human world? These human roots are both individual and relational; they are both personal and familial; they are both singular and cultural. One's "spirit" drinks heavily from these roots of humanity. In this regard, P. Fransen wrote: "The more intensive is our humanization, the more radical is our divinization; and the more total our divinization, the more profound is our humanization."[1] Human life itself is a major root of personal identity and personal spirituality.

Secondly, our identity as a Christian is rooted in gospel discipleship, the common matrix of all believers. Our life as part of the people of God, as a *christifidelis,* as a member of the priesthood of all believers, provides us with our personal identity. What one's baptism, confirmation, and eucharist give to a person is a continuous source of personal nourishment. The sharing in the *tria munera* of Jesus himself becomes a part of our personal Christian identity. The way in which a Christian, on a day to day basis, is teacher/preacher, is sanctifier, is leader, both within the church community and within the wider cultural community, shapes and forms one's identity and one's spirituality.

Thirdly, but only in this tertiary position, can one speak of an identity as an "ordained servant-leader," as a "vowed religious," as a "sacramentalized husband or wife," as a "sacramentalized mother or father," as a "vocational lay minister." Too often it is these strands alone which one claims as one's personal identity, disregarding the identity as a human being and the identity as a gospel disciple. When this happens, with either an ordained person, a vowed religious person, or a person in a specific lay ministry, the identity of an individual is skewed and narrowly defined. When this happens, one often sees neither a richly human person nor a richly gospel person, but an impoverished "ecclesiocrat."

Twenty-first century spirituality has already begun to sing the praises of human identity and gospel identity, and only when these two strong melodies are heard can one also begin to hear the counterpuntal melody of servant-ministry in any of its varied forms.

3. A PROFILE OF THE BAPTIZED CATHOLIC CHRISTIAN AT THE BEGINNING OF THE THIRD MILLENNIUM

The inward rush of the tide is still with the Christian communities at the beginning of the third millennium. The last one thousand years have seen a steady inward flow, with moments of explosive surge as well. The shape of the coastline has been sharply redefined, with no possibility of rearranging it into the contours it once had. Nor can it be claimed that the inward tide has spent itself and a changing of the tide outward has begun.

In the Roman Catholic Church there are some Christians, including some who are in clerical ministries and some who are in lay ministries, who view this rearrangement not as a benefit but as a disruptive moment. In their view the bishops at Vatican II did indeed set solid goals, but men and women, after Vatican II, have attempted to run too far with these same goals and have instead run amok. Many of these people are in highly influential leadership positions, and either they themselves or others with similar views will remain a part of the Roman Catholic profile at the beginning of the third millennium.

A rarely cited letter of John Paul II to Cardinal Ratzinger offers an important appreciation for this segment of the Christian profile:

> There have appeared tendencies which create a certain difficulty in putting the council into practice. One of these tendencies is characterized by a desire for changes which are not always in harmony with the teaching and spirit of Vatican II, even though they seek to appeal to the council. These changes claim to express progress, and so this tendency is given the name "progressivism."

> The opposite tendency, which is usually called "conservatism" or "integralism," stops at the past itself, without taking into account the correct aspiration toward the future which manifested itself precisely in the work of Vatican II.

> While the former tendency seems to recognize the correctness of what is new, the latter sees correctness only in what is "ancient," considering it synonymous with tradition.[2]

John Paul II goes on to say that the council unleashed an aspiration for renewal, and in the very word "renewal" there is included something "new," an element of "novelty." Excess might take place, but an opposition to the "new" can also lead to "another deviation" which opposes growth in the church. What John Paul II wants to urge is, of course, a balance. There is clearly room for a conservative stance in any profile of Christian men and women, but this must be a balanced conservative stance, not a one-sided, obstinate, and therefore deviant conservatism.

The "progressive" Christian must evidence a similar balance, for part of the wonder and mystery of the Christian community is its rootage and origin, and its long, historical development. The balance is found in the sorting out of tradition and traditions. For such a task of sorting out criteria are needed, and fundamental to all criteria are:

a. christology;

b. gospel discipleship.

These form the basic hermeneutic for a determination of what might be tradition and what might be traditions. Both christology and a study of gospel discipleship, however, employ a number of other auxiliary but necessary hermeneutical methods, many of which one finds in both biblical and historical scholarship. Nonetheless, both a solidly established christology and a solidly established scriptural understanding of gospel discipleship remain the primary tasks for those who wish to be credible disciples of Jesus at the beginning of the third millennium.

A third millennium disciple of Christ, whether of conservative or progressive stance, will, in my view, evidence the following characteristics:

1. An untiring effort to clarify the meaning of a God who is creator of all, and therefore loves each and every human person in an equal way.

2. An untiring effort to clarify the meaning of the human Jesus: his message, his ministry, his identity and his life. This will focus on the issue of "God's reign" which is the center of Jesus' message and ministry, and also on the issue of the gospel message of salvation for the poor, the marginated, and the dispossessed. This kingdom will not be seen as co-extensive with the church, and the marginated will include not only those in society who are on the edges, but also those in the church itself who are likewise considered on the edges. Since the gospel says that such marginated people will enter the kingdom ahead of the acceptable others, third millennium Christians will severely question the social and ecclesial leadership by the "acceptable others."

3. The third millennium Christian will take at face-value the equality of all human beings, regardless of gender, ethnicity, social status, or religious involvement. Christian communities which are not attuned to the fundamental equality and dignity of each and every human person will be seen as anti-gospel.

4. Given the growing ecumenical movement, Roman Catholic third millennium Christians will continue to raise serious questions on the absoluteness of the Roman Catholic claim. Not only will some of these Roman Catholic Christians raise questions, but in ecclesial life, they will as well, either permanently or from time to time, find "church" within non-Roman-Catholic communities.

5. Third millennium Christians will not accept at face value statements made by clerical leadership which state that the "lay person" has

come of age, that the post-Vatican II period of church history is a major moment for the "lay person."

> In the modern era, the great state of the reawakening of the laity's responsibility to the mission of the church has to a great extent coincided historically with the rapid pace of scientific progress, the development of democratic culture and the emergence of new social problems resulting from the expansion of an urban-industrial civilization.[3]

Such a statement does not take into account that for centuries a form of church leadership has not encouraged the "lay person" to be such an active member of the church. To place all the reasons in external, historical factors and to pass over in silence the internal suppression of the "lay person" in the structuring of the church is no longer acceptable.

6. Such a position as described in n. 5 indicates that the baptized-eucharistic Christian cannot be addressed as a "child." No church leader should use such a phrase as "My sons and daughters." The baptized-eucharistic Christian is the primary disciple in the church, is mature enough to be entrusted by none other than the Lord himself with the *tria munera,* and is consequently able to make decisions in the social order, in the moral order, and in the spiritual order. These decisions are made in virtue of *communio,* of course, but the third millennium Christian sees himself or herself as part and parcel of the very process whereby a community called church arrives as such decisions, and not simply as the recipient of decisions made by others.

7. The third millennium Christian will search out better ways to understand the church within this pluralistic world. The continued struggle to maintain a *regnum et sacerdotium* momentum will be seen as anachronistic. Rather, the very term *sacerdotium* will be replaced by the term *ecclesia,* "people of God," and the very term *regnum* will be replaced by the term "a pluralistic world." It is no longer a question of a *sacerdotium* standing over and against a *regnum,* but rather a community called church within a larger community called a pluralistic world.

8. Above all else, however, the third millennium Christian will return to the gospels again and again, seeking to establish in his or her personal and social life the very meaning of gospel discipleship. If Jesus is indeed the *lumen gentium,* metaphorically the mystery of the sun, then each third millennium Christian will attempt to be, metaphorically, part of the mystery of the moon. Only if and when he or she reflects Jesus, at whatever level the person might be either in the church or in society at large, will he or she be truly church. Whenever this mystery of the moon

begins to wane during this same third millennium, then the church and those in the church who cause this waning will be seen as, and in reality be, non-church. When, however, this mystery of the moon begins to wax during this third millennium, then the church and whoever in the church brings about this waxing phase will be seen as, and indeed be, the church. Gospel discipleship is that wonderful sharing in the life of God. As Jesus once said: "The one who sees me sees God as well." Discipleship of Jesus means: "Anyone who sees a credible disciple of Jesus sees Jesus as well, which can only mean that one begins to see in such an encounter the contours of a credible God."

Notes

1. The First Point of Departure: The Origin and Significance of the Terms, Lay/Cleric, in the Early Christian Churches

1. Y. Congar, *Jalons pour une théologie du laïcat* (Paris: Unam Sanctam, 1953); cf. also idem, *Sacerdoce et laïcat devant leurs tâches d'évangélisation* (Paris: Unam Sanctam, 1962).

2. Cf. Wolfgang Nauck, "Probleme des frühchristlichen Amtsverständnisses," *Zeitschrift für die neutestamentliche Wissenschaft,* 48 (1957) pp. 200–220.

3. W. Foerster, "Kleros ktl," *TWNT;* ET: *Theological Dictionary of the New Testament,* ed. G. Kittel and G. Friedrich (Grand Rapids: Eerdmans, 1964–1976) v. 3, pp. 758ff.

4. Foerster, op. cit., p. 761.

5. For the deeper meaning of this entire pericope, and particularly the use of Psalm 22:16–18, cf. D. Senior, *The Passion of Jesus in the Gospel of Matthew* (Wilmington: M. Glazier, 1985) pp. 129–130.

6. E. Haenchen, *Die Apostelgeschichte* (Göttingen: Vandenhoeck & Ruprecht, 1965) p. 121. Such a list of names might indicate that the pericope in Acts recounts an historical event. This might not be the case. Luke may be presenting a non-historical description in historical garb. The historicity/non-historicity of the passage should not be center stage; rather, what should be center stage is the fact that the pericope includes women as well as men. Cf. also K. Schäfer, *Gemeinde als "Bruderschaft": Ein Beitrag zum Kirchenverständnis des Paulus* (P. Lang: Frankfurt am M., 1989) pp. 21–26 "adelphos und adelphe bei Paulus."

7. The Jerusalem Bible at this verse notes: Brothers = "The term for Christians, usually the laity as distinct from apostles and elders." There is

610

absolutely nothing, either in the text or the context, to warrant such a comment. By "brothers" the author appears to mean all of those assembled. To call the brothers "laity" is rampant eisegesis. In the text, the term "brothers" refers to the eleven as well, but the Jerusalem Bible implies that the eleven were not "lay." Haenchen believes that the women were not included in this title of address, which may or may not be the case. Cf. also J. Beutler, "Adelphos," *Exegetisches Wörterbuch zum Neuen Testament*, ed. by H. Balz and G. Schneider, v. I (Stuttgart: Kohlhammer, 1980), 67–72.

8. Haenchen, op. cit., p. 125.

9. This is the preferred reading; some manuscripts, namely, the Sinaiticus, the Ephraemi Rescriptus (C^e), the codex at Basel (E) and a few numbered uncials use the word "kleros" rather than "topos." Again, the one term (later) clarifies the meaning of the other.

10. Foerster, op. cit., mentions that in 67 A.D. the Zealots chose a new high priest by lot, appealing to an ancient tradition. Josephus and Philo also attest to this method of determining such candidates.

11. Cf. Nauck, op. cit., p. 212. For Hippolytus, cf. *Apostolic Tradition* III, 5.

12. Ibid., pp. 212–213.

13. Cf. K. Osborne, *Priesthood* (N.Y.: Paulist, 1989) pp. 42–44.

14. The material is vast on this particular subject: cf. O. Giacchi, *Lo Stato laico. Formazione e sviluppo dell'idea e delle sue attuazioni* (Milan: A. Giuffrè, 1947).

15. Y. Congar, *Jalons pour une théologie du laïcat;* idem, *Sacerdoce et laïcat devant leurs tâches d'évangélisation.* Cf. also E. Lanne, "Le laïcat dans l'Église ancienne," *Verbum Caro* 18 (1964) pp. 105–126.

16. Congar, *Jalons pour une théologie du laïcat,* p. 19: "Notre mot 'laïc' se rattache donc à un mot qui dans le langage juif, puis chrétien, désignait proprement le peuple consacré par opposition aux peuple profanes: nuance qui a été présente aux esprits, là du moins où l'on s'exprimait en grec, pendant les quatre premiers siècles ou même davantage."

17. I. de la Potterie, "L'Origine et le sens primitiv du mot 'laïc'," *Nouvelle Revue Théologique,* 80 (1958) pp. 840–853.

18. J.B. Bauer, "Die Wortgeschichte von 'Laicus'," *Zeitschrift für Katholische Theologie,* 81 (1959) 224–228. Bauer emphasizes that *laikos* is always (*immer*) related to cult in the passages from Aquila Symmachus and Theodotion (p. 224). Bauer also corrects de la Potterie's citations from Preisigke. Bauer stresses the difference between Egyptian citizens and the "others," *die Behörde* (p. 226).

19. Cf. de la Potterie and S. Lyonnet, *La vie selon L'Esprit* (Paris, 1965).

20. F. Wulf, "Über die Herkunft und den ursprünglichen Sinn des Wortes 'Laie'," *Geist und Leben*, v. 32 (1959) pp. 61–63.

21. A. Barruffo, "Il significato cristiano della parole 'laico'," *La Civiltà Cattolica*, 113/2 (1962) pp. 157–160.

22. M. Jourjon, "Les premiers emplois du mot laïc dans la littérature patristique," *Lumière et Vie* (1963) 37–42. Cf. also G.H. Williams, "The Role of the Layman in the Ancient Church," *Greek, Roman and Byzantine Studies*, 1 (1958) 9–42; W.H.C. Frend, "The Church of the Roman Empire, 313–600," *The Layman in Christian History* (London, 1963) 28–56; E. Lanne, "Le laïcat dans l'Église ancienne," *Verbum Caro, 18* (1964) 105–126. Earlier studies on the laity include: P. Dabin, *L'Apostolat laïque* (1933); followed by *Le sacerdoce royal des fidèles dans les livres saints* (Gembloux: J. Ducolot, 1940) and *Le sacerdoce royal des fidèles dans la tradition ancienne et moderne* (Brussels: L'Édition universelle, 1950); E. Niebecker, *Das allgemeine Priestertum der Gläubigen* (Paderborn, 1936); N. Rocholl, *Vom Laienpriestertum* (Paderborn, 1940); E. Rösser, *Die Stellung der Laien in der Kirche nach dem kanonischen Recht* (Würzburg, 1949); B. Schultze, "Die byzantinisch-slawische Theologie über den Dienst der Laien in der Kirche," *Ostkirchliche Studien* V (1956) 243 ff.

23. J. Hervada, "La definición nominal del laico (Etimologia y uso primitivo)," *Ius Canonicum* v. 8 (1968) pp. 471–533. This was reprinted in *Tres estudios sobre el uso del término laico* (Pamplona: Universidad de Navarra, 1973).

24. L. Pizzolato, "Laicità e laici nel cristianesimo primitivo," *Laicità, problemi e prospettive, Atti del XLVII corso di aggiornamento culturale dell'Università Cattolica* (Milan: Vita e Pensiero, 1977) pp. 57–83; G. Picasso, "La laicità nel medioevo," ibid. pp. 84–99.

25. Pizzolato, op. cit., p. 58.

26. G. Wingren, "Der Begriff 'Laie'," *Von Amt des Laien in Kirche und Theologie*, ed. H. Schrörer and G. Müller (Berlin: Walter de Gruyer, 1982) pp. 3–16.

27. G. Magnani, "Does the So-Called Theology of the Laity Possess a Theological Status?" *Vatican II: Assessment and Perspectives* (N.Y.: Paulist Press, 1988) v. I, pp. 568–633. Cf. P. Bonet, "The *Christifidelis* Restored to His Role as Human Protagonist in the Church," ibid., pp. 540–567.

28. Magnani, op. cit., p. 583; cf. also p. 585, n. 8.

29. A. Faivre, *Les laïcs aux origines de l'Église* (Paris: Le Centurion, 1984).

30. Ibid., p. 38.

31. J. Chapa, "Sobre la Relación: *Laos - Laikos*," *La Misión de Laico*

en la Iglesia y en el Mundo, ed. by A. Sarmiento, T. Rincon, J.-M. Yanguas, A. Quiros (Pamplona: Ediciones Universidad de Navarra, 1987), pp. 197–212.

32. H. Strathmann and R. Meyer, *TWNT,* (ET) v. 4, pp. 29–57.

33. Ibid., p. 57.

34. F. Preisigke, *Fachwörter der öffentlichen Verwaltungsdienstes Ägyptens in den griechischen Papyrusurkunden* (Göttingen: Vandenhoeck und Ruprecht, 1915), p. 116.

35. Cf. N. Lewis, *Life in Egypt Under Roman Rule* (Oxford: Oxford Univ. Press, 1983) p. 90.

36. F. Preisigke, *Wörterbuch der griechischen Papyrusurkunden* (Berlin: Selbstverlag der Erben, 1927), c. 2, "Laikos, den ägyptischen Zivilisten betreffend (im Ggs zum kgl Beamten, Lebensträger, Staatspächter usw)." Notice that Preisigke places Egyptian citizenship in the main part of his sentence, and the state of dependence in parentheses. Preisigke says the same thing in *Griechische Papyrus,* v. I (Leipzig: J.C. Hinrichs'che Buchhandlung, 1912) p. 39 note 4. "Das *laikos* bezieht sich auf die ägyptischen Zivilpersonen, im Gegensatze zu den kgl. Lehensträgern, kgl. Pächtern usw." Only Egyptians are called *laikoi.* This is the basis for its use; secondarily, in opposition to the Egyptian priestly and royal class, etc. The papyri which are cited for this position are: Lille, 10, 4, 7; Strassburg, 93, 4; Zenon 59394, 13, 18; BGU 1053 II, 10 (Ia). Cf. also P.W. Pestman, *Greek and Demotic Texts from the Zenon Archive* (Leiden: E.J. Brill, 1980) p. 159. It is noteworthy that in F. Preisigke's *Wörterbuch der griechischen Papyrusurkunden* (Berlin: Selbstvertrag der Erben, 1925), v. 1, under *klerikos,* cc. 802–807, there is no mention of *laikos.* The usage in the many Greek texts he cites refer to (1) Los, Verlosung, Auslosung (a casting of dice, a raffle); (2) Das durch das Los Zugefallene, der Anteil, z.b. (a) Erbgut, Erbstück; and (b) connected to the Greek word *meris;* (3) Lehenland, and from the Roman times on, Ackerstück, Ackergut, Grundstück.

37. Chapa, op. cit., p. 201 attempts to correlate the use of the term *laos* to an authority, and as a consequence sees in the term *laos* a sense of superiority/inferiority. *Laos,* when used of the Israelites, has an authority referent: Yahweh; *Laos,* when used of the general "mass" of people, has an authority referent: the leader or the priest. In the OT, the term *laos* is a translation, usually, of *'am,* not *le'om* (*ethnos*). The Israelites were called by Yahweh out of a scattered and not necessarily homogenous group to be a people (*'am* = *laos*). In contrast, the human authority figure or priest does not, by his or her call, form a people. His argument: "En ambos casos *laos* mantiene vigente su sentido de clase diferenciada de la autoridad," does not appear to be logical and cogent.

38. Cf. also C.D. Buck and W. Peterson, *A Reverse Index of Greek Nouns and Adjectives* (Chicago: University of Chicago Press, 1940) pp. 638–677 for endings in "kos-kon." Among these endings is, of course, *ikos,* an ending which both de la Potterie and Magnani emphasize as meaning "belonging to." In this lengthy section from Buck and Peterson, there are hundreds of Greek words listed, which end in *ikos,* most of them adjectives. It would, however, be difficult to say that the majority of them indicate a "belonging to" inference, which is precisely de la Potterie's and Magnani's argument. Cf. also P. Chantraine, "Le suffixe grec '-ikos'." *Études sur le vocabulaire grec* (Paris, 1956) pp. 97–171. J. Chapa relies heavily on Chantraine.

39. Cf. F. Field, *Origenis Hexaplorum quae supersunt* (Oxford, 1875). Cf. Chapa, op. cit., pp. 206–207.

40. Cf. A. Tkacik, Ezekiel, *The Jerome Biblical Commentary* [henceforth *JBC*] (Englewood Cliffs: Prentice Hall, 1968) [21:92].

41. Ibid., [21:54].

42. The conclusions which Francisco Varo draws from the Acts of the Apostles, cf. "Formulas Determinantes de la Condición Laical en los Hechos de los Apóstoles," *La Misión del Laico en la Iglesia y en el Mundo,* pp. 247–267, though interesting, remain very conjectural. Varo notes that there are sixty-two named individuals in Acts who are Christians. Twenty-four of these are presented with details of birth, family, geography and profession. Varo investigates all twenty-four and notices that with some there is a "call" to ministry; with the remainder, there is no call, but a clear statement that they continued to ply their trade. On this basis, Varo sees the "cleric" and the "lay" and even deduces a scriptural basis for lay/cleric from this distinction between those who went back to their trades and those who did not; namely, "[una] distinction específica entre el servicio a la communidad eclesial (la Jerarquía y sus colaboradores) y otros que tienen como función específica impregnar de espíritu cristiano la sociedad en la que viven, siendo uno más de los ciudadanos corrientes, y santificar el trabajo ordinario en medio del mundo (los laicos)" (p. 266). These conclusions seem to be more than the texts in Acts can truly bear.

43. Cf. J. Galot, *Theology of the Priesthood* (San Francisco: Ignatius Press, 1984) trans. R. Balducelli; G. Martelet, *Deux mille ans d'église en question* (Paris: Les Éditions du Cerf, 1984) v. I; M. Guerra, "La 'plebs' y los 'ordines' de la sociedad romana y sus traspaso al pueblo cristiano," *Teología del sacerdocio,* 4 (1972) 255–293.

44. Cf. Osborne, *Priesthood,* pp. 70–75.

45. Cf. A.H.M. Jones, "The Social Background of the Struggle between Paganism and Christianity," *The Conflict between Paganism and*

Christianity in the Fourth Century (Oxford: Oxford Univ. Press, 1963) ed. A. Momigliano, pp. 16–37; Jones points out that as the Roman empire moved into the third and fourth centuries, senators were drawn not merely from aristocratic and blue-blood lines, but from the army, the merchant class, and even from the peasantry. So, too, *episkopoi* came from a variety of classes and were classified as an *ordo.*

46. Cf. St. W.J. Teeuwen, *Sprachlicher Bedeutungswandel bei Tertullian* (Paderborn: F. Schöningh, 1926) p. 69: "Ordo hieß im römischen Recht 'der Stand, die Klasse', speziell aber 'der Senatorenstand'. In der christlichen Sprache wurde das Wort auf die verschiedenen kirchlichen Körperschaften angewendet, so z.B. auf den 'ordo viduarum', . . . Besonders wurde mit diesem Ausdruck, nach Analogie von 'ordo senatorius', der 'ordo ecclesiae', 'ordo ecclesiasticus', 'ordo sacerdotalis' bezeichnet. d.h., die geistliche Obrigkeit den Laien gegenüber: 'Differentiam inter ordinem et plebem constituit ecclesiae auctoritas' (*De. Cast.* 7)."

47. T. O'Meara, "Order and Ordination," *The New Dictionary of Theology,* ed. J. Komonchak, M. Collins, D. Lane (Wilmington: M. Glazier, 1987) p. 724.

48. Ibid.

49. Ibid.

50. Ibid., pp. 724–725.

51. B.D. Dupuy, "Theologie der kirchlichen Ämter," *Mysterium Salutis* 4/2 (Einsiedeln: Benziger, 1973) p. 505. Cf. also the remark of J. Magne, *Tradition apostolique sur les charismes et diataxeis des saints apôtres* (Paris: Laballery et Cie, 1975): "L'analyse du statut de l'ordination épiscopale, qu'à cause de sa difficulté nous avons réservée pour la fin, nous fera remonter à une époque et à une Église où le peuple chrétien non seulement élisait son évêque, mais le consacrait par une imposition des mains silencieuse, en sorte qu'on peut se demander si ce sont bien les Apôtres qui ont institué les évêques, ou si ce ne seraient pas plutôt les évêques, les presbytres, les prophètes, les docteurs et les évangélistes qui auraient imaginé les Apôtres" (p. 10).

52. For further discussion of this issue, cf. K. Osborne, "The Meaning of Lay, Laity, and Lay Ministry in the Christian Theology of Church," *Antonianum,* 53 (1988) 227–258.

53. Cf. Gérard Philips, *La Chiesa e il suo mistero* (Milan: Ed. Jaca Book, 1975); cf. F. Klostermann, "The Laity," *Dogmatic Constitution on the Church,* in *Commentary on the Documents of Vatican II,* v. 1, (N.Y.: Herder and Herder, 1967) pp. 231–236.

54. This section on Jesus as the foundational sacrament and the basis of all Christian ministry and mission is treated in detail in Osborne, *Priesthood,* pp. 3–29.

55. J. Galot, "Christ: Revealer, Founder of the Church and Source of Ecclesial Life," *Vatican II: Assessment and Perspectives,* v. I, pp. 385–406.

56. Ibid., p. 388.

57. Ibid., p. 393.

58. Ibid., pp. 393–400. Galot presents a very conservative picture of the development of the various ministries in the New Testament. His position on this matter has been considered in the book *Priesthood.*

59. G. Philips, *La Chiesa e il suo mistero,* pp. 136–139.

60. Ibid., p. 138: "Non si è voluto evitare il problema della terminologia. La lunga lista delle expressioni citate potrebbe dare l'impressione che i teologi s'abbandonano a discussioni oziose. Ma la questione del vocabolario, a cui abbiamodedicato tanto spazio, presentava l'occasione di describere più da vicino il significato dogmatico della vocazione cristiana, e di analizzarlo a fondo. Solo dopo matura riflessione il Concilio ha deciso di scegliere i termini che se avvicinano di più alla Rivelazione, cioè el sacerdozio commune, edificato sulla base del battesimo [one might add eucharist], e il sacerdozio ministeriale o gerarchico, fondato sull'ordinazione sacramentale in vista del servizio organizzato."

61. Cf. Osborne, *Priesthood,* pp. 3–29.

2. The Second Point of Departure: The Use of Lay/Cleric in Roman Catholic Canon Law

1. Cf. Innocent III, *Cum contingat* (1210); Hugh of St. Victor, *De sacramentis* II, 3, c. 1, 2, 3, 4; S. Many, *Praelectiones de Sacra Ordinatione* (Paris: Letouzey et Ané, 1905) pp. 37–40.

2. Cf. Many, op. cit., pp. 40–44.

3. Trent did not settle the issues which divided the various schools. The issue of the sacramentality of minor orders was not specifically confronted by Trent, with the result that their statements left the theological discussion on this matter an open one.

4. The canon from the code of 1917 is patently inaccurate, and this is one of the reasons why it has been revised. Canon law, however, is not a source of theology. The laws in a code embody a pre-existing theology; the laws do not establish a theology. In this way, one could say that the theological validity of each and every canon depends not on its own position within a code, but on the theological arguments which stand behind the various canons. To cite canon law as though such a citing provides in itself conclusive theological evidence for a given position is a misuse of canon law. This present canon, 107, is a case in point.

5. P. Wernz - P. Vidal, *Ius Canonicum* (Rome: Gregorian Univ., 1928,

2^{ed}) v. II, "De Personis," p. 58. The authors devote twenty pages, pp. 46–66, to this topic of lay/cleric.

6. Ibid., p. 58. The exception, which the authors allude to, is to the celebrated case of a lay person elected to the papacy. By his election, he has immediately supreme jurisdiction over the entire church, even though he has not yet been ordained. There are many disputed issues on this "case" by canonists.

7. Ibid., p. 59: "... neque ullam potestatem sacrificandi et sanctificandi, docendi et regendi in Ecclesia Catholica habeat."

8. A. Ledesma, *La condición jurídica del laico del C.I.C., al Vaticano II* (Pamplona, 1972) p. 181, cited by J. Fornes, "El Laico en el ordenamiento canónico (del código de 1917 al código de 1983)," *La Misión del Laico en la Iglesia y en el Mundo* (Pamplona: Ediciones Universidad de Navarra, 1987) ed. A. Sarmiento, T. Tincon, J.-M. Yanguas, A. Quiros, p. 589.

9. Fornes, op. cit., p. 590: "Sin embargo, el panorama cambió radicalmente, como es bien sabido, con el Vaticano II." Cf. also, P. Rodriguez, "La Identidad Teológica del Laico," *La Misión del Laico en la Iglesia y en el Mundo,* pp. 71–111, esp. pp. 82–85.

10. *Code of Canon Law: Text and Commentary* (N.Y.: Paulist Press, 1985).

11. Ibid., p. 131. J. Corriden authored most of this section of the commentary.

12. Ibid.

13. Ibid.

14. Cf. the articles of both Fornes and Rodriguez, which analyze the new code from the standpoint of the documents of Vatican II. Fornes particularly notes the two documents: *LG* and *AA*. In the same volume, the articles by Miguel Facäo "La Noción del Laico en el Concilio Vaticano II," pp. 309–316; by A. Viana "Algunos Aspectos de la Doctrina del Concilio Vaticano II sobre los Laicos," pp. 317–323; by M.B. Plans, "La Misión Específica de las Laicos: Estudio de los Términos en los Documentos del Concilio Vaticano II," pp. 325–335, present the background for this change in the new code.

15. *Code of Canon Law: Text and Commentary,* p. 132.

16. Cf. J. Komonchak, "Clergy, Laity, and the Church's Mission in the World," *The Jurist,* 41 (1981) 422–447.

17. *Code of Canon Law: Text and Commentary,* p. 133.

18. Many of the articles in *La Mision del Laico en la Iglesia y en el Mundo* take the stand that the secular character of the lay person is the specific quality of "lay." Cf. e.g. A. Maroza, "Apostolado Laical Individual," "Es un apostolado secular. Su nota específica frente al apostolado de

los religiosos viene dar pro su modo de ser en la Iglesia, por su modo de ser Iglesia: 'viviendo en el siglo, es decir, en todos y cada uno de los deberes u ocupaciones del mundo, y en las condiciones ordinarias de la vida familiar y social con los que su existencia "quasi contextitur" (p. 666).

3. The Third Point of Departure: The Meaning of Discipleship in the New Testament Writings

1. The eleven times in which the word "kleros" appears in the NT do not remotely refer to what a later Christian community will designate by the term "cleric."

2. D. Harrington, "The Gospel according to Mark," *The New Jerome Biblical Commentary* (Englewood Cliffs, N.J.: Prentice-Hall, 1990), 41:4. Hereafter cited as *NJBC*.

3. Ibid.

4. Ibid.

5. Ibid.

6. Ibid.

7. Cf. G Theißen, *Lokalkolorit und Zeitgeschichte in den Evangelien: Ein Beitrag zur Geschichte der synoptischen Tradition* (Göttingen: Vandenhoeck und Ruprecht, 1989) pp. 246–261. "Milieukolorit, traditionsgeschichtlicher Ort, geographische Angaben lassen sich eher verständlich machen, wenn man es im südlichen Teil Syriens entstanden sein läßt—in jenem Teil, der später offiziell 'Syrophönikien' gennant wurde" (p. 261). Cf. also p. 270.

8. On this subject, cf. R. Brown, "The Twelve and the Apostolate," *NJBC*, 81:135–157.

9. Ibid., 81:137. Cf. also J. P. Meier, "Jesus," *NJBC*, 78:26.

10. Cf. e.g. W. Schmithals, *Das kirchliche Apostelamt* (Göttingen: Vandenhoeck und Ruprecht, 1961); Eng. trans. by J.E. Steely, *The Office of Apostle in the Early Church* (Nashville: Abdington, 1969); J.H. Charlesworth, *Jesus Within Judaism* (N.Y.: Doubleday, 1988); P. Vielhauer "Gottesreich und Menschensohn in der Verkündigung Jesu," *Festschrift für Gunther Dehn*, ed. W. Schleiermacher (Neukirchen: Verlag der Buchhandlung des Erziehungsvereins, 1957); E.P. Sanders, *Jesus and Judaism,* (Philadelphia: Fortress, 1985).

11. Brown, op. cit., 81:146.

12. Meier, op. cit., 78:26: "It was not Jesus' intention to found a new sect separated from Israel."

13. Harrington, loc. cit., 41:40.

14. Ibid.

15. For this question of the "brothers and sisters" of Jesus, cf. R. Brown et al., *Mary in the New Testament* (N.Y.: Paulist, 1978).

16. Harrington, ibid., 41:61.

17. Some make note that in the text "fathers" are given up, but there is no hundred times repayment of fathers, as there is such a repayment of other relations. Whether this can be interpreted as a statement for a "non-patriarchal" situation now and in the age to come might be, indeed, an over-interpretation of both the text and the context.

18. Cf. on this matter J.R. Donahue, *Are You the Christ? The Trial Narrative in the Gospel of Mark* (Missoula, Mt: SBLDS, 1973).

19. Cf. on this matter, ibid.

20. Cf. Harrington, loc. cit., 41:3.

21. J. Fitzmyer, *The Gospel according to Luke* (Garden City, N.Y.: Doubleday & Co., 1981), Anchor Bible Series, p. 143.

22. H. Flender, *St. Luke: Theologian of Redemptive History* (Philadelphia: Fortress, 1967).

23. I.H. Marshall, *Luke: Historian and Theologian* (Exeter: Pater Noster, 1970).

24. E. Franklin, *Christ the Lord: A Study in the Purpose and Theology of Luke-Acts* (Philadelphia: Westminster, 1975).

25. Fitzmyer, op. cit., p. 58.

26. R. Karris, "The Gospel according to Luke," *NJBC,* 43:2–3, presents a number of views on the addressees of this gospel. He himself opts for a community in Syrian Antioch somewhere between 85 and 90.

27. Fitzmyer, op. cit., p. 57.

28. R. Dillon, "Acts of the Apostles," *NJBC,* 44:4.

29. Fitzmyer, op. cit., pp. 144–162.

30. Cf. Karris, op. cit., 43:56, for the listing of citations.

31. This is particularly evident in the "speeches of Acts." Luke presents these various speeches as models of early Christian teaching. Cf. Haenchen, op. cit., and also such authors as Dibelius, C.H. Dodd, Plümacher, and Wilckens.

32. Ibid., p. 300. In this section Fitzmyer discusses the various identities of this honored Theophilus, and comes to the conclusion that he was a catechumen or neophyte, rather than a non-believer or a Roman of great power in the civil community.

33. Ibid., p. 615.

34. The parallel passage in Mark 4:10 has "those who were with him along with the twelve." In both Luke and Mark the "disciples" in this passage include both the twelve and others.

35. It seems clear that the interpretation of the parable of the sower does not as such go back to Jesus, but to the interpretation of the early church. Already Mark presents the parable and its interpretation; Matthew clearly links it to the LXX; Luke makes modifications of his

own. Thus, Luke does not create this interpretation; he has inherited it. He has, however, modified it.

36. Ibid., p. 723. Cf. as well 11:27–28: "Blessed is the womb that bore you and the breasts that nourished you," and also Acts 1:14.

37. Ibid., p. 725. Fitzmyer disagrees with J.M. Creed, *The Gospel according to Luke*, who simply says that Luke lessens the disharmony between Jesus and his relatives, and also E. Ellis, *The Gospel of Luke*, who parallels Mark and Luke. Rather, Fitzmyer argues that even though physical descent by itself guarantees nothing, "In Luke Jesus makes those of physical descent models for those who hear the word of God and keep it."

38. Ibid., p. 752.

39. The later eisegetical interpretation of the twelve representing *episkopoi* and the seventy (-two) representing *presbyteroi* has no foundation in Luke.

40. Karris, op. cit., 43:197: "We have a fresh story. . . ."

41. The subtitle in the Jerusalem Bible just prior to 24:36 is: "Jesus appears to the apostles"; and just prior to 15:44: "Last instructions to the apostles." Given Luke's penchant for restraining the term "apostle" to the twelve, the editors of this translation would be hard pressed to justify these subtitles. Not only are the eleven the addressees, but also "their companions" (24:34 JB translation) and the two disciples who had just returned. Nowhere in the text can we find a justification for making the apostles, or the eleven alone, the reference to the term "they" in 24:36, 41, 43, 44. Nowhere is the reference to the term "you" (14:37, 38, 39, etc.) limited to the eleven, the apostles.

42. Ibid., p. 254.

43. Cf. Osborne, *Priesthood*, pp. 30–39, in which I have argued that authors address certain passages, such as these in the Lucan gospel and Acts, with an ecclesiological presupposition. As a result, such passages are interpreted differently. The answer to Fitzmyer's questions, then, often reflects not the text or the context of the scripture itself, but rather the ecclesiological presupposition.

44. It would be of interest to compare this Lucan notion of faith on the one hand with the presentation of faith in Augustine, the major scholastic theologians and Trent, on the other hand, with the presentation of faith by Luther, Calvin (or even Seripando). The Roman Catholic Church has never officially addressed the reformation understanding of faith in a forthright way: cf. H. Vorgrimler, "Der Kampf des Christen mit der Sünde," *Mysterium Salutis* (Einsiedeln: Benziger, 1976) pp. 429–430.

45. Karris, op. cit., 43:9.

46. Ibid., 43:73.

47. Ibid., 43:84.

48. R.J. Dillon, "Acts of the Apostles," *NJBC,* 44:19.

49. Karris, op. cit., 43:93.

50. Ibid., 43:178.

51. The mention of sword in this verse should be connected to the passage just above in 22:36: "If you have no sword, sell your cloak and buy one." The sword is not to be taken literally, and Jesus' rejection of the sword in 22:51 indicates this. The sword in 22:36 must be taken figuratively.

52. Osborne, *Priesthood,* pp. 40–85.

53. R. Dillon, "Acts of the Apostles," *NJBC,* 44:7.

54. B. Viviano, "The Gospel According to Matthew," *NJBC,* 42:6.

55. Ibid., 42:7.

56. Cf. Bultmann, *The History of the Synoptic Tradition* (Oxford: Blackwell, 1968), Eng. trans. J. Marsh.

57. Viviano, op. cit., 42:145.

58. R.E. Brown and J.P. Meier, *Antioch and Rome* (N.Y.: Paulist, 1983) pp. 45–72.

59. Ibid., p. 58.

60. For the "synoptic question," cf. J.S. Kselman and R.D. Witherup, "Modern New Testament Criticism," *NJBC,* 70:1–84.

61. Meier, op. cit., p. 61. Jewish writers today bristle at this approach, but it seems to be the approach which one finds in Matthew. Even if one attempts to nuance the situation by proposing that the school of Matthew is contesting the Pharisees for leadership of the "genuine Israel," there is still in Matthew a position that the church (i.e. the followers of Jesus) has supplanted any Jewish group which does not accept Jesus. One cannot reinterpret Matthew in a way which might agree more with contemporary ecumenical endeavors but which falsifies the text itself. Nor can one reinterpret Jewish anti-Christian texts of a former age in a way which agrees with contemporary ecumenical endeavors, but which falsifies these texts as well.

62. On the use of the term "Pharisees," it should be noted that the text of Matthew's gospel uses the term in a rather blanket way (which I follow in my own text in presenting the material from Matthew). However, current christological investigations stress the fact that not all Pharisees can be judged in such a negative way. The same is true for the use of Jewish priests and scribes in the gospel material.

63. Meier, op. cit., p. 65.

64. Cf. R. Brown, *The Birth of the Messiah* (N.Y.: Doubleday, 1979) pp. 107–109.

65. The "school of Matthew" which Stendahl advocated might also be identified with this leadership group at Antioch.

66. Meier uses this phrase; cf. p. 70.

67. Cf. Meier, op. cit., p. 66.

68. For this entire matter of Peter in Matthew's gospel, the literature is super-abundant. Cf. R. Brown et al., *Peter in the New Testament* (N.Y.: Paulist, 1973).

69. Cf. Meier, op. cit., p. 59.

70. Ibid., p. 64.

71. In Luke, as we saw, Jesus is presented as the one who names the twelve "apostles"; in Matthew it is the author himself who calls the twelve "apostles."

72. Cf. Viviano, op. cit., 42:168.

73. Cf. R. Brown, *The Birth of the Messiah,* pp. 71–74.

74. P. Perkins, "The Gospel according to John," *NJBC,* 61:9.

75. Cf. Brown, *The Community of the Beloved Disciple* (N.Y.: Paulist, 1979) pp. 66–67.

76. Perkins, op. cit., 61:12.

77. R. Brown, *The Community of the Beloved Disciple,* pp. 59–91; summarized on pp. 168–169.

78. F. J. Moloney, "Johannine Theology," *NJBC,* 83:13.

79. Perkins, op. cit., 61:11.

80. Perkins, op. cit., 61:171.

81. Pharisees however are mentioned in 11:46–47 and they are clearly implicated in the plans by Jewish leadership to bring about the death of Jesus. The instigators for the death of Jesus, in the Johannine writings, are not merely the Roman authorities, but also key and leading members of the Jewish leadership at that time.

82. The identity of this beloved disciple remains a matter of dispute. Certainly he is not the apostle John, son of Zebedee. On the other hand, who he is either historically (if he is historical) or symbolically (if that is the author's intention) remains an open question.

83. Perkins, op. cit., 61:206.

84. Perhaps the author of the gospel reduces the number of women to a single individual, a literary device which the author uses on other occasions as well.

85. There is some connection with this unknown placement of the body with the "fear of the Jews" found in 19:38 and 20:19, 26.

86. Cf. P. Moreno-Jiménez, "El discípulo de Jesu Cristo según el evangelio de San Juan," *Estudios bíblicos,* 30 (1971) 269–311.

87. Cf. Brown, *The Community of the Beloved Disciple,* p. 81, n. 150.

88. Cf. Brown, op. cit., pp. 99–103.

89. J. Murphy-O'Connor, *St. Paul's Corinth: Texts and Archaeology* (Wilmington: M. Glazier, 1983).

90. W.A. Meeks, *The First Urban Christians: The Social World of the Apostle Paul* (New Haven: Yale Univ. Press, 1983).

91. H. Koester, *Einführung in das Neue Testament im Rahmen der Religionsgeschichte und Kulturgeschichte der hellenistischen und römischen Zeit* (Berlin: De Gruyer, 1980).

92. V. Branick, *The House Church in the Writings of Paul*, (Wilmington: M. Glazier, 1988).

93. G. Theissen, *The Social Setting of Pauline Christianity: Essays on Corinth* (Philadelphia: Fortress, 1982), trans. J.H. Schütz.

94. M. Hengel, *Between Jesus and Paul: Studies in the Earliest History of Christianity* (Philadelphia: Fortress, 1983).

95. H. Doohan, *Paul's Vision of the Church* (Wilmington: M. Glazier, 1989), pp. 170–193.

96. Cf. J. Fitzmyer, "Pauline Theology," *NJBC*, 82:24–80 for a discussion of many other views of contemporary scholarship on the key to Pauline thought.

97. Ibid., 82:37–48.

98. Ibid., 82:81–137.

99. Ibid., 82:138–151.

100. In v. 5 the term is *presbyteros;* in v. 7, the term is *episkopos.* These two "names" are, at this period of church history, interchangeable.

101. W.J. Dalton, "The First Epistle of Peter," *NJBC*, 57:5.

102. E. Käsemann, "An Apology for Primitive Christian Eschatology," *Essays on New Testament Themes* (London: SBT, 1964), pp. 169–196.

103. J.H. Neyrey, "The Second Epistle of Peter," *NJBC*, 64:3.

104. T.J. Leahy, "The Epistle of James," *NJBC*, 58:4.

105. R. Schnackenburg, *Baptism in the Thought of St. Paul: A Study in Pauline Theology* (Oxford: Basil Blackwell, 1964).

106. B. Witherington, *Women in the Earliest Churches* (Cambridge: Cambridge Univ. Press, 1988), esp. pp. 5–23. His references are particularly helpful on this matter of the role of women within the various cultural groupings of that period.

107. Ibid., p. 125.

108. Ibid.

109. Ibid., p. 182. For Luke, cf. his intriguing diagram on p. 129. Witherington uses the term "a reformed patriarchy" as a goal of the gospel writers (p. 182). To some this might be an inadequate phrase, but when placed into the portrait of women within the Mediterranean cultures, it has a strong value.

110. Ibid., p. 182.

111. Cf. for instance F. Blanke and F. J. Leenhardt, *Die Stellung der*

Frau im Neuen Testament und der alten Kirche (Zurich: Zwingli, 1949); R. Gryson, *The Ministry of Women in the Early Church* (Collegeville: Liturgical Press, 1976); J. Leipoldt, *Die Frau in der antiken Welt und im Urchristentum* (Leipzig: Koehler und Amelang, 1955); L. Swidler, *Women in Judaism: The Status of Women in Formative Judaism* (Metuchen: Scarecrow, 1976); G.H. Tavard, *Women in Christian Tradition* (South Bend: University of Notre Dame Press, 1973); R. Ruether and E. McLaughlin, eds., *Women of Spirit—Female Leadership in the Jewish and Christian Traditions* (N.Y.: Simon and Schuster, 1979).

4. The Patristic Period: The Apostolic Church to 325 A.D.

1. Cf. J.A. Sanders, "Torah and Christ," *Interpretation,* 24 (1975) pp. 372–396; ibid., *Torah and Canon* (Philadelphia: Fortress Press, 1974); W.A. Meeks, *The First Urban Christians* (New Haven: Yale University Press) 1983. In contemporary study, the complexity of Jewish pluralistic thought during the period of the second temple has been studied intensively, particularly through research on the apocrypha, the pseudepigrapha, the Dead Sea Scrolls, the Elephantine papyri, and the Tanaitic literature.

2. An exciting way to read the comprehensive study by B. Cooke, *Ministry to Word and Sacraments* (Philadelphia: Fortress, 1976), is not to read it page by page, but rather to read it segment by segment, that is, apropos to the theme of this chapter, to read at one sitting all the sections which the author has on the ante-Nicene developments. In this way, one catches a picture of the churches at that particular period of time. In these sections Cooke offers us a window-vision of Christian life from the time of the earliest non-canonical writings down to the year 325.

3. At the Second Vatican Council the bishops clearly distinguished between the official ministry of clerics, which was called *ministerium,* and the acceptable ministry of lay men and women, which was called *apostolatus.* Clerical church leadership became, over the centuries, possessive of its prerogatives, and official church documents continually represent the "ministry" of lay people in a secondary way. Even Catholic Action was consistently referred to by the official church as the cooperation of the laity in the work of the hierarchy. The division of the church into cleric/lay clearly had repercussions on the way in which Christian ministry was theologically defined.

4. I. de la Potterie, op. cit., p. 847.

5. Cf. G. Magnani, op. cit., pp. 571–572. One might note as well that it is *only* this section of the letter of I Clement which is included in Den-

zinger, *Enchiridion Symbolorum, Definitionum, et Declarationum* (Freiburg i. Br.: Herder, 1958) 101.

6. Cf. A. Faivre, op. cit., pp. 28–36.

7. R. Brown and J.P. Meier, *Antioch and Rome* (N.Y.: Paulist, 1983).

8. J. Fuellenbach, *Ecclesiastical Office and the Primacy of Rome* (Washington, D.C.: The Catholic University Press, 1980) is a study on current scholarship regarding the letter of Clement. Fuellenbach presents an overview of almost every recent Protestant and Catholic author of note who has contributed to Clementine studies. Pp. 1–24 offers a summation of such thought on date, author, occasion, purpose, etc.

9. Cf. Robert M. Grant, *The Apostolic Fathers*, v. I: *An Introduction* (N.Y.: Thomas Nelson & Sons, 1964) pp. 36–47; R.M. Grant and H. Graham, *The Apostolic Fathers*, v. II: *First and Second Clement* (N.Y.: Thomas Nelson & Sons, 1965) pp. 3–13 for pertinent manuscript information and a review of various studies and commentaries on the letter. Cf. Osborne, *Priesthood*, pp. 93–97, for a summation of Clement's position on priestly ministry.

10. O. Knoch is the first major Catholic scholar to opt for a collegial leadership at Rome, of which the author was a member. Cf. Knoch, "Die Ausführungen des I. Clemensbriefes über kirchliche Verfassung im Spiegel der neueren Deutung seit R. Sohm und Harnack," *Theologische Quartalschrift*, v. 141 (1967) pp. 202–210; idem, *Eigenart und Bedeutung der Eschatologie im theologischen Aufriß des ersten Clemensbriefes* (Bonn: P. Hanstein, 1964). Knoch has been followed on this matter by most Catholic authors: Stuiber, Quasten, Clarke, Lawson, Zollitsch. For background on Corinth, cf. J. Murphy-O'Connor, *St. Paul's Corinth, Texts and Archaeology* (Wilmington: M. Glazier, 1983); Barbara E. Bowe, *A Church in Crisis* (Minneapolis: Fortress, 1988), pp. 7–32; W. Meeks, *The First Urban Christians*.

11. At a later date of history, namely, in Irenaeus, Clement is called an *episkopos*, but this could easily be reading backward. At the time of Irenaeus, the more common name for the main spiritual leader of the Christian community was *episkopos;* still at the time of Clement and with particular reference to Rome, there is no historical verification that this either was the case at all or that it can be presumed to be the case.

12. E. Schüssler-Fiorenza, *In Memory of Her* (N.Y.: Crossroad, 1983) 291–293, indicates that some of the dissidents might have been women. B. Bowe, *A Church in Crisis* (Minneapolis: Fortress, 1988) pp. 19–20, notes that women might have been among those deposed and concludes (p. 20): "While this thesis [Schüssler-Fiorenza] does not contradict what is stated in I Clement and it is just as likely that women, as well as men,

might have been instigators of the troubles, the gender of the dissidents does not seem to be at issue."

13. Bowe, op. cit., p. 21.

14. Cf. K. Beyschlag, "I Clemens 40–44 und das Kirchenrecht," *Reformatio und Confessio: Festschrift für D. Wilhelm Maurer* (Berlin: Lutherisches Verlagshaus, 1965), ed. F. Katzenbach and G. Müller, p. 12.

15. Cf. Bowe, op. cit., pp. 22–23. This is the thesis of her entire work, which she summarizes in her conclusion, pp. 155–158. The arguments for her case are, of course, found in the body of her book.

16. Text is from Grant-Graham, op. cit., p. 70.

17. Ibid., p. 69.

18. Cf. de la Potterie, op. cit., p. 848; A. Faivre, op. cit., p. 35.

19. Faivre, op. cit., p. 34.

20. Faivre, op. cit., p. 31: "L'homme laïc de la liturgie vétéro-testamentaire trouve-t-il son correspondant exact dans le culte chrétien? Le texte ne dit rien de semblable."

21. Ibid., p. 36. "En fait, l'homme laïc de la lettre de Clément n'est pas chrétien, mais juif. Ou, plus exactement, c'est une créature hybride et synthétique. L'homme laïc nous est présenté comme exerçant une fonction spécifique dans le cadre du culte juif, ce qui est totalement artificiel et correspond uniquement à l'image du simple baptisé qui, lui, participe réellement au culte chrétien en y apportant l'offrande spirituelle d'une vie réglée selon l'idéal chrétien. De la sorte, il existe une distorsion de l'image vétéro-testamentaire par la réalité chrétienne et l'homme laïc est ainsi placé en porte-à-faux." Cf. also Brown-Meier, *Antioch and Rome*, p. 162, where Brown indicates that the community at Rome had a strong loyalty to its Jewish heritage, and a Roman such as the author of this letter would have easily used a Jewish background.

22. A. Harnack, *Sitzungsberichte der preussischen Akademie der Wissenschaften* (1894) pp. 261–273.

23. Cf. Faivre, op. cit., pp. 35–36; de la Potterie, op. cit., p. 849.

24. Cf. B. Bowe, op. cit., pp. 144–153 for an analysis of Clement's understanding of office.

25. Ibid., p. 39.

26. R.A. Norris, *God and World in Early Christian Theology* (N.Y.: Seabury, 1965), p. 44.

27. Cf. Eusebius, *Eccl. Hist.* 5, 21, 2–5, for a resume of these *acta*.

28. P.F. Bradshaw, *Ordination Rites of the Ancient Churches of East and West* (N.Y.: Pueblo, 1990) p. 3, wisely cautions that the text might have been reworked by fourth century hands, so that "it is dangerous to draw the conclusion that other Christian communities in the third cen-

tury would necessarily have followed a similar practice to that described here [in the *Apostolic Tradition*]." G. Martelet, *Deux mille ans d'Église en question,* v. 2 (Paris: Éd. du Cerf, 1990) in his chapter on the *Traditio apostolica* (pp. 175–218) is neither as cautious nor as scholarly as Bradshaw.

29. Cf. D.M. Power, *Gifts That Differ: Lay Ministries Established and Unestablished* (N.Y.: Pueblo, 1980) pp. 60–66. Power underscores the difference between ordination and mere installation. The reason for ranking, he states, is threefold: appointment, charism and personal choice. "Ordination, not charismatic gift, becomes the definitive distinguishing mark in the church and the stamp of authority" (p. 65).

30. Cf. ibid., p. 64, where Power states that not all widows have the rank (*ordo*) of widow. On this matter of early ordination, cf. R. Gryson, *The Ministry of Women in the Early Church* (Collegeville: Liturgical Press, 1976), trans. J. Laporte and M.L. Hall. One should confer as well P. Bradshaw, *Ordination Rites of the Ancient Churches of East and West,* p. 84: "The debate between A.-G. Martimort and Roger Gryson as to whether deaconesses were here thought of as receiving a sacramental ordination and as being part of the clergy may not only be anachronistic but also oversimplistic: the categorization of the liturgical ministries of the early Church cannot be reduced to a simple division between clergy and laity."

31. Eng. trans. from Bradshaw, op. cit., p. 112.

32. It is interesting to note that with the motu proprio *Ministeria quaedam* (1972) and the *Codex iuris canonici* (1983) the term "cleric" applies only to bishop, presbyter and deacon. All other ministries are considered lay. In the *Traditio apostolica* one finds at least a patristic basis for this distinction, but one cannot apply to the *Traditio apostolica* the same technical and juridical finesse of language which either the motu proprio or the 1983 code employs.

33. Eusebius, *Eccl. hist.,* 4, 2.

34. Cf. W. Bauer, *Orthodoxy and Heresy in Earliest Christianity* (Philadelphia: Fortress, 1971), Eng. trans. R. Kraft and G. Krodel; he addresses all the problematic areas of early Alexandrian Christianity on pp. 44–60.

35. *Clemens Alexandrinus* (Berlin: Akademie Verlag, 1985), ed. O. Stählin, L. Früchtel, U. Treu, v. II, *Stromata,* Buch I–VI, p. 237.

36. Ibid., p. 347.

37. *Clemens Alexandrinus* (Berlin: Akademie Verlag, 1972), ed. O. Stählin and U. Treu, v. I, *Protrepticus und Paedagogus,* p. 213.

38. L. Pizzolato, "Laicità e laici nel cristianesimo primitivo," *Laicità, problemi e prospettive,* pp. 58–60. Cf. also H. Chadwick, ed., *Alexandrian*

Christianity (Philadelphia: Westminster Press, 1954): G.W. Butterworth, *Clement of Alexandria* (Cambridge: Harvard Univ. Press, 1968); G.W. Griggs, *Early Egyptian Christianity* (Leiden: E.J. Brill, 1990).

39. Cf. Osborne, *Priesthood,* pp. 111–114.

40. Cf. J. Quasten, *Patrology* (Westminster: Newman Press, 1953), v. II, pp. 34–35. Quasten cites precisely this section, *Strom.* III, 12, 82 and 84. Cf. also T. Mackin, *The Marital Sacrament* (N.Y.: Paulist, 1989), pp. 102–105.

41. Cf. de la Potterie, op. cit., p. 848.

42. Origen, *Homilies on Jeremiah;* a critical edition of these homilies can be found in *Origenes Werke,* Bd. III, *Jeremiahomilien, Klagelieder-kommentar, Erklärung der Samuel- und Königsbücher,* ed. E. Kloster-mann (1901) and re-edited by P. Nautin (Berlin: Akademie-Verlag, 1983), pp. 1–194.

43. Until Demetrios (190–233) became the bishop of Alexandria, there is shadowy evidence about Christian leadership in this area of the world. Even with Demetrios, who appears as a single *episkopos,* there remains a question concerning the acceptability of Demetrios' own ordination. Per-haps his lack of a clear claim to ordained status prompted him and his followers to stress his status as sole *episkopos.* On the other hand, was he selected by the presbyters to serve as one of a group, a presider-*episkopos?* This appears to be what Jerome implies (*Epistle* CXLVI, 1). Chadwick, op. cit., p. 175, notes that perhaps "during the long reign of office of Demetrios (190–233), things at Alexandria were already moving towards such a system of monarchical episcopacy and encouraged Demetrios to emphasize his authority." Cf. Griggs, op. cit., pp. 61–63.

44. In the same homilies, e.g., cf. *Homilies on Jeremiah XI,* op. cit., pp. 80, 12, 16, 17, and 21.

45. Cf. Osborne, *Priesthood,* pp. 111–114. Cf. also Theo Schäfer, *Das Priester-Bild im Leben und Werk des Origenes* (Frankfurt a. Main: Peter Lang, 1977).

46. Cf. *Contra Celsum,* 8, 73.

47. *Homilies in Leviticus* 12, 1.

48. *Homilies in Joshua,* 13, 1.

49. *Exhortation to the Martyrs,* 33.

50. *Contra Celsum,* 8, 17; *Homilies on Numbers,* 11, 8; 24, 2; *Homilies on Leviticus,* 6, 2; 6, 5; 9, 9; cf. also J. Lécuyer, "Sacerdoce des fidèles et sacerdoce ministériel chez Origène," *Vetera Christianorum,* 7 (1970), pp. 253–264. "Nous avons trouvé chez Origène un riche enseignement sur le sacerdoce des chrétiens et sur le sacerdoce ministériel. . . . Aucune théologie du sacerdoce ne peut se désintéresser d'un tel témoignage" (p. 264). In the same volume, cf. G. Otranto, "Il sacerdozio comune dei fedeli

nci riflessi della 1 Petr. 2, 9 (I e II secolo)," which studies Clement of Rome, Ignatius, the Didache, Justin, Barnabas and Clement of Alexandria. Otranto writes (p. 245): "Nessuno degli autori da noi studiati considera metaforico il sacerdozio de 1 Petr. 2.9"; and again (p. 246): "I Padri da noi esaminati avevano piena coscienza del sacerdozio comune."

51. Cf. Schäfer, op. cit, p. 50; also J. Scherer, *Entretien d'Origène avec Héraclide (Sources chrétiennes)*, n. 67 (Paris: Éditions du Cerf, 1960).

52. Cf. Schäfer, op. cit., p. 54; also H.J. Vogt, *Das Kirchenverständnis des Origenes, Bonner Beiträge zur Kirchengeschichte*, ed. E. Dassmann, E. Hegel, B. Stasiewski, v. IV (Cologne-Vienna: Böhlau, 1974), p. 70.

53. Origen, *Homilies on Jeremiah*, XI, 3, 9–29. Greek text is in *Origène: Homélies sur Jérémie*, with a French translation by P. Husson and P. Nautin (Paris: Éditions du Cerf, 1976), 418–420. The English translation is my own. *Kleros* throughout this section of the French rendition is translated by "function" (which I have kept) with the one exception in line 19: *tines en klero* is translated by the term "clergé," which I have translated as "those in the function," retaining the non-personal use of *kleros*, and thereby reserving the personal reference to the term *tines*. This seems to be more in line with Origen's use of *kleros*, since in his day there was no term which corresponded to the later term "clergy." It is also important to note that Origen combines both *kleros* and *topos* in this passage.

54. Cf. Origen, *Homilies on Ezechiel*, 1, 11; *Homilies on the Canticle of Canticles*, I; *Homilies on Exodus*, 9, 3.

55. Origen also uses the word *tagma*, which occurs in the LXX. Cf. *Homilies on Jeremiah*, 8, 6; 20, 4. He also uses the term *time* in a collective sense; cf. *Commentary on John*, 32, 12.

56. Jerome translates Origen's use of *taxis* by *ordo clericatus;* cf. *Homilies on Jeremiah*, 11, 3. Cf. Origen, *Homilies on Numbers*, 2, 1; 21, 2.

57. Cf. Schäfer, op. cit., p. 199; also his diagram on p. 153.

58. *Homilies on Numbers*, 10, 1.

59. Faivre, op. cit., p. 92; Schäfer, op. cit., pp. 170–177.

60. English text of the fragment of the epistle of Alexander to Demetrios is in *Ante Nicene Fathers* (Grand Rapids: Eerdmans, 1957), v. VI, p. 154: "And he—i.e. Demetrius—has added to his letter that this is a matter that was never heard of before, and has never been done now—namely, that laymen should take part in public speaking, when there are bishops present. But in this assertion he has departed evidently far from the truth by some means. For, indeed, wherever there are found persons capable of profiting the brethren, such persons are exhorted by the holy bishops to address the people. Such was the case at Laranda, where Evelpis was thus exhorted by Neon; and at Iconium, Paulinus was thus exhorted by Celsus;

and at Synada, Theodorus also by Atticus, our blessed brethren. And it is probable that this is done in other places also, although we know not the fact."

61. Faivre, op. cit., pp. 84–89; cf. also the carefully constructed appraisal of H. von Campenhausen, *Ecclesiastical Authority and Spiritual Power* (Stanford: Stanford University Press, 1969), trans. J.A. Baker, pp. 248–250. One finds an account of Demetrios' reaction in Eusebius, *Hist. eccl.* VI, 19, 17–18.

62. Cf. *Homilies on Isaiah,* 17, 2; *Homilies on Leviticus,* 5, 3; 6, 6; *Homilies on Numbers,* 5, 1; 11, 1; *Commentary on Matthew,* 14, 22; *Discussion with Heraclides,* sec. 4.

63. Faivre, op. cit., p. 91; also von Campenhausen, op. cit., p. 252; *Homilies on Genesis,* 16, 6; *Homilies on Numbers,* 11, 1 ff; *Homilies on Leviticus,* 3, 6.

64. Cf. Tertullian, *De Monogamia,* 11, 12; Clement, *Stromata,* 3, 18, 108, 2; Origen, *Homilies on Numbers,* 11, 4, states that virginity is not the criterion for church leadership, but faith; in the *Fragments on 1 Cor. 37,* marriage is called a value-neutral reality. The difficulty for Origen is remarriage, and it is from his view on remarriage that even first marriage begins to appear suspect; cf. *Homilies on Luke,* 17.

65. Faivre, op. cit., p. 94.

66. Cf. G. Schöllgen, *Ecclesia Sordida? Zur Frage der sozialen Schichtung frühchristlicher Gemeinden am Beispiel Karthagos zur Zeit Tertullians* (Münster: Aschendorfsche Verlagsbuchhandlung, 1984) pp. 10ff.

67. Cf. Gösta Claesson, *Index Tertullianeus A-E* (Paris: Études augustiniennes, 1974), for a computerized list of Tertullian's use of the word *clerus,* which is used primarily in but one of his writings: *De monogamia* XII. The term *laicus* is found eight times in this same work but is found only four other times in all his other works. The fact that these terms are not found in any extensive way throughout Tertullian's writings indicates that, in his age and locale, these terms had not yet gained a generalized usage.

68. Trans. by S. Thelwall, *Ante-Nicene Fathers,* v. III (N.Y.: Christian Literature Co., 1896), ed. by A. Roberts and J. Donaldson, p. 677. Cf. *Tertulliani Opera,* v. I: *Opera Catholica adversus Marcionem* (Turnholt: Brepol, 1954), XVII, 1–2, p. 291, ed. J.G. Ph. Borleffs: "Dandi quidem summum habet ius summus sacerdos, si qui est, episcopus; dehinc presbyteri et diaconi, non tamen sine episcopi auctoritate, propter ecclesiae honorem quo salvo salva pax est. Alioquin etiam laicis ius est: quod enim ex aequo accipitur ex aequo dari potest—nisi [si] episcopi iam aut presbyteri aut diaconi vocabantur discentes domini!—id est ut sermo non debet abscondi ab ullo, proinde et baptismum, aeque dei census, ab omnibus

excrcceri potest. Sed quanto magis laicis disciplina verecundiae et modes-
tiae incumbit cum ea [quae] maioribus competant, ne sibi adsumant [di-
catum] episcopi officium."

69. Eng. trans. by William P. LeSaint, *Tertullian: Treatises on Marriage and Remarriage* (ACW) (Westminster: Newman, 1951), pp. 53–54. Cf. *Tertulliani Opera*, v. II, *Opera Montanistica* (Turnholt: Brepol, 1954), pp. 1024–1026, ed. Aem. Kroymann: "Vani erimus, si putaverimus quod sacerdotibus non liceat laicis licere. Nonne et laici sacerdotes sumus? Scriptum est: Regnum quoque nos et sacerdotes deo et patri suo fecit. Differentiam inter ordinem et plebem constituit ecclesiae auctoritas et honor per ordinis consessus sanctificatos deo. Ubi ecclesiastici ordinis non est consessus, et offers et tinguis et sacerdos es tibi solus; scilicet ubi tres, ecclesia est, licet laici. Uniusquisque enim, secundum quod et apostolus dicit, vivit fide sua, nec est personarum acceptio apud deum, quoniam non auditores legis iustificantur a domino, sed factores. Igitur si habes ius sacerdotis in temetipso ubi necesse est, habeas oportet etiam disciplinam sacerdotis nec ubi necesse est habere ius sacerdotis. Digamus tinguis? digamus offers? Quanto magis laico digamo quod ad salutem capitale erit agere pro sacerdote, cum ipsi sacerdoti digamo facto auferatur agere sacerdotem. . . . Unus deus, una fides: una sit et disciplina, usque adeo nisi et laici ea observent, per quae presbyteri alleguntur, quomodo erunt presbyteri, qui de laicis alleguntur? Ergo pugnare debemus ante laicum iussum a secundo matrimonio abstinere, dum presbyter esse non aliud potest laicus quam semel fuerit maritus."

70. Eng. trans. by R. Arbesmann, E.J. Daly, E.A. Quain, *Tertullian: Disciplinary, Moral and Ascetical Works* (N.Y.: Fathers of the Church, Inc, 1959), pp. 296–297. Cf. *Tertulliani Opera*, v. II, XI, 48, pp. 1148, ed. J.J. Thierry: "Sed cum ipsi actores, id est ipsi diaconi et presbyteri et episcopi, fugiunt, quomodo laicus intelligere poterit, qua ratione dictum sit: 'Fugite de civitate in civitatem'?"

71. *The Writings of Quintus Sept. Flor. Tertullianus*, vol. III, ed. A. Roberts and J. Donaldson, trans. by S. Thelwall (Edinburgh: T. & T. Clark, 1870), p. 43; cf. also *Tertulliani Opera*, v. II, XI, 4, p. 1244, ed. E. Dekkers: "Si vult nos iterare coniugia, quomodo semen nostrum in Isaac semel marito auctore defendit? Quomodo totum ordinem ecclesiae de monogamis disponit, si non haec disciplina praecedit in laicis, ex quibus ecclesiae ordo proficit?"

72. Ibid., p. 47. For the Latin, cf. loc. cit. XII, 5, pp. 1247–1248: "Si enim suam habent episcopi legem circa monogamiam, etiam cetera quae monogamiae accedere oportebit episcopis erunt scripta. Laicis vero, quibus monogamia non convenit, cetera quoque aliena sunt."

73. Eng. trans. P. Holmes, *Ante Nicene Fathers*, v. III, p. 263. Cf. *Ter-*

tulliani Opera, vol I, p. 222, ed. R.F. Refoulé: "Itaque alius hodie episcopus, cras alius; hodie diaconus qui cras lector; hodie presbyter qui cras laicus. Nam et laicis sacerdotalia munera iniungunt."

74. M. Jourjon, "Le premiers emplois du mot laïc dans la littérature patristique," *Lumière et Vie,* 12 (1963), p. 41. Jourjon also attempts to see a *iure divino* status to the term *laikos* as it is used in Clement of Rome. This appears to be an overburdening of the text.

75. Cf. Schöllgen, op. cit., pp. 17–98, for a detailed description of the economic rise of Carthage and its concomitant socially structured development. The statistics are taken from A. Deman, "Matériaux et réflexions pour servir à une étude du développement et du sous-développement dans les provinces de l'empire romain," *Aufstieg und Niedergang der römischen Welt,* ed. H. Temporini (Berlin: De Gruyter, 1975), pp. 3–97. Cf. Also W.H.C. Frend, *The Donatist Church,* and Osborne, *Priesthood,* pp. 114–117.

76. Cf. P. Bouet, Ph. Fleury, A. Goulon, M. Zuinghedan and P. Dufraigne, *Cyprien: Traités Concordance* (N.Y.: Olms-Weidman, 1986).

77. *Cyprian, Epist.* 66, 8. Cf. *Epist.* 33, 1; 3, 3. The ranking position of the *episcopus* is clear from Cyprian's writings. Cyprian's statements on baptism and to some degree eucharist indicate the high regard he has for the baptized, but this is based theologically on his position that "outside the church there is no salvation" (*Epist.* 73, 21; 55, 24).

78. Cyprian's ideas on the new life of the baptized, ideas which other fathers of the church also expressed in their own writings, indicate that there is—to use the language of a later generation—an "ontological difference" between the baptized and the non-baptized. This makes much more sense than the later attempts to describe in theological terms an "ontological difference" between the ordained and the non-ordained. In the documents of Vatican II, there is a step away from such theological argumentation, for the documents deliberately use the phrase "essential difference" rather than "ontological difference," when they attempt to distinguish the ordained from the non-ordained. However, the bishops at Vatican II merely used this term without any attempt to define it. Several theological attempts were described in various presentations to the bishops at Vatican II, but none of these various attempts were adopted. The bishops used the term and left the entire issue "open."

79. Cf. E. Bourque, *Histoire de la Pénitence-Sacrement* (Québec: Bibliothèque Theólogique de Laval, 1947), pp. 98–105; J. Favazza, *The Order of Penitents* (Collegeville: Liturgical Press, 1988), pp. 210–211.

80. R. Brown and J.P. Meier, *Antioch and Rome,* pp. 15–86. Cf. also W. Bauer, op. cit., pp. 61–94.

81. Cf. R.H. Connolly, *Didascalia apostolorum* (Oxford: Clarendon

Press, 1919), p. xci. The English citations from the *Didascalia* used in the text are from this edition.

82. Connolly, op. cit., p. xl.

83. Ibid., p. xli.

84. Ibid., p. 147.

85. A. Robinson, in *The Ministry of Deaconesses*, cited by Connolly, op. cit., pp. xlii–xliii.

86. Connolly, op. cit., p. 44.

87. Ibid., p. 60.

88. Ibid., pp. 85–86.

89. Ibid., p. 93.

90. Ibid., p. 101.

91. Ibid., pp. 122–124.

92. *Conciliorum Oecumenicorum Decreta* (Freiburg im. B.: Herder, 1962), p. 6. The subsequent references to these canons are taken from this same source, pp. 5–15.

93. Cf. E.A. Clark, *Women in the Early Church* (Wilmington: M. Glazier, 1983), pp. 77–114, for the texts from various apocryphal Acts and accounts of martyrdom, which present Christian women as the heroines. Clark notes, pp. 77–78: "By no means are the women of the Apocryphal Acts the docile housewives commended in I Timothy: these determined women are willing to risk social disapproval and life itself to uphold their faith."

94. Cf. W.H.C. Frend, *The Donatist Church*, pp. 19–20, 49, 149–150, 164, etc.

95. Cited by Origen, *Contra Celsum*, III, 55; Eng. trans. from G.H. William, "The Role of the Layman in the Ancient Church," loc. cit., p. 42.

96. K.S. Latourette, *A History of the Expansion of Christianity* (N.Y.: Harper and Bros., 1937), v. I, p. 117.

97. Williams, op. cit., p. 10.

98. Clark, op. cit., besides the material on women martyrs referred to above, includes only a brief paragraph from Irenaeus' *Adversus haereses* (p. 38); several paragraphs from Clement's *Stromata* (pp. 47–54) which deal with marriage; two brief paragraphs from Tertullian's *De cultu feminarum* (p. 39), two from his *Ad uxorem* (p. 70), a fairly lengthy section from his *De exhortatione castitatis* (pp. 147–151), a brief section from his *De monogamia* (pp. 151–152), and a paragraph from *De baptismo* (p. 173). Hippolytus' *Syntagma* merits one paragraph (p. 160). The references to the deaconesses which one finds in *Can. 19* from the Council of Nicaea and the lengthier references to deaconesses in the *Apostolic Constitutions* are also cited (pp. 176–181). Once these citations are spelled

out, one can only conclude that the resultant data on women in the patristic writings of that period must be described as meager and spotty. When compared to the writings on men during the same patristic period, these few citations witness to an overbearing male bias.

99. Cf. Frances and Joseph Gies, *Marriage and the Family in the Middle Ages* (N.Y.: Harper & Row, 1987), p. 28. This entire section presents an overview of the marriages of that period of time: *cum manu* and *sine manu*. Aristocratic Roman women were to a degree quite free and at times equal to their male counterparts. On the other hand, it is clear that a male bias undergirded much of the Graeco-Roman world of that time.

100. W. Schneelmecher, ed., in E. Henneck, *New Testament Apocrypha*, v. 1 (London: Lutterworth Press, 1963), p. 63, trans. by G. Ogg.

101. Ibid., pp. 63–64.

102. Cf. Elisabeth Schüssler-Fiorenza, *In Memory of Her*, p. 265.

103. Ibid., p. 305. Cf. Schneelmecher, p. 247, for the English translation of the pertinent text of the *Sophia Iesu Christi.*

104. Ibid., p. 305.

105. Cf. pp. 492–493 for text.

106. Cf. W. Bauer, *Orthodoxy and Heresy in Earliest Christianity*, pp. 1–43.

107. Schneelmecher, op. cit., p. 64.

108. Schüssler-Fiorenza, op. cit., p. xix and passim.

109. The final section of Schüssler-Fiorenza's book on "Tracing the Struggles: Patriarchy and Ministry," pp. 243–334, recounts this exclusionary process from the women's side. If one adds to this exclusionary process, the exclusion of non-*ordo* Christians, both male and female, one has the compounded picture which seemed to have occurred. This process, however, did not occur uniformly throughout the Christian world. Once again, one finds evidence of a non-monolithic or non-unified form of Christian communal life. At the end of the third century and the beginning of the fourth century, however, the evidence does show that fewer women are found in ecclesiastical office than earlier on, but a total exclusion of women from office in the episcopally directed churches had not yet taken place.

110. Cf. Williams, op. cit., pp. 30–48; for our present purposes adaptations have been made in the naming of his categories.

111. Tertullian, *De paenitentia, 7.*

112. Cyprian, *Ep. 59, 15.*

113. Origen, *Homilies on Leviticus, 3.* The only extant text is the Latin, and the key words are "sacerdos" for the church leader (which at this time primarily meant *episkopos*), and "populus" for the Christian non-ordained community.

114. Cyprian, *Ep.* 67, 5. In *Ep.* 10, 8, he mentions that Cornelius of Rome had been made *episkopos* by both the presbyters and the people (*plebs*).

115. Cyprian, *Ep.* 67, 3.

116. Cf. P.F. Bradshaw, *Ordination Rites of the Ancient Churches of East and West*, pp. 21–24. Bradshaw makes note of the gradual separation of these two acts: election and imposition of hands, and of the way in which the "real" act of ordination came to be seen in the laying on of hands, and "as the means by which the gift of the office itself was bestowed on the candidate, and election merely as a preliminary to it" (p. 22). Prior to this separation, however, the "real" act of ordination included the election by the Christian community, not simply a hierarchical laying on of hands.

117. Irenaeus, *Adversus haereses,* II, 32, 4; cf. also Aristides, *Apologia,* 15; Dionysius of Alexandria, *Letter to the Brethren,* c. 252.

118. *Entretien d'Origène avec Héraclide,* J. Scherer.

119. Williams, op. cit., p. 39.

120. The issues vis-à-vis Judaism and the Graeco-Roman world, as also the centrality of Jesus and one's discipleship in the name of Jesus, were matters of life and death for the Christians of that period, often in a literal way. Inner-church structuring was secondary, which, however, does not mean lacking in importance.

121. Lanne, op. cit., p. 124: "La frontière entre laïcat et cléricature est très floue (elle l'est encore aujourd'hui, dans une certain mesure) en raison de l'existence de charismes ministériels."

122. One of the major issues of society which faced the western world, and therefore the church, was that of the plagues and resultant poverty. The ways in which the church leadership rose to meet these issues were imbued with a sense of discipleship and were nourished by gospel ideals. Although the issues of poverty and the poor are present in the period prior to Nicaea, it is in the period after 325 that the ecclesial and governmental response rose, on many occasions, to heroic proportions; at the same time there were occasions when the response was less than exemplary. Cf. M. Mollat, *The Poor in the Middle Ages: An Essay in Social History* (New Haven: Yale University Press, 1986), Eng. transl. A. Goldhammer, pp. 1–23.

5. The Lay Person in the High Patristic Period
324 to 731 A.D.

1. Cf. J. Richards, *The Popes and the Papacy in the Early Middle Ages: 476–752* (London: Routledge and Kegan Paul, 1979) p. 305.

2. C. Straw, *Gregory the Great, Perfection in Imperfection* (Berkeley: University of California Press, 1988) p. 71, with ref. to *Dial.* 1.4.1f; also C. Dagens, *Saint Grégoire le Grand* (Paris: Études augustiniennes, 1977) p. 17. It might also be noted that in 604 with the death of Gregory, the clergy of Rome staged a backlash to this monasticizing personnel program of Gregory, so that Roman clergy once again began to take over the curial positions.

3. An example of the socio-historical method can be found in M. Mollat, *The Poor in the Middle Ages: An Essay in Social History* (New Haven: Yale University Press, 1986), trans. by A. Goldhammer. On p. 25 he writes: "The main sources for the history of the Merovingian era are ecclesiastical. Compared with monastic translations of relics, works of theology, sermons and conciliar canons, the importance of royal charters, formularies, and literary works is only secondary. Clerics were the authors of all the documents, however."

4. Cf. P.R. Coleman-Norton, *Roman State and Christian Church. A Collection of Legal Documents to A.D. 535* (London: SPCK, 1966) v. 1. One can document Constantine's openness by his *Letter on the Restitution of Property to the Church* [313] pp. 27–28; *Letter of Constantine I and Licinius of Restoration of the Church* [313] pp. 30–35; *Letter of Constantine I on State Subsidies to Churches and on Seducers of Christians* [313] pp. 41–43; *Letter of Constantine I on Clerical Exemption from Public Duties* [313] pp. 43–46; the *Letters of Constantine I regarding the Donatist Schism* [313–314] pp. 46–62; the *Mandate of Constantine I on Jewish Molestation of Christians* [315] pp. 66–67; plus several other instances of Constantine's favor for Christians.

5. K. Baus, "The Development of the Church of the Empire within the Framework of the Imperial Religious Policy," *The Imperial Church from Constantine to the Early Middle Ages,* ed. K. Baus, H.-G. Beck, E. Ewig, H.J. Vogt (N.Y.: Seabury Press, 1980). Eng. trans. A. Biggs [henceforth: *HC*] v. 2, p. 7.

6. Eusebius, *De Vita Constantini,* 2, 26–27, 42; cf. I. Heikel, *Eusebius Werke* Bd. I: *Über das Leben Constantins,* [*GCS*] (Leipzig: J.C. Hinrichs'sche Buchhandlung, 1902).

7. Cf. A. Momigliano, "Christianity and the Decline of the Roman Empire," *The Conflict between Paganism and Christianity in the Fourth Century* (Oxford: The Clarendon Press, 1964) pp. 1–16.

8. J. Herrin, *The Formation of Christendom* (Princeton: Princeton University Press, 1987) p. 19.

9. The number of church councils held during this period, both locally and ecumenically, attest to the many variants in christology and trinitarian theology. Even at these councils, the bishops and others who attended

struggled to find a correct or "orthodox" terminology. Politics, as well, entered into these conciliar discussions, and inter-patriarchal rivalry also played a role. For the christological situation, cf. A. Grillmeier, *Christ in Christian Tradition*, v. 1 (Atlanta: John Knox Press, 1975), Eng. trans. J. Bowden, pp. 104–105, 148–149, for a description of the groping character of christology up to Origen; from Origen to Nicaea, cf. p. 218: "We find quite different 'christologies,' which can hardly be brought together under the same heading."

10. Grillmeier, op. cit., p. 272: "In the christological controversies over Ephesus and Chalcedon, the Nicene creed *retrospectively* acquired the reputation of being a fundamental statement in the church's interpretation of the incarnation." Italics added, but Grillmeier stresses in other texts the slow acceptance, retrospectively, of the Nicene position.

11. Hippolytus, *Commentary on Daniel*, IV, 9.

12. Melito of Sardis, *Homily on the Pasch;* cf. W. Schneelmecher, "Heilsgeschichte und Imperium. Meliton von Sardes und der Staat," *Kleronomia*, 5 (1973) pp. 257–275, esp. 272.

13. Origen, *Contra Celsum*, II, 30.

14. Grillmeier, op. cit., p. 251.

15. Letter of Gregory II to Leo III, in E. Caspar, "Gregor II. und der Bilderstreit," *Zeitschrift für Kirchengeschichte*, 52 (1933) pp. 29–89.

16. J. Herrin, *The Formation of Christendom*, particularly parts I and II, pp. 19–290.

17. This pattern of church-government relationship did not disappear from church history with the death of the Saxon dynasty. In many lingering ways, one finds that church officials still acted or tried to act on its premises even into the nineteenth century. The ways in which some church leadership responded to both the French and American revolutions offer examples of the manner in which this early ideology lingered in church history. The arguments by some bishops at Vatican II, on the issue of religious freedom, reechoed this same ideological stance.

18. Jones, "The Social Background of the Struggle between Paganism and Christianity," *The Conflict between Paganism and Christianity in the Fourth Century*, p. 22, describes the peasantry of the Roman empire as a "vast inert and passive, if stubborn, mass." There may be some correlation between this inertia and passivity of the Roman peasantry and its translation to the ordinary "lay" person in the church. Still, the church became established originally in city-structures, where the shopkeeping and mercantile classes, as also the lower military class, were more predominant. These latter groups were neither passive nor inert.

19. Faivre, op. cit., p. 140.

20. Faivre, op. cit., p. 160.

21. Cf. e.g. the two *Apologies* of Eunomius of Cyzicus (307 and 308 A.D.), and that of Appolinaris of Laodicea, as also John Chrysostom's *De S. Babyla contra Julianum et Gentiles* and the *Contra Judaeos et Gentiles quod Christus sit Deus*. A few other examples of post-Constantinian *Apologies* could be cited as well. The majority of these later apologies are directed against the then contemporary platonists, and the apologies are written from a position of social and political strength, while the earlier apologies were written from a position of social and political weakness, pleading a case that Christians might be able at least to live within the then current social and political world.

22. Cf. Baus, op. cit. [*HC*] p. 90: "The extraordinary close union of the two was not questioned, especially since in the thought of the day an alternative to it was not known and could scarcely be understood."

23. Cf. B. Kriegbaum, *Kirche der Traditoren oder Kirche der Märtyrer?* (Vienna: Tyrolia-Verlag, 1986) p. 83 writes: "Est ist bereits deutlich geworden, daß die traditio mancher Bischöfe zu Spannung mit ihren Gemeinden oder wenigstens mit bestimmten rigoristischen Gruppen in den Ortskirchen führen mußte."

24. W.H.C. Frend, *The Donatist Church. A Movement of Protest in Roman North Africa* (Oxford: Oxford Univ. Press, 1985). This last edition makes note of the work of C. Lepelley, S. Lancel, and J. Divjak, which appeared after the second edition of Frend's work (1971).

25. P. Monceaux, *Histoire littéraire de l'Afrique chrétienne depuis les origines jusqu'à l'invasion arabe* (Paris, 1920; reprinted at Brussels: Culture and Civilization, 1960). Cf. Kriegbaum, op. cit., pp. 28–29 for a criticism regarding the objectivity of Monceaux.

26. Frend particularly emphasizes this aspect, so that there was a correlation between the Donatist sense of church as the separated and morally pure church, on the one hand, and, on the other, a basic North African hostility toward Rome. This independent stance of the North African church toward all others, Rome included, remained part of the North African church until its demise.

27. Most recently, we see this kind of ecclesiological stance toward governments in the two-perfect-kingdoms-theory, officially stated in the encyclical of Pius XII, *Mystici Corporis,* and semi-officially taught by a number of theologians who followed the ideas of S. Tromp.

28. The formation of Catholic enclaves in the United States throughout the nineteenth and early twentieth centuries, the episcopal resistance to the overtures of such men as Isaac Hecker and Orestes Brownson to a more open co-existence with the government of the United States, the wary stance of the majority of Catholics in the United States between

World War I and World War II to the "Protestant government"—in all of these one sees reflections of the Donatist position vis-à-vis the government. The opposition of some twentieth century liberation theologians to the entrenched and oppressive governments, together with their critique of the coziness of an "official" or even hierarchical church structure with such oppressive governments, has an echoing of this early-church stance toward entrenched governmental structures. So, too, is there an echo of this Donatist position in the stance of Pius XII, as expressed in *Mystici Corporis,* with its two perfect societies, a stance which made Roman Catholic opposition to the Third Reich extremely problematical.

29. P. Brown indicates that Augustine himself, even after the publication of *Civitas Dei,* moved to some degree toward the option of separation rather than interrelationship of church and government. Cf. Brown, *Augustine of Hippo* (Berkeley: University of California Press, 1967) pp. 419–426. The issue is more strongly stated by A. Schindler, "Die Theologie der Donatisten und Augustins Reaktion." *Internationales Symposion über den Stand der Augustinus-Forschung,* ed. C. Mayer and K.H. Chelius (Würzburg: Augustinus Verlag, 1989) pp. 131–147.

30. Grillmeier, op. cit., p. 251: "A *political* note intervenes in the Eusebius of the years 314–320: the incarnation is put in the context of the civilization of the empire as the embodiment of peace and order. A historico-political theology emerges: the appearance of the Messiah and imperial peace, Christianity and the empire, are bound together in an indissoluble unity by the idea of providence." The term "indissoluble" should be noted, for it is a highly charged theological term.

31. Cf. P. Caron, "Les 'seniores laici' de l'Église africaine," *Revue Internationale des Droit de l'Antiquité,* 6 (1951) pp. 7–22; W.H.C. Frend, "The Seniores Laici and the Origins of the Church in North Africa," *Journal of Theological Studies,* 12 (1961), pp. 280–284.

32. Cf. Optatus, *De Schismate* 1, 17:*PL* 11, 918.

33. Cf. *Gesta apud Zenophilum, CSEL* 26, 189.

34. Cf. *Codex canonum ecclesiae Africanae* c. 91 (Hard I, 914; Bruns I, 180, ed. Joannou, 341).

35. Cf. *Acta Purgationis Felicis, CSEL,* 26, 198.

36. W.H.C. Frend, op. cit., p. 63.

37. Ibid., p. 65.

38. Cf. H. Chadwick, "Faith and Order at the Council of Nicaea," *History and Thought of the Early Church* (London: Variorum Reprints, 1982) pp. 171–195, esp. 181–188.

39. Ibid., p. 175.

40. Herrin, op. cit., p. 39. She mentions not only the code of 529, its

revision in 534, and the subsequent *Novellae,* but also the building program of Justinian in both east and west and his deliberate disregard for the rebuilding of Rome.

41. U. Stulz, *Die Eigenkirche als Element des mittelalterlichen germanischen Kirchenrechts* (1895).

42. *Concilium Romanum* II, *PL.* 59, 183, B.

43. Cf. Herrin, op. cit., p. 40; R.M. Harrison, "The Church of St. Polyeuktos in Istanbul and the Temple of Solomon," *Okeanos, Harvard Ukrainian Studies,* 6 (1983) pp. 276–279.

44. Palladius writes about Olympias in his *Lausiac History* (56). John Chrysostom wrote seventeen extant letters to her during his time of exile. There is a "Life of Olympias, Deaconess," in John Chrysostom, *Lettres à Olympias* (Paris: Les Éditions du Cerf, 1947), *Sources Chrétiennes,* 13 bis. ed. A.M. Malingrey.

45. Baus, op. cit., p. 89.

46. Ibid., p. 90.

47. Ibid.

48. J.N.D. Kelly, *Early Christian Doctrines* (London: Adam & Charles Black, 1965) p. 401.

49. Ibid., p. 416.

50. This closeness accounts for many other historical developments: the relationship to Pippin and then to Charlemagne; the entire concept of the Holy Roman Empire; the effort to make the pope, even *in temporalibus,* supreme over all the western rulers; the *cuius regio illius religio* of the reformation period; the explicitly enunciated role of the laity in the late nineteenth and early twentieth century as key to the reinstatement of the pre–French revolution church-state relationship; and finally the difficulty of many bishops at Vatican II to understand the meaning of "freedom of religion" which some bishops and theologians were propounding and which eventually was expressed in the decree *Dignitatis humanae.*

51. Basil, *In divites,* 7.39 PG 35, 880.

52. *The Pilgrimage of Etheria* (London: SPCK, 1919) ed. M.C. McClure and C.L. Feltoe (London: SPCK, 1919) p. 30.

53. *Codex Theodos.* XVI, 2:20. Cf. *Codex Theodosianus,* translation and commentary by Clyde Pharr, Theresa Sherrer Davidson and Mary Brown Pharr (Princeton: Princeton University Press, 1952).

54. Jerome, *Ep.* 52, 6; *PL* 22, 532.

55. Neill, op. cit., p. 70.

56. Cf. Herrin, pp. 73–74.

57. W.H.C. Frend, "The Church of the Roman Empire, 313–600," *The Layman in Christian History,* p. 59.

58. Marius Victorinus, *Adv. Arium, PL* 8.

59. Cf. E.A. Clark, op. cit., pp. 165–168.

60. E. Clark, op. cit., pp. 24–25; cf. also, p. 156.

61. Ibid., p. 204.

62. The magisterial and theological discussion of the role of the papacy and its connection to the New Testament is not the focus of this particular section. In this section I am presenting only certain key figures and their writings which spelled out in a significant way the position of papal monism.

63. Cf. W. Ullmann, *The Growth of Papal Government in the Middle Ages: A Study in the Ideological Relation of Clerical to Lay Power* (London: Methuen, 1970) pp. 2–14. Cf. also Ullmann, *Principles of Government and Politics in the Middle Ages* (N.Y.: Barnes and Noble, 1961). Ullmann's writings present a clear "bias" toward papal monism, and as a result he reads and evaluates historical data from this standpoint, sometimes with over- and perhaps mis-interpretation of texts. For a critique of Ullmann, cf. F. Kempf, "Die päpstliche Gewalt in der mittelalterlichen Welt," *Saggi storici intorno al papato (Miscellanea historica pontificie,* XXI, 1959) pp. 117ff.

64. P. Batiffol, *Cathedra Petri: Études d'histoire ancienne de l'église* (Paris: Les Éditions du Cerf, 1938) p. 89.

65. Gelasius I, *Ep.* 14, c. 9: ". . . satisque conveniens sit, ut totum corpus ecclesiae in hac sibimet observatione concordet, quam illic vigere conspiciat ubi Dominus ecclesiae totius posuit principatum."

66. K.F. Morrison, *The Two Kingdoms: Ecclesiology in Carolingian Political Thought* (Princeton: Princeton University Press, 1964) p. 258; cf. *MGH Epp.* iv, n. 93, p. 137.

67. *MGH, Epp.* v, n. 2, p. 91; n. 8, pp. 66 ff; n. 2, p. 91.

68. Cf. Pope Leo I, *Sermo* 3, cap. 4, had designated the bishop of Rome as the vicar of St. Peter, and this had been a *new way* of describing the pope. In his view, the spiritual aspect of the papacy was considered higher, of course, than the governmental aspect of the emperor. Gregory IV, however, went far beyond Leo I or any of his predecessors by claiming supremacy even in temporal matters. Gregory IV added something *new* as well.

69. *MGH*, n. 10, p. 589.

70. *PL,* 115, 692 ff.

71. Cf. Ullmann, *The Growth of Papal Government in the Middle Ages,* pp. 202ff. Morrison, op. cit., p. 260, nuances Ullmann's assertions regarding Nicholas I and John VIII.

72. Gelasius I, *Tractatus II,* c. 8. Cf. Ullmann, op. cit., pp. 15–27.

73. Cf. Ullmann, op. cit., pp. 414–446.

74. The *Dictatus Gregorii VII* is used only as illustrative, for there are

many medieval sources in which this view can be found, both in the writings of popes mentioned previously, and in the writings of the theologians also already mentioned.

75. The view of papal monism has never totally disappeared. During the turbulent reformation period, popes attempted to use this kind of power, but for the most part their efforts proved futile. During the time of Vatican I, at the end of the nineteenth century, with the proclamation of the infallibility of the pope, the position of the pope again came to the fore, and particularly as regards the issue of his relationship (and therefore the Church's relationship) to sovereign states. During the time of Vatican II, the issue of the lay person vis-à-vis the *sacerdotium* raised once again many of the same issues. We see this, for instance, in the efforts of some church leaders and scholars, first to delimit the lay person's activity to the "secular" sphere and the ordained person's activity to the "ecclesial" sphere, and then, secondly, following the axiom of earlier "Catholic action" movements: namely, only those lay activities which are under the *sacerdotium* can be considered "Catholic action." We see something of this in episcopal and papal intrusions into the world of politics, often with the threat of severe denunciations, even excommunications, at least for lay Christians who might presume to act publicly within the *res publica* in ways which are in apparent opposition to church teaching. On what basis, people ask, do bishops and popes intrude into the sphere of the *res publica?*

76. J. Aufhauser, "Die sakrale Kaiseridee in Byzanz," *La Regalitá Sacra* (Leiden: Brill, 1959) pp. 531–542; in the same volumes the articles by K. Goldammer, "Die Welt des Heiligen im Bilde des Gottherrschers," pp. 513–530, and Margaret Murral, "The Divine King," pp. 595–608.

77. The precise role that Sigismund played in arranging this council is disputed. It is true that on December 9, 1413, John XXIII issued a bull convoking the council to Constance, a place which Sigismund had really determined. However, since John XXIII is a rival claimant to the papal throne, and since Gregory XII is the Roman claimant, there is surely a question of a *titulus coloratus* as regards the very jurisdiction of John XXIII. Although the actual numbering of popes does not conclusively adjudicate the situation, it is of no little importance that in the twentieth century a pope not only chose the name John, but also counted himself as John XXIII. Where does this leave the fifteenth century pope John XXIII who "convoked" the council? Gregory VII at a later date also "convoked" the council as well, even though it was already de facto in session. Gregory's claim to the papacy, however, is itself tainted, and as in the case of John XXIII there was a *titulus coloratus* to his own papal legitimacy. All of this leaves the question "Who legitimately convoked the council?"

quite open. The emperor clearly was the one who de facto brought it about.

78. K.A. Fink, "The Western Schism and the Councils," *HC*, v. IV, p. 424. He cites some telling phrases from the conciliar literature of that era: *quod omnes tangit, ab omnibus approbari debet*, and: *major est auctoritas totius orbis quam urbis alicuius.*

79. Fink, op. cit., p. 425, sagely remarks that the variety of views regarding a council indicate that "it will not do to speak of an exclusively correct 'divinely willed monarchical structure' of the Church in the late Middle Ages." Papal monism, particularly extreme papal monism, was one view among several.

80. The various papal convocations of this council have to be seen as a sort of grandstanding, in an effort to validate their respective claim to papal power. Still, these various "convocations" indicate a clash between papal monism and imperial monism.

81. An example of this can be seen in the religious symbolism of the Third Reich which has been well documented. The Protestant-dominated government of the United States in the nineteenth century gave rise to anti-Catholic demonstrations, and the attempt by Roosevelt to establish official ties to the Vatican raised, even within governmental departments, enormous official counter-activity.

82. In the United States, for example, there is today a growing sense of an "imperial presidency," replete with a theory of untouchableness.

83. Cf. Morrison, op. cit. Morrison spends most of his book delineating this position, and indicates that it was held by a majority of Gallic bishops. Thus, there was a clear division of thinking between the Roman, papal approach and the Gallic approach. This caused considerable strain between these churches as time went by, and had repercussions at both Vatican I (the infallibility issue) and Vatican II (the issue of religious freedom).

84. Morrison, op. cit., p. 243.

85. For the medieval church's approaches toward the Muslims, cf. B. Kedar, *Crusade and Mission* (Princeton: Princeton University Press, 1984). Since the medieval church leadership was well aware of many aspects of the Islamic world, many questions are raised by the material in this volume regarding the claims made by the proponents of papal monism. Nowhere do we find popes deposing Islamic rulers, although they were well aware of their existence and there were in some areas Christians who lived among them. Nowhere was there any officially endorsed attempt to convert them. In what way, then, were they part of the world, the *societas Christiana*, as it was then thought to exist?

86. Cf. Morrison, op. cit., p. 239.

87. This idea of conquering and baptizing can be seen in the Spanish and Portuguese expeditions into the Americas, after the time of Columbus. This idea can be seen as well in some of the colonization of the African states, by both Catholic and Protestant countries, in the eighteenth to early twentieth centuries.

88. K. Baus, "The Development of the Church of the Empire within the Framework of the Imperial Religious Policy," op. cit., p. 3.

89. Cf. ibid., p. 5, for an enumeration of such legislative acts.

90. Cf. ibid., p. 7.

91. Coleman-Norton, op. cit., in his introduction, notes that the drafting of imperial instruments, particularly if the topics were ecclesiastical in nature, were probably drafted by Christian clerics who shaded the text in favor of the Christian position, or in favor of a particular Christian position; cf. p. xxxix.

92. The emperor Gratian renounced the title *Pontifex maximus,* and only then was it gradually taken up by the bishop of Rome as a papal title.

93. There is no little difference of scholarly opinion on the exact reference of this phrase: bishop to the "ektos."

94. K. Baus, op. cit., p. 14.

95. Cf. Coleman-Norton, op. cit., p. xli. The author in his footnote to this section is well aware of the controversy over the term "bishop" applied to Constantine, p. lvii. The emperor is not presented so much in an episcopal or clerical mode of operation, but in a way consonant with Hellenistic philosophy, which Eusebius of Caesarea utilized in his description of the emperor as a uniquely and divinely appointed instrument to bring about unity within the civilized world.

96. Cf. Sozomon, *Historia ecclesiastica,* VI, 7. Cf. also H. Rahner, *L'Église et l'État dans le christianisme primitif* (Paris: Éditions du Cerf, 1964).

97. Cf. Coleman-Norton, op. cit., v. 1, pp. 300–341. Of particular interest is the letter of Valentinian I, Valens and Gratian on consubstantiality, written in 375. Using his imperial power, Valentinian imposes a position regarding consubstantiality on the entire Christian empire; cf. ibid., pp. 336–341.

98. Ambrose, *Ep. 21. PL,* 16, 953–955. Eng. trans. *St. Ambrose: Letters (Fathers of the Church)* (N.Y.: Fathers of the Church Inc., 1954), trans. M. Bejaha, pp. 52–56.

99. Ambrose, ibid.

100. The controversy over rebaptism raised the issue of who was to be rightfully considered within the Christian community and who was to be considered outside the Christian community. If a "first" baptism was

useless, then rebaptism was needed to bring such people into the Christian church.

101. E. Ewig, "The papacy's alienation from Byzantium and rapprochement with the Franks," *HC*, v. 2, p. 18.

102. Ibid., p. 19.

103. J.B. Bury, *History of the Later Roman Empire* (N.Y.: Dover Publications, 1958) v. 2, p. 360.

104. Gelasius, *PL* 56, 634–635; 59, 42–43; 128, 436–437; 129, 1216; 130, 958–959.

105. Gelasius, *PL*, 58, 935. In this letter he tells Zeno: "You should desire to subject, not to exhibit, the royal will to Christ's bishops [*sacerdotes*] and to learn through their holy presidents [*praesules*] rather than teach most holy matter; to follow the Church's decision, not to prescribe." In another letter written five years later (489), the curial official Gelasius writes: "The emperor is a son, not a president [*praesul*] of the Church; it befits him to learn, not to teach, what belongs to religion. . . . God has willed the things which must be administered by the Church to pertain to bishops, not to the world's powers; and if these are loyal Christians, he has willed these to be subject to his Church and to the bishops." *PL* 58, 950.

106. Optatus of Mileve, *CSEL* 26, 74.

107. Ambrose, *Serm. contra Auxentium*, 36. *PL* 16, 1049–1062.

108. K. Baus, "Inner Life of the Church between Nicaea and Chalcedon," op. cit., p. 334.

109. Ibid., p. 334.

110. *Apostolic Constitutions*, III, 57, 4–5; Synod of Laodicea, can. 19.

111. Cf. Victricius, *Liber de laude sanctorum* 2–3. *PL* 20, 443–458.

112. *Council of Elvira*, can. 38.

113. Baus, op. cit., p. 335.

114. B.Z. Kedar, *Crusade and Mission*, p. xii.

115. The edict of Galerius on toleration of Christians (311) offered protection of Roman law for the freedom of Christians to worship. It did not offer Christians any exclusive claim on religious worship in the empire. The famous so-called "Edict of Milan," or more accurately the letter of Constantine I and Licinius on the restoration of the church, was an edict in which there was toleration for religion generally. "It declares for the first time the doctrine that full freedom in the realm of religion belongs as a right to everyone" (Coleman-Norton, op. cit., p. 30). The same attitude of toleration, not exclusivity, must be read in the edict of Constantine on behalf of Christians (324); cf. Coleman-Norton, op. cit., p. 106.

116. Cf. E.A. Thompson, "Christianity and the Northern Barbarians,"

The Conflict between Paganism and Christianity in the Fourth Century,
pp. 60–61. Thompson notes that Frumentius had missionized mostly to
the Roman traders, not the barbarians. Once he had become bishop, he
extended his missionary activity to the non-Romans. Thompson also
notes that in such places as Axum missionary activity proceeded in a way
quite different from the missionary work sponsored by Gregory the Great
to the English, or that of Ansgar among the Danes and Swedes or that of
Louis the Pius as regards Hamburg.

117. Cf. Herrin, op. cit., pp. 75–89.

118. Cf. John Chrysostom, *Cat. ad illum,* I, 1; *In Joh. hom.* 18, 1; *In
Act. hom.* 23, 4; *In ep. ad Cor. hom.* 2, 6; Basil, *Hom. in s. bapt.* 7; Gregory
of Nyssa, *De iis qui bapt. differunt;* Ambrose, *Expos. in Luc.* 7, 220, 225;
De Hel. et jej. 22, 83–85; *De Noe,* 25; *Epp.* 79 and 80.

119. Mollat, op. cit., p. 19.

120. Ibid.

121. C. Straw, *Gregory the Great: Perfection in Imperfection,* pp. 4–27.

122. Ibid., p. 6.

123. Ibid., passim, 6–17. Straw also cites such authors as F. Gastaldelli,
L. Weber, J. Leclercq, R. Gillet, J. LaPorte, P. Aubin, C. Dagens, R.
Bélanger, and M. Doucet. All of these have made serious contributions to
the literature on Gregory the Great and have avoided the neo-scholastic
approach which has generally characterized studies on Gregory. Cf.
Straw, pp. 17–18.

124. Gregory, *Mor.* 9, 5.5 (*CCL* 143, 458).

125. Straw, op. cit., p. 83.

126. Ibid., p. 85; cf. Gregory, *In Lib. I Reg.* 2, 125, and 129; *Mor.* 35,
14–28; 32, 20, 37.

127. Cf. for instance the list of citations of Gregory used in Peter Lombard's *Libri IV Sententiarum* (Quarrachi, St. Bonaventure, 1916) v. II, p.
1053. Cf. P.E. Schramm, "Gregor der Große und Bonifaz," *Beiträge zur
allgemeinen Geschichte,* v. I (Stuttgart: Anton Hiersemann, 1968) pp.
86–89, "So ist er [Gregor] bis in das 11. Jahrhundert der geistliche Lehrer
des Mittelalters geblieben. Erst die Scholastik hat ihn wieder in den Shat-
ten Augustins zurücktreten lassen" (p. 89).

128. Cf. Straw, op. cit., pp. 70, 71, 72 and 87.

129. Ibid., p. 3, and the correspondence of Gregory to Brunhilda, p. 87.

130. Ibid., p. 72. Gregory, *Dialogues,* 1.1.6.

131. Ibid., p. 73; Straw refers not only to the *Dialogues,* but also to
Sulpicius Severus. P. Rousseau, "The Spiritual Authority of the Monk-
Bishop," *Journal of Theological Studies,* 22 (1971), p. 407, is also cited as
one who sees this trend of correspondence between spirituality and ecclesiastical office as fairly general for the west by the fifth century.

132. Gregory, *Moralia,* 9.5.5. "For he who marvelously created all things ordered all creation so that it would harmonize with itself."

133. The term "exarch" first appeared in 584. Cf. T.S. Brown, *Gentlemen and Officers* (Rome, 1984) pp. 48–53, who presents the background for the use of this term.

134. H.-G. Beck, "The Early Byzantine Church," *The Imperial Church from Constantine to the Early Middle Ages,* p. 491.

135. For background on Dionysius, cf. R. Roques, *L'Univers dionysien* (Paris, 1954); W. Völker, *Kontemplation und Ekstase bei ps.-Dionysius Areopagita* (Wiesbaden, 1958); M. de Gandillac, Fr. trans. *Oeuvres complètes du Pseudo-Denys l'Aréopagite* (Paris, 1980).

136. A. Louth, "Denys the Areopagite," *The Study of Spirituality,* ed. by C. Jones, G. Wainwright, E. Yarnold (Oxford: Oxford University Press, 1986) p. 186.

137. Dionysius Areopagita, *Celestial Hierarchy,* III, 1, 164. D.

138. There are many similarities between Dionysius Areopagita and Proclus. Whether Dionysius is dependent on Proclus or whether both draw from similar sources remains a moot question. Proclus (412–485), an Athenian neoplatonist, attempted to move beyond Plotinus, but yet remained within the same Plotinian framework. For him existence is a passage into various levels (orders) of perfection.

139. A. Meredith, "Proclus," *The Study of Spirituality,* p. 101.

140. Aristides, *Apology,* n. 15, in *Ante-Nicene Fathers,* v. IX (N.Y.: Christian Literature Company, 1896) trans. from both Greek and Syriac, pp. 263–279. N. 15 is found in both the Greek and the Syriac texts. Cf. *Aristides,* ed. J. Giffken, *Zwei griechische Apologeten* (Hildesheim: Olms, 1970).

141. Athenagoras, *Presbeia peri Christianon, PG* v. 6, esp. n. 8.

142. *Epistle to Diognetus, 5–6,* in *Ancient Christian Writers,* v. 6 (Westminster: Newman Press, 1948), trans. and ed. by J. Kleist, pp. 138–140.

6. *Monasticism to 600 A.D.*

1. For a history of monasticism, cf. especially Baus, op. cit., pp. 794–800 for a lengthy bibliography on almost every aspect of monastic life; Ivan Gobry, *Les Moines en Occident: De saint Antoine à saint Basile* (Paris: Arthème Fayard, 1985), *Les Moines en Occident: De saint Martin à saint Benoit* (Paris: Arthème Fayard, 1985).

2. The term "ontological" is deliberately selected, for in much of post-reformation Catholic theology, the cleric, at least the cleric in major orders, was considered to be "ontologically" distinct from all other

members in the church. It is in this sense that there is an "ontological *klerikos/laikos* model" of the church.

3. Cf. Origen, *Homiliae in Ez.* 4, 4–8.

4. Cf. G. Folliet, "Les trois catégories de chrétiens," *Augustinus Magister,* v. II (Paris, 1954) pp. 631–644; H. de Lubac, *Exégèse médiévale,* I-2 (Paris: 1959) pp. 571ff; G. Penco, "Temi ed aspetti ecclesiologici della tradizione monastica," *Medioevo Monastico* (Rome: Pontificio Ateneo S. Anselmo, 1988) p. 244.

5. Anon., *Expositio in Cant. Cantic.* Prol, *PL* 172, c. 519: "Tres ordines sunt in Ecclesia: Noe, Job, Daniel. Noe doctores, Job coniugati, Daniel contemplativi."

6. Abbone di Fleury, *Apologeticus, PL* 139, 463 a/b. Cf. Penco, op. cit., pp. 245–249 for other medieval citations on this threefold representation of Christian life.

7. Cf. A. Veilleux, *La Liturgie dans le cénobitisme pachômien au quatrième siècle* (Rome: Pontificium Institutum S. Anselmi, 1968) pp. 171–174. This is a key work on Pachomian monasticism.

8. Cf. P. Gobillot, "Les origines du monachisme chrétien et l'ancienne religion de l'Égypte," *Recherches de Science Religieuse* (1920–1922), v. 10, pp. 303–364; v. 11, pp. 168–213; v. 12, pp. 46–68.

9. R. Reitzenstein, *Historia monachorum und Historia Lausiaca* (Göttingen: Vandenhoeck und Ruprecht, 1916).

10. K. Heussi, *Der Ursprung des christlichen Mönchtums* (Tübingen: J.C.B. Mohr, 1936); cf. A. Vööbus, *History of Asceticism in the Syrian Orient, CSCO,* v. 184 (Louvain, 1958–1988).

11. E.E. Sutcliffe, *The Monks of Qumran as Depicted in the Dead Sea Scrolls* (Westminster: Newman, 1960); I van den Ploeg, "Les Esséniens et les origines du monachisme chrétien," *Il Monachesimo orientale* (Rome, 1958).

12. Cf. Adalbert de Vogüé, in *Pachomian Koinonia: The Lives, Rules and Other Writings of Saint Pachomius and His Disciples,* trans. by Armand Veilleux (Kalamazoo: Cistercian Publications, 1980), who sees, p. xvii, the rootage for Pachomian cenobitism in "the secular church and anchoritism; the charity of Christians at Themebes and the monastic ascesis of Paloman." In the lives of Pachomias, we find that the teaching of Paloman is rooted in Old Testament figures.

13. Cf. H. Bacht, "Mönchtum und Kirche," *Sentire Ecclesiam* (Freiburg: Herder, 1961) pp. 114–123; also Veilleux, op. cit., pp. 192–195. Veilleux mentions W. Bousset and H. Rahner as two authors who attempt to stress an early antagonism not only with the socio-political world, but also with the clerical world. Bousset speaks of "die anfänglichen Ge-

gensätze zwischen Klerus und Mönchtum," and Rahner uses the term: "Kirchenferne."

14. J.A. McGuckin, "Christian Asceticism and Alexandria," *Monks, Hermits and the Ascetic Tradition* (London: Blackwell, 1985), ed. W.J. Sheils, p. 31; cf also Clement of Alexandria, *Paedagogos*, 3, 7, and 8.

15. Cf. J.M. Rist, *Stoic Philosophy* (Cambridge: University Press, 1969) pp. 22–53.

16. Ibid., p. 26.

17. This idea of monastic perfection still appears even after Vatican II. Cf. e.g. I. Gobry, *Les Moines en Occident: De saint Antoine à saint Basile*, p. 26: "Cependant, d'après la doctrine traditionelle de l'Église, la voie des conseils, ajoutant aux précepts et mettant tout en oeuvre pour les accomplir en perfection, exprime un amour plus total et est en elle-même une voie plus parfaite." Gobry, in this same section, indicates that this view is the traditional teaching of the Roman church. It is traditional, in the sense that many theologians have held it, and it has often appeared in official documents of the church. That this doctrine is part of the "official magisterium" of the church cannot be held after Vatican II. Vatican II deliberately avoided this approach to religious life, and viewed Christian baptismal/eucharistic holiness itself as perfection. Cf. *LG*, ch. V, "De universali vocatione ad sanctitatem in Ecclesia."

18. Veilleux, op. cit., p. 205.

19. Cf. M. Viller, *La spiritualité des premiers siècles chrétiens* (Paris: Bloud and Gan, 1930); K. Holl, *Enthusiasmus und Bußgewalt beim griechischen Mönchtum. Eine Studie zu Symeon dem neuen Theologen* (Hildesheim: C. Olms, 1963); A Veilleux, op. cit., pp. 176–177.

20. Cf. P. Rousseau, "The Desert Fathers, Antony and Pachomius," *The Study of Spirituality*, p. 123: "A whole range of texts recounts how monks would escape into town, sleep with prostitutes and others, even knowingly sire children, and yet be received again in their communities. The power of repentance was more highly regarded than the danger of lust." Rousseau makes reference to *The Desert Fathers* by Helen Wadell (N.Y.: Sheed and Ward, 1942) pp. xxvii, xxviii, and F. Nau, "Histoire des solitaires Égyptiens," *Revue de l'orient chrétien*, passim 1908–1913.

21. Cf. Henry Chadwick, "The Ascetic Ideal in the History of the Church," *Monks, Hermits and the Ascetic Tradition*, p. 14: "That in Augustine's time the vows included renunciation of property and of marriage is certain. That they included obedience in set terms is not attested." The very same conclusion can be found in Veilleux, op. cit., pp. 213ff.

22. John Chrysostom, *On the Priesthood*, 3, 4. Cf. also Ivo Auf der

Maur, *Mönchtum und Glaubensverkündigung in den Schriften des hl. Johannes Chrysostomus* (Freiburg: Paulusdruckerei, 1959) pp. 25–32; Auf der Maur compares the monk and the ordained minister (p. 30), and in a special way he discusses later in his book the opinion of some authors such as L. Meyer and R. Heiss, who believed that Chrysostom thought that priesthood and monastic status were incompatible (pp. 154–157).

23. Chadwick, op. cit., p. 11.

24. Ibid., pp. 12, 16.

25. Even the bishops at Vatican II found the canonical distinction, lay/cleric, inadequate for their needs and used instead a threefold distinction: lay, religious, cleric, which they called a pastoral description of church structure. Cf. *LG*, n. 31.

26. Rousseau, op. cit., p. 125.

27. Cf. the lengthy geographical discussion in Baus, op. cit., pp. 343–393, 518–523, 690–707.

28. Cf. Athanasius, *Vita S. Antoni*, 51–53. Cf. *PG* 26, 835–976.

29. Contemporary with Antony was the development of the baptismal liturgy, with its many exorcisms against the devil. Cf. H.A. Kelly, *The Devil at Baptism* (Ithaca: Cornell University Press, 1985).

30. This rule is preserved in Jerome's Latin translation. The Coptic sources (cf. *Vies coptes*, 67–69) do not offer more than a vague glimpse of this rule.

31. Baus, op. cit., p. 348.

32. Cf. Vogüé, op. cit., p. xiv.

33. In the *Life of Pachomias*, we even read that Pachomias himself abandoned the ministry to the poor, since this was the work for the "clerics."

34. Cf. John Chrysostom, *Epp.* 49, 53, 54, 123, 126. Cf. *PG*, 52.

35. Theodore of Cyrus, *Historia religiosa seu ascetica vivendi ratio*, n. 26. Cf. *PG* 82, 1283–1496.

36. Cf. Sozomen, *Historia ecclesiae*, Bk. 1, 14. Cf. Greek text, ed. by J. Bidez: *Sozomène: Histoire Ecclésiastique* (Paris: Éditions du Cerf, 1983).

37. Cf. Straw, op. cit., p. 71. Noteworthy in these references is Gregory's use of the term *vir*, which in Latin is one-sidedly masculine. Should there not also be a *mulier Dei, mulier sancta, mulier venerabilis?*

38. Ibid., p. 181.

39. Ibid., pp. 45–46.

40. Cf. P. Rousseau, *Pachomius: The Making of a Community in Fourth-Century Egypt* (Berkeley: University of California Press, 1985); R. Van Dam, *Leadership and Community in Late Antique Gaul* (Berkeley: University of California Press, 1985).

41. Straw, op. cit., p. 101.

42. Cf. J. Pelikan, *Jesus through the Centuries* (New Haven: Yale Univ. Press, 1985), esp. "The Monk Who Ruled the World," pp. 109–121.

43. Cf. K. Hallinger, "Papst Gregor der Große und der heilige Benedikt," *Studia Anselmiana*, 42 (1957) pp. 231–319.

44. The rule which Teodomar sent was copied at Aachen in the early ninth century, and it is this manuscript which is preserved at St. Gall. More than any other manuscript this seems to be the closest to the original from Benedict himself.

45. Cf. I. Gobry, *Les Moines en Occident: De saint Martin à saint Benoit*, pp. 377–406.

46. Ibid., p. 395.

47. C.H. Lawrence, *Medieval Monasticism*, p. 24. Cf. Gobry, op. cit., pp. 394–395.

48. Lawrence, op. cit., p. 26.

49. Cf. e.g., *The Rule of S. Benedict*, ch. 60 and 61. Cf. K. Seasoltz, "Monastery and Eucharist: Some American Observations," *Living Bread, Saving Cup* (Collegeville: Liturgical Press, 1987).

50. Cf. Gennadius of Marseilles, *De vir. ill.* 23, *PL* 58, 1052–1120; Bachiarius, *Liber de fide*, 2, *PL* 20, 1015–1062.

51. Augustine, *De Ordine*, 1, 31–33.

52. Augustine, *De beata vita*. The fact that notaries were present, and that the discussion was held in such a festive situation provides us with a small window into an urbane form of monasticism which one would not find in the Pachomian or Syrian forms of the cenobitic life.

53. Augustine, *Sermo* 355, 2.

54. H. Chadwick, "The Ascetic Ideal in the History of the Church," *Monks, Hermits and the Ascetic Tradition*, p. 16.

55. Ibid.; cf. also Augustine, *De sancta virginitate*, 12 and 54.

56. Cf. Augustine, *De civitate Dei*, 19, 27.

57. Cf. Augustine, *Ennaratio in Ps.* 147, 9.

58. Perhaps the insights of Marcuse in *One Dimensional Man* could be, *mutatis mutandis*, applied to monasticism as well. In Marcuse's view, the regnant society absorbs the opposition, making it a part of its own dimension. So, too, the regnant Christian socio-economic world of the middle ages absorbed monasticism into its own dimensions, thus depriving it of its original counter-culture stance.

59. Cf. note above.

60. H. Bacht, "Die Rolle des orientalischen Mönchtums in den kirchenpolitischen Auseinandersetzungen um Chalkedon (431–519)," *Das Konzil von Chalkedon*, ed. A. Grillmeier and H. Bacht (Würzburg: Echter-Verlag) v. II, 1959, pp. 299–307.

61. Cf. Ueding, op. cit., p. 600: "Als die Freizügigkeit der Mönche so ungewöhnliche Maße annahm, daß daraus ein Vagantentum wurde, als zudem das Mönchtum ein Machtfaktor für oder gegen christliche Lehre oder Disziplin wurde, weil es durch die Hochachtung des Volkes eine ungewöhnlich hohe moralische Bedeutung gewonnen hatte. . . ." The author refers as well to the way in which the monks in Asia Minor and Syria opposed the teaching of Apollinarius. Cf. Sozomen, *Hist. eccle.* VI, 27.

62. The word "jurisdiction" might be misused in this early period of church history. It certainly does not have the canonical meaning which developed from the twelfth century onward. Cf. L. Ueding, op. cit., pp. 597–676. Ueding is well aware of this difficulty, although at times he tends to describe the situation from a standpoint of episcopal jurisdiction, which better conforms to a later understanding of this term. Throughout this patristic period, various groups in the church were emerging and therefore the juridical interrelationships were (a) not settled and (b) not uniform throughout the Christianized empire. H. Bacht, "Die Rolle des orientalischen Mönchtums," *Das Konzil von Chalkedon*, pp. 302–303, notes that many episkopoi, presbyters and deacons were taken from the ranks of the monks, and that as time went on many clerics entered monasteries and did rise to positions of leadership within the monastic communities. Indeed, in the sixth century and onward the monastic communities often became the "seminaries" for episkopoi (p. 302).

63. Cf. Bacht, op. cit., p. 301.

64. Baus, op. cit., p. 365.

65. Cf. John Chrysostom, *In 1 Tim. hom.* 14, 4. Cf. *PG,* 62, 663–700.

66. Theodoret, *Hist. rel.* 2, 3. Cf. *PG,* 82, 1283–1496.

67. Bacht, op. cit., pp. 307–308 makes a case for the theological acumen of the monks, but even with his more positive aspect, monasticism cannot be seen, in its earlier patristic period, as strongly academic or as a vanguard of theological investigations.

68. Cf. E. von Severus, "Das Monasterium als Kirche," *Enkainia: Festschrift zum 800-jährigen Weihegedächtnis der Abteikirche Maria Laach* (Düsseldorf: 1956); A. de Vogüé, "La monastère, Église du Christ," *Commentationes in Regulam S. Benedicti* (Rome: Herder, 1957); A. Kassing, "Die Mönchsgemeinde in der Kirche," *Geist und Leben,* 34 (1961) pp. 190–196; S. Benz, "The Monastery as a Christian Assembly," *The American Benedictine Review,* 17 (1966) pp. 166–178; A. Veilleux, op. cit., pp. 181–323; L. Ueding, op. cit., pp. 569–676.

69. Y. Congar, "Conscience ecclésiologique en Orient et en Occident du VIᵉ au XIᵉ siècle," *Istina,* 6 (1959) p. 190.

70. Veilleux, op. cit., p. 183.

71. Ibid., pp. 189–195.

72. Ueding, op. cit., pp. 570–600.

73. Cf. Bacht, op. cit.; Ueding, op. cit.; for the theological issues, cf. Grillmeier, *Christ in the Christian Tradition,* v. I (Atlanta: John Knox Press, 1975) trans. J. Bowden, pp. 488–554.

74. Ueding, op. cit., p. 617. It is noteworthy that Ueding says: "Von der Kirche her . . . vom Mönchtum her. . . ." This kind of language continues the false understanding of an opposition between "church" and "monk," i.e. the church on the one hand, and the monks on the other. Actually, it would have been clearer had he used the term "church leadership," rather than simply "church." Monks were, indeed, part of the church and considered themselves in a very ecclesial way. They were attempting to live in a way similar to the apostolic church. The problem with this church-monk language is that one finds it repeated here and there, throughout church history, even in quasi-official documents, in which "church" is used with reference to "church leadership" (i.e. pope, bishops, priests), while others such as monks and lay people are set in opposition to "church." E.g., the church prays for all the faithful . . . the church shows concern in a special way for the many religious men and women. Such language is open to a view of church which borders on the heretical.

75. One should note that both civil and ecclesiastical disturbances are united in this canon, indicating, indirectly, that church leadership and government were indeed involved at that time in some sort of close union.

76. Ueding, ibid., p. 607. Ueding cites Zonara, *PG,* 137, 402.

77. H. von Campenhausen, *Asketische Heimatlosigkeit im altkirchlich-frühmittelalterlichen Mönchtum* (Tübingen: J.C.B. Mohr, 1930).

78. Cf. Ueding, p. 609. He disagrees with H.R. Bittermann, "The Council of Chalcedon and Episcopal Jurisdiction," *Speculum,* 13 (1938) pp. 198–203, who claimed more jurisdiction for bishops than these canons allow.

79. Ueding, op. cit., pp. 620–676.

80. Ibid., p. 643.

81. Veilleux, op. cit., pp. 198–225.

82. Ibid., p. 198: "L'un des traits les plus charactéristiques de la physionomie du monachisme pachômien, c'est précisément qu'on y recevait, au monastère, des païens qui y faisaient leur catéchuménat au sein de la communauté."

83. Ibid., p. 207.

84. Ibid., p. 212; n. 60 presents a respectable bibliographical list on this subject.

85. Ibid., p. 219.

86. Ibid., p. 225.

87. Ibid., pp. 226–248.

88. There is, for instance, the current struggle between some major religious orders (OFM, OFM Cap) and various Vatican officials on the issue of the non-ordained religious, holding positions of jurisdiction within their respective communities. There is, as well, the manner in which the Jesuits were ruled after the general. Fr. Arrupe, relinquished his power. There is, again, the struggle in which some contemporary women religious find themselves as regards decision making within their own religious communities and the imposed requirement to refer various issues to Rome for final decision. This applies in a particular way to the details of religious constitutions.

89. This conflict of rhythms became noticeable for women religious in the nineteenth and early twentieth centuries; the monastic horarium, which many religious communities strongly maintained, conflicted in very profound ways with the ministerial tempo, which these same communities also strongly maintained.

90. The way in which Ignatius of Antioch, for instance, speaks of the *episkopos* as a reflection of God, and the way in which an abbot at times has been portrayed as a reflection of God, have many theological similarities.

7. The Lay Person in the Medieval Frankish Church: 700 to 1000 A.D. The Turning of the Tide

1. Cf. B. Ramsey, "Fathers of the Church," *The New Dictionary of Theology* (Wilmington: Glazier, 1987) p. 387: "The uncertain terminal point in the West only serves to illustrate what is true of the East as well, namely that such cut-off dates are rather arbitrary."

2. J.M. Wallace-Hadrill, *The Frankish Church* (Oxford: Clarendon Press, 1983).

3. E. Amann and A. Dumas, *L'Église au pouvoir des laïques 888–1057* (Paris, 1948).

4. Wallace-Hadrill, op. cit., p. 113.

5. Ibid., p. 162.

6. The Latin reads: "De regibus in Francia, qui illis temporibus non habentes regalem potestatem, si bene fuisset an non?"

7. Wallace-Hadrill, op. cit., p. 166.

8. Ibid.

9. Ibid., p. 304.

10. One instance of a theory preceding practice can be found in the determination of the sequence of minor orders. A sequence was suggested by *Statuta Ecclesiae Antiquae*, and this sequencing became popular and

then canonically established for the western church and subsequently provisioned with theological justification. Cf. Osborne, *Priesthood,* p. 198.

11. Eng. translation of the *Dictatus Gregorii VII* can be found in E. Lewis, *Medieval Political Ideas* (London: Routledge & Kegan Paul, 1954) v. II, pp. 380–381. Lewis cites É. Voosen in the introductory statement, with reference to Voosen's book *Papauté et pouvoir civil à l'époque de Grégoire VII* (p. 71).

12. Ibid., p. 381.

13. E. Lewis, op. cit., v. 1, p. 140. The term "state" did not appear in the western world until the fourteenth century, but it did not appear out of nowhere. Even without this specific term, "state," there is a history to its fourteenth century appearance. Cf. P.E. Schramm, "Die 'Herrschaftszeichen', die 'Staatssymbolik' und die 'Staatspräsentation' des Mittelalters," *Kaiser, Könige und Päpste* (Stuttgart: A. Hiersemann, 1968); ibid., p. 45: "Das Wort, 'Staat' formt sich erst im 14. Jahrhundert. Aber der Staat selbst hat es lange vorher gegeben. Wer seine Geschichte schreiben will, muß sich mit der Mittelalterlichen Staatssymbolik befassen."

14. E. Ewig, "The Papacy's Alienation from Byzantium and Rapprochement with the Franks," *The Church in the Age of Feudalism* (N.Y.: Herder and Herder, 1969) p. 4.

15. Herrin, op. cit., p. 295.

16. Ibid.

17. Ibid., p. 297, citing I. Goldziher, *Muslim Studies,* v. 2 (London, 1971), Excursus 2, "Hadith and the New Testament," pp. 346–362.

18. Wallace-Hadrill, op. cit., p. 185.

19. Ibid., p. 186. Herrin, op. cit., p. 296, makes a similar judgment as regards Pippin and Pope Stephen II. Pippin "did not embark on a policy of expansion into the Italian peninsula to safeguard the Christian republic of Rome simply out of respect for St. Peter and his power to loose and bind on Judgement Day. Rome's legitimation of his dynasty would also assist in consolidating his authority over the semi-independent regions adjoining his Frankish territories, in establishing Frankish leadership of Christian missionary work among the pagans and thus his own domination of the emerging political culture of northern Europe."

20. Cf. Schramm, "Karl der Große als Kaiser (800–814) im Lichte der Staatssymbolik," op. cit., pp. 264–300, esp. pp. 268–273.

21. Cf. Wallace-Hadrill, op. cit., p. 185. Already in June 774, when Charles the Great had overcome the Lombard Desiderius, he assumed the Lombard crown, styling himself *rex Francorum et Langobardorum.*

22. Already in 799 Alcuin wrote in one of his letters that the pope, Leo III, was a refugee. The Byzantine emperor Constantine V had been deposed by his own people. The only hope for the *populus Christianus* was

Charles the Great. At the same time Alcuin begins to use the phrase *imperium Christianum* not in reference to the Byzantine empire, but to the western world, i.e. Charles' empire. "Alcuin's point was clear as it stood: only one man had the power and authority to rescue the papacy, and that man already exercised *imperium* over most of western Europe. Moreover, that *imperium* was not merely political but spiritual in the sense that the king was God's chosen instrument for the establishment of a Christian society." Cf. Wallace-Hadrill, op. cit., p. 187. Cf. as well the *Paderborn Epic,* probably written by Alcuin in the year 799, again prior to the Roman coronation.

23. Wallace-Hadrill, op. cit., p. 231.

24. Cf. Schramm, "Der Ablauf der deutschen Königsweihe nach dem 'Mainzer Ordo' (um 960)," *Kaiser, Könige und Päpste,* v. III, pp. 59–107. Schramm, in *Anhang I,* includes a critical edition of the Latin text, pp. 87–103.

25. Cf. ibid., p. 84. After a sketch and commentary of the liturgical-sacramental rite itself (pp. 62–81), Schramm presents an analysis of "Die 'Königstheorie' des 'Mainzer Ordo' " (pp. 81–87).

26. Schramm, ibid., p. 87.

27. Cf. Herrin, op. cit., pp. 352–353. Gregory's letters to Charles on this matter contained veiled threats of eternal damnation.

28. Herrin, op. cit., p. 356, notes that ever since Leo I, bishops of Rome had been involved in socio-political activities on the part of the Byzantine emperor. The instances involving Gregory III and Zachary indicate a distinct development, namely, the enhanced socio-political position of the popes in Italy, in and for a strictly western area.

29. Schramm, "Die Anerkennung Karls des Großen als Kaiser (bis 800)," op. cit., p. 231, for text on the mosaic, and p. 369 for a reproduction of the mosaic. Schramm notes that G. Ladner considers the presentation of a king within the apse, which was clearly a sacred area, quite extraordinary.

30. Ibid., pp. 231–232; reproduction of the mosaic is found on pp. 367 and 368.

31. *MGH Epist. (Alcuini Epistolae),* n. 174, p. 288.

32. Ewig, op. cit., p. 93.

33. Cf. chapter 5 of this volume.

34. Kempf, op. cit., p. 202.

35. Ibid., p. 202. Kempf refers to Schramm, "Die Krönung in Deutschland bis zum Beginn des salischen Hauses," *Zeitschrift der Savigny-Stiftung für Rechtsgeschichte, Kanonistische Abteilung,* 55 (1935) p. 319. Also cf. C. Erdmann, *Forschungen zur politischen Ideenwelt des Frühmittelalters* (Berlin, 1951), pp. 52–91.

36. In the year 1000 theology and law were not as totally separated as they would become in the thirteenth century. Cf. O. Capitani, "Episcopato ed ecclesiologia nell' età gregoriana," *Le Instituzioni Ecclesiastiche della "Societas Christiana" dei Secoli XI–XII* (Milan: Vita e Pensiero, 1974) pp. 347–348. Also J. Gilchrist, "'Simoniaca haeresis' and the problem of orders from Leo IX to Gratian," *Proceedings of the Second International Congress of Medieval Canon Law* (Vatican City, 1965) pp. 234–235.

37. Cf. M. Reydellet, *La royauté dans la littérature latine de Sidone Apollinaire à Isidore de Séville* (Rome, 1981) pp. 556–595. Also, Herrin, op. cit., pp. 232–249.

38. Herrin, op. cit., p. 242.

39. R.W. Southern, "The Church of the Dark Ages," *The Layman in Christian History*, pp. 102–103.

40. C.H. Lawrence, *Medieval Monasticism*, p. 82. Lawrence also notes that in the ninth century one finds the earliest commentaries on the rule of St. Benedict, namely, those of Smaragdus and Hildemar.

41. Ewig, op. cit., p. 170.

42. Cf. T. Mackin, *Divorce and Remarriage* (N.Y.: Paulist, 1984) pp. 238–257; ibid., *What Is Marriage?* (N.Y.: Paulist, 1982), pp. 145–152.

43. Kempf, "Renewal and Reform from 900 to 1050," *The Church in the Age of Feudalism*, p. 332.

44. Cf. Lawrence, op. cit., p. 82.

45. G. Macy, *The Theologies of the Eucharist in the Early Scholastic Period* (Oxford: Clarendon Press, 1984) pp. 21ff. Macy's reinvestigation of this eucharistic discussion is surely the finest to date.

46. Cf. Kempf, op. cit., pp. 337–338 for bibliographical details on history and correspondence.

47. Gregory the Great, *In Ez.*, II hom. 7, 3: *PL* 76, 967. Cf. G. Picasso, "Laici e laicità nel medioevo," *Laicità: problemi e prospettive*, p. 86.

48. Cassian, *Instituta* xi, 18 *CSEL* 17, 203; Cf. also *Collationes* 1, 20 *CSEL* 13, 31. The counsel to flee from bishops was a counsel to avoid being chosen for bishop.

49. *Vita S. Romani* in *Vie des pères du Jura*, ed. F. Martine (Sources chrétiennes, 142, Paris: Éditions du Cerf, 1968), p. 262.

50. *Gregorii I Papae Registrum Epistolarum* (*MGH:* Berlin, 1891) ed. P. Ewald and L.M. Hartmann, pp. 281–282.

51. Lawrence, op. cit., p. 114. Isidore of Seville recruited well-educated monks into leading positions within the church, which in turn contributed to the clericalization of such monks. Cf. Herrin, op. cit., p. 234.

52. Isidore of Seville had helped bring about a uniform liturgy for Visigothic Spain, later becoming the Mozarabic rite.

53. Cf. Kevin Seasoltz, "Monastery and Eucharist: Some American Observations," *Living Bread, Saving Cup* (Collegeville: Liturgical Press, 1987) p. 265.

54. Cf. M. Bateson, "The Origin and Early History of Double Monasteries," *Trans. of the Royal Historical Society NS,* xii (1899), pp. 137–189. Also G.A. Rohan Chabot, *Les Cryptes de Jouarre* (Paris, 1971).

55. Lawrence, op. cit., p. 52.

56. The use of the term *ordo* in this official local church document should not go unheeded; it indicates the lingering wider usage of the term, rather than the later limited, intra-ecclesiastical, canonical use of the term *ordo* only for clerics. It also indicates that in some areas at least, monks/nuns formed an *ordo.*

57. The prestige of abbots remained in the church throughout the middle ages. At the various Lateran Councils, the number of abbots who attended these gatherings almost rivaled the number of bishops. At the Council of Trent, on the other hand, bishops dominated, although some major superiors of religious groups, including some abbots, were in attendance. Historically, one finds a virtual equation, in many ways, between bishop and abbot in the early middle ages and an exclusionary factor as regards abbots in the pre- and post-reformation periods.

58. Cf. Kempf, op. cit., p. 320.

59. In today's church there remains on the part of some a strong claim that religious life should involve papal exemption. Cf., e.g., J.W. O'Malley, "Priesthood, Ministry and Religious Life: Some Historical and Historiographical Considerations," *Theological Studies,* 49 (1988) pp. 223–257. In speaking of the mendicants, O'Malley says: "The *ministry* of the friars was exempt from the supervision of the episcopacy" (p. 236). Cluniac exemption, on the other hand, was, he states, for the inner-monastic life alone (p. 235). Again, p. 237: "The mendicants had their warrant from the bishop of Rome." After a lengthy discussion of the rise of the Jesuit Order and the Council of Trent, O'Malley turns to Vatican II and notes that *PO,* as well as other Vatican documents, views the ordained presbyter in one way only: "the priest-minister is in hierarchical communion with his bishop" (p. 251). In discussing the fourth vow of the Jesuits (p. 242) he notes that it is the bishop of Rome, not the local bishop, who centers the Society's ministerial life. One can legitimately ask, however, the following question: If religious priesthood is to be centered on exemption from the local bishop (because of the special ministry of religious, as O'Malley argues) and if it is consequently to be centered instead on the bishop of Rome, thus preserving the theologically important presbyteral-episcopal link, is not the logical outcome of such a program of exemption a group such as *Opus Dei,* which exists within a diocese almost as an "alternate

diocese"? I would find the logic of O'Malley's position somewhat discon-certing, if it were pursued to such alternative diocesan structures as *Opus Dei* within a given diocese.

60. Kempf, op. cit., p. 454. Cf. K. Hallinger, "Woher kommen die Laienbrüder?" *Analecta S. O. Cist.,* 12 (1956) pp. 1–104.

61. Ibid., p. 457.

62. Many of these variant liturgies, however, did not disappear; liturgi-cal life even at the height of the Carolingian reform was not monolithic. The richness of variant liturgies continued to co-exist, though marginally, alongside the dominant Gallic-Roman form of liturgy.

63. Cf. B. Poschmann, *Penance and the Anointing of the Sick* (N.Y.: Herder and Herder, 1964) trans. by F. Courtney, p. 139: "About 800 Theodulf of Orleans testifies that in Gaul confession at the beginning of Lent is general practice (*Capitulare,* I, c. 36)." Poschmann also cites the *Penitential of Egbert* and the instruction *Praemonere debet*. The interpo-lated *Rule of Chrodegang,* c. 900, urges monks to confess every Saturday.

64. Cf. *Synod of Frankfurt,* 794 A.D., *MGH Capit.* no. 28.

65. Cf. Jungmann, "The Sacraments and the Mass," *The Church in the Age of Feudalism,* p. 305.

66. Ibid., p. 306.

67. It was Alexander II (1061–1073) who made a single mass per day the norm.

68. Power and greed certainly played major roles in this issue of si-mony, but there was also the Germanic notion of the proprietary church. Roman law focused on function, with property an appendage; Germanic law focused on property, with function as an appendage, which of course made the priest or bishop secondary. Cf. Kempf, op. cit., p. 342.

8. *The First Millennium of the Christian Community and the Role of the Lay Person: An Evaluation*

1. C. Volz, *Pastoral Life and Practice in the Early Church* (Minneapo-lis: Augsburg, 1990).

2. Ibid., p. 36.

9. *The Later Medieval Period*

1. B. Hamilton, *Religion in the Medieval West* (London: Edward Ar-nold, 1986) p. 17. Hamilton is describing in this passage a pope at the end of the first millennium, not a pope during the entire first thousand years. Some of the papal prerogatives which he mentions had been acquired only in the course of time and not always without a struggle. Some of

these prerogatives remained on paper only, and in regional practice some of them were totally disregarded. Hamilton's description indicates, however, that at the end of the first millennium there was evidence of an ongoing mind-set on the part of many popes and on the part of many papal theologians as regards the powers, privileges, prerogatives, and duties of a pope. It is this mind-set, with all its theological and political overtones and implications, which was picked up in a fierce way by Gregory VII as he struggled to reform the papacy and the church.

2. S. Ozment, *The Age of Reform, 1250–1550: An Intellectual and Religious History of Late Medieval and Reformation Europe* (New Haven: Yale University Press, 1980) p. 9. He is citing from E. Gilson, *The Christian Philosophy of St. Thomas Aquinas* (N.Y.: Random House, 1956).

3. Ibid., p. 12.

4. Cf. E.A. Moody, *The Logic of William of Ockham* (N.Y.: Russell and Russell, 1965); Philotheus Boehmer, *Collected Articles on Ockham* (St. Bonaventure: Franciscan Institute Publications, 1958); A.S. McGrade, *The Political Thought of William of Ockham: Personal and Institutional Principles* (Cambridge: Cambridge University Press, 1974); William J. Courtenay, "Nominalism and Late Medieval Religion," *The Pursuit of Holiness* (Leiden: Brill, 1974), eds. C. Trinkhaus and H.A. Oberman, pp. 26–58. Courtenay is of particular value, since he presents an excellent overview of the historical development of nominalism in the late medieval period as well as the revision of nominalistic thinking by scholars and historians in the twentieth century.

5. Ozment, op. cit., p. 17; cf. D. Trapp, "Augustinian Theology of the Fourteenth Century: Notes on Editions, Marginalia, Opinions and Book-Lore," *Augustiniana*, 6 (1956) pp. 146–274; cf. also G. Leff, *The Dissolution of the Medieval Outlook* (N.Y.: Harper & Row, 1976), who seems to accept some of Trapp's views, even though he remains quite tied to Gilson's assessment of the middle ages.

6. Cf. A. Wolter, "The 'Theologism' of Duns Scotus," *The Philosophical Theology of John Duns Scotus* (Ithaca: Cornell University Press, 1990) pp. 209–253. In this essay, Wolter argues rather cogently against the views of Gilson.

7. Hamilton, op. cit., p. 17.

8. Edward Peters, *Inquisition* (N.Y.: Macmillan [The Free Press] 1988) pp. 35–36.

9. In the text I have referred to the Gregorian reform as the "so-called Gregorian reform," since (a) the movement associated with Gregory began before his papal tenure; (b) the movement associated with Gregory was only one among many reform movements of that time, and these

other movements were often only tangentially influenced by Gregory's reform goals; (c) the goals of Gregory were often papally subservient, while the goals of several other movements were much more focused on the *vita evangelica*.

10. Cf. Robertus de Arbrisello, *Praecepta Recte Vivendi, PL,* 162, 1058ff., esp. 1061–1062. Also H. Grundmann, *Religiöse Bewegungen im Mittelalter* (Hildesheim: G. Olms, 1961) pp. 45ff.

11. Cf. J. von Walter, *Die ersten Wanderprediger Frankreichs: Studien zur Geschichte des Mönchtums* (Leipzig: Dieterich, 1906). *Vita B. Bernardi Tironensis, PL,* 172, 1367–1446; *Vita B. Geraldi de Salis, Acta SS.* (Paris: Victor Palmé: 1869) Oct., v. X, pp. 254–267. *Vita B. Vitalis Saviniacensis, Analecta Bolland.* I, pp. 356–390.

12. For Bruno of Cologne, cf. "Lettres," *Sources Chrétiennes* (Paris: Ed. du Cerf, 1962) v. 88.

13. For Stephen of Thiers-Muret, cf. *Vita S. Stephani, PL* 204, 1005–1046; also Gerard of Gratia's other writings on Stephen, ibid., 1046–1071, 1071–1086. Cf. J. Leclercq, F. Vandenbroucke, and L. Bouyer, *La Spiritualité du moyen âge* (Paris: 1961), pp. 316ff.

14. For Norbert of Xanten, cf. F. Petit, *Norbert et l'origine des Prémontré* (Paris: Ed. du Cerf, 1981); *Norbert von Xanten: Adliger, Ordensstifter, Kirchenfurst* (Cologne: Wienand, 1984) ed. K. Elm.

15. Cf. for Bénézet of Avignon, *Acta Sanctorum,* April, v. 2, pp. 254–263.

16. S. Classen, "Poverty Movement," *New Catholic Encyclopedia* (N.Y.: McGraw-Hill, 1967–1979). For the Beguines and Beghards, cf. C.W. Bynum, *Holy Feast and Holy Fast* (Berkeley: University of California Press, 1987); ibid., *Fragmentation and Redemption: Essays on Gender and the Human Body in Medieval Religion* (N.Y.: Zone Books, 1991).

17. F. Kempf, "The Church in the Age of Feudalism, History of the Church," *HCH,* v. III (N.Y.: Herder and Herder, 1969), separates both physically and descriptively the "heretical and reform movements among clergy and laity (1000 to 1050)," pp. 339–348, from "the '*Vita Evangelica*' movement and the appearance of the new orders," pp. 453–465. In the latter section Kempf makes no mention of the earlier reform movements, giving the impression that the latter arose without any connection to the former. This is certainly a debatable position.

18. In many ways the ecumenical council of Lateran I in 1123, the first attempt at an ecumenical council since Constantinople IV (869–870), attempted to mark an end to these reform movements, since it changed in many ways the manner in which popes determined church policy as regards promotion to hierarchical office and even to ordination itself, namely by attempting to reserve all hierarchical promotions to papal in-

stallation and to validate ordinations only by those who were so installed. In practice, of course, this was disregarded. Cf. canons 1–6 in *Conciliorum Oecumenicorum Decreta*, p. 166.

19. The literature on this subject is rather abundant: cf. H. Grundmann, *Religiöse Bewegungen im Mittelalter;* also ibid., "Ketzergeschichte des Mittelalters," *Die Kirche in ihrer Geschichte*, eds. K.D. Schmidt and E. Worl (Göttingen, 1960ff.); R. Morghen, *Medioevo cristiano* (Bari: Laterza, 1958) pp. 212–286; A. Dondaine, "L'Origine de l'hérésie médiévale," *Rivista di storia della chiesa in Italia*, v. 6 (Rome, 1952) pp. 47–78.

20. R. Morghen, op. cit.; also "Movimenti religiosi popolari nel periodo della riforma della Chiesa," *X Congresso Internazionale de Scienze Storiche*, III (Florence, 1935). Also J.B. Russell, "Interpretations of the origins of medieval heresy," *Mediaeval Studies*, 25 (1963) pp. 26–53.

21. A. Dondaine, op. cit. However, J.V. Fearns, "Peter von Bruis und die religiöse Bewegung des 12. Jahrhunderts," *Archiv für Kulturgeschichte*, v. 48 (1966) pp. 311–335, has argued fairly conclusively that it is only with the Petrobrusians that there is any clear evidence of eastern influence prior to 1140.

22. A. Borst, *Die Katharer* (Stuttgart: Hiersemann, 1953).

23. H. Grundmann, *Religiöse Bewegungen im Mittelalter*, offers a more careful analysis of cause.

24. Cf. Russell, op. cit., for a discussion of this issue.

25. C. Brooke, "Heresy and Religious Sentiment: 1000–1250," *Medieval Church and Society* (London: Sidgwick and Jackson, 1971), p. 147: "A preacher will start as some kind of revivalist, but in intention Catholic, and will end, either with the founders of Tiron and Savigny and Prémontré, by founding a great monastic community, and retreating, respectably, from the world, or, like Peter of Bruis and Henry of Lausanne, by becoming a heresiarch." J.B. Russell, *Dissent and Reform in the Early Middle Ages* (Berkeley: University of California Press, 1965) pp. 241–246, notes that this reform movement tended to appear in strength in the "Fertile Triangle of the Rhineland, the Low Countries and northern France, but that it can be found in almost every part of Europe, with the exceptions of Scandinavia, Scotland, Ireland, and to some degree England." He also argues, and rightfully (pp. 247–249), that reform movements extended from the eighth to the twelfth centuries, and do not start at the turn of the century. However, the reform movements from 1000 onward, coupled with other issues, produced a climate that substantially changed the role of the lay person in the church, and for this reason I have focused on those which date from 1000 onward. In chapter 5, Russell

provides us with a clear picture of the various meanings of "heresy" in this medieval period, and how these various meanings developed.

26. Christopher Brooke, "Heresy and Religious Sentiment: 1000–1250," op. cit., pp. 139–140.

27. For the early Waldensians, cf. K.-V. Selge, *Die Ersten Waldenser* (Berlin: Walter de Gruyter, 1967) p. 35: "Wir wollen die Idee des Waldes bestimmen. Sein Bekenntnis und sein Propositum geben uns nur Material hierfür: Waldes wollte orthodox sein, er hatte der Welt entsagt, er hatte auf sein Eigentum verzichtet, um nicht für den anderen Tag zu sorgen, sondern—unstet wandernd—von den Gaben der Frommen zu leben; er wollte die Räte befolgen: er berief sich auf Worte Jesu, namentlich der Bergpredigt und der Aussendungsreden." One sees in this summary the criterion of discipleship, which I have stressed, as well as the repossession of the scriptural words, which served as the basis both for Waldes' own conversion and for his plan of Christian perfection.

28. The literature on the mendicant orders is vast; cf. as representative such works as A. Fortini, *Francis of Assisi* (N.Y.: Crossroad, 1981), trans. by H. Moak, esp. the assembly of bibliographical materials, pp. 671–699. Also J. Moorman, *The History of the Franciscan Order* (Chicago: Franciscan Herald Press, 1988); Duncan Nimmo, *Reform and Division in the Medieval Franciscan Order* (Rome: Capuchin Historical Studies, 1987); Théophile Desbonnets, *De l'Intuition à l'institution* (Paris: Éditions Franciscaines, 1983); *Archivum Franciscanum Historicum* (Florence and Quaracchi, 1908ff); *Archivum Fratrum Praedicatorum* (Rome, 1931ff); W.H. Hinnebusch, *The History of the Dominican Order* (Staten Island: Alba, 1973) 2 vols.; G. Bedouelle, *Saint Dominic* (San Francisco: Ignatian Press, 1987), trans. M.T. Noble; D. Berg, *Armut und Wissenschaft* (Düsseldorf: Pädigogische Verlag Schwann, 1977); A. Perini, *Bibliographia Augustiniana* (Florence, 1929–1935); *De scriptoribus scholasticis saeculi XIV ex ordine Carmelitarum* (Louvain, 1931); G. Wessels, ed., *Bibliotheca Carmelitana* (Rome, 1927). *Ephemerides Carmeliticae* (Roma, 1947ff); *Monumenta Ordinis Servorum S. Mariae* (Brussels and Florence, 1897–1930).

29. It should be noted that Alexander of Hales, a diocesan priest, had influenced the theological world in very key ways, quite prior to his entry into the Franciscan Order.

30. Cf. L. Landini, *The Cause of the Clericalization of the Order of Friars Minor* (Chicago, 1983).

31. Cf. André Vauchez, *Les laïcs au Moyen Age* (Paris: Les Éditions du Cerf, 1987) pp. 15–35.

32. H. Wolter, "The Threats to the Freedom of the Church, 1153 to

1198," *HCH*, v. 4 (*From the High Middle Ages to the Eve of the Reformation*) p. 104.

33. Cf. Selge, op. cit., p. 313: "Das Waldensertum ist entstanden aus dem Gefühl eines geistlichen Notstandes in der Christenheit des 12. Jahrhunderts. Die Kirche stellte sich unbeschadet der Theologie, die von ihr durchweg als von der *Universitas fidelium* sprach, wesentlich als von der Hierarchie repräsentierte und beherrschte Kirche des Sakraments und des orthodoxen Glaubensbekenntinisses dar; das Christenvolk aber empfand im Gefloge der Kirchenreform des elften Jahrhunderts und der mannigfachen, von Mönchen, Kanonikern, charismatischen Einzelgestalten und Häretikern als Licht gezogenen und propagierten Ideale urchristlichen, evangelisch-apostolischen Lebens immer mehr die Diskrepanz zwischen den neuentdeckten christlichen Normen und der eigenen Lebenswirklichkeit im Rahmen jener klerikalen Sakramentsanstalt." Russell, op. cit., p. 103, after discussing the eccentric reformer Adelbert and the attraction of his gospel message on the ordinary people, notes: "Nothing could be more indicative of the failure of the Church of that time to provide adequate instruction and inspiration to the people." The enthusiastic response which Tanchelm of Antwerp received is also indicative of this need by ordinary people for models of gospel discipleship (ibid., pp. 56–68, but esp. pp. 67–68).

34. Cf. B. Hamilton, *Religion in the Medieval West,* op. cit., pp. 68–69: "Arguably the greatest defect in the organization of the medieval church was the lack of any provision for training the secular clergy. . . . Before 1100 most ordinands were trained by the parish priests. . . . They could read Latin liturgy, but they could not understand what they read. . . . The standard of education [after 1200] among the secular clergy varied a great deal. . . . Their knowledge of the Latin language and of church doctrine was very unequal, and a significant proportion of priests was ill-educated and ignorant, although this was undoubtedly a more general problem before 1100 than later." Cf. also Russell, op. cit., pp. 136–143, who provides many historical instances of the precedence for a married clergy in the west up to Lateran IV. It was a concubinate clergy which contributed to the call for reform in the church. A legitimately married clergy, such as one finds in the eastern churches, is one thing; a clandestinely married or openly concubinate clergy, such as one found in the western church of the middle ages, was quite a different thing. A married/non-married clergy seems not to have been the issue; rather, it was a clergy which was by church law supposed to be unmarried, but which in public opposition to church law lived as though married, but which at the same time called for lay obedience to church law. A preacher, whether episcopal or presbyteral, who preached obedience to law should himself live this obedience to

law. In the issues of simony and concubinate clergy, the "evil" was clearly the patent falsification of gospel discipleship, not simply greed or illicit sexuality.

35. Cf. Kempf, op. cit., p. 339: "The heretics took their religious and moral requirements to a great extent from the New Testament and did not hesitate to attribute their scriptural interpretation to the inspiration of the Holy Spirit. The essential point of the Gospels—faith in Christ, Son of God and Saviour—definitely took second place to the personal striving to lead a pious life and could even disappear entirely from one's mental horizon." Kempf, in spite of his negative approach to these movements, does see them rooted in a return to the gospel. Actually, the essential point of the gospels (Kempf's phrase) is discipleship, which certainly involves a personal striving to lead a pious life. Kempf, it seems, uses a different criterion in judging these movements: namely, the criterion which governed Gregory VII and the other reform popes—that is, an orthodox faith which corresponds to the orthodox interpretation which the papacy accepts. This is clear from the way he presents the Gregorian reform.

36. F.B. Artz, *The Mind of the Middle Ages: An Historical Survey A.D. 200–1500* (Chicago: The University of Chicago Press, 1980) p. 421. There are as well many instances of "eccentric mysticism," i.e. religious fanatics who also had a following. He describes Adalbert and Theuda, prior to 1000, with the bizarre episode of the "ship of fools" at Saint Truiden from 1133–1136, and slightly later Eudo of Loudéac; cf. also Russell, op. cit., pp. 101–124, for historical descriptions of such eccentric mysticism.

37. Cf. Kempf, op. cit., p. 368. In comparing Gregory VII with Arnold of Brescia, Russell, p. 99, notes: "It was Gregory's design to increase the independence and spiritual influence of the Church by increasing its political and economic power. It was Arnold's contention that it was precisely this worldly power that was the source of corruption. Both Reformer and Reformist desired to remold the Church in the image of Christ but differed in their notions of how to go about it." In spite of Arnold's problems of dissidence, it should be remembered that Arnold's position and that of Bernard of Clairvaux were very similar, namely a church which was not entangled in political and economic issues.

38. Henry III claimed a right for the Saxon dynasty to participate in papal elections, which had been established under Otto I, although it had not been used since Otto III; he also conferred with the Roman delegates, and he had received the title from the Romans of *patricius*. In so many ways, Henry III wanted his involvement to be invulnerable against any challenge.

39. Kempf, op. cit., p. 359, notes: "What made it impossible to eradicate simony was its involvement with the contemporary world . . . bound

up with the proprietary church system. Selecting the chief cause, then, Humbert [of Silva Candida] condemned lay investiture as an unlawful abuse and as a perversion of the proper relationship between priests and laity." Humbert noted that the assent of the prince was given first and that of the metropolitan was last. In the middle was the assent of the electors. The struggle on this issue was a lay/cleric issue, but also one which saw an abuse in the very structure of the religious and political world of the middle ages. Cf. ibid., p. 360. Russell, op. cit., pp. 130–131, indicates the way in which simony came to be considered heresy, and therefore strengthened the role of church religious leadership against church lay leadership. This issue is indeed a tangled web, and simplistic positions, such as church/lay, are inexcusably short-sighted.

40. Cf. Osborne, *Priesthood,* pp. 179–188.

41. Ibid., pp. 209–210.

42. Kempf, op. cit., p. 360.

43. Cf. Brooke, op. cit., pp. 59–60.

44. It must be candidly stated, however, that Gregory spent comparatively little time living as a monk in his monastery.

45. H.E.J. Cowdrey, *Popes, Monks and Crusaders* (London: The Hambledon Press, 1984), nn. IV and V.

46. On the issue of the *Dictatus papae,* cf. E.G. Robison, "Dictatus Papae," *Dictionary of the Middle Ages* (N.Y.: Charles Scribner's Sons, 1984) pp. 177–178; H. Morder "Dictatus Papae," *Lexikon des Mittelalters,* v. 3 (Munich: Artemis, 1986) pp. 978–981.

47. Augustinus Triumphus in *Summa de Potestate Ecclesiastica,* for instance, describes the difference between the pope and the bishops as follows: "We shall say that the prelates of the church compare with the pope as a boy compares with a mature man." Such a view reduces episcopacy to a ludicrous level of immaturity. Cf. the English text in E. Lewis, *Medieval Political Ideas* (London: Routledge & Kegan Paul, 1954) v. 2, p. 388. If the bishops are described as boys, then the lay people must be infants. Only the pope is mature enough to explain to the "boys" and the "infants" what discipleship, i.e. Christian maturity, is all about.

48. Kempf., op. cit., p. 402.

49. Ibid., p. 440. This entire section of Kempf leans heavily toward an equation of church with cleric; everyone else is secular. It is precisely this kind of writing which must be faulted as theologically unacceptable. The "secular" area of the *societas Christiana* of that era was very much a part of the church. The attempt to equate church with clergy, especially the higher clergy, is a denial of the basic tenets of ecclesiology.

50. Ibid., p. 349.

51. The famous instance of Henry IV at Canossa has been described by many church historians as a triumph of the church over the secular—a very odd description of the actual ecclesiology of that time. Nor is the second excommunication and deposition in 1080 by Gregory VII of Henry IV an example of church over the state. Rather, what we find in both instances is a crucial moment in the struggle of *regnum et sacerdotium*. Both the kingdom and the priesthood are essential parts of the *societas Christiana* of that time. Still, certain church historians, often it seems more interested in furthering the papal approach to this struggle, offer us, the readers, a theologically indefensible ecclesiology. From a review of historical data, it might be more correct to say that Henry IV gained far more than Gregory VII because of this incident at Canossa.

52. *Gesta Francorum et aliorum Hierosolymitanorum: The Deeds of the Franks and Other Pilgrims to Jerusalem* (London: T. Nelson, 1962), ed. and trans. Rosalind Hill, p. 1.

53. Cowdrey, op. cit., "The Genesis of the Crusades," XIII, 11.

54. Cf. *Gesta Francorum* etc., p. 62.

55. Cf. canon one of the Council of Narbone (1054).

56. C. Erdman, *Die Enstehung des Kreuzzugsgedankens* (Stuttgart: W. Kohlmanner, 1935), pp. 24–26, 72–78, 326–335.

57. Cf. *Vita Geraldi Aur. PL,* 133; Eng. trans. in G. Sitwell, *St. Odo of Cluny* (London: Sheed and Ward, 1958).

58. Cf. *Chanson de Roland* (Harmondsworth: Penguin, 1957), trans. by D.L. Sayers.

59. Cowdrey, op. cit., XIII, 18.

60. Ibid., XIII, 20.

61. Cf. *Gesta Francorum et aliorum Hierosolymitanorum.* Cf. also Guibert of Nogent, *Historia Hierosolymitana* in *Historiens Occidentaux* (1844–1895) II, iv, pp. 137–140. Cf. S. Runciman, *A History of the Crusades* (Cambridge: University Press, 1951) v. 1, p. 108.

62. Cowdrey, op. cit., XIII, 24.

63. Ibid., XIII, 27.

64. Cf. the work *On Fevers,* translated by Constantine the African (d. 1087), and Adelard of Bath (1150) who translated the *Arithmetic* of al-Khwarizmi, the *Elements* of Euclid, and the *Natural Questions.* Robert of Chester (1106) translated the *Koran,* a text on alchemy and the *Algebra* of al-Khwarizmi.

65. Thomas de Vio Cajetan's *Commentary* on the *Summa* of St. Thomas played a major role in Roman Catholic thought on the develop-

ment of ecclesiology. Though not the first commentary on St. Thomas, it became the prototype of such literature; cf. U. Horst, *Papst—Konzil—Unfehlbarkeit* (Mainz: Matthias-Grünewald, 1978) pp. 24ff.

66. Names abound, such as Leonard of Pisa, Buridian, Oresme, Robert Grosseteste, and Roger Bacon, and universities such as Paris, Bologna and Oxford contributed to these studies in a major way.

67. Cf. e.g. Y. Congar, "The Idea of the Church in St. Thomas Aquinas," *The Thomist*, 1 (1939) pp. 331–359; ibid., *Sainte Église* (Paris: Éditions du Cerf, 1963); ibid., " 'Ecclesia et populus (fidelis)' dans l'ecclésiologie de s. Thomas," *St. Thomas Aquinas 1274–1974. Commemorative Studies* (Toronto: PIMS, 1974), pp. 159–174. T.M. Käpelli, *Zur Lehre des h. Thomas von Aquin vom Corpus Christi Mysticum* (Freiburg, 1931); George Sabra, *Thomas Aquinas' Vision of the Church* (Mainz: Matthias-Grünewald, 1987).

68. M. Grabmann, *Die Lehre des heiligen Thomas von Aquin von der Kirche als Gotteswerk. Ihre Stellung im thomistischen System und in der Geschichte der mittelalterlichen Theologie* (Regensburg: C.J. Manz, 1903), p. 2. Sabra, op. cit., p. 20, rightly notes that there are many instances of theological discussion in the writings of St. Thomas on a particular theme, which appeared even though there was no specific historical problem or cause for such a discussion.

69. Ibid., p. 10. Cf. also Max Seckler, *Das Heil in der Geschichte, Geschichtstheologisches Denken bei Thomas von Aquin* (München: Kösel, 1964), p. 219, who tends to agree with Grabmann.

70. Congar, "The Idea of the Church in St. Thomas Aquinas," op. cit., p. 332. Cf. also Sabra, op. cit., pp. 19–33 for an overview of this debate.

71. R. Busa, *Index Thomisticus: Sancti Thomae Aquinatis operum omnium indices et concordantiae* (Stuttgart: Friedrich Fommann, 1975) 44971–44978.

72. Cf. e.g. Thomas' reference to the church as *navis* (*In Io.* c. vi, 1, 3); *arca* (*In I Thess.* prol; *In Rom.* prol; 6); *castra* (*In Col.* prol.); *turris* (*In Symb.* a. 9); *torcular* (*In Ps.* 8, 1); *Eva* (*In II Cor.* c. xi, l. 1); *sponsa* (*In Ps.* 45, 7; *IV Sent.* d. 49, q. 4, a. 3).

73. Sabra, op. cit., pp. 34–71.

74. Cf. *In Eph.* c. ii, 1, 6; ibid. c. iv, 1, 2; *In Ps.* 45, 3.

75. Cf. *In Io.* c. xiv l, 1; *In Matt.* c. vii, 1, 2; *In Ps.* 35, 4.

76. Sabra, op. cit., pp. 46–47.

77. Cf. A. Darquennes, "La Définition de l'Église d'après S. Thomas D'Aquin," *Études présentés à la commission internationale pour l'Histoire des Assemblées d'Etats*, v. 7 (Paris, 1943) pp. 1–53.

78. This is Sabra's argument; cf. op. cit., pp. 55–58.

79. Literature on this subject is extensive: cf. T. Käpelli, op. cit.; J. Anger, *La Doctrine du Corps Mystique de Jésus-Christ d'après les Principes de la Théologie de s. Thomas* (Paris: Beauschesne, 1929); E. Mersch, *La Théologie du Corps Mystique* (Paris: Desclée, 1949).

80. Cf. H. de Lubac, *L'Eucharistie et l'église au moyen âge* (Paris: Aubier, 1949).

81. For Thomas, however, the church cannot be seen as a continuation of the incarnation itself, as some contemporary authors have attempted to do.

82. Sabra, op. cit., p. 196.

83. R. Silic, *Christus und die Kirche, Ihr Verhältnis nach der Lehre des heiligen Bonaventura* (Breslau, 1938); D. Culhane, *De corpore mystico doctrina Seraphici* (Mundelein: St. Mary of the Lake, 1934); Bruno Korosak, "Il Mistero della Chiesa in S. Bonaventura," *Icontri Bonaventuriani* (Benevento: Montecalvo Irpino, 1968) pp. 25–34; Pasquale Caporale, "Il Popolo di Dio in S. Bonaventura," ibid., pp. 35–48; Antonio Blasucci, "La costituzione gerarchica della Chiesa in S. Bonaventura," ibid., pp. 49–68.

84. Bonvanture, *In Sap.* 16, 2; 16, 5; *In Io.* 8, 14.

85. Bonaventure, *IV Sent.* d. 4, dub. 1.

86. Bonaventure, *In Hexaem,* 1, 2.

87. Bonaventure, *III Sent.,* d. 1, a. 2, q. 2; *Vitis mystica,* 10, 2; *De perfectione evangelica,* q. 4, a. 3; *In Luc.,* 24, 13; *In Io.,* 10, 16; *De S. Matthia sermo II.*

88. Blasucci, op. cit., p. 68.

89. Bonaventure, *IV Sent.* d. 24, p. 1, a. 2, q. 1, ad 1.

90. Bonaventure, *Expositio super Reg. FF. Min.,* n. 2. In this approach he relies on Ps. Dyonisius, *De caelest. Hierarchia,* c. 3, par. 2; *De Eccles. Hierarchia,* c. 1, par. 3. It is with this perspective that one must read, e.g., *Exp. Reg. FF. Min.,* c. 9, n. 4: "Cura pastoralis non est dominium, sed dispensatio et officium ecclesiasticae potestatis. Unde hierarchia, secundum Dionysium, est potestas ordinata ad disponendum omnia sacrae potestati subiecta."

91. Caporale, op. cit., pp. 47–48.

92. Cf. P. Rosini Ruggero, "La suprema distinzione tra Dio e il mondo in Duns Escoto," *Homo et Mundus: Acta Quinti Congressus Scotistici Internationalis* (Rome: Societas Internationalis Scotistica, 1984) pp. 345–353; also G. Bloch, "La posición natural de hombre según Duns Escoto y Teilhard de Chardin," ibid., pp. 145–157.

93. Allan B. Wolter, "Duns Scotus on the Will and Morality," *The Philosophical Theology of John Duns Scotus* (Ithaca: Cornell University Press, 1990), ed. Marilyn McCord Adams, p. 186.

94. Ibid., pp. 195–202; cf. Scotus, *Ord.* IV, d. 46; *Ord* I, d. 44.

95. Scotus, *Ord.* IV, d. 46.

96. Cf. Osborne, *Justification and Reconciliation* (N.Y.: Paulist, 1990) pp. 126ff; cf. A. Wolter, op. cit., pp. 42ff.

97. Heiko Oberman, *The Harvest of Medieval Theology* (Cambridge: Harvard University Press, 1963) p. 473. Also cf. E. Randi, "A Scotist Way of Distinguishing between God's Absolute and Ordained Powers," *From Ockham to Wyclif* (Oxford: Blackwell, 1987) pp. 43–50. Randi spells out the difference between Scotus' presentation of these two powers and the presentation by Ockham. Cf. also Scotus, *Ordinatio,* I d. 44, q. un. *Opera omnia,* ed. C. Balic, VI (Rome, 1950) pp. 363–365.

98. Ozment, op. cit., p. 36.

99. E. Lewis, op. cit., p. 506.

100. Pierre Dubois, *De Recuperatione Terrae Sanctae,* Eng. trans. W.I. Brand (N.Y.: Columbia University Press, 1956).

101. Anon., *Établissements de St. Louis.*

102. Georges de Lagard, *La naissance de l'esprit laïque au déclin du moyen âge* (Saint-Paul-Trois-Chateaux, 1942). Cf. also J.R. Strayer, "The Laicization of French and English Society in the Thirteenth Century," *Speculum,* XV (1940) pp. 76–86.

103. Cf. R.W. and A.J. Carlyle, *A History of Mediaeval Political Theory in the West* (N.Y.: Barnes and Noble, 1953) 6 vols.; Jean Rivière, *Le problème de l'église et de l'état au temps de Philippe le Bel* (Paris: Champion, 1926).

104. E. Lewis, op. cit., p. 434.

105. Cf. B. Tierney, *Foundations of the Conciliar Theory* (Cambridge: Cambridge University Press, 1955), pp. 141–149. Tierney's discussion of *plenitudo potestatis* includes (a) its use in describing both episcopal and papal power, (b) Huguccio's use of the term for both pope and emperor, and (c) the Decretists' use of the term for both pope and bishop. In Innocent III's writings, however, *plenitudo potestatis* "was not only cited time and again to vindicate the Pope's universal powers of jurisdiction and administration, his right to intervene in the affairs of all the churches, but it was also presented as the source of all other authority in the Church. Moreover according to Innocent III, the Pope's *plenitudo potestatis* not only set him above all other prelates, but also above the law, *supra ius.*" Innocent IV asserted "that the possession of *plenitudo potestatis* enabled

the pope to exercise temporal power as well as spiritual power, and that it gave him authority over infidels as well as over Christians. The ground was thus well prepared for the concept of *plenitudo potestatis* as an illimitable and all-embracing sovereignty which becomes so familiar in the writings of the fourteenth-century papal publicists" (p. 147; cf. also p. 243).

106. Cf. H. Wolter, op. cit., p. 141; his conclusion, however, is not really justified, namely: "The *plenitudo potestatis* was understood by Innocent, just as it had been taught by his mentor Huguccio, as a *plenitudo potestatis ecclesiasticae,* not as a fullness embracing all spiritual and secular power whatever. It must be regarded as a defining of what is today termed the primacy of jurisdiction of the Bishop of Rome." Today's papal position cannot be read backward into Innocent III's views, since in the interim the entire relationship of *regnum et sacerdotium* has been radically changed. Aegidius Romanus in *De potestate ecclesiastica,* pt. 3, cc. 4–8, stresses this aspect of universal papal jurisdiction. Cf. also Tierney's assessment in the preceding note, with specific references to Huguccio and Innocent III.

107. Boniface VIII, *Clericis laicos,* Eng. trans. from O.J. Thatcher, *A Source Book for Mediaeval History,* p. 311.

108. Boniface VIII, *Unam sanctam,* Denzinger, 873.

109. Marsiglio of Padua, *Defensor pacis,* II, ii, 3. This definition is similar to that of Hugh of St. Victor, *De sacramentis,* II, ii, 2; Thomas Aquinas, *Sent.* L. iv. d. 20, q. 1, a r. qu. i. Cf. also A. Gewirth, *Marsilius of Padua: the Defender of Peace* (N.Y.: Columbia University Press, 1951).

110. William of Ockham, *Dialogus,* P. III, t. 1, 1. 11.

111. John of Paris, *De Potestate regali et papali,* c. iii.

112. E. Iserloh, "The Concept of the Church and the Idea of the State in the Polemics of the Fourteenth Century," *HCH,* p. 363.

113. J. D'Amico, *Renaissance Humanism in Papal Rome: Humanists and Churchmen on the Eve of the Reformation* (Baltimore: The John Hopkins University Press, 1983), p. 216.

114. Ibid., pp. 220–226.

115. Artz, op. cit., p. 447.

116. The study on the renaissance and humanism has been very intensive and extensive. Interesting studies include: J. D'Amico, op. cit., who points out that there was a sort of "clericalization" of humanism in Rome during the fifteenth century. The humanist call for reform was, he notes, both formal and ultimately ineffective (p. 213), and it was thought that whatever reform the papacy initiated would automatically be effective (p. 215). Neither of these situations aided the reforms needed for the church.

Cf. also the series of articles in *Itinerarium Italicum* (Leiden: Brill, 1975), ed. H. Oberman and T. Brady.

117. The "official" list of popes, which the Vatican maintains, should be considered as an "official list" and not as a definitive list. The mere fact that certain popes have been listed, particularly those during the western schism but also several other popes, does not determine the historical validity of those so officially listed. Current scholarship on various claimants during the western schism, for instance, indicates that each claimant had, to some degree, a title to be considered the legitimate pope, and each claimant had enough duplicity and chicanery in his respective election process to have an illegitimate claim to the papacy.

10. The Reformation and Tridentine Churches and Their Aftermath: 1500 to 1800 A.D.

1. E. Gordon Rupp, "The Age of the Reformation: 1500–1648," *The Layman in Christian History* (Philadelphia: Westminster, 1963) p. 135.

2. Martin Schmidt, "The Continent of Europe: 1648–1800," ibid., p. 151.

3. Peter Meinhold, "Modern Europe: 1800–1962," ibid., p. 170.

4. Stephen Neill, "Britain: 1600–1780," ibid., p. 191.

5. E. Erikson, *Young Man Luther* (N.Y.: Norton, 1958).

6. Cf. G. Lindbeck, "Erikson's Young Man Luther: A Historical and Theological Reappraisal," *Soundings* (1973) pp. 210–217; Roger A. Johnson, ed., *Psychohistory and Religion: The Case of Young Man Luther* (Philadelphia, 1977); S. Ozment, op. cit., pp. 223–244.

7. M. Luther, *Disputation Against Scholastic Theology, Weimar Ausgabe* [*WA*] (Weimar: H. Böhlau, 1883), v. 1, pp. 221–223.

8. D. Steinmetz, *Luther in Context* (Bloomington: Indiana University Press, 1986) pp. 23 and 28.

9. J. Pelikan, *Spirit Versus Structure: Luther and the Institutions of the Church* (N.Y.: Harper and Row, 1968) p. 5.

10. Ibid., p. 30.

11. Ibid., p. 32.

12. Luther, *On the Papacy in Rome, Luther's Works* [*LW*] (Philadelphia: Fortress, 1970), v. 39, ed. E. Gritsch, pp. 49–104.

13. D. Bagchi, " 'Eyn mercklich Underscheyd' Catholic Reactions to Luther's Doctrine of the Priesthood of All Believers," *The Ministry: Clerical and Lay*, ed. W.J. Sheils and D. Wood (Oxford: Basil Blackwell, 1989), p. 155.

14. Ibid., pp. 160–161, nn. 28 and 29 for detailed bibliographical references.

15. John Chrysostom, *De sacerdotio*, III, 1.

16. Ibid., III, 2.

17. Ibid.

18. Ibid., III, 5.

19. Bagchi, op. cit., p. 158.

20. Luther, *Concerning the Ministry*, in *Church and Ministry*, v. II (*LW*), v. 40, p. 35.

21. Cf. R. Kolb, "The Doctrine of Ministry in Martin Luther and the Lutheran Confessions," *Called and Ordained*, ed. T. Nichol and M. Kolden (Minneapolis: Fortress, 1990) p. 53, citing H. Lieberg *Amt und Ordination bei Luther und Melanchthon* (Göttingen: Vandenhoeck & Ruprecht, 1962) pp. 24–39.

22. B. Lohse, *Martin Luther: An Introduction to His Life and Work* (Philadelphia: Fortress, 1986), trans. R.C. Schultz, pp. 183–184.

23. Cf. Osborne, *Reconciliation and Justification*, pp. 157–197, in which I analyze the Tridentine statements on the sacrament of reconciliation and the decree on justification. In much of the argumentation presented by the Tridentine bishops, the issue was a defense of ecclesiastical authority rather than a defense of the theological issues involved in the process of reconciliation.

24. H. Jedin, *A History of the Council of Trent* (St. Louis: B. Herder Book Co., 1961), trans. by E. Graf, v. 2, p. 42. In v. 1, pp. 446–581, Jedin describes at great length the tug-of-war between the pope and the emperor as well as various secular princes, just to convoke a council. This is a continuation of the *regnum et sacerdotium* issue, but it is also a continuation of the role of the lay person generally within the church. In the citation in the text, the issue is not simply the struggle about the authority of the council vis-à-vis the papacy, although this is part of the scenario. Lay people were involved, along with the bishops and abbots, at Trent, so that the role of the lay person was involved, but included in this is the authority of bishops vis-à-vis the bishop of Rome.

25. Lohse, op. cit., pp. 179–180, 182–186. Cf. also J.A. Burgess, "An Evangelical Episcopate?" *Called and Ordained*, pp. 137–150; p. 137: "Lutherans can of course adopt any form of church structure, up to and including the papacy, as long as the primacy of the gospel and Christian freedom are allowed."

26. Ibid., pp. 174–177, is titled: "The absence of any ecclesiological program in Luther's thinking." On p. 175, the author states: "Neither side in these sixteenth-century controversies—most certainly not Luther—was working out of a coherent set of ideas [on the church]."

27. Most contemporary Roman Catholic theologians do not accept the medieval understanding of *plenitudo potestatis.* That the idea lingers even

in modern times in the wings of some areas of Roman Catholic dreams can be seen, e.g., in the "world vision of Leo XIII" and the repercussions of this "world vision" on subsequent popes.

28. Luther, *Temporal Authority: To What Extent it Should be Obeyed, WA*, v. 11, pp. 245–280.

29. Lohse, op. cit., pp. 186–193. Cf. also J.M. Headley, *Luther's View of Church History* (New Haven: Yale University Press, 1963).

30. H. Lesètre, "Ordre," *Dictionnaire de la Bible* (Paris: Letouzey et Ane, 1908), ed. F. Vigouroux, v. 4, c. 1855.

31. "Priestertum: Allgemeines," *Lexikon für Theologie und Kirche* (Freiburg: Herder, 1963), v. 8, pp. 753–756.

32. J. Galot, *Theology of the Priesthood* (San Francisco: Ignatius Press, 1984), Eng. trans. R. Balducelli, p. 118. Italics added.

33. Cf. R. Schwartz, *Servant Leaders of the People of God* (N.Y.: Paulist, 1989), which cites in detail statements of various bishops of the United States on the issue of *ordo* and ontological distinction, a view which the author himself considers central to the sacrament of priestly ministry. Cf., for example, pp. 126–128, 190–193.

34. N. Ring, "Heresy," *A New Dictionary of Theology,* ed. J. Komonchak, M. Collins, D. Lane (Wilmington: M. Glazier, 1987) p. 461, notes: "Who, then, are those who contribute to the conditions which lead to heresy? First, they may be . . . the majority within the ecclesia who historically endorse the *status quo.*" An endorsement of the status quo of a position which is clearly based on certain unproven theological and philosophical positions, such as the advocacy of *ordo* as the basis for ordained priesthood, is clearly a situation which in this description can lead to heresy.

35. Cf. H. Lieberg, op. cit.; W. Stein, *Das kirchliche Amt bei Luther* (Wiesbaden: F. Steiner, 1974); R. Schäfer, "Allgemeines Priestertum oder Vollmacht durch Handauflegung," *Von Amt des Laien in Kirche und Theologie* (Berlin: Walter de Gruyter, 1982), ed. H. Schröer and G. Müller, pp. 141–167.

36. Lieberg, op. cit., pp. 50ff. R. Schäfer, op. cit., p. 144, describes this approach as follows: "Die eine Linie beginnt in der Lehre vom allgemeinen Priestertum, welches durch die Taufe empfangen wird und jedem Christen die grundsätzliche Befähigung zum Dienst an Wort und Sakrament verschafft. Für das Amt der Leitung des öffentlichen Gottesdienstes bedarf es deswegen keiner zusätzlichen geistlichen Ausrüstung mehr, sondern nur noch der geordneten Beauftragung (Berufung, Vokation) durch die Gemeinde."

37. Lieberg, op. cit., p. 235.

38. W. Stein, op. cit., pp. 202ff.

39. W.J. Bousma, *John Calvin: A Sixteenth-Century Portrait* (Oxford: Oxford University Press, 1988) p. 214.

40. J. Calvin, *Institutes of the Christian Religion* (Philadelphia: Westminster, 1950), ed. by J.T. McNeill, trans. by F.L. Battles, 2 vols.

41. Bousma, ibid., p. 214.

42. Calvin, *Institutes*, pp. lxi–lxxi. The author of this introduction uses phrases such as "doctrine of the ministry" and "well-ordered treatise," but in actuality we cannot really find an "ecclesiology" in this section of Calvin's work.

43. B.C. Milner, Jr., *Calvin's Doctrine of the Church* (Leiden: E.J. Brill, 1970) p. 194. Cf. also P. Barth, "Calvins Verständnis der Kirche," *Zwischen der Zeiten*, v. 8 (1930) pp. 216–230; W. Kolfhaus, *Christusgemeinschaft bei Johannes Calvin* (Neukirchen: Kr. Moers, 1939).

44. E.A. Dowey, Jr., *The Knowledge of God in Calvin's Theology* (N.Y.: Columbia University Press, 1952).

45. Milner, op. cit., p. 193.

46. A. Ganoczy, *Ecclesia Ministrans: Dienende Kirche und kirchlicher Dienst bei Calvin* (Freiburg: Herder, 1968), Ger. trans. by H. Sayer, p. 140.

47. Ibid., p. 174.

48. Ibid. Cf. *Institutes*, 4.1.1, and 4.1.4.

49. *Institutes*, 4.1.3.

50. Ibid.

51. Ibid., 4.1.7.

52. Ibid., 4.1.8.

53. Ibid., 4.1.10.

54. Ibid., 4.1.12.

55. Cf. G. Yule, "Calvin's View of the Ministry of the Church," *The Ministry: Clerical and Lay*, pp. 167–184. Yule writes that "Calvin's view of the ministry is dependent on his view of the Church and his view of the Church is itself controlled by his Christological emphasis" (p. 167). However, "scholastic Calvinism," which had dominated Calvinistic thought prior to liberal Protestantism, did not honor this christological base; rather, for scholastic Calvinism doctrine was "formulated by the exact verbal precepts and prescriptions of the Bible of which the doctrine of Christ was seen to be only one, though admittedly a major one." "The Bible was a book of divine truths and propositions" (ibid., passim).

56. Calvin, "Reply by John Calvin to the Letter by Cardinal Sadolet to the Senate and People of Geneva," *Calvin: Theological Treatises* (Philadelphia: Westminster, 1954), Eng. trans. by J.K.S. Reid, pp. 221–256, Cf. esp. pp. 232–233. In the *Institutes*, 3.1.1, Calvin reiterates this connection of word, Spirit and church.

57. Ibid., p. 229.

58. Ibid., p. 253.

59. *Institutes,* 4.1.10.

60. H. Schützeichel, "Calvins Kritik der biblischen Begründung des Papstamtes," *Katholische Beiträge zur Calvinforschung* (Trier: Paulinus-Verlag, 1988) pp. 49–70; cf. Gonozcy, op. cit., pp. 338–342.

61. Calvin, *Ioannis Calvini Opera quae supersunt omnia* (Brunswick and Berlin: Schwetschke, 1863–1900), eds. G. Baum, E. Cunitz and E. Reuss, v. 7, p. 611.

62. Calvin, ibid., v. 47, p. 453.

63. Bowsma, op. cit., p. 220, citing Calvin, *Comm. Acts,* 5:32. Milner, op. cit., reinforces this view with his continuous emphasis on the principle of order in Calvin, an order which derives from God, not from the human will.

64. Calvin, "Draft of Ecclesiastical Ordinances September & October, 1541," *Calvin: Theological Treatises,* pp. 58–72. H. Schützeichel, op. cit., p. 46, mentions that in the *Institutes* of 1543 Calvin has three orders of ministry, combining pastor and teacher.

65. Yule, op. cit., p. 175. Yule notes that scholastic Calvinists regarded both as clerical.

66. *Institutes,* 4.3.11.

67. Ibid., 4.3.15.

68. H. Schützeichel, op. cit., p. 48.

69. Bouwsma, op. cit., spends three chapters, namely 3, 4, and 5, on the issue of order in Calvin's thought, pp. 49–98.

70. Calvin, *Confession de la foi,* in *Ioannis Calvini Opera quae supersunt omnia,* v. 9, p. 69.

71. Bowsma, op. cit., citing Calvin, *Comm. Acts,* 20:20 and *Comm. II Cor.* 11:20.

72. Calvin, *Institutes,* Introduction, p. lxii.

73. U. Stutz, *Der Geist des Codex juris canonici* (Stuttgart: 1918) cited by M. Keller, "Theologie des Laientums," *Mysterium Salutis* (Einsiedeln: Benziger, 1973), v. IV/2, p. 397.

74. Cf. Gordon J. Spykman, "Sphere-Sovereignty in Calvin and the Calvinist Tradition," *Exploring the Heritage of John Calvin* (Grand Rapids: Baker Book House, 1976), ed. D. Holwerda, pp. 163–208. Also, J.T. McNeill, *The History and Character of Calvinism* (N.Y.: Oxford University Press, 1962).

75. Émile Léonard, *A History of Protestantism* (London: Nelson, 1967), v. 2, Eng. tr. by R.M. Bethell. Léonard does not hesitate to use the term caesaro-papism on many occasions as he discusses the controversies

between the leaders of the Calvinist churches and the leaders of the various cities and regions.

76. Cf. ibid., p. 147, for a listing of lay people attending the various national assemblies from that of Figeac (1579) to Montpellier (1598). Roughly forty percent of the delegates were lay at all these assemblies.

77. Ibid., p. 394.

78. Ibid., pp. 394–395.

79. Ibid., p. 174.

80. C.J. Blaisdell, "Calvin's and Loyola's Letters to Women: Politics and Spiritual Counsel in the Sixteenth Century," *Calviniana: Ideas and Influence of Jean Calvin* (Kirksville: Sixteenth Century Journal Publishers, 1988), ed. R.V. Schnucker, pp. 235–253.

81. W.P. De Boer, "Calvin on the Role of Women," *Exploring the Heritage of John Calvin,* pp. 236–272.

82. A. Biéler, *L'homme et la femme dans la morale calviniste* (Geneva: Labor et Fides, 1963); N. Roelker, "The Appeal of Calvinism to French Noblewomen in the Sixteenth Century," *Journal of Interdisciplinary History,* 2 (1972) pp. 391–418.

83. Cf. Gonzague, *Histoire ilustrée de la femme* (Paris: Plon, 1940–1941), v. 1, p. 199.

84. Cf. R.H. Bainton, *Women of the Reformation in Germany and Italy* (Minneapolis: Augsburg, 1971) p. 55.

85. Cf. Calvin, *Commentary on Genesis: Commentary on 1 Tim.; Sermon on 1 Cor.; Commentary on 1 Cor.*

86. Calvin's arguments against women in church ministry have an affinity to the *Declaration on the Question of the Admission of Women to the Ministerial Priesthood.*

87. Claire Cross, *Church and People, 1450–1660: The Triumph of the Laity in the English Church* (Atlantic Highlands: Humanities Press, 1976) p. 9.

88. Ibid., p. 20.

89. Recent historiography on the English reformation and the Catholic position has changed radically in recent times. Rather than a defensive and confessional approach, both Anglican and Catholic authors today present a far more cautious and historical approach. Cf. M.J. Havran, "The British Isles," *Catholicism in Early Modern History: A Guide to Research,* ed. J. O'Malley (St. Louis: Center for Reformation Research, 1988) pp. 69–82. An excellent bibliography is appended to Havran's essay.

90. Cross, op. cit., p. 63.

91. Cross, op. cit., pp. 43–80, presents a fairly comprehensive view of

the many factors behind the Henrician reform: economic, political, social and religious. The same approach can be found in J.J. Scarisbrick, *Henry VIII* (Berkeley: University of California Press, 1968), and ibid., "Clerical Taxation in England, 1485–1547," *Journal of Ecclesiastical History*, v. 9 (1960) pp. 41–54; cf. also the bibliographical study by C. Cross, op. cit., pp. 252–254.

92. Cross, op. cit., p. 53.

93. H. Tüchle, *Réforme et Contre-Réforme* (Paris: Éditions du Seuil, 1968) p. 101: "C'était là l'expression d'une structure ecclésiastique nationale et absolue et d'un humanisme anti-romain; cette déclaration devait être le fondement de la Réforme anglaise." It is difficult to find in the historical data for the English reform that the declaration of 1534 was the "foundation of the English reform." Tüchle appears to be reading into the data a theological stance on the papacy developed at a later historical period. On p. 102 Tüchle states: "Le schisme anglais ne recontra aucune resistance dans le peuple; le pape et la curie ne jouissant pas de grandes sympathies." If there was no resistance to the reform and if the papacy was not held in high esteem, which seems to be the opinion of other contemporary historians as well, it is difficult to see that the "papal issue" was the foundation of the English reform, particularly since the English reform movement had been going on long before the question of Henry VIII's marriage, and since Henry's declaration of ecclesial supremacy met with little resistance.

94. Ibid., p. 112.

95. Ibid., p. 242.

96. F.H. Littell, "The Radical Reformation," *The Layman in Christian History*, p. 261.

97. Ibid., p. 273.

98. Cf. G. Alberigo, "The Council of Trent," *Catholicism in Early Modern History: A Guide to Research*, pp. 211–226, for a scholarly overview of current studies on the interpretation of the Council of Trent.

99. J.M. Weiss, "Council of Trent," *The New Dictionary of Theology*, p. 1045.

100. H. Vorgrimler, "Der Kampf des Christen mit der Sünde," *Mysterium Salutis* (Zürich: Benziger, 1976), v. 5, pp. 429–430.

101. Osborne, *Reconciliation and Justification*, pp. 185–197.

102. Ibid., pp. 159–161.

103. H. Tüchle, op. cit., p. 183.

104. *Conciliorum Oecumenicorum Decreta* (Freiburg i. Br.: Herder, 1962), p. 636: "ad reformationem cleri et populi Christiani." The separa-

tion of cleric from the people of God is the troublesome theological issue, since clergy are a part of the people of God, not an entity over against the people of God.

105. Jedin, op. cit., v. 2, p. 490. It should be mentioned, however, that some influence of the political world was accomplished in a different way, for the three and only French bishops (Aix, Clermont and Agde) never made a major decision on an issue which had any political consequence without prior consultation with the French king; ibid., p. 488.

106. J. Grootaers, "The Roman Catholic Church," *The Layman in Christian History*, p. 305, with reference to A. Duval, *La Vie Spirituelle, Supplément*, 1949, p. 359.

107. Jedin, op. cit., p. 492.

108. E. Delaney, "Laity in the Middle Ages," *The New Catholic Encyclopedia* (N.Y.: McGraw-Hill, 1967) pp. 331–335.

109. G. Alberigo, op. cit., p. 212.

110. Y. Congar, *Lay People in the Church*, p. 47.

111. J.M. Weiss, op. cit., p. 1046.

112. Cf. Congar, *Lay People in the Church*, pp. 312–323, for details of this battle over scripture.

113. J. Jungmann, *The Mass of the Roman Rite* (N.Y.: Benziger, 1951), Eng. tr. F. Brunner, pp. 107–109.

114. Ibid.

115. In the German area, residency for prince-bishops did not become normative until the prince-bishops themselves were removed with the secularization of 1803. Cf. R. Bireley, "Early Modern Germany," *Catholicism in Early Modern History: A Guide to Research*, pp. 11–30.

116. J. Weiss, "Counter Reformation," *The New Dictionary of Theology*, p. 242. Cf. also the classical work on the subject of the term "counter-reformation," H. Jedin, *Katholische Reformation oder Gegenreformation?* (Lucerne, 1946); also J.C. Olin, *The Catholic Reformation* (N.Y.: Harper and Row, 1969); J. Delumeau, *Catholicism Between Luther and Voltaire: A New View of the Counter Reformation* (London, 1977). The study by P. Chaunu, *Eglise, culture et société* (Paris, 1981), improves on Delumeau's positions.

117. On recent scholarship regarding the *Catechismus Romanus*, cf. G. Bellinger, *Der Catechismus Romanus und die Reformation* (Paderborn: Bonifacius, 1970); P. Rodriguez and R. Lanzetti, *El Catecismo Romano: Fuentes e historia del texto y de la redacción. Bases críticas para el estudio teológico del Catecismo del Concilio de Trento* (Pamplona: Ediciones de la Universidad de Navarra, 1985).

118. *Catechism of the Council of Trent for Parish Priests* (N.Y.: J.F. Wagner, 1934), Eng. trans. A. McHugh and C.J. Callan, pp. 96–112.

119. Citations are found ibid., pp. 97–102.

120. J. Grootaers, op. cit., p. 306.

121. G. Alberigo, op. cit., p. 220.

122. Ian Green, " 'Reformed Pastors' and *Bons Curés:* The Changing Role of the Parish Clergy in Early Modern Europe," *The Ministry: Clerical and Lay,* p. 251. This is a very informative article on the question of ministry in this post-reformation space and time.

123. Cited by R. Birely, op. cit., p. 12.

124. I. Green, op. cit., p. 252.

125. Ibid.

126. Cf. Peter Burke, "Popular Piety," *Catholicism in Early Modern History,* pp. 113–131. There are still many lacunae as regards this theme of "popular piety" which make conclusions somewhat tentative.

127. Kathryn Norberg, "The Counter Reformation and Women: Religious and Lay," *Catholicism in Early Modern History,* p. 133. Other studies on this subject include J.-M. Aubert, *La Femme: antiféminisme et christianisme* (Paris: Éditions du Cerf, 1975); N. Davis, *Society and Culture in Early Modern France* (Stanford: Stanford University Press, 1975); N. Davis and J. Conway, *Society and the Sexes: A Bibliography of Women's History in Early Modern Europe, Colonial America and the United States* (N.Y., 1981); S. Ozment, *The Reformation and the Family* (New Haven: Yale University Press, 1984).

128. M. De Certeau, *La Fable mystique XVIᵉ–XVIIᵉ siècle* (Paris: Éditions du Cerf, 1982).

129. Norberg, op. cit., p. 142. Cf. also P. Hoffman, *Théories de la fémininité aux XVIIᵉ et XVIIIᵉ siècles: de Descartes à Cabanis* (Paris, 1975); Marc Venard, *L'église d'Avignon au XVI siècle* (Lille, 1980).

130. Congar, *Lay People in the Church,* p. 359.

131. The use of the term "pathological" is deliberate. This term has been used by A. Görres, in "Pathologie des katholischen Christentums," *Handbuch der Pastoraltheologie* (Freiburg: Herder, 1966), v. 2/1, pp. 277–343, and there was no backlash at all by ecclesiastical authority. However, L. Boff, in *The Church: Charism and Power* (N.Y.. Crossroad, 1985), uses this term, "pathological," in ch. 6, pp. 65–88, and there was a major response by ecclesiastical authority.

132. Cf., e.g., the *Praenotanda* for the revised ritual for the sacrament of reconciliation, n. 2.

133. Cf. L. Boff, op. cit.; also P. Granfield, *The Limits of the Papacy* (N.Y.: Crossroad, 1987).

11. The French and American Revolutions and Their Influence on the Role of the Laity in the Roman Catholic Church

1. Cf. J. Hennesey, *American Catholics* (N.Y.: Oxford University Press, 1981) pp. 55–100.

2. It was basically French presbyters, not bishops, who sided with the people during the early stages of the revolution. The bishops almost unanimously sided with the king and the nobility.

3. Sacred Congregation for the Doctrine of the Faith, *Instruction on Certain Aspects of the "Theology of Liberation"* (Rome: Vatican Press, 1984).

4. Sacred Congregation for the Doctrine of the Faith, *Instruction on Christian Freedom and Liberation* (Rome: Vatican Press, 1986).

5. *De Vocatione et missione laicorum in ecclesia et in mundo viginti annis a concilio Vaticano II elapsis,* English and Latin text (Rome: Vatican Press, 1987).

6. John Paul II, *Mulieris dignitatem* (1988), Eng. trans. (Washington, D.C.: USCC, 1988).

7. Pius XII, "Address to the World Congress of the Lay Apostolate on Its Need Today," presented at Rome, October 14, 1951, Eng. trans. in *Official Catholic Teachings: Clergy and Laity,* ed. Odile M. Liebard (Wilmington: Consortium Books, 1978) pp. 88–97. Future references to this volume will be cited as *Clergy and Laity.*

8. Cf. Congar, *Lay People in the Church,* p. 48, footnote n. 1, for a lengthy listing of early occasions when an "ecclesia clericorum" was proposed.

9. Ibid. p. 46. Basing himself on the work of F.X. Arnold, Congar writes: "The idea of the Church as it appears in catechisms and works of pastoral theology during the second half of the eighteenth century and the first half of the nineteenth . . . have the same defects as some of the Counter-Reformation controversialists—they do not say a word about the Church's mystical aspect, they are concerned only with her organization as a society and the exercising of her hierarchical powers. They do not point out that it is the whole Church quickened by the Holy Spirit, the whole faithful people, that co-operates in the work of sanctification and praise of God; they talk only about the priest and the hierarchy, and the believing, praying people appears to be passive in a church that it does not affect and is not expected to affect." Besides Arnold, Congar mentions others as well on which he bases this view: M. Ramsaur, M.J. Congar, H. de Lubac.

10. Burke, "Popular Piety," op. cit., pp. 120–121; cf. esp. p. 119, note 26, for a list of authors who have currently studied this question of confraternities.

11. Ibid., p. 122; cf. B. Arditi, *Diario dell'esodo,* ed. R. Cantagallo (Florence: Vallecchi, 1970); A. Lottin, *Vie et mentalité d'une Lillois sous Louis XIV* (Lille, 1968).

12. Cf. Burke, ibid., pp. 113–131. In this essay, Burke surveys contemporary historical studies from Trent onward on the theme of popular piety, one of which was this movement of various associations into confraternities. Historical data today does not allow the view which Pius XII so generically makes.

13. Cf. K. Norberg, "The Counter Reformation and Women: Religious and Lay," *Catholicism in Early Modern Church History,* pp. 133–146. This is another essay covering the bibliographical material of recent scholarship on this subject of women in the post-Tridentine period. Norberg's analysis makes it difficult to agree with Pius XII's conclusions.

14. J. Hennesey, *American Catholicism,* pp. 69–100.

15. Ibid., p. 77.

16. C.H. Hayes, *A Generation of Materialism* (N.Y.: Harper & Row, 1963) p. 48.

17. Cf. T. Bokenkotter, *A Concise History of the Catholic Church* (N.Y.: Doubleday, 1990) p. 270.

18. Cf., for instance, the difference in historical writing between J. Janssen's *Geschichte des deutschen Volkes seit dem Ausgang des Mittelalters* (Freiburg i. Br.: Herder, 1882), and L. Pastor's *Geschichte der Päpste seit dem Ausgang des Mittelalters.* Cf. as well Leo XIII, *Saepenumero,* August 18, 1883 (*Acta Leonis,* v. III, pp. 259–273) in which he states clearly what he expects from Catholic historians: "a defense against accounts of the papacy written *in mendaci colore.* He trusted that the *incorrupta rerum gestarum monumenta,* if studied without prejudice, would successfully defend the Church and papacy *per se ipsa.*" O. Köhler, op. cit., p. 321. In 1884 Leo said: "non abbiamo paura della pubblicità dei documenti," calling the skeptics around him "small minds." Leo, and Pastor to a great extent, did not understand the meaning and implications of the historical method.

19. R. Aubert, *The Church in a Secularized Society* (N.Y.: Paulist, 1978), Eng. trans. by J. Sondheimer, p. 5 (*The Christian Centuries,* v. 5).

20. Ibid., pp. 56–69; cf. Colton, op. cit., pp. 604–605.

21. Ibid., p. 7.

22. O., Köhler, "The World Plan of Leo XIII: Goals and Methods," *The Church in the Industrial Age (HC)* (N.Y.: Crossroad, 1981), pp. 3–25.

23. Ibid.

24. Ibid., p. 6. Cf. Leo XIII, *Immortale Dei* (1885), in which Leo describes his world vision of the socio-political world and the world of true religion. In this encyclical, Leo sees the root of discord in the "harmful and lamentable rage for innovation which rose to a climax in the sixteenth century," and from "all those later tenets of unbridled license, which, in the midst of the terrible upheavals of the last century, were wildly conceived and boldly proclaimed as the principles and foundation of that new jurisprudence. . . . Among these principles the main one lays down that as all men are alike by race and nature, so in like manner all are equal in the control of their life." Eng. trans. in *Readings in Church History*, ed. C.J. Barry (Westminster: Newman Press, 1965), p. 99.

25. Cf. Köhler, ibid., p. 18. In *Immortale Dei*, the middle ages are extolled by Leo as an ideal time: "There was once a time when states were governed by the principles of Gospel teaching. . . . Christian Europe has subdued barbarous nations, and changed them from a savage to a civilized condition, from superstition to true worship" (ibid., p. 98). Cf. also Leo XIII, *Libertas praestantissimum* (1888), which offers a similar judgment.

26. Cf. Köhler, ibid., p. 19.

27. Ibid., p. 20.

28. Ibid., p. 21. It should be recalled that the title *vicarius Christi* was a title for the emperor, not the pope, until the last part of the first millennium. Only in the struggle for supremacy over the emperor did popes claim to be *vicarius Christi*, not merely *vicarius S. Petri*. Once this claim of *vicarius Christi* became a customary title for the pope, an entire area of papal theology was developed, as we have seen, which made the pope a most singular individual.

29. Cf. Köhler, ibid., p. 22. When Leo sent Francesco Satolli to be his representative at the Plenary Council of Baltimore in the United States, his reception as apostolic delegate was not all that welcome by key American bishops.

30. Besides *Rerum novarum, Immortale Dei* must also be seen as a statement of this revised worldview, and above all his apostolic letter *Praeclara gratulationis* (1894), which Harnack called "the testimonial of Leo XIII," and which Köhler, op. cit., p. 24, describes as follows: "The world design of Leo XIII found its most magnificent expression revealing its innermost moments in the apostolic letter *Praeclara gratulationis* of June 1894. It is one of those utopias without which historical greatness is not possible."

31. Cf. Leo XIII, *Libertas praestantissimum* (1888), in the section "De libertate conscientiae et de tolerantia." *Acta Leonis*, viii, 241.

32. Cf. *Acta Leonis*, viii, 341, 229–234, 235.

33. Cf. Leo XIII, *Longinqua oceani spatia* (1895).

34. Cf. among others R. Fülöp-Miller, *Leo XIII* (Zurich, 1935); R. Aubert, *Leone XIII: I cattolici italiani dall' 1800 ad oggi* (Brescia: 1964); E.T. Gargan, ed., *Leo XIII and the Modern World* (N.Y., 1961).

35. Cf. L. Scheffczyk's essay, "Main Lines of the Development of Theology Between the First World War and the Second Vatican Council," pp. 260–298, and E. Iserloh's essay, "Movements within the Church and their Spirituality," pp. 299–336, in *The Church and the Modern Age* (*HC*) (N.Y.: Crossroad, 1981), Eng. trans. A. Biggs.

36. Cf. as well Leo XIII, *Est sane molestum* (1888), in which the pope focused on the lay person in the church. Leo stresses that there are two orders in the church quite distinct from one another: the shepherds and the flock. The shepherds (pope and bishops) have the duty to teach, govern, guide and fix rules; the flock is to submit to the shepherds, to obey, to carry out its orders and to pay honor. Criticism of bishops, who are in communion with Rome, is disallowed, with the only exception that recourse in case of serious need can be made to the pope himself.

37. Pius X, *Pascendi gregis* (1907).

38. Cf. Pius X, *Il fermo proposito* (June 11, 1905), Eng. trans. in *Clergy and Laity*, pp. 17–18.

39. Ibid., p. 18. For Pius X's understanding of Catholic Action, cf. J.-G. Vaillancourt, *Papal Power: A Study of Vatican Control over Catholic Elites* (Berkeley: University of California Press, 1980), pp. 41–45, 177–183.

40. Cf. Pius X, *Il fermo proposito*, in *Clergy and Laity*, p. 12.

41. M. Bendiscioli, "Italian Catholics between the Vatican and the Quirinal," *The Church in the Industrial Age* (*HC*), p. 88.

42. Pius X, *AAS*, 2 (1910) pp. 607–633.

43. R. Aubert, op. cit., p. 475.

44. Vaillancourt, op. cit., p. 42.

45. Pius X, *Quam singulari, AAS*, v. 2, pp. 577–583; cf. also clarification of the Congregation of the Council, *De quotidiana SS. Eucharistiae sumptione, AAS*, 2 (1910) pp. 894–898.

46. Vaillancourt, op. cit., p. 42.

47. Hennesey, op. cit., p. 190, citing M. Adele Gorman.

48. Ibid.

49. Ibid., 190–191, citing J.T. Ellis, *Life of Gibbons.*

50. Ibid., p. 191, citing *Progress of the Catholic Church in America and the Great Columbian Catholic Congress of 1893.*

51. Cf. J.P. Chinnici, *Living Stones: The History and Structure of*

Catholic Spiritual Life in the United States (N.Y.: Macmillan, 1989) pp. 150–153.

52. Hennesey, op. cit., p. 191.

53. Ibid., p. 192.

54. It is interesting to note that in the book *Clergy and Laity* (referred to above) which is advertised as the part of the series on "official Catholic teachings," no excerpt from the writings of Benedict XV is included. After selections from Pius X, one moves immediately to selections from Pius XI. Nor are there included any selections from the writings of John XXIII. One moves directly from Pius XII to Paul VI and official documents from Vatican II.

55. Cf. J. Chinnici, op. cit., p. 122.

56. Ibid., pp. 122–136.

57. Ibid., p. 136.

58. Jean-Guy Vaillancourt, op. cit., p. 271.

59. Ibid.; cf. esp. his introduction in which he states his thesis, pp. 1–16, and his resume, pp. 263–297.

60. Congar, op. cit., pp. 362ff, indicates that Catholic Action, which Pius XI advanced to a strong degree, was really rooted in the nineteenth century, from Pius IX and Leo XIII as key papal figures, even though the term "Catholic Action" became the *lingua franca* only with Pius XI onward.

12. Vatican II and Post-Vatican II Theology of the Lay Person

1. Cf. G. Martina, "The Historical Context in Which the Idea of a New Ecumenical Council Was Born," *Vatican II: Assessment and Perspectives* (N.Y.: Paulist, 1988), ed. R. Latourelle, trans. by L. Wearne, pp. 1–73. Martina notes that Pius XII had considered a council, but had discarded the idea. John XXIII moved in a conciliar direction only ten weeks after his election (p. 4). The immediate response by church leadership to John XXIII's call for a council was not overwhelming.

2. D. Power, *Gifts That Differ: Lay Ministries Established and Unestablished* (N.Y.: Pueblo, 1980) pp. 11–32, relates some of the post-Vatican II developments in lay ministry to inner-church issues which took place prior to the council.

3. Cf. D. Tardini, *Pio XII* (Vatican City, 1960) pp. 72–74.

4. Martina, op. cit., p. 16.

5. Ibid., p. 16.

6. R. Aubert, *La théologie catholique au milieu du XXe siècle* (Tournai, 1954).

7. O. Rousseau, "La Costituzione ne quado dei movimenti rinnovatori de teologia e di pastoral degle ultime decenni," *La Chiesa del Vaticano II* (Florence: Vallechi, 1965), ed. G. Baraúna and S. Olivieri, p. 112.

8. Ibid., p. 123.

9. Martina, op. cit., pp. 7–8.

10. This question was first stated by Cardinal Suenens, and then repeated by Paul VI in his opening words to the second session of the council.

11. Cf. B. Kloppenburg, *The Ecclesiology of Vatican II* (Chicago: Franciscan Herald Press, 1974), Eng. trans. M.J. O'Connell, pp. xii–xiii, describes the deep division on ecclesiology, evident in the studies of the bishops of the Brazilian church. What Kloppenburg writes is typical of many areas of the church in various parts of the world.

12. Kloppenburg, op. cit., p. 9 writes: "The contemporary way, since Vatican II, has obviously been changing rapidly from the way of the anti-Protestant, post-Tridentine age. This is, in my opinion, the main point on which those who style themselves 'traditionalists' (in a certain sense we all want to be, and must be, traditionalists!) must reflect calmly, attentively, and sympathetically. *An important shift in emphases took place at the Council and has continued to take place ever since*" (emphasis that of Kloppenburg).

13. A compilation of Vatican II texts on the lay person can be found in F. Hengsbach, *Das Konzilsdekret über das Laienapostolat* (Paderborn: Bonifacius Druckerei, 1967). Besides text and commentary on *Apostolicam actuositatem*, the additional citations can be found on pp. 153–188.

14. Cf., however, G. Ghirlanda, "Universal Church, Particular Church, and Local Church at the Second Vatican Council and in the New Code of Canon Law," *Vatican II: Assessment and Perspectives*, Eng. trans. (N.Y.: Paulist Press, 1989) p. 234: "The church is the sacrament of the communion of mankind with God who is one and three, and of men with one another. This means that the church signifies this communion and brings it about: anybody who enters into communion with God is also in communion with his brethren; and all those who are united to God are united to one another." There is no mention of Jesus in this statement; no mention of the light of the world; no christology. In Ghirlanda's entire essay, an appreciation of christology is noticeably missing. Ghirlanda's approach seems to be a voice "cantans extra chorum."

15. Cf. Kloppenburg, op. cit., p. 19.

16. Ibid., p. 21.

17. Ibid., pp. 19–20.

18. Ibid., p. 21.

19. Cf. Osborne, *Priesthood*, pp. 30–39. This small chapter is in many ways the most important chapter of this book, for from the way that one reads the christology of the New Testament, one will also deduce the role of church leadership, both ordained and unordained.

20. An example of this can be found in official interpretations given to the Vatican II texts which treat of the origin of episcopacy. These interpretations are made on the basis of a christological presupposition, namely the connection of Jesus to the apostles or twelve, and the connection, intended by Jesus, of apostleship to episcopacy. New Testament data does not warrant either of these assumptions. A dogmatic form of christology, however, does postulate such relationships. Another example centers around the many interpretations given to the word *subsistit* in n. 8 of the first chapter of *Lumen gentium*. The various authors who defend an interpretation of this term do so because of their christological presupposition, i.e. to what extent did Jesus during his lifetime "found" a Church? When *subsistit* is taken to mean exclusively the Roman Catholic Church, neither text nor context can warrant such an interpretation. A presupposed dogmatic christology, however, can be seen as the basis of such an exclusivity.

21. Chapter 5 of *Lumen gentium* on holiness in the church also states that there is only one basic holiness in the church. Just as there is not a distinct way of gospel discipleship for the various "orders" in the church, so, too, there is not a distinct form of holiness for various "orders" in the church. Gospel discipleship is fundamentally one and the same for all; holiness in the church is fundamentally one and the same for all.

22. Cf. R. Sugranyes de Franch, "Apostolado Laical," *Estudios sobre el Concilio Vaticano II* (Bilbao: Mensajero, 1966) pp. 341–356. He was a lay auditor at the council itself. On p. 347 he mentions that a key moment in the council was the day on which the bishops decided to place the chapter on the people of God prior to the chapter on the hierarchy.

23. *Lineamenta: The Formation of Priests in Circumstances of the Present Day*, Eng. trans. (Washington, D.C.: USCC, 1989).

24. Paul VI, *Sacrum Ordinatus Ordinem*, Motu proprio, June 18, 1967.

25. Paul VI, *Homily to the Third World Congress of Lay Apostolate*, Eng. trans. from *Clergy and Lay*, p. 291.

26. *Called and Gifted: The American Catholic Laity* (Washington, D.C.: USCC, 1980). It should be noted that in this same document the bishops write: "The Church is to be a sign of God's Kingdom in the world. The authenticity of that sign depends on all the people: laity, religious,

deacons, priests and bishops." Obviously, the term "people" is used in a multi-valent way. This is the precise point I wish to make: the term "people of God" has not been completely accepted as the best term for the "common matrix." The term "people of God" is still used as a term for those other than and distinct from the hierarchy, and hence the term is not always accepted to mean the basis of gospel discipleship common to all.

27. In the Latin text of the code, the phrase "in the world," *in mundo*, refers not to the baptized Christian but to the church itself: "quam Deus Ecclesiae in mundo adimiplendam concredidit." This canon cannot be cited to claim that the mission of the *tria munera* is to be exercised in the world, i.e. a strictly secular vocation, as distinct from the inner-church vocation of the clergy. Such a view would mutilate the intent of the Latin text.

28. Congregation for Divine Worship, *Circular Letter Concerning the Preparation and Celebration of The Easter Feasts* (Washington, D.C.: USCC, 1988).

29. John Paul II, *Christifideles laici* (1988), Eng. trans. (Washington, D.C.: USCC, 1989). The introduction itself indicates this division: "To bishops; to priests and deacons; to women and men religious; to all the lay faithful." Or in n. 2: "The call is a concern not only of pastors, clergy, and men and women religious. The call is addressed to everyone: lay people as well are personally called by the Lord, from whom they receive a mission on behalf of the Church and the world." It is clear that the common matrix, under whatever name, is not the focus of the pope's post-synodal apostolic exhortation.

30. A lengthy bibliography is given in G. Philips, *La Chiesa e il suo Mistero* (Milan: Jaca, 1975) pp. 131–132.

31. Ibid., pp. 136–137.

32. A very helpful volume on this issue is H.-M. Barth, *Einander Priestersein: Allgemeines Priestertum in ökumenischer Perspektive* (Göttingen: Vandenhoeck & Ruprecht, 1990). Not only does one find in this volume a discussion of the term on the basis of Protestant-Catholic, but also a chapter on a theme which is not often treated: orthodox-western, namely, chapter VI, pp. 161–187.

33. In 1978, many years after Vatican II, the form of dispensation used by the Sacred Congregation for the Doctrine of the Faith included the phrase: "N. petiit reductionem ad statum laicalem. . . ." And in the listing of conditions and effects of this dispensation, one reads: "Per se sacerdos ad statum laicalem reductus. . . ." In a later form (1988) of the same kind of dispensation from the same Roman congregation the initial wording has been changed to read: "N. petiit dispensationem a sacerdotali coeli-

batu. . . ." In the list of conditions and effects of the dispensation, the word "lay" is not used. This indicates that even the official church administration does not change its language immediately.

34. Cf. K. Osborne, "The meaning of lay, laity and lay ministry in the Christian theology of church," *Antonianum*, 63 (1988) pp. 227–258.

35. Cf. similar discussions on this theme: O. Semmelroth, "La Chiesa, nuovo popolo di Dio," *La Chiesa del Vaticano II*, pp. 439–452; É.J. de Smedt, "Il sacerdozio dei fedeli," ibid., pp. 453–464; B. van Leeuwen, "La partecipazione comune del popolo di Dio all'ufficio profetico di Christo," ibid., pp. 465–490; A. Ciappi, "De praesentia Domini in communitate cultus ratione characteris baptismalis," *Acta Congressus Internationalis de Theologia Concilii Vaticani II* (Rome: Typis Polyglottis Vaticanis, 1968), ed. E. Dhanis, pp. 272–282; J.R. Scheifler, "La Iglesia, 'Pueblo de Dios,' " *Estudios sobre el Concilio Vaticano II*, pp. 71–157.

36. Scheifler, op. cit., p. 85, states the case, as found in the documents of Vatican II, in unequivocal terms: "Dentro de esa concepción estrictísima, es claro que 'pueblo de Dios' no se identifica en manera alguna con los 'laicos' o el 'laicado.' "

37. This methodological approach—Jesus/church/individual sacrament—has been presented at length in my other books on the sacraments: *Sacramental Theology: A General Introduction; The Sacraments of Initiation: Baptism, Confirmation and Eucharist; Priesthood; Reconciliation and Justification.* In each of these works, I have not only presented and used this methodology, but indicated that this is the methodology used by Vatican II documents and by many subsequent official documents of the Roman Catholic Church.

38. Cf. *Inaestimabile donum, AAS,* v. 72 (1980) p. 338; *Liturgicae instaurationes, AAS,* v. 62 (1970) pp. 692–704.

39. Cf. *AAS,* 62 (1970) pp. 692–704. For a discussion on this matter. cf. J. Huels, *Disputed Questions in the Liturgy Today* (Chicago: Liturgy Training Publications, 1988) pp. 27–38.

40. *Missale Romanum, Instructiones generales,* n. 70.

41. Cf. as well John Paul II, *Mulieris dignitatem,* op. cit., nn. 17–22, in which he focuses on "two particular dimensions of the fulfillment of the female personality" (n. 17). He states that motherhood "gives an essential indication of what it means to be human, while emphasizing the value of the gift of self, the gift of the person" (n. 18). And "by freely choosing virginity, women confirm themselves as persons, as beings whom the Creator from the beginning has willed for their own sake" (n. 20). What is striking in this chapter is not so much what is said, but what is not said. No mention is made of a major event in the life of a women, namely, her marriage to a man. Certainly, being a wife is as prominent a vocation in

life as motherhood and virginity. No mention is made of professional women, of single women who do not "take a vow" of chastity, of women in major careers in society. The vocation of a male would not be described only in terms of fatherhood and celibacy. More than likely, the calling to priesthood would be mentioned, which has a "career" tonality about it. One asks: Why are there so many *lacunae* in this description of a woman's fundamental vocation?

42. "Place of Women in the Liturgy" (February 14, 1971), *Thirty Years of Liturgical Renewal: Statements of the Bishops' Committee on the Liturgy* (Washington, D.C.: USCC, 1987), ed. F. McManus, p. 137.

43. *Lumen gentium*, n. 30, states clearly: "Quodsi omnia quae de Populo Dei dicta sunt (i.e., chapter 2) ad laicos, religiosos et clericos aequaliter diriguntur, (note the term equality) laicis tamen, viris et mulieribus (women were deliberately mentioned), ratione condicionis et missionis, quaedam particulariter pertinent."

44. For background on the *tria munera*, cf. L. Schick, *Das Dreifache Amt Christi und der Kirche: Zur Entstehung und Entwicklung der Trilogen* (Frankfurt a. M.: Peter Lang, 1982); Y. Congar, "Sur la trilogie Prophète-Roi-Prêtre," *Revue des sciences philosophiques et théologiques,* 67 (1983) pp. 97–115; J. Fuchs, "Origines d'une trilogie ecclésiologique à l'époque rationaliste de la théologie," *Revue des sciences philosophiques et théologiques,* 53 (1969) pp. 185–211; T. Potvin, "Le baptême comme enracinement dans la participation à la triple fonction du Christ," *Le Laïcat: les limites d'un système* (Montréal: Éditions Fides, 1987) pp. 141–190.

45. This gathering of Vatican II documents is based on those found in Kloppenburg, op. cit., pp. 263–264.

46. F. Klostermann, "Chapter IV *Lumen Gentium," Commentary on the Documents of Vatican II* (N.Y.: Herder and Herder, 1967) v. 1, p. 240.

47. A lengthy study of the *tria munera*, in both its historical development and its detailed use in the documents of Vatican II, can be found in the essay by T. Potvin, "Le baptême comme enracinement dans la participation à la triple fonction du Christ," *Le laïcat: les limites d'une système*, op. cit., pp. 141–190.

48. F. Klostermann, "Dogmatic Constitution on the Church," *Commentary of the Documents of Vatican II,* v. 1, p. 241.

49. In *Lumen gentium*, c. 2, ¶ 13, there is no explicit mention of the people of God sharing in the kingly office of Christ. This royal office of all Christians is, however, mentioned elsewhere in the documents of Vatican II.

50. Already the *schemata* on the church, developed for Vatican I, used such a trilogy: "magisterium, ministerium, et regimen." Kleutgen's

Schema 2 used the terms "Sacerdotes, Iudices, Doctores/Rectores." Leo XIII in *Satis cognitum* used the same sort of trilogy. Pius XII mentions this trilogy in both *Mystici corporis Christi* and *Mediator Dei.* The use of the *tria munera* at Vatican II was, therefore, not something new. The way the *tria munera* was woven into the very fabric of Christian life by the bishops at Vatican II was indeed new.

51. U. Beste, *Introductio in Codicem* (Naples: D'Auria, 1961) p. 171.

52. Ibid. The bold print and the italics are in Beste's text itself.

53. Potkin, op. cit., p. 161: "Avec Vatican II, l'utilisation de la trilogie atteint un nouveau palier, et cela à l'interieur d'une ecclésiologie qui est consciemment basée sur la conviction que l'Église est une 'mystère'."

54. *Lumen gentium,* 10, 27.

55. Cf. W. Hryniewicz, "Theologischer Dialog und ökumenische Hoffnung," *Im Dialog der Wahrheit* (Vienna: Tyrolia, 1990) pp. 140–142. In this essay, Hryniewicz provides a resume of the dialogue between Roman Catholic and Orthodox theologians, which took place in June 1985 at Oppeln, Poland. It was during these dialogues that Orthodox theologians raised substantive criticisms of the *tria munera* presentation of priestly ministry, based primarily on the inadequacy of such an approach. They suggested that the *tria munera* approach needed to be enriched by an understanding of "icon."

56. The term "Catholic Action" was at first only accepted in Italy; not until the time of the First World War does one begin to find this term used north of the Alps.

57. Cf. *Apostolicam actuositatem,* n. 20, in which the phrase "Catholic Action" is used by the bishops at Vatican II. This use of the phrase is referred basically to an organized activity with the four characteristics named in the document. It is not a generalized term for the role of the baptized-confirmed as regards their mission and ministry in the *tria munera.* Such a role does not conform to the four characteristics, nor is it given to the baptized by the hierarchy. On the issue of the relationship of hierarchy and laity as expressed in *Lumen gentium,* 3, cf. Power, op. cit., p. 44.

58. In the documents of Vatican II, one finds that the baptized-confirmed Christian has an "apostolate," while the ordained Christian has a "ministry." The documents attempted through these separate terms to reinforce the "essential" difference between all Christians, on the one hand, and the specific task of the ordained, on the other. In post-Vatican II documents, even from the highest level, this distinction has been disregarded. The term "ministry" is used again and again, even in official documents, for both unordained and ordained ministerial activity.

59. Kloppenburg, op. cit., p. 309.

60. Ibid., p. 312.

61. Cf. Osborne, "The Meaning of Lay, Laity and Lay Ministry in the Christian Theology of Church," pp. 225–258.

62. Cf. F. Hengsbach, *Das Konzilsdekret über das Apostolat der Laien,* pp. 30–37.

63. G. Magnani, op. cit., p. 590, citing Klostermann, op. cit., pp. 236–238.

64. Ibid., p. 593.

65. Ibid., p. 627.

66. This approach was particularly stressed by the *VIII Simposio Internacional de Teología de la Universidad de Navarra.* Cf. G. Lo Castro, "La misión cristiana del laico," *La Misión del Laico en la Iglesia y en el Mundo* (Pamplona: Universidad de Navarra, 1987), eds. A. Sarmiento, T. Rincón, J.M. Yanguas, A. Quiros, pp. 441–463; Lo Castro summarizes his position on p. 462: "Laico es el cristiano . . . que vive la dimensión de la secularidad, a la cual está ontológica y específicamente llamado." In the same volume, cf. A. Maroza, "Apostolado laical individual," pp. 659–673, especially p. 666, in which he states: "Notas características del Apostolado laical . . . se trata, en primer lugar, de un apostolado *no ministerial:* una actividad personal y privada. A diferencia del apostolado público, no actúa el laico *nomine Christi capitis,* ni, consiguientemente, *cum ipsius potestate.* . . . Es un apostolado secular. Su nota específica frente al apostolado de los religiosos viene dada por su *modo de ser* en la Iglesia, por su modo de ser Iglesia: 'viviendo en el siglo, es decir, en todos y cada uno do los deberes y ocupaciones del mundo, y en las condiciones ordinarias de la vida familial y social, con las que su existencia *quasi contextitur'* (*LG* 31b)." This symposium was clearly directed by Opus Dei and reflects the views of Opus Dei.

67. G. Philips, op. cit., p. 348. The uncharacteristic length given to this section, 31 a/b, in Philips' commentary indicates that there was a strong need for explanation, because there had been—and still is—a major degree of unclarity about the passage.

68. Cf. Power, op. cit., pp. 44–46. He also indicates that the "secular" aspect of the non-ordained ministry is not that clearly presented by the documents of Vatican II. He indicates that the reason for the ambiguity lies in the issue of church and world: "Perhaps what the Council had not clarified in a way sufficient to allow it to speak differently was the relationship of the church to the world." *Regnum et sacerdotium* remains a highly influential issue with ramifications on the way in which the *sacerdotium* relates in an inner-church way to the role and presence of the non-ordained. Cf. also a similar view in Hengsbach, op. cit., p. 31.

69. Cf. also *Lumen gentium* 33, 3: "Praeterea aptitudine gaudent [bap-

tizati Christiani] ut ad quaedam munera ecclesiastica, ad finem spiritualem exercenda, ab Hierarchia adsumantur"; 36, 1 speaks of a power: "Quam potestatem discipulis communicavit. . . ." This is the only time in the documents of Vatican II, however, that the word *potestas* is used for the baptized. Cf. Potvin, op. cit., pp. 167–168.

70. John Paul II, *Christifideles laici,* also emphasizes this secular dimension of the lay person. Cf. n. 9. When he has discussed the common matrix under the rubric of the *tria munera* (n. 14), the pope then moves without any change of name to the secular character of the "lay people" (n. 15): "The world thus becomes the place and the means for the lay faithful to fulfill their Christian vocation." The ministry of the *tria munera,* however, has a far more fundamental arena of ministry and mission within the church, and it is this more profound meaning of the *tria munera* which one looks for in vain throughout *Christifideles laici.*

71. T. Bokenkotter, op. cit., p. 390.

72. Cf. the lengthy and documented explanation by M. Martin, *The Keys of This Blood* (N.Y.: Touchstone, 1990), pp. 620–652.

73. Robert Schwartz, *Servant Leaders of the People of God,* p. 33. Cf. *Presbyterorum ordines,* 2: "Officium Presbyterorum, utpote Ordini episcopali coniunctum, participat auctoritatem qua Christus Ipse Corpus suum exstruit, sanctificat et regit. Quare sacerdotium Presbyterorum initiationis christianae Sacramenta quidem supponit, peculiari tamen illo Sacramento confertur, quo Presbyteri, unctione Spiritus Sancti, speciali charactere signantur et sic Christo Sacerdoti configurantur, ita ut in persona Christi Capitis agere valeant." Cf. also *Lumen gentium,* n. 10; Pius XII, *Magnificate Dominum, AAS* 46 (1954) p. 669; *Mediator Dei, AAS* 39 (1947) p. 555.

74. Schwartz, ibid., p. 33.

75. Cf. J. Galot, *La nature du caractère sacramentel* (Paris: Desclée de Brouwer, 1958); Osborne, *Sacramental Theology,* pp. 111–112.

76. One can, for instance, find the same line of "ontological" and "essential" thinking in the article by Ghirlanda cited above.

77. Schwartz, op. cit., p. 37.

78. *LG* used the phrase *in persona Christi* or its equivalent six times, 10, 2; 11, 2; 21, 2; 25, 1; 27, 2; 28, 3; *PO* uses it three times, 2, 2; 2, 3; 2, 4; *SC* once, 7, 1.

79. Schwartz, op. cit., p. 41.

80. Ibid., p. 42.

81. Ibid.

82. T. Bokenkotter, op. cit., p. 401.

83. Cf. Ghirlanda, op. cit., pp. 245ff, in which the author argues that union with the bishop of Rome is an essential characteristic of episcopal

hierarchy. If this is true, the recognition of episcopacy in the non-uniate churches becomes a major problem, since evidently something "essential" is missing. However, the Roman Catholic Church leadership acknowledges that non-uniate bishops are valid bishops, and therefore nothing "essential" can be lacking to them as far as episcopacy is concerned. Ghirlanda's argumentation in this section is theologically inconclusive.

84. The bibliography has become both extensive and profound. Cf., e.g., M. Dwyer, ed., *New Woman, New Church, New Priestly Ministry* (Rochester: Women's Ordination Conference, 1980); E. Schüssler-Fiorenza, *In Memory of Her* (N.Y.: Crossroad, 1984); R. Radford Ruether, *New Woman/New Earth: Sexist Ideologies and Human Liberation* (N.Y.: Seabury, 1975); ibid. *Women-Church* (San Francisco: Harper & Row, 1985); M. Kolbenschlag, ed., *Women in the Church* (Washington, D.C.: Pastoral Press, 1987); A. Carr, *Transforming Grace* (N.Y.: Harper-Collins, 1990); M. Giles, *The Feminist Mystic and Other Essays on Women and Spirituality* (N.Y.: Crossroad, 1982); M. Grey, *Feminism, Redemption and the Christian Tradition* (Mystic: Twenty-Third Publications, 1990); M. Reilly and N. Sylvester, *Trouble and Beauty: Feminist Meets Catholic Social Teaching* (Washington D.C.: Center of Concern, 1991).

85. F. Wulf, "Decree on the Ministry and Life of Priests," *Commentary on the Documents of Vatican II* (N.Y.: Herder and Herder, 1969) v. 4., p. 225. This section of *PO* is particularly important for this theme, since it is in this section that the text reads *in persona Christi capitis*. Even with this description, the relationship between the "general" and "special" priesthood remains unclear.

86. Ibid., pp. 225–227; Wulf cites *LG* 4, a. 32; *PO* 9, 1.

87. Cf. P. Bradshaw, *Ordination Rites of the Ancient Churches of East and West*, pp. 83–92; cf. especially the relevant Byzantine text on pp. 137–139.

88. Cf. Osborne, *Priesthood*, pp. 336–337.

89. G. Philips, *La Chiesa e il suo Mistero*, p. 111.

90. A. Grillmeier, "The Mystery of the Church," *Commentary on the Documents of Vatican II*, v. 1, pp. 149–150.

91. Sullivan, "The Significance of the Vatican II Declaration That the Church of Christ 'Subsists' in the Roman Catholic Church," *Vatican II: Assessment and Perspectives*, v. 2, pp. 272–287.

92. Grillmeier, op. cit., p. 149. Sullivan, op. cit., p. 284, expresses the same judgment: "To sum up: the point of this article has been to show that, beginning with the change of wording from *est* to *subsistit in*, the Second Vatican Council introduced a way of thinking about the Catholic Church and about the other Christian churches that is substantially differ-

ent from the view put forward in the schema *De Ecclesia* drawn up by the Preparatory Commission and presented to the council fathers in the opening session of 1962. No subsequent statement can be a correct interpretation of the mind of Vatican II, if it means a return to the exclusive claim made in that schema that only the one church that is Roman Catholic has the right to be called church." Sullivan is clearly concerned about the interpretation given to this passage by the Congregation for the Doctrine of Faith; cf. pp. 280–283.

93. Ibid., p. 150, n. 29.

13. Looking to the Future

1. P. Fransen, "Das neue Sein des Menschen," *Mysterium Salutis* (Einsiedeln: Benziger, 1973) v. 4/2, p. 922: "Je intensiver unsere Vermenschlichung ist, desto radikaler ist unsere Vergöttlichung, und je totaler unsere Vergöttlichung ist, desto tiefgreifender wird auch unsere Vermenschlichung sein." Fransen prefers this way of speaking as a basic methodological statement on grace over the usual: grace builds on nature: *gratia supponit naturam.*

2. John Paul II, "Letter to Cardinal Ratzinger," *L'Osservatore Romano,* April 18, 1988, p. 2.

3. *De Vocatione et missione laicorum in ecclesia et in mundo viginti annis a concilio Vaticano II elapsis,* n. 12.

Selected Bibliography

This bibliography is meant to be indicative only.

EDITIONS AND COLLECTIONS

ACO   *Acta conciliorum oecumenicorum,* Strasbourg, 1914–.

CCSL   *Corpus christianorum. Series latina,* Turnhout, 1953–.

CDD   *Constitutiones, decreta, declarationes: sacrosanctum oecumenicum concilium Vaticanum II,* Rome, 1966.

COD   *Conciliorum oecumenicorum decreta,* Rome, 1962.

CSCO   *Corpus scriptorum christianorum orientalium,* Paris, 1903–.

CSEL   *Corpus scriptorum ecclesiasticorum latinorum,* Vienna, 1866–.

DS   *Enchiridion symbolorum, definitionum, declarationum,* Freiburg i. Br., 1963.

Mansi, J. D.   *Sacrorum conciliorum nova et amplissima collectio,* Florence, 1759–1798.

MGH   *Monumenta Germaniae historica: Epistolae,* Berlin, 1891–.

PG   *Patrologia graeca,* Paris, 1857–1866.

PL   *Patrologia latina,* Paris, 1878–1890.

SC   *Sources chrétiennes,* Paris, 1940–.

BOOKS

Artz, F.B., *The Mind of the Middle Ages: An Historical Survey A.D. 200–1500,* Chicago: The University of Chicago Press, 1980.

Athanasius, *Vita S. Antoni,* [PG], 26, 835–976.

Aubert, R., *The Church in a Secularized Society,* N.Y.: Paulist, 1978.

———, *La théologie catholique au milieu du XXᵉ siécle,* Tournai: 1954.

———, *Le Pontificat de Pie IX (1864–1878),* Paris: Bloud & Gay, 1963.

Auf der Mauer, I., *Mönchtum und Glaubensverkündigung in den Schriften des hl. Johannes Chrysostomus,* Freiburg: Paulusdruckerei, 1959.

Bainton, R.H., *Women of the Reformation in Germany and Italy,* Minneapolis: Augsburg, 1971.

Baraúna, G. and S. Olivieri, *La Chiesa del Vaticano II,* Florence: Vallechi, 1965.

Barth, H.-M., *Einander Priestersein: Allgemeines Priestertum in ökumenischer Perspektive,* Göttingen: Vandenhoeck & Ruprecht, 1990.

Bauer W., *Orthodoxy and Heresy in Earliest Christianity,* Philadelphia: Fortress, 1971.

Berman, H.J., *Law and Revolution: The Formation of the Western Legal Tradition,* Cambridge: Harvard University Press, 1983.

Biéler, A., *L'homme et la femme dans la morale calviniste,* Geneva: Labor et Fides, 1963.

Blanke, F. and Leenhardt, F.J., *Die Stellung der Frau im Neuen Testament und der alten Kirche,* Zürich: Zwingli, 1949.

Bokenkotter, T., *A Concise History of the Catholic Church,* N.Y.: Doubleday, 1990.

Bousma, W.J., *John Calvin: A Sixteenth Century Portrait,* Oxford: Oxford University Press, 1988.

Bowe, B., *A Church in Crisis,* Minneapolis: Fortress, 1988.

Bradshaw, P.E., *Ordination Rites of the Ancient Churches of East and West,* N.Y.: Pueblo, 1990.

Branick, V., *The House Church in the Writings of Paul,* Wilmington: M. Glazier, 1988.

Brooke, C., *Monasteries of the World,* N.Y.: Crescent Books, 1982.

Brown, P., *Augustine of Hippo: A Biography,* Berkeley: University of California Press, 1967.

————, *Society and the Holy in Late Antiquity,* Berkeley: University of California Press, 1982.

Brown, R., *The Community of the Beloved Disciple,* N.Y.: Paulist, 1979.

Brown, R. et al., *Peter in the New Testament,* N.Y.: Paulist, 1973.

Brown, R., and Meier, J.P., *Antioch and Rome,* N.Y.: Paulist, 1983.

Brown, R., Fitzmyer, J., Murphy, R., *The New Jerome Biblical Commentary,* Englewood Cliffs, N.J.: Prentice-Hall, 1990.

Buck, C.D., and Peterson, W., *A Reverse Index of Greek Nouns and Adjectives,* Chicago: University of Chicago Press, 1940.

Bury, J.B., *History of the Later Roman Empire,* N.Y.: Dover Publications, 1958.

Butterworth, G.W., *Clement of Alexandria,* Cambridge: Harvard University Press, 1968.

Bynum, C.W., *Holy Feast and Holy Fast,* Berkeley: University of California Press, 1987.

————, *Fragmentation and Redemption,* N.Y.: Zone Books, 1991.

Calvin, J., *Institutes of the Christian Religion,* Philadelphia: Westminster, 1950, ed. J.T. McNeil.

Campenhausen, H. von, *Asketische Heimatlosigkeit im altkirchlich-frühmittelalterlichen Mönchtum,* Tübingen: J.C.B. Mohr, 1930.

Canon Law Society of America, *Code of Canon Law: Text and Commentary,* N.Y.: Paulist Press, 1985.

Carlyle, R.W., and A.J., *A History of Mediaeval Political Theory in the West,* N.Y.: Barnes and Noble, 1953.

Chadwick, H., ed., *Alexandrian Christianity,* Philadelphia: Westminster, 1954.

————, *History and Thought of the Early Church,* London: Variorum Reprints, 1982.

Chadwick, O., *The Popes and the European Revolution,* N.Y.: Oxford University Press, 1981.

Charlesworth, J.H., *Jesus Within Judaism,* N.Y.: Doubleday, 1988.

Chinnici, J.P., *Living Stones: The History and Structure of Catholic Spiritual Life in the United States,* N.Y.: Macmillan, 1989.

Clark, E.A., *Women in the Early Church,* Wilmington: M. Glazier, 1983.

Clement of Rome, *Clemens Alexandrinus,* Berlin: Akademie Verlag, v. I, 1972 and v. II, 1985, ed. O. Stählin, L. Früchtel, U. Treu.

Coleman-Norton, P.R., *Roman State and Christian Church: A Collection of Legal Documents to A.D. 535,* London: SPCK, 1966.

Congar, Y., *Jalons pour une théologie du laïcat,* Paris: Unam Sanctam, 1935.

————, *Sacerdoce et laïcat devant leurs tâches d'évangélisation,* Paris: Unam Sanctam, 1962.

————, *Sainte Église*, Paris: Éditions du Cerf, 1963.

Connolly, R.H., *Didascalia Apostolorum*, Oxford: Clarendon Press, 1919.

Cooke, B., *Ministry to Word and Sacraments*, Philadelphia: Fortress, 1976.

Cowdry, H.E.J., *Popes, Monks and Crusaders*, London: The Hambledon Press, 1984.

Cross, C., *Church and People, 1450–1660: The Triumph of the Laity in the English Church*, Atlantic Highlands: Humanities Press, 1976.

Crossan, J.D., *The Historical Jesus: The Life of a Mediterranean Jewish Peasant*, San Francisco: Harper, 1991.

Dagens, C., *Saint Grégoire le Grand*, Paris: Études augustiniennes, 1977.

Dam, R. van, *Leadership and Community in Late Antique Gaul*, Berkeley: University of California Press, 1985.

D'Amico, J., *Renaissance Humanism in Papal Rome: Humanists and Churchmen on the Eve of the Reformation*, Baltimore: The John Hopkins University Press, 1983.

Dolan, J., *The American Catholic Experience: A History from Colonial Times to the Present*, Garden City: Doubleday, 1985.

Doohan, H., *Paul's Vision of the Church*, Wilmington: M. Glazier, 1989.

Doohan, L. *The Lay-Centered Church: Theology and Spirituality*, Minneapolis: Winston, 1984.

Dudden, F.H., *Gregory the Great: His Place in History and in Thought*, N.Y.: Russell and Russell, 1967.

Dvornik, F., *The Idea of Apostolicity in Byzantium and the Legend of the Apostle Andrew*, Cambridge: Harvard University Press, 1958.

Dwyer, M., ed., *New Woman, New Church, New Priestly Ministry*, Rochester: Women's Ordination Conference, 1980.

Empie, P.C., and Murphy, A., *Papal Primacy and the Universal Church*, Minneapolis: Augsburg, 1974.

Erdmann, C., *Forschungen zur politischen Ideenwelt des Frühmittelalters*, Berlin: 1951.

Faivre, A., *Les laïcs aux origines de l'Église*, Paris: Le Centurion, 1984.

————, *Naissance d'une hiérarchie: Les premières étapes du cursus clérical*, Paris: Beauchesne, 1977.

Fitzmyer, J., *The Gospel according to Luke*, Garden City: Doubleday & Co, 1981.

Flender, H., *St. Luke: Theologian of Redemptive History*, Philadelphia: Fortress, 1967.

Fortini, A., *Francis of Assisi*, N.Y.: Crossroad, 1981.

Franklik, E., *Christ the Lord: A Study in the Purpose and Theology of Luke-Acts*, Philadelphia: Westminster, 1975.

Frend, W.H.C., ed. *The Layman in Christian History*, London: 1963.

Frend, W.H.C., *The Rise of Christianity*, Philadelphia: Fortress, 1984.

———, *The Donatist Church*, Oxford: Clarendon Press, 1952; revised edition: Oxford University Press, 1985.

Fuellenbach, J., *Ecclesiastical Office and the Primacy of Rome*, Washington, D.C.: The Catholic University of America Press, 1980.

Galot, J., *Theology of the Priesthood*, San Francisco: Ignatius Press, 1984.

Gargan, E.T., ed., *Leo XIII and the Modern World*, N.Y.: Sheed and Ward, 1961.

Gilson, E., *The Christian Philosophy of St. Thomas Aquinas*, N.Y.: Random House, 1956.

Gobry, I., *Les Moines en Occident: De saint Antoine à saint Basile*, Paris: Arthème Fayard, 1985.

———, *Les Moines en Occident: De saint Martin à saint Benoit*, Paris, Arthème Fayard, 1985.

Grant, R.M., *The Apostolic Fathers*, v. I, *An Introduction*, N.Y.: Thomas Nelson & Sons, 1964.

———, *Augustus to Constantine: The Thrust of the Christian Movement into the Roman World*, N.Y.: Harper & Row, 1970.

Grant R.M., and Graham, H., *The Apostolic Fathers*, v. II, *First and Second Clement*, N.Y.: Thomas Nelson & Sons, 1965.

Griggs, G.W., *Early Egyptian Christianity*, Leiden: E.J. Brill, 1990.

Grillmeier, A., *Christ in Christian Tradition*, Atlanta, John Knox Press, 1975.

Grundmann, H., *Religiöse Bewegungen im Mittelalter*, Hildesheim: G. Olms, 1961.

Gryson, R., *The Ministry of Women in the Early Church*, Collegeville: Liturgical Press, 1976.

Haenchen, E., *Die Apostelgeschichte*, Göttingen: Vandenhoeck & Ruprecht, 1965.

Hamilton, B., *Religion in the Medieval West*, London: Edward Arnold, 1986.

Hengel, M., *Between Jesus and Paul: Studies in the Earliest History of Christianity*, Philadelphia: Fortress, 1983.

Hennesey, J., *American Catholics*, N.Y.: Oxford University Press, 1981.

Herrin, J., *The Formation of Christendom*, Princeton: Princeton University Press, 1987.

Huizinga, J., *The Waning of the Middle Ages*, London: Penguin Books, 1955.

Jedin, H., *A History of the Council of Trent*, St. Louis: B. Herder Book Co., 1965–1981.

———, *Ecumenical Councils*, N.Y.: Paulist, 1961.

Jedin, H., and Dolan, J., *Handbook of Church History*, N.Y.: Herder and Herder, 1962–1979.

Käpelli, T.M., *Zur Lehre des h. Thomas von Aquin vom Corpus Christi Mysticum*, Freiburg, 1931.

Kedar, B., *Crusade and Mission*, Princeton: Princeton University Press, 1984.

Kelly, J.N.D., *Early Christian Doctrines*, N.Y.: Longman, 1981.

Kloppenburg, B., *The Ecclesiology of Vatican II*, Chicago: Franciscan Herald Press, 1974.

Knowles, D., *Christian Monasticism*, N.Y.: McGraw-Hill, 1969.

———, *The Evolution of Medieval Thought*, N.Y.: Longman, 1988.

Knowles, D., and Oblensky, D., *The Middle Ages*, N.Y.: Paulist, 1983.

Koester, H., *Einführung in das Neue Testament im Rahmen der Religionsgeschichte und Kulturgeschichte der hellenistischen und römischen Zeit*, Berlin: De Gruyer, 1980.

Kriegbaum, B., *Kirche der Traditoren oder Kirche der Märtyrer?* Vienna: Tyrolia Verlag, 1986.

Landini, L., *The Cause of the Clericalization of the Order of Friars Minor*, Chicago, 1983.

La Porte, J., *The Role of Women in Early Christianity*, N.Y.: E. Mellen Press, 1982.

Latourelle, R., ed., *Vatican II: Assessment and Perspectives*, N.Y.: Paulist, 1988.

Lawrence, C.H., *Medieval Monasticism: Forms of Religious Life in Western Europe in the Middle Ages*, N.Y.: Longman, 1989.

Leff, G., *The Dissolution of the Medieval Outlook*, N.Y.: Harper & Row, 1976.

———, *Medieval Thought: St. Augustine to Ockham*, Atlantic Highlands: Humanities Press, 1983.

Leipoldt, J., *Die Frau in der Antiken Welt und im Urchristentum*, Leipzig: Koehler und Amelang, 1955.

Léonard, É., *A History of Protestantism*, London: Nelson, 1967.

Lewis, E., *Medieval Political Ideas*, London: Routledge & Kegan Paul, 1954, 2 vols.

Lewis, N., *Life in Egypt under Roman Rule*, Oxford: Oxford University Press, 1983.

Lieberg, H., *Amt und Ordination bei Luther und Melanchthon*, Göttingen: Vandenhoeck & Ruprecht, 1962.

Lohfink, G., *Jesus and Community*, N.Y.: Paulist, 1984.

Lohse, B., *Martin Luther: An Introduction to His Life and Work*, Philadelphia: Fortress, 1986.

Lubac, H. de, *Exégèse médiévale*, Paris: Aubier, 1954–1964.

————, *L'Eucharistie et l'église au moyen âge,* Paris: Aubier, 1949.

Luther, M.D., *Martin Luthers Werke,* Weimar: H. Böhlau, 1883–1967; *Luther's Works,* St. Louis: Concordia/Philadelphia: Fortress, 1960–1986.

MacMullen, R., *Christianizing the Roman Empire. A.D. 100–400,* New Haven: Yale University Press, 1986.

Macy, G., *The Theologies of the Eucharist in the Early Scholastic Period,* Oxford: Clarendon Press, 1984.

Martelet, G., *Deux mille ans d'église en question,* Paris: Éditions du Cerf, 1984.

McNeill, J.T., *The History and Character of Calvinism,* N.Y.: Oxford University Press, 1962.

Meeks, W.A., *The First Urban Christians: The Social World of the Apostle Paul,* New Haven: Yale University Press, 1983.

Meier, J.P., *A Marginal Jew: Rethinking the Historical Jesus,* N.Y.: Doubleday, 1991.

Mollat, C.M., *The Poor in the Middle Ages: An Essay in Social History,* New Haven: Yale University Press, 1986.

Momigliano, A., ed., *The Conflict Between Paganism and Christianity in the Fourth Century,* Oxford: Clarendon Press, 1970.

Moody, E.A., *The Logic of William of Ockham,* N.Y.: Russell and Russell, 1965.

Morrison, K.F., *The Two Kingdoms: Ecclesiology in Carolingian Political Thought,* Princeton: Princeton University Press, 1964.

Murphy-O'Connor, J., *St. Paul's Corinth: Texts and Archaeology,* Wilmington: M. Glazier, 1983.

Neill, S., *A History of the Christian Missions,* Harmondsworth: Penguin Books, 1986.

Nichol, T., and Kolden, M., *Called and Ordained,* Minneapolis: Fortress, 1990.

Norman, E., *The English Catholics in the Nineteenth Century,* N.Y.: Oxford University Press, 1984.

Oberman, Heiko, *The Harvest of Medieval Theology,* Cambridge: Harvard University Press, 1963.

Origen, *Origenes Werke,* ed. P. Nautin, Berlin: Akademie Verlag, 1983.

Osborne, K., *The Christian Sacraments of Initiation,* N.Y.: Paulist, 1987.

————, *Sacramental Theology,* N.Y.: Paulist, 1988.

————, *Priesthood,* N.Y.: Paulist, 1988.

————, *Reconciliation and Justification,* N.Y.: Paulist, 1990.

Ozment, S., *The Age of Reform, 1250–1550: An Intellectual and Religious History of Late Medieval and Reformation Europe,* New Haven: Yale University Press, 1980.

Pelikan, J., *Jesus Through the Centuries*, New Haven: Yale University Press, 1985.

———, *Spirit Versus Structure: Luther and the Institutions of the Church*, N.Y.: Harper and Row, 1968.

———, *The Christian Tradition: A History of the Development of Doctrine*, Chicago: The University of Chicago Press, 1971.

Philips, G., *La Chiesa e il suo mistero*, Milan: Ed. Jaca Book, 1975.

Power, D.M., *Gifts That Differ*, N.Y.: Pueblo, 1980.

Preisigke, F. *Fachwörter der öffentlichen Verwaltungsdienstes Ägyptens in den griechischen Papyrusurkunden*, Göttingen: Vandenhoeck & Ruprecht, 1915.

———, *Griechische Papyrus*, Leipzig: J.C. Hinrichsche Buchhandlung, 1912.

Quasten, J., *Patrology*, 4 vols., Westminster: Newman, 1962–86.

Reydellet, M., *La royauté dans la littérature latine de Sidone Appolinaire à Isidore de Séville*, Rome: 1981.

Richards, J., *The Popes and the Papacy in the Early Middle Ages: 476–752*, London: Routledge and Kegan Paul, 1979.

Rousseau, P., *Pachomius: The Making of a Community in Fourth-Century Egypt*, Berkeley: University of California Press, 1985.

Ruether R. and McLaughlin, E., eds., *Women of Spirit—Female Leadership in the Jewish and Christian Traditions*, N.Y.: Simon and Schuster, 1979.

Runciman, S., *A History of the Crusades*, Cambridge: University Press, 1951.

———, *The Sicilian Vespers. A History of the Mediterranean World in the Later XIII Century*, N.Y.: Cambridge University Press, 1982.

Russell, J.B., *Dissent and Reform in the Early Middle Ages*, Berkeley: University of California Press, 1965.

Sabra, G., *Thomas Aquinas' Vision of the Church*, Mainz: Matthias-Grünewald, 1987.

Sanders, E.P., *Jesus and Judaism* Philadelphia: Fortress, 1985.

Sarmiento, A., Rincon, T., Yangua, J.-M., Quiros, A., eds., *La Misión del Laico en la Iglesia y en el Mundo*, Pamplona: Ediciones Universidad de Navarra, 1987.

Scarisbrick, J.J., *Henry VIII*, Berkeley: University of California Press, 1968.

Schäfer, K., *Gemeinde als "Bruderschaft": Ein Beitrag zum Kirchenverständnis des Paulus*, Frankfurt am M.: Peter Lang, 1989.

Schäfer, T., *Das Priester-Bild im Leben und Werk des Origenes*, Frankfurt a. M.: Peter Lang, 1977.

Scherer, J., ed., *Entretien d'Origène avec Héraclide,* Paris: Éditions du Cerf, 1960.

Schick, L., *Das Dreifache Amt Christi und der Kirche: Zur Entstehung und Entwicklung der Trilogen,* Frankfurt a. M.: Peter Lang, 1982.

Schmithals, W., *Das kirchliche Apostelamt,* Göttingen: Vandenhoeck & Ruprecht, 1961.

Schneelmecher, W., ed., *New Testament Apocrypha,* London: Lutterworth Press, 1963.

Schnucker, R.V., ed., *Calviniana: Ideas and Influence of Jean Calvin,* Kirksville: Sixteenth Century Journal Publishers, 1988.

Schöllgen, G., *Ecclesia Sordida? Zur Frage der sozialen Schichtung Frühchristlicher Gemeinden am Beispiel Karthagos zur Zeit Tertullians,* Münster: Aschendorfsche Verlagsbuchhandlung, 1984.

Schröer, H., and Müller, G., *Von Amt des Laien in Kirche und Theologie,* Berlin: Walter de Gruyter, 1982.

Schüssler-Fiorenza, E., *In Memory of Her,* N.Y.: Crossroad, 1983.

Schwartz, R., *Servant Leaders of the People of God,* N.Y.: Paulist, 1989.

Secretaria Generalis, *Sacrosanctum Oecumenicum Concilium Vatican II: Constitutiones Decreta, Declarationes,* Vaticanum: Typis Polyglottis, 1966.

Senior, D., *The Passion of Jesus in the Gospel of Matthew,* Wilmington: Glazier, 1985.

Sheils, W.J., ed., *Monks, Hermits and the Ascetic Tradition,* London: Blackwell, 1985.

Sheils, W.J. and Wood, D., *The Ministry: Clerical and Lay,* Oxford: Blackwell, 1989.

Silic, R., *Christus und die Kirche. Ihr Verhältnis nach der Lehre des heiligen Bonaventura,* Breslau, 1938.

Sozomen, *Sozomène: Histoire Ecclésiastique,* Paris: Éditions du Cerf, 1983, ed. J. Bidez.

Spitz, L.W., *The Protestant Reformation, 1517–1559,* N.Y.: Harper & Row, 1985.

Steinmetz, D., *Luther in Context,* Bloomington: Indiana University Press, 1986.

Straw, C., *Gregory the Great, Perfection in Imperfection,* Berkeley: The University of California Press, 1988.

Swidler, L., *Women in Judaism: The Status of Women in Formative Judaism,* Metuchen: Scarecrow, 1976.

Tavard, G.H., *Women in Christian Tradition,* South Bend: University of Notre Dame Press, 1973.

Teeuwen, St. W.J., *Sprachlicher Bedeutungswandel bei Tertullian,* Paderborn: F. Schöningh, 1926.

Tertullian, *Tertulliani Opera*, ed. A. Kroymann, Turnholt: Brepol, 1954.

Theissen, G., *The Social Setting of Pauline Christianity: Essays on Corinth*, Philadelphia: Fortress, 1982.

Tierney, B., *Foundations of the Conciliar Theory*, Cambridge: Cambridge University Press, 1955.

———, *Crisis of Church and State, 1050–1300*, Toronto: University of Toronto Press, 1976.

———, *Religion, Law and the Growth of Constitutional Thought, 1150–1650*, N.Y.: Cambridge University Press, 1982.

Ullmann, W., *The Growth of Papal Government in the Middle Ages*, London: Methuen, 1970.

———, *Principles of Government and Politics in the Middle Ages*, N.Y.: Barnes and Noble, 1961.

Vaillancourt, J.-G., *Papal Power: A Study of Vatican Control over Catholic Elites*, Berkeley: University of California Press, 1980.

Vauchez, A., *Les laïcs au Moyen Age*, Paris: Éditions du Cerf, 1987.

Veilleux, A., *La Liturgie dans le cénobitisme pachômien au quatrième siècle*, Rome: Pontificium Institutum S. Anselmi, 1968.

Vogüe, A. de, *Pachomian Koinonia: The Lives, Rules and Other Writings of Saint Pachomius and His Disciples*, Kalamazoo: Cistercian Publications, 1980.

———, *History of Asceticism in the Syrian Orient* [*CSCO*], v. 184, Louvain, 1958–1988.

Volz, C., *Pastoral Life and Practice in the Early Church*, Minneapolis: Augsburg, 1990.

Vorgrimler, H., ed., *Commentary on the Documents of Vatican II*, N.Y.: Herder and Herder, 1967.

Wadell, H., *The Desert Fathers*, N.Y.: Sheed and Ward, 1942.

Wallace-Hadrill, J.M., *The Frankish Church*, Oxford: Clarendon Press, 1983.

Williams, G.H., *The Radical Reformation*, Philadelphia: Westminster, 1962.

Wolter, A., *The Philosophical Theology of John Duns Scotus*, Ithaca: Cornell University Press, 1990.

ARTICLES

Alberigo, G., "The Council of Trent," *Catholicism in Early Modern History: A Guide to Research*, ed. J. O'Malley, St. Louis: Center for Reformation Research, 1988.

Bacht, H., "Die Rolle des orientalischen Mönchtums in den kirchenpolitischen Auseinandersetzungen um Chalkedon (431–519)," *Das Kon-*

zil von Chalkedon, eds. A. Grillmeier and H. Bacht, v. 2, Würzburg: Echter-Verlag, 1953, 193–314.

Barruffo, A., "Il significato cristiano della parole 'laico'," *La Civiltà Cattolica* 113/2 (1962) 157–160.

Bauer, J.B., "Die Wortgeschichte von 'Laicus'," *Zeitschrift für Katholische Theologie*, 81 (1959) 224–228.

Beutler, J., "Adelphos," *Exegetisches Wörterbuch zum Neuen Testament*, eds. H. Balz and G. Schneider, Stuttgart: Kohlhammer, 1980, v. 1, 67–72.

Beyschlag, K., "I Clemens 40–44 und das Kirchenrecht," *Reformatio und Confessio: Festschrift für Wilhelm Maurer*, Berlin: Lutherisches Verlagshaus, 1965.

Bonet, P., "The *Christifidelis* Restored to His Role as Human Protagonist in the Church," *Vatican II: Assessment and Perspectives*, N.Y.: Paulist, 1988, v. 1, 540–567.

Brooke, C., "Heresy and Religious Sentiment: 1000–1250," *Medieval Church and Society*, London: Sidgwick and Jackson, 1971.

Caron, P., "Les 'seniores laici' de l'Église africaine," *Revue Internationale de Droit de l'Antiquité*, 6 (1951) 7–22.

De la Potterie, I., "L'Origine et le sens primitiv du mot 'laïc'," *Nouvelle Revue Théologique*, 80 (1958) 840–853.

Dondaine, A., "L'Origine de l'hérésie médiévale," *Rivista di storia della chiesa in Italia*, v. 6, Rome, 1952.

Dupuy, B.D., "Theologie der kirchlichen Ämter," *Mysterium Salutis*, Einsiedeln: Benziger, 1973, v. 4/2.

Foerster, W. "Kleros ktl," *TWNT;* ET *Theological Dictionary of the New Testament*, eds. G. Kittel and G. Friedrich, Grand Rapids: Eerdmans, 1964–1976, v. 3.

Folliet, G., "Les trois catégories de chrétiens," *Augustinus Magister*, v. 2 Paris (1954), 631–644.

Gobillot, P., "Les origines dans le cénobitisme chrétien et l'ancienne religion de l'Égypt," *Recherches de Science Religieuse*, 10 (1920) 303–364; 11 (1921) 168–213; 12 (1922) 46–68.

Goldie, R., "Laity: A Bibliographical Survey of Three Decades," *The Laity Today*, 26 (1979) 107–143.

Hallinger, K., "Papst Gregor der Große und der heilige Benedikt," *Studia Anselmiana* 42 (1957) 231–319.

Hervada, J., "La definición nominal del laico [Etimología y uso primitivo]," *Ius Canonicum*, 8 (1968) 471–453.

Jourjon, M., "Les premiers emplois du mot laïc dans la littérature patristique," *Lumière et Vie* (1963) 37–42.

Käsemann, E., "An Apology for Primitive Christian Eschatology," *Essays on New Testament Themes,* London: SBT, 1964, 169–196.

Knoch, O., "Die Ausführung des I Clemensbriefes über kirchliche Verfassung im Spiegel der neueren Deutung seit R. Sohm und A. Harnack," *Theologische Quartalschrift,* 141 (1967) 202–210.

Komanchak, J., "Clergy, Laity and the Church's Mission in the World," *The Jurist,* 41 (1981) 422–447.

Lanne, E. "Le laïcat dans l'Église ancienne," *Verbum Caro* 18 (1964) 105–126.

Magnani, G., "Does the So-Called Theology of the Laity Possess a Theological Status?" *Vatican II: Assessment and Perspectives,* N.Y.: Paulist, v. 1 (1988) 568–633.

Momigliano, A., "Christianity and the Decline of the Roman Empire," *The Conflict between Paganism and Christianity in the Fourth Century,* Oxford: The Clarendon Press, 1964, 1–16.

Moreno-Jimenez, P., "El discípulo de Jesu Cristo según el evangelio de San Juan," *Estudios bíblicos,* 30 (1971) 269–311.

Morghen, R., "Movimenti religiosi popolari nel periodo della riforma della Chiesa," *X Congresso Internazionale de Scienze Storiche,* III, Florence: 1935.

Nauck, Wolfgang, "Probleme des frühchristlichen Amtsverständnisses," *Zeitschrift für die neutestamentliche Wissenschaft,* 48 (1957) 200–220.

O'Meara, T., "Order and Ordination," *The New Dictionary of Theology,* Wilmington: Glazier, 1987.

Osborne, K., "The Meaning of Lay, Laity and Lay Ministry in the Christian Theology of Church," *Antonianum,* 53 (1988) 227–258.

Picasso, G., "La laicità nel medioevo," *Laicità, problemi e prospettive,* Milan: Vita e Pensiero (1977) 84–99.

Pizzolato, L., "Laicità e laici nel cristianesimo primitivo," *Laicità, problemi e prospettive,* Milan: Vita e Pensiero (1977) 57–83.

Potvin, T., "Le baptême comme enracinement dans la participation à la triple fonction du Christ," *Le laïcat: les limites d'une système, Actes du Congrès canadien de théologie,* Montréal: Fides, 1986.

Randi, E., "A Scotist Way of Distinguishing Between God's Absolute and Ordained Powers," *From Ockham to Wyclif,* Oxford: Blackwell, 1987.

Rosini Ruggero, P., "La suprema distinzione tra Dio e il mondo in Duns Escoto," *Homo et Mundus: Acta Quinti Congressus Scotistici Internationalis,* Rome: Societas Internationalis Scotistica, 1984.

Rousseau, P., "The Spiritual Authority of the Monk-Bishop, *Journal of Theological Studies,* 22 (1971).

Schramm, P.E., "Die 'Herrschaftszeichen', die 'Staatssymbolik' und die 'Staatspräsentation' des Mittelalters," *Kaiser, Könige und Päpste,* Stuttgart: A. Hiersemann, 1968.

Schützeichel, H., "Calvins Kritik der biblischen Begründung des Papstamtes," *Katholische Beiträge zur Calvinforschung,* Trier: Paulinus-Verlag, 1988.

———, "Karl der Große als Kaiser (800–814) im Lichte der Staatssymbolik," *Kaiser, Könige und Päpste,* Stuttgart: A. Hiersemann, 1968.

———, "Der Ablauf der deutschen Königsweihe nach dem 'Mainzer Ordo' (um 960)," *Kaiser, Könige und Päpste,* Stuttgart: A. Hiersemann, 1968.

Trapp, D., "Augustinian Theology of the Fourteenth Century: Notes on Editions, Marginalia, Opinions and Book-Lore," *Augustiniana* 6 (1956) 146–274.

Ueding, L., "Die Kanones von Chalkedon in ihrer Bedeutung für Mönchtum und Klerus," *Das Konzil von Chalkedon,* v. 2, ed. A. Grillmeier and H. Bacht, Würzburg: Echter Verlag, 1959, 569–676.

Vogüé, A. de, "La monastère, Église du Christ," *Commentationes in Regulam S. Benedicti,* Rome: Herder, 1957.

Williams, G.H., "The Role of the Layman in the Ancient Church," *Greek, Roman and Byzantine Studies,* 1 (1958) 9–42.

Wingren, G., "Der Begriff 'Laie'," *Von Amt des Laien in Kirche und Theologie,* eds. H. Schrörer and G. Müller, Berlin: Walter de Gruyer, 1982, 3–16.

Wulf, F., "Über die Herkunft und den ursprünglichen Sinn des Wortes 'Laie'," *Geist und Leben,* 32 (1959) 61–63.

Index of Authors

709